Inclusive Teaching

Creating Effective Schools
for All Learners

J. Michael Peterson
Wayne State University

Mishael Marie Hittie
*MacArthur Elementary School,
Southfield Public Schools*

Boston ▪ New York ▪ San Francisco
Mexico City ▪ Montreal ▪ Toronto ▪ London ▪ Madrid ▪ Munich ▪ Paris
Hong Kong ▪ Singapore ▪ Tokyo ▪ Cape Town ▪ Sydney

Executive Editor: Virginia Lanigan
Developmental Editor: Alicia Reilly
Editorial Assistant: Robert Champagne
Marketing Manager: Amy Cronin Jordan
Editorial-Production Administrator: Annette Joseph
Editorial-Production Service: Omegatype Typography, Inc.
Text Designer: Carol Somberg

Photo Editor: Katharine S. Cook
Electronic Composition: Omegatype Typography, Inc.
Composition Buyer: Linda Cox
Manufacturing Buyer: Megan Cochran
Cover Administrator: Linda Knowles
Cover Designer: Susan Paradise

For related titles and support materials, visit our online catalog at www.ablongman.com.

Between the time website information is gathered and then published, it is not unusual for some sites to have closed. Also, the transcription of URLs can result in unintended typographical errors. The publishers would appreciate notification where these errors occur so that they may be corrected in subsequent editions.

Library of Congress Cataloging-in-Publication Data

Peterson, Michael (J. Michael)
    Inclusive teaching : creating effective schools for all learners / J. Michael Peterson,
  Mishael Marie Hittie.
        p. cm.
    Includes bibliographical references and index.
    ISBN 0-205-29628-9
        1. Inclusive education. I. Hittie, Mishael Marie. II. title.
LC1200 .P48 2003
371.95'2—dc21

                                                                    2002071179

Printed in the United States of America

10 9 8 7 6 5   RRD-VA   07

To Georgie Ellen Peterson and Todd A. Hittie, without whose love and support this book would not have been possible

Contents

5 Support and Collaboration:
Getting Help and Building a School Community   121

PART TWO: Inclusive Teaching

The Foundations

Academic Instruction

9 Adapting Academic Instruction:
   Strategies for Meeting Special Needs   **255**

Social and Emotional Learning

Sensory–Physical Needs and Learning

15   **Making Environmental Accommodations and Using Assistive Technology:** *Tools That Extend Human Capacity and Promote Learning*   **447**

PART THREE: Leading Change

16 Teacher Leadership for Innovation and Change toward Inclusive Schooling:
Creating the Schools All Children Need

 *Special Features*

 *Voices*

Our Collaborative Journey

In this book we call you to join a traveling company on a journey toward becoming an *inclusive teacher*: a teacher who intentionally seeks to build a learning community composed of children of diverse abilities. Our goal is to move beyond "inclusion" to *inclusive teaching*—to help you learn how to teach in such a way that all your students, including children with mild through severe disabilities, children who are gifted, and children from diverse cultural and ethnic groups, *learn together well*. Being an inclusive teacher means genuinely understanding and committing yourself to building heterogeneous learning communities. We use the metaphor of a journey because it fits the experience of many people who have helped to develop inclusive schools and have become inclusive teachers. Few of us had experiences in inclusive schools growing up, so learning about inclusive teaching truly *is* a journey.

We also take a new approach to the way we think about teaching children with differences. Rather than accepting the way schools are as a given and "including" such students as we can, we seek to design our teaching and schools—from the beginning—so that all children learn well together, are challenged at their own levels of ability, and receive the support they need within a community of learners to which they know they belong. We call this *designing for diversity*. We will find that inclusive teaching improves learning and growth not only for students with special needs but for *all* students. By the end of our quest together, we think you will find that this perspective makes a great deal of sense—and that you may never think about teaching in the same way again.

Much of the information we share in *Inclusive Teaching* derives from our own action research experiences in schools and from our reading of the experience of others, including many teachers, parents, and children themselves. We have particularly drawn from an intensive qualitative study of fifteen inclusive schools that was conducted through the Whole Schooling Research Project, a three-year study funded by the U.S. Department of Education that explored inclusive teaching on a daily basis (Peterson, Tamor, Feen, & Silagy, 2002). Our understandings have been further

---

Beyond "Inclusion" to Inclusive Teaching

The unique purpose of this book is captured in the following question, which we hope you will carefully ponder:

How can we teach so that children with dramatically different academic, social–emotional, and sensory–physical abilities learn well together?

This is what being an *inclusive teacher* and creating an *inclusive school* is all about.

deepened as we have worked to connect schools in urban, suburban, and rural areas to promote effective learning for all students as part of the Whole Schooling Consortium (see **www.coe.wayne.edu/CommunityBuilding/WSC.html**).

Organization of the Book

As we begin Part I, "Inclusive Schools and Community," we seek to understand historical movements in school and community—from exclusion and segregation toward inclusion and support (Chapter 1). We then are challenged to envision the type of school for which we would hope; in Chapter 2 we visit classes and outline a holistic image of inclusive classrooms and schools, the concepts on which they are founded, and the research that supports them. In Chapter 3 we explore the partnerships with parents and community resources that are essential to an inclusive school. Chapter 4 discusses planning overall instruction and special accommodations and supports for students with special needs; Chapter 5 examines the roles of effective support and collaboration.

Part II, "Inclusive Teaching," opens with a foundational chapter on key instructional strategies for inclusive teaching—what we call the *four building blocks* (Chapter 6). We then head into the substance of inclusive teaching: academic instruction, social and emotional learning, and sensory–physical needs and learning. In Chapter 7 we discuss students with differing academic abilities; in Chapter 8 we discuss exemplary academic instruction that allows students to learn at their own levels of ability without being separated into ability groups; Chapter 9 explains adaptations for academic learning. Chapter 10 examines students who present behavioral and social challenges; Chapter 11 discusses community and social supports as a way to prevent social and emotional problems and describes a community of learners in a classroom and school; Chapter 12 presents proactive approaches to teaching students with behavioral challenges. Chapter 13 covers students who have differing physical and sensory abilities; in Chapter 14 we explore concepts, strategies, and resources that can help us design our class so it naturally attends to the differing sensory and physical needs of children; Chapter 15 presents a wide range of accommodations and assistive technologies for extending the sensory and physical capacities of students with disabilities.

Finally, Part III, "Leading Change," addresses our leadership as teachers. As Chapter 16 argues, to create inclusive schools, to be an inclusive teacher, we cannot wait for others to tell us what to do but must seek allies and create positive change. In many ways, in fact, this call for action is a theme for the entire book.

Chapter Features

Each chapter includes a mix of (1) theory and research; (2) concrete stories that help you visualize and feel the emotional impacts of issues and approaches; and (3) practice—applied strategies that can be used in the classroom. Each chapter also seeks to paint a picture of the sometimes painful realities we see in schools, realities that often sharply contrast with best practices. Our hope is that the mix of vision, theory, research, story, and practice will help you learn at a deeper level, to understand the why and how, and ultimately to link emotional and cognitive intuition with systematic, practical action. Each chapter contains some or all of the following special features:

- *Traveling Notes:* Reflective questions that appear early in each chapter to help you think deeply about the information and issues
- *Voices:* Accounts from teachers, parents, and students in their own words
- *Tools for the Trek:* Specific strategies and teaching approaches that can be used in the classroom
- *Schools to Visit:* Brief profiles of real schools—with contact information provided—that are seeking to include all children in learning together
- *Stepping Stones:* Practical strategies for promoting schoolwide acceptance and enthusiasm for inclusion
- *Learning Expeditions:* Ideas for activities to extend your understanding
- *Cartoons* by Michael Giangreco that bring humor and truth to our theme
- *Pencil drawings* by Martha Perske that wonderfully illustrate inclusion. We are grateful to Martha for these pieces, which convey so gracefully the reality and the spirit of inclusive teaching.

Supplements for Students and Teachers

Instructor's Manual/Test Bank. Written by Michael Peterson, the Instructor's Manual includes a wealth of interesting ideas and activities designed to help instructors teach the course. For each chapter in the text, the Instructor's Manual provides: goals and objectives; a variety of classroom discussion topics and activities; student assignments and classroom handouts; case studies; and video and Internet resources. The Test Bank contains hundreds of challenging questions in multiple choice, true/false, and essay formats along with an answer key.

Computerized Test Bank. The printed Test Bank is also available electronically through our computerized testing system, TestGen EQ. You can use TestGen EQ to create professional-looking exams in just minutes by selecting from the existing database of questions, editing questions, or writing your own.

PowerPoint Presentation. Ideal for lecture presentations or student handouts, the PowerPoint presentation created for this text provides dozens of ready-to-use graphic and text images (available on the Web at **www.ablongman.com/ppt**).

Companion Website. Students who visit the Student Learning Center of the Companion Website that accompanies the text (**www.ablongman.com/petersoninclusive**) will find many exciting features and activities to help them in their studies. Students can take part in online discussion events and chat rooms; read fascinating stories from inclusive teachers around the country; access exclusive video footage of the classroom;

expand their knowledge through Web links and learning activities; and test their knowledge using challenging practice tests for each chapter of the text. The website will also have regular online forums chaired by the authors, teachers, parents, and recognized leaders where instructors and students can dialogue about inclusive teaching.

The Companion Website also includes a Faculty Resource Center that has many teaching resources for faculty: downloadable files that include syllabi, student class projects, examples of student work, chapter-by-chapter in-class learning activities, and key Internet links.

VideoWorkshop for Special Education CD-ROM. Available as a "value package" item with the *Inclusive Teaching* text, this multimedia student supplement is a CD-ROM packed with specially selected digitized video clips of children with disabilities and their teachers, accompanied by an accompanying Student Study Guide. The Study Guide contains all the materials needed to help students get started and features before, during, and after viewing activities. An Instructor's Teaching Guide is also available to provide ideas and exercises to assist faculty in incorporating this convenient supplement into course assignments and assessments. (Go to **www.ablongman.com/videoworkshop** for more details).

Professionals in Action Videotape: Teaching Students with Special Needs (© 2000, 120 min. in length). This *Professionals in Action* video consists of five 15–30 minute modules presenting viewpoints and approaches to teaching students with various disabilities, in general education classrooms, separate education settings, and various combinations of the two. Each module explores its topic via actual classroom footage, and interviews with general and special education teachers, parents, and students themselves. The five modules are:

1. Working Together: The Individualized Education Program (IEP)
2. Working Together: The Collaborative Process
3. Instruction and Behavior Management
4. Technology for Inclusion
5. Working with Parents and Families

The "Snapshots" Video Series for Special Education

Snapshots: Inclusion Video (© 1995, 22 minutes in length) profiles three students of differing age levels and with various levels of disability in inclusive class settings. In each case, parents, classroom teachers, special education teachers, and school administrators talk about the steps they have taken to help Josh, Eric, and Tonya succeed in inclusive settings.

Snapshots 2: Video for Special Education (categorical organization) (© 1995, 20–25 minutes in length) is a two-video set of six segments designed specifically for use in the college classroom. Each segment profiles three individuals, their families, teachers, and experiences. You'll find these programs to be of high interest to your students; instructors who have used the tapes in their courses have found that they help in disabusing students of stereotypical viewpoints, and put a "human face" on course material. The topics explored are:

- behavior disorders*
- learning disabilities*
- mental retardation*
- traumatic brain injury
- hearing impairment
- visual impairment

Allyn & Bacon Transparencies for Special Education 2002. This package includes 100 full-color acetates.

Digital Media Archive for Special Education. This CD-ROM for Windows and Macintosh contains a variety of media elements that you can use to create electronic presentations in the classroom. It includes hundreds of original images, as well as selected art from Allyn and Bacon special education texts, providing instructors with a broad selection of graphs, charts, and tables. For classrooms with full multimedia capability, it also contains video segments and Web links.

About the Authors

For us, writing this book has also been a journey. We are a father–daughter, university professor–teacher team.

Michael Peterson is a professor in the College of Education at Wayne State University in Detroit, where he has taught courses in inclusive education since 1994; before this he directed the Developmental Disabilities Institute. He has more than thirty years of experience working with children and adults with disabilities and teachers and service providers. In 1997 Michael and colleagues organized the Whole Schooling Consortium, a school renewal network based on a framework in which inclusive education is a central component. The Whole Schooling Consortium works with schools in urban, suburban, and rural settings.

Mishael Hittie began her teaching career in 1997 as a support teacher in an inclusive school. She has taught third and fourth grade, looping with her children, and a grade 3–5 multiage class. In her classes she's had children with mental retardation, children with learning disabilities, highly gifted children, children of different ethnic groups, and children from low- and high-income backgrounds all learning together. She participated in the Whole Schooling Research Project, in which the researchers studied her school and classroom to understand and document effective inclusive teaching practices.

We've been excited about our own journey—about learning, writing, thinking, and exploring together. Our goal is to share our discoveries with you and to help prepare you for your own trek of development and growth. We hope you find the path enjoyable, rewarding, and valuable as you seek to be an effective teacher of highly diverse children learning *together*.

*this segment available with closed captioning for individuals with hearing loss

Acknowledgments

Michael: I would like to thank the first teachers who taught me about inclusive community, my parents J. W. and Juanita Peterson. Together they have modeled inclusion, support, and care. My wife Georgie taught me about good teaching as she taught our children and about community as we built a family. My son Shawn has helped me understand the importance of critical reflection, perseverance, and caring relationships. Joyful has been the opportunity to learn with and from my colleague and daughter Mishael, who has become a passionate leader toward inclusive teaching.

Mishael: I would like to thank my parents for their demonstration of how to live in and create inclusive communities wherever they go. My mother Georgie taught me how to love with my whole heart and soul and that learning is a joyous part of daily life, not confined to school. I get my love of learning and reading from her. My father Michael taught me to persevere and to always strive to improve. From him I get my passion for teaching. He has become a friend and confidant who has challenged me in my teaching.

My husband, Todd, has been supportive and loving throughout countless dinners discussing teaching and writing. I love him for his loving patience, willingness to give of his time, and ideas for making learning interesting. He knows more about teaching than he realizes. Shawn Peterson, my brother, and long-time friends Jim Ford and Sarah Melamed have always been there for me. Dana Gress, my church choir director and a teacher himself, and Vivienne Collinson and Jim Gallagher of Michigan State University have helped me learn.

The children in my classes have influenced me the most. They taught me to make learning fun, to leave my comfort zone, to encourage them to think and grow, to give of myself, and to always keep their best interests in mind. They have touched my heart, and the lessons I have learned from them grace this book in many ways.

We both have many colleagues who have influenced and supported us in learning about inclusive teaching. These include:

- Members of the Whole Schooling Consortium: Rich Gibson, Greg Queen, Katy Landless, Stacey Lindsey, Amber Goslee, Bill Boyer, and many more.
- Wonderful educators and parents we've come to know online: teachers in Fresno, California; Sigamoney Naicker, Director of Inclusive Education in South Africa; and Jen Snape, parent of a child with a severe disability in Australia.
- Colleagues at Wayne State University: Gerry Oglan, Marshall Zumberg, Mark Larson, Karen Feathers, Kathi Tarrant-Parks, Assistant Dean Sharon Elliot, and Dean Paula Wood.
- Administrators: Jan Colliton, Assistant Superintendent of the Farmington Public Schools; Terry Patterson, former Principal of MacArthur Elementary; Barbara Mick, Principal of Ausable Primary; Carla Harting, Special Education Director of Wyandotte Public Schools; and Carloz Lopez, Detroit Public Schools.
- Teachers: Nancy Creech, Tanya Sharon, Sandy Widmer, Melissa Silagy, Jim Anderson, Deb Badrak, Dodie Harris, Sue Huellmantel, Halina Leary, Maureen Girty-Andrews, Brenda Vaughn, Tricia Coger, Sasha Roberts-Levi, Jon Chisek, Holly Koscielniak, Denise White, Vitas Underys, Chris Horrocks, and Nancy Barth.
- Parents of children with disabilities: Bev Crider, Orah Raia, Janice Fialka, and Lynne Tamor, an amazing parent, professional, friend, and colleague who was first an educator then a parent seeking inclusive education for her son, Isaac.

Over the years we have learned from and been inspired and challenged by many people who've led the way in working to include all children in effective schools and communities: Kim Beloin, Doug Fisher, Bill Henderson, Cheryl Jorgensen, Norm Kunc, Barbara LeRoy, Diane Ryndak, Jacqueline Thousand, and Rich Villa. We particularly honor the memory of Marsha Forrest, an international heroine and model extraordinaire of inclusion, courage, and care, and her amazing circle of friends that included Jack Pearpoint, Shafik Asante, John O'Brien, John McKnight, and Judith Snow.

We would like to thank this book's reviewers:

Robin S. Barton, Armstrong Atlantic State University

Mitchell Beck, Central Connecticut State University

Cora Coulter Bolden, Miami University

Peggy B. Gill, Stephen F. Austin State University

Christine Givner, California State University, Los Angeles

Martha Jane Harris, Texas A&M University–Texarkana

Delores D. Liston, Georgia Southern
    University
Ruth Marsh-Thomson, Edinboro
    University of Pennsylvania
Darcy Miller, Washington State
    University
Chris Ormsbee, Oklahoma
    University
Ernest L. Pancsofar, Central
    Connecticut State University
Carol Melvin Pate, Chestnut Hill
    College

Philip Patterson, California State
    University, Dominguez Hills
Melinda Rice, Elon University
Tara Stevens, University of Illinois,
    Springfield
Teresa A. Taber, Purdue University
Phillip Waldrop, Middle Tennessee
    State University
Helen J. Wyatt, Alcorn State
    University.

Finally, we owe a great debt to our editors and staff in developing this book.
Virginia Lanigan, Executive Editor, and Alicia Reilly, Developmental Editor, assisted
by Erin Liedel and Robert Champagne, worked long and hard helping us to shape,
deepen, clarify, and strengthen our message. We've learned much from them and
appreciate the sensitivity and competence of their work.

CHAPTER GOAL

Understand how inclusive teaching relates to the ongoing social struggle to develop communities in which difference is valued and celebrated.

CHAPTER OBJECTIVES

1. Understand how communities respond to people who are different in terms of ethnicity, culture, socioeconomic status, sexual orientation, or ability.

2. Explore the functions of labels for people with disabilities.

3. Understand the treatment of people with disabilities and the movement from segregation to inclusion and community.

4. Describe laws related to the education and the rights of individuals with disabilities.

5. Trace the growing movement toward inclusive education in the United States and the world.

People with Disabilities in School and Society

Welcome

We welcome you on a quest to improve schooling and learning for *all* children through inclusive teaching. We begin in this chapter with the question: "How does society deal with people considered 'different,' particularly people with disabilities?" We will explore the gradual shifts in treatment of children and adults with disabilities and will explore similarities to the way in which people with other differences are addressed—people who are different in terms of race/ethnicity, gender, culture, language, sexual orientation, or socioeconomic status.

To start, we ask you to close your eyes and picture inclusive teaching with us. Can you imagine teaching in a school where students with dramatically different academic, social–emotional, and sensory–physical abilities learn well together? Can you imagine classrooms where children who are gifted learn with children who have severe mental retardation; where no student leaves to get special help and support teachers come into the class; where students are not grouped by ability; where children work at their own levels of ability, no longer bound by a one-size-fits-all curriculum? Can you picture a school where children with behavioral challenges are rarely medicated and the school community is so strong that no one would think of sending a child to a segregated program because of emotional problems? A school in which students with severe physical disabilities, returned from a segregated center school, have become an integral part of the school community and made friends? Can you imagine a school where children are evaluated by how much each one has progressed?

Such schools are not imaginary. In schools all over the world, inclusive teachers are creating a quiet revolution, discovering new energy and excitement as they learn how to teach very different children well together. Teachers *can make a difference*. We have important choices. We do have the power to create classrooms where difference is celebrated, embraced, and valued. We can intentionally seek to become inclusive teachers.

So let's begin. As we travel, we encourage you to think deeply, take notes, seek colleagues who will support you and with whom you can talk. We are off.

𝒫ictures in Time: Shifting Possibilities

It is late August of 1950 in a small Texas town populated largely by immigrant farm workers from Mexico. The heat is sweltering as Juanita Garcia walks to enroll her son Lorenzo in school. Young Juanita has worried about Lorenzo ever since his birth. Her doctor says he has cerebral palsy and mental retardation.

Together they walk down the hall to the office of the principal, Mr. Foster. "Come in, Mrs. Garcia," he says briskly. "What can I do for you today?" "I have come to enter Lorenzo in school," she says, looking down in respect, wishing her husband Juan were here. Mr. Foster shifts uncomfortably. Clearing his throat, he says cautiously but firmly, "I am sorry. I thought you knew that children like Lorenzo do not come to school. He should go to the institution in the city. I am surprised your doctor did not tell you." Juanita is stunned. Indeed, the doctor did tell her, but her family felt that her child belonged with them, not in a large segregated place for people with disabilities. She leaves dismayed.

> Jeffrey Regan became the first person with Down syndrome to graduate with a regular high school diploma from Kempsville High School in Virginia in June 1999.

Lorenzo grew up without a day of schooling. Each morning he watched the children get on the school bus. As a young adult, he learned to read, write, and talk, although he still walked awkwardly and had speech difficulties. He liked reading about sports and enrolled in an adult education program. He wanted to get his G.E.D.

We fast-forward to Sunday, June 20, 1999. Jeffrey Regan is graduating from Kempsville High School. Jeffrey is the first person with Down syndrome to receive a regular diploma in his school, part of a national trend. Elizabeth Simpson of the *Virginian Pilot* talks with Jeffrey.

"I had to work really, really hard," Jeffrey says, shoveling in bites of mashed potatoes. "All kinds of study, homework, tests, back to back." He shakes his head. . . .
"Your teachers say you're very conscientious. That
true?" He puts his fork down, pushes his hands in
two directions, Egyptian-style, one at head level,
one at his waist. "That's me!" (Simpson, 1999,
p. E1)

Indeed, Jeffrey did work hard. He attended summer
school and did homework every night for two hours. He
was school basketball team manager, "drawing applause from the crowd by taking a jog around the court
after collecting balls."

At the Virginia Beach Pavilion, he stands amid a sea
of blue graduation robes and straightens his tassel
as he waits to walk in. . . . The moment arrives—
"Jeffrey Thomas Regan"—and he strides across the
stage to applause . . . that's as thunderous as any
valedictorian or class president will receive. (Simpson, 1999, p. E1)

At home
Jeffrey relaxes
playing pool.

After finishing high school Jeffrey planned to attend classes in a technical program at
Old Dominion University and to live in an apartment with his friend Ian (Simpson,
1999, p. E1).

Much and little has changed in the education of students with disabilities, as these
two stories suggest. Segregation is still a common practice. At a growing number of
schools, however, students with disabilities and other differences are learning well
together.

Lorenzo and Jeffrey's stories illustrate a dramatic change in schools and a struggle to open education to people with disabilities. The stories also illustrate the substantial difference that socioeconomic status can make, for students who are
members of minority groups or have parents of low socioeconomic status are still
most likely to be educated in segregated classrooms. Yet the stories also show the
potential for a new vision. How much has changed? How might we move toward a
society in which more people have Jeffrey's experience?

Dealing with Difference
The Opportunity to Build Community

If we seek to be inclusive teachers, our ultimate goal is to help create a society in
which people with ethnic, cultural, linguistic, sexual, gender, and socioeconomic
differences value, support, and care about one another. The community would focus

on the strengths and gifts of each person, valuing people with differences as human beings.

Across the world we see a picture of this type of **inclusive community** emerging. People with disabilities and their allies are at the forefront in this movement. Children with disabilities who previously attended only separate classes are being welcomed into schools. Young people are becoming friends with people with disabilities (Amado, 1993). Individuals with significant disabilities who once lived in institutions are living in their own homes and apartments; participating in civic activities; being welcomed by churches, temples, and synagogues into religious life (Nisbet, 1992). Recreation departments in local cities are including people with significant disabilities in regular programs, moving beyond separate "handicapped swimming" classes. Employers are hiring individuals with disabilities and finding that they make good employees (Hagner & Dileo, 1993). Communities are becoming stronger in the process (Peterson, 1996).

However, it remains true that societies have difficulty dealing with those seen as different—with what sociologists call "the other" (Grabb, 1997). Norm Kunc (2000), a person who has cerebral palsy and is an international spokesperson for disability civil rights and social justice, identified four "stages" of responses to people with differences, each a step from barbarism to humanity (Figure 1.1). This four-stage framework helps us think about how people with differences are treated. Although people from specific groups face specific difficulties, all groups considered "different" are treated in many similar ways and have related issues.

Extermination

The most extreme approach, of course, is to simply kill those considered different, or to cause such people not to be born at all. In early Rome, children with disabilities were left exposed to die (Kroll & Bachrach, 1986; Piers, 1978); in Germany in the 1940s, people with disabilities were the first sent to extermination camps (Disability Rights Advocates, 1999). In the early twentieth century in the United States, states passed laws to sterilize people with disabilities to reduce numbers of undesirable individuals (Brantlinger, 1995). The issue lives on through assisted suicide, the use of "do not resuscitate" (DNR) orders for children with significant disabilities, and genetic engineering practices that augur a growing devaluation of lives deemed imperfect. Can you think of other examples showing that views of the value of people with disabilities actually affect their chances of survival?

Segregation

As societies decide that extermination of people with differences is inhumane, they typically develop segregated places for such people apart from the mainstream. As in the townships of South Africa or on the numerous reservations for Native Americans, entire geographical regions have sometimes been set apart. In the deep South, segregation of black and white people was enforced through separate water fountains, schools, places to sit, stores, and churches. For people with disabilities a host of separate places exist—segregated schools, classrooms, workplaces, and living places (Heal, Haney, & Amado, 1988).

Figure 1.1

Four Key Stages in Human Responses to Others Perceived as Different	
RESPONSES TO PEOPLE CONSIDERED DIFFERENT	**RATIONALE AND EXPLANATIONS FOR THESE RESPONSES**
Stage 1: Extermination People who are different are killed—by banishment, exposure, direct slaughter.	*To protect society.* People who are different are considered a threat or menace, often not viewed as human.
Stage 2: Segregation People who are different are segregated into "special places"—ghettos, inner cities, segregated schools, homes for aged.	*To protect society.* People are isolated and segregated for the express and overt purpose of protecting the larger society from their harmful influence. *To protect special people and allow them to be with "their own kind."* People are isolated to protect them from harm in the larger society and to allow them the comfort of being with "their own kind." *To provide specially designed, professional services based on the unique needs of a group.* People are isolated so that they can be in specially designed places served by a professional trained in meeting the unique needs of this group of people.
Stage 3: Benevolence People who are different are accepted into the community to be helped by their "betters," to receive charity and assistance.	*To provide special help to people who can't function.* People are not considered to be capable of being real friends or to have skills or gifts to offer the community. Those providing the help have the opportunity to feel they are caring while at the same time having a position of power or superiority.
Stage 4: Community People who are different are accepted as members of the community with the capacity to contribute as well as to receive.	*To benefit everyone; everyone has a gift, and the community is less when such gifts are not recognized.* All in the community are recognized as having differences. Each difference contributes to the total, and all people are needed to make a strong community.

What is the rationale for segregation? One goal has been to protect the larger community from unwanted influences. Thus the Jewish ghettos in Europe (Prager & Telushkin, 1983), racial segregation in the United States in the 1800s and 1900s (Hacker, 1992), and the growth of institutions for persons with disabilities in the early twentieth century (Katz, 1985).

More recently, advocates of segregation argue that it is in the best interest of those being segregated, who need to be with others like themselves (Hacker, 1993; Orfield, 2001; National Law Center on Homelessness and Poverty, 2000). Some groups themselves argue for separation, often as a result of forced segregation. Examples include some groups among the deaf community (Cogswell, 1984; Sacks, 1989) and some African Americans, who state that racial integration is not realistic and call for business, culture, and community by and for black people (Hacker, 1992; West, 1993).

Finally, some say people with differences need segregated environments specifically designed for them: environments in which they can receive services from trained professionals (Katz, 1986). In this viewpoint, a special education classroom, residential facility, or vocational training program can more efficiently offer help in one location (Adams, Swain, & Clark, 2000; Kavale, 1990; Lance, 1976). In the 1970s, many states built schools for students with moderate to severe disabilities that featured swimming pools, accessible classrooms, and other specially designed services (Taylor & Searl, 1987). Proponents also argue that specialists are needed for second-language learners and for students who are gifted and talented.

Clearly, segregating individuals with differences because they are seen as inferior or evil is very different from segregating them in order to meet their needs. Many well-meaning, concerned people have established separate places for such individuals to learn, work, and live, often because other options were not clear.

For many, however, the issue of segregation is about values. Segregation presents questions regarding civil and human rights and the type of community in which we wish to live—one that separates people by characteristics of color, ethnicity, socioeconomic status, gender, sexual orientation, and ability, or one in which difference and diversity are valued.

Have you experienced segregation in your own life? How were you affected? Do you see segregation in your community? What do you think is the impact of segregation on children?

Benevolence

Benevolence occurs when people are tolerated but not considered as equals; treated patronizingly; seen as lower in ability, status, and prestige. When people act benevolently, they are not cruel or rejecting. Rather, they seek to help. In so doing, however, the recipients of benevolence may become charity cases, people to pity; the recipients are not considered as potential partners or friends, do not share power, and are often not considered as contributing members. Benevolence thus can become another method of exclusion, a way of preventing real human interaction (Adam, 1978). Benevolence occurs, for example, when a teacher assigns students to help a classmate with a disability but never allows that classmate also to help others, or when a wealthy community donates goods to a low-income community but does not enter into relationships and partnerships. Adam (1978) and Grabb (1997) found that benevolence often allows helpers to maintain a sense of self-esteem by seeming to confirm that they are "at least better than this person."

Donald uses a wheelchair and can neither talk nor use his hands effectively. It's not clear how smart Donald is, though he sometimes seems to understand much. His eyes are alive and his laughter and enjoyment make others want to be around him. Some students in Donald's seventh-grade biology class have attended school with him since kindergarten. Visiting Clover Middle School, we assumed that Donald and other students spent time together outside school. "I like Donald a lot," said Jeremy as he put his hand on Donald's wheelchair. "I help him in class." "So what do you do together on the weekend?" we asked. Jeremy looked confused, and it became clear he had never asked Donald over. Later that year we talked with Donald and his class about their experience in building a community. They were enthusiastic, and we were happy to hear that Donald had begun to be involved socially with his fellow students. Was this friendship or benevolence? We weren't sure.

Think about how benevolence can be hurtful, even with good intentions. How might this occur in a classroom? How do we teach children the difference between benevolence and friendship?

Traveling Notes

As we begin each chapter, we will visit teachers, students, and parents and be part of their story. These stories will embody many issues. We'll be asking questions in our traveling notes to help prompt thinking, helping you notice important details along the path. Lorenzo and Jeffrey's stories illustrate the trend away from exclusion and segregation of students with disabilities and toward inclusion and community. This chapter explores how individuals with disabilities have fared in this country over the last two centuries and surveys the growing movement toward inclusive communities and schools. As we travel, think about the following questions:

1. What has changed over time? How much?

2. In what ways are individuals with disabilities segregated? Why?

3. What is the relationship of segregation by race/ethnicity, gender, culture, language, sexual orientation, socioeconomic status, and ability?

4. What does all this mean for teachers?

Toward Community

Judith Snow's story powerfully illustrates the interplay of the various approaches to people with differences. Judith lives in Toronto. Some describe her as a deep philosopher on the meaning of life. She travels throughout the world with colleagues, helping people struggle to overcome differences that separate human beings. She lives in a cooperative living apartment and has been particularly

Artwork reprinted by permission of Martha Perske from *Perske: Pencil Portraits 1971–1990* (Nashville: Abingdon Press, 1998).

JUDITH SNOW AND HER CIRCLE OF SUPPORT

helpful in describing how circles of friends assist vulnerable people and how all participants grow stronger in the process.

Judith also has a **severe disability:** She gets around in a wheelchair, which she directs with a "puff and sip" switch. She relies on paid assistants to bathe, dress, and move; she has very limited capacity to move her arms and hands, and she cannot walk.

Judith's life shows what is possible when inclusion, community, care, and a willingness to challenge come together. In downtown Toronto in 1995, a hundred people paid tribute to Judith's parents. Her dad, a World War II veteran, spoke with deep emotion of Judith's childhood, describing how she attended a typical school (unheard of at the time) and how he and Judith's mother strove to nurture, challenge, and support Judith.

All that did not stop Judith from almost dying. In her twenties she moved out of her parents' house to go to college, but she had to live in a nursing home to receive needed support services. She went to school and engaged in disability advocacy work during the day and returned to the nursing home at night. The care was poor, however, and Judith's health began to deteriorate. One day in 1976 there was a crisis. Her friends concluded that if something were not done, Judith would die. What could they do?

Quickly pulling together a support group she dubbed the Joshua Committee, after Joshua in the Bible who led the Israelites around the city of Jericho to conquer it, Judith's friends convened to address a complex question: "How can Judith have the life she wants?" Judith slept exhausted in bed as they met. Ultimately, Judith's circle convinced authorities to provide individualized funding to hire people to support her in her own apartment. Since then many people in Ontario and the United States have begun receiving such supports. Judith was the first.

Judith's circle continues to meet to support her and to enjoy one another's company. Judith's circle has influenced many people, particularly the late Marsha Forest, a dynamic individual who was a remarkable champion of inclusion for all. It was Marsha who made famous the sayings that "together we are better," "inclusion means *with,* not just *in,*" and "the only requirement for inclusion is breathing." (See **www.inclusion.com/C-Marsha.Forest.Centre.html**.)

Judith's story illustrates how segregation and benevolence can even threaten existence, and how the power of community can make a dramatic difference. While not everyone will be known by people as a leader and philosopher, the lessons of Judith's story repeat themselves over and over: When people are supported in being part of the community, all benefit. We'll learn this lesson as inclusive teachers.

What Do We Call People with Disabilities and Why?
Labels and Their Uses

A particularly important issue for children and adults with disabilities is the way we label and categorize groups of people. In the nineteenth and twentieth centuries, psychologists developed methods to identify, test, and categorize people—a process fraught with controversy, as labels often have lifelong consequences. Different approaches to categorizing disabilities include those based on etiology, the part of the body affected, or the functional impact. The categories from the Individuals with Disabilities Education Act (IDEA), which we will discuss in detail in later chapters, are as follows:

- Specific learning disability (Chapter 7)
- Speech or language impairment (Chapter 13)
- Mental retardation (Chapter 7)
- Emotional disturbance (Chapter 10)
- Multiple disabilities (Chapter 13)
- Hearing impairment (Chapter 13)

- Orthopedic impairment (Chapter 13)
- Other health impairment (Chapter 13)
- Visual impairment (Chapter 13)
- Autism (Chapter 10)
- Deaf-blindness (Chapter 13)
- Traumatic brain injury (Chapter 7)

Impairment, Disability, and Handicap

According to the World Health Organization (WHO), understanding the differences among the words *impairment, disability*, and *handicap* is important (Wood, 1981). An **impairment** is a physical, cognitive, or psychological abnormality—such as Down syndrome, a defective limb, or brain damage. A **disability** describes the functional impact of an impairment in performance of human activities—such as difficulty in walking, speaking, or doing math. A **handicap** is a problem resulting from difficulties in performing a social role—such as work, parenting, or friendship.

Michael Oliver (1990), a sociologist with a disability, suggests that these distinctions focus exclusively on the individual with the disability and do not adequately consider the interaction of the person with the community. During the twentieth century many conditions became "medicalized": physicians began taking the lead role in diagnosis and treatment, accompanied by a growing array of specialists—offering, for example, special education, rehabilitation, occupational therapy, and physical therapy. With this therapeutic focus on individual impairment, the first question is often "What specialist does this person need to see?" rather than "How can we include this person in our community?"

The medical model seeks to diagnose problematic conditions that are directly connected to treatment strategies; as such, the model has influenced special education dramatically. Following this model, many disciplines seek to identify deficits and treatments to address them. Unfortunately, only deficits may be seen. The strengths, capacities, and gifts of people with disabilities may not be recognized, and community capacity to include, support, and value people may not be addressed. As a result, this focus on deficits has tended to be correlated with segregated education and human services (McKnight, 1995; Oliver, 1990; Schwartz, 1992).

An *ecological perspective*, in contrast, sees human development as a function of the interaction of the person and the environment (see Chapters 3 and 9 for more discussion on this), and disability becomes a community rather than only an individual issue (Amado, 1993; Bradky, 1994; Bronfenbrenner, 1979; Oliver, 1990). In schools, rather than focusing only on problems of individual children, an ecological perspective asks: "How can our classroom community include and support all children? How can individuals with disabilities contribute to our classroom?" (Goleman, 1995; Kohn, 1996; Peterson, 1992).

The Functions of Disability Labels

What are the functions of disability labels? Answers vary. From a professional perspective, labels describe conditions that call for specific treatment and indicate

THE MOST APPROPRIATE LABEL IS
USUALLY THE ONE PEOPLE'S PARENTS
HAVE GIVEN THEM.

eligibility for services. In this view, labeling is a necessary step toward obtaining help. Over time, the number of conditions, diagnoses, and professional services has expanded dramatically. Some see this as scientific progress.

Other individuals, however, have a more critical view. McKnight (1995) and others (Braithwaite & Thompson, 2000; Oliver, 1990; Susman, 1994) see labels as a way of expanding the influence of specialized human services. Sociologists studying the stigmatizing impact of disability labels find that communities often separate those perceived as deviating from the norm; difference is negatively valued, so labeling facilitates setting apart the "other" (Braithwaite & Thompson, 2000; Oliver, 1990; Susman, 1994).

Alternative methods for establishing service eligibility have been developed. For example, the Center for Special Education Finance (Parrish, 1993) has recommended that funding for special education be based on the number of children in a school system and the degree of poverty in the community. Florida has established eligibility based on functional assessment of needs and on the type and intensity of services required, departing from a traditional system based on disability labels. Relatedly, a growing number of parents are refusing to have their children tested and labeled with categories such as "mental retardation," believing that such processes yield no useful information and focus only on their children's deficits (Ninness, McCuller, & Ozenne, 2000). Conversely, other parents seek diagnoses for children to establish eligibility. Diagnosis and labeling presently represent a double-edged sword for those seeking to build inclusive schools (Ninness, McCuller, & Ozenne, 2000).

Finally, labels play an everyday role in relationships with people with disabilities. People with disabilities and their allies have championed the use of *people-first language*. Rather than calling people by their disability (e.g., "the handicapped," "the blind," or more disparagingly, "retards"), we recognize people with disabilities are people first and use language that expresses this. So we discuss a person with mental retardation or cerebral palsy, a friend who is blind, a singer who is deaf. We avoid language that implies that disability, in itself, connotes a lower form of humanity. For example, rather than saying a person is "confined to a wheelchair," we say this person "uses a wheelchair." The point here is to realize that language is powerful: Language both expresses and shapes our thoughts.

From Institutions to Segregated Community-Based Programs
The First Step toward Community Participation

In this and the next section we will explore the unfolding story of people with disabilities in U.S. society, moving from segregation and benevolence toward community membership.

In 1978 Jim sat on the concrete steps of the factory where he worked and talked with Margaret, a social worker. Jim had lived his life in an institution for persons with mental retardation. Jim's parents had put him there when he was little, even though he was not classified as mentally retarded. "My parents were poor and I had epilepsy," Jim explained. Two years earlier he had moved out of the institution. He now worked in a sheltered workshop and lived in a group home. He had never even gone to school. Many people have been institutionalized because basic reasonable assistance in the community was not provided. Jim's story, like Lorenzo's at the beginning of this chapter, illustrates much about the history of people with disabilities in our country.

Institutions: From Reform to Abuse

In the earliest years of the United States, children and adults with disabilities often had accepted community roles, working on farms or at other menial tasks. By the beginning of the nineteenth century, however, as towns and cities grew with industrialization, people who could not care for themselves were put in poorhouses. These were residences where poor people worked for their keep—families with children, persons with mental illness, people with mental retardation, and older persons abandoned by their families (Katz, 1985; Taylor & Searl, 1987).

Beginning in the mid-nineteenth century, community reformers opposed poorhouses and proposed two solutions. First, they established specialized **institutions** for particular groups; second, they promoted the training of specialists. Many professional specializations, such as occupational and physical therapy, were established in institutions (Katz, 1985).

Dorothea Dix, a social crusader in New England, became particularly concerned regarding people with mental illness. She conducted investigations in twenty states and championed the establishment of asylums to provide care, support, and training (Brown, 1998). Similar programs were established for persons with mental retardation, adolescents, and young children with sensory and physical impairments. Although Dix and her fellow reformers hoped that vocational training would allow people to become functioning members of society, the goals of training were nevertheless quite limited—often involving skills such as beadwork and broom making (Blum, 1968; Katz, 1985).

Gradually, many residential institutions were built. By the early twentieth century asylums had changed dramatically—from small, family-oriented programs to huge edifices housing thousands of people. Their purposes shifted from training to custodial care and protection of the community from people viewed as menaces. This trend mushroomed as the *eugenics movement* in the early twentieth century sought to promote a "pure" genetic strain. Beginning in Indiana in 1907, seventeen states mandated involuntary sterilization of persons with disabilities in institutions (Katz, 1985; Rothman, 1990; Scotch, 1984; Shapiro, 1993). Eugenics was discredited and died as a major movement after the Nazis killed millions of people in World War II in an effort to establish a pure master race.

In the 1960s, reformers exposed shocking conditions in institutions. In 1966 Burton Blatt, accompanied by photographer Fred Kaplan with a hidden camera, toured back wards of institutions and published a pictorial exposé entitled, *Christmas in Purgatory.* This book graphically documented naked men and women herded in groups, standing in their own excrement (Blatt, 1966; Shapiro, 1993). In the 1970s, Geraldo Rivera aired a television series that exposed conditions at the Spofford facility in New York City. Similar exposés occurred in other states.

Out of the Institution

As abuses in institutions were exposed, the public was outraged. In seminal court cases in New York, Pennsylvania, Alabama, and Michigan, judges found that conditions violated constitutional protections of life, liberty, and the pursuit of happiness. Gradually, a controversial movement developed to move children and adults with disabilities out of institutions and into the community. Despite the fact that such programs often were still segregated, they provided the first move toward community membership. Courts required improvements in living conditions, qualified personnel, and services further establishing key legal principles:

1. *The right to treatment:* People's needs should be addressed through individual treatment plans.
2. *The right to services in the least restrictive environment:* People had a right to participation in the community and services in the most typical setting possible.
3. *The right to due process:* Formal procedures designed to protect individual rights must be adhered to.

These actions occurred at a time when the rights of many oppressed people were being addressed—the rights of members of minority groups, women, older people, gay individuals, and others. In this context a movement developed to deinstitution-alize people with mental retardation and mental illness. The Community Mental Health Facilities and Construction Act was passed in 1963 to assist states in developing community-based programs. Many people moved from institutions into group homes and worked in sheltered workshops, where they received training and minimal wages (Katz, 1985; Taylor & Searl, 1987).

Wolfensberger (1972) articulated an intellectual foundation for this movement through the concept of **normalization,** a highly influential philosophy throughout the world that promoted the opportunity for people with disabilities to live normal lives. In 1967 normalization principles were incorporated into Danish law (Winzer, 1993). From 1977 to 1992 the number of people living in institutions in the United States dropped from 149,681 to 77,618, with proportionate increases in community-based programs. In 1996 New Hampshire was the first state to complete the closing of its state institutions. Yet many people still live in institutions nationwide. The state of Mississippi, for example, has actually increased the number of people institutionalized in recent years (Braddock, Hemp, Fujiur, & Batchelder, 1995).

Parent Advocacy

Following World War II, parents of children with disabilities organized and greatly influenced policies and services. As parents struggled to prevent their children from being institutionalized, they developed numerous organizations through which to focus their efforts. These included the United Cerebral Palsy Association, the Muscular Dystrophy Association, and the Association for Retarded Children (now simply the ARC) (Sheereneberger, 1983; Taylor & Searl, 1987).

The central concern of most parents was education. In the mid-nineteenth century, complex circumstances had led to the creation of compulsory public education. These early public schools had little place for children who had obvious disabilities (Katz, 1995). Even in the late twentieth century, however, many children with disabilities stayed home and simply did not attend school. In community after community, parent groups established classes and schools, often held first in church basements and community centers, later supported by school districts. In 1966 Congress established a bureau to fund training of special education teachers and improvement projects for the education of children with disabilities. In 1973 Marian Wright Edelman, founder of the Children's Defense Fund, noted that some 750,000 children in the census were not attending public school. These were not the children of minority parents; most were children with disabilities from predominantly white communities (Shapiro, 1993) who had been turned away, as with Lorenzo, by schools. This information fueled a movement requiring that all children with disabilities receive a free public education. By 1975 parent groups were successful in mobilizing the passage of the Education for All Handicapped Children Act, a groundbreaking law (to be discussed shortly). Parent groups have continued to play a critical role in instigating amendments to this law as well as in local and state advocacy efforts for children with disabilities (Shapiro, 1993; Sheereneberger, 1983).

Segregated Schools and Classes:
They're in the Trailer behind the School

In 1954 the Supreme Court mandated racial desegregation in schools through *Brown v. Board of Education*. Following this Supreme Court ruling, increasing numbers of students from minority groups entered white middle-class schools, often based on desegregation plans. However, important events occurred to stall the movement toward racially integrated schools. In 1974 the Supreme Court overturned an earlier decision in *Milliken v. Bradley*, a case from Detroit that sought to desegregate schools across the entire metropolitan area, both the city of Detroit and its suburbs. This ruling and the subsequent desegregation of Detroit exacerbated white flight from the city to the suburbs throughout the United States (Kozol, 1991). In California advocates concerned about overrepresentation of children with language differences in special education, particularly Mexican and Chinese Americans, pursued precedent-setting litigation. As of 2001 racial segregation in schools throughout the United States was again increasing (Orfield, 2001).

Along with racial desegregation efforts, some public schools began to accept responsibility for the education of students with disabilities. Initially, classes for children with disabilities were in segregated schools or classes. Special schools were often separated from typical school buildings; in one community, for example, a special school was sited near the city dump and small industrial businesses on a street at the edge of town. In other situations, students were taught in trailer houses at the back of the school (Katz, 1985; Taylor & Searl, 1987).

The Growth of Special Education and the Education
for All Handicapped Children Act (PL 94-142)

During the 1960s, President John F. Kennedy, whose sister had mental retardation, brought national attention to the issue of mental retardation. Concerned advocacy groups pushed for the rights of citizens with disabilities and filed numerous lawsuits. The 1971 class action suit *Pennsylvania Association for Retarded Citizens (PARC) v. Commonwealth of Pennsylvania* established requirements for a **free and appropriate public education (FAPE)** for all children with mental retardation within the federal court jurisdiction. *Mills v. Board of Education of the District of Columbia* (1972) extended the right of education to all children with exceptional educational needs. These cases established legal precedents for movement toward inclusive education (Berres & Knoblock, 1987; Shapiro, 1993).

Public Law 94-142, the **Education for All Handicapped Children Act,** passed in 1975 and amended in later years, established rights, protections, and entitlements for students with disabilities. The act requires that students be educated in the **least restrictive environment (LRE)**—that is, with typical students to the greatest degree possible and appropriate—and that a **continuum of placement options** be available.

Following the passage of PL 94-142, two approaches were used for educating students with disabilities. For students with mild disabilities, the model of choice was (and still largely is) the **resource room,** a special education class where students went to obtain special help. Students who needed some assistance with reading, writing, math, or science left the general education classroom to obtain individualized help from a specially trained teacher who had a smaller number of students (Allington, 1991, 1994; Moody, Vaughn, & Hughes, 2000; Spear-Swerling & Sternberg, 1998). Students with moderate to severe disabilities were most often educated in separate schools or classes—an approach based on the assumption that the special needs of these students could not be met in a general education class.

By the 1980s, however, special education had grown dramatically into what some termed a second system. The combined resources offered by special education and other classes that pulled children out of the regular class almost equaled the resources available in the mainstream school (Allington, 1993). Researchers and educators began noting that students attending resource rooms lost valuable instructional time in the regular class, that teachers in resource rooms were seldom able to coordinate their activities with those of the general education class, and that special education students often were stigmatized (Allington, 1994; McIntosh, Vaughn, Schumm, Haager, & Lee, 1993; Moody, Vaughn, & Hughes, 2000; Vaughn, Moody, & Shumm, 1998). Also, children from certain minority groups were placed in special education programs at a rate disproportionate to their representation in the overall school population. For example, African American students make up 16 percent of the student population, but 21 percent are classified as having a disability (Individuals with Disabilities Education Act, 1997).

Toward Community Membership
Civil Rights, Inclusion, and Self-Advocacy

Although community-based programs for people with disabilities were improvements over institutional care, they continued to be based on the paradigm of separation—special places for special people. According to Schwartz (1992), as time went by, community-based programs were no longer considered innovative, and problems of abuse and neglect again emerged. Simultaneously, new approaches were developed to provide persons with severe disabilities opportunities to live in typical apartments and homes, participate in community activities, work in typical jobs, and have a degree of control over their own lives (O'Brien & O'Brien, 1992).

The Independent Living Movement

People with disabilities themselves have been increasingly active in organizing politically to create opportunities. By 1973 related movements for independent living and disability civil rights had emerged. Ed Roberts, along with other friends with disabilities, initiated the independent living movement. Roberts barely survived polio in high school, had quadriplegia, used a wheelchair, and needed much assistance in daily living tasks. He entered the University of California at Berkeley in 1962; with struggle and support, he obtained housing on campus and an electric wheelchair, and he requested funding for attendants to assist him in daily tasks. By 1967 twelve other students with significant disabilities were living with Roberts in a dorm. They organized to request expanded services, established a program to support their education, and, in 1970, obtained a federal grant to establish the Physically Disabled Students' Program (Berkowitz, 1987; Shapiro, 1993).

This program was the first of a network of university support services and centers for independent living for people with disabilities. Roberts's program also became the center of a national movement to promote a new philosophy of independent living. Key elements of this philosophy:

- People with disabilities can live independently with appropriate supports.
- People with disabilities should direct the organization of independent living services.
- Integration and social inclusion is an issue of social justice.
- Political activism is necessary.

In 1973 independent living was included as part of the federal rehabilitation act (PL 93-112) (Berkowitz, 1987; Shapiro, 1993). And in 1975 Roberts was appointed director of California's Department of Rehabilitation, an agency which refused him assistance because he was evaluated as unable to work. He used agency resources to expand independent living services.

Civil Rights at Last: Section 504 of the Rehabilitation Act of 1973

Although Section 504 of the Rehabilitation Act of 1973 was the first civil rights act for people with disabilities, the regulations to implement this law were delayed. In response, people with disabilities came in large numbers to demonstrate in Washington, D.C., in 1977. Activists took over the office of Secretary of Health, Education, and Welfare (HEW) Joseph Califano and the HEW office in California. Because of this political activism, regulations were developed and plans to create separate facilities for people with disabilities were halted (Califano, 1982; Scotch, 1984; Shapiro, 1993).

Figure 1.2

Section 504 of the Rehabilitation Act of 1973: Key Components

Discrimination on the basis of disability is prohibited in programs receiving federal aid for "qualified" handicapped persons.

- Programs must be accessible to persons with disabilities.
- Reasonable accommodations are required for access to service programs and employment.

Section 504 of the Rehabilitation Act of 1973 (PL 93-112) prohibited discrimination against qualified handicapped persons by any public organization receiving federal funds. The key concepts of Section 504 (Figure 1.2) were also incorporated later into the Americans with Disabilities Act (discussed later in this chapter).

In schools, Section 504 requires that all students with disabilities be educated in the least restrictive environment with reasonable accommodations. Most schools develop a written plan. It covers students who have disabilities but are not eligible for special education, such as students diagnosed with attention deficit/hyperactivity disorder and students in wheelchairs who need only assistance or adjustments in the physical environment (PL 93-112).

Supported Community Living

Now with new legal rights, and parallel with the movement toward inclusive education, people with significant disabilities increasingly have begun to live, work, and participate in typical community activities with support.

Tim's story is illustrative. Tim lives in a midwestern state and was classified as moderately mentally retarded. He reads at a second-grade level, speaks haltingly and with a small vocabulary, and has difficulty managing his own affairs without help. However, Tim is a likable person who is now an integral member of his community, owns his own house, and lives with a roommate who assists him.

In 1989, as Tim was graduating, his parents wanted options other than a group home and sheltered workshop. They sought help. First, with the help of community mental health and a local foundation, they bought a house in Tim's name and advertised for a roommate to live with him. Second, Tim and his friends invited people to form a **circle of support,** a group who agreed to meet with Tim and provide him with help (see Chapter 11). As of 1997, 120 other individuals with severe disabilities had circles and were living in their own apartments and homes with individualized support.

In the late twentieth century, innovative leaders worked to assist persons with disabilities in becoming community members. Thanks to a national **supported employment** movement that began in the 1980s, intensive training and ongoing supports are provided to help individuals with disabilities obtain and maintain employment (Bellamy, Rhodes, Mank, & Albin, 1988; Hagner & Dileo, 1993). Innovative funding strategies have allowed people with disabilities to combine public assistance with other income to purchase homes. Human service agencies have piloted arrangements whereby the person chooses services and providers. Neighbors, family, and community members are acting as mentors for individuals. Circles of support have harnessed energies and commitment (Mount, Beeman, & Ducharme, 1988).

Disability Civil Rights and the Americans with Disabilities Act

In 1983 Bob Kafka and colleagues founded Americans Disabled for Accessible Public Transit (ADAPT). ADAPT organized civil disobedience actions protesting discrimination and pushing for supports to facilitate independence. Hundreds of people participated in the Wheels of Justice March in March 1990 in Washington, D.C., an effort that helped promote the passage of the Americans with Disabilities Act in that year. People with disabilities discarded their wheelchairs and crawled up the steps of the White House, symbolizing daily barriers they face. The next day 150 people with disabilities entered the Capitol rotunda, insisting on hearings with key legislators. After being carried off one by one by police, demonstrators blocked subway entrances to the Capitol. In court, the demonstrators told their stories for the first time to an authority who listened. The judge, choking back tears, said, "The rightness of your cause is a big one." Imposing minimal fines, he "stepped down from the bench and went around the courtroom, shaking the hand of each of the activists" (Shapiro, 1993, pp. 135–140).

The **Americans with Disabilities Act (ADA)**, signed by the first President Bush on July 26, 1990, expanded civil rights for persons with disabilities. The ADA articulated rights in employment, public services, public accommodations, and telecommunications (Americans with Disabilities Act, 1990; Gostin & Beyer, 1993; Wehman, 1993). First, employers cannot discriminate in the hiring process on the basis of disability. Disability can be considered in the hiring process only if it relates to a person's ability to perform essential functions of a job with reasonable accommodations, which employers are required to provide. However, providing accommodations cannot pose an "undue hardship" involving significant difficulty or expense (Gostin & Beyer, 1993).

Also, ADA protects access to all public services in communities. These include public programs such as public schools, mental health services, and welfare programs as well as privately owned settings such as businesses and offices open to the public. If a program or business serves the general public, it must also provide access and support for persons with disabilities. In practice, restaurants, for example, must provide assistance so blind people can understand what is on the menu; theaters must provide seats that are accessible to people with physical disabilities; grocery stores must provide assistance to individuals in shopping.

Finally, the ADA requires accessibility in telecommunications and transportation. For example, the ADA requires that telephone companies provide access to relay operators: A relay operator, hired by the phone company, receives messages typed on TDD devices by persons who are deaf and acts as an intermediary with individuals with typical hearing who may not have equipment to access these messages. The act also requires public transportation authorities to make their vehicles accessible or to provide alternative transportation services to persons with disabilities (Americans with Disabilities Act, 1990; Wehman, 1993).

People First: Self-Advocacy by Persons with Developmental Disabilities

By 1980 people with developmental disabilities were creating a different type of disability rights movement. Composed of people who in many cases had been in institutions, group homes, and sheltered workshops, the *self-advocacy movement* encouraged people often considered unable to direct their own lives to speak out for their rights. At one organizational meeting, for example, the group passed resolutions calling for the closing down of all state institutions for people with retardation; sick leave, vacation time, and holidays at job sites and sheltered workshops; and recognition of the right to have sexual relationships. Typically supported by nondisabled facilitators, self-advocacy chapters were started throughout the country. Increasingly, their demands have been recognized.

Disability Culture

As people with disabilities have become politically active, many have viewed disability itself in new ways, conceptualizing the experience of disability as providing a common experience and bonding across disability categories—what some have described as a culture of disability. Writers and artists with disabilities are illustrating the perspective of people with disabilities on the human experience and in 1994 founded the Institute on Disability Culture (Institute on Disability Culture, 2001).

The Growing Movement to Inclusive Schools: These Are All Our Children

Shifts in approaches to schooling of students with disabilities and other special needs have occurred interactively with these civil and human rights movements. The move is away from segregated models of learning and toward schools designed to educate all children together.

The Regular Education Initiative and Integrated Education.   In the 1980s parents and professionals began to question the effectiveness of separate special education programs. Madeline Will (1986), assistant secretary of the Office of Special Education and Rehabilitative Services (OSERS) and herself the parent of a child with a disability, developed the federal **Regular Education Initiative (REI)** calling for special and general educators to share responsibility for the education of children with disabilities. One organizational model during this time was *class merging,* in which a whole special education classroom of students with mild disabilities merged with a regular education class where teachers cotaught (Lipsky & Gartner, 1997).

At the same time, TASH, formerly the Association for Persons with Severe Handicaps (TASH) and others advocated for placement of students with severe disabilities in neighborhood schools. These advocates were particularly concerned about the lack of positive outcomes from separate schools and the degree to which these schools cut children off from relationships with others. A new organizational approach for special education services was developed for students with moderate to severe disabilities—**integrated education,** in which students were enrolled in a special education classroom in a regular school and had opportunities for integration at lunch, recess, or "specials" (art, music, etc.).

Inclusive Education: Welcome to Our Class.   In the late 1980s, President George H. W. Bush called a governors' summit conference on education. Following publication of a highly critical report on public education, *A Nation at Risk,* this conference called for substantial restructuring (National Commission on Excellence in Education, 1983), for active learning approaches, and for the use of **push-in services** instead of **pull-out programs** for children at risk of educational failure. These ideas built on a growing base of research showing the negative effects of tracking children in homogenous ability groups (Lipsky & Gartner, 1997; Oakes, 1985; Ogle, Pink, & Jones, 1990; Wheelock, 1992).

Two students in a fifth-grade class, one with a severe disability, study maps of their state. In this class all students pair at different times with the child with a severe disability. "We have learned so much by his being in our class," several students said one day in a class discussion about diversity.

In this fertile climate, inclusive education was developed. Initially championed by advocates, parents, and educators of children with the most severe disabilities, **inclusive education** heralded a new and very different paradigm:

1. Inclusion of *all* students, with mild to severe disabilities, in general education classes.
2. Provision of supports and services within the general education class for both teachers and students (push-in services).

As schools began to implement inclusive education, researchers began to find that youngsters with disabilities were learning more effectively; that these youngsters were not hindering the learning of other students; and that in fact all students were learning more effectively (LeRoy, 1990a, 1990b, 1995; Stainback, Stainback, Moravec, & Jackson, 1992). The federal government funded a series of systems change grants to states to help local schools implement inclusive education. Beginning in small states such as New Hampshire and Vermont in the mid-1980s, by the end of the twentieth century inclusive education was implemented in some schools throughout the United States (Lipsky & Gartner, 1997).

Inclusive Schools: We All Can Learn Together. As inclusive education has become a reality in some schools, educators have begun to understand its connection to whole school reform. Inclusive education, like other significant school reform efforts, has been controversial. For example, Fuchs and Fuchs (1994) argued that what they call *full inclusionists* do not pay adequate attention to the individual needs of children with disabilities. They believe that general education teachers will not accept students with disabilities, that students with disabilities may detract from the learning of other students, and that schools may use inclusive education as an excuse to reduce funding and legal protection for students with disabilities. The American Federation of Teachers (1993) similarly called for a ban on inclusive education until adequate supports are provided.

Stepping Stones

To Inclusive Teaching

Although many schools are including students with different abilities, not all are. We may well find ourselves in a school that largely segregates children with special needs. In such a school we may get little support for practices we describe in this book. Yet *we always have choices:* We can do what we can to move toward inclusive teaching, even if the steps are small. In each chapter we will highlight a few practical efforts you can undertake. Following are a few beginning steps.

What is happening? Find out what is happening in your school and district related to inclusive schooling. How is special education structured in your school? Are students included or pulled out? What about students who are gifted, second-language learners, at-risk students?

Allies in your school? Are there people in your school who are really good with children and/or parents with challenges? Might they be interested in inclusive teaching? If your school is not inclusive, might the special education teacher be willing to work with you with a couple of students?

What about your community? What happens in the community in relation to people with differences? Do people with disabilities have support to live in their own apartments and work in regular jobs, or are they mostly in group homes and sheltered workshops?

What do you think? Think about what you believe at this point. Don't worry about being "right". Just identify your own opinions and feelings. If you are feeling negative about inclusive schooling, ask yourself why. If you are positive, again ask why. Journal about your own feelings and perceptions.

These simple actions will give you a base for understanding where you are and why, and where your school and community is. Knowing is always the basis for doing. It puts any action we take in a context. It's a first step.

Numerous educational organizations, however, have developed papers and position statements supporting inclusive schooling. In a nationally acclaimed report for *Newsweek* magazine, Joseph Shapiro (1993, p. 10) discussed the rising cost of special education and segregation of children with disabilities and stated that "we are spending billions on special education which is having little impact." In 1994 the National Association of School Boards of Education (NASBE) published *Winners All* and called on school boards to embrace inclusive education. Other organizations articulated similar statements of support, among them TASH, United Cerebral Palsy Association (1993), and the Council for Exceptional Children (CEC) (1993).

IDEA (Individuals with Disabilities Education Act)

As mentioned earlier, Congress passed the **Individuals with Disabilities Education Act (IDEA)** in 1997 as an update to PL 94-142 as passed in 1975. Let's look more closely at the requirements of the law as passed in 1975 and at changes in reauthorizations, many of which strengthen the move toward inclusive education (see Figure 1.3).

Figure 1.3

Strengthening the Law for the Education of Children with Disabilities

EDUCATION FOR ALL HANDICAPPED CHILDREN ACT (1975) (PL 94-142)

- Students are eligible for special education services if they have a disability that substantially interferes with their learning and education.
- All students with disabilities must receive a *free and appropriate public education (FAPE)* . . .
- In the *least restrictive environment (LRE)* . . .
- Based on an *Individualized Education Plan (IEP)*.
- Where needed, *supplementary services and supports* are provided.
- A *continuum of services*, ranging from less to more intensive, must be available to respond to individual needs of students (IDEA 1997 changed the language to *continuum of placement options*).
- Parents are integrally involved in planning educational goals and services.
- *Nondiscriminatory assessment* is used to aid in establishing eligibility and plan an educational program.
- *Due process* must be followed. Plans may be appealed legally by the family or school through an impartial hearing officer. Beyond this process, cases may be taken to federal court.

EAHCA OF 1986 (PL 99-457; 94-142 AS AMENDED)

- Early intervention services for infants 0–3 based on . . .
- Individualized Family Services Plan (IFSP).

INDIVIDUALS WITH DISABILITIES EDUCATION ACT OF 1990 (IDEA) (PL 100-476; PL 94-142 AS AMENDED)

- Changed name of the law, replacing the word *handicapped* with *with disabilities*, using person-first language.
- Transition plan and services for students aged 14 and older.
- Assistive technology as service.
- Added autism and traumatic brain injury to list of eligible disabilities.
- Student "stays put" during due process hearings.

INDIVIDUALS WITH DISABILITIES EDUCATION ACT OF 1997 (IDEA)

- Access to the general education curriculum.
- Increased role of general educators in the IEP.
- Opportunity to be involved in all state-mandated tests.
- Manifest determination reviews.
- Functional assessment and behavioral intervention plans.

INDIVIDUALS WITH DISABILITIES EDUCATION IMPROVEMENT ACT OF 2004 (PL 108-446)

- Emphasis on *early intervening services* allowing 15% of funds to help students who need additional academic and behavioral support.
- No longer requiring the IQ-academic achievement discrepancy in identifying students with learning disabilities.
- Elimination of short-term objectives except for students with severe disabilities who will take alternative assessments.
- Accountability for most students to be based on performance on the state standardized exam as required in the No Child Left Behind Act 2001.
- Required transition planning at age 16 instead of 14.

First, the law guarantees that all children with disabilities are entitled to a *free and appropriate public education (FAPE)*. All students with disabilities, ranging from those with mild challenges to those with the most severe disabilities, must be educated by public schools. Following enactment of PL 94-142, many children who were in institutions returned to their homes and received services in schools.

Second, education must be provided in the *least restrictive environment (LRE)*, which means that "to the maximum extent possible, children with disabilities must be educated with nondisabled children." A *continuum of placement options* requires that services be available to meet the needs of the student (see Chapter 5).

Third, the law requires that an **Individualized Education Plan (IEP)** be developed based on each individual student's needs (see Chapter 4). Schools are required to involve parents in educational decisions and the development of the IEP. This plan is a legal contract between the school and the parents regarding educational services.

Fourth, the law recognizes that students with disabilities may need specialized *supplementary and related services*. Such related services are stipulated to help students succeed in general education classes.

Finally, the act establishes processes to handle disagreements regarding the individualized education plan. If conflicts cannot be resolved at the IEP meeting, the parents and/or the school may take the case to an impartial hearing officer, often a lawyer or a university professor. Such officers are charged with hearing arguments and making a decision. This decision may be appealed to federal court by a dissatisfied party. As the number of hearings and court cases have risen, **mediation** programs have been developed in which trained individuals attempt to work out solutions.

In 1986, PL 99-457 amended PL 94-142 (see Figure 1.3) to extend services to infants and toddlers through collaborations among human service agencies. The law requires that family centered services (see Chapter 3) be based on an **Individualized Family Services Plan (IFSP)**; it encourages serving children in natural environments. Additionally, 99-457 utilizes a noncategorical approach to services for young children. All this has served to lay the groundwork for encouraging such children to move into inclusive education as they grow older.

In 1990 the act formally changed its name to the Individuals with Disabilities Education Act (IDEA), recognizing the importance of people-first language. This reauthorization required that an Individual Transition Plan be developed for students with disabilities aged fourteen and older. Two disability categories were added—autism and traumatic brain injury. (Advocates sought unsuccessfully, however, to have attention deficit/hyperactivity disorder [ADHD] added to the list of identified disabilities.) Finally, for the first time, IDEA specified that assistive technology must be considered in the IEP.

The 1997 amendments added the following components supporting movement toward inclusive education (Gartner & Lipsky, 1998):

- Requirements for "access to the general education curriculum"
- Involvement of a general education teacher on the IEP team if the student is participating in a general education program

- Requirement that the IEP describe annual goals, objectives, and services addressing the student's needs in general education
- PL 108-446, the Individuals with Disabilities Education Improvement Act was passed in December 2004. See Figure 1.3 on page 23 for key changes in the law. Most notable is the emphasis on early intervention services, the change in the required definition of learning disabilities, and the elimination of short-term objectives for most children with disabilities in the IEP.

The law continues to grow and change, reflecting increased knowledge as well as evolving political and social perspectives.

Litigation: Strengthening the Move toward Inclusion

Lawsuits have established a legal basis for inclusive education. Although some courts have ruled in favor of segregated placements (*D. F. v. Western School Corp*, 1996; *Hudson v. Bloomfield Hills School District*, 1995; *McWhirt by McWhirt v. Williamson County School*, 1995) most have ruled in favor of inclusive education.

Figure 1.4 summarizes key court cases upholding the right to education in the least restrictive environment.

Court rulings have been based on the following focal points: (1) Schools must, in good faith, consider inclusive placement of all students, no matter the severity of the disability; (2) students and teachers must be provided supports and supplementary services; (3) although costs, amount of teacher time, and impact on other students

Figure 1.4

Building Case Law Supporting Inclusive Education	
Roncker v. Walter (1983).	In this case the court established strong language regarding congressional presumption. In cases in which a segregated special education class is shown to be superior to a general education class, "the court should determine whether the services which make that placement superior could be feasibly provided in a non-segregated setting. If they can, the placement in the segregated school would be inappropriate under the Act."
Daniel R. R. v. Board of Education (1989).	Case involving a child with mental retardation. Court established test for determining appropriate placement: (1) Determine whether the child can be educated satisfactorily in a regular classroom with supplementary aids and services, how this compares to benefits a child will receive from a special education classroom, and the possible negative on other students in the classroom. (2) Has school "taken the steps to accommodate the child in the regular classroom?" The school is required to provide supports and adaptations to include the child in the regular classroom.
Greer v. Rome City School District (1991).	Christy Greer was a kindergarten student with a severe cognitive disability. The court used the *Daniel R. R.* test, stating that the district must consider the use of supplementary services and supports.
Oberti v. Board of Education (1993).	The court held that there was no reason established that the behavior problems of a child could not be dealt with in a general education classroom and that "inclusion is a right, not a privilege of a select few."
Sacramento City School Dist. v. Rachel H (1994).	In this case, parents of an 8-year-old child with mental retardation, Rachel Holland, sought placement in a general education class. The court ruled that Rachel's IEP objectives could be met in the general education class, that significant nonacademic benefits would come from involvement with typical peers, and that the school failed to show that the special education class was superior.
Corey H. (1992).	On May 22, 1992, Corey and three other students with disabilities, along with their parents, filed a class action lawsuit in federal court on behalf of all students with disabilities in the Chicago Public Schools, alleging that students with disabilities were not being educated in the least restrictive environment. On September 24, 1997, the Chicago School Reform Board of Trustees agreed to settle and to establish policies, services, and staff development to end segregation of students with disabilities. See **http://home.sprintmail.com/~ory64/ advocat_coreyh.htm.**
McLaughlin v. Board of Education (2001).	In this case, an inclusive placement was sought for a child. The court upheld that the student could be educated effectively in the neighborhood elementary school.

may be considered, the standards for these factors are so high that denial of an inclusive placement based on these issues is rarely supported (Lipsky & Gartner, 1997).

Where are we now in the movement from segregated to inclusive schooling? The answer varies greatly from state to state. Some states, such as New Hampshire and Vermont, have been leaders. In other states inclusion is very limited. The increased sophistication and political clout of parents with high socioeconomic status has often created more opportunities for their children. Cities with high concentrations of low-income minority populations have the highest degrees of segregation (Office of Special Education Programs, 1998, 2000b). Even in these situations, however, change is occurring. In Chicago in 1992, the *Corey H.* class action suit resulted in a court order requiring inclusive education. Cities such as Boston, Pittsburgh, and San Francisco are implementing inclusive education as part of overall school reform (Lipsky & Gartner, 1997; McLaughlin & Rouse, 2000; Office of Special Education Programs, 2000).

Although numerous schools throughout the country continue to segregate many children with disabilities (Office of Special Education Programs, 2000), more schools are embracing inclusive education as their philosophy for all their students—gifted, disabled, bilingual, and at risk—and in a growing number of schools faculty have come to think of inclusive education as simply "how we do business in our school" (Fisher, Sax, & Grove, 2000).

Inclusive Schools throughout the World

The movement toward inclusive education is worldwide. In 1994 a United Nations conference developed the Salamanca Statement (UNESCO, 1994), which outlined goals and strategies for inclusion of people with disabilities in school and society. With increased diversity of children in schools throughout the world, old models of separating students by various categories and labels have increasingly been seen as unfeasible and oppressive (Booth & Ainscow, 1998; Vitello & Mithaug, 1998). International projects sponsored by the United Nations have promoted growth of inclusive schooling in countries all over the world, including Belgium, Great Britain (Ainscow, 1999), Germany (Hinz, 1996), Italy (Balboni, Giulia, & Pedrabissi, 2000; Berrigan, 1994); various African nations (Miles, 1999; Naicker, 1999), India, and China (Booth & Ainscow, 1998). Italy has become recognized as a leader in inclusive education, and as early as 1977 Italy passed National Law 517 requiring inclusion of students with disabilities, elimination of classes tracked by ability, and team teaching by general and special education teachers (Berrigan, 1994).

More recently, South Africa, a country in which apartheid has existed for many years, has begun implementing a national inclusive education initiative as part of its efforts to transform its postapartheid educational system (Naicker, 1999).

Calling for Support
Toward Respect and Community Participation

Justin Dart, a Reagan appointee to the National Council on Disability in 1985 and a successful Texas businessman, said that the treatment of people with disabilities

A Credo for Support

By Norm Kunc

Throughout history,
people with physical and mental disabilities
have been abandoned at birth,
banished from society,
used as court jesters,
drowned and burned during the Inquisition,
gassed in Nazi Germany,
and still continue to be segregated, institutionalized,
tortured in the name of behaviour management,
abused, raped, euthanized, and murdered.

Now, for the first time, people with disabilities are taking their rightful
place as fully contributing citizens. The danger is that we will respond with
remediation and benevolence rather than equity and respect. And so, we offer you . . .

A Credo for Support

Do Not see my disability as the problem.
Recognize that my disability is an attribute.

Do Not see my disability as a deficit.
It is you who see me as deviant and helpless.

Do Not try to fix me because I am not broken.
Support me. I can make my contribution to the community in my way.

Do Not see me as your client. I am your fellow citizen.
See me as your neighbour. Remember, none of us can be self-sufficient.

Do Not try to modify my behaviour.
Be still and listen. What you define as inappropriate
may be my attempt to communicate with you in the only way I can.

Do Not try to change me, you have no right.
Help me learn what I want to know.

Do Not hide your uncertainty behind "professional" distance.
Be a person who listens, and does not take my
struggle away from me by trying to make it all better.

Do Not use theories and strategies on me.
Be with me. And when we struggle
with each other, let that give rise to self-reflection.

Do Not try to control me. I have a right to my power as a person.
What you call non-compliance or manipulation may
actually be the only way I can exert some control over my life.

Do Not teach me to be obedient, submissive, and polite.
I need to feel entitled to say No if I am to protect myself.

Voices

Continued

Do Not be charitable towards me.
The last thing the world needs is another Jerry Lewis.
Be my ally against those who exploit me for their own gratification.

Do Not try to be my friend. I deserve more than that.
Get to know me. We may become friends.

Do Not help me, even if it does make you feel good.
Ask me if I need your help. Let me show you how you can best assist me.

Do Not admire me. A desire to live a full life does not warrant adoration.
Respect me, for respect presumes equity.

Do Not tell, correct, and lead.
Listen, Support, and Follow.

Do Not work on me.
Work with me.

Dedicated to the memory of Tracy Latimer. 1995 © Norman Kunc and Emma Van der Klift. Distributed by Axis Consultation & Training Ltd., 250-754-9939. Used with permission. Available on video at www.normemma.com/credwait.htm.

is a window on the health of a society (Dart, 1987). Norm Kunc captured the challenge and opportunity to create a healthier community in a poem called "A Credo for Support." He calls on us to prevent exclusion and segregation, to move beyond benevolence, to support inclusion, and simply to accept people with disabilities as human beings. As teachers, we are key people in helping such a goal become reality. Our journey toward inclusive teaching is part of creating a better world—and a better place for children in that world.

Key Points

- The movement toward inclusive schooling is providing new opportunities for students with disabilities and other special needs.

- Parents, people with disabilities, and their allies have struggled to move from segregation in special institutions, schools, and group homes to full participation in inclusive schools and communities.

- Their struggle parallels the struggle of other groups for civil rights, integration, and equality.

- Laws passed since the early 1960s provide a legal basis for civil rights and inclusion.

- PL 94-142, passed in 1975, updated over the years, and renamed in 1990 as the Individuals with Disabilities Education Act, guides the delivery of special education services in schools and mandates that students be educated in the least restrictive environment possible.

■ Throughout the world, increasing numbers of students with more severe disabilities are suc-

cessfully being educated in general education classes with support.

 Learning Expeditions

Following are some ideas that may extend your learning.

1. Investigate the history and present status of institutions for persons with mental retardation and mental illness in your state. What has been the experience of people moving from institutions into the community?

2. Locate someone in your relationship network who has a developmental disability and is older than fifty. Interview the person and learn his or her life story. How does it fit into themes in this chapter?

3. Contact the Developmental Disabilities Council of your state government. Get from the council a list of projects sponsored over the last ten years. What are the council's priorities for people with developmental disabilities in your state? Why?

4. Locate someone in your network who has a disability and went to public schools. Interview this person and, if possible, his or her parents regarding the person's experiences in school. What do their stories tell you about

trends in education in your area, and how do they relate to themes in this chapter?

5. Visit three local schools. Interview the principals regarding inclusive education. What has changed, and in what direction is each school going?

6. Find a local attorney involved in special education cases or a parent who has been involved in a hearing or court case. Interview the person regarding how local conflicts are being handled with parents and schools. What are the issues and needs you hear described?

7. Go to links of a website for the Salamanca Statement (**www.unesco.org/educationeduc progsne/salamanc/index.html**). What are the issues?

8. Consider what you really feel and believe about difference and inclusion in our society. What do you believe? How comfortable are you with people with various types of differences—different disabilities, different sexual orientation, different cultural or ethnic backgrounds?

CHAPTER GOAL

Envision effective inclusive schools and understand research, principles, and practices on which they are based.

CHAPTER OBJECTIVES

1. Understand principles and practices of quality inclusive teaching and schooling.

2. Evaluate the research about segregated and inclusive education.

3. Develop an awareness of practices that may lead to educational problems and segregated education for some children.

4. Develop a mental picture of effective inclusive schools.

Envisioning an Inclusive School

Schools That Educate All Children Together Well

with contributions by Douglas Fisher

In this chapter we will begin to create a picture of how teachers can teach, how schools can be, so that children with significant disabilities can be part of our school community. This picture will leave behind the factory model and will move beyond segregation and benevolence to community membership. We will visit classes, evaluate research on inclusive education, and visit effective inclusive schools. We'll pay careful attention to what we see.

What Is Wrong Here? The Frustrations of Coping with Diverse Children in a "Factory School"

We enter Lafayette Elementary School, where we'll be visiting several classrooms today. As we walk down the hall, we first observe Amanda, a child with mental retardation who attends a special education class in the morning and Head Start in the afternoon. John, the special education teacher, greets us; he introduces the paraprofessional, Jan, and the speech therapist, Audrey, who is in the class once a week. These specialists have fourteen children in three groups, each working on skills—colors, naming letters, cutting with scissors. Jan is working with Amanda one-on-one at a table. "She really needs individual attention," John explains.

In the afternoon Amanda goes to Head Start. The teacher there, Brenda, has activity centers at which her twenty-four children are engaged. We are intrigued as we watch other children pull Amanda into the center activities, helping her select colors of paper and cut. Curiously, we see Amanda attending and performing in ways that John and Jan thought not possible.

Next, we walk to the resource room at the end of the hall, a class for students with learning disabilities. We are warmly greeted by Gayle Horton. "Hi. Come in!" She is using reading and math worksheets with ten students. After a while Gayle tells us about Robie, a student who "comes to me two hours each day for reading and math. I use a special curriculum so that he can have some success." We ask if she helps Robie with the reading and math in his regular class. "No," she says. "That is much too hard for him, and besides, there's no way I can keep up with all the different materials the different teachers are using."

Gayle then expresses her frustrations and the pressures she feels. "They are on so many different levels!" she exclaims. "It's really hard to get to all the students. All are at different levels in every subject, and they are not able to help one another. So I do the best I can. It's really hard." She goes on to explain that it is virtually impossible to coordinate with the six teachers who send her students. "They are all at different places in the curriculum, using different materials. I am in this class all day with students and have no time to work with them." We ask Gayle what she thinks about having these students in the general education class full time. "Oh no!" she says. "They could never keep up. They would be lost and left behind! Also, the teachers would never want another teacher in their class."

Finally, we visit Jim Bridges's fifth-grade social studies class. The upper elementary grades are departmentalized, and Jim shares seventy-five students with two other teachers. He's been quite bothered with Lamar, a student classified as "educable mentally retarded." Lamar goes to Mrs. Horton's resource room for one hour daily but is in Jim's class the whole period. "Lamar can't function in my class at all," Jim says. "His academics are far too low, and he is always causing trouble. I have to spend so much of my time with this one child that I can't give other children what they deserve."

As we come in, Jim is passing out textbooks. "Turn to page 53 and begin reading about the Bill of Rights, then go to the questions on your worksheet." We look around at the class. The children are seated at tables in groups of four or five. A few commercial posters about social studies are on the wall; the only books in the room are the textbooks.

Indeed, Lamar is acting upset. He looks at the book, fidgets, and goes over to the trash can and throws something in it. "Lamar, sit down!" says Jim. Lamar returns and stares at the book.

Jim keeps a watchful eye on Lamar. "See, he won't do his work," says Jim. We ask if Lamar is able to read the textbook. "No, that's the problem. The textbook is at a fourth-grade reading level and Lamar is at a first-grade level." We ask Jim if he has books at a lower level and if he's paired Lamar with another student and let them read aloud together. Jim explains that he has no books Lamar can read and doesn't have the money to buy any. He further observes that students must do their own work and that pairing students for work is a bad idea. "We've got to do everything we can to get the test scores up," he points out. "So they need to do their worksheets on their own."

We leave for the car, deep in thought. In the two special education classrooms teachers are working hard, but the situation creates dynamics that appear to directly hamper the learning of the children. In Jim's class some obvious approaches that might help Lamar simply aren't being tried. Unfortunately, we are aware that Lafayette Elementary is too typical. Can it be different?

Toward Inclusive Schooling
A Glimpse of Teaching Practices That Honor All Children

We take our questions to another school, Thomas Jefferson Middle School. This school has children from many different ethnic groups and from both low and high socioeconomic backgrounds. The district has adopted a focus on both inclusion and improvement of instruction. As we walk in, students in the hall are noisy but not loud. There is an engaged, excited hum and periodic jovial outbursts. The phrase "learning noise" comes to mind.

Our first class is Bob Stephen's World Cultures class. At Lafayette Elementary the students were all seated at their desks, and the teachers put a lot of energy into keeping the students quiet and working. This class is different. Bob is discussing a project with a small group of students. The rest of the class is a buzz of activity—some students are standing, some sitting, some moving around the room, all engaged.

Bob points out a student to observe. Jonathan, he comments, has low reading and writing abilities and can be disruptive. However, he is very interested in learning and works very hard when he is engaged. He is also very good at singing and playing baseball.

The fourth-hour bell rings. Jonathan, restless, wanders to the back of the room, drumming his pencil on desks along the way. Bob watches Jonathan but says nothing. "Get in your work groups," he says, and Jonathan and the other students gather in circles. Jonathan's group is working on bartering; today he is the banker, tracking items his group receives in trade and money they have. He works very well and is totally engaged. Later we notice a paraprofessional working with Jonathan's group. Bob walks throughout the class, helping, encouraging, and coaching students. At the end of the activity, Jonathan reports the money and items to his group. He beams with pride.

Bob has been teaching the World Cultures class for eight years. He uses teaching strategies such as cooperative learning, simulations, lectures, computer, video, reading supplements, and text reading. For assessment he uses rubrics for research projects, reports, papers, essay tests, oral presentations, and group projects (Peterson, 1999).

We ask him how including students with learning challenges has affected his class. Bob admits it was difficult at first but concludes that it has benefited everyone. "I have the support of a great special education department," he says. "The inclusion of students with special needs has really improved my teaching."

We next walk down the hall to Annette Smith's literacy class. Annette and her students are gathered in the rug area of the room. She is sitting in a chair reading a story to the students. The students listen intently. We wander around the room looking at learning projects: *books read list; places we've been map; book recommendations* (an envelope where students suggest books another student might like); *personal "memoirs" projects* (shoe boxes containing various personal archives and belongings that help explain students' lives); *published books* (three-ring binders filled with poems and writings of students—and of some parents as well).

As the next class comes in, Annette asks them to gather on the carpet. She asks for two or three volunteers. She reminds the other students how hard it is to go first and quietly encourages them to be supportive. Annette then exclaims, "Ladies and gentlemen! We now present Sharon." Sharon stands and faces the class, showing a picture drawn to illustrate a scene in the book she is reading. She explains what is happening in the scene. Two other students present scenes using characters made of paper or small dolls. Annette then passes out grading rubrics to all of the children. These have the key elements of the story scenes presentation: title, author, pages, presentation of setting, description of characters, the problem in the story, and how the problem was dealt with. She asks students to describe what they liked about the presentations and make suggestions for improvement. The presenting students call on those who raise their hands. We are amazed at their thoughtfulness.

Following a substantial amount of time on this activity and much clapping and appreciation, Annette directs the students to various projects—reading a "just right" book, working on memoirs, or doing group projects on the carpet. The children sort themselves with a bit of flurry but soon settle down to concentrate.

Annette talks with us and notes that among the students are children labeled ADHD, children diagnosed as learning disabled, and one child with severe brain damage. We are amazed that we simply did not notice these children in the classroom. The choices given, the requests for engagement that allowed for a range of ability levels, the respect for all children—all made the learning differences in this class invisible to us as outside observers.

A special education teacher leads a heterogeneous group in a reading lesson in a multi-age, inclusive classroom while a teacher and paraprofessional teach other children in small groups elsewhere in the class.

We leave thoughtful and amazed. At Lafayette, even though teachers work hard, they don't know how to meet the multiple styles, abilities, and challenges of their students. Therefore, many students are referred to special education. At Thomas Jefferson Middle School, in contrast, each of the teachers we have seen is using engaging, interesting learning activities that allow students to work at their own level and encourage students to help one another. Although what we have seen at Jefferson is not perfect, it does represent what is both possible and needed.

What made the difference in these two schools? Engaging teaching techniques? A commitment to educating diverse children together? Supporting children in regular classrooms rather than in separate special education classrooms? Collaboration of teachers and specialists in the classroom? School administrative policies that support teachers? In these two schools we saw the difference between effective inclusive teaching and some of the problems associated with segregated special education, themes we will return to many times on our journey.

Traveling Notes

1. What did you feel as you observed in Lafayette Elementary and Thomas Jefferson Middle School? What did you notice?

2. Do you know classes that are like the classes in these two schools? Think a bit about what they are like.

3. A key question: Do schools and classes that successfully include all children use different teaching strategies? Are they more caring, supportive, fun places? If so, what makes them so? If not, what *is* the difference?

4. We know that some schools and some teachers respond proactively to children with a wide range of social and emotional needs. Others do a poor job of this. What are the differences?

Make notes along the way about these fundamental questions.

Research and Inclusive Schooling
The Effectiveness of Inclusive versus Segregated Education

What does research show regarding inclusive education? Does it work to have students of such differing abilities learning together? Can schools and teachers implement effective inclusive schooling? Let's discuss the promise of segregated special education classes, review data on how this promise has been delivered, then consider the hopes for inclusive education and research findings to date. (See McGregor & Vogelsberg, 1998, for a comprehensive review.) Figure 2.1 summarizes research on comparative academic and social outcomes of students in special and general education classes. You'll note that Figure 2.1 does not have a column headed "Segregated Classes Best." This is because no research to date has found better outcomes when comparing segregated and inclusive education. Figure 2.2 provides a summary of academic and social outcomes of students with varied levels of disability in inclusive education.

Academic Achievement

Educators have thought that segregated special education classes with smaller class sizes and additional adult resources would allow teachers to individualize instruction and focus on the learning styles and needs of each student, thus leading to improved learning. However, research overwhelmingly indicates that this has not occurred. For example, when Vaughn, Moody, and Shumm (1998) and Moody, Vaughn, and Hughes (2000) studied instruction in resource rooms, their findings validated the literature they had reviewed—literature concluding that these programs constitute "broken promises" and are a "setup for failure" for students with disabilities. In both of these studies teachers taught mostly through whole class instruction; gave the same level of reading materials to students at obviously different levels of ability; used basals as the primary source of reading material; and used very little individualized, small group, or differentiated instruction. Others have reviewed instruction in special education classrooms with similar findings (Allington, 1991, 1993, 1994; McIntosh, Vaughn, Schumm, Haager, & Lee, 1993).

Advocates of inclusive education have hoped that greater academic expectations, a richer learning environment, more effective teaching strategies, and modeling by more able peers would enhance learning. With few exceptions, the research strongly supports these hopes. Again, note that no research findings in Figure 2.1 indicate segregated education is more effective. As early as 1968, Dunn questioned separate special education classes (Dunn, 1968). Waldron and McLeskey (1998), summarizing research related to segregated special education programs, indicated that "there is some controversy regarding whether separate class placement is *ever beneficial* for students with mild disabilities." Carlberg and Kavale (1980), Wang and Baker (1986), and Baker (1994) each conducted a meta-analysis, a statistical procedure by which findings from different studies are combined, of seventy-four studies; results showed that students with disabilities had more positive academic learning in integrated settings. Likewise, several studies found that achievement of IEP goals was stronger in inclusive education (Brinker & Thorpe, 1984; Hunt, Farron-Davis, Beckstead, Curtis, & Goetz, 1994; Hunt, Goetz, & Anderson, 1986; Kaskinen-Chapman, 1992). Freeman and Alkin (2000) conducted a comprehensive review of research over the preceding twenty-five years concerning integration of children with mental retardation; they concluded that studies showed that the more time these children spent in general education, the more their academic growth improved.

Figure 2.1

Comparative Impacts of Inclusive and Segregated Education

INCLUSIVE EDUCATION BEST	MIXED RESULTS
Carlberg and Kavale (1980): Meta-analysis of 50 studies showed more positive academic learning in integrated settings.	
Brinker and Thorpe (1984) and Hunt, Goetz, and Anderson (1986): Greater integration associated with more IEP goals met.	
Wang and Baker (1986). Meta-analysis of 11 studies showed more positive academic learning in integrated settings.	Affleck, Madge, Adams, and Lowenbraun (1988): Study found no difference in academic performance; integrated education was more cost-effective.
Cole and Meyer (1991): Children in inclusive settings showed greater social competence, spent more time with peers and less time alone.	
Baker (1994): Meta-analysis of 13 studies showed more positive academic learning in integrated settings. Hunt, Farron-Davis, Beckstead, Curtis, and Goetz (1994): Students with severe disabilities had more engagement, higher-quality IEP's, and higher levels of social interaction in inclusive education.	Baker and Zigmond (1995): 50 percent of students with LD made equal progress to classmates. Students with more severe LD made equal progress in both special education and general education classes.
Fryxell and Kennedy (1995) and Kennedy, Shulka and Fryxell (1997): Studies showed larger social networks, substantial social benefits, interactions with general education students.	Marston (1996): 240 students with LD made better progress in partial pull-out than in full-time inclusion or pull-out only.
Waldron and McLeskey (1998): Mild LD students gained in reading in inclusive class, were equal in math; those with severe LD made equal progress in both inclusive and segregated settings.	Manset and Semmel (1997): Reviewed 11 studies but could not conclude that either segregation or inclusion was more effective. Recommended best practice teaching strategies in general education.
Buysse and Bailey (1993) and Hundert, Mahoney, and Mundy (1998): Children with severe disabilities in segregated preschools showed less developmental progress than comparable children in integrated settings. Freeman and Alkin (2000): Comprehensive review of studies for students with mental retardation concluded that the more students were integrated, the higher were their academic performance and social skills.	

Figure 2.2

	ACADEMIC	SOCIAL
Students with mild disabilities	Students with mild disabilities make better gains in inclusive programs than in pull-out programs (Banerji & Dailey, 1995; Deno, Maruyama, Espin, & Cohen, 1990; Fishbaugh & Gum, 1994; Jenkins, Jewell, Leicester, O'Connor, Jenkins, & Troutner, 1994; National Center for Educational Restructuring and Inclusion, 1995).	There is more active student engagement (Saint-Laurent & Lessard, 1991). Students develop enhanced social competence and improved behavior more than in segregated classes (Baker, Wang, & Walberg, 1994; Cole & Meyer, 1991; McLeskey, Waldon, & Pacchiano, 1993; Saint-Laurent & Lessard, 1991). Students with mild disabilities are less often accepted and are more likely to be rejected because of their behavior than nondisabled students (Roberts & Zubrick, 1992).
Students with moderate to severe disabilities	The quality of Individualized Education Plans is improved (Brinker & Thorpe, 1984; Hunt & Farron-Davis, 1992; Hunt, Farron-Davis, Beckstead, Curtis, & Goetz, 1994; Hunt, Goetz, & Anderson, 1986; Kaskinen-Chapman, 1992). For students with moderate to severe disabilities, achievement is enhanced or at least equivalent in inclusive versus segregated settings (Cole & Meyer, 1991; Giangreco, Dennis, Cloninger, Edelman, & Schattman, 1993; National Center for Educational Restructuring and Inclusion, 1995; Ryndak, Downing, Jacqueline, & Morrison, 1995; Saint-Laurent & Lessard, 1991).	Friendships and social interactions for students with disabilities expand in school and carry over to after-school contexts (Fryxell & Kennedy, 1995; Hall, 1994; Hunt et al., 1994; McDonnell, Hardman, Hightower, & Kiefer-O'Donnell, 1991; Ryndak et al., 1995; Salisbury, Palombaro, & Hollowood, 1993; Staub, Schwartz, Gallucci, & Peck, 1994). Students with severe disabilities have many social interactions, though these are often assistive. Over the course of the year, the numbers of interactions decrease but become more natural. Teachers can facilitate increased reciprocal interactions between students with and without disabilities (Hunt, Alwell, Farron-Davis, & Goetz, 1996).

Outcomes of Inclusive Education

Figure 2.2

Continued		
	ACADEMIC	SOCIAL
Students without disabilities	There is no evidence that academic progress is impeded in inclusive classes, and in some cases it consistently increases (Fishbaugh & Gum, 1994; Hunt, Staub, Alwell, & Goetz, 1994; Kaskinen & Chapman, 1992; Odom, Deklyen, & Jenkins, 1984; Saint-Laurent, Glasson, Royer, Simard, & Pierard, 1998; Scruggs & Mastropieri, 1994; Sharpe, York, & Knight, 1994; Wang & Birch, 1984). Engaged time is not diminished (Hollowood, Salisbury, Rainforth, & Palombaro, 1995; McIntosh, Vaugh, Schumm, Haager, & Lee, 1993; Peck, Carlson, & Helmstetter, 1992; Pugach & Wesson, 1995). Problem-solving skills are acquired (Biklen, Corrigan, & Quick, 1989; Salisbury, Palombaro, & Hollowood, 1993).	Students view their involvement with peers with disabilities positively (Altman & Lewis, 1990; Helmstetter, Peck, & Giangreco, 1994; McLeskey, 1993; Pugach & Wesson, 1995; Stainback, Stainback, Moravec, & Jackson, 1992). There is an increased appreciation and understanding of diversity (Fisher, Pumpian, & Sax, 1998; Helmstetter et al., 1994; Peck et al., 1992; Scruggs & Mastropieri, 1994). Self-esteem and behaviors improve. (Staub, Spaulding, Peck, Gallucci, & Schwartz, 1996).

A small number of studies (see Figure 2.1) have been less clear. Affleck, Madge, Adams, and Lowenbraun (1988) and Manset and Semmel (1997) found neither segregated or inclusive education to be more effective. Baker, Zigmond, and colleagues (Baker & Zigmond, 1995; Zigmond, Jenkins, & Fuchs, 1995) showed that some 33 to 64 percent of students with mild learning disabilities in inclusive classes in three states made gains comparable to those of their general education peers. For those with more severe learning disabilities, however, progress was minimal and no differences in progress existed between general and special education. The researchers concluded that "general education settings produce achievement outcomes for students with learning disabilities that are neither desirable nor acceptable" (Zigmond, Jenkins, & Fuchs, 1995, p. 539). However, these conclusions are far too broad to be supported by the data. The studies showed that in *particular* schools using *particular* instructional and support strategies, results were disappointing. However, they did not indicate that pull-out programs were superior. Their results would appear to call into question the specific instructional approaches used rather than placement in general education. Waldron and McLesky (1998) replicated the research and found similarly that 48 percent of students with learning disabilities made gains comparable to those of their general education peers. However, Waldron and McLesky saw the glass as half full: They were quite encouraged that approximately half of these students made progress equal to that of students without disabilities, and they suggested that the criterion for success cannot be "cure" but should be progress in learning.

Social and Emotional Well-Being

Socially, the promise of segregated special education classes has been twofold. On the one hand, parents and educators have sought a place to protect students with cognitive and physical disabilities from feared ridicule or direct harm. On the other hand, segregated programs for students with behavioral difficulties have allowed greater control and promised more nurturing environments in which trained specialists can help students improve emotionally and socially.

Those calling for inclusive education, however, have been concerned about the isolation of children with disabilities from their neighborhood communities. Students in special education classes often go to a different school than neighborhood children, limiting opportunities for relationships. Parents of children in special schools typically come from a wide geographical area, making development of mutually supportive relationships difficult. Advocates of inclusive education hope that attending regular education classes, with needed support, will help children develop relationships, become a meaningful part of their community, and improve their self-esteem.

For students with behavioral problems, inclusive educators have been concerned that schools do not build a supportive learning community when students are removed—and that the self-esteem of such students is severely damaged. Kauffman, Lloyd, and Baker (1995) argue that general educators are not prepared to meet the behavioral challenges of students with emotional disturbances and that separate programs staffed by specially trained professionals are needed. However, problems in outcomes of segregated programs for students with emotional and behavioral problems are clear. Follow-up data indicate that once students are placed in a segregated program, the chances that they will drop out of school, be arrested, be imprisoned, and/or be unemployed all increase (Berg, 1989, p. 10B; Cheney & Harvey, 1994; Garbarino, Dubrow, Kostelny, & Pardo, 1992; Kay, 1999; Lantieri & Patti, 1996; Zionts, 1997). Researchers in this field hope that schools will work to develop nurturing communities that help prevent emotional problems and will use proactive strategies to help children learn social skills when problems do occur. Guidelines for practice resulting from research and demonstration efforts have been documented (Cheney & Muscott, 1996; Knoff & Batsche, 1995; March & Sprague, 1999; Meadows, 1996; Reavis & Andrews, 1999; University of Oregon, 1999; Zionts, 1997).

For students with academic and physical challenges, the social and emotional results of inclusion have been particularly positive. Inclusive education provides many more opportunities for interactions, development of relationships, and social skill enhancement (Fryxell & Kennedy, 1995; Hall, 1994; Hunt, Farron-Davis, Beckstead, Curtis, & Goetz, 1994; McDonnell, Hardman, Hightower, & Kiefer-O'Donnell,

1991; Ryndak, Downing, Jacqueline, & Morrison, 1995; Staub, Schwartz, Gallucci, & Peck, 1994).

Research has also documented challenges and questions. With students who have more severe disabilities, typical students may provide help and assistance rather than playing or socializing (Salisbury, Palombaro, & Hollowood, 1993). Not surprisingly, students with disabilities, whether mild or severe, often have poorer social skills and are less often accepted and more often rejected (Freeman & Alkin, 2000; Salend & Duhaney, 1999), particularly because of behavioral problems, than students without disabilities. Studies have also shown, however, that teachers and other staff can facilitate relationships as part of community building, and that problem solving, conflict resolution, and social skills development can be effectively integrated into classes across the grade levels (Freeman & Alkin, 2000; Hunt, Alwell, Farron-Davis, & Goetz, 1996).

Research and Change

Many studies make it clear that proactive efforts to create an inclusive school can be effective, even invigorating for students and teachers. Some researchers, however, argue that educators are neither willing nor able to develop the innovative practices necessary to make inclusive teaching successful; these researchers have documented problems that include (1) poor planning and preparation, (2) inadequate supports for students and teachers, and (3) negative and adversarial attitudes of educators (Baines, Baines, & Masterson, 1994; McGregor & Vogelsberg, 1998; Salend & Duhaney, 1999; Zigmond & Baker, 1995).

Although change is always slow, increasing numbers of schools are successfully moving towards inclusive schooling. When change efforts involve faculty training, administrative leadership and support, in-class assistance, and other special services, the attitudes of teachers are positive (Phillips, Alfred, Brulli, & Shank, 1990; Villa, Thousand, Meyers, & Nevin, 1996; Werts, Wolery, Snyder, & Caldwell, 1996). Some teachers see inclusive schooling as building on positive teaching practices they already have in place (Fisher, Sax, Rodifer, & Pumpian, 1999; Rainforth, 1992). Teachers may fear having students with severe disabilities at first—but as teachers have come to know these students, they have engaged them and have been willing to have them again (Giangreco, Dennis, Cloninger, Edelman, & Schattman, 1993).

Despite the fact that much segregated education still exists, many schools are gradually moving toward inclusive education, as several comprehensive studies have documented. Among these are O'Hearn Elementary School in Boston (Henderson, 2000), Souhegan High School in New Hampshire (Jorgensen, 1998), and Purcell Marion High School in Cincinnati (Bauer & Myree-Brown, 2001). The National Center for Educational Restructuring and Inclusion (1995) conducted a national study of hundreds of schools throughout the United States that were implementing inclusive education.

Implications of Research

Research to date provides a solid foundation on which to expand inclusive schooling. Legally and ethically, students should not be segregated unless there is clear evidence of superiority for segregated classes and programs. The most important research questions for the future are not *whether* we should seek to build inclusive schools but *how* we may do so well. Clearly, as Zigmond and Baker (1995) state, for inclusive teaching to be successful, "business as usual" is not possible.

Inclusive Teaching
Key Elements of Schooling for All Children

Based on the research, what would an effective **inclusive school** look like? Below we'll sketch a picture of an inclusive school and inclusive teaching practice. (The following is adapted from Peterson, 2000.)

For us, inclusive teaching is quite simple: We seek to educate *all children together well.* For us, "all" really does mean "all." As inclusive teachers, committed to the growth and development of all children, we see a quality school as a school that combines a focus on excellence and equity; that sees excellence and equity as mutually reinforcing, not as mutually exclusive. For us, teaching all children *together* is a cornerstone of good teaching and schooling.

In most schools a move to inclusive teaching will mean shifting special education, gifted, at-risk, and other students from separate classes into general education; identifying students now in separate special education or gifted schools who would typically attend our school and inviting them back; and redesigning the roles of specialists to provide support for inclusive teaching.

Rather than separating children by abilities or other characteristics in special education classes, clustering them in general education classes, or grouping them according to ability within a class, inclusive teachers intentionally seek to have children of very different cultures, languages, and academic, social–emotional, and sensory–physical abilities learn *together.* Staff are committed to **heterogeneous grouping** across and within classes. Fewer students are referred for special education services because teaching and individual support structures are in place and available to all students, based on their needs, consequently reducing the stress of referral and evaluation and freeing up more resources to provide direct assistance to children.

In an inclusive school, literally every type of child attends and learns with other children. Inclusive schools follow both the spirit and the letter of IDEA: The general education classroom is the first choice for all students, and such classrooms are designed to meet the individualized educational needs of all students as they learn together. For example, activities in an inclusive classroom might include the following:

A student of the highest ability works on a project involving a study of the polar ice caps in a small group that includes a student with severe mental retardation. Each of the students contributes to the total project at their own ability level; each is benefiting based on individual needs.

A student who uses a wheelchair partners in science lab with a student who has immigrated recently from another country.

A child who is blind intrigues his classmates with talking software on his laptop. A student who is deaf is aided by a signing interpreter; ninety students join the "Sign Language Club," and the music teacher incorporates sign language into school musical productions.

Students with social and emotional problems get help and support from a staff committed to helping them learn social skills, develop relationships, and know they are cared for and belong.

Circles of support meet for different types of students throughout the school—one for a little boy who does not understand English, another for a child who just lost both parents in a car accident, another for a child who was abused in the past and has many emotional and behavioral problems.

Inclusive schools spend much time putting in place practices in the classroom and schoolwide supports and instructional practices to make this possible. What are these practices? Here's a brief summary:

- Reaching out to parents of all children; paying particular attention to helping parents of children with special needs to know that their children are welcome and are part of the school community.
- Providing support for teachers and children in general education classes.
- Offering authentic, multilevel instruction specifically designed to engage children in meaningful activities in which they learn together at different ability levels; this may involve making adaptations and modifications in academic instruction.
- Building a community among children, staff, and parents: a community in which all feel welcome, all belong, emotional intelligence and social skills are taught, and relationships are nurtured. Part of building this community is responding

Artwork reprinted by permission of Martha Perske from *Perske: Pencil Portraits 1971–1990* (Nashville: Abingdon Press, 1998).

proactively to the needs of children who have behavioral and emotional problems and challenges.

- Designing the physical environment of the classroom and school to promote learning and growth among children with diverse sensory and physical characteristics; adapting the environment and using assistive technology to help children learn more effectively.
- Demonstrating leadership and learning through dialogue and democratic decision making.

Does inclusive teaching mean that we *never* have students in separate classes or ability groups? We believe the evidence is clear that schools can and must work toward including all students in heterogeneous learning groups, in classes for all children. At the same time, we recognize that sometimes we just can't figure out how to make it work with a child. We recognize that when this happens, we've failed to create the type of school community to which we are committed, and we realize that our failure may have a negative impact on this child's life. Sometimes, however, that's the best we can do. In other situations, we may well find a school where the instruction in general education classes is ineffective for all students—and where the instruction in the segregated special education class is wonderful. In such a situation, we know we have a school that is not working for many of the children, a school that needs great improvement. For the time being, however, we may agree that a particular child would be better off, this semester, in the special education class. Yet, rather than negating the goal of inclusive teaching, these situations underscore the importance of working to improve it.

What about ability grouping or clustering students who are gifted in one class? Do we never do this? Our goal is that we meet the needs of all our students. We intentionally group children heterogeneously across classes; students labeled as gifted or having a disability are not grouped or clustered in a class. We use ability groups only for short-term, nonrecurring groupings for minilessons for specific skills or activities. We are very careful that such groupings are not stable ability groups but rather are flexible and have constantly shifting membership or methods of organization—by interest, topic, or type of project. No student in our class should be able to identify who is in the "low" group and who is in the "high" group.

Let's now look in greater detail at what makes an effective inclusive school.

Partnering with Parents

Parents of children with special needs have typically gone through much. In traditional schools, such parents receive frequent negative feedback. However, we know that strong parent support is critical. Therefore, in an inclusive school we turn this pattern around through the following types of actions:

- Parents are *immediately* invited to have their children in inclusive classes.
- We meet with parents and listen carefully to their thoughts about their children, seeking to understand each child's gifts, strengths, needs, and interests from the parents' perspective, as well as to identify strategies that work with the child.

■ We invite parents into the school and into class, making them feel welcome and a part of the school family and community.

In an inclusive school family members are often seen in the building. They read to classes, help during writing time, cut out materials, and demonstrate things they have learned in their career. Even parents whose work does not give them the flexibility to join the class during the day are often willing to do something at home for the class. They can read and record books on tape, put together books from a publishing center, or arrange for a field trip that involves touring their workplace. Family fun nights allow children and parents to engage in learning activities together in the evening. In an inclusive school parents are allies, discuss concerns freely and often, and see themselves as working as a team.

Providing Support for Teachers, Students, and Parents

Supporting teachers in working with students at multiple ability levels, students who have emotional and social challenges in their lives, or students with sensory–physical differences is critical. Just as children need to feel safe and comfortable, so do adults. Teachers who are used to teaching at only one level sometimes have difficulty teaching to multiple levels and need help learning new ideas.

At most schools a range of specialists are available to deal with special needs and problems of children—social workers, special education teachers, bilingual teachers, psychologists, nurses, occupational therapists, speech therapists, and others. In a traditional school most of these people work on their own, with limited consultation from others, pulling children out of class for services. In an inclusive school, however, specialists work to support the general education classroom teacher as part of a *team*. Students are heterogeneously grouped in all classes and not ability grouped within classes. Support staff and the general education teacher work together with the whole class, and students with special needs are not taught at the side or at the back of the class.

Support teams often meet weekly to discuss the needs of children with special problems and brainstorm ideas for handling the issues, and planning meetings are scheduled at least every two weeks between the general education teacher and specialists who support the classroom. Special education teachers and other specialists—Title I teachers, speech therapists, occupational therapists—collaborate and support general education teachers in their classes. Teachers or **paraprofessionals** work with all the students in the class while ensuring that the students with special needs receive the help they need; such teachers often supervise small groups of children with mixed abilities who are engaged in different projects—centers, inquiry projects, and more. Teachers meet regularly in book study groups to learn new strategies.

Offering Authentic, Multilevel Instruction

A seventh-grade boy spends his time in English class struggling to read at a beginner's level. A girl at a nearby desk with her nose in a book could tackle a Harvard literature class. Seated in between is a youngster who's a whiz at math, but takes a whole period to write three English sentences because he is much more comfortable writing sentences in his native Spanish. (McAdamis, 2001, p. 48)

Schools are typically structured by grade levels and teach using standardized materials aimed at a middle ability level. However, we know that children of the same age do not necessarily learn at the same rate or level. In fact, any class, whether attempting to be inclusive or not, contains children functioning three to six grade levels apart. Therefore, inclusive teaching means **designing for diversity** from the beginning, rather than thinking of each type of special student as a separate challenge. Inclusive teachers use the growing understanding of differentiated instruction and **universal design** to:

- Design lessons at multiple levels
- Challenge students at their own level
- Provide support to push children ahead to their next level of learning
- Engage children in learning via activities that relate to the real world—to their lives at home and in the community
- Engage the **multiple intelligences** and **learning styles** of children so that many pathways for learning and demonstrating achievement are available
- Involve students in collaborative pair or group work in which children draw on each other's strengths

Many exciting methods of teaching may easily accommodate many levels of ability. These methods are part of what we call **multilevel teaching:** good teaching practices that actively engage children in real-world, problem-based projects. For example, a teacher may teach writing by having all students write about the same topic, but at different levels, expecting very different results from different children. The teacher helps students edit their work and provides specific instruction in needed skills via minilessons with individuals or with small groups that have similar needs cropping up in their writing. Instead of everyone's reading the same book, children choose books at their personal level, not too hard and not too easy. They read with a partner who is reading a similar book, or sit near a student who is at a higher level for ease of help with words. Teachers read with individual learners or sit in on a discussion group.

Teachers also help children draw from the knowledge and skill of their

CLEARING A PATH
FOR PEOPLE WITH SPECIAL NEEDS
CLEARS THE PATH FOR EVERYONE!

peers. The children know whom to ask for spelling advice, guidelines on quotation marks, or funny ideas for stories. They know who will allow them to practice reading out loud and always give positive feedback. Everyone, no matter what his or her ability level, has a needed role. Gifted children grow in their relationships with others through working with special education students, and lower-functioning students may encourage a gifted but underachieving friend to improve his or her work. Students with mental retardation have models and a rich learning environment, picking up much by incidental learning yet benefiting from explicit, systematic instruction on needed skills. As children are expected to recognize each person's strengths and needs and to help one another achieve their goals, they rise to the occasion.

Building Community and Meeting the Needs of Children with Behavioral Challenges

If children are to learn, they must feel safe, secure, and cared for. When they don't, learning diminishes or ceases. Yet many children are at risk in our society. Teachers and schools are challenged to fill this void by providing comforting support structures. *Building community* in the school is critical, and intentional tools and strategies are needed. This is a complex process, however. Its many dimensions may include:

- Cultivating collaborative, supportive, respectful relationships among staff, parents, and the community—creating study groups, school teams that focus on different issues, team teaching, and so on.
- Building structures among children in the classroom so students can help one another—peer partners; circles of support; conflict resolution; and sharing of lives and feelings in conversation, writing, the arts, class meetings, and more.
- Giving children choices and teaching them responsibility—for example, letting children go to the bathroom on their own (rather than lining up a whole group); offering selection among several classroom activities; allowing students to sit, stand, move around, lie on the floor, and so on as they study or work together.

In an inclusive classroom, children are amazing in the way they know the strengths and problems of everyone in the classroom and are willing to share their own strengths and be guided in overcoming their challenges. They learn to share feelings with one another: "Please don't do that. It hurts me." Teachers help students learn how to brainstorm cooperative play activities so that some do not feel left out and how to include all in both play and academic work. Children are quick to point out positive attributes of their peers and have strategies for dealing with a classmate who is having a bad day. Students know if peers are upset and can request that the teacher call a class meeting to address their concerns. Students learn it is safe to take risks and to try more difficult work, knowing that others will not laugh at them and the teacher will not give them a bad grade for not getting it right. They know that all behavior involves choices and that they can make peaceful ones.

In such classes, behavior problems are much less frequent. Children know they belong; they have choices and do not feel constrained, yet are systematically taught responsibility. Of course students still cause problems. However, staff respect children and work to develop proactive solutions, involving the children in the process.

The way in which inclusive teachers (and the total school staff) approach problem behavior is perhaps most important. Too often, in their attempts to eliminate misbehavior without considering the underlying causes, schools actually *create* behavior problems. Inclusive teachers work to foster a culture that meets students' needs. They understand that *all behavior communicates a message.* When a child acts out, this is his or her way of telling staff about a need. Teachers understand that motivation must come from inside the child—must be what psychologists call *intrinsic motivation*—rather than constantly being controlled by external forces through punishments or rewards *(extrinsic motivation).* Teachers in inclusive schools know that they must seek to understand the needs of the child and must identify and teach alternative strategies for helping the child meet his or her need in a positive way. Together with parents they ask questions: "What occurs before, during, and after the problematic behavior?" "What is going on in the child's life?" Together with the child and parents, staff then design strategies to meet the child's needs in positive ways. The aim is to help the child understand that the behavior is not good; that people care, but that there are other ways for a person to get what he or she needs.

Most centrally, inclusive teachers and their colleagues do their very best to avoid the use of rewards and punishments; and they do their very best to keep a child in their school and classroom, resisting the frequent pressure and temptation to send children with behavior problems to separate classes or schools. They work hard to build a caring culture, help children support one another, learn about their own needs, and devise positive behavioral strategies for meeting them.

Inclusive School and Classroom Design

In inclusive schools, whether newly constructed or older buildings, we do our best to take the multiple needs of children and staff into account in the way we use physical space and resources. We work to create places of beauty, peace, and fun; spaces where all have a place to belong and that respond to the different learning styles of children. Technology plays a key role in providing children expanded tools for learning and sources of information. In all this, we use **assistive technology,** whether simple devices such as nonskid desk pads that help a child with cerebral palsy place materials on his desk, software that reads words aloud or provides spelling and writing assistance, or more sophisticated electronic communication devices.

Empowerment, Leadership, and Democracy

Given the amount of segregation in our society based on race, class, culture, and ability, it is not surprising that building an inclusive school is a very challenging task and must be intentional, requiring a different way of thinking about teaching children. It takes a staff commitment that all students will be welcomed. For this commitment to become part of the culture of the school, the total staff must see inclusion as a value for children, must be able to articulate the reasons for their belief, must be willing to defend their work to those voicing concern, and must be willing to struggle when the inclusive approach doesn't seem to be working for a particular child. Effective inclusive schools, then, are also models of democratic practice. In them teachers and parents, supported by administrators, take responsibility both for leading and for listening, involving children in creating a school and classes where children learn together (Apple, 1995; Banks, 1990; Edelsky, 1999; Kozol, 1991).

School Reform and Inclusive Schools

In recent years much effort has gone into developing whole school models of reform and renewal. Some models have been successful in responding to the needs of diverse children and families and are very consistent with inclusive education (Tyack & Cuban, 1995). A few of the most effective models for working with diverse children and families are the following.

The **Accelerated Schools** approach (Hopfenberg, Levin, & Associates, 1993) promotes the use of challenging and engaging teaching, typically reserved for gifted students, for all students, particularly those with learning challenges. The goal is to accelerate, not slow down, learning for *all* students through exciting, authentic teaching techniques—"powerful learning." The Accelerated Schools program engages teachers, administrators, parents, and community members who work together in teams to develop improved learning strategies for all students.

The **Coalition for Essential Schools** (Sizer, 1996) is based on ten principles. Schools move away from the fifty-minute class period in high schools and develop larger blocks of instructional time, in which teachers work as interdisciplinary teams to engage students in substantive learning activities. Students demonstrate learning through portfolios and yearly demonstrations to parents, other students, and the larger community.

The **Comer School Development Program** brings another important perspective. According to James Comer (1987, 1997), a psychiatrist, children need not only a sense of safety and security but also a sense that they are welcomed if they are to learn. In the Comer School Development Program, schools develop teams to facilitate partnerships with parents and communities and set up an interdisciplinary mental health team consisting of teachers, a psychologist, a social worker, and others to deal with holistic needs of both students and families.

In 1997 a new school reform model was initiated that intentionally and centrally made inclusive education a central component (Peterson, Beloin, & Gibson, 1997). Called **Whole Schooling,** this approach is based on five principles that link overall school reform to effective learning for students from a wide range of cultures, languages, and abilities:

1. *Include all:* All children learn together across culture, ethnicity, language, ability, gender, and age.
2. *Partner:* Educators build genuine collaboration within the school and with families and the community; engage the school in strengthening the community;

Becoming an Inclusive Teacher: A Statement of Intent

I start by taking care of myself—emotionally, intellectually, physically.

I think about what kind of teacher I want to be and why, who will be welcomed into my class, the type of teaching I will seek to provide.

I actively seek opportunities for students with differences to be in my class. If special education students are not included by policy, I go to the special education teacher and ask that they be in my class as much as they can or that we work together coteaching our students.

As school begins, I welcome all students into my class.

I look for ways that each child can find his or her entry into the class and make contributions to the group.

I do my best to ensure that all children receive cognitive, emotional, and physical supports so they feel they belong and are successful.

I build community in my classroom, a community in which students respect and care for one another and in which we are all teachers and colearners together.

I design my curriculum so that students work at multiple levels, challenged at their own level of learning. This includes arranging choices and presenting learning tasks at various levels of difficulty.

I seek to have students always challenged but equipped with enough background knowledge and support to move successfully to the next level.

I manage my day and resources—time, support and coteaching staff, volunteers, students working together and helping one another—to make this a reality.

I constantly monitor my students' learning, paying special attention to how students are feeling and whether I think they are showing me what they know.

When I identify students who are not learning, I design ways to help them by (1) changing the way I teach—using other "intelligences," allowing for other learning styles, emphasizing more active learning, connecting learning to their own lives; (2) adapting the lesson to meet them at their own level; (3) marshaling support systems such as students helping students, support personnel, my own teaching strategies, and special assistance.

I reach out to parents and community members, bringing them in and taking us out to the larger world, making all a part of my class as a living learning laboratory.

I make my class interesting, often even fun! When learning is not, then we all stop and understand why and get on with the fun again.

and provide guidance to involve students, parents, teachers, and others in decision making and in the direction of learning and school activities.

3. *Provide multilevel, authentic instruction for learners of diverse abilities:* Teachers design instruction for diverse learners that promotes active learning through meaningful, real-world activities; teachers develop accommodations and adaptations for learners with diverse needs, interests, and abilities.

4. *Build community and support learning:* The school uses specialized school and community resources (special education, Title I, gifted education) to build support for students, parents, and teachers; builds community and mutual support within the classroom and school; and provides proactive supports for students with behavioral challenges.

5. *Empower citizens for democracy:* Educators work to build a culture of empowerment and democracy in the school at all levels—school decision making and classroom instruction.

(See **www.coe.wayne.edu/CommunityBuilding/WSC.html** for detailed information on Whole Schooling.) This model provides a schoolwide process for creating an inclusive school that connects with other exemplary educational practices. Your author guides have been involved in developing and utilizing Whole Schooling principles in schools associated with the Whole Schooling Consortium, a coalition of schools and individuals dedicated to improving schools.

Visiting Two Inclusive Schools

Let's now visit an effective inclusive elementary school and high school. What is their experience related to the principles and practices of inclusive schooling we have outlined? How do they deal with the issues identified in research?

Gilman Elementary School

Gilman Elementary School is located in a small rural community. Many students ride buses a significant distance in order to attend school. Many people in Gilman have very limited incomes. There are few resources to assist families in the community. In recent years racial tensions have risen among white people, Native Americans who live on reservations, and a growing number of Asian American immigrants. Despite the idyllic and beautiful countryside, community life in this rural area can be both challenging and isolating for children and their families.

Despite these barriers, Gilman Elementary School is known as an effective inclusive school. Inclusive education began at Gilman Elementary in 1989 when the principal, Al Arnold, began a principal's math challenge class. The group needed space in the building, but the only space available was the special education resource room. On the first day of the challenge class, Al noticed that the children were very reticent. They did not want to sit and would not touch anything in the classroom. "What is going on?" Al asked. With a bit of questioning, he discovered that students were afraid because this was the special education room. Al was shocked. That evening he received phone calls from parents concerned that their children were being placed in special education. Al felt he had to take action: "If this is how general education students feel about a special education classroom, how do they feel about their classmates with disabilities?" He and a few teachers developed a school vision and plan in which all students could learn within the general education classroom.

As we walk into Gilman Elementary today, children with and without disabilities are learning together in the same classrooms. There are no special education rooms. The special education teacher, paraprofessionals, and other related service personnel teach in general education classrooms. As we walk around the school with Al, we notice that children are engaged in very exciting learning activities. There is a positive, busy atmosphere about each class and a comfortable, relaxed sense of respect between the principal and the teachers, children, and parents with whom we come in contact.

Al talks with us about how inclusive schooling is being implemented at Gilman Elementary. "Inclusion for us at Gilman," he says, "has several parts. First, we seek to deliver instruction to all students in a manner that meets individual needs and gives students the opportunity to develop to their full potential, academically and socially. Second, we do this by utilizing the team teaching of general and special teachers, who work together using diverse teaching strategies. We seek to respond to diverse learning styles, using individualized instruction and flexible grouping."

"To make these goals a reality," Al continues, "the school is using five key strategies to provide support to students and teachers." First, the staff designed a structure in which one specialist is assigned to each grade-level team as a support to all students with special needs. The specialists include a Title 1 teacher, gifted coordinator/reading specialist, guidance counselor, speech/language therapist, and one special education teacher (with cross-categorical experience). These specialists team-teach every day for a minimum of one-half day per week in each class.

Second, teams composed of two general educators and one specialist provide support to students. Each team member has equal responsibility for every student at their grade level. In essence, these three teachers are individually and collectively responsible for approximately fifty to sixty students. The grade-level teaching team is responsible for the success of their students with disabilities and all other students.

Third, the teaching staff redesigned the schoolwide schedule in order to create a daily block of *"sacred time"* during which there are absolutely no interruptions. During sacred time the grade-level classrooms have 100 percent of their students for 100 percent of the time. No music, art, physical education, or computer classes are scheduled. Sacred time is for grade-level teaching teams to go full speed ahead in teaching the core subject material without interruptions.

The fourth program feature involves *planning time* for grade-level teaching teams and the team of specialists. Thanks to the creation of the block schedule, each grade-level team now has ninety minutes of planning time each week, *in addition to* the designated amount of preparation time each teacher receives as specified in his or her teaching contract. Specialists also have a weekly sixty-minute planning block in which they meet as a team to discuss specific students' needs, goals, and progress.

Fifth, to guarantee that students will never again identify a classroom as stigmatizing, Al explains, Gilman Elementary has implemented a system of flexible instructional grouping and utilization of instructional space. The staff change instructional groupings continually to eliminate the possibility of stigma becoming associated with a group. Similarly, all students work with each of the three teachers, so no stigma is associated with special teachers. The same is true of space usage. There is nothing unusual about a student's learning in any particular room or space, as all students work in those rooms at one time or another. The three teachers rotate and teach in each of the rooms (including the specialist's small room or office) so that the students will not associate a certain teacher with any specific room or space. (Figure 2.3 summarizes these five strategies.)

As we finish our tour, Al leads us to a classroom at the end of the hall. There we see a general and special education teacher leading a rehearsal for a play students will present in an assembly for parents in the coming week. We see a child who typically experiences significant behavioral outbursts at the center of a small group of children singing a song. They are all holding hands, and the child smiles, making everyone in the room laugh. The teachers wave. We walk to our car wishing we could stay. (Account adapted from Arnold, 1998, and Beloin, 1998.)

Graham High School

"Urban high school"—in our mind's eye we picture security gates, metal detectors, graffiti, and gangs. However, we understand that Graham High School has developed an exemplary program for meeting the needs of all students, and we have been looking forward to visiting the school.

A junior named Thuy Nguyen greets us and tells us he will be our guide. Walking across the campus, we notice a group of students in the courtyard, one of whom is using a wheelchair. Thuy says they are ninth graders working on a science project, creating their own measuring system. They are using Paulo's wheelchair as their measuring system, they explain: A full rotation of the wheel counts as one unit, and they are measuring the perimeter of the school.

We ask Thuy to introduce us to the special educators at the school. Again he looks puzzled; he says he doesn't know any special educators. We describe teachers who team-teach or who help students with disabilities in their classes. "Oh, you mean the resource teachers," he says. Then he asks, "for which department?" "English," we reply, feeling that this would be a safe bet in a high school. Thuy responds, "Do you mean humanities?"

Following more awkward interactions in which we discover that traditional stereotypes don't necessarily apply here, we meet Greg Allen, a member of the science team who coaches football and is the "advocate" for twenty-seven students with disabilities. Graham High serves some 2,200 students and is organized into knowledge base groups, and all teachers in a knowledge base work together on curriculum and instruction. One member sits on the school curriculum council to negotiate schoolwide instructional themes and essential questions (see Jorgensen, 1998). All categorically funded teachers (special education, Title I, bilingual education, reading specialists, and migrant education), Greg explains, are called "resource teachers" and are members of knowledge base groups.

The school is organized into two divisions. Division I encompasses ninth and tenth grade and provides all students with a core curriculum. Classes are ninety minutes long on the block/quarter system. Division II is organized into

Figure 2.3

Inclusive Strategies in an Elementary School

- A specialist, drawn from several categorical programs, is assigned to each grade-level team to provide in-class support for teachers.
- Teachers and specialists work together as a team to assist all children at a grade level.
- "Sacred time" is established to create uninterrupted academic learning.
- A ninety-minute planning block is set aside for grade-level teams and an additional sixty-minute planning block with specialists each week.
- Flexible instructional groupings ensure heterogeneous grouping and prevent stigmatization of students.

curricular clusters: business, technology, engineering, communicative and fine arts, and human services. Within each cluster, students have classes that cover many disciplines.

We ask Greg about his role with students who have disabilities. He tells us that in addition to his role as a support teacher in science, he communicates regularly with each student and his or her family and chairs (or cochairs with the student) the IEP meeting. "I do not see all my students every day. If one is not in science this term, I may not see him or her very often. I rely on colleagues to provide support. I know the science curriculum quite well, and I support every student who has a disability in his or her science class. My colleagues support students in humanities, technology, communicative and fine arts, and other areas."

Greg says that every student with a disability who lives in the school catchment area attends Graham and that each student with a disability receives all special education supports and services within the general education classroom. Students with disabilities are not grouped by category, and no teacher has advocate responsibilities for a specific type of student disability (e.g., blindness, mental retardation).

We continue our tour and Thuy takes us to the technology cluster area where he attends class. We enter the humanities class for the Division II technology group and find two teachers and thirty-five students—a diverse group in terms of ethnicity, gender, age, and language background. Both adults look up from their tables and smile.

We talk with Felicia Conway, one of the two resource teachers in the humanities knowledge base. "I spend time two days a week with Ginger

Four middle school students conduct a science experiment. A lowered table allows the student in a wheelchair to participate fully.

Ferrara working at learning centers, providing all students feedback and instruction on their writing." Four students in this section of humanities have IEPs, and every class in the school has a natural proportion of students with and without disabilities. Approximately 10 percent of the students in any class receive special education services. Felicia tells us that the school decided on this approach "many years ago, to avoid the idea that there were just a few 'inclusion classes' in which special education teachers and aides spent their time." We ask her what it took to ensure that all teachers were ready to teach all students. She shows us a list of interview questions used for all new teachers. Several of these questions make it clear that the ability to teach an inclusive, diverse group of students is a prerequisite for faculty. "I am a member of the professional development committee, and our staff development efforts focus on differentiating instruction," Felicia continues. Interestingly, she tells us that they have never done an "inclusion training." All staff development providers are selected based on their ability to share information about quality instruction for all students.

Our tour guide introduces us to his girlfriend, Jessica, who tells us about her fourth-block class. During that ninety-minute period, Jessica is a peer tutor in a math class; she does not get math credit for the period but does receive an elective credit. "I provide assistance to any student in the class who needs it," she says. For example, Anthony "learns a bit different, moves his eyes to communicate, and uses a switch to talk. He has modified work that I help with, but mostly I make sure that he's involved with peers and stuff." Jessica tells us that she is in the technology cluster because she wants to be a teacher and knows that technology will be very important for teachers.

As we leave the technology cluster, we ask Thuy about how students get extra help if they need it. He tells us about the learning center. Thinking we've found the special education room, we walk into the learning center—a room off the library/media center—and see students tutoring other students and teachers working with individuals and small groups of students. Students come in and out of the learning center.

Barbara Samimi coordinates the learning center. She is also the "coordinator of family and community involvement" for the school. Title I funds are used to support the learning center. Barbara is a bundle of energy, and every student seems to know her. We first ask her about attendance. She tells us that teachers "do all kinds of activities in their classes, and sometimes students just need a place to go and get caught up. The learning center is here for that." She adds that students come before or after school "to do homework without the pressure or to make sure that they're getting it done right."

We inquire about students with disabilities, asking her if, as happens in other schools, the learning center becomes a dumping ground for students the teachers don't want in their classrooms. Barbara looks troubled by our question. "A dumping ground?! The learning center is not there for that! We are a place for students to get help; anyone can get help; not just students who have special needs. About your teachers not wanting kids . . . they shouldn't be teachers. Graham High School is a school for everyone—we figure it out and make sure that every student is provided the opportunity to be successful."

As we leave we consider the successes experienced by the students at this school. Figure 2.4 provides an overview of the inclusive practices at Graham High School, which typify exemplary approaches used in both middle and high schools. We realize that these practices are good for all students and serve to ensure that students feel welcomed and respected within the school walls.

Figure 2.4

Inclusive Practices in a High School

- Every student can access teachers—general and special education—for assistance, mentoring, or conflict resolution.
- Special education teachers provide in-class support and assistance for all students.
- Classes are structured to encourage peer support and a spirit of collaboration and collegiality among students.
- Special education and other categorical services are organized according to the overarching school governance structure (e.g., departments, knowledge base groups, academic families, academies).
- Class time is longer (ninety minutes), allowing students to process information more deeply and ensuring that teachers get to know students well.
- Curriculum is planned and organized for all students, and accommodations and modifications are provided for those students who need them.
- Teachers are provided with the professional development resources they need to be successful.

Stepping Stones

To Inclusive Teaching

1. Find at least one school in your area that is trying to be inclusive and visit it. Compare this school's practices to what happens at your school. How did the inclusive school get started? What do you notice? What are your feelings about this school?

2. It all starts with one teacher who cares enough about all children to say, "I want to have a student with special needs in my class. I think they belong here and I want to learn how." In your school is there one special education student whom you could take into your class—perhaps part-time at first and building on this as you, the child, and the special education teacher feel comfortable?

3. If you are in a school that is inclusive, explore *how* inclusive it is. Are children with moderate to severe disabilities in general education classes in your school? Or only students with slight differences such as learning disabilities? If the latter, where are those other students?

Onward in Our Journey
The Sun Is High, the Road Is Wide

As we have begun our journey together, we have visited real schools and classrooms to see how an inclusive classroom and school looks; we have looked at the research and have introduced the principles and practices on which inclusive teaching is based. We hope that you are beginning to see how inclusive education can work and are excited about the possibility of being an inclusive teacher. Now, more than ever, in the midst of social change, children and families need good schools and effective education. Most of all they need caring teachers who reach out and welcome all children.

A former university student said this about a teacher who was working with students with special needs in her math class:

> The teacher sincerely believes that every student in her classroom has the ability to be successful and to learn. Her obligation is to discover how each student learns best and use that information to the student's advantage. . . . Her secret joy is defying visitors to correctly identify the "included" students. (Ceifetz, 1997, p. 5)

Before we continue, we invite you to reflect a few minutes. Think about your images of schools, families, and children with special needs. Think about your own experiences as a young child and as a student. Think about your experiences with people who are different from you. Think about the possibilities of a school where all learn, all achieve, and all value one another. Think about the roles you might play in teaching in such a school and even in helping to create one.

 Key Points

- Many students are referred for segregated special education programs because of ineffective teaching and schooling practices.

- Research comparing inclusive and segregated education of students with disabilities consistently shows that inclusive education produces better academic, social, and emotional outcomes.

- Inclusive education has many benefits for students both with and without disabilities, and no evidence exists that inclusive education has harmed the learning of students without disabilities.

- Effective inclusive schools make a commitment to include all students in heterogeneous classes with limited to no clustering or ability grouping.

Such schools work to develop an inclusive culture through interacting principles and practices:
  - ✓ Partnering with parents and the community
  - ✓ Providing support services for teachers and students
  - ✓ Offering authentic, multilevel instruction
  - ✓ Building community and responding positively to the needs of students with behavioral challenges
  - ✓ Designing the school and classroom to respond to differing learning abilities and styles
  - ✓ Empowerment, leadership, and democracy

- Inclusive teaching and schooling is both possible and fun, as illustrated by real schools.

 Learning Expeditions

Following are some ideas that may extend your learning.

1. Visit a segregated class or school for children with disabilities. Observe children and interview staff about their opinions about inclusive education. Talk with a parent. Think critically about the reasons behind the responses you get.

2. Visit a general education classroom that includes children with types of disabilities similar to those represented in the separate class you observed (question 1). Observe the teaching and support provided in the regular classroom. Interview both the general and special education teacher as well as students and parents. Ask them about their feelings about what is happening. Again, think about the reasons behind the responses you get. How do your two observations compare?

3. Interview an adult with a disability. Ask about the person's public school experience and present life circumstances. What did the person feel about the help, support, and accommodations he or she received in school? What is the person's opinion of inclusive education? Explore the reasons for the answer the person gives. What do these responses tell you?

4. Interview a parent of a child with a disability who is being included and supported in a general education classroom. Ask about the parent's experiences with the child, the professionals, and the schools. Ask about his or her own experience in inclusive education—what is working and what is not. Again, explore the reasons for the answers the parent gives. What do these responses tell you?

5. Develop a checklist based on the information presented in this chapter regarding characteristics of an effective inclusive school. Use this checklist in visiting a school. What questions or conclusions does this experience generate?

CHAPTER GOAL

Grasp theoretical and practical aspects of partnering with families in the education of students with special needs.

CHAPTER OBJECTIVES

1. Become more sensitive to the challenges facing families and develop strategies for working effectively with families of children with special needs.

2. Utilize strategies for communication, collaborative problem solving, and support of families.

3. Understand system-, child-, and family-centered approaches to services.

4. Identify ways to connect with community resources that support families and teaching.

Partnering with 3 Parents and the Community

Building Relationships for Learning

few years ago, a teacher made the following comment at the conclusion of a class focusing on partnering with families: "Before I took this class, I thought that I would be teaching math, science, reading, and social studies. Now I know that I will be teaching children, and with children come families." If we are to be effective teachers of *all* children, understanding parents is critical.

We are visiting with a parent support group, part of a state-funded parent-to-parent network of families of children with special needs who meet periodically.

We arrive at the home of Jan, the group's facilitator, and find fifteen parents sitting on the living room floor. We're struck immediately by the diversity represented. Although most participants are women, they come from many different ethnic groups. Some, we are told, have very low incomes; others have moderate to high incomes.

After a welcome from Jan, Frieda begins. "I am excited about how Melanie's high school drama teacher is reaching out to my daughter," she says with a big smile. Melanie has a severe learning disability and has had trouble with teachers who would not try to help her. "Mr. Kizewski really went out of his way to include Melanie in the school play. With his encouragement she is really blossoming!" she exclaims. "He met with Melanie to make suggestions about how she might practice and how we could help at home. She is having so much fun. It has brought out a side of her we have never seen. Amazingly, this new confidence is spilling over into some of her other courses."

Jan, the group facilitator, draws a lesson. "We need to look for teachers who develop partnerships with parents," she said. "They need our support. However, others have stories that we need to hear tonight."

"Yes," said John, one of the two fathers at the meeting. "We are very frustrated and would appreciate your support." Looking burdened and with a sigh, John describes his efforts to get his son Matt, a fourteen-year-old with Down syndrome, into regular academic and industrial arts courses at high school. John became convinced that Matt should be in a regular class after attending conferences and obtaining information from other parents about how much their children were learning.

"We just don't know what to do," John says. "We met with the special education director, principal, and special education teacher. We visited some classes. The industrial arts teacher was encouraging, but he seemed nervous. The special education director told us that inclusion is inappropriate for Matt because Matt's abilities are too low. He says that Matt's special needs can be met only in a special education class. He doesn't even consider, it seems, how much Matt can learn by being with other children. The special education director will not even visit schools that are doing this successfully. We really do not want to take them to a hearing. We also do not want to have to sell our house and move to another district like some other families we know. What are we to do?"

Jan asks for feedback from the group: "What ideas do you have?" They ask John additional questions and share other stories of frustration. Throughout the next two hours, parents discuss concerns and experiences, some of them tearfully. As we leave, we are amazed at the degree of openness, emotional support, and practical advice and help these parents provide to one another. Some stories fill us with hope; others with despair. We ponder how these stories reflect both good and bad practices.

Traveling Notes

Parents and teachers may find themselves at odds about how to teach children—and particularly children with special needs. Conversations in teachers' lounges often revolve around this problem.

1. What were your reactions to the stories told in the gathering at Jan's home? What do you think should be done to help John in his frustration with the school?

2. What are the many concrete ways in which teachers can connect with and support families?

3. Do you know other teachers who have helped parents in the ways that Jeanette and Frieda described? How did these teachers manage to offer this kind of support while teaching children all day?

4. Why do parents feel welcome in some schools and classes but not in others?

5. The sense of relationship and personal connection seemed important to the parents in this meeting. Yet in schools you often hear people say that "you can't get parents to come to a meeting unless you give them food or raffle a prize." Think about this. How can we communicate with parents about difficulties their children are having academically or behaviorally in our classes and yet build a relationship with them?

Toward Family-Centered Education
Building Genuine Partnerships

Research clearly demonstrates that if children are to learn and grow, teachers must reach beyond the classroom to partner with families and community members (Ballen & Moles, 1994; Barnett, 1997; Becher, 1984; Epstein, 1994). This is particularly true of children who have learning, social, and/or physical challenges (Bishop, Woll, & Arango, 1993; O'Shea, O'Shea, Algozzine, & Hammitte, 2001; Turnbull, Turnbull, Bronicki, Summers, & Roeder-Gordon, 1989). In this part of our journey, we explore ways to connect with parents of students with special needs and harness the power of family partnerships.

The U.S. Department of Education (Ballen & Moles, 1994) has championed the strengthening of partnerships between schools and families by providing grant funds for demonstration programs, helping develop publications that promote effective parent–school partnerships, and encouraging research. Despite this national thrust on partnering with parents, however, parents of children with special needs often find their problems compounded by difficult interactions with teachers and school staff (Fialka & Mikus, 1999; Turnbull & Turnbull, 1997). Parents often sense that teachers do not care about their children. They often receive ongoing negative feedback that makes them feel unwelcome and unsupported. Even the most informed, educated, and committed parents often struggle to get help for their child. In virtually every school district, when parents of children with disabilities talk together, they share stories of pain and struggle like John's story (Turnbull & Turnbull, 1997). Parents from low-income or minority backgrounds who have children with special needs are particularly likely to have difficulties (Comer, 1988; Moles, 1993; Villa & Thousand, 1996; Villa, Thousand, Stainback, & Stainback, 1992).

Some teachers and schools do not share this mindset, however. In many communities schools serve as potent centers of the community, reaching out to parents in partnership. These same schools are engaged in effective teaching practices and in active reform efforts.

Family and Community Challenges

What is a family? In the twentieth century we thought mostly about the nuclear family—mother and father with children. Grandparents, aunts, and uncles are the extended family. For most of history (and prehistory), however, "family" meant the full village—mother and father, extended family, neighbors, and friends. Everyone in a local community considered children "theirs" and saw themselves as having personal responsibilities to these children. The focus on the nuclear family is recent.

Today, in response to the need for stable relationships and support systems, people are finding new ways of forming social bonds. This trend is causing the definition of what constitutes a family to broaden and shift. If we understand the family of each child as a network of people who are intimately connected to and responsible for one another, we can then more naturally connect with the whole range of people in the life of a child—grandparents, family friends, and mentors (Dunst, 1987; Kagan & Weissbourd, 1994; O'Shea, O'Shea, Algozzine, & Hammitte, 2001).

Local communities face many challenges, as do the families who live in them. Some of the problems are reported in the newspaper on a daily basis—teenage pregnancy, violence, crime, poverty, unemployment, divorce, illiteracy, disease, substance

A child with special needs shows her work to her parents and teacher in a student-led conference.

abuse, illness, and disability. People are isolated and often have few resources to draw upon. Neighbors may know little if anything about one another and may have infrequent interactions (Perin, 1988; Rankin & Quane, 2000).

As a result of these dynamics, when families encounter problems—such as the loss of a job, divorce, or serious illness—they often feel overwhelmed and alone. For example, perhaps a child with mental retardation is born. Families with children who have disabilities or other health issues may have few resources to call on for support. Human service agencies are often too understaffed and overburdened to provide the level of assistance needed to those encountering these difficulties (Kagan & Weissbourd, 1994; Turnbull & Turnbull, 1997).

Typically, too, such stressors do not occur in isolation. Poor families may occupy substandard housing, have trouble getting employment with a living wage, and live in environments that can contribute to children's learning problems or other disabilities. For example, lead poisoning, long known to damage the learning ability of children, is far more prevalent in housing in low-income neighborhoods (Schmidt, 1999). Many schools in low-income areas are in great disrepair, sometimes causing health and learning problems for children (Agron, 1998; Fraser, Clickner, Everett, & Viet, 1991; Grubb & Diamantes, 1998). Another kind of difficulty faces the executive who lives in a "nice neighborhood": He or she may be under great pressure to maintain the family's standard of living and may therefore spend little time at home. Also, children in families under stress are more vulnerable to abuse or neglect (Barnett, 1997; Bishop, Woll, & Arango, 1993; Coleman, 1994; Dunst, 1987). As we deal with parents of children with disabilities and other special needs, we must bear all this in mind, trying to understand the world from their point of view.

The Importance of Family and Community for Child Development: An Ecological Framework

For many years the importance of total family and community interactions, the "life ecology" of children, was not well understood. Researchers studied learning in controlled clinical settings, focusing at most on mother–child interactions, rather than seeking to understand the complex influences of family and community. Urie Bronfenbrenner (1979) developed a widely utilized theory, an adaptation of which is graphically presented in Figure 3.1, that broke with this tradition and posited an ecological model of human development. This ecological framework posits that all aspects of the environment have an impact on child development and growth. A hierarchy of interacting influences is apparent. Those most critical are in inner circles—family, intimate relationships, close friends, and community mentors. For optimum growth and development, a child will be supported by this inner circle—which is, in turn, supported by key community institutions—such as church, synagogue, school, or the business community. When this framework breaks down, children have problems.

The implications of this ecological theory for teachers and schools are substantial. What are teachers and educators to do if a child does not have a caring social support system? Comer (1997) and others (Ballen & Moles, 1994; Becher, 1984; Hyde, Burchard, & Woodworth, 1996; Moles, 1993) suggest that the school must become a caring community where children are nurtured and where adults and other children

Figure 3.1

Ecological Framework for Child Development

COMMUNITY (Microsystem)

Circle 1 Inner circle: family, close friends, spouse
Circle 2 Friends and acquaintances
Circle 3 Participation: acquaintances in local stores, community groups, or associations

PAID HELPERS (Mesosystem)

Circle 4 Paid helpers: doctors, teachers, dentists
Circle 5 Special human services: vocational rehabilitation, welfare caseworkers

ADMINISTRATION AND POLICY (Exosystem)

Policymakers and administrations: city council and school board, state legislature, U.S. Department of Education

SOCIETY AND CULTURE (Macrosystem)

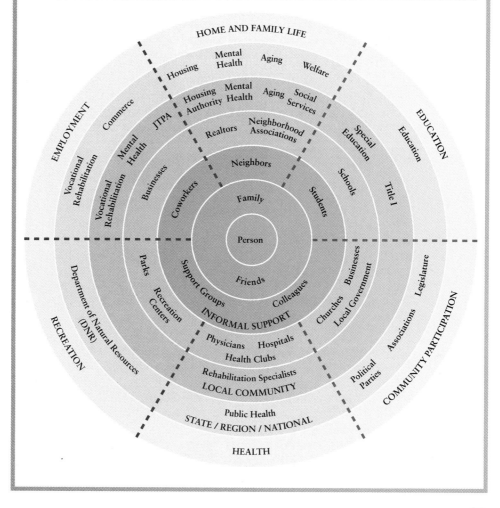

become a support system for the child. McKnight (1993) suggests that the school develop partnerships with the community to link community resources to parents; providing support for parents, in turn, can make them better able to care for their children. We will find that our approach to parents of children with special challenges is key to building a truly caring learning community for all families and their children. Let us consider, then, the needs and challenges of such parents.

Being a Parent to a Child with Special Needs

When we speak of families of children with special needs, we recognize that in one sense these families are like all other families. That is, all children are "special," presenting their own unique gifts and needs. On the other hand, some children place greater demands on the resources of the family, community, and school than others.

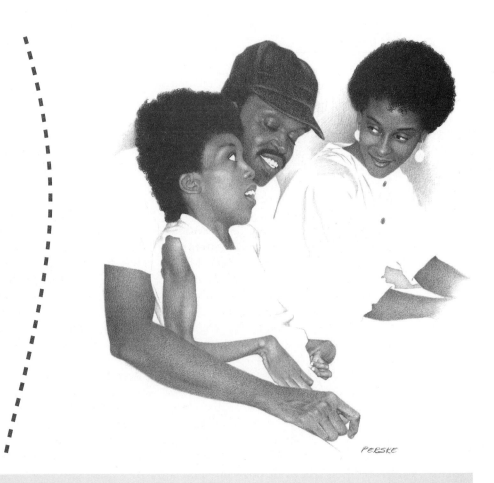

Artwork reprinted by permission of Martha Perske from *Perske: Pencil Portraits 1971– 1990* (Nashville: Abingdon Press, 1998).

Responding to a Child with Special Needs. Being a parent is always challenging and exciting, and this is true of raising a child with special needs as well. Parents respond to a child with a disability in many ways, depending on their own personality, resources, and support. Some will be overwhelmed and angry; some will be thoughtful and reflective, gleaning insights into the challenge of human living. Some will be active advocates; others will cope by withdrawing. However parents may respond, they have much to share with us, and we can do much to support them.

Children with disabilities come into families in many different ways. Some have observable disabilities from birth. Some have a special need that may not be identified until the child enters school or later. Some families adopt children with special needs. For other families, a disability may occur as a result of a tragic accident.

Guilt. Families often struggle with guilt and issues of self-esteem. When a disability results from an accident, particularly from an accident that involved negligence, this can be particularly difficult. For example, one young father and his son were out fishing and the boat capsized. The boy survived but suffered severe brain damage. When genetic factors cause the disability, both parents may feel responsible for the struggles their child experiences (Fialka, 1997; O'Shea, O'Shea, Algozzine, & Hammitte, 2001; Perske & Perske, 1981).

If the child has a severe disability, the family may take responsibility for home-based medical care requiring that they learn the use of medical equipment and obtain assistance from family, friends, and medical personnel. Daily routines of bathing, feeding, and play take more time and energy. Coupled with therapies and doctors' appointments, these substantial new responsibilities tax families' time, energy, emotions, and finances (Featherstone, 1980; Knoll, 1994).

Cycle of Grief. Families of children with disabilities often experience a cycle of grief that is not unlike dealing with death. All parents hope to have children who are bright, able, and talented. Most of us have to deal with the fact that our children have limitations. For parents of children with disabilities, however, this realization is often intensified. For example, the parents of a boy with severe mental retardation, whose language development by the first grade is very limited, know that he will not be a doctor, lawyer, or teacher. They also know that he will need significant support and assistance all his life. Such a family must allow the original desired image of their child to literally die so that they can accept their child as he is and rejoice in his strengths and capacities (Fialka, 1997; Turnbull & Turnbull, 1997).

Some family researchers, however, question the degree to which the experience of grieving is either typical or necessary. "It is misleading to describe parental reactions without also considering how professionals share the diagnosis," say Turnbull and Turnbull (1997, p. 137). O'Halloran (1995) takes a different approach. She describes a "celebration process" in which the emotions prompted by a diagnosis can be connected with deep reflections regarding hope for the future; the positive contributions of people with disabilities; and the capturing of negative emotions as a catalyst for energy, persistence, and learning.

The Tragedy of Abuse. Parents of children with disabilities develop strategies to cope with the stress of raising their children. Given the lack of support for parents, we sometimes see patterns emerge that limit or even directly harm children. Some 25 percent of the caseloads of welfare agencies dealing with abused children, for example, involve children with disabilities (Finkelhor & Hashima, 2001; Sobsey & Doe, 1991). Some parents believe that their children cannot learn, do not expect anything of them, and reinforce negative behaviors. As such children grow older, they sometimes are violent when their wants are not met immediately; parents may then withdraw, intimidated (Ammerman, Van Hassett, & Hersen, 1988; Finkelhor & Hashima, 2001; Sobsey & Doe, 1991).

Informal Support for Families. Parents of children with disabilities find themselves coping with other problems. Babysitters are often very difficult to find. In some cases, having a child with a disability is seen as a great shame to the family. Some families have experienced increased social isolation as neighbors and friends are uncomfortable being around a child with a disability. People may even make hurtful comments, clearly indicating that the child with disabilities is not accepted. In such situations the weakened bonds of community and neighbor relationships represent a dwindling support network just when families face increased responsibilities (Fialka, 1997; Knoll, 1994; O'Shea, O'Shea, Algozzine, & Hammitte, 2001; Perske & Perske, 1981).

However, families and their allies also are developing alternative social supports to help them cope. The type of parent support meeting we described at the beginning of this chapter is one powerful example. Networks of family support groups and parent-to-parent connections are growing throughout the country (Bishop, Woll, & Arango, 1993; O'Shea, O'Shea, Algozzine, & Hammitte, 2001). Circles of support that bring people together around children with special needs also provide enormous assistance to families (Falvey, Forest, Pearpoint, & Rosenberg, 1998; O'Brien & O'Brien, 1996). Parent-based advocacy organizations help parents connect with others who face similar challenges (Turnbull & Turnbull, 1997).

Professional Services and Supports. Professionals in medical, educational, and other social service agencies can make an enormous difference in the lives of families, and an expanding network of support programs now exists (Knoll, 1994). A growing number of physicians have training related to the disabilities of children (Society for Developmental and Behavioral Pediatrics, 2001). Mental health programs help families locate resources and provide **respite care,** a service that allows the family to leave their child with trained caregivers and have some time to themselves. Although these programs are generally inadequately funded, they do provide needed support to families (Knoll, 1994; Perske & Perske, 1981; Shelton, Jeppson, & Johnson, 1992).

Yet professionals often display attitudes, ignorance, and disrespect that greatly increase the stress on the families of children with disabilities (Turnbull & Turnbull, 1997). To be sure, these families encounter many professionals whom they deeply respect and appreciate; still, virtually all such families have dealt with a significant number of professionals who have caused serious problems.

Consider Brenda's story. Brenda's child, Monica, was born in 1984 with severe physical and mental disabilities. Brenda received training in the hospital to provide care for Monica, who used a respirator and other medical equipment. This was difficult, but she and her husband were committed to raising their child at home. As Brenda prepared to leave the hospital, the chief neurologist approached her. "I know what you should do with your child," he said. Brenda paused. This is a renowned physician, she thought. Maybe he knows something someone else missed. "What is it?" she queried anxiously. "You should put your child in an institution and get on with your life," he said, then quickly walked down the hall to complete his rounds. Brenda was shocked. When she recovered, she had the doctor paged and confronted him. "How dare you say to me what you did? This is my child. Her place is in my home. You have no right to use your position to give such devastating messages to parents." Eventually, Monica became the first child considered "medically fragile" to enter a public school in her state (Crider, 1998).

Many families continue to receive such messages from many kinds of professionals, despite gradual changes and the move away from the practice of institutionalizing young children. After experiences like Brenda's, a parent may naturally come to be cautious and defensive. As teachers, we must bear this in mind. When we communicate with the families of children with disabilities, we must seek to understand the experiences of the family.

Rethinking Life and the Road to Inclusion. In the midst of all these challenges, many parents of children with special needs rethink their view of life. They learn to look at strengths differently. They also ask difficult questions about where their child belongs in their community—and in school. Many professionals and extended family members suggest that their children belong in special places with other children who are "like them," hoping they will be protected from rejection, safe from harm, and able to find friendship with other children with disabilities. Parents of children in segregated schools often develop close and mutually supportive bonds with one another. In many locations, in fact, segregated schools were initially developed by parents' groups and have been virtually the only option available.

A growing number of parents, however, are beginning to question segregated special education. They often come across the idea of inclusive education by happenstance—in a talk with another parent or at a local conference. In school districts where inclusive education has become part of the natural order, parents are given much support in understanding inclusive education as well as other placement options on the continuum. Schools that have not embraced inclusive education, however, typically provide little information and often resist efforts by parents to have their children in general education full time. Some parents report that embracing inclusion means giving up their connection with and support from other parents of children with disabilities, who are fearful of having their child leave a segregated class or school. Yet the opportunity for their child to grow, learn, and become a real member of the community helps these parents continue to push for inclusion and to seek allies and support from others (Fialka & Mikus, 1999; Hampel, 2000; Turnbull & Turnbull, 1997).

Advocacy and Parents. The difficulty of caring for their children while meeting—too often—with frustrating responses from professionals has often thrust parents into a new role as advocates for their children. Over time parents have had enormous impact on policy. Parent advocacy, however, is in the midst of a substantive paradigm shift. Parent advocacy is torn between advocacy for inclusion and support in the mainstream and provision of special services.

The initial efforts of parent advocates were to develop special, segregated programs for their children in education, mental health, and rehabilitation—special education schools, separate classes, sheltered workshops, group homes. Many parents became convinced that the only way their children could be safe and that the families could have a life of their own was through segregated programs.

However, a growing number of parents are seeing a new vision of community life for their children that begins with being part of the regular school (Fialka & Mikus, 1999; Hampel, 2000; Ryndak, Downing, Jacqueline, & Morrison, 1995; Turnbull & Turnbull, 1997), and new advocacy efforts have emerged that have taken several tracks. Most centrally, parents work very hard to advocate for their own child—interacting with teachers, principals, even school board members. A growing number of court cases have resulted from such individual advocacy efforts. However, parents also network with one another for support, often seeking to build collaborative efforts to have impact on the policies of a local school, district, or state. Nationally, TASH, which developed as a coalition of parents and university faculty, has been a major force for inclusive education since the early 1980s. Many other organizations have joined in this effort, and many state networks of parents working toward inclusive education have been established.

The Gift Teachers Have for Parents. All this means is that when parents come to our class, they often bring a long history of struggles, learning, isolation, and dreams for a better day. What they want most of all is a teacher they can trust who will welcome their child into the class, seeking to teach their child effectively and willingly. We have a special opportunity and responsibility to parents of children with disabilities. Rather than merely tolerating such parents and their children, we can reach out, helping parents understand that our class, our school is theirs also. We can help break the cycle of isolation, rejection, and hurt. We can come together with our principal and other teachers to say that our school is for *all children,* communicating this message in multiple ways:

- We can help develop brochures about the school that highlight our commitment to children of difference learning together, specifically stating that children of different colors, cultures, economic resources, and abilities are welcome. We might give an example of a child with autism who has succeeded in our school, along with children from different ethnic groups.

- We can distribute this information to offices of physicians, agencies, and parent advisory councils for special education in our district and county.
- We can incorporate students with disabilities and their parents into literally every aspect of school life.
- We can help parents obtain information and make connections.

Our potential for having dramatic impact on children, parents, and the total culture of our school is very high as we welcome parents into the life of our school. Let's discuss principles and practices by which we can be supportive of families of our students.

Principles and Practices for an Inclusive, Family-Centered School

Our goal is to make the family the center of learning where services are available and easily accessible. What do we mean by this? Understanding the differences among system-centered, child-centered, and family-centered approaches, as summarized in the Tools for the Trek feature, gives us a framework to answer this question.

System-centered services are organized for the convenience of the system—for the organization providing services and those in it rather than for the child or the family. This is both the most typical and the least desirable approach. Each of the three examples given in Tools for the Trek is driven by the needs and requirements of the system rather than by those of the family. In some cases, as with the example of the requirement for assessment, the original intent may have been to provide more effective services for children. However, such requirements often develop into inflexible bureaucratic procedures that no longer serve the child or family well.

Child-centered services focus on the needs of the child, usually without looking at the child in the context of the total family unit. In the examples in Tools for the Trek, service providers give directives to a family to assist their child, but without dialogue or consideration of family circumstances. For example, if library books are sent home and the parents themselves are marginally literate, these books will not be read and the child may receive negative feedback about reading. If a communication device is sent home without the involvement of the family, family members may not know how to use it.

Family-centered services, on the other hand, focus on the total family unit. The child is considered in the context of the entire family. Families are given choices for meeting times and choices regarding services for their children that fit into their overall structures and needs. They are given support and assistance (e.g., child care provided by the school) so they can attend meetings. Families can meet with school people based on their convenience, so it is unnecessary to leave work to attend an important meeting. These strategies, of course, require that schools and other organizations rethink how they provide services. The fact is that in most systems the customers fit the system's needs, rather than the system's serving the customer—which in this case is the family. Yet the impact this can make on the lives of children can be enormous. One parent of a middle school student shared with us her frustration at not being able to get in touch with her child's teacher. "I work late, and

Tools *for the* Trek

System-, Child-, and Family-Centered Services

TYPE OF SERVICE	DEFINITION	EXAMPLES
System-centered	The strengths and needs of the system drive the delivery of services.	An interdisciplinary assessment of psychological, cognitive, personality, and motor skills is required before a student can receive special education services and assistance. An education plan is given to the parent to sign at a meeting regarding the child.
Child-centered	The strengths and needs of the child drive the delivery of services.	The speech therapist orders an augmentative communication device that will be used both at home and school. Children with special needs are sent home with books to read, but the family is not consulted.
Family-centered	The priorities and choices of the family drive the delivery of services.	Child care is provided while a parent and child have a conference with the teacher. The school provides space for parent-to-parent support groups to meet at night or during the day. A teacher and parent together develop a plan to have a child do grocery lists for the family to help the child improve in writing.

when I get off she is never here. She has no method of weekly communication, like Friday folders or assignment books; she does not return my phone calls, and I am very worried about my daughter's reading. I can't just take off work to come talk to her." The system was failing this parent (Allen & Petr, 1995; Kagan & Weissbourd, 1994; Knoll, 1994; Shelton, Jeppson, & Johnson, 1992).

In sum, system-, child-, and family-centered services represent very different perspectives on education and other human services. Family-centered services are the most effective, recognizing the needs of the entire family unit and the important influence of the family in the life of the child. Several principles provide guidance as we develop family-centered education practices. From these principles flow a series of practices that schools can use to effectively engage parents as they educate children.

Engage Families as Partners. Partnership between two or more parties implies equality of power. As representatives of the school system, we hold great power. For a partnership to work, then, we must make conscious efforts to equalize the power between schools and parents. This is difficult but very rewarding. As described earlier in this chapter, rather than making demands of parents, we must seek their suggestions and ideas, offer choices, and invite them to participate in their child's school (Allen & Petr, 1995; Dunst, 1987; Knoll, 1994). One teacher shared a beautiful example of how valuable parents' suggestions can be. She was very worried about a little boy labeled "trainable mentally retarded" in her fifth-grade classroom. In talking with the mother, the teacher commented that the boy was having great difficulty settling down and keeping his hands to himself. "I just couldn't understand what the problem was. He never used to be this difficult." The boy's mom explained that he had not been able to run and play for the last six weeks because of an air cast on his ankle. "It was hidden by his clothing, so I had forgotten it. Suddenly his behavior made sense."

Affirm and Build on Family Strengths and Gifts. All families have strengths. It is our job to see, understand, and draw on those strengths. This is sometimes very difficult, for we live in a culture that focuses on people's deficits. For example, a mother may be a drug addict, live in an apartment in great disrepair, and not have worked in two years. Some people, unable to see beyond her problems, might say she doesn't care about her children. However, as you confer with her you see how she talks about her son, see how hard she is trying to do better. You can find many strengths on which to build (Bishop, Woll, & Arango, 1993; Dunst, 1987; Knoll, 1994).

Honor Cultural Diversity. Truly honoring cultural diversity is much easier to say than to do. We must develop a sense of who we are, an understanding of our own culture and of how it has influenced our thinking and values. A mistake we often make is to fail to understand how our own cultural perceptions actually differ from those of others and to assume that our own judgments are unbiased or that they even transcend cultural mores.

We also must recognize that our school has its own culture and expectations—which are often different from the culture of the child. This "cultural mismatch" can be very problematic. Faltis (1997), for example, tells of a teacher who was concerned about a girl who did not engage in movement and choice activities and would never share in partner time. The teacher discovered, however, that in the girl's family culture, children were expected to talk little and to listen much when around adults. Once the teacher understood this, she and the parents were able to talk about ways that the student could share what she was thinking in the class. At first the student did this through writing in a journal, which she shared with a classmate. It often happens that as we understand the culture of a child's family, we can create conditions in our classroom that match better, thus increasing our capacity to know what the child's responses mean and providing a link between learning at home and the school. Families can and will often be our teachers in this regard if we let them (Bishop, Woll, & Arango, 1993; Dunst, 1987; Faltis, 1997; Knoll, 1994).

Virtually all cultures have their own ways of viewing children with disabilities. In some cultures, great shame is brought on the family. In others, the family sees the child as a special person from God and seeks to build a nurturing (though often heavily protective) circle around the child. In the former case, we have to help the parents see the strengths of the child and model acceptance through our own behavior. In the latter, we can draw from the caring tradition of the family, yet suggest and model ways that the child can become more independent (Turnbull & Turnbull, 1997).

Treat Families with Respect and Dignity. Particularly when families are experiencing difficulty or when they challenge us, teachers can feel threatened and react in unhelpful ways. When a mother living in poverty is concerned for her child's safety in her neighborhood but is also frightened of the school, she may be angry and defensive with the teachers. When a parent is concerned about her child's treatment by teachers, she may act suspicious or hostile. All of this requires that we try and understand why. We look for the strengths of families and are firmly grounded in a commitment to listen to families and treat them with respect, seeking to put ourselves in their shoes. As we take the initiative to reach out and communicate, we will often encourage trust and may have opportunities to see assets as well as problems. When we do this, we will earn families' respect (Bishop, Woll, & Arango, 1993; Turnbull & Turnbull, 1997).

Promote Family Choices. Providing choices is particularly important for families of children with disabilities or other special needs. Too often families have been given very restrictive choices and have been pressured by schools to accept the recommendations of educators with little or no consultation. This is particularly likely to occur when children are identified by the school as having academic or behavioral difficulties (O'Shea, O'Shea, Algozzine, & Hammitte, 2001; Turnbull & Turnbull, 1997).

These principles ground us in our mission to develop effective family-centered services and lead us to partnership with families. You should note that these principles and practices relate to parents of all students, not only to those identified as having "special needs." However, family-centered education is particularly important for these families. With special students we particularly need inclusive family partnerships—so that their special needs and issues can be addressed not in separate meetings and structures but in the context of other parent partnership activities. Let's now consider specific practices through which we can partner with and support parents of children with special needs in our teaching.

Welcome Parents into the School as Partners. Schools that support families look for ways to welcome families as genuine partners in the life of the school. As teachers we are an important part of this process. Welcoming can be as simple as a friendly greeting in the hall when we encounter parents—or as complex as inviting elected representatives to serve on the local school board with authority to hire and fire the principal or on the school improvement committee. For all parents, coming into a school can be unsettling. This is particularly true of low-income parents and of parents who themselves did poorly in school (Ballen & Moles, 1994). They may remember feelings of rejection or hurt. However, even parents who have high status may feel that they are entering another world, a world they only partially understand. Reaching out to

"FAMILY-CENTERED APPROACHES"
GONE BAD.

welcome people, making people comfortable, helping them to feel ownership is important (Barnett, 1997; Coleman, 1994; Epstein, 1994).

Welcome and Care about Children with Special Needs. Although it may seem simplistic, a most important element in working with parents who have children with disabilities is to welcome their children into our classrooms and show that we care about them. The experience of many families of such children is that teachers and other professionals reject their children because they feel untrained, fearful, or disinterested (University of Alberta, 2000). When we simply welcome these children into our classes and communicate to families, we can make a difference to that child and family in many positive ways.

For example, in Helen's third-grade class (Hittie, 1999b), Adam was having problems with behavior. Constantly in motion, he frequently broke things and periodically fought with other children. His previous teacher simply could not control him, and she and the school psychologist believed that he had ADD (attention deficit disorder). They suggested that Adam's mother ask her pediatrician to evaluate him for medication. The mother did not want her child "put on drugs," and Helen agreed with her. She sought instead to help Adam develop responsibility for his own behavior. She taught differently than the last teacher, trying to engage children in interesting activities while being both firm and respectful. Adam still had trouble periodically, but Helen thought he was doing fine. However, Adam's mother had become so frustrated with pressure from other staff that she was considering withdrawing Adam from school. One day Helen sent the following note home in Adam's assignment book:

> Mrs. Smith, I am going to continue to do my best with Adam. I have a new idea to try. I want him to pick one goal each day. What do you think? Give me some time with him before you give up on us.

Helen received the following response from this parent—a person described as "difficult" by others in the school:

> Thank you! So much. This is the only good thing that has been said to me. Yes, please, whatever you can do to help me. I will be glad to see ideas you

have. Goals sound good. Let us go that way. Please write or call me at any time. [She then gave three phone numbers.] I'm really trying hard. I'm in tears almost every night for my son. Thank you again.

In this example, a simple act of communication on the part of this teacher made an enormous difference for this parent. Throughout the year Adam's mother worked with Helen. Adam, her son, continued to do better in this class than in any prior year. This story powerfully illustrates the impact that a simple welcome can have on a parent. It also illustrates the pressure that educators sometimes put on parents to obtain medication for their children—and suggests that a more effective approach may be working with the child and trying new strategies.

Communicate Effectively with Families. One of our most important jobs as teachers is communicating with families of the children with whom we work. We may have difficulty responding to parents who get angry, appear unreasonable, or want us to cure the problems their child is having. It is easy to feel scared and to get defensive, return the anger, or blame the parents. In fact, too often this is what parents experience from teachers. We need strategies that will enable us to communicate effectively. This is particularly important when we need to talk with parents regarding concerns we are having about their children. Next we discuss helpful strategies.

Explain how our teaching works and helps children learn. If we are using best practice teaching strategies (discussed in Chapters 6, 8, 11, and 14), it is highly probable that what goes on in our class looks very different from what the parents of our children experienced. We will need to be able to explain to parents what we are doing and why, helping parents to understand the theory of learning that undergirds our approach. As we do this, parents will become our best supporters and will also be learning how to be better partners with us in helping their children learn (Oglan, 1997).

Be a resource and support for families. We must expand our role from being solely centered in the classroom to caring about the whole lives of the children we teach. Teachers are constantly aware of needs, and we often encounter opportunities to serve as resources, even within a limited amount of time. As teachers assist families in these broader ways, we gain credibility among parents and community members (Epstein, 1994).

The following story illustrates how one principal played a key role in the life of one family. It was John Davis's first day as a principal of an elementary school that served many low-income children. John was told to watch out for Jim, a young boy who had started a fire in the office last year, and he decided to make a home visit to talk with Jim's parents. As he drove down the dirt road to the dilapidated mobile home, he saw Jim's father step out looking as if no one had set foot on his property in years. Jim's father yelled, "What do you want?" John replied, "I'm the new principal. Just came by to chat a bit." Jim's father replied, "You wanna talk, come down to the barn." So John and the entire family walked down to the barn and sat on bales of hay among the pigs and talked. After an hour of conversation, John drove home. Jim continued to have some minor problems at school over the next few years, but nothing as drastic as setting a fire.

Almost three years later John answered the phone at his home one evening. Jim's father said somberly, "Mr. Davis, my wife just shot herself, and I'm not sure what to tell the children. If you could come and sit with us for awhile, we sure would appreciate it." John drove back out to the mobile home to sit, talk, and support Jim and his family (Arnold, 1998).

Listen reflectively. We recently visited a high school on parent–teacher conference night and overheard several conversations between parents and teachers.

"We have been getting such negative notes about Andrew in school. Why can't you tell us something positive?" we heard a parent ask tenth-grade teacher Rosa Sanchez. "Mrs. Rodriguez, you know your son has not been turning in his homework and has been causing trouble in the lunchroom," said Rosa. "It has just got to stop. You must control your son." Mrs. Rodriguez became more angry.

Shortly we came upon a similar conversation. Mr. Hall was speaking to the English teacher Randy Brookes. "You called last night expressing concern that my daughter Shirley has missed several classes and did not turn in an important paper. We did not know about this! Why have you not called before now?" Randy responded, "Mr. Hall, I am so glad you came in. Last night I was checking my records and realized I did not have her paper and called right away. You seem concerned about Shirley." Mr. Hall visibly seemed to relax and settled in the chair. They continued to talk.

These two anecdotes illustrate, respectively, poor and good reflective listening. We must seek to listen carefully to parents (and children) as they talk with us. We must first attend to what they say, and second understand the feelings and deeper meanings underneath the spoken words. A simple but powerful communication technique involves several steps (Benjamin, 1981; Carkhuff, 2000):

1. Listen carefully to the person.
2. Check your accuracy by summarizing what the person says.
3. Probe for additional information or depth.

In the first example above, Rosa Sanchez defended her own actions rather than really listening to the parent and probing what was happening. In the process she created an adversary rather than a partner. Randy Brookes, on the other hand, simply explained his actions and reflected back to Mr. Hall his observation that the father seemed concerned about Shirley. Mr. Hall continued talking about his daughter in the spirit of trust that Randy had begun to build through this simple response.

Rosa might have responded similarly: "Mrs. Rodriguez, I appreciate your coming to talk to me. I know it must be hard hearing that Andrew is having trouble. I have been concerned about him, and I am sorry if you've only heard bad things. Let's talk together."

As we work with families of children with disabilities, we will have many occasions to listen reflectively. Parents are trying to help their children, cope with stress at home and work, and deal with unfriendly schools and services, and they may become frustrated. If we listen reflectively and let parents know that we hear them and care about their children, we can build trust and provide support to parents. Of course, we must be genuine as we do so, not just acting as if we care. Parents will quickly recognize artificiality and withdraw (O'Shea, O'Shea, Algozzine, & Hammitte, 2001; Turnbull & Turnbull, 1997).

Communicate positively about children. Many children with disabilities have academic or social difficulties in the classroom—typically either doing poorly in their academic work or demonstrating problematic behaviors. As a result, unfortunately, families often receive repeated negative feedback from teachers that makes them feel defensive, creating conditions in which it is hard to engage in positive planning discussions. This does not mean that teachers should not address problems, but it does mean that we should do so in a way that recognizes the strengths and interests as well as the needs of the child. Here are some simple but effective guidelines for communicating positively with parents:

1. Frequently communicate positive strengths of the child—through notes home, comments to parents as they pick the child up in the afternoon, parent–teacher conferences, or telephone calls. Such actions build up an "emotional bank account" of positive rapport that makes dealing with problems much easier.
2. When a problem arises that needs to be communicated, do it as personally and as positively as possible. Ask for the family's input.
3. Develop a plan that involves a partnership between parent and teacher in which both have input. Establish a time and method for communicating progress.

Ask for input, ideas, and involvement of families. Families know more about their children than anyone and can provide us with some very valuable information if we ask and listen respectfully and carefully. As we develop teaching strategies for children, asking for the input and ideas of families regarding learning goals and strategies is invaluable. The caution, however, is to refrain from expecting parents to solve the problems about which we are concerned.

Engage in parent–teacher conferences and planning meetings. Key times for teachers and parents to talk together are the times virtually all schools set aside for parent–teacher conferences. Many schools are using innovative approaches to these conferences, involving students and parents in more active and positive roles. **Student-led conferences** are particularly powerful ways to help parents see what has been occurring in class and student learning (see Chapter 8). For children with special needs, teachers will often have special conferences with parents that involve an **interdisciplinary team,** a group of professionals who help support a student; these teams often include a teacher, a psychologist, a social worker, an occupational therapist, a speech therapist, and others. The intent of these meetings is to provide an

A teacher discusses the growth and progress of a child with his mother. The child is proud and smiles.

opportunity to review progress and develop plans for students. These include Individualized Education Plans (IEPs) for students who have been identified as having disabilities and who qualify for special education services and 504 plans for students with disabilities who do not qualify for special education (see Chapter 4). At other times, meetings may be called with the parents and children that bring together teachers and support staff who are concerned about a particular student. Ultimately, the aim is the same as the typical parent–teacher conference. They provide an opportunity to develop needed supports and accommodations in greater depth with the input of multiple professionals. Ongoing, informal communication with parents, however, is critical to make these meetings effective. If teachers and parents are communicating on an ongoing basis, they will be working together to arrive at many of the goals and strategies that will be formalized with other professionals in a meeting.

Linking Parents, School, and Community
Resources for Learning and Family Support

A most critical element in working with parents is linking home, school, and community learning. Let's survey some examples of ways to link home and classroom learning (Ballen & Moles, 1994; Epstein & Salinas, 1998).

Linking Home and Classroom Learning

Home Learning Activities. Teachers can collaborate with parents to identify tasks that are part of the family routine and that children can perform as learning activities at home. This allows parents to help children develop skills using authentic tasks that

Voices

A Miracle of a Teacher

Leia's son, Sean, is a second grader who has epilepsy and autism. Leia is excited about what happened at the recent support team meeting.

We have been pushing for inclusion since we moved to this district last year. They have been doing a good job this year. During the meeting many wonderful positive things were said! You could tell that Sean had really found a place in the hearts of his team. The second-grade teacher said her dream for Sean was that he be in her class without a para-educator. Wow! On the one hand this is exciting. On the other hand it is scary. Sean has behavioral issues, and when he is done with something he is ready to leave. The teacher is a miracle. She and Sean have connected. She has a sister with autism and is able to see Sean in a different light. With her on Sean's side this year, full inclusion is a real possibility.

Source: Holly (2000).

fit into the daily functioning needs of the family. For example, as families engage in various activities together (from going grocery shopping to taking family trips), a child can collect artifacts, take pictures, and write or tape-record a description of the activity that becomes part of a family-focused educational portfolio.

Meaningful, Engaging Homework. Homework can become a powerful tool for linking home and school learning. Typical homework often involves completion of worksheets of math problems, spelling words, or additional reading. In contrast, authentic homework that links to family and community life can provide an opportunity for children and parents to engage in an enjoyable, educational project together at the child's own level of ability. For example, one teacher asked students to do a project that lasted several weeks and focused on heroes in their lives. One student interviewed an aunt who was a singer and produced a poster. Another student met with a friend of the family who was a photographer, and together they took pictures and made a display. Students presented their projects in class. Several had their heroes come to the class with them. Other examples of such meaningful homework might include:

- Writing out the grocery list and shopping with a family member to obtain items. While shopping, the child can be responsible for adding up the prices of the items and helping to decide how much money should be available for weekly grocery shopping.
- Helping to prepare dinner, including reading recipes, measuring, and cooking.
- Researching historical community events and developing a presentation.

Reading Together. Families can be asked to read to and with their children. We must be careful, however, to ascertain the ability of the parent. If a parent cannot read well, this activity may be embarrassing and the parent may unintentionally discourage the child. Teachers can suggest and make available simple books that can be read aloud to children, or can provide books on tape for loan to a family.

Connecting with Community Resources

If we are to be effective teachers, we must also help families access resources and supports in the community. This becomes much easier if our school is committed to community partnerships. As we develop outreach relationships between the school and the wider community, we identify a wide range of possible resources for teachers, children, and families. By understanding the interests, needs, and skills of our families and their children and knowing about resources in the community, we can help link families to community. Schools and teachers who are effective use three key approaches:

1. Bring resources—people, organizations, materials—*into the school* to support learning and provide support for children and families.
2. *Connect learning* to the local community.
3. Engage children and the school community in activities that strengthen the neighborhood and community.

Let's see how this works in a process developed by McKnight and Kretzmann (1993).

Map Resources in the School. First, we can identify school resources that might be used in partnership with others in the community. What resources does our school possess? How might we make these available in new ways to families and the community? The most valuable resource of all is people—teachers; students in classes, who have enormous gifts to bring to the community; and families of students. Schools also have many other resources: space to be used for people to meet, office equipment, and so on. It can be helpful to compose a written list of all potential resources.

Map Community Resources Surrounding the School. Learning to view the assets, rather than deficits, of neighborhoods, families, and children is the key to what McKnight and Kretzmann (1993) call **assets-based community development (ABCD).** Too often, particularly in low-income communities, only the deficits and problems are reported. However, any community is rich in positive resources. For a community to become stronger, people must identify and build on strengths rather than trying to repair deficits. A critical starting point is simply to identify what is good about a community. Notice that this way of thinking closely parallels suggestions earlier in this chapter that we build on the strengths of families, an approach that applies directly to students with special needs as well.

Each community is composed of four key building blocks (McKnight & Kretzmann, 1993):

1. Individuals (children, youth, elderly, people with disabilities).
2. Associations (formal clubs, church choirs, the local garden club).

3. Institutions (schools, hospitals, welfare offices, mental health services).
4. Businesses (stores, law offices, etc.).

Associations, according to Kretzmann and McKnight (1993) are the most powerful resources. Whereas schools often gravitate toward the large organizations in their communities—government officials, businesses, hospitals, and the like—smaller-scale associations bring people together voluntarily based on their interests. This is their power and contribution, because they can connect people who have interests and gifts to contribute with other people with similar interests. A local garden club might involve a class of students in planting flowers on the school grounds and invite specific students who are interested in plants to be part of their monthly meetings. A local block club might work with a class to investigate their block—interviewing residents, doing presentations on the history of the block, helping clean up a vacant lot, or researching why the city had not cleaned it. As students learn to see the rich resources available in their community, they come into contact with positive role models and acquire ideas about productive ways to grow and learn.

As teachers we can identify concrete ways for adults in the community to help children and their families. As we gather information, we will begin to build relationships with various community people. We can, for example:

1. Conduct interviews of local residents regarding their skills, interests, and so on. Have students conduct these interviews in pairs and develop reports of what the people said.
2. Draw maps and take photographs or draw pictures of the local community.
3. Divide the class into teams to explore each of the building blocks of a community—individuals, associations, businesses, and institutions. Have each team collect information about the resources and assets of its "building blocks."
4. Invite five to ten community leaders to the school and hold a focus group with teachers and students serving as the interviewers. Record this on tape and video.
5. Send a survey to community associations asking them what they do, what they think needs to be done to make the community better, and what one thing they could do that is not a part of their normal activities. Students could draft, compile, and interpret this survey with assistance from local community people.

We can use our findings in many ways: compile them into a book, make a bulletin board with changing components, or publish sections in the newsletter. This project itself could be published by a local community association after being illustrated with art, photography, and written work by students.

Develop School–Community Partnerships. As schools gather information about what they have to offer and the resources in the community, teachers can develop specific partnerships with community people. The possibilities are infinite. The key is to start small, have fun, and build trust. It starts when people get together and explore how to link the interests, needs, and gifts of people or organizations with one another (Kretzmann & McKnight, 1993).

■ A teacher invites a local artist to school to share her work. They discuss ways in which the class and this artist might be involved with each other. One student who wants to be an artist is invited to see the studio of the artist.

Schools to Visit

Listening to Families and the Community

Puesta del Sol Elementary
450 Southern Blvd., SE
Rio Rancho, NM 87124
Phone: 505-994-3305
Principal: Connie Chene
**www.rrps.k12.nm.us/elementa/puesta/
About%20Our%20School/index.htm**

One school that listens to families is Puesta del Sol Elementary. The school serves a moderate- to middle-income group of families representing a cross section of New Mexico's ethnic diversity and is one of the eleven collaborating schools involved with the Dual License Program of the University of New Mexico, a teacher education program in which student teachers are certified in both general and special education to support inclusive teaching. As a member of the Coalition of Essential Schools, Puesta consciously practices the philosophy of building an inclusive community.

The principal, Connie Chene, came to Puesta with both an appreciation for special education and an awareness of the need to do things differently. Her previous experience, as an assistant principal in a school that served students with severe disabilities by teaching them on separate sides of the campus, opened her eyes to the issues of segregation. When she began at Puesta del Sol, a hundred students were schooled in the main building and in thirty-two outside portable buildings. All the special education programs were outside. Connie said the special education students and teachers "had been made second-class citizens just by the physical placement of the programs." Connie listened to her teachers, parents, and children.

Teachers helped provide the impetus for change. They wanted to team-teach, to talk to one another, and, most importantly, to make special education more a part of the school. "The reform efforts began here with special education knocking on the door and insisting that we open," Connie said; it was inclusion before Connie and her faculty had a name for it. The initial idea was to share resources, to be aware that everyone had something to offer someone else, and to know that there was a lot more that they could do.

The voices of parents advocating for their individual children catalyzed more change. Of the children who were bused to schools outside of the community, one boy with Down syndrome received maximum special education services. His mom wanted him to attend Puesta and learn to socialize with other children. Connie arranged to have him attend Puesta with the following conditions: The people involved (teacher, parent, administrator, and special education department) communicated almost daily, and a dual certified teacher worked with him in the general education classroom. The voices and caring behavior of the twenty-five general education children in the room demonstrated to this student how school works; they played with him and he taught them. The next year, a general and special educator team taught. Staff took a hammer to a separating wall in a double-wide portable classroom and broke down the barrier. This became the first inclusive classroom at the school, and many others have become a reality since that time.

By Liz Keefe and Pam Rossi, University of New Mexico.

- A local family support group is created to help parents deal with the problems and challenges of being a parent.
- The members of the school support team (psychologist, special education teachers, Title I teachers) meet with three local block clubs to discuss how they might work together to build circles of support in neighborhoods for families.

- The school sponsors a meeting of local block clubs to talk about how they can work together.
- When the city recreation department holds a community planning meeting for a local park, the school takes a group to provide ideas.

Develop Connections for Families and Children in the Community. Once we have identified resources in the community, we are in a position to connect children and families with these resources. First, we identify the gifts, interests, and needs of the child or family. As we get to know children, we will also get to know their families. We can have special nights when children and families come together and share their gifts and interests with one another.

We then match the interests or gifts of the family and child to community resources. We can have an evening workshop for families, teach them how to identify community resources, and encourage them to assist one another in locating such resources. Individually, we can look for resources throughout the year and work to make connections with families.

Get Help from Community Guides in the Area. In every neighborhood and community there are wonderful people known by many in the community. McKnight (1995) called these individuals **community guides:** trusted community members who know the neighborhood inside and out and who can be invaluable sources of information and connections for the school, children, and families. McKnight (1995) identified their key traits. Community guides are first and foremost people who see gifts in their community and the gifts in people. They see possibilities more than problems. Such people are also very connected to and involved in their community. They know many people and are, in turn, trusted and respected. This gives them access to a great number of people and resources in the community. Not surprisingly, they see their community as a caring, welcoming place and are willing and able to help connect people who need support and welcome. If we can locate these individuals, we can tap into a valuable resource for our school, our children, and their families. For example, they can help build a mentoring program, establish circles of support in a local community center, or run potluck dinners where families gather for fun and recreation in the school.

Community Agency Resources for Families

Numerous human service agencies have been established to provide assistance for families. Some specifically target families of children with special needs. We should be aware of agencies that may be helpful. Figure 3.2 provides a listing of comprehensive family support services available through one or more agencies.

Parent Training and Support Programs. Most states have programs that organize parent-to-parent help. A growing number of programs in the country also provide parent support groups. Such programs often have a staff of parents of children with disabilities who facilitate and coordinate a statewide network of support groups for parents of children with disabilities and special health care needs (Briggs, 1996; Briggs, Koroloff, Richards, & Friesen, 1993).

Figure 3.2

Components of a Comprehensive Family Support System

RESPITE AND CHILD CARE

SPECIAL NEEDS
Transportation
Special diet
Special clothing
Utilities
Health insurance
Home repairs
Rent assistance

INFORMATION AND RESOURCES
Information and referral
Advocacy
Futures and financial planning
Training

EMOTIONAL SUPPORT
Family counseling
Family support groups
Sibling support groups
Individual counseling

IN-HOME ASSISTANCE
Homemaker
Attendant care
Home health care
Chores

ENVIRONMENTAL ADAPTATIONS
Adaptive equipment
Home modification
Vehicle modification

RECREATION
Accessible recreation services
Day and summer camp

DEVELOPMENTAL SERVICES
Behavior management
Speech therapy
Occupational therapy
Medical/dental care
Physical therapy
Nursing

CASE MANAGEMENT AND SERVICE
COORDINATION

FINANCIAL ASSISTANCE
Direct cash subsidy
Allowances
Vouchers
Line of credit

Source: Adapted from Knoll (1994).

The U.S. Department of Education funds a national network of **parent training centers** that provide information to parents regarding their rights under special education law. Sometimes these centers also provide parent advocates who will attend IEP meetings with a family, sponsor a variety of informational seminars, or conduct other types of family support programs (Office of Special Education Programs, 2000a).

Early Intervention and Family Support. **Public Law 99-457** provided funds for **early intervention** assistance to babies and young children through age three who show clear signs of disability or who are at risk for developmental delay. States have developed interagency coordination plans to provide services based on the family-centered principles. That is, services must be developed in the context of the needs of the total family and documented in an Individualized Family Services Plan (IFSP) (see

Chapter 4). In each area of the country, one agency will be designated as the coordinating agency from which services and assistance can be requested. Teachers working in early childhood programs may contact the local agency for more information (Bishop, Woll, & Arango, 1993; O'Shea, O'Shea, Algozzine, & Hammitte, 2001).

Protection and Advocacy. Each state also operates a program funded by the federal Developmental Disabilities Act whose intent is to protect the rights of children and adults with developmental disabilities or mental illness. Typically housed in the state's department of mental health or mental retardation, **protection and advocacy** agencies provide training and can be called on for legal assistance when violations of state or federal laws occur (National Association of Protection and Advocacy Systems, 2000).

Family Financial Assistance. Some programs provide financial assistance to families who need help coping with the high medical and care needs of children with severe disabilities. In an increasing number of states, a **family support subsidy** provides a flat fee for parents of certain children with more severe disabilities whose income does not exceed a certain level. A Medicaid-funded program, usually called a **Medicaid Waiver** plan, also provides funds for the health care and related needs of children with severe disabilities. Both of these funding sources are most often coordinated by a local mental health agency (Bishop, Woll, & Arango, 1993; O'Shea, O'Shea, Algozzine, & Hammitte, 2001).

Community Mental Health Services. Numerous therapists provide family therapy, in which counseling is provided for the family unit. Family therapists view the family as a system and see family members' emotional difficulties as a function of the family dynamic and relationships rather than as the problem of individual members. Supportive family therapists can give important assistance to families. In addition, community mental health agencies can provide additional practical services—respite care, to give families a chance to get away from the care of children with high needs; information and referral; adaptive equipment; assistance with therapies; summer camps; and parent training on many issues (Knoll, 1994).

Neighborhood Family Resource Centers. In many communities centers have been established to provide a range of family services under one roof. The most effective of these function as community centers, combining activities for children with supportive services for families. Parents obtain counseling while their children receive tutoring and are involved in arts and recreational activities. Oftentimes, parent-to-parent support groups will meet in such centers (Kretzmann & McKnight, 1993).

Wraparound Services. Public family services fall under the jurisdiction of multiple federal, state, and local agencies. Nonprofit organizations receive government funds to operate services and often compete for clients in local areas. Private family services typically are funded by payments from individuals with higher levels of income or insurance. This multiplicity of organizations has made the provision of coordinated services difficult. Numerous efforts have been made over the years to promote interagency coordination. One of the most recent and most promising attempts is the model of **wraparound services.** In this model multiple agencies commit to work as a team around a specific family—to "wrap their services around" the family. In addition, this model is based on family-centered principles and provides flexible access to funds and resources based on the practical needs of the family. Such programs will also work to partner with informal resources in the community. Wraparound services are governed by a family–professional board that attempts to develop an effective partnership between public agency resources and the resources of the local community (Hyde, Burchard, & Woodworth, 1996; Melaville, Blank, & Asayesh, 1993; Yoe, Santarcangelo, Atkins, & Burchard, 1996).

Full-Service Schools. Schools are at the center of every family's life until the family's children are about eighteen. Yet schools have often been isolated from the larger community and from other service organizations that assist families. Many schools throughout the country have made a commitment to function as a community center for families, to house multiple services that can provide assistance to families—in other words, to be **full-service schools.** Such schools, in partnership with other human service agencies, include many services on-site (Dryfoos, 1994).

Welcome Home

In this chapter we have described family-centered teaching and schooling. Rather than seeing the community and the family as helping schools, we need to do the opposite. We must see ourselves and our school as both supporting and learning from families, as building a "village" in which people care for one another. These are vastly different practices and entail a huge paradigm shift. As educators we can implement new ideas for involving parents and families in the educational process. We can serve not only as partners in the children's education but also as friends and members of the community. So we have begun our journey into inclusive schools by thinking about the community and parents—the two driving forces for the existence of schools in the first place.

●●●●●●●●●●● Stepping Stones ●●●●●●●●●●●

To Inclusive Teaching

1. Have a conference with the parent of a student in your room who is not doing well. Engage the parent in collaborative problem solving. Assure the parent that you really care about the child and will work together.

2. Attend a meeting of a parent-based advocacy organization for children with disabilities—ARC, Autism Society, or others. Listen to their concerns. Tell people you want to be an inclusive teacher. Get their advice on starting.

3. Have a joint meeting with the special education teacher and a parent of a special education student to talk about the possibility of the student's joining your class.

4. Conduct a neighborhood map, involving children and parents together in the process. Use the information to help make a connection between a community resource and the needs of one family.

 Key Points

- Partnership between families and teachers is critical for all children, and especially so for children with special needs.

- Raising a child with a disability is both rewarding and challenging. Often families have had previous difficulties with other teachers or professionals, and they bring that history into their relationship with us.

- We want to teach children with awareness of the centrality of families, putting families at the center rather than focusing primarily on the needs of the school (a system-centered approach) or the child alone (a child-centered approach).

- We can offer many gifts to parents that will strengthen our relationship with them. It is particularly important that we make a commitment to welcome all children to our class; that we work in partnership with families; and that we effectively teach each child, explaining to parents the how and why of our instruction.

- As teachers we can also reach out to community resources that strengthen students' learning and provide helpful resources for both parents and children.

- Many service agencies are available to provide assistance to families, including early intervention for young children with special needs.

 Learning Expeditions

Following are some ideas that may extend your learning.

1. Interview a parent of a child with a disability in the family's home. Ask the parents to tell his or her story of the child and of past interactions with professionals.

2. Spend an evening with a family and a child with a disability. Accompany them on an outing or go with them to a community event. Take notes regarding family interactions, how the family responds to the child, issues that come up.

3. Locate a teacher who has a reputation for partnering effectively with parents. Interview this teacher and ask about his or her philosophy and practices with parents. Join the teacher at a planning meeting for a child with a disability.

4. Identify an adult with a disability who is successful in his or her career. Ask to hear this person's story, particularly emphasizing the person's relationship with his or her parents and the interactions between the person's parents and school. What do the person's responses tell you?

5. Attend a support group meeting for parents of children with special needs. What do the parents discuss? What stories or issues do they bring up that have to do with interactions with teachers and other professionals?

6. Contact a local organization for people with disabilities that provides family support and advocacy. Interview a staff person: What does the staff do? What do they feel are the key issues facing families of children with disabilities and other special needs?

7. Identify a local school that has a reputation for exemplary practices in partnering with parents. Interview the principal and observe some school activities. What do faculty and staff do? What is the role and place of students with disabilities and their families in this school?

Visualize a framework for planning inclusive instruction and understand how to develop individualized plans for students with
special needs.

CHAPTER OBJECTIVES

1. Acquire and apply a framework
   to use in designing instruction and
   classroom management for students with widely diverse abilities.

2. Understand procedures for developing specialized plans to improve
   learning and obtain assistance for
   students having difficulties.

3. Know the procedures for referral and
   for developing Individualized Education
   Plans (IEPs) for students with disabilities
   in special education.

4. Develop an awareness of related planning
   processes, including MAPs and service plans
   for adult service agencies.

Planning Instruction 4 for Diverse Learners

A Framework for Inclusive Teaching and Meeting Needs of Challenging Students

It's the week before school begins. Teachers are unpacking boxes, organizing, decorating class-rooms, and poring over the curriculum for the year. How do teachers plan for students with differing abilities as school begins? We visit Maria, who teaches a grade 3–5 multiage class. She will have students of even more diverse abilities this year. As we enter, she has just stapled bright green bulletin board paper on the wall. These blank bulletin boards will provide a place for student work to be displayed; this strategy helps students feel ownership of the class-room and gain confidence. Speaking about her range of students, Maria says, "I've looked at our curriculum, clustered topics into themes, and am developing learning projects involving real-world activities to allow my stu-dents to work together." In language arts, for example, she uses reading and writing workshop, in which students read materials they choose and write stories, letters, or other authentic products at their own level of ability, helping one another (see Chapter 8).

"I've had the most difficulty with math," Maria continues. After a lot of thinking, however, she has come up with an idea. She is using the six math topics from the district curriculum to organize her lessons. Each topic is written at different levels of ability for students in grades 3–5. For example, the unit on fractions extends to basic concepts, adding, reducing, or multiplying. Students will choose the topic they feel matches their ability level and work in groups. "They can all work on fractions at different levels, helping one another and doing projects together. It is going to be fun!" We're impressed with Maria's creativity and promise to return after classes get started.

We next visit George, a high school English teacher. In his class this year George will have some seniors with moderate and severe mental retardation and with limited reading and writing abilities as well as several students with learning disabilities. George also will have two students who are unusually gifted in writing. He is excited about using many of the strategies in *You Gotta BE the Book* by teacher Jeffrey Wilhelm (1995).

Like Maria, George plans to have students work in groups in his literature class, reading, writing, reflecting, and developing skits based on different books. He thinks that reading aloud together in small groups and talking about books will be helpful for all his students. In addition, the special education department purchased several tape recorders and books on tape that are available to all students. Those with the lowest reading levels will read books via tape, following along as they read. These techniques will allow students to begin reading at their own level, gaining confidence and interest. George knows he must engage students who are convinced that reading is not for them. "I am really looking forward," he explains, " to involving students in thinking about the meaning of books. We will do short skits, discussions, and art projects related to key points."

We are encouraged. These teachers are not only using terrific teaching practices but also thinking seriously about how to include students with different abilities. We'll enjoy seeing this creativity play out in Maria and George's classes.

Designing and Adapting Instruction for Learners of Diverse Abilities
Expecting Diversity from the Beginning

How do we plan our instruction? Do we plan to have students with a wide range of cognitive, social, and physical abilities, or does our planning reflect a **one-size-fits-all curriculum**? How do children see themselves and their future? How does all this come together? In this chapter we will explore these issues. We will first develop a framework for designing teaching for students of diverse abilities. We will then discuss specific planning procedures to be used when students need special help, particularly Individualized Education Plans (IEPs).

𝒯raveling 𝒩otes

Teachers traditionally have been frustrated when not all their students were "at grade level." Yet we know that people simply don't develop at standard rates. Some teachers are amazingly successful at structuring their classes so that students with different abilities are all challenged at their own levels.

1. Do you know some teachers who work well with students at different levels? Teachers who don't? Are there common elements between these two types of teachers?

2. Do the ideas presented in the first half of this chapter help you begin to develop images of how inclusive teaching can occur? Make some notes. Imagine you are teaching in an inclusive class. Describe what you are doing, what you see, and what you feel.

We've seen some real differences in how teachers instruct students with diverse abilities. For some teachers, including children with multiple ability levels is challenging. These teachers tend to favor traditional methods—straight rows of desks, heavy use of worksheets, an emphasis on keeping students quiet, and a prohibition on students' sharing their work. These teachers often have great difficulty accepting minor deviations from the established order. Other teachers, however, accommodate children with widely varying abilities—"slow learners" through "gifted"—more naturally. These teachers engage children in active learning through a range of strategies such as cooperative learning, community projects, research, and drama. What is going on? What is the relationship between teaching practices and the successful education of children with diverse abilities, cultures, ethnic backgrounds, and levels of family and community support?

Designing for Diversity from the Beginning

How do we think about designing instruction for diverse learners? First, we *plan* to have students with a wide range of abilities, learning styles, talents, gifts, interests, and intelligences in our classes, oftentimes intentionally inviting students with special needs into our class. We *design for diversity* (a practice sometimes called *universal design*). Second, when we encounter students whose abilities, interests, problems, and needs do not fit our original plans, we make adaptations—changes that help students be successful. However, we do not stop there. We ponder how we might redesign our instruction next time.

Sitting at the Subway: A Lesson in Designing for Diversity. A story illustrates the implications of designing for diversity. In 1977 thousands of people with disabilities and their allies gathered in Washington, D.C., to force the federal government to develop regulations for Section 504 of the Rehabilitation Act of 1973, the first civil rights act for people with disabilities. They held sit-ins at the Capitol building, halted traffic, and visited the offices of Congress.

Washington, D.C., had just constructed the newest and most efficient and modern subway system in the country. The system was not, however, accessible to persons with physical disabilities. Protesters parked their wheelchairs in front of the busy entrances to key subway stops, effectively preventing their use by commuters.

Within a year the federal government published the regulations for Section 504 of the Rehabilitation Act of 1973, which included requirements that all new construction built with federal funds must be accessible. Shortly elevators were installed in D.C. subway stops. This was very expensive, because parts of the original construction had to be torn apart. Which would have been less expensive—to design accessible subways in the first place or retrofit them? Obviously, to design for diversity in the first place would have cost less.

When we design for diversity, all people often benefit. For example, many architects and designers now incorporate ramps, easy-to-open doors, and electric doors into their designs. Although these adaptations originally were designed for people with mobility difficulties, many people benefit from doors that are easier to open—among them mothers carrying children, older people with limited strength, and young children. Similarly, voice activation for computers is a critical adaptation for people who cannot use their hands well. Yet researchers are finding that other people also enjoy this type of computer interface and that it increases efficiency and accuracy.

The same phenomenon occurs in learning. When we design instruction for students with special needs, all students benefit. For example, a particular student moves around all the time and finds it difficult to stay in his seat. We decide to change our teaching so that movement within reasonable boundaries is encouraged. Now, as students make a model of the world, they move about, interacting with other students and helping one another. Such active learning helps not only the student who needs to move but many other students as well. Our "gifted" students excel by delving deeper into a topic in order to help other students. Students whose motivation has been low begin to be excited about coming to school.

Inclusion and Learning: More Lessons about Designing for Diversity. When students with moderate to severe disabilities were first included in general education classes in the mid-1980s, many people thought their presence would detract from the learning of typical students. In 1989, at a meeting in Washington, D.C., we met a researcher from Hawaii who had been working with schools involved in inclusion for more than ten years. "What impact did inclusive education have on typical students?" we asked. The researcher replied that scores on the California Achievement Test at schools that had been most involved in inclusion showed a steady rise (Kishi, 1989). Clearly, at least based on these results, students had not been educationally harmed; but had they been helped? Why had test scores actually risen? Inclusive education was implemented concurrently with other efforts to improve instruction, helping teachers design instruction for the total class more effectively. Good teaching and inclusion appeared to have reinforced each other.

Key Domains in Designing for Diversity: Academic, Social–Emotional–Behavioral, and Sensory–Physical

As we design our class for diverse learners, we do so in three key areas—academic, social–emotional–behavioral, and sensory–physical. This is the organizing schema of Part II of this book. Figure 4.1 illustrates the interaction between designing for diversity, adapting, and revising teaching in each area. We first develop strategies that incorporate the best of what we know about cognitive learning. We do this while simultaneously building a caring classroom community, providing emotional support, and teaching social skills. In addition, we design the learning environment for multiple ways of learning and think ahead about students who have physical or sensory disabilities. When we design instruction for diversity, more students learn

Figure 4.1

	Designing and Adapting for Diverse Learners in Three Key Domains		
	ACADEMIC *Cognitive growth and development*	SOCIAL–EMOTIONAL *Relationships, community, and behavioral challenges*	PHYSICAL *The learning environment*
Design for Diversity	Provide authentic instruction Promote project learning Build a microsociety Recognize multiple intelligences Devise multilevel lessons *Chapters 6, 7, 8*	Build community Promote caring Encourage friendships Teach social skills and "emotional intelligence" *Chapters 10, 11*	Implement heterogeneous grouping Provide space for wheelchairs Use multiple learning modalities Design space for authentic teaching *Chapters 13, 14*
Adapt	Offer advanced projects Reduce difficulty Use drama to teach social studies Provide additional help and support Read stories to students with reading difficulties *Chapter 9*	Identify interests Understand needs and communication Provide positive alternatives Encourage peer support Foster circles of friends *Chapter 12*	Obtain a talking computer for a blind student Rearrange books so a student in a wheelchair can reach them Set aside areas to be alone or to get help *Chapter 15*
Evaluate and Revise	Read stories to all students Incorporate drama and art in all subjects	Use circles of friends to build community	Use talking computers for all students

and we can handle wider ranges of abilities and learning styles. We will also have fewer behavioral problems and greater energy and interest in our classroom.

However, some students will continue to challenge us. We then adapt for these students—sometimes on a moment-by-moment basis, at other times more systematically. When students learn much more than we anticipated, we develop learning activities that stretch them to go farther and deeper. When students have difficulty understanding, we give them simpler tasks, a reduced amount of work, and additional help. Other students bring emotional stress from home to the school and act out or fight with other students. For such students we use positive approaches, seeking to understand them, listening, giving them alternative ways to express themselves, and helping build support systems for them. Some students need help in physical and sensory arenas. A child who is deaf or hard of hearing uses an interpreter. For a child who is blind or partially sighted, we need to obtain a computer with talking software. In each of these cases, we are adapting.

Once we adapt, we consider whether our adaptations, even if uniquely designed for an individual student, may not be incorporated into our ongoing teaching. For example, perhaps we begin reading aloud to one student whose reading abilities are low—but then decide that reading to all our students would be beneficial. Or we decide that a circle of friends, a group of students who originally volunteered to provide assistance to a student with cerebral palsy, is a powerful tool to strengthen community for many students in our class (see Chapter 11). Or, having purchased talking software for use by a blind student, we decide that this could be helpful to many students, including students with learning disabilities.

A View from the Classroom

Herbert Kohl once provided a powerful illustration of teaching diverse children. He arrived at a school in Harlem where he was assigned the lowest-functioning group. His classroom was a shambles, complete with an old piano on which old records were stacked. As a first-year teacher, he grappled with how to teach children with few resources. "During the first two weeks of school," he writes, "my students put me to the test with the piano. It was irresistible to two children in particular: Larry and Ellen. *Everything* seemed irresistible to Larry, except for sitting in his desk and working. During the course of a morning his unbolted desk would migrate from one side of the room to the other and often make a stop next to the piano, where he'd sneak a tune" (Kohl, 1998, p. 23).

To Kohl's credit, he paid attention to the interests of his students. It started with the piano. Larry could play a bit. Ellen could sing. In fact, she was always singing and humming. Kohl let these interests and talents become part of his class. "I was not prepared for Larry's tunefulness, Ellen's singing, or the articulate way in which my students asked me to do reasonable things that . . . were not part of the sixth-grade curriculum. . . . I acted on intuition and curiosity and asked Larry to play and sing a tune for the class, and helped the students plan a time for Ellen to sing and for them all to listen to music in the classroom" (Kohl, 1998, p. 23).

We've provided guidelines for planning inclusive teaching (see Tools for the Trek feature). These are the big ideas that provide a base—something to come back to, build on, and revise. In later chapters, we will explore each of these in depth. A good way to start is literally to sketch our approach to academic instruction, social/emotional/behavioral growth, and the physical structure of the learning environment. Figure 4.2 provides a simple but useful form for this preliminary sketch. First, what is our general approach to teaching? Will we use primarily lectures with some lab work? Community-based projects organized around themes? How do our ideas compare with the guidelines summarized in the Tools for the Trek list?

Similarly, how will we deal with interactions of students? How can we build a sense of connection, community, or care in the class? Do we try to build community in the class, or do we see each student as "on their own"? What happens when students become angry or act out? What gets students in trouble? What strategies should we use to respond?

Finally, how is the class laid out and organized? What learning resources do we have that accommodate different learning styles and abilities? When we ask such questions, constantly revising and seeking to do better, we will gradually develop good ideas and specific plans.

Tools *for the* Trek

Guidelines for Planning Inclusive Teaching

ACADEMIC LEARNING FOR ALL

- Engage students in authentic activities that relate community issues and present and future life roles.
- Involve students in active, collaborative learning through hands-on, exploratory, inquiry-based learning.
- Design instruction for multiple ability levels.
- Provide multiple pathways for learning.
- Help students find their entry into, and ongoing active engagement in, the learning process.
- Support student choices and empowerment in learning.
- Use authentic assessment.

BUILDING COMMUNITY IN THE CLASS

- Build a caring community and provide emotional learning and support in the classroom.
- Provide multiple opportunities for participation and learning with other students.
- Use in-class support people.

INCLUSIVE LEARNING ENVIRONMENTS

- Design learning environments that meet diverse physical, sensory, emotional, and intellectual needs of students.

Figure 4.2

Planning an Overall Approach to Teaching

What are my strategies for grade 9 social studies?

Academic Learning for All
Weekly journals to one another regarding personal life or
   news event.
Study project with seniors about issue in the community—
   identify, research, interview community people, prepare
   presentation and portfolio for class.
Weekly discussion and dialogue groups.
Assignments—optional. Reading, internet research, listening
   to tapes of books, going to community meetings or conferences, interviewing community experts.

**Social–Emotional–Behavioral Issues
and Building Community**
Cooperative work groups—teach how to work collaboratively.
Peer group "peacemakers" training for student leaders.
Circles of support—teach students how circles work and
   encourage participation; include in reflective journals.

Learning Environment
Room arranged in tables of 4.
Computers for internet, graphics, and word processing
   next to wall.
Corner for small group and 1–1 conferencing and conflict
   resolution sessions.
Space to move around.
Music available—classical, jazz, rock, blues, folk. Use this
   to highlight periods.
Art examples from places and periods we are studying.

**How do they fit the beginning
ideas for inclusive teaching?**

_X_ Connections to student's lives,
   community, and social issues

_X_ Instruction at multiple levels

_X_ Multiple intelligences

_X_ Learning styles

_X_ Heterogeneous grouping

_X_ Student choices

_X_ Student reflection on learning

_X_ Building a caring community

___ Learning environment for
   people with diverse abilities
   and styles.

Need to improve on this!!

_X_ Use of in-class supports—
   peers, coteachers, volunteers,
   related services personnel

Special education coteacher 2× per week

Planning for Students with Special Needs
Getting Help, Services, and Supports

Students always cause us challenges. We cannot anticipate the difficulty some students will have with certain lessons. We may not yet know how to challenge a student with high abilities while students with lower abilities also work at their own
level. As we begin to identify students with whom we may have difficulty, we may

want assistance in developing teaching strategies. We may find it useful to refer students for special education to obtain additional assistance and resources.

Identifying Student Strengths and Needs

Anyone who works with a student can identify concerns. Parents may worry about academic or emotional problems. A paraprofessional may notice that a student is having trouble completing assignments. Problems typically fall into the three key domains we have already discussed: (1) academic performance, (2) social and emotional needs, and (3) physical well-being and health.

As we become concerned about a student, it's important to focus on both strengths and needs. Every person has important strengths, even a person with severe disabilities. The danger is that we literally can see only a student's problems, not the whole child. Teachers often send negative notes home with increasing frequency. When parents receive only negative feedback, they begin to be defensive and wary and trust breaks down. Increasingly, a teacher may see a student as a problem and the student may react by withdrawing or acting out. In turn, the teacher may grow more frustrated and the parents more and more angry and afraid. In effective inclusive classes and schools we develop relationships with parents, communicate about both the strengths and the challenges we discern in their children, and ask for input.

A team of teachers meets for consultation regarding a child who is having difficulties.

We cannot progress by focusing on problems. We can try to make problems go away, but this doesn't necessarily promote positive growth. Growth happens only if we can build on strengths (Falvey, Forest, Pearpoint, & Rosenberg, 1998). When we are concerned about a student's academic performance, we should step back and ask, "What are the strengths of this student?" Then we ask, "How can we use this student's strengths to help him or her deal with problems? How can we build on those strengths in a way the student likes?" For example, Julie sometimes acts out and disrupts class, but she also has a talent for making her classmates laugh, and she has shown leadership skills. Perhaps she could be given a responsible role in an oral reading lesson.

This leads us to think about "needs." Need is a powerful word. Asking the question "What do I need?" requires that we also ask the related question "For what?" The needs of students are tied to goals they want to accomplish. For example, a student may *need* to learn math skills because he wants to own a bicycle repair shop. Another student may *need* to improve her reactions to criticism because she wants to have friends.

However, the word *need* is often used to express adults' wishes for a student to be or act a certain way. We then hear statements like "Mark, you *need* to do your homework. You *need* to sit in your seat." These things are more *our* needs than those of the student. As we talk with students, it's very helpful to *own* our needs—"Mark, *I need* you to sit down right now! I am very frustrated." You may find it helpful to write down notes about the strengths and needs of the child related to school as well as home and community.

Prereferral Strategies and Collaborative Consultation: Getting Ideas and Trying New Approaches

In traditional schools the only way we have to get help for students and ourselves is to refer students to be evaluated for special education. Most often referral has meant placement in a segregated special education class, despite the least restrictive environment requirements of IDEA. As referrals have multiplied, efforts have been made to reduce referrals to special education. Requirements have been instituted for **prereferral strategies:** Teachers are expected to try different approaches with a student, often in consultation with a specialist, before referring the student for evaluation for special education. The language itself is telling; as it suggests, many teachers have viewed this requirement as one additional bureaucratic hoop before a referral to a separate special education class is processed.

In effective inclusive schools, in contrast, specialized support staff (special education teachers, gifted consultants, bilingual teachers, and aides) provide ongoing assistance in the general education classroom (see Chapter 5) regardless of referrals (McCarney, 1993; Michigan Department of Education, 1999; Parent Education Project, 1998a). Thus, teachers in inclusive settings have daily opportunities to talk with staff about a special student, brainstorm ideas, and develop collaborative strategies. Specialists are often assigned a caseload of students who have IEPs, but they also work with struggling students who have not been referred—a change allowed in the 1990 amendments to IDEA. Such an approach provides the equivalent of ongoing "prereferral strategies," as teachers constantly strategize and experiment with different approaches to meeting children's needs.

Another useful preventive approach is **collaborative consultation,** in which we work together with one or more professionals to explore strengths, needs, and strategies for a student. Sometimes a team of teachers and specialists meet on a regular basis to discuss children's needs. In other cases, individual teachers and support staff talk one-on-one.

How does collaborative consultation work? Figure 4.3 provides an example. First, we identify the resources and strengths of the student. Next, we focus on barriers and problems, listing these so we can be specific. We want to break the problem down so we can see it in detail rather than making global statements. Is the student having trouble reading? If so, what specifically do we mean—is the problem understanding text (orally or via print), reading at a certain level, knowing certain types of letter combinations, not wanting to read? At this point, we prioritize issues, asking the question: "What one or two things could we do to make the most difference?" These become a plan of action, describing who will do what, when, and how progress will be assessed. This process provides a valuable base for developing an IEP (see below) if further referral and intervention is needed. However, special education referral rates often decline in schools using collaborative consultation (Hiibner & Fracassi, 1999; Idol, Paolucci-Whitcomb, & Nevin, 1994).

Individualized Education Plans (IEPs)
Referral and Planning for Special Education Services

We may decide to refer a student for special education services. In inclusive schools this is most often done to help the student qualify for specific assistance and resources not already provided. Given that in inclusive schools special education and other support resources work effectively with all students, referral rates are much lower in such schools, often ranging from 2 to 5 percent rather than the 11 percent that is now the national average (Peterson, Tamor, Feen, & Silagy, 2002; Office of Special Education Programs, 2000).

Referral for Special Education Services

Special education in a school *can* operate as a wonderful support for students, teachers, and families. Services that can be accessed through special education are numerous—essentially consisting of whatever a student needs to be successful in school. The specific procedures for referral vary across school districts and states. In some schools we complete a simple referral form and document strategies we have tried and the student's response. In other schools we may complete a comprehensive checklist of behaviors and other types of information (Parent Education Project, 1998a; Riester, 1998).

Interdisciplinary Evaluation

Once a student is referred for special education, an interdisciplinary team of professionals conducts a formal assessment to determine if the student has a disability

Figure 4.3

Collaborative Consultation Action Planning

Student Name: Sasha Levine   Birthdate: Date:
School: Bernard Middle School   Teacher: Horton   Grade: 7
Team members: Horton, Juanita (school psychologist), Barry (special education teacher), Beth
(social worker), Jameson (general education teacher), Mona (grandmother).
Initial concern: Reading and behavioral problems

STRENGTHS/RESOURCES	BARRIERS/PROBLEMS/NEEDS
When knows she's being listened to will work hard.	Easily distracted.
Less impulsive lately.	*Textbook in social studies is too hard for her and she gets angry.
Likes hands-on activities.	*Has difficulty making friends.
Enjoys reading and learning about astronauts and astronomy.	Gets upset when someone talks about her.
Has a strong sense of family.	*Taking medications and seems to get worse when she does not take them.
Loves animals and small children.	

TARGET GOAL(S)

(Select one or more barriers from above to identify a target goal and devise a plan of action that
builds on strengths and resources of the student.)

Help Sasha get materials to read in areas of her interest on her own level that are still age appropriate.
Help her to connect with friends and deal with anger.
Evaluate her medication dosage.

PLAN OF ACTION

What	Who	When	Assessment
Circle of friends.	Social worker and parent help Sasha to get a meeting after school.	Within one month.	Sasha's self-report about her feelings and others' observations of relationships
Get trade books regarding social studies and areas of interest to be included in the curriculum.	General and special education teacher.	This week. More throughout the year. Begin having these types of books for all students.	Record of books read. Observations of Sasha's reading behavior and skills.
New physician visit. Consider effect of medications, whether they are making the problem worse.	Grandmother contact Dr. Diller. Support from social worker if needed.	Within two weeks.	Whether contact was made. Evaluate impact of any changes on behavior and initiative.

and needs special services. Typically, an evaluation will, at minimum, include an individualized intelligence test and a standardized test of academic achievement, teacher reports, and information from parents. Specialized evaluations from various professionals also may be included—speech and language evaluation, occupational and physical therapy assessments, psychiatric evaluation, and more. For students aged fourteen and above, assessment must also consider the transition needs of the student related to employment, independent living, and community participation (Procedures for Evaluation and Determination of Eligibility, 1999).

In most states professionals with special training in individualized assessment conduct and coordinate these evaluations. These individuals' professional titles vary by state—in Michigan, for example, school psychologists do evaluations; in Texas, educational diagnosticians. Evaluations must not discriminate against students from different cultural and ethnic backgrounds. Tests must be given in the primary language or other mode of communication, such as sign language, of the student.

The team develops a formal report describing the student's present levels of performance, the needs of the student for services and assistance, and the eligibility of the student for special education services. Eligibility is based on two factors: (1) whether the student has a disability in the categories identified in the federal law and (2) whether the student needs special education services. Parents have the right to receive a copy of this evaluation report and to have input into the decision regarding student eligibility for services and must agree with the decision to provide special education services. Whether the multidisciplinary team actually meets depends on local and state procedures. If the team does meet, however, the parent must be invited to participate (Michigan Department of Education, 1999; Parent Education Project, 1998b; Riester, 1998).

Individualized Education Plan

Once the evaluation team declares the student eligible for special education services, a different team is convened to develop an Individualized Education Plan (IEP) for the child, a document intended to address the unique educational needs of the child. Figure 4.4 describes the legally required members of the team. Parent participation is particularly important; in addition, starting at age fourteen, when appropriate, students are required by law to attend. Many educators recommend that students participate at

Figure 4.4

Individualized Education Plan Team

The law requires that the following individuals participate in the development of the IEP. Other people *may* participate—family, friends, peers of the student, and others.

- The *parents* of a child with a disability
- At least one *regular education teacher* if the child is, or may be, participating in the regular education environment
- At least one *special education teacher*
- *Administrator:* A representative of the local educational agency who is qualified to provide, or supervise the provision of, specially designed instruction to meet the unique needs of children with disabilities
- *Evaluator:* An individual who can interpret the instructional implications of evaluation results
- *Other individuals* who have knowledge or special expertise regarding the child, including related services personnel
- *The child with a disability* (whenever appropriate)

Source: Individuals with Disabilities Education Act (1997).

all ages, suggesting that their presence encourages those attending to focus more directly on the needs of the child. Parents also may invite other participants such as a **parent advocate,** a university professor, or staff of the state protection and advocacy agency (see Chapter 3) (Gibb & Dyches, 2000; Michigan Department of Education, 1999; Parent Education Project, 1998a; Riester, 1998; Seyler & Buswell, 2001).

Figure 4.5 describes the required components of an IEP from the Individuals with Disabilities Education Act (IDEA). In the IEP we:

1. Identify goals for children with special needs, select services to help them reach such goals, and decide how they will be involved in general education;
2. Specify the placement of the student, particularly related to participation in general education;
3. Describe the services to be provided in terms of amount, frequency, and duration; and
4. Develop a plan for evaluating the student's progress (Federal Register, 1999).

An IEP is a legal contract between the school and the parents. We have the responsibility of helping to plan and carry out the services described in the IEP. The legal mandate for IEPs was created, as with all laws, to solve a problem. In this case the problem was that schools were simply putting children in special education without consultation with parents, oftentimes in programs that did not attend to the unique needs of the child.

Figure 4.5

What Is Required in an IEP? What the Law Says

The term *individualized education plan* or *IEP* means a written statement for each child with a disability that . . . includes:

- A statement of the child's *present levels of educational performance,* including—how the child's disability affects the child's involvement and progress in the general curriculum
- A statement of measurable *annual goals*
- Short-term objectives for students with more severe disabilities who will take an alternate assessment
- A statement of the *special education and related services and supplementary aids and services*
- An explanation of *the extent,* if any, *to which the child will not participate with nondisabled children in the regular class*
- A statement of any individual modifications in the administration of state or districtwide *assessments of student achievement*
- The *projected date* for the beginning of the services and modifications . . . and the anticipated frequency, location, and duration of those services and modifications
- Beginning at age 16, and updated annually, an individual *transition* plan
- A statement of *how the child's progress toward the annual goals . . . will be measured;* and *how the child's parents will be regularly informed*

Source: Individuals with Disabilities Education Act (1997).

IEPs can provide powerful opportunities for parents and educators to work collaboratively to develop strategies for supporting a student with special needs. In addition, IDEA provides parents a powerful tool for seeking inclusive education for their children. Parents can go to court to request placement in the least restrictive environment and services that will provide help for the teacher and student so that inclusion is successful. The number of such legal actions, on the one hand, demonstrates that many schools resist inclusive education. On the other hand, the courts are increasingly clear in supporting the move toward inclusive education. Yet parents often feel caught in a bind. Legal action is time-consuming and emotionally draining. Although IDEA requires that schools pay legal costs if the parents win, parents must foot the bill until such a decision is made, and sometimes they lose. Further, forcing a school to comply with a law or regulation often works against parents, as the goodwill and support of teachers and school staff are critical.

We talk with Cathy and Steve about their experience with their son Michael and his IEP meeting. Cathy explains that Michael, who is diagnosed as having mental retardation, had a hard time in first grade. He had attended an inclusive kindergarten program, so "we just assumed he would continue to receive his education in a general education class," Cathy says. Unfortunately, this assumption was incorrect. In Michael's first year in first grade, the teacher did not expect him to learn anything. "In a meeting before the end of the school year, a few members of the IEP team felt Michael should receive his education in a special education class and be 'included' only for music, PE, lunch, and recess. We couldn't believe it!" she exclaims, the tears welling up. "We finally had to tell them that it was not Michael who was failing. Rather, we had failed him. The expectation was that Michael should 'fit in' instead of being accepted for who he is."

Cathy and Steve educated themselves about their legal rights, "arming ourselves with every bit of information we could get our hands on about inclusion." In addition Cathy put together what she called "The Michael Book," a collection of pictures and stories illustrating her son's positive attributes. She hoped that the educators would look beyond Michael's Down syndrome. She presented the book to his new first-grade teacher along with other books and articles on inclusion and Down syndrome.

"At our first IEP meeting for the new year we decided to bring a parent advocate with us," she says. "Fortunately for us, staff had changed and the people who were pushing for a segregated classroom were gone."

Cathy and Steve were wary and cautious as they walked into a room full of unfamiliar people, only a few of whom even knew Michael. "We were totally prepared to battle," Cathy recalls, "but to my surprise and delight, they never even talked about having Michael in a separate class! Instead we all talked about our expectations for Michael, his strengths, and roles for each of us." The general and special education teacher used an "IEP matrix" to match Michael's learning goals to the curriculum. They looked at units of study—for example, America: community formation, community contributors, early settlements, animal habitats, and environment—and identified learning goals for Michael, using the matrix to plan lessons in which Michael could participate. Cathy says ecstatically, "I never in a million years thought I'd see that level of commitment to do what ever it takes. Michael

Teachers read books with preschool children. Children with special needs learn from modeling and benefit from supportive relationships.

is doing so well. He loves school, he adores his teacher, and his classmates think the world of him. In fact, Michael came home yesterday and told me 'Tiffany . . . wow!' " The delight on his face fills the room with warmth.

Michael's story richly illustrates both what can go wrong and what can go right as we work with students with special needs. The first IEP team had difficulty looking beyond Michael's disability and seeing a whole child. The second group worked collaboratively with the family and were able to see Michael's strengths and capabilities as well as his needs.

At best, all IEP meetings should be like this: meetings where educators and parents positively look at the needs *and* the strengths of a child. In Figure 4.6 we list a few practical steps to help you prepare for participating in an IEP. In fact, these are the same steps to consider for any child who is having difficulty in your class. First, develop a good picture of the student's strengths, challenges, and needs. Second, make notes on any other information that would be helpful. Finally, identify ideas for working with the student, including supports and assistance you need as a teacher. If you and others bring this kind of thinking to the meeting, you will be able to pool ideas and identify ways to work together. Focus on how this student can be successful in your class. Be open and honest about your concerns, and ask for help and input (Ford, Fitzgerald, Glodoski, & Waterbury, 1997; Gibb & Dyches, 2000).

Figure 4.6

Steps in Preparing for an IEP

1. Identify the student's strengths and needs in your class.
2. Identify questions you have so as to understand the student's needs and potential strategies in greater depth.
3. List ideas to meet student needs—teaching practices, support, adaptations, etc.

Parents often experience IEP meetings as extremely intimidating, which may cause them to become angry or withdrawn. If we come to a meeting frustrated, aiming to remove a child from our class or feeling the need to blame parents, we will make the process very difficult for all. One key strategy is to begin meetings by giving people the opportunity to state and own how they are feeling.

In terms of the framework described in Chapter 3, these meetings can either be family- and child-centered or system-centered. System-centered approaches are typically built around defending what the school has in place rather than responding to needs of the child and family. Complex reports, provided in the technical language of a professional discipline, can be overwhelming and confusing to parents, adding to their sense of powerlessness. On the other hand, IEP meetings can be used to develop partnerships between families and school personnel. *In the poorest IEP meetings, educators come with everything typed out, expecting parents simply to listen and sign.* In an effective meeting, in contrast, the components of the IEP serve as the agenda, and parents, the child, peers, and other educators bring their own ideas and make decisions collaboratively. As we discuss aspects of IEPs you may want to review Figure 4.7, which shows a partially completed IEP. However, the goal of the IEP meeting is not to complete a form but to develop a genuine plan to help the student.

Present Levels of Performance: Strengths and Needs. After introductions, the person facilitating the IEP meeting asks the team to review the present functioning of the student. In some meetings individual specialists report one at a time. In more effective meetings, however, team members address key areas of functioning together: academic, emotional–social, and physical across environments in which the student functions. For example, the facilitator might ask people to give brief summaries of Jenny's academic strengths and needs. In response, classroom teachers first share work samples of the student that show Jenny's skill level and needs for improvement. The parents share their observations regarding Jenny's use of academic skills at home. The facilitator may ask the child herself to add comments: "How do you use reading, writing, and math at home, Jenny? What are some things you would like to do better?" These discussions would be followed by specialists' testing reports and observations related to academic performance. Similar discussion would address other key areas in turn—social, emotional, sensory–physical, and more (Parent Education Project, 1998a; Williams, Fox, Monley, McDermott, & Fox, 1989).

Annual Goals and Measurable Objectives. The IEP must describe annual learning goals for most students and short-term objectives for each goal for students with severe disabilities who will take an alternative assessment to the state achievement test.

Figure 4.7

Individualized Education Plan (IEP)

Student Name   Fred Borden   **Date of Meeting**   April 23

Present Levels of Educational Performance

How does the child's disability affect the child's involvement and progress in the general curriculum; or, for preschool children, how does the disability affect the child's participation in appropriate activities?

> Fred is fourteen. Fred is able to read at a third-grade level but can understand at a higher level than he reads. He likes to read but is hesitant to write or express himself. He can do basic math functions and has begun to keep a checking account but would like to learn more daily math skills. He likes electric motors and machines and spends time with his dad at his car garage. Fred likes to be around people, but his oral communication skills are limited. He has a few friends but often seems awkward socially.

> Fred is not sure what he wants to do when he graduates from high school. He could use exploration of the community and job options, thinking about where he might like to live. A MAP might be useful with his friends and family to provide input into his transition plan and IEP.

Eligibility

Does the student have a disability and need special education and related services?

> Fred is diagnosed as mentally retarded.

Measurable Annual Goals and Short-Term Objectives

How will these goals enable the child to be involved in and progress in the general curriculum or, for preschool children, to participate in appropriate activities? What other educational needs result from the child's disability? What services or interagency linkages are needed for transition, including instruction, related services, community experiences, employment, postschool adult living, daily living skills, and functional vocational evaluation?

Annual goal: Improve Fred's ability to read and express himself effectively in writing and with other tools.

Objective	Service/Person	Assessment
Over the semester Fred will read six books he enjoys and will develop interesting responses and share key ideas and issues in each of the books.	1. Fred will participate in a literature circle where he will be part of sharing group. 2. Special education teacher will coteach literacy class twice a week and monitor Fred's progress and provide support as needed. 3. Peer partner in the literacy group will work together with Fred in designing a project reporting on book via a play, computer graphic, or art. 4. General and special education teacher with librarian will help Fred pick out books at his level that he finds interesting. 5. Parent and Fred go to library together once a month.	General and special education teacher observation, Fred's self-report, summary record sheet for each book (location, main characters, plot, key message). Actual reporting project. Criteria: number of books read, Fred's evaluation of these books, rubric on report and reporting project.

Figure 4.7

Continued

Objective	Service/Person	Assessment
Fred will learn to express himself in writing and through other tools, using his own life and other topics of interest.	1. General education teacher will use writing workshop approach in English class for development of written pieces. 2. Fred and small group will work together reviewing and editing one another's pieces, providing encouragement. 3. Special education teacher will work with Fred and the group to help them use tools for expression to focus and expand their writing, such as stick figures and graphics as a tool for storytelling, Inspiration software for graphic organizers, PowerPoint, use of movies with I-Move to go with text.	General and special education teacher observation, Fred's self-report, rubric on written stories (teacher and student evaluation) and related expression products.

How Child's Parents Will Be Regularly Informed of Child's Progress

Regular report cards, parent conferences, and biweekly notes of learning activities and progress from the special education teacher.

Placement

What percentage of the time will the child be in general education or in a special education setting? What is the rationale for placement?

Location	% of time	Rationale
General education (specify) Fred will be involved in a schedule of classes that fit his interests and IEP goals. Special education (specify)	100%	Fred has been included in general education full time his entire school career. Teachers are working hard to teach at multiple levels and modify instruction to meet his needs.

Special Education and Related Services

What services, modifications, and supports are needed to help the child advance appropriately toward attaining the annual goals, be involved and progress in the general curriculum, participate in extracurricular and other nonacademic activities, and be educated and participate with other children with and without disabilities?

Service or Support	Start Date	Location	Frequency	Duration
MAP facilitated by social worker.	9-3	Fred's home	Once per year	Time necessary
Coteaching support by special education teacher in language arts.	8-15	Language arts class	2 classes per week	Year

(continued)

Figure 4.7

Continued

Supplementary Aids and Services/Interagency Linkages

Service or Support	Start Date	Location	Frequency	Duration
Refer to vocational rehabilitation for job exploration summer program.	November	Counselor's office	NA	NA

Program Modifications or Supports for School Personnel

Modifications or Supports	Start Date	Location	Frequency	Duration
Allowing Fred to read and write at his own level in language arts class.	8-15	Language arts class	Ongoing	Year
Modified grading in machine shop based on project rubric designed with special education teacher.	9-15	Machine shop class	Each card marking	Year

Extent, If Any, to Which Child Will Not Participate with Nondisabled Children

None.

State and Districtwide Assessments

In what state and district assessments will the student participate? What individual modifications are needed? What alternative assessment, if appropriate, will be used?

Fred does not want to participate in the statewide assessment, and his parents support this decision.

Source: Adapted from Office of Special Education and Rehabilitative Services (2000).

These requirements are intended to help ensure accountability, and part of our responsibility will be to document the progress of a child related to these goals and objectives.

From time to time, educators have developed highly detailed and sometimes trivial goals in order to state objectives in measurable terms. For example, one might find statements in IEPs such as, "Lamar will learn to spell all words with 95 percent accuracy; Lamar will complete oral sentences correctly 90 percent, and respond to criticism appropriately 80 percent, of the time." However, there are several problems with these types of goal statements. On the one hand, their specificity and detail makes them difficult to document. In addition, while they lead to lists of skills and subskills that are immediately observable, they do not tend to evaluate complex cognitive, emotional, and physical learning goals. We see many examples of pseudobehavioral language in IEPs, and too few examples of goals that consist of complex skills.

However, we can develop more effective goal statements that fit best teaching practice and relate to critical skills. For example, in some cases we can use curriculum guidelines in our own lesson plans to target skills for which our lessons are designed, generating goals that focus on meaning, practical application, and the ability to use skills in authentic community settings. Here are some examples:

1. Improve reading abilities and enjoyment of reading.
2. Develop basic math skills and apply these in simple daily money management.
3. Increase oral expression abilities.

Typically, measurable objectives are subunits of the overall goal. For the first goal above, for example, we might identify the following objectives:

1.1. Manuel will learn to monitor whether the text is making sense to him as he reads.
1.2. Manuel will discover meaning-based strategies for figuring out words.
1.3. Manuel will participate in oral storytelling based on stories he has read (Rhodes & Dudley-Marling, 1996).

In other cases, IEP goals will be directly related to the student's disability and to provision of specific special education services. If a student has difficulties in articulation of words, a speech therapist may target improvement of articulation as a goal. If a student needs to learn how to use a piece of assistive technology, such as a talking calculator, this can be identified as a goal with appropriate objectives (see Chapter 15).

MRS. BAKER EXPERIENCES "OPTION PARALYSIS."

IN PLANNING YOUR DAUGHTER'S IEP, WE'D LIKE YOU TO CHOOSE FROM THIS COMPREHENSIVE LIST OF 13,941 LEARNING OUTCOMES.

© 1999 MICHAEL F. GIANGRECO. ILLUSTRATION BY KEVIN RUELLE PEYTRAL PUBLICATIONS, INC. 612-949-8707

Curriculum Matrix: Connecting the IEP to the Classroom. The **curriculum matrix** provides a useful tool that answers the question, "How do goals and objectives designated on an IEP relate to the work of the class?" Figure 4.8 illustrates a sample curriculum matrix for a high school student. Key goals for the student are listed in the left column. The curriculum units and school activities are listed across the top. For an elementary class a typical daily schedule might include beginning activities, math, centers time, and so forth. The curriculum matrix helps us plan how to maximize learning for the student in the existing curriculum and helps us identify gaps and appropriate adaptations. For example, if John is working on improving social interaction skills, we can target particular times when this area needs

Figure 4.8

Curriculum Matrix

FRED BORDEN
FRESHMAN, HILLSDALE HIGH SCHOOL

			SCHOOL DAY		
IEP GOALS	Math	Social Studies	Physical Education	Language Arts	Machine Shop
Read six books he enjoys over the semester.		X		X	X
Express himself in writing and through other tools, using his own life and other topics of interest.		X		X	
Learn to use math skills to make daily purchases, manage bank account, and pay bills.	X				
Increase ability to express himself orally.	X	X	X	X	X
Increase positive interactions with peers.	X	X	X	X	X
Improve stamina by walking two miles each week.			X		

attention. In recording progress regarding each goal, the curriculum matrix again helps us focus: We can make notes on the matrix daily or weekly regarding specific progress. We may find a particular unit or class that has no goals or has a goal not adequately addressed. If this occurs we can revise our plans. The matrix can help identify such gaps (Ford, Fitzgerald, Glodoski, & Waterbury, 1997).

Special Education and Related Services. **Related services** are services—such as occupational therapy, physical therapy, speech therapy, counseling, and so on—that provide needed assistance to a student. If a student is to receive in-class support from a special education coteacher or paraprofessional, this will be written in the IEP. As appropriate, the IEP must also address issues of language acquisition, assistive technology, behavioral interventions, and other special needs.

One of the key questions we must address in this part of the IEP is: "How much assistance and of what type does the student need to be successful in the general education classroom?" In poorly planned sessions, there is an automatic assumption that a particular disability means a particular type of service. For example, teacher aides may be routinely assigned to every student with mental retardation. What is more helpful, however, is to consider the school day from start to finish and develop specific plans for supports and adaptations. We should ask, "What is going on at this hour? What problems are apparent? How will we solve these?" When we do this, we anticipate problems, work out satisfactory solutions, and clearly identify the specific types of assistance needed. The **individual class schedule** can be a helpful tool for this purpose. Figure 4.9 shows an example; note that we've included the schedule for home activities to help the team see the connection between school and home.

When we work step by step as a problem-solving group, we often find multiple options to difficult challenges. Take the example of a student with multiple disabilities who uses a wheelchair. We want her to come to school like everyone else. However, neither the school bus nor the school is wheelchair accessible. What might we do? The team brainstorms solutions. In difficult situations like this, having the student and peers there can also make a huge difference. Often they are able to identify solutions not at first apparent (Ford, Fitzgerald, Glodoski, & Waterbury, 1997; LeRoy, England, & Osbeck, 1994).

Students' Ownership of Their IEPs. Often we tend to focus primarily on how *teachers* use the IEP, but we also can help students themselves understand and own their plans. When we promote student ownership, we shift the dynamic. Rather than representing parents' and school personnel's telling a student what to do, the IEP becomes a tool to help a student meet his or her own goals, a plan in which the student has some degree of control and input. Participating in IEP meetings can help promote students' making choices for their lives and strengthening their own self-determination (Field, Martin, Miller, Ward, & Wehmeyer, 1998; Hughes & Agran, 1998).

When students are present at their own IEP meetings, the occasion gives us a wonderful opportunity to demonstrate to the child that people care, as well as to teach the child to take responsibility. In addition, a student can use the IEP to track his or her own learning, with support by teachers and other professionals. We may want to take the IEP and develop a booklet with the child that identifies goals and provides a way to record progress. This can easily become part of the class portfolio. This makes the IEP a living instrument, owned by the person it is intended to benefit, rather than a bureaucratic document.

Placement: The Degree of Involvement in General Education. Historically, the most controversial decision in IEP meetings has involved the **educational placement** of the student with a disability—the type of class or school where the student will be educated. Referral to special education has often meant a separate special education classroom. Since the passage of PL 94-142, however, the legal presumption has been that students would be educated in the general education class. When this does not occur, the IEP team must justify that decision. In almost all cases the needs of the child *can* be met in general education when, as the law requires, appropriate services

Figure 4.9

Individual Class Schedule with Accommodations and Supports

Linda Donatello's Schedule
7th grade, McConnell Middle School

Linda has mild cerebral palsy but can walk and speak understandably. She is very pleasant and well liked by her classmates. However, she also has learning disabilities. Her reading and math abilities are at a fifth-grade level, but she's had good instructors and she is enjoying learning.

TIME	ACTIVITY	SUPPORTS AND ADAPTATIONS
7:30	Come to school	Assistance from bus driver in getting safely off bus.
8:00	World cultures	John, a classmate, will make a copy of his notes for her. She will use a tape recorder as well.
9:00	Social studies—literacy team	She will use a computer with a typing guard to do her work. The special education support teacher, Janice, will be available for special assistance as needed.
10:30	Science—math team	Cooperative work groups on projects—take parts of the project she can do.
12:00	Lunch	None.
1:00	Physical education	Once a week the physical therapist will come and help the PE teacher include PT exercises for Linda in his class.
2:00	Technology studies	The class will explore various assistive technology devices, including talking software, as part of the curriculum. Meet with special education support teacher briefly before leaving school.
3:30	After school: Synchro swimming club	Randi will buddy with Linda.
4:30	Goes home	Randi and Linda's parents will carpool.
6:00	Dinner and family time	
8:00	School studies	John, Lisa, and Janeen will team study once per week. Self-monitoring checklist developed with special education support teacher Janice.
10:00	Bedtime	

Artwork reprinted by permission of Martha Perske from *Perske: Pencil Portraits 1971–1990* (Nashville: Abingdon Press, 1998).

and supports are provided. The questions then involve politics, how resources are used, and the willingness of schools to include students. For every student with a disability who is denied inclusion, there is most often a comparable student in another school who thrives academically and is a valued member of the classroom. In truly inclusive schools, placement is not often an issue. The child with a disability is part of the general education class like everyone else. What changes is not the location of the student but the degree of support and assistance provided in that class to aid both the student and the teacher (LeRoy, England, & Osbeck, 1994; Parent Education Project, 1998a; Saha, Enright, & Timberflake, 1996).

There are still a small number of students whose needs are so complex that educators have not yet come up with ways to include them successfully. Other programs, such as separate schools, may be seen as the best alternative. Our goal, however, should be to include all students. If we are committed to inclusive teaching, it is painful when we find we do not, today, know how to include a student. Yet such instances offer us opportunities to reflect. "How can we do better? How might we have helped this student if things had been different in our school?" These are critical questions that will, we hope, lead to better answers in the future.

Evaluation of Progress. The law requires that educators report the progress students make on the goals and objectives identified in their IEPs. Evaluation criteria and tools need to be clear, so that we can track and report on a student's progress. If we incorporate goals for the student into the structure of our curriculum, and if we use assessment that is the same as or similar to what we use with all our students, this process is much easier to manage. We may need to make adaptations, but most often we should evaluate progress toward IEP goals in the same way that we evaluate progress made by other children. Most students with disabilities take the state standardized test that is required by the No Child Left Behind Act of 2001 while a small number who have more severe disabilities will take an alternative examination.

Mediation, Hearings, and Appeals. Sometimes school personnel and parents cannot agree on the IEP. Federal law has established procedures for the appeal of decisions. However, jurisdictions also encourage *mediation,* a process by which parents and school representatives come together with an individual who facilitates dialogue and discussion. Many states have established formal mediation services to achieve more amicable outcomes and reduce legal costs.

If parents and the school continue to disagree, however, the first level of appeal is an **impartial hearing.** This is a quasi-judicial meeting at which a court-appointed hearing officer, most often a university professor or a lawyer, hears the sides presented by the parents and the school system and makes a decision. If either side disagrees with this decision, the case can be appealed to federal court. Special education law is now a subspecialty of law practice. In every state multiple hearings are conducted yearly. This is costly and emotionally stressful for parents.

Behavioral Intervention Plan. If students have behavioral challenges a **Behavioral Intervention Plan (BIP)** should be part of the IEP. In 1997, a multistep process was written into law. First, if a student with disabilities displays dangerous actions and the school wants to expel the student, a multidisciplinary team must conduct a **manifest determination review**—a review to determine whether or not the behavioral issues were directly related to the disability of the student. If the actions were related, the school must develop a BIP as part of the IEP (Riester, 1998) (see Chapter 12 for details).

Individual Transition Plan (ITP) and High School. The transition of students with disabilities from school to adult life has been a concern for many years. Students with disabilities often have much higher rates of unemployment and more difficulty accessing postsecondary educational opportunities than their peers. Students with mild to severe disabilities may spend years on waiting lists for adult service systems. The **Individual Transition Plan (ITP),** a required component of the IEP starting at age sixteen, is a central tool; it requires that schools work with adult service agencies to develop collaborative services to assist students with disabilities (Ludlow, Turnbull, & Luckasson, 1988). According to IDEA, the purpose of the ITP to is promote

movement from school to postschool activities, including postsecondary education, vocational training, integrated employment (including supported employment), con-

Voices

Advice for Professionals Who Must Conference Cases

Janice Fialka

Before the case conference,
I would look at my almost five-year-old son
And see a golden haired boy
Who giggled at his new baby sister's attempts
    to clap her hands.
Who charmed adults by his spontaneous hugs
    and hello's,
Who captured his parents with his rapture with
    music and
His care for white-haired people who walked
    a walk
A bit slower than younger folks,
Who often became a legend in places visited
    because of his
Exquisite ability to befriend a few special
    souls,
Who often wanted to play "peace marches,"
And who, at the age of four
Went to the Detroit Public Library
Requesting a book on Martin Luther King.

After the case conference
I looked at my almost five-year-old son.
He seemed to have lost his golden hair.
I saw only words plastered on his face.
Words that drowned us in fear and revolting
    nausea.
Words like:
Primary expressive speech and language
    disorder
Severe visual motor delay
Sensory integration dysfunction
Fine and gross motor delay
Developmental dyspraxia and RITALIN now.

I want my son back. That's all.
I want him back now. Then I'll get on with
    my life.
If you could see the depth of this wrenching pain.
If you could see the depth of our sadness
Then you would be moved to return
Our almost five-year-old son
Who sparkles in the sunlight despite his faulty
    neurons.

Please give me back my son
Undamaged and untouched by your labels,
    test results,
Descriptions and categories.
If you can't, if you truly cannot give us back
    our son
Then just be with us quietly,
Gently and compassionately as we feel.
Just sit patiently and attentively as we grieve
    and feel powerless.
Sit with us and create a stillness
Known only in small, empty chapels at sundown.
Be there with us
As our witness and as our friend.

Please do not give us advice, suggestions,
    comparisons or
Another appointment. (That's for later.)
We want only a quiet shoulder upon which to
    rest our too-heavy heads.
If you can't give us back our sweet dream
Then comfort us through this nightmare.
Hold us. Rock us until morning light creeps in.
Then we will rise and begin the work of a
    new day.

Source: Taken from *It Matters: Lessons from My Son,* Janice Fialka, 10474 LaSalle Boulevard, Huntington Woods, MI 48070. www.danceofpartnership.com copyright Fialka, 1997. Used with permission.

tinuing and adult education, adult services, independent living, or community participation [that is] based on the individual student's needs, taking into account the student's preferences and interests; and . . . includes—(i) Instruction; (ii) Related services; (iii) Community experiences; (iv) The development of employment and other postschool adult living objectives; and (v) If appropriate, acquisition of daily living skills and functional vocational evaluation. (Individuals with Disabilities Education Improvement Act, 2004, Section 300.42)

Many human service agencies provide specific services to adults and children with disabilities. Many students will receive services from these agencies. Each agency must, like schools, develop their own written plan of services. The ITP and these services should be developed collaboratively and should work in concert. In each state a *vocational rehabilitation agency* employs counselors who coordinate services designed to help youth and adults with disabilities obtain employment or increase their ability to live independently. For each client vocational rehabilitation agencies are required to develop an **Individualized Written Rehabilitation Plan (IWRP)** that describes employment, independent living goals, services to be provided, and evaluation mechanisms. Mental health agencies also require individualized plans, most often governed by state law and/or accreditation standards rather than by federal law. Plans associated with these agencies go by many names—**Individual Program Plan (IPP)**, Individual Plan of Services (IPOS), and Individual Habilitation Plan (IHP), among others.

Parents and the IEP Meeting. Federal law assures **due process** and mandates that parents be involved in all decision making and have access to information about their children. As educators we must understand the authority and power that we bring into an IEP meeting and be very sensitive interacting with parents. Too often IEP meetings are devastating for parents, who do not feel cared for or supported by school personnel. Janice Fialka wrote the poem in the Voices feature here after the first individualized planning meeting for her young son, Micah (Fialka, 1997). This moving statement makes it ever so clear that listening and simply being with a family as caring people is the most fundamental and important part of developing an IEP.

MAPS—A Student-Centered Planning Process
Dreams Drive the Plans of Friends, Professionals, and Family

In the early 1980s, allies of both adults and children with disabilities became concerned about the system-centered approaches used in planning for people with disabilities. These advocates recognized, however, that bringing people together could be an important source of support. They created a new form of gathering: the *circle of support,* a group that would engage in person-centered planning and harness the resources of the group to help an individual, a "focus person," achieve his or her dreams and goals (see Chapter 11). The approach used most often in schools is **Making Action Plans (MAPS)** (Falvey, Forest, Pearpoint, & Rosenberg, 1998; O'Brien & O'Brien, 1998; Snow, 1998b). (Many books, videos, and articles on this process are listed at **www.inclusion.com.**)

The MAPS process is simultaneously simple, complex, and powerful. MAPS can be conducted as a way to develop the IEP. MAPS includes the planning requirements of an IEP but goes much farther. Alternatively, a family or student may meet with a circle of support and develop a MAPS statement that identifies what they need from the school and/or other human service organizations. A person or family might subsequently ask a member of their circle to attend the IEP meeting.

MAPS meetings include individuals invited by the student, such as family, friends, community members, educators and other professionals. While MAPS sessions can be conducted anywhere, they are most effective in informal, welcoming, and comfortable settings. MAPS have been held in homes, community centers, churches, and restaurants, as well as schools. At a MAPS gathering, as at an IEP meeting, one person acts as facilitator to help the group answer questions, ensure that all have a chance to talk, and keep the focus on the dreams of the individual. Another person acts as a graphics recorder and documents what individuals say through a combination of words and pictures on a flip chart or long piece of paper on the wall. This use of graphics and color in recording the session helps create a person-friendly dynamic and opens up the more creative, intuitive parts of people's brains. Recording all responses on the wall helps people vividly see ideas and words communicated all at once.

Figure 4.10 outlines the overall agenda for the MAPS meeting. The facilitator first introduces the group, saying something like "We are here to help Mary describe a dream for her life and develop an action plan to move toward that dream." She then leads the group through each of the questions shown in Figure 4.10, always allowing the focus person to speak first, followed by others who add to the question based on their own experience. "Mary, tell us your story. What has happened in your life?" the facilitator may begin. As Mary begins to talk, the facilitator summarizes. When Mary is finished, she asks others to add their perspectives.

The power of the MAPS process derives from the fact that as the group addresses each question, group members often bond over common understandings and deep feelings. Telling the story of the person from multiple perspectives brings the group together. We see the person, not just the disability.

Figure 4.10

Questions for a MAPS Meeting

1. *Story:* What is your history and experience?
2. *Dreams:* What are your dreams?
3. *Nightmares:* What are your nightmares?
4. *Who:* Who are you?
5. *Strengths:* What are your strengths?
6. *Needs:* What are your needs?
7. *Action:* What is the action plan?

The "nightmares" discussion allows the person and the group to name and identify what would happen if the worst occurred. In this very important part of the process, the unspoken is confronted directly. Naming nightmares allows the person, family, and circle to face their fears and removes some of those fear's destructiveness.

In a typical MAP, members of the circle give one-word answers to the question "Who is Mary?" This is an amazing time, because the group almost always describes the positive essences of the person. It's encouraging and strengthening.

Schools to Visit

Turning around to Include All Children

Thompson Elementary School
1110 18th Ave. SW
Vero Beach, FL 32960
Phone: 561-564-3240
Principal: Martin O'Neal
www.indian-river.k12.fl.us

Through collaborative work within the school and with external critical friends, Thompson Elementary school has made major changes so as to include its many children with varied disabilities. Thompson Elementary is located in a low-income area of town and has 402 students, of which 22 percent are African American, 2 percent Hispanic, and 76 percent Caucasian; 67 percent are on free or reduced lunch. Martin O'Neal became principal of Thompson Elementary after working as a teacher and assistant principal in the district for twenty-three years. He relished the challenge of including children and improving learning outcomes for all.

The district adopted Quality Designs for Instruction (QDI), a process developed by Stetson and Associates, and Thompson Elementary was one of the first schools to sign up for the training, which was facilitated by Dr. Terri Ward and Susan Benner from the Florida Inclusion Network. QDI helps schools examine staffing patterns and adjust roles of personnel to better meet the needs of students in general education classrooms.

Mr. O'Neal first worked to build teamwork. A special education teacher was assigned to each grade level and attended weekly meetings. Common planning time was established to allow special and general education teachers to meet consistently to plan curriculum and to identify accommodations. Staff participated in coteaching training through a program called FUSE. (Florida

Uniting Students in Education), led by Dr. Deborah Harris of the University of South Florida. The first step was to establish a cotaught K/1 multiage classroom. That proved to be a tremendous success, with significant academic and social gains made by both general and special education students. Thompson next planned a 2/3 coteaching model and began plans for a 4/5 multiage class.

The school created an Inclusion Task Force composed of the principal, general and special education teachers, paraprofessionals, parents, the district inclusion coordinator, and critical friends from the Florida Inclusion Network (FIN) and the University of Florida. The group meets monthly to look at barriers, issues, and next steps; helps the school move from being reactive to being proactive; and establishes policies that effectively deal with issues.

Staff recognized that the inclusion of students with significant disabilities would require outside assistance and obtained on-site modeling and training through the CAFE (Curriculum Access For Everyone) in curriculum and instructional strategies and assistive technologies. Other resources have included a summer conference conducted by the southeastern regional Comprehensive System of Personnel Development (CSPD); support from the Assistive Technology Education Network (ATEN); and training for paraprofessionals related to their roles in providing academic, behavioral, and physical supports, provided by Dr. Diane Ryndak of the University of Florida with the assistance of the district's inclusion specialist.

Thompson Elementary continues to change and grow, utilizing support from both outside and inside and recognizing the importance of developing a team capable of including all children.

By Rick Reardon, Program Specialist, Indian River County Schools; **Rick.Reardon@indian-river.k12.fl.us.**

Then the group talks about strengths and needs. We ask, "What *needs to happen* for Mary to reach her goals?" The answer might involve Mary's improving skills or getting support and assistance from a peer or teacher. She might need to gain friends so as to feel comfortable in the classroom.

Finally, the circle articulates an action plan—steps toward the realization of Mary's dreams. This is the phase on which typical IEP meetings spend most of their time. What people discover in a MAP, however, is that often the action plan goes quickly, building on the previous discussion. During this phase, we prioritize needs. We can use additional tools such as the curriculum matrix (Figure 4.8) and individual class schedule (Figure 4.9) to develop an action plan regarding what happens in our classes.

The information from the MAP can be translated into the formal documentation required by the IEP. Needs statements can easily be translated into more formal goals and objectives on a typical IEP form. Sometimes a separate short meeting is held to translate the MAP ideas into more specific plans within the school and classroom (Knowlton, 1998).

MAPS are often used in schools to plan for students with great life challenges. However, MAPS can be used in many other ways as well. One fifth-grade teacher in Wisconsin divided her class into small groups as circles of support, and over the course of the year each circle did a MAP on each student. This was done as part of a required curriculum on career guidance. Another teacher used circles and MAPS when students were having problems in her class and needed help and support (Knowlton, 1998; Peterson, Tamor, Feen, & Silagy, 2002).

Other Individualized Plans for Students with Special Needs
Families and 504 Plans

Students with disabilities and their families may be served under other agencies that require individualized service plans that will expand on and be coordinated with the IEP. Much of the discussion regarding an IEP can be directly related to each of these planning processes. Let's discuss these briefly.

Individualized Family Services Plan (IFSP)

With the passage of Part H of PL 94-142, special education began to provide early intervention services for young children with identified disabilities or children at risk of having such disabilities. Such services coordinate multiple service agencies—education, welfare, medical, and others—in providing assistance to children and their families to reduce the impact of disabling conditions and to promote increased health and skills. Federal legislation requires an *Individualized Family Services Plan (IFSP)* that articulates how integrated services will assist families and their children with special needs. The IFSP seeks to provide family-centered assistance to children (McGonigel, Kaufmann, & Johnson, 1991). IFSPs include the following components:

1. A statement of the child's present level of functioning
2. A description of the status and needs of the family
3. Goals selected by the family and other professionals collaboratively
4. Services, including frequency and duration
5. Evaluation methods to determine whether goals were met

Section 504 Plans

Section 504 of the Rehabilitation Act of 1973 requires that all organizations receiving public funds provide equal access to persons with disabilities. Section 504 requires that students have access to the least restrictive environment and be provided with accommodations to enable them to participate in the general education class or to engage in formal assessment programs, such as standardized tests. Schools are required to develop **504 plans** to document the accommodations that they provide. Unlike IDEA, however, Section 504 does not provide funding assistance or prescriptive guidelines for how these plans are developed or documented. Typically, schools develop 504 plans for students with ADHD, as well as for students with other disabilities that do not qualify them for special education services.

Getting Started and Going On

We've explored how to design our classes for all students and have surveyed ways to develop individualized support plans. Let's connect with DeMarcus, a beginning biology teacher and see how things are going. . . .

Well, it's the end of the first week of school. It's been a good week. My strategy for teaching eighth-grade biology this year combines several practices that are new for me, exciting but scary at the same time. We still have the district's required text, and my principal insists that we target our instruction within the state's curriculum framework. However, I have decided I am not going to "cover" these objectives week by week in the textbook. No, I am going to involve my students in real, authentic experiences. First, I am involving my students in planning the class. This week we spent half our time discussing what they want to learn in biology this year. We brainstormed ideas on the board. There were a lot. Then we spent time organizing the ideas around learning themes and activities. That was a good beginning. Following this, the students and I together compared the state curriculum objectives to what we had done in our own planning. This helped us focus on certain activities we wanted to do. It was amazing how much we had addressed based on their own interests. I then taught them about multiple intelligences and the need to have students work at different levels. Together we came up with fun, thought-provoking lessons that will include

Stepping Stones

To Inclusive Teaching

1. Design one lesson plan that involves learning activities for students with very diverse abilities, in which children can work together but at different levels. What did you learn? How might you work toward teaching all your lessons this way?

2. Participate in an IEP meeting for a student with a disability. Bring to the meeting a description of the strengths of the student, some key needs, and ideas for ways you can meet those needs in your classroom. Help the team state goals and objectives that fit with good teaching practices.

3. Investigate how your school brings together resources to help children and teachers who are facing challenges. How are referrals made for special education in your building? What happens afterward? What percentage of students are labeled in your school? What do you think all this means? Identify two practices you'd like to see changed to better support students and teachers, and talk with another teacher about these ideas.

4. Do a MAP with a circle of friends. Use this process to gain assistance for a student from his or her peers. Incorporate these strategies into the student's IEP at your next meeting.

5. Have a meeting with the parents of a student who is having difficulty. Get their priorities for their child's learning and their input into how the child learns best. Suggest some strategies for learning that they could use at home. Consider including these in the IEP.

working in groups with different abilities (we talked about how to ensure each person was responsible and what would happen if they were not); developing our own experiments; using drama, art, and music to portray concepts; and conducting community projects both during and after school. The kids seem excited and so am I.

"I was worried about the students with disabilities in my class. However, as we planned together, I asked the students to come up with ideas to ensure that everyone was learning and could participate. We will work these plans out in more detail as we go, but they had some terrific suggestions. In fact, I took their concepts into the IEP meeting for Joe, my student who is mentally retarded and has cerebral palsy. You should have seen the parents. They actually looked shocked. They smiled and came up to me after the meeting. The dad shook my hand heartily and the mom hugged me! They both had tears in their eyes. Wow! Makes me glad I am a teacher. At least today" (D. Thomas, personal communication, September 2001).

 Key Points

- Teaching is easier and more effective if we start with the understanding that our students will have wide ranges of abilities. This understanding is vital if we're to be an inclusive teacher.

- We can *design for diversity* in three interactive domains: (1) academic, (2) social–emotional, and (3) sensory–physical.

- We can *adapt* as needed in one or more of these domains, using the lessons we learn to design differently the next time around.

- If students have difficulty in our classes, we may want to *refer* them to be evaluated to see if they have a disability and can benefit from special education services.

■ We can use *collaborative consultation* to obtain ideas for working with a student.

■ If the student has a disability, we will serve on a team to develop an Individualized Education Plan (IEP), which specifies goals, objectives, placement, services, and evaluation criteria. We take our ideas to the IEP meeting to contribute to a plan that works for our class.

■ Other planning approaches such as MAPS (Making Action Plans) are valuable and involve a circle of support composed of friends and family as well as teachers and other professionals.

 Learning Expeditions

Following are some ideas that may extend your learning.

1. Look for examples in your own neighborhood and community that illustrate "designing for diversity" and "adaptations."

2. Take about fifteen minutes and sketch ideas for how you might teach students with wide ranges of ability this year. Discuss your ideas with other teachers or parents.

3. Present the basic ideas of designing for diversity at a workshop for teachers and have them brainstorm new ways to work toward meeting the guidelines (see Figure 4.1).

4. Observe in a classroom and pay particular attention to one student that is having problems. How might changes in the design of teaching and the culture of the classroom make a difference with this student? What adaptations might be useful?

5. Use the student profile with a student in a class you teach or can observe who is having some difficulties. Focus on identifying the student's strengths and needs. What ideas might help build on strengths and meet needs?

6. Obtain a copy of an IEP, observe the student for whom the IEP was written, and talk with the family. How useful is the IEP as a working plan for the student? What strengths and weaknesses do you see?

7. Participate in an IEP meeting. What occurred, and how did you feel about it? To what degree did this meeting seem "system-centered" or "child- and family-centered"? Why?

8. View a video about a MAP. How does this compare to your observation of an IEP?

9. Interview a family or an individual that has been the focus of a MAP or similar person-centered planning process. What happened in the meeting, and what resulted from the process? How did the person or family feel about the process?

10. Interview community agencies that work with people with disabilities about their individualized planning processes. What do they do that is similar to and different from the IEP process? Do they use person-centered planning? If so, how? What relationship do they have with schools, and how do they mesh their required planning with the school's IEPs?

CHAPTER GOAL

Understand how the concept and practice of support for teachers and students works in effective inclusive schools to strengthen learning and the school community.

CHAPTER OBJECTIVES

1. Understand effective methods of grouping students and ways in which students may provide assistance to one another with teacher guidance.

2. Develop skills in collaborating with other professionals in the classroom in teaching students with a wide range of abilities and needs.

3. Recognize the roles of various support staff in working in the general education classroom.

4. Comprehend practices and principles of effective support for inclusive teaching.

Support and Collaboration

Getting Help and Building a School Community

When we think about having students of truly different abilities in our classes, students who may not be able to talk, who may read far below (or far above) grade level, who may have seizures or use a wheelchair, or who may be unable to see, we may feel overwhelmed. How can we manage? Our teaching methods make a great difference. However, we also need *support*. As we shall see in this chapter, support involves multiple forms of assistance from others— the emotional sustenance afforded by a listening ear, ideas to help us improve our teaching or deal with challenging students, solutions to problems with parents, and more. When we are asked to perform a task in which we are unsure of our abilities, we often ask, "How can I get help? Can someone help me learn how to do this? Can someone help me feel like I am not alone?" This is natural. Support is critical in successful inclusive teaching. Let us visit a classroom where teachers are getting help in teaching students with special needs.

121

Monica has begun her twentieth year as a middle school science teacher with excitement and trepidation. Last year she attended workshops on project-based learning and decided to take a risk and organize her teaching around problem-based projects, using textbooks only as a reference. She and the social studies teacher, Mark, are teaming to link science and social issues. It's been hard work but has gone pretty well so far.

Monclair Middle School is also including special education students, even bringing two students with severe mental retardation back from a segregated school. Teachers met at the end of last year and planned carefully to place students in heterogeneous groups; they made sure not to cluster students with academic or behavioral problems in any one class and to ensure a distribution of races and genders, even matching students to teachers based on their personalities. One student with severe mental retardation, Jennifer, was in Monica's class. Terrified at first, Monica was relieved to have the full-time help of a paraprofessional, Jan, and part-time support from the special education teacher, Bob. However, she became increasingly concerned as Jan and Bob both worked with Jennifer on separate activities at the back of the class, isolating her from the other students. What to do? One day she talked with Bob. "I am wondering," she said, "could you help Mark and me design our lessons so that Jennifer can participate?" This idea was foreign to Bob and Jan. "We don't really know your curriculum," they said.

However, they decided to try, and the situation is slowly improving. For example, last week they studied the environmental impact of pollution, and the class divided into two groups. One group took water samples from the pond next to the school. Another interviewed local environmentalists. Jennifer chose to go with classmate Amy in the interview group. The children and their teacher discussed how to include Jennifer and decided to videotape the session. Jennifer would turn the videotape on and off. The school technician helped them connect the camera to a switch. Jennifer ran the camera with some help from Amy. She was so proud! "Since this first time, we daily figure out ways to include Jennifer and meet her IEP goals. It's funny that before we had no clue."

Monica has avoided some problems we've sometimes seen. She proactively, respectfully brought the special education teacher and paraprofessional into the class curriculum, simultaneously ensuring that Jennifer could participate at her own level. She took responsibility for Jennifer, rather than leaving this to the special education staff, while also inviting collaboration. She has set up a situation where all can be part of the classroom community.

At Eubanks Elementary School, arriving for a visit in Hannah Smith's fourth-grade classroom, we find country music playing loudly and children milling about the room. "This is a transition time," Hannah says, "when the kids unwind a bit." Hannah's room is designated as the "inclusion classroom": All fourth graders with disabilities are in her class—four children labeled as having learning disabilities, two with mental retardation, and one with emotional disturbance in a class of twenty-five. Usually a paraprofessional works in the class in the morning and a special education teacher in the afternoon. Today, however, both are in the class together. Students sit at tables arranged in a U. Nathan, however, has a desk at the side of the room.

After Hannah shuts off the music, we are surprised to see the students divide into three obvious ability groups. One group is working with the special education teacher on forming letters in colored sand. Another group is reading a short book together as the paraprofessional follows a scripted lesson on phonics. The final group is in the hall with Hannah, reading an interesting book together and sharing stories written from the perspective of a character in the story. Nathan continues to work on a puzzle, totally separate from the other students.

Coteachers collaboratively assist students as they work on projects about whales. Both work together to support students with special needs and teach the entire class.

We are concerned. We've seen other schools where teachers have students of different ability levels working together, learning skills such as letter recognition and phonics as they are reading and writing. Hannah clearly doesn't know how to do this, however. The special education teacher and paraprofessional are re-creating the equivalent of segregated special education within this classroom. Those with lower abilities don't have the benefit of interacting with higher-ability students, and the more able children themselves are not learning leadership skills.

Support and Teaching

Support is important. Teachers need support from peers, principals, and families. As Joan, a high school teacher, said about her collaboration with a special education teacher, "The kids love having help when and where they need it. For me, it has been so wonderful because it gives me more comfort in knowing I have support. I don't feel so alone any more" (Peterson, 1999). In this chapter we explore how we can obtain support as inclusive teachers. As you journey with us, think carefully about support you might need in order to teach children with different academic, social–emotional, and sensory–physical abilities.

Traveling Notes

Learning to collaborate with other professionals in supporting children with real differences in our classroom is a new skill for most of us. Monica worked through some issues, but Hannah clearly was re-creating a special education island in her classroom.

1. How can we as teachers make use of assistance to ensure that students get the help they need without stigmatizing them in our own classes?

2. What roles do different support professionals play?

3. How does our relationship develop with them?

4. Who is in charge, and who does what?

These are important questions. In fact, as schools are becoming more inclusive, teachers and support staff are constantly experimenting with answering these questions.

Figure 5.1 lists nine principles of effective inclusive support. First and foremost, effective support promotes and strengthens inclusion in our classes—it helps us group children heterogeneously, distribute children with special needs across classes, and teach children of differing abilities together rather than pulling children out to a resource room or to the back of the classroom. Inclusive support helps us build community to deal with behavioral challenges rather than to focus only on a specific child. Support specialists help us design instruction at multiple levels, teach collaboratively with us, and help track each child's progress and needs, coordinating services so that we do not have specialists doing parallel activities. Such support implies the building of a culture of community and care for one another, as well as for children, within the school (Carpenter, King-Sears,

Figure 5.1

Principles of Support for Inclusive Teaching

1. *Inclusive classrooms:* Students are grouped heterogeneously, pull-out services are minimized, and segregation is not re-created in the general education classroom.

2. *Building community and meeting behavioral challenges:* Teachers are assisted in building a classroom community in which children help one another.

3. *Multilevel, authentic instruction:* Faculty and staff design and implement multilevel, authentic, challenging, and scaffolded instruction.

4. *Adaptations:* Teachers and support staff design and use needed instructional adaptations.

5. *Child services coordination:* Support staff coordinate services across multiple classes and professionals.

6. *Teacher support coordination:* Multiple services in a teacher's room are coordinated to ensure consistency of approach.

7. *Professional growth:* Teachers are given opportunities for collaborative growth and learning.

8. *Emotional support:* Teachers have forums through which they can get emotional support, opportunities to share with one another, and a time and place for all this to happen.

9. *Teacher empowerment:* Support staff seek to empower rather than to displace teachers in working with special students.

Source: Adapted from Peterson, Tamor, Feen, & Silagy (2002).

Tools *for the* Trek
Strategies of Support for Inclusive Teaching

STUDENTS HELPING STUDENTS
- Peer buddies
- Peer tutoring
- Mentors
- Circles of support

TEAMING
- Building child study teams
- Teacher and support staff teams
- Coordination of student services
- Collaborative consultation
- Consultation and collaboration with community agencies

SCHOOL SUPPORT PROGRAMS
- Learning support centers
- Counseling

COLLABORATIVE TEACHING
- General education team teaching
- In-class collaborative teaching by support teachers and specialists
- In-class team instruction
- In-class support by paraprofessionals
- Community volunteers

PROFESSIONAL DEVELOPMENT AND GROWTH
- Professional development inquiry and dialogue groups
- Teacher support networks—in person and online
- Critical friends
- Professional organizations and conferences

& Keys, 1998; Giangreco, 1996; Peterson, Tamor, Feen, & Silagy, 2002). The Tools for the Trek feature lists key support strategies built on these principles. The remaining sections of this chapter will expand on many of these strategies .

Inclusive Grouping of Children for Support
Starting with an Inclusive School Community

Since the beginning of compulsory education, schools have sorted children many ways—by age (thus the creation of grades), by ability, by language, and, for many years, by race. The theory for such sorting is seldom articulated and little researched, despite its prevalence as a fundamental organizing premise. When public schools were first developed in rural areas, children of all ages learned together in one-room schoolhouses. As schools grew, however, experts began using the factory as a model for educational design, and these heterogeneous classes disappeared. Children were organized by age-bound grades. Curriculum was developed based on narrow expectations at each grade, and special programs were created for those who did not fit. This is the basic model by which schools are still organized (Smith, F., 1998; Tyack & Cuban, 1995).

However, children don't all develop at the same rates (Bredekamp & Copple, 1997). As with adults, their abilities vary dramatically. In any typical school classroom, reading abilities, for example, will range across four to six theoretical grade levels (Allington, 1994; Peterson, Tamor, Feen, & Silagy, 2002). Recognizing this problem, schools have begun to group children in ways that keep with children's natural development. The move toward inclusive schooling is consistent with this effort. Effective inclusive schools develop strategies for **inclusive grouping:** grouping across and within classes in heterogeneous groups of children with different abilities, styles, ethnicity, and other characteristics. Schools are seeking ways to allow students and teachers come to know one another well and to foster continuity across several years. Such connection and support is particularly important for students with special needs.

Multiage Teaching

In **multiage teaching,** students from two to three typical grades learn together in one classroom, using the same curriculum and staying with that teacher for two to three years. Teachers engage students in projects that explore questions and facilitate mutual helping by older and younger students. In a multiage classroom students work in pairs or small groups as the teacher moves from group to group or conferences with students.

Research has shown that multiage settings offer substantial academic and social advantages compared to single-age classrooms, not only for students with special needs but also for all other students (Feldman & Gray, 1999; McClellan, 1994; McClellan & Kinsey, 1999). Vygotsky (1978) based his influential work on the idea that children learn best from others who differ in ability and that "by playing and working with older and more competent partners, children are able to engage in and master more difficult tasks than they can handle alone" (Feldman & Gray, 1999, p. 508). Younger children learn from older children, and older children learn skills of teaching and nurturing. Students have opportunities to seek out a wider range of styles, interests, and expertises: Sometimes very able younger students are ready to be challenged by older students; at the same time, less able older students have the opportunity to deepen their own skills by leading and helping younger students. Such instruction also naturally enhances social and emotional learning and the development of a sense of community (Chase & Doan, 1994; Feldman & Gray, 1999; McClellan & Kinsey, 1999; Miller, 1995).

Looping

The term **looping** refers to a teacher's moving from one grade level to another along with his or her students. For example, Nancy is a third-grade teacher who is looping with her children and will continue to be their teacher in the fourth grade. The following year she will drop back to third grade and start the same process with another group of children. The effect of looping is that, as in multiage classes, a teacher spends two or more years with the same group of students. This allows the teacher to build a strong relationship with students and parents and to start off each new year more seamlessly. Students and teachers alike find this practice emotionally supportive as well as beneficial to learning (Gaustad, 1998; Grant, 1996).

School within a School

A **school within a school** is another helpful strategy. Large schools can create a sense of anonymity in which students often feel literally lost in the crowd. To counter this, some schools, particularly middle and high schools, divide the school population into smaller groups in order to build a sense of community, collaboration, and support among teachers and students. A group of one to two hundred students go through their school careers together, often assigned to teachers who work with students over several years. These groupings go by different names in different schools—pods, families, houses, universities, and the like (Peterson, 1992; Sergiovanni, 1994).

Clustering and Ability Grouping: Re-Creating Segregation on the Road to Inclusive Schooling

Every school has a wide variety of children with special needs. These may include students in the following broad categories: (1) disabled, (2) gifted and talented, (3) at-risk, and (4) bilingual (second language learner). Of course, any given student also may fall into two or more of these categories. Historically, schools have created special segregated classes for each of these groups. Inclusive schools, in contrast, seek to have all students in general education classes where they receive the support and assistance they need. However, schools sometimes re-create segregation in the midst of a general education class by (1) **clustering** students with certain types of characteristics in certain classrooms and/or (2) **ability grouping** students within a class.

Support staff—special education teachers, bilingual or gifted teachers, speech therapists—believe clustering helps them organize their efforts, minimizing the number of classes in which they work. Harmon Middle School, for example, assigns all students with learning disabilities to one class, second language learners to another class, and gifted students to yet another class. Similarly, Oakdale Elementary School uses a common pattern in which students with special needs are in only one of the four classes at each grade level; a special education teacher works with only two of the four classes. In Eagle Mountain Elementary School, a special education teacher is in the general education class in the morning and is replaced by a paraprofessional in the afternoon. In a variation of clustering, an entire special education class (usually ten to fifteen students) may be merged with a general education class and two teachers may teach the class together.

Despite perceived administrative benefits of clustering for support staff, the practice violates the underlying educational theory of inclusive schooling, replicating the kinds of practices that led to segregated education in the first place. Even with professional support, overloading one classroom with a disproportionate number of students with special needs can mean fewer opportunities for students to model learning, thus creating overtaxed, highly stressed teachers (Blanksby, 1999). Some teachers do not have students with special needs; therefore, some teachers feel overburdened. Other teachers may receive no support even though many unidentified students in their room need assistance. We've seen teachers essentially bartering for who "gets" special students. Classes with special students may become labeled and stigmatized. Coteachers of these classes, too, may experience the type of stigma that has typically occurred in segregated classes in schools (Peterson, Tamor, Feen, & Silagy, 2002).

Heterogeneous Grouping of Students: The Better Path

Effective inclusive schools group students systematically across and within classes. In inclusive elementary schools teachers may complete brief profiles of students in terms of a few basic variables. Two schools we have studied used the following categories:

1. Academic abilities
2. Behavioral and social challenges and needs
3. Socioeconomic status
4. Race
5. Gender

In a placement meeting, taking into consideration all these factors, faculty members construct compatible but heterogeneous classes. They also think about how children relate to one another and consider the match of child and teacher personality. Once students have been distributed, support staff develop a plan with the general education teachers for how and when they will provide support. Table 5.1 illustrates how such a distribution looks (Peterson, Tamor, Feen, & Silagy, 2002; Walther-Thomas, Korinek, McLaughlin, & Toler Williams, 2000).

Table 5.1

Heterogeneous Student Distribution: An Example

	CLASS 1	CLASS 2	CLASS 3
Academic Ability			
High	4	5	4
Medium	15	13	16
Low	6	7	5
Behavior			
Excellent	8	7	6
Average	12	14	13
Poor—high support needs	5	4	6
Socioeconomic Status			
High	5	2	5
Middle	14	15	13
Lower	6	8	7
Total in Class	**25**	**25**	**25**

In middle schools or high schools, scheduling is more complex, because students no longer remain in one classroom all day. An inclusive secondary school eliminates tracked classes—lower-level and upper-level English and biology, for example. Similarly, it does not have special classes for students with special needs–students with disabilities, gifted students, and so on. Students select classes based purely on graduation requirements and their interests. The elimination of tracked and separate special classes most often ensures a heterogeneous mix of students. When schools find clusters of students developing, they initiate efforts to recruit students from underrepresented categories or to deal with underlying issues. For example, if groups of students with disabilities were signing up for one class, the school staff would want to understand why. Similarly, if classes became racially segregated, this would be a sign of issues to be addressed.

An Inclusive Continuum of Services: From Place to Process

As we seek to mix students heterogeneously, we also attend to the federal legal requirement that schools provide a *continuum of placement options* to meet the needs of children with disabilities. These options must include instruction in regular classes, special classes, special schools, home instruction, instruction in hospitals and institutions, and provision for supplementary services in the general education classroom (IDEA, 2004). Figure 5.2 provides an illustration of this continuum of placement options as first popularized by Deno (1970).

The model assumes that the more intensive a service, the more segregated the placement. Frequently, the need to maintain this continuum has been used as one argument against inclusive education. Taylor (1988) suggested alternatively that linking intensive services with segregation is not necessary. Services at very different levels of intensity may be delivered in general education classrooms. Virtually any support service can be effectively delivered in general education. In Figure 5.3 we've provided an illustrative example of an **inclusive continuum of services.** What changes is not the physical location where the student spends his or her time. Rather, the type, intensity, and duration of various supports and services change based on the needs of the student and teachers. Thus any particular place, including a general education class, could have intensive services. This model has important implications for both practice and policy.

Students Helping Students
The Power of Peers

In inclusive schools we intentionally group children heterogeneously to build a sense of community and support. Students themselves can be the most valuable resource for student support. Teachers often take responsibility for helping students and don't create structures whereby students are taught to support one another in learning. Students can support one another, however, and several strategies help make this possible. We discuss these strategies in detail in Chapter 11.

Figure 5.2

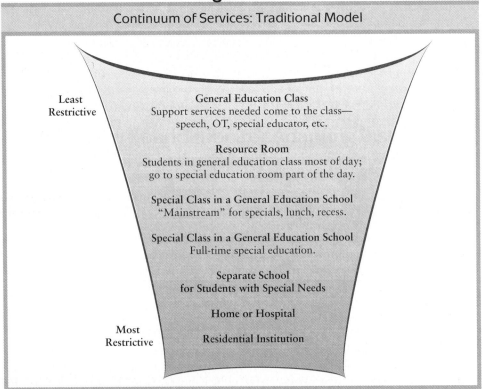

Continuum of Services: Traditional Model

Least
Restrictive

General Education Class
Support services needed come to the class—
speech, OT, special educator, etc.

Resource Room
Students in general education class most of day;
go to special education room part of the day.

Special Class in a General Education School
"Mainstream" for specials, lunch, recess.

Special Class in a General Education School
Full-time special education.

**Separate School
for Students with Special Needs**

Home or Hospital

Most
Restrictive   **Residential Institution**

Source: Adapted from Deno (1970).

Collaborative Teams
Gathering the School Community

Effective inclusive schools build a culture of mutual help and support among all
staff—teachers, secretaries, support staff, custodians. Helping children is the over-
riding aim, but all concerned understand that helping one another is a prerequisite
for this to occur. Within such a culture, staff and volunteers work in collaborative
teams. Let's explore teams we see in inclusive schools.

Collaborative Teacher Teams

Collaborative teams involve two or more teachers who work together at various levels of intensity, from periodic collaboration on a learning activity to teaching lessons
collaboratively to a larger group of students. A special education teacher and/or
other support person is an integral member of the team. Traditionally, teachers have
been organized by grade levels in elementary schools and by departments (e.g., science and math, English and social studies) in secondary schools. As looping and

Figure 5.3

Continuum of Services: Inclusive Model

Greatest supports and services	All services listed below plus any additional consultative or direct services (e.g., therapist for child and family, psychiatrist).
	In-class support coteacher works more than half to full time. Circles of support/friends.
	Paraprofessional aide works part to full time.
	Specialist assistance: Speech therapy, occupational therapy, rehabilitation teachers, orientation and mobility, etc.
	In-class support coteacher provides periodic in-class assistance in adapting lessons and instructs special students or the whole class. Intentional assistance from classmates.
	Collaborative consultation: Periodic consultation with teacher either in or out of class. Building relationships in the classroom.
Least supports and services	Collaborative team planning: General and special education, parents, other professionals.

multiage classrooms become more prevalent, however, it makes less sense to cluster teachers by grade levels. In elementary schools, teachers often think of themselves as "early elementary" and "upper elementary" and work in formal and informal teams. In other schools, classes at different grade levels are intentionally placed next to one another so that faculty can develop collaborative, multiage instruction, linking activities in their classes. Innovative secondary schools often use **interdisciplinary teams of teachers:** Social studies, literacy, math, science, and special education teachers work together rather than within separate subject departments (Fisher, Sax, & Pumpian, 1999; Walther-Thomas, Korinek, McLaughlin, & Toler Williams, 2000). Teacher teams often use themes to link the subjects and to bring their classes together in learning (Kovalik & Olsaen, 1997; Manning, Manning, & Long, 1994). In one school, for example, a team of teachers, including special education and **Title I support teachers,** used a yearlong theme of oceans and space as an organizer for many activities. They met across grade levels to plan instruction throughout the year (Peterson, Tamor, Feen, & Silagy, 2002).

Teacher Support Teams

Inclusive schools organize **child study teams** through which teachers can bring concerns regarding a child to the attention of other staff. Such teams often meet either weekly or biweekly and are attended by the teacher who has referred the student, other teacher representatives, the principal, parents and family members, and support

Artwork reprinted by permission of Martha Perske from *Perske: Pencil Portraits 1971–1990* (Nashville: Abingdon Press, 1998).

staff in the building—often a special education and Title I teacher (if applicable), counselor, social worker, or psychologist. These teams are called by many names: child study teams, prereferral intervention teams, student and teacher support teams, and more. Sometimes children attend these meetings as well. When the child is present, the team tends to focus more positively on communicating with both child and parent. The child is given responsibility for being part of decision making.

In some cases support teams are built around specific needs and respond to crises, behavioral challenges, or student academic problems. Increasingly, however, to use staff time and energy more efficiently, schools are creating one team that will deal with multiple issues, recognizing that problems are often linked (Fisher, Sax, & Pumpian, 1999; Walther-Thomas, Korinek, McLaughlin & Toler Williams, 2000).

A key purpose of effective team meetings is to provide assistance to a teacher or staff member who is concerned about an issue in his or her class. This is the process referred to as *collaborative consultation* (see Chapter 4), in which a teacher presents an issue and obtains assistance from others. One teacher, for example, was concerned about Randy, a child in her class who had diabetes. Randy's blood sugar level was not stabilized, and he frequently needed to stop work and ask the teacher to help him administer a simple blood sugar test. The teacher was particularly worried

EXTREME TEAM

DREAM TEAM

about the rest of the class and felt a need for backup from others. She obtained input from other teachers, two nurses who attended the meeting, and support staff—a psychologist, a special education teacher, and the principal. She went away from the meeting with commitments from support staff to help her monitor Randy's situation and deal with the class (Idol, Paolucci-Whitcomb, & Nevin, 1994; Peterson, Tamor, Feen, & Silagy, 2002).

Individual Student Teams

As we discussed in Chapter 4, teams are also built around students with special needs as part of an Individualized Education Plan (IEP) or a Section 504 plan. The more intense such needs, the more people may be involved to provide support and assistance. For example, Elizabeth, a student with a mild learning disability, has the special and general education teachers and the school psychologist on her team. Jonathan, a student with a complex medical condition and severe mental retardation who uses a wheelchair and a computerized communication device, has a large team—special education teacher, speech therapist, occupational therapist, assistive technology consultant, general education teacher, and nurse. A support staff person is assigned to coordinate services across multiple classes and provide some direct support (Bauwens & Hourcade, 1998; Ford, Fitzgerald, Glodoski, & Waterbury, 1997; Giangreco, 1996; Noell & Witt, 1999).

Support Staff Teams

In effective inclusive schools, the *support staff*—special education teachers, Title I and bilingual teachers, counselors, social workers, psychologists, and others—work as a collaborative team to develop a comprehensive system of support. In Jamestown High School, for example, specialists meet together frequently to discuss children, the needs of teachers, and strategies for particular students. They develop coordinated schedules of support in classes, sometimes intentionally working together in a class, and at other times arranging to be in different classes, depending on teacher and student needs. Similarly, in Three Rivers Elementary, support staff meet formally early in the morning twice each week to discuss students and coordinate schedules (Noell & Witt, 1999; Snell & Janney, 2000; Walther-Thomas, Korinek, McLaughlin, & Toler Williams, 2000).

In less effective schools, in contrast, specialists tend to work in parallel, seeing only the children assigned to their own caseloads and scheduling separately from one another. For example, in one school the special education support teacher and the gifted education specialist both work with children in one fifth-grade class, but they do not coordinate their services or talk together about how to support the teacher in instructing students with such differing abilities (Noell & Witt, 1999; Snell & Janney, 2000; Walther-Thomas, Korinek, McLaughlin, & Toler Williams, 2000).

Volunteer Support and Community Agency Collaboration

Finally, the larger community can provide wonderful sources of support for schools and teachers. In many schools parents not only volunteer for projects such as baking cookies but also operate parent resource centers, read stories to the class, or mentor individual students during or after school. Community agencies may also bring specialized resources to the school. (Kretzmann & McKnight, 1993). Nationally, for example, Communities in Schools helps connect schools to community resources. At Merrill elementary school a hospital sends interns into classes on a weekly basis to teach students science lessons related to the body. A violence prevention organization called Common Ground brings a special program into schools to provide emotional support via group meetings with students and to train students in conflict resolution (Peterson, Tamor, Feen, & Silagy, 2002).

Schoolwide Student Support Services
Using Our Resources for Teachers and Students

Most schools employ support staff to provide services to children and families, and these staffers often provide direct and indirect support to teachers as well.

Counselors, Social Workers, and Psychologists

Counselors, social workers, and psychologists consult with teachers regarding student academic and emotional needs, suggest strategies, and provide helpful information. They can provide direct individual or group counseling, contact families, serve on a crisis team, and provide in-class support. For example, a psychologist might offer advice to teachers about self-esteem and conflict resolution. A psychologist–social worker team may facilitate circles of support (Bowen & Glenn, 1998; Carpenter, King-Sears, & Keys, 1998; Quigney & Studer, 1999).

Media Specialists

Media specialists can be invaluable in locating written materials at various levels of difficulty, in providing assistance to individuals and groups of students engaged in research projects, and in training students in the use of computers and other media. Media specialists are increasingly becoming skilled in helping teachers design authentic, multilevel instruction and in working with students with special needs (Peterson, Tamor, Feen, & Silagy, 2002).

Learning Support Centers

Learning support centers, or simply learning centers, are physical locations in schools where any student, not just those with special needs, may obtain assistance for academic, emotional, or physical needs. Centers are staffed by one or more teachers, and students may visit these centers for help or hang out during their lunch period. A laid-back style often makes a learning center a preferred gathering place for students. For some students, time in the learning support center may be scheduled as a daily class. However, students should *choose* to come.

Collaborative Teaching
Partnerships for Student Learning

Collaborative teaching, by which we mean working collaboratively with support staff as we help students learn, is one key source of support. Collaborative teaching involves making important changes as we decide to move beyond being a "lone ranger" and to work with others. In effective inclusive schools, teachers have choices regarding collaboration and professional supports. For example, Nancy is a seventh-grade teacher who teaches children with very different abilities together in creative ways. However, she neither asks for nor wants additional staff support in her classroom. She is able to manage just fine, enjoys teaching by herself, and successfully facilitates mutual support among her students. Jane, on the other hand, teaches sixth grade and thrives on teaming with support staff, collaboratively planning and implementing instruction, and using the strengths of others to complement her own abilities. For Jane collaboration is the lifeblood of teaching. The point is that there is no one way to be an effective inclusive teacher. The key is to know ourselves, our working style, and our desire or need for additional support. If we do seek support, developing our collaborative skills will be critical.

The Purpose and Practice of Collaborative Teaching: Four Approaches

There are four key approaches by which support staff provide support to teachers, each based on different goals and strategies (Peterson, Tamor, Feen, & Silagy, 2002). Understanding these approaches will help us decide how we want to work with support staff in our class.

Pull-Out Remediation. Remediation aims to improve student functioning in identified deficit areas. The assumption is that students possess within themselves either a deficit or a special ability that cannot be met in the regular classroom and that services must be provided elsewhere by a specialist. In most cases special instruction is provided in a separate classroom or therapy room. Such approaches may become self-reinforcing, perpetuating rather than diminishing a student's need for special services. As students are withdrawn from typical activities in the classroom, they often fall farther behind, creating the perception that they need even more remedial education (Spear-Swerling & Sternberg, 1998; Sternberg & Grigorenko, 1999).

Adaptations. Alternatively, support staff may work with children in the regular classroom, developing any needed adaptations to instruction. An adaptation involves a strategy, specifically selected for an individual student, that varies from typical instruction and is designed to help the student succeed (see Chapter 9). In adapting curriculum, support staff typically works within the existing curriculum and instructional approach (Ford, Fitzgerald, Glodoski, & Waterbury, 1997).

Support for Teacher Needs. All teachers have both strengths and needs, and support staff can help us strengthen areas in which we need improvement. In one situation, for example, the support teacher for at-risk students was skilled in teaching science—so she led the science lesson two or three times a week while the general education teacher worked with students who were having difficulty. This provided both support and teacher development. In another case a teacher wanted to use a running record (a systematic analysis of errors in a reading sample) for each child but needed to learn better how to employ the strategy. The reading clinician spent thirty minutes twice a week demonstrating lessons in the class and mentoring the teacher (Peterson, Tamor, Feen, & Silagy, 2002).

Inclusive Multilevel Teaching. In the fourth approach support staff work with general education teachers to design and implement multilevel curriculum and instructional activities (see Chapter 6). The assumption is that instruction can be designed and implemented manageably for very diverse ability levels so that all students benefit. In this approach support staff assist teachers in designing and implementing authentic, multilevel learning activities.

Methods of Organizing Collaborative Teaching

There are many types of staff with whom we may have the opportunity to teach collaboratively. As we work with specialists, we can use one of several methods of organizing our work together.

Team Teaching. Perhaps the most common method of collaborative teaching is team teaching between two or more general education teachers. In one elementary school two multiage classes (grades 2–3) adjoin, and the teachers engage in collaborative instruction. At MacNeilson elementary school two teachers decide to teach together in a larger room and combine their two classes for one year; other teachers work together on units organized by themes or collaborate in teaching particular subjects. At Dellian High School, interdisciplinary teams of science, social studies, language arts, and special education teachers have adjoining rooms and work together on projects throughout the year. One high school class reads and writes with students in grades 1–3 once each month, visiting the elementary school for two hours in the morning. Similarly, many upper elementary classes pair with students in grade 1 for buddy reading and special projects. All these arrangements provide additional support and collaborative opportunities for both students and teachers (Fisher, Sax, & Pumpian, 1999; Peterson, Tamor, Feen, & Silagy, 2002; Walther-Thomas, Korinek, McLaughlin, & Toler Williams, 2000).

In-Class Collaborative Teaching by Support Teachers. Many teachers who specialize in a particular student population may work in a given school. These specialists, who previously taught students in separate rooms, now often work in the general education classroom, helping us teach. These teachers are typically associated with specially funded programs that include:

- Special education
- Title I (federal funds for schools with high concentrations of low-income students)
- Bilingual education
- Gifted and talented education

Special education and bilingual teachers will have specific students assigned to their caseload, for whom they are responsible. However, they are also allowed to work with the total class as long as the individual needs of the students are met (see Figure 5.4) (Dover, 1994). In one classroom, for example, Susan, the special education teacher, and Janet, the general education teacher, plan and teach collaborative lessons. They trade roles in leading the class, helping groups work on projects, and providing direct skills instruction to individuals or small groups as needed.

In-Class Collaborative Teaching by Related Services Specialists. Many other specialists provide what IDEA calls *related services:* "transportation and such developmental, corrective, and other supportive services as are required to assist a child with a disability to benefit from special education" (CFR 300.24; IDEA, 1999; Snell & Janney, 2000; Thomas, Correa, & Morsink, 1995).

- *Sign language interpreters* help students who are deaf to understand what is happening in the class and communicate with others.
- *Speech therapists* help students with difficulties in producing sounds and communicating effectively.
- *Audiologists* evaluate hearing ability and make recommendations to maximize students' ability to hear and understand sounds.
- *Rehabilitation teachers* assist students who are blind or visually impaired in using accommodations, adaptive equipment, and materials for daily living and communication.
- *Orientation and mobility specialists* aid persons who are blind or visually impaired in using adaptive strategies to move around from place to place—canes, guide dogs, and so on.

Figure 5.4

Roles of Support Teachers

1. Plan with the principal and teachers for new approaches to providing learning supports:
   - Organize in-service training.
   - Work with consultants.
   - Serve on inclusive education planning committee.

2. Plan for individual students:
   - Facilitate person-centered planning/IEPs.
   - Consult with individual families and attend parent meetings.
   - Advocate on behalf of individual students and families.

3. Assist in multilevel instruction and adaptations for students:
   - Take leadership in promoting collaborative teaching and cooperative learning.
   - Work with teachers to identify strategies for accommodating students.
   - Develop or acquire needed materials.
   - Help general education teachers coordinate with related services in the classroom.
   - Provide direct support and instruction with the general teacher.

4. Facilitate community connections and family involvement:
   - Facilitate involvement of students in school-sponsored extracurricular activities.
   - Contact Boy Scouts/Girl Scouts, community recreation.
   - Connect families to one another to provide support.

Source: Adapted from Tashie, Shapiro-Barnard, Donoghue-Dillon, Jorgenson, & Nisbet (1993).

- *Occupational therapists* help students improve fine motor coordination and use of the upper extremities to accomplish functional tasks.
- *Physical therapists* help people improve their gross motor abilities—walking, gait, and so on.
- *School nurses* provide assistance related to health issues and coordinate in-school services with medical services outside the school.

In most of these specialties there is controversy over whether to provide the service in the context of a general education class or in a clinic. For example, speech therapists traditionally work with individual students on speech articulation and other communication strategies in a separate room. In inclusive education models, however, speech therapists come into the classroom and assist students in class communication activities. The therapist often works with a small group and sometimes with the whole class, helping promote language development of all the children while targeting the specific needs of a student with special needs. For example, a speech therapist may work with a student or small group of students on the articulation and production of specific sounds as the children sing a song or read text aloud. The same IEP goals and objectives can be practiced during literature circles or small group discussions. Peers serve as fluent role models and supporters for students with speech/language challenges, naturally reinforcing and expanding the assistance provided by the speech therapist.

Specialists very often benefit the total class. For example, students at Garland High School take sign language courses from sign language interpreters and earn foreign language credit. At Hamilton Elementary School, an interpreter facilitates communication between a child who is hard of hearing and her classmates. The interpreter and the child cotaught a weekly sign language class to all seventy-five students at that grade level. Classmates quickly discovered that learning a new language is challenging and fun. The classmates' parents were pleased that their children were learning sign language, and many children taught family members basic signs.

Other professionals also assist the total class while meeting the needs of the student with special needs. While helping a student who is blind learn how to get around the school, an orientation and mobility specialist teaches the whole class how to function as a "sighted guide." Classmates explore interactions of body, space, and sensation as they learn how the student navigates the school without seeing. An assistive technology specialist identifies a communication device and simultaneously trains the student user and the rest of the class. Special services thus give the class new opportunities for learning, and the student with special needs has an opportunity to shine in front of his or her peers (Etscheidt & Bartlett, 1999; Friend & Bursuck, 1999; Giangreco, 1996).

According to Szabo (2000), related services specialists today provide direct services in the general education classroom as well as indirect, consultative services to assist the teacher. Professional organizations have endorsed these approaches as good standards of practice. Such a framework for inclusive related services is illustrated in Figure 5.5.

In-Class Team Instruction. In some schools teams of support staff collaborate to support teachers. In some elementary schools, for example, teams in the lower grades assist classroom teachers in intensive literacy instruction. At Harper Elementary School a reading specialist supervises a team of one teacher and three paraprofessionals—individuals who are not certified as teachers but are hired to provide instructional assistance—who spend forty-five minutes each day in the first- and second-grade classes working with the classroom teacher. They break the children into small groups for reading and writing instruction. At MacNeilson Elementary School the speech therapist and special education teacher team with the classroom teacher to do whole class and small group literacy instruction.

In-Class Support by Paraprofessionals. Paraprofessionals provide support in many schools. Their roles and relationship with teachers, however, must be carefully defined, and care must be taken to avoid some common problems. As teachers we take responsibility for all students, and we should expect the paraprofessional to work with all students as well as to attend to a student with special needs. A paraprofessional must be supervised by a teacher who is responsible for instruction and

Figure 5.5

Related Services: Inclusive Models	
DIRECT SERVICES	
One-on-one therapy	*Small group therapy*
The therapist works with the student during a classroom activity to facilitate his or her participation. Therapy can also occur during activities in the gymnasium, on the play-ground, or at a community site.	The therapist works with the student with special needs and a group of classmates on an activity that promotes a therapeutic goal for the student with special needs; such as a craft project involving fine motor manipulation for all students that meets needs of the special student.
INDIRECT SERVICES	
Consultation	*Monitoring*
The therapist recommends and instructs other professionals to carry out therapeutic programs, including instructional or environ-mental modification, activity enhancement, adaptation of materials, routine or scheduling alterations, or training.	The therapist maintains contact to monitor status, including scheduling checkups on a regular basis in the classroom.

Source: Adapted from Szabo (2000, p. 16).

student support. We should plan with the paraprofessional at least once a week, defining his or her role in instruction. Paraprofessionals may (McVay, 1998):

1. Lead small group instruction.
2. Provide assistance for personal care and other physical needs.
3. Assist students in completing directions given by the teacher (*all* students, not just a student with special needs).
4. Facilitate interactions among students.
5. Adapt lessons under the teacher's guidance.
6. Implement other needed tasks.

At best, the teacher and paraprofessional share responsibility for all students within the class. The best paraprofessionals learn about the culture of the classroom; find ways to help under the guidance of the teacher; and figure ways to subtly en-courage interactions, providing needed support but drawing back to encourage child-to-child engagement. Such paraprofessionals move throughout the classroom, helping all students so that a casual visitor would not see them as assisting primarily one student. The teacher and the paraprofessional constantly look for ways that chil-dren can support one another; they coach classmates in ways of being of assistance,

...SO I DON'T FEEL PREPARED TO TEACH A CHILD WITH DISABILITIES

PRINCIPAL

© 1998 MICHAEL F. GIANGRECO. ILLUSTRATION BY KEVIN RUELLE. PEYTRAL PUBLICATIONS, INC. 612-949-8707

DESPITE HAVING A MASTER'S AND 18 YEARS OF EXPERIENCE, MRS. SNIPPETT TRIES TO CONVINCE MR. MOODY THAT THE STUDENT WITH DISABILITIES IN HER CLASS WOULD BE BETTER SERVED BY AN ASSISTANT WITH NO EXPERIENCE.

consider peers as members of a student's team, and seek to facilitate independence on the part of children with special needs (Doyle, 1997; Friend & Bursuck, 1999; Marks, Schrader, & Levine, 1999; McVay, 1998).

Sometimes, however, problematic practices occur. Giangreco (1997) and Marks, Shrader, and Levine (1999) found that many paraprofessionals spent much of their time close to a student with a disability. These paraprofessionals further perceived a major portion of their job as ensuring that the student was not a bother to the teacher and assumed the role of functioning as the expert on the student, oftentimes taking major responsibility for instructional decisions. In such situations the teacher had little responsibility for student instruction or for supervision of the paraprofessional. In some cases the paraprofessional and the student literally worked together in a separate place in the classroom, effectively creating their own isolated environment. Parents may request a paraprofessional to assist with inclusion, assuming that this will give their child support and ensure success—and often treating the paraprofessional as the person most knowledgeable about their child. Similarly, a teacher may welcome the paraprofessional, initially seeing the person as taking responsibility for the child off their shoulders. We will need to work proactively to use best practices and prevent such problems.

Consultation. A **teacher consultant** may visit a class, observe students, and consult with the classroom teacher regarding effective strategies. A consultant may also obtain materials, facilitate referrals to other services, and coordinate communication with parents. However, a teacher consultant does not often engage in actual instruction. In many situations consultation is provided in response to a short-term need to solve a problem (e.g., inability to complete class work, aggressive behavior) (Boudah, Schumacher, & Deschler, 1997; Idol, Paolucci-Whitcomb, & Nevin, 1994). However, the long-term goal is to empower the classroom teacher to solve similar problems in the future (Friend & Cook, 1996; Noell & Witt, 1999).

Considerations for Success

How can we be effective in collaboration? Collaborative relationships are much like a marriage. They can be heaven; they can be hell. As in marriages, however, we have considerable power to shift direction. A lot will depend on how we decide to work together.

In some cases styles, ways of thinking, and methods of communication between teachers click so well that we fall into a terrific working relationship almost effortlessly. In other cases we are so different that we must work very hard to make the relationship productive. Figure 5.6 summarizes findings by Friend and Cook (1996) regarding characteristics of good collaboration and barriers that sometimes get in our way.

Keeping Children First. Sometimes adults get caught up in their own issues—hurts with roots in childhood or anxiety and fears of incompetence. If we can acknowledge these feelings while at the same time keeping our focus on children, we will be more likely to find common ground. This is actually more difficult than it seems, because adults must recognize when their behavior has to do more with their own needs than with the needs of children.

Power. Who is in control of what? At best, we come together with support staff and cede some control, developing a shared decision-making approach in which the opinions and perspectives of each person are respected. Differences in competence, philosophy, personal style, and needs can dramatically affect how this plays out. We must seek to develop effective collaborative relationships. However, we will not cede control when we feel that our partners will not or cannot use best practice approaches. At best, both parties identify and share what we see as our areas of strength and learn from and with one another.

What are the areas in which power is most important? At bottom line is the decision about what is to be done, when, where, with what materials, and using which instructional approach. The issue of whose discipline is perceived as more important may also be evident. For example, if our school has a reading clinician who is providing support to teachers in reading, do we defer and follow that person's

Figure 5.6

Collaboration: Success and Barriers

CHARACTERISTICS OF SUCCESSFUL COLLABORATION	BARRIERS TO COLLABORATION
▪ Collaboration is based on voluntary relationships. ▪ Collaboration involves a mutual goal. ▪ Each person is equally valued. ▪ Each has equal decision-making power. ▪ Responsibilities, accountability, and resources are shared.	▪ Time for planning is insufficient. ▪ Administrative support is lacking. ▪ Scheduling problems exist. ▪ Personal misunderstandings occur. ▪ Roles are unclear. ▪ Power struggles and hidden agendas exist.

Source: Friend & Cook (1996).

A teacher and two students, one with a severe disability, read together at Patrick O'Hearn Elementary School.

direction, or do we engage with the clinician as equal partners in dialogue, expecting that we bring equal perspectives to the table? These are issues we may have to work through with both patience and strength.

Philosophy. Some teachers aim toward innovative teaching philosophies and approaches (see Chapters 6 and 8); others stand by traditional teaching methods such as worksheets, lectures, and fill-in-the-blank or multiple-choice tests. Many incorporate elements of both in their teaching. In collaborative relationships we may have to work through differences in philosophies. In some cases, we may give very specific directions to support staff regarding what we would have them do in our classroom, mentoring support staff and helping them learn innovative teaching techniques. In other cases, support staff will teach us new strategies and will have unique and important knowledge that strengthens our understanding of students with special needs. As we work together, both partners in a collaboration must be flexible and yet clear regarding our own approaches to teaching.

Balancing and Sharing Competence. All of us have areas of strength and need. Sometimes we are aware of these, sometimes not. The balance between collaborating partners can go either way. A support staff person may be the more skilled teacher. If this is the case, such an individual can be a mentor and professional development guide. In one school, for example, teachers were having difficulty teaching math at multiple levels using a new math program. The district hired a support teacher who worked half time in the building and taught a thirty-minute demonstration lesson each week. The regular teachers thus learned new skills that they used throughout the week.

If we understand ourselves, we know how we can contribute in a partnership and we know where to ask for help. The concept of multiple intelligences (see Chapter 6) can help us think about our own strengths, needs, and styles, as well as about those of our students. As we talk with our partner in collaboration, it is helpful to recognize these different styles, strengths, and needs and to express a respect for the differences between us. If we can develop trust and ask for help in our weaker areas, we will build a bond as a foundation of our work together. We can both contribute to and draw from strengths of others in collaborative teaching.

Beyond Disciplinary Territory. We will likely work with specialists from different disciplines—special educators, counselors, social workers, and more. Traditionally, different aspects of human beings have been claimed as the territory of different disciplines. In an interdisciplinary model, the team looks together at all the needs of the individual as a totality. In practical terms, all would look together at literacy, behavioral, social, and sensory–physical needs. This approach brings the wisdom of the total team into play and enhances the capacity of the team to engage in needed work.

Collaborative Teaching Strategies

What is it that support people actually *do* to help us? As we discussed earlier, this will vary greatly depending on our personal approach to including and supporting diverse students in our classroom, our philosophy, and our associated strategies. The framework on which this book is based would lead to the following roles for support people:

1. Designing curriculum, instruction, physical layout, and resources for students with diverse abilities
2. Team teaching
3. Building a community of learners
4. Developing needed adaptations
5. Addressing behavioral challenges, physical and sensory needs, communication, and assistive technology
6. Evaluating students

Depending on our needs and the resources available in the school, this support might involve direct work with students, indirect consultation and assistance, and intensive or mild assistance. As we develop our teaching style over the years, our skills at teaching multiple levels and building a community will grow, and we may find that we need less support.

Friend and Cook (1996) identified several methods of collaborative instruction that are briefly described in Tools for the Trek. The major differences boil down to answering the question, Is our collaborating partner "teaching with" us or "helping" us? In most of the effective inclusive classrooms we've observed, collaborating

Tools *for the* Trek
Methods of Teaching Together

- *One teach, one observe:* One teacher is responsible for the instruction while the other observes one student, a small group, or the entire class to monitor learning and develop strategies to improve instruction. Teachers alternate teaching and observing roles.
- *One teach, one drift:* One teacher is responsible for instruction while the other teacher circulates to answer questions, bring students back to attention, or provide minilessons and assistance. Teachers may alternate roles.
- *Station teaching:* Students are arranged at "stations" around the room. Each teacher delivers instruction to one small group. One group may work independently. Groups switch from one station to another.

- *Parallel teaching:* The class is split in two groups, and two teachers work simultaneously, each teacher with one group.
- *Alternate teaching:* One teacher manages the majority of the class while the other teacher pulls a small heterogeneous group aside to preview, review, assess, or provide enrichment. The purposes and membership of this small group change constantly.
- *Teaching together:* Two teachers manage and instruct the class at the same time, flexibly interacting in the various instructional formats being used—small groups, partners, individual work, centers.

Source: Friend & Cook (1996).

teachers use *all* of these strategies at one time or another. Sometimes it's helpful to have one person stand back and observe or help a few students. Sometimes we break students into small cooperative groups or "centers," and both of us rotate throughout the room. Sometimes we divide the class into two groups and actually teach the same content in these smaller groups. Truly collaborative coteachers switch in and out of these various roles frequently, often shifting with minimal conversation, as a glance or request will do. Other times, teachers very intentionally plan roles for the day or week and stick to these (Tashie, Shapiro-Barnard, Donoghue-Dillon, Jorgenson, & Nisbet, 1993; Wood, 1998).

In effective collaborative instruction each teacher takes responsibility for all students in the room. Each teacher also has input into grading and contact with parents. The general education teacher takes responsibility for all students in the class; the special education teacher does not grade only students on his or her caseload. Teachers communicate to parents and students alike that there are two teachers in the room for all children. At best, students do not understand that one is a "special education" or "bilingual" teacher. They know only that they have two teachers in the room. This does not mean, however, that students do not know that their peers have some learning challenges. In a good inclusive classroom this is explicitly understood, as are the needs of all the students in the class (Patriarcha, Freeman, Hendricks, & Swift, 1996; Snell & Janney, 2000; Tarrant, 1993; Vaughn, Schumm, & Arguelles, 1997; York, Kronberg, Medwetz, & Doyle, 1993).

To get a sense of how this works, let's hear Erin Herold, a fifth-grade teacher, describe how she and her special education coteacher work together in her classroom. Erin explains (Herold, 1998):

> I have been co-teaching for two years. It has been a successful experience. Here are a few things that we do to create a positive learning environment for all our students.
>
> *Planning:* We meet every Thursday morning to go over the next week's schedule. I usually come up with the topic and the general assignments and projects, and she will give feedback. We decide who will teach which component during this planning time. . . . We spend a bit of time talking about which student may have trouble with the assignment and how we can modify it. All the modification plans are prepared beforehand, but we both know that we can adapt on the spot if needed. This seems like it takes a long time, but it doesn't! . . . Approximate time: 30 minutes.
>
> *Teaching:* My coteacher leads the starter activity. . . . I then go over the daily agenda. Either one of us will lead the lesson. When one is teaching, the other is either standing in the back, monitoring behaviors, or else sitting with individual students. Occasionally, we will pull out individual kids to work with either of us one on one. Once a week, we try to do some type of bounce back and forth where she will talk, then me, then her, etc.
>
> *Review of students:* Once every few weeks we discuss each individual student. We focus on their progress, strengths, weaknesses, behaviors, etc. My coteacher put together a guide of each student's goals for the year, and every few months we review these goals during our whole team meeting to see if and how we are helping them meet these goals.
>
> *Writing:* We came up with a personal goal that we wanted one strong, solid piece of writing from each of the students on her caseload. We worked together with her students and walked them through answering an essay question from start to finish. We met with each student individually, either after school, before school, or during lunch. Once their piece was finished, we made copies as an example of their best writing. This was put in their IEP record as well.
>
> These are just some of the things that we do that have been successful. The one thing I can say is that teachers involved in co-teaching really have to make it their own. They have to develop their own style with which they are most comfortable.

In Figure 5.7 we've listed a few practical dos and don'ts for collaborative teaching. We've seen firsthand both very successful and very unsuccessful practices. The key for inclusive collaborative teaching is this: All children should be a part of the class working at their own level. When people enter our class, if they can easily find students with special needs doing different things in different places from the other children, we have a problem. Relatedly, if a visitor can observe our room and immediately know that a collaborating professional is there for specific students, we have a problem. In both instances we are sending powerful, deep messages to children that they don't belong to the class and that the collaborating professional is not a real teacher. In the process, we are laying the foundation for ongoing problems of acceptance and community in our classrooms (Peterson, Tamor, Feen, & Silagy, 2002).

Scheduling and Collaborative Teaching

As collaborating partners start working together, we need time for planning. Effective inclusive schools have developed strategies that allow teachers time for collaborative

Figure 5.7

Principles and Practices for Inclusive Coteaching

DOS	DON'TS
Really, you can do this! We've seen many teachers collaborating in these ways.	*Really, these are practices we've seen in some actual schools! We hope you don't do them.*
Consider students with special needs as full members of your class.	Cluster all the students with disabilities in one place in the room—at the back, on one side of the room, in their own row.
Work with your coteacher as a real partner, negotiating and sharing all aspects of work in the class.	Have the coteacher act as a teacher helper, copying or filling out forms.
Collaborating staff share responsibility for all students in the class. Students know that there are "two [or more] teachers" in the room.	Have the coteacher, aide, or other specialist work only with students with disabilities or with other students who are on his or her "caseload" separately from the rest of the class in the back or in a corner of the room.
Make sure that students with special needs are part of all aspects of the class so that outsiders find it difficult or impossible to identify the "special kids."	Enclose an "included" student within a wall of file cabinets to keep behaviors in check.
Work together to design teaching at multiple levels that includes all students. Spend 90 percent of your collaborative time this way and 10 percent of your time doing accommodations and adaptations.	Use the coteacher or other professional primarily to develop adaptations to your lessons; ignore (or refrain from asking for) advice on how to teach differently for all students.

planning (Agnew, Van Cleaf, Camblin, & Shaffer, 1994). Monroe Elementary School schedules "specials" (art, music, gym) at the same time so that teams of teachers can meet together. Hernandez Elementary School blocks specials for all lower elementary teachers in the morning, for upper elementary in the afternoon to allow for collaborative planning time. Still another school, Napoleon High School, closes early one day each week to allow a half day for teacher planning time and in-service development. Incorporating time for collaboration is critical for success.

Collaborating support teachers who work with several general education teachers develop their schedule to address both the needs of classroom teachers for support and the practical limitations of their own timetable. Support teachers are often assigned to teams of teachers. In elementary schools that use multiage teaching, one support teacher might be assigned to "lower el" (K–2) and another to "upper el" (3–5). In a middle or high school that is using interdisciplinary teams, a support teacher might work with one team of four teachers (Wiedmeyer & Leyman, 1991). In a traditional departmentalized high school, on the other hand, a support teacher might be assigned to each department—math, science, language arts, and so forth (Boudah, Schumacher, & Deschler, 1997).

Collaborating teachers and other staff can help design our teaching for diverse students. We can talk together about our students, about the curriculum, about teaching and support strategies that use multiple intelligences, various learning styles, and multilevel teaching. For example, Marvin felt unprepared to teach science in his fourth-grade classroom. He and Mary, the support teacher, developed a plan in which Mary designed and taught the science lesson each day, as she had strong skills in this area. During this time Marvin assisted the support teacher and helped students with special needs. In another situation, a high school English teacher knew he would have several students in his fourth period who were well below "grade level." He and the special education teacher agreed that she would come to the class for this whole period throughout the first weeks of school. Later, as the semester developed and he gained confidence in his ability to work with these students, she shifted her schedule to another time slot. Figure 5.8 provides a picture from the point of view of the classroom teacher and shows classroom activities, support from a special education teacher and a speech therapist, and the involvement of community members in the classroom.

Professional Development and Growth
Building a Professional Community of Learners

As we begin inclusive teaching, we will likely ask for as much help as we can get. That's a natural reaction. As we develop skills and confidence, however, we will often need less assistance, or at least different types of assistance. That's why support for professional growth and development is a critical piece of inclusive teaching. If all goes well, we will become master inclusive teachers who can then provide support to other new teachers coming on board, sharing our learning at conferences, on listservs, and in daily informal conversations with other teachers. What are key ways we can obtain support to grow and develop as teachers? We'll describe a few exemplary strategies and structures.

Professional Development Inquiry and Dialogue Groups. Many are increasingly critical of the typical one-shot staff development workshops in which a consultant comes in for an afternoon or a day, gives a talk, and then leaves. Little real growth occurs from such events. More effective are professional development strategies that enable teachers to study and reflect on their own practice.

All over the country, different structures are being developed by which small groups of teachers meet to learn together in their own schools. For example, in three elementary schools in Detroit, teachers and a faculty member from a local university meet together once a month, read a book regarding exemplary teaching practice, and discuss instructional strategies. In another school a professional development coordinator initiated similar teacher study groups. In still other schools teachers engage in collaborative teaching and demonstrate a new strategy directly in the classroom (Vargo, 1998).

Figure 5.8

Sample Schedule for a Day of Collaborative Teaching in an Elementary Classroom

TIME	TEACHER	PROFESSIONAL SUPPORT	COMMUNITY PARTNERS IN THE CLASS
8:30	Choice time.	Teachers share ideas for multilevel teaching.	Volunteers read with selected children.
9:00	Writers' workshop—rove, help edit, small group minilessons, and assess.	Special education teacher and speech therapist work with groups. All teachers collaborate in supporting all students.	Peer relations program teaches social skills once a week.
10:00	Readers' workshop, read with individual children and small group minilessons.	Special education teacher goes with class to library once a week.	
10:45	Read-aloud.		Several parents or community volunteers per month read books.
11:10	Class meeting.		
11:30	Specials.		
12:10	Lunch/Recess.		
1:00	Math—one of two groups, same math skills. Student experts.	Class divides in two with special needs student in special education teacher's group. Few minutes one-on-one.	
2:00	Theme study—integrate literacy, science, and social studies.	Share content. Get ideas for multilevel teaching.	Residents from local hospital talk to class once a month.

Support Networks of Teachers—Gatherings and Online. In many communities teachers, parents, and university faculty have come together to provide mutual support and work together to improve schools and influence policy. Teachers are increasingly using listservs and chat rooms online to share successes, ask questions, and engage in dialogue about best practices. The Inclusion listserv out of the University of Alberta, with members all over the world, is a forum for daily intense discussion among parents, teachers, and university faculty regarding strategies for

Schools to Visit

Making Teamwork Fun

Theodore Roosevelt High School
540 Eureka
Wyandotte, MI 48192
rhs.wyandotte.org/
Contact: Carla Harting, Special Education
    Director, Wyandotte Public Schools
Phone: 734-246-1008 x2409
hartinc@wy.k12.mi.us

Roosevelt High School is located in Wyandotte, Michigan, a southwest suburb of Detroit, known as "Downriver." Most of the 1,300 students come from blue-collar, working-class families. In 1987 Roosevelt began its journey towards inclusive education. The school developed a process of team teaching by general and special education teachers to provide support in general education for students with mild to moderate disabilities. Beginning with a small number of teachers, the program has grown. Certain classes are identified as team-taught classes. The general and special education teachers have, over the years, worked out very positive relationships and enjoy their work together. The special education teachers see themselves as supporting all students in the class. They've also been about team building in the school. The special education office, centrally located in the school, serves as a planning cen-

ter for teachers but also as the setting for parties and celebrations for all involved in the coteaching effort.

In recent years Roosevelt has hosted a special class of students with severe and multiple disabilities that come from sixteen school districts in the county. The school has sought to integrate these students as much as possible into general education classes throughout the school. The special education class is located in the center of the school, and many general education students volunteer in the class, receiving service-learning credit; they also help the special students participate in general education classes.

Roosevelt has a strong program of vocational–technical education and a strong art program. A horticulture program helps students apply biology knowledge through a school-run greenhouse and florist shop. Students with special needs have found such programs particularly helpful.

Recently, in concert with an initiative by the superintendent of the school system, general and special education staff have begun to work together to expand hands-on, activity-based learning throughout the school curriculum. Special education staff are developing a catalogue describing many practical active learning methods that better meet the needs of students with special needs and other students as well.

inclusive teaching of students with special needs. (Go to **www.quasar.ualberta.ca/ddc/incl/intro.html**.) Many teachers have found both live gatherings and online communication to be valuable sources.

Critical Friends and Consultants from Outside the School. An external partner, often called a "critical friend," is important in facilitating positive change and growth in a school. Such an individual comes to know the school well, pulls in additional resources and people, and acts as a supportive critic. For example, Jorgensen (1998) describes working with Souhegan High School and providing assistance in planning and implementing an approach to inclusive schooling. Many faculty at universities have developed partnerships with schools, often supported by grants or contracts. Regional support centers also provide a range of services to schools—video and other media resources, consultants and in-service trainers on various topics, information regarding grants and collaborative opportunities, and professional development programs.

Support for the Road

We hope by now you are beginning to have a few concrete pictures regarding how support is provided in inclusive schools. We also suspect that you may be having a range of reactions. You may be feeling: "This is a fairy tale. No school does these things. Certainly it won't happen in my school!" It is certainly true that the supports we've described don't yet exist fully in every school. However, in most areas some schools are working hard to put such systems in place. You may also be feeling: "Wow! This is wonderful. I had no idea schools were doing work like this to support teachers and students." If so, we confirm that yes, they are. Support is a foundation for inclusive teaching. When supports are effectively provided, the whole teaching enterprise is strengthened; teachers feel new energy and engagement (Pugach & Johnson, 1995; Rankin et al., 1994); and students increase their learning (Saint-Laurent, Glasson, Royer, Simard, & Pierard, 1998). In Part 2 of this book we will build on the ideas, strategies, tools, and information in this chapter. You will meet teachers, other professionals, parents, and community groups all collaborating in various aspects of supporting students in inclusive classes.

Stepping Stones
To Inclusive Teaching

1. Find out how support services are delivered in your school. Where are the special education teachers, and what do they do? What about other specialists—speech therapists, psychologists, gifted educators, social workers?

2. Identify a student with special needs in your class who is presently being pulled out of your class to obtain assistance. Talk with a support person about how he or she might provide support in your room instead. Start very small if need be.

3. If you already have support staff in your room, how well is the collaboration working? What model of support is being used? How would you like to see this collaboration improved? Set up a time to talk with support staff about collaborative teaching in your room and how improvements might be made.

4. Together with a special education teacher or other specialist from your school, visit another school where collaborative teaching is occurring. Discuss what you see and think about how you might do this in your building.

Key Points

- All teachers and children need support; support is not just about students with special needs. Also, we obtain support in many ways, not just through another adult in our class.

- Inclusive grouping of children helps build a community in which children help one another; specific strategies include multiage teaching, looping, the "school within a school" approach, peer tutoring and mentoring, circles of support, and cooperative learning.

- Intensive help and support for students with high needs can most often be delivered better in a general education classroom than in a segregated class or clinic.

- Teachers can work together in collaborative teams to discuss students and to obtain assistance in dealing with issues and challenges.

- Many support professionals can work with students and teachers in the classroom, including special education and Title I teachers, paraprofessionals, speech therapists, and others.

- In an effective collaborative partnership with support staff, all adults in the room are responsible for all the children and work in collaboration with all while ensuring that individual needs are met.

- Most support staff work in several rooms and develop a schedule that they can adjust to best utilize their time and services.

Learning Expeditions

Following are some ideas that may extend your learning.

1. Explore the meaning of "support" in your own life. Keep a journal for a week regarding the types of support you get and do not get each day. Write down what happened, how you felt, the impact of support or of its absence. What are the implications for students with special problems?

2. Interview someone who has successfully dealt with a great challenge. This might be an adult with a disability who has a good job, someone who was once on welfare, or someone who suffered the death of a very close friend. Talk with the person about his or her experiences. What types of support did the person

receive? From whom? What difference did the support make? Why?

3. Visit two classrooms, one in which effective in-class supports are operating and the other in a school that has a reputation for not supporting teachers and where special education uses a pull-out model. Talk with the teachers and students. Ask the teachers about problems and challenges with students. What support do they receive, and what is the impact?

4. Contact an agency that provides assistance to the families of children with special needs. Interview a caseworker and ask about the types of challenges that families face and the supports available to them. What do you think the caseworker's responses imply for teachers and schools?

The Four Building Blocks of Inclusive Teaching

Strategies to Reach All Students

Sheila Howell is a sixth-grade teacher at Bloomington Middle School. She has several students with learning disabilities in her class, as well as Donald, who uses a wheelchair and whose cognitive abilities are not totally understood. The school psychologist thinks he has severe mental retardation. His parents think his abilities are much higher. Either way, it's amazing to watch the students and Sheila make Donald a part of the class.

We talk with Sheila during her planning period. "I love children like Donald," she says with an energetic twinkle in her eye. "I seek them out. He's a delight. Donald is in my room for a second year because his parents have been so happy with what he's getting from my class." She goes on to talk about how she ensures that all her students are learning. "I try to keep all the students involved. I never really lecture. I intentionally pair students with higher and lower abilities to read with each other and answer questions. This allows the students with lesser abilities to gain from the other students' strengths, and the more able students strengthen their skills by helping another student."

As the next class begins, the energy in the classroom is infectious. One student reads a short paragraph, then Sheila poses questions. "Come on. What do you think? Why did they do that?" she says. Hands shoot up. Afterward, the students break into pairs, and two students, one labeled as gifted, the other learning disabled, work together. Rather than being intimidated by students with special needs, Sheila requests that they be in her class. She feels they help her strengthen her teaching skills.

As we think about students we hope to teach, we likely imagine students eager to learn, well fed, well-mannered—students who make us feel good. When we go to real classes with real children, we're often shocked. For many of us that shock never goes away. Recently we talked with a teacher who had transferred from an inner-city school to a school in one of the wealthiest suburbs in the country. "Now I can actually teach," she said. The implication of her statement is clear: We can't teach unless we have children who appear near perfect.

A few organizations oppose inclusion of students with disabilities in general education classes. Their reasons are very telling: They don't believe general education teachers have the ability or willingness to teach students with disabilities, even with the help of a collaborating special education teacher. For example, Justine Maloney of the Learning Disabilities Association said:

> Too often regular education teachers have been taught to teach curriculum, not students. They are uncomfortable with another adult in the classroom, are under pressure to cover course material within a given period of time, and are judged by the test scores of their students, not by how much the student has learned in the classroom. (Maloney, 1994/1995)

Children have tremendous differences in needs and abilities, and thus we are challenged to improve instruction for *all* students. Although the law now requires schools to include students with special needs in general education classes "to the maximum extent possible" (IDEA, 2004), ultimately, individual teachers make their own decisions about whether to become inclusive teachers. *First,* we decide if we want to teach all students. *Then* we decide how we do it.

In this chapter we explore building blocks for teaching diverse children together well. We first discuss the limitations of traditional instruction. Second, we explore brain-based research and its implications for teaching. Third, we discuss the emerging consensus regarding best practices in teaching and learning. We then investigate the **four building blocks** of inclusive teaching: (1) multilevel teaching, (2) scaffolding, (3) multiple intelligences, and (4) learning styles. The four building blocks denote concepts and practical strategies that provide a foundation for inclusive teaching.

Traveling Notes

The idea that teachers might actually *seek out* students with substantial challenges may be new to us. However, a growing group of inclusive teachers sees this as an important goal.

1. What was your reaction as you read about Sheila and Donald? How do you interpret your reaction?

2. What strategies did we see Sheila using that made her class a class well suited for children with very different abilities?

3. What do you think about Justine Maloney's statement that many teachers "teach curriculum, not students"?

As we explore the four fundamental building blocks of inclusive teaching in this chapter, pay attention to how you feel, and create mental images of a class with children with very different abilities.

Worksheets, Lecture, and Seatwork
The Limitations of Traditional Teaching

Early in the twentieth century, the "factory" model of schooling—in which students sit in straight rows, listen to lectures, fill out worksheets, read from texts under the watchful eye of the teacher, and are tested by filling in blanks, responding to multiple-choice items, or answering true-or-false questions—was questioned and challenged, most notably by John Dewey. Dewey (1938, 1943) argued that rote study promoted shallow thinking and a dislike for learning; experience in meaningful, real situations, he claimed, was the key to learning.

These critiques continue. For example, F. Smith (1998) described what he called official and classic theories of learning. The "official" view says that learning is occasional, hard work, limited, dependent on rewards and punishment, based on

Two students play a game called "seal hop" in Mishael Hittie's fourth-grade class. They have been studying frozen worlds as a year long theme and this game is played by Eskimo children in Alaska. This game provides an opportunity to move while deepening their academic understanding.

effort, individualistic, easily forgotten, and assured by testing and memorization. However, Smith points out that students are learning all the time, even though this

> is a frightening thought for many teachers . . . and the students can't help it. They even learn things they might be better off not learning. The problem in school is not that many students aren't learning but what they are learning. . . . If they leave thinking that "school things"—such as reading, writing, mathematics, or history—are boring, difficult, and irrelevant to their lives and that they are "dummies," . . . they learn to be nonreaders or . . . nonspellers or that they can't do mathematics. (Smith, F., 1998, p. 10)

According to the classic view of learning, in other words, people are learning all the time. Learning is continual, effortless, independent of rewards and punishment, and social. Very simply, says Smith, "you learn from the company you keep . . . you *become* like them. . . . And this is learning that is *permanent*. We rarely forget the interests, attitudes, beliefs, and skills that we acquire simply by interacting with the significant people in our lives" (Smith, F., 1998, p. 9).

None of the individual elements of traditional teaching is ineffective in itself. Worksheets, lectures, and textbooks all can have an effective place in a best practice class. The problem, however, is that such strategies often form the bulk of instruction. As a group they fit together into a paradigm—an integrated overall approach that, according to Kohn (1999) and Haberman (1998), has the following problems:

- The emphasis on memorization engenders little understanding of the meaning of events, mathematic operations, or scientific data. This leads to shallow understanding and lack of motivation.
- Mastery of certain skills—mathematical algorithms, spelling, writing conventions—is seen as separate from the use of such skills in applied, authentic, meaningful situations. As a consequence, teachers seldom have students use these skills for real-world purposes.
- Teaching materials are largely textbooks written at one particular level. Little deviation from that level occurs, so students for whom the material is too difficult and students for whom it is too simple are both frustrated.
- Instruction occurs largely through lecture and videotapes with periodic field trips, all strategies that put students in passive roles. Many students simply disengage.
- Schoolwork is seen as an individual rather than a social effort. Students most often sit at desks in straight rows and get in trouble if they talk. Consequently, school fails to help students learn critical social skills—and simultaneously ignores a powerful source of learning.
- As students get frustrated and bored, they often find ways to make the class more interesting. Some act out, playing jokes or getting in fights. Others simply withdraw. As a result, teachers spend much time maintaining classroom control.
- Evaluation largely occurs through tests that emphasize short-term memorization—multiple-choice, fill-in-the-blank, or true/false exams. Such exams don't require students to demonstrate meaningful understanding of material or use of skills in real-world situations.

Despite these and other ongoing critiques, traditional schooling practices continue unabated—in large part, according to Tyack and Cuban (1995), because this is the mental image people have of what "school is." For example, Public Agenda (1997) conducted a national survey of high school students. They explored two over-all questions: (1) What could teachers do to help you in your learning? (2) Do your teachers do these things? The answers were both revealing and troubling. Students wanted teachers to know their subject, use engaging learning approaches, and present information in an interesting way. Yet only a small percentage of students reported that their teachers did so.

These results correspond with those of another major study of U.S. schools in which researchers found, for example, "a repetitive reinforcement of basic skills . . . throughout the twelve grades—a heavy emphasis on mechanics, textbooks, workbooks, and quizzes emphasizing short answers and the recall of specific information" (Goodlad, 1984, p. 207). More recently, Haberman (1998) and Hale (2001) report that such ineffective instructional approaches continue to be the norm, particularly in schools that serve low-income, urban children of color: a situation that these researchers challenge educators to change.

How Do People Learn?
How Should We Teach?

If traditional practices in schools are not effective, how should we teach? It is here that we begin to see effective instruction for all children and inclusive teaching come together. Alfie Kohn (1998) described an effective inclusive classroom as well as pointing out practices that should cause us concern (Figure 6.1). Using a concept called Universal Design for Learning, the Center for Applied Special Technology (2002; see **www.cast.org**) suggests that we can design engaging instruction for all students learning together, a concept similar to what we have described as "designing for diversity."

Brain-Based Learning

In recent years many scientists have conducted research on how the brain actually learns, what some call **brain-based learning** (Caine & Caine, 1991, 1994; Goleman, 1995; Jensen, 1995, 1998). The implications of these findings on education are enormous and exciting. Quina (1995) synthesized these findings as follows.

First, *the brain is a parallel processor,* meaning that it simultaneously makes connections between multiple ideas and engages in many activities and thought processes at once. Based on these findings, the step-by-step lecture and worksheet design of most U.S. schools simply inhibits meaningful learning. Brain-based teaching, in contrast, facilitates deeper learning by building connections between multiple stimuli; for example, storytelling and drama to enhance learning, body sculpture to teach syntax, and metaphorical stories read to music.

Second, *the brain processes parts and wholes at the same time.* The "left brain," which breaks content into parts, and the "right brain," which sees wholes, interact constantly. This is how the brain builds patterns and connections for learning. Thus, the typical focus only on parts—skills, phonics, multiplication tables—reduces learning. Students, therefore, need much more practice to process facts and skills

Figure 6.1

What to Look for in a Classroom

	GOOD SIGNS	POSSIBLE REASONS FOR CONCERN
Furniture	■ Chairs around tables to facilitate interaction ■ Comfortable areas for learning	■ Desks in rows or chairs all facing forward
Walls	■ Covered with student projects ■ Evidence of student collaboration ■ Signs, exhibits, or lists created by students rather than teachers ■ Information about and mementos of those who spend time together in the classroom	■ Bare ■ Decorated with commercial posters ■ Lists of consequences for misbehavior ■ List of rules created by an adult ■ Stick or star chart or other evidence that students are rewarded or ranked ■ Student assignments displayed but they are (a) suspiciously flawless, (b) only "the best" students' work, or (c) virtually all alike
Sounds	■ Frequent hum of activities and ideas being exchanged	■ Frequent periods of silence ■ Teacher's voice the loudest or most often heard
Location of Teacher	■ Typically working with students so that it takes a moment to find	■ Typically front and center
Teacher's Voice	■ Respectful, genuine, warm	■ Controlling and imperious ■ Condescending and saccharine sweet
Student's Reaction to Visitor	■ Welcoming and eager to explain or demonstrate what they are doing or to use the visitor as a resource	■ Either unresponsive or hoping to be distracted from what they are doing
Class Discussion	■ Students address one another directly ■ Emphasis on thoughtful exploration of complicated issues ■ Students ask questions at least as often as the teacher	■ All exchanges involve (or directed by) teacher; students wait to be called on ■ Emphasis on facts and right answers ■ Students race to be first to answer teacher's "Who can tell me?" queries
Tasks	■ Different activities take place at the same time	■ All students usually do the same thing
Around the School	■ Inviting atmosphere ■ Students' projects fill hallways ■ Bathrooms in good condition ■ Faculty lounge warm and comfortable ■ Office staff welcoming toward visitors and students ■ Students helping in lunchroom, library, and with other school functions	■ Stark, institutional feel ■ Awards, trophies, and prizes displayed, suggesting emphasis on triumph rather than community

Source: Kohn (1996) pp. 54–55. Used with permission.

taught in isolation than those taught in context. A brain-based teacher incorporates into lessons a focus on both wholes and parts.

Third, *the search for meaning is automatic and basic to the human brain.* The brain needs the familiar *and* the novel simultaneously. Therefore, we should build into every lesson (1) security (the familiar) and (2) novelty (the search for new connections and possibilities).

Fourth, *emotion and cognition are linked in the hard wiring of the brain.* Emotion and thinking cannot be separated. When we teach, we must deal with both together. The brain will "downshift" under threat; when students feel threatened, emotionally or physically, thinking and learning literally stop. We must build a sense of community, safety, and support in the classroom if learning is to occur.

Caine and Caine (1991, 1994, 1995) worked with staff of the Dry Creek Elementary School to develop approaches built on these findings of brain researchers. They articulated three simple but powerful principles for brain-based teaching:

1. *Ensure a state of* relaxed alertness *in a challenging but nonthreatening environment.* "Relaxed alertness" is a condition in which children feel comfortable, safe, and at ease, on the one hand, but engaged, interested, involved, and curious, on the other. This combination creates the psychological state that is conducive to most effective learning.

2. *Orchestrate immersion in complex experience.* The brain thrives on complexity, seeking naturally to create its own sense of order out of the multiple inputs it receives. When students are given a structure imposed from the outside, rather than being allowed to organize their own ideas, learning is reduced. To maximize learning, we maximize experience, looking simultaneously at the big picture and small parts. We do *not* break learning down into small segments and present these in a sequence. Teachers guide, shape, and orchestrate experiences so that needs for order, safety, and novelty are met.

3. *Continuously engage in active processing of ongoing changes and experiences to consolidate emergent mental models.* To help the brain create its own structure and mental models, reflection, talk, and dialogue about experience is critical. Classroom discussions, journal writing, e-mail groups with other students in other schools, small group discussions—all these provide ways of helping learners process, understand, and remember what they've learned.

Best Practices: Emerging Standards for Teaching and Learning

In recent years, propelled by highly controversial school reform efforts, national professional organizations have engaged in substantive study to understand best practices. Amazingly, across all fields, a common consensus regarding **best practices for teaching and learning** is emerging that is consistent with brain-based learning, Smith's classic approach, and Kohn's picture of an effective classroom. Classrooms, this consensus holds, *can* be engaging, caring places where learners of different races, cultures, abilities, and learning styles draw from one another. In addition, these national reports mirror research findings in regard to many specific groups— students with learning disabilities, gifted students, students with mental retardation, and others (Cline, 1999; Faltis, 1997; Freeman & Alkin, 2000; Vaughn, Gersten, & Chard, 2000).

Figure 6.2 summarizes the common recommendations (Zemelman, Daniels, & Hyde, 1998). The reports call for less emphasis on traditional lecture–text–test–grading and more emphasis on learning that is active, cooperative, authentic, and inclusive. In such classes students work on real issues that integrate several subjects at once. Classes are abuzz with activity, work, and noise as students take responsibility for projects from start to finish—developing ideas, finding information, developing products and methods of presentation. Evaluation is based on actual evidence of learning—presentations, writing, plays—rather than on traditional tests.

Figure 6.2

Common Recommendations of National Curriculum Reports

LESS OF . . .

- Whole class, teacher-directed instruction (e.g., lecturing)
- Student passivity: sitting, listening, receiving, and absorbing information
- Presentational, one-way transmission of information from teacher to student
- Prizing and rewarding of silence in the classroom
- Classroom time devoted to fill-in-the-blank worksheets, dittos, workbooks, and other "seatwork"
- Student time spent reading textbooks and basal readers
- Attempts by teachers to thinly "cover" large amounts of material in every subject area
- Rote memorization of facts and details
- Emphasis on competition and grades
- Tracking or leveling students into ability groups
- Use of pull-out special programs
- Use of and reliance on standardized tests

MORE OF . . .

- Experiential, inductive, hands-on learning
- Active learning in the classroom, with all the noise and movement of students doing, talking, and collaborating
- Diverse roles for teachers, including coaching, demonstrating, and modeling
- Emphasis on higher-order thinking: understanding of a field's key concepts and principles
- Deep study of a smaller number of topics, so that students internalize the field's way of inquiry
- Reading of real texts: whole books, primary sources, and nonfiction materials
- Transfer to students of responsibility for their work: goal setting, record keeping, monitoring, sharing, exhibiting, and evaluating
- Choice for students (e.g., choice of their own books, writing topics, team partners, and research projects)
- Enacting and modeling of the principles of democracy in the school
- Attention to affective (emotional) needs and the varying cognitive styles of individual students
- Cooperative, collaborative activity; the classroom as an interdependent community
- Heterogeneously grouped classrooms where individual needs are met through individualized activities, not through segregation of bodies

Source: Zemelman, Daniels, & Hyde (1998).

Figure 6.3

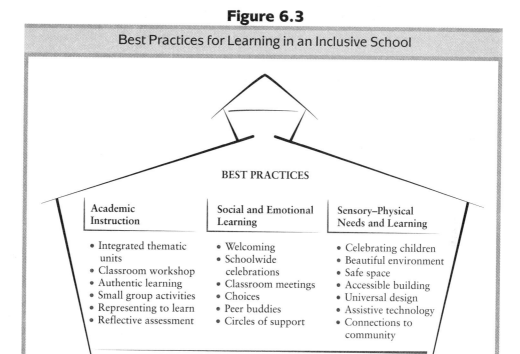

Best Practices for Learning in an Inclusive School

BEST PRACTICES

Academic Instruction	Social and Emotional Learning	Sensory–Physical Needs and Learning
• Integrated thematic units • Classroom workshop • Authentic learning • Small group activities • Representing to learn • Reflective assessment	• Welcoming • Schoolwide celebrations • Classroom meetings • Choices • Peer buddies • Circles of support	• Celebrating children • Beautiful environment • Safe space • Accessible building • Universal design • Assistive technology • Connections to community

Four Building Blocks of Inclusive Teaching

1. Multilevel teaching
2. Scaffolding
3. Multiple intelligences
4. Learning styles

Figure 6.3 lists some examples of active learning strategies that are based on an emerging consensus about best practices.

Classes that use best practices create space for students of differing abilities, learning styles, and strengths to flourish. Authentic learning activities let students of different abilities work together on the same project. In a class at one school, for example, students were studying the construction of space stations. A student with severe mental retardation carried materials and learned some key words. When time came to build the mock space station, he helped color key parts and copied letters for signs. What better way to meet his IEP goals of following sequences, learning his letters, and increasing dexterity? How different from doing isolated drills over and over.

Similarly, Mari-Jane Medenwaldt (2000) tells how a child who simply couldn't sit still flourished in such a class. Children were making puppets and preparing for a play. Paul, who would be in constant trouble in a traditional class, was simply a part of the active scene. He had made his puppet very fast and was now playing, but dropped in right on time when he was to say his lines.

The Four Building Blocks of Inclusive Teaching
Strategies for Differentiated Learning

Let's now explore the four building blocks of inclusive teaching, a set of concepts that provide a foundation for brain-based learning and implementation of best practices. As introduced earlier, the four building blocks are:

1. Multilevel teaching
2. Scaffolding
3. Multiple intelligences
4. Learning styles

Figure 6.3 illustrates how the four building blocks operate as the foundation upon which instruction of diverse children is built. In *multilevel teaching* we challenge and engage all students at their individual levels, breaking away from the one-size-fits-all curriculum. Students are not separated into ability groups but learn together, each working at his or her own level. Teachers *scaffold* or support student learning, helping students engage in activities they could not do without assistance. Our learning activities build on students' *multiple intelligences*, the many different ways in which human beings are smart. Finally, we organize our learning environment so that it accommodates different *learning styles* of students and respects individual choices. These four building blocks undergrid and interact with academic, social–emotional, and sensory–physical components of learning. When we incorporate these ideas into instruction, we witness amazing learning and growth. Let's now spend some time with each of these building blocks of inclusive teaching.

INCLUSIVE EDUCATION:
DOING IT WRONG DOESN'T MAKE IT WRONG.

Multilevel Teaching

In multilevel teaching we design our teaching so that students of very different abilities can learn together, each at his or her own level of ability. When we base our teaching on brain-based learning and thematic, interdisciplinary instruction, our classes provide many *opportunities* for students to learn at multiple levels together. However, we must intentionally take advantage of these opportunities (Harris & Graham, 1994; Hopfenberg, Levin, & Associates, 1993; Peterson, Tamor, Feen, & Silagy, 2002; Tomlinson, 1999).

Teaching at multiple levels simultaneously is a critical part of best practices for several reasons. First, for students, the challenge of working with classmates of truly diverse abilities is an important "complex experience" all by itself. At an inclusive middle school, we once met with several eighth graders who had been a circle of friends for May, a student with Down syndrome. As these young people shared their experiences, we were amazed at their critical thinking and problem-solving skills. Working with May had provided them with an authentic course of study in critical thinking, management, and social issues, leading to deep learning.

Second, because students vary dramatically in their abilities, if we do not teach in a way that supports students at their own levels, we exclude students who cannot "keep up." School becomes a place of competition, of winning and losing, rather than a place of support and refuge. Learning is literally shifted downward, and the emotional reactions of fear, anger, and hostility became more prevalent. So multilevel teaching is a critical component of helping all students learn at the highest possible levels (Caine & Caine, 1995).

Vygotsky (1978) described an important concept for multilevel teaching, the **zone of proximal development**—the range of tasks just beyond a student's present level of ability that the student cannot yet perform independently but can perform with the help and guidance of others. We seek to take students where they are, provide support and assistance for tasks they can not accomplish on their own, and challenge them to go to the next level. Thus, multilevel teaching does not mean that some have it "easy" and others must work "harder."

Now contrast this scenario with what is more typical. Traditional schooling has all children learning the same material at the same level and at the same pace. In a traditional class we often hear people saying things like "He just can't do eighth-grade work. I think he should be referred to special education." In that same class we also usually observe some students who never study at all and yet always get A's. The first student daily experiences the message "I cannot learn" and probably comes to believe it. The other student thinks, "I am so smart I don't have to work."

Learning Goals and Activities. As we plan instruction, we naturally think interactively about learning goals and activities. We typically first identify *learning goals*. What are we seeking to help students learn? What are their interests? What are the goals outlined in the school district curriculum guide? Are there IEP goals to incorporate? We will develop broad learning goals from our students' interests in a particular subject and the school curriculum guide. This gives us a broad starting place.

Next, we suggest a simple four-step process to guide the development of multilevel teaching units and lessons. We suggest using three levels of learning goals and roles in learning activities. You can use this process formally, actually completing the forms, or use this process to stimulate your thinking, simply jotting a few notes to follow. Figure 6.4 presents a sample group learning activity from the Jason Project (Hittie, 1999a), showing differing levels of learning goals, tasks, and individual learning activities at differing ability levels. It also illustrates how different subjects may be integrated in this kind of interactive unit.

Step 1: Identify the learning goals for a unit that you can reasonably expect of your *highest-ability* student while bearing in mind the interests, characteristics, and even IEP goals of your lower-ability students.

Step 2: Design learning activities that help your highest-ability students by allowing students to either *(a)* work in groups on meaningful tasks, taking roles that let them function at different levels of ability, or *(b)* work alone or in pairs on related tasks using materials at differing levels of ability. Note that we do not ability-group students.

Step 3: Develop average and lowest-level learning goals. These additional levels are only approximate, but they help us think about ways we can have students functioning at different levels. If we already know our students, we can think about specific students as we identify these.

Step 4: Consider individual students with special needs. We will want to check our initial ideas against the reality of our specific students. For example, by looking at a student's IEP in relation to a curriculum matrix (see Chapter 4, Figure 4.8), we identify ways the IEP goals can be incorporated into the activity. After a while, of course, we do this almost automatically. We also think more carefully about our highest-ability students. Thinking of a few students who represent differing ability levels will help us make any needed revisions to ensure that activities work for these students.

A level 1 learning goal (see Figure 6.4), designed for students whose abilities are the most limited, would involve the simplest type of learning. Theoretically, there is no bottom level. However, we will most often target the lowest-functioning students in our class as we develop these goals, noting that we can always adjust the levels as needed. We examine the amount of reading and writing required as well as simplifying the concepts and complexity. A level 2 goal focuses on the writing, reading, and reasoning skills achievable by most students in the class. A level 3 activity extends opportunities for deeper engagement, using more complex activities, thought processes, and concept extensions. However, all levels are related to the same learning activity and can be done together, without necessitating separation of students.

The key in effective multilevel teaching is the use of learning goals that truly challenge children to think at deeper levels of ability. Bloom's taxonomy of educational outcomes (Bloom, 1956) has for many years been used for this purpose (see Figure 6.5). Our goal is to have children move from the lowest levels of thinking toward capacities for application, analysis, synthesis, and evaluation. Bloom's taxonomy helps us consider ranges of abilities and ways to develop lessons that use higher-level functions. Lessons geared to these higher levels of ability, however, involve students in complex tasks that also provide a place for students operating at lower levels in different roles. Looking at examples in this and other chapters, you'll notice that students are involved in projects in which they are studying complex events, often using engaging, hands-on activities. For students whose abilities are lower, however, there are many opportunities to work on skills at their own level as part of a complex project. Said another way, complex thinking always uses and builds on simpler forms of knowledge and understanding.

Many teaching approaches can be used to structure learning at differing levels. For example, in **writing workshop** (see Chapter 8) we develop an understanding of the present knowledge of children and increase their writing skills by having them write pieces that are meaningful to them—a journal entry about their daily life, a letter to a parent, or a story about a character in a book. Students learn multiple

Figure 6.4

Multiple Levels of Teaching Goals: Example from "Going to the Extremes"

Unit Theme: *Science: Human beings living in extreme conditions—in outer space and deep in the ocean.*

Learning Activity: Small groups conduct a hydroponic experiment (growing plants without soil as scientists are doing in space), record multiple data, and compare results of data from two different sources.

LEARNING GOALS	MULTILEVEL ROLES IN THE LEARNING ACTIVITY	INTEGRATED LEARNING IN LANGUAGE ARTS, ART, PHYSICAL EDUCATION
Level 3 Teamwork and leadership skills Measurement Methods to record multiple data Compare results of data from two different sources. Develop an analysis report.	*Level 3* Take leadership roles in organizing the team and solving problems. Record data. Help the team compare their results with those of the scientists. Write an analysis report.	1. Read books about plants. 2. Read chapter books about children in science fairs. 3. Write scientific reports in writers' workshop to share progress. 4. Create artwork to demonstrate the growth of the plant. 5. Create a play acting out the life of a plant. 6. Explore what people use plants for and how we care for plants. 7. Write songs about plants to familiar tunes.
Level 2 Learn how to work as a team, plant seeds, record growth, and write simple conclusions.	*Level 2* Plant seeds. Record plant growth. Describe conclusions in journal.	
Level 1 Help set up materials, work in a team, and do basic recording of the responses of the plant.	*Level 1* Help set up materials. Draw picture of plant each day.	

Source: Adapted from Hittie (1999a).

skills at one time. The teacher keeps informal notes. In one classroom, for example, Bobby is working on capital letters and periods and can create stories a few sentences long with a lot of perseverance and effort. In the same classroom, Julie writes nicely edited stories but needs to tap her creative and descriptive skills. Both students can help the other: Bobby listens for ideas to add to Julie's story, and she helps him edit for spelling (Calkins, 1994).

The same idea works with **reading workshop**; in which the teacher helps each student learn to pick a "just right" book using the five-finger rule. The rule goes like this: Read the first page. Put one finger up every time you miss a word. If you miss

Figure 6.5

Bloom's Taxonomy of Educational Outcomes

COMPETENCE	SKILLS DEMONSTRATED
Knowledge	Recalling facts, terms, basic concepts, and answers *Question cues:* List, define, tell, describe, identify, show, label, collect, examine, tabulate, quote, name; who, when, where, etc.
Comprehension	Demonstrating understanding of facts and ideas by organizing, comparing, translating, interpreting, giving descriptions, and stating main ideas *Question cues:* Summarize, describe, interpret, contrast, predict, associate, distinguish, estimate, differentiate, discuss, extend
Application	Solving problems by applying acquired knowledge, facts, techniques, and rules in a different way *Question cues:* Apply, demonstrate, calculate, complete, illustrate, show, solve, examine, modify, relate, change, classify, experiment, discover
Analysis	Examining and breaking information into parts by identifying motives or causes; making inferences and finding evidence to support generalizations *Question cues:* Analyze, separate, order, explain, connect, classify, arrange, divide, compare, select, explain, infer
Synthesis	Compiling information together in a different way by combining elements in a new pattern or proposing alternative solutions *Question cues:* Combine, integrate, modify, rearrange, substitute, plan, create, design, invent, compose, formulate, prepare, generalize, rewrite, explore "what if"
Evaluation	Presenting and defending opinions by making judgments about information, the validity of ideas, or the quality of work based on a set of criteria *Question cues:* Assess, decide, rank, grade, test, measure, recommend, convince, select, judge, explain, discriminate, support, conclude, compare, summarize

Source: Adapted from Bloom (1956), Fowler (1996), and Counseling Services Learning Skills Program (2001).

two to four words, the book is just right. Missing more than four means the book is too hard right now, and missing one is too easy. Children learn how to pick work that is challenging but in which they can be successful. They learn strategies and skills in small groups or individual conferences.

Other multilevel teaching strategies appear in the Tools for the Trek feature on page 208. Let's briefly discuss a few of these approaches (Peterson, Tamor, Feen, & Silagy, 2002).

- *Conduct individual reading, writing, and spelling conferences* during workshop time. Teachers identify skill needs for minilessons and record students' progress, learning strategies, and interests (Graves, 1983; Tomlinson, 1999; Zemelman, Daniels, & Hyde, 1998).
- *Have children keep journals* in which they record their thinking about books and school topics. Use this writing to facilitate discussion groups. Journal writing provides insight into students' learning and helps them think about what they are reading.
- *Give homework projects* related to what the children are learning that can be done at multiple levels. For example, students may interview a parent about their childhood and write a report to share in class.
- *Foster a community* in which children are *expected* to help one another. Students understand that in a real community they both increase their own skills and encourage everyone to do well (see Chapter 11).
- *Regularly have students choose a question to research.* Teach students to find material at their level to answer their questions.
- *Group students in many different ways* for lessons—by topics, by count-off, by particular skill, in guided reading groups. *Group heterogeneously* most of the time. *Never* have stable, ongoing ability-based groups.
- *Gear read alouds to higher reading levels.* Have students share copies of the read-aloud book with the more able students following words with their finger for the less able readers.
- *Have students meet in groups to share* what they are reading about. This invites conversation no matter what their reading levels.
- *Teach topics in themes* so that children can choose different parts on which to work. This way, all students work on a related topic at their own level.
- *Teach students to use mind mapping* to organize information and take notes. Mind mapping is like webbing (see Chapter 8), only it uses colorful pictures and a few key words. Because color stimulates the brain, students remember information better.

Although students choose many aspects of their activities, they need us as teachers to follow up. Many teachers have systems for tracking student choices for different activities or projects. One teacher showed us a notebook with a tab section for each child. In their sections children fill out contracts specifying when and how each book, writing assignment, or project will be completed.

Demonstrating Learning. When teaching at multiple levels, we must assess students continually so as to know if they are being challenged at their level of success (Armstrong, 1994). If we do not know that all students are being challenged, then we do not know if they are all learning. When students are making a choice that is too easy or too hard, we discuss it with them. Does it stretch their abilities? Are they finishing too quickly? If they decide a new choice is in order, then we commend them for thinking it through. Given the proper support, students often make good choices.

In Chapter 8 we will discuss a range of strategies for demonstrating learning. Effective assessment is based on students' production of authentic learning activities—reading real books at their own levels, producing a range of materials (drawing, building a model, writing a song or reflective poem) that demonstrate deep understanding

Tools *for the* Trek
Strategies for Multilevel Teaching

LITERACY	SCIENCE	MATH	SOCIAL STUDIES
Choice of books at different levels	Experiments with different group roles identified	Math games	Projects that allow students different roles
Buddy reading	Note taking using graphic organizers such as webbing (see Chapter 8)	Learning groups based on student interest and readiness	Dramatic role play of social and historical situations
Read alouds		Math projects with multiple types of tasks and levels to choose from	Writing of songs, poems, stories, etc. that show learning
Individual writing goals			
Stick-figure drawing to write a story line	Informational reading at many levels	Whole class interest-related community projects	Involvement with local people through interviews, visits, and projects
Individual spelling lists	Heterogeneous work groups help each other with assignments	Heterogenous practice groups	
Writing poetry			

ACROSS SUBJECT AREAS
- Art to convey meaning
- Choice of inquiry project at differing ability levels
- Partial participation in learning activities
- Cooperative learning groups (with differing levels of activities to contribute to the total group)

- Support and scaffolding to enable students to complete activities not possible independently
- Student-led portfolio conferences
- Pair–share information
- Heterogeneous partners for projects
- Student choice of own topics within broader theme

of content, writing real stories, or participating in a student-developed play about a historical event. All these authentic forms of assessment allow students to demonstrate learning at their own level without requiring us to create a different test for every child in our class (Neill, Bursh, Schaeffer, Thall, Yohe, & Zappardino, 1995; Tomlinson, 1999; Wolf, 1989).

Avoiding Pitfalls. We need to avoid several traps as we work toward multilevel teaching. Let's first talk about situations we've seen in which students have been locked rigidly into specific ability levels. Any level planning is simply a template that changes as students grow and we better understand their abilities. It is also vital that we teach children to choose for themselves developmentally appropriate work that stretches their thinking. When we provide different levels of an activity, we do not preselect and assign students to an ability level. They will make mistakes that we will need to discuss, but that is all part of the learning process.

Some teachers do, in fact, lock students in and limit their abilities by creating elaborate leveling and management systems for different subject areas. One teacher codes books by colored stickers and assigns students their color to read. Another teacher uses blocks with different activities on the various faces and assigns each child a particular face (Kronberg, 1999). One teacher gives her children three choices of activities but designates these as A, B, and C activities for each particular child. These designations represent the highest grade that child could get in each activity, even if the work was at the child's level (Nunley, 1998). In all of these approaches students have no knowledge of how to choose appropriate work when the teacher is unavailable; nor do they have strategies for completing work that is more difficult by relying on those around them.

Schum, Vaughn, and Leavell (1994) suggest a pyramid for planning at three levels (1) what *all* students should learn; (2) what *most* but not all students will learn, and (3) what *some* students will learn (the highest level and the top of the pyramid). This approach helps us differentiate learning for students with higher abilities. However, this strategy may be problematic for teaching that includes students with severe disabilities, depending on how we define "what all students should learn." If, for example, teachers routinely identify learning targets that are beyond the capabilities of a student with severe disabilities, what is to be done? At worst, this could easily result in the conclusion that the general education classroom is inappropriate for this student. At best, the process simply provides no guidance. You will notice that in our multilevel lesson planning approach (see Figure 6.4), we too identify three levels. However, instead of specifying the lowest level as what all students will learn, we suggest simply that this is the lowest level of ability for which we are targeting the lesson, a level that can be adjusted as we need.

As we design instruction, we also must not develop automatic and stereotypical approaches based on disability categories. There is no formula. Each student is unique, and our planning of multilevel instructional adaptations will be unique for each student.

The Meaning of Fair. How do we handle the situation that occurs when we have different expectations for different students—when one student may get an A for work that is clearly not as sophisticated as the work that earns a C for another student? How do we respond when some students turn in very sophisticated and complex projects and another student turns in only a simple drawing? What about when one student reads three complex chapter books and another three simple picture books? How do we explain this to students and parents? Some people will say that this is not fair.

We'd like to respond by telling a story. We go to the playground and watch the children playing baseball. To our surprise we see a boy in a wheelchair at the batter's box. We've heard of students with disabilities' being involved with typical children in sports. The boy hits the ball over first base and begins wheeling as fast as he can go. He manages to get to first base before the ball is thrown. Yet the umpire shouts "Out!" The crowd yells in anger. The umpire explains, "He is supposed to run to first base. He used a wheelchair. That is not fair."

This is obviously not a true story. Yet we think it illustrates the point. Using his wheelchair was not unfair at all. In fact, it was quite the opposite. The wheelchair helped this child perform more equally. We can state a simple guiding principle about fairness: *Fairness is not about providing the same thing but about providing what each student needs.* We can think of other obvious examples. When people who are blind use braille, tape recorders, or readers, they are engaging in a task in

Artwork reprinted by permission of Martha Perske from *Perske: Pencil Portraits 1971– 1990* (Nashville: Abingdon Press, 1998).

a different way that helps equalize their opportunity; the same is true when people who are deaf use sign language interpreters, or students who speak Spanish have texts in Spanish to read in class.

In an inclusive class we help students understand how they are each different. As we have differing options and standards based on individual capacities and needs, students understand that we provide what each student needs rather than expecting all to be the same. We will be surprised how much students understand and appreciate this approach. In fact, if we provide the same curriculum and expectations to all people despite their different intelligences, learning styles, and ability levels, *this* is unfair (Tomlinson, 1999; Zemelman, Daniels, & Hyde, 1998).

Scaffolding

When we have children of differing abilities learn together, we provide them support and assistance to reach to the next level of learning—Vygotsky's (1978) "zone of proximal development." The term **scaffolding** is often used to refer to this kind of support, in which teachers, other adults, or more competent students help students

Tools *for the* Trek

Literacy Scaffolding in the Inclusive Classroom

- Daily modeling writing procedures, verbalized thinking in math, and so on
- Demonstration of key words: who, what, why, first, next, finally, and so on
- Word banks/picture dictionaries that students continually add to
- Cognitive maps to organize reading and writing processes
- Reader response logs to share thoughts
- Choral and partner reading, writing, spelling practice
- Flexible grouping (large group, small group, pairs, individual)
- Developmental spelling
- Structures that encourage participation, inquiry, and student talk
- Motivating activities that create desire to learn about a topic
- Guided reading strategies groups

- Choral reading in which teacher sits slightly behind students so they hear words and inflections
- Readers' Theater to interpret readings
- Heterogeneous groups doing jigsaw reading and sharing with other groups.
- Preteaching of vocabulary, content, and questioning
- Marking points in reading where students refer to questions to encourage thinking
- Semantic maps or time lines to organize information
- Deep content materials at different levels (e.g., books, Internet access, books on tape, videos, community resources)
- Student "apprenticeships" in effective strategies used in a discipline.

Source: Adapted from Tarrant (1999b).

perform tasks that are within their zone of proximal development (Ormrod, 2000). Morocco and Zorfass (1996) describe effective scaffolds as (1) multilevel, (2) inclusive, (3) promoting higher-level thinking, and (4) dynamic and evolving.

Construction crews use scaffolds to support a building while it is being constructed. Scaffolds in the classroom are similar. Teachers provide supports and assistance so that a student can perform a task or activity *just beyond* their actual level of ability. Therefore, scaffolding engages students in work at a higher level while simultaneously supporting their learning and achievement. The teacher (or other helper) can provide the support before the activity to help activate student background knowledge, during the activity to build concept understanding, afterward to extend thinking, or a combination of all three (Graves & Graves 1994; Berk & Winsler, 1995). Scaffolding helps us avoid lowering our expectations—whether of gifted students or of students with special needs—to the point where children are not learning in our class, just occupying space (Graves & Graves, 1994).

What are some examples? Kathi Tarrant-Parks conducted research investigating scaffolding strategies that promote inclusion in literacy instruction. Tarrant (1999a,b) identified a range of manageable scaffolds that are applicable in most educational disciplines; these are listed in the Tools for the Trek feature here. Some additional examples include the following:

- A teacher or student reads a book to a student that the student likes but could not read independently.
- As a student reads, a more competent reading buddy reads along and helps with words the student doesn't know.
- One student records in the math journal for another student who has difficulty writing.
- A teacher arranges spaced blanks for words in a sentence for a child who has difficulty writing and separating words. The child then writes each word on its blank.
- A teacher provides a pictorial guide for a student to use in conducting a student-led conference. The teacher remains available to help the student, if needed, in conducting the conference.
- New vocabulary in a reading assignment is pretaught and then highlighted for the student, so it is easily identified.
- Students act out an emotional scene in a novel to understand concepts.
- The teacher or another student reads a student's work aloud so the student can hear which words are missing.

Morocco and Zorfass (1996) describe a project that illustrates how scaffolding and authentic learning build student strengths. In a middle school, an interdisciplinary team of teachers decided to engage in a "we-search" unit (Macrorie, 1988) organized around the theme of water ecology. The unit used an adaptation of the authoring cycle involving four phases: (1) identifying thematic questions for exploration, (2) developing a search plan, (3) gathering and integrating information, and (4) drafting, revising, and "publishing" a product.

First, teachers and students explored the topic. Teachers worked as an interdisciplinary team. Activities included viewing a video on water pollution, using a computer simulation on pollution and the environment, listening to an invited speaker from the local water commission, reading Spanish and English comic books about waterborne diseases; in addition, the teachers took one hundred students on a hike to the local river to collect and test water samples.

To ensure active involvement and learning for all, the teachers broke the students into cooperative learning groups, and each teacher (social studies, science, English, and special education) coached five to six groups, monitoring their progress. Scaffolds included worksheets to track progress as well as teacher discussions with each group regarding what they knew, what they wanted to know, and how they could obtain information. All teachers ensured that all students, including students with learning challenges, were an integral part of the project.

As the learning groups identified questions, they developed a plan to answer their questions. The teachers required each group to gather information in four ways: reading, watching, asking, and doing. They helped the groups develop a logistical plan and made sure that the groups established responsibilities and gave each group member support for doing his or her task.

As the groups began to gather information, the teachers recognized problems in students' interactions. Some were not taking responsibility. Others were dominating the groups. They decided that the special education support teacher, who was very skilled at dealing with emotional frustrations, would work with each group and "teach them how to discuss their frustrations constructively, using 'I' statements instead of fighting" (Morocco & Zorfass, 1996, p. 173). All the teachers helped students solve problems, using one another as resources. Teachers helped students identify interview questions for speakers and develop an interview guide for telephone interviews. Robert, a student with learning disabilities, was one student who conducted phone interviews. At one point, with help from the teacher, his group conducted a group interview with a speakerphone. This demonstration provided a model for Robert, who then rehearsed with support from the teacher and classmates. Though he was nervous and unsure at first, by the end of the rehearsal sessions his voice became confident. He learned much as he attempted to talk to people in government offices.

Finally, students used word processors to develop their reports. Again, teachers provided a detailed guide. Periodically a teacher would conduct a minilesson regarding a particular skill—grammatical structure, how to develop a lead, and so forth. Robert had great difficulty writing, so he talked about what he had discovered while another student wrote down his comments. Students invited more than 200 people to hear them as they shared their findings and made recommendations for how to solve some real ecological problems facing their community.

In this example, students were challenged at multiple levels and teachers used a range of constantly changing scaffolds. They modeled, conducted skill lessons, worked in small groups to further understanding, and arranged for a student to write for a peer who had difficulty. By participating in an engaging and meaningful problem-solving task, students who began at different levels arrived at a shared understanding. Robert could not have done this complex an activity on his own. With support from teachers and his peers, however, he was able to record his findings about water, conduct a phone interview, and learn about government bureaucracy. However, scaffolding should be thought of not as a teaching technique for struggling students but as a key strategy for all students. It extends students' zones of proximal development and gives them common experiences to talk about, write about, and share (Graves, 1994; Berk & Winsler, 1995).

Multiple Intelligences

Howard Gardner (1993) developed the idea of multiple intelligences in response to his dissatisfaction with typical intelligence tests. He posited that there are seven forms of human intelligence, or ways of being smart; later he added an eight form. Figure 6.6 provides a simple description of these intelligences, indicators of each, and sample teaching techniques for each. As we focus on the ways students think, what they love, and what they *need*, we dramatically improve learning.

For example, students who have strong spatial intelligence think in images and pictures; love designing, drawing, visualizing, and doodling; and *need* art, movies, imagination games, mazes, illustrated books, and trips to art museums. Students with high levels of kinesthetic intelligence think through bodily sensations; love dancing, running, jumping, building, and touching; and *need* role play, drama,

Figure 6.6

Multiple Intelligences		
INTELLIGENCES AND DESCRIPTIONS	THINKS . . . LOVES . . . NEEDS . . .	TEACHING MENU (A FEW IDEAS)
1. *Linguistic:* The capacity to use language to express ourselves and to understand other people. Examples: poet, writer, orator, lawyer, teacher.	Thinks in words. . . . Loves reading, writing, telling stories, playing word games. . . . Needs books, tapes, writing tools, paper, diaries, dialogue.	Use storytelling to explain. . . . Conduct a debate on. . . . Write a poem, legend, short play, or news article about. . . . Conduct an interview about. . . .
2. *Logical–mathematical:* Ability to use numbers effectively and to reason well logically. Examples: mathematician, accountant, computer programmer, scientist.	Thinks by reasoning. . . . Loves experimenting, questioning, figuring out logical puzzles. . . . Needs things to explore and think about, science materials, manipulatives.	Translate a . . . into a math formula. Design and conduct an experiment on. . . . Make up syllogisms to explain. . . . Describe patterns of symmetry in. . . .
3. *Spatial:* Competence to represent the spatial world internally in our mind and to use materials to impact the environment. Examples: hunter, scout, artist, architect, inventor.	Thinks in images and pictures. . . . Loves designing, drawing, visualizing, doodling. . . . Needs art, video, movies, imagination games, mazes, illustrated books, trips to art museums.	Chart, map, or graph. . . . Create a slide show, video, or photo album of. . . . Create a piece of art that illustrates. . . . Draw, paint, sketch or sculpt. . . .
4. *Bodily–kinesthetic:* Expertise in using our whole body to express ideas and feelings and ability to use our body to make or change things. Examples: actor, athlete, sculptor, mechanic, surgeon.	Thinks through bodily sensations. . . . Loves dancing, running, jumping, building, touching. . . . Needs role play, drama, movement, construction, activities, sports, hands-on learning.	Create a sequence of movements to explain. . . . Build or construct. . . . Plan and attend a field trip to. . . . Bring hands-on materials to demonstrate. . . .
5. *Musical:* Ability to think in music; to hear patterns, recognize them, remember them, manipulate them. Examples: singer, songwriter, composer, music critic.	Thinks via rhythms and melodies. . . . Loves singing, whistling, humming, tapping feet. . . . Needs sing-along time, music playing, musical instruments, music.	Give a presentation on . . . with musical accompaniment. Sing a rap or song that explains. . . . Explain how the music of a song is similar to. . . . Make an instrument and use it to demonstrate. . . .

Figure 6.6

	Continued	
INTELLIGENCES AND DESCRIPTIONS	THINKS . . . LOVES . . . NEEDS . . .	TEACHING MENU (A FEW IDEAS)
6. *Interpersonal:* Ability to understand thoughts, feelings, motivations of other people and to interact well with them. Examples: politician, salesperson.	Thinks by talking with other people. . . . Loves leading, organizing, talking, mediating, partying. . . . Needs friends, group games, social events, mentors.	Conduct a meeting to address. . . . Participate in a service project to. . . . Teach someone about. . . . Practice giving and receiving feedback on. . . .
7. *Intrapersonal:* Understanding of ourself—of our feelings, and reactions to others—and ability to act on that understanding. Awareness of inner moods, capacities for self-discipline and deep reflection. Examples: philosopher, poet, counselor.	Thinks by reflecting deeply inside self. . . . Loves setting goals, meditating, dreaming, being quiet. . . . Needs secret places, time alone, self-paced projects, choices.	Describe qualities you have that will help you. . . . Develop a plan to. . . . Describe a personal value about. . . . Write a journal entry on. . . . Assess your own work in. . . .
8. *Naturalist:* High sensitivity and responsiveness to living beings (plants, animals), the natural world, and the environment. Examples: "street smart" student, hunter, farmer, botanist.	Thinks by interacting with nature and the environment. . . . Loves camping, moving around the community, organizing the environment. . . . Needs time in nature or the community, organizing events.	Create observation notebooks of. . . . Describe changes in the local community. . . . Care for pets, wildlife, gardens, or parks in. . . . Draw or photograph natural objects or the community.

movement, construction projects, sports, and hands-on learning. If students truly do *need* these types of activities, what does it mean when they do not have them? Clearly, they will learn less, be less motivated, and probably create problems. Certainly not only these students but also their teachers and classmates will have lost opportunities to benefit from others' abilities (Armstrong, 1994).

If we take seriously the argument that students with various intelligences *need* particular experiences, then we must pay attention to this need. For example, in the kinesthetic example, allowing students to stand or lie on the floor while reading is a good start, but we could do more. Acting out parts of the text, having students represent concepts through art or illustrations, creating quick "body figures" that portray a key emotion or idea—such experiences stretch the whole community's thinking, stretching our comfort levels so that we have to reach inside ourselves and learn along with our students. (Armstrong, 1994).

Student–Teaching Mismatch. There is often a mismatch between the multiple intelligences of students and typical instruction in schools. Teachers have estimated that 75 to 90 percent of the learning in schools relies heavily on the first two intelligences—linguistic and logical–mathematical. Yet, as we look carefully at the characteristics of students, teachers have found that a minority of students excel in these intelligences. An estimated 60 percent of children in schools today have high abilities in visual–spatial intelligence, in part because of the increasing prevalence of media in our lives. As children spend more and more time watching TV, playing video games, and surfing the Internet, this percentage continues to rise. Approximately 33 percent express their learning through music, while around 17 percent are strongly bodily–kinesthetic in ability and another 17 percent are interpersonal (Gardner, 1993; Jensen, 1998).

Given this reality it is interesting to note that the number of children in schools identified as having learning disabilities has grown rapidly since the early 1980s. The areas in which these children tend to have the most difficulty are language and mathematics, the two intelligences on which schools focus the most (Armstrong, 1994; Campbell & Campbell, 1999). We also know that these same students often

Coteachers help students create costumes to act out essays. Such active learning helps all students use multiple intelligences and strengthen learning.

have highly developed abilities in one or more of the other intelligences. For example, at age fourteen Brad was identified as having a learning disability and doing poorly in school. He felt stupid. Yet at home he had an amazing ability to design and build shelves and cabinets and a gift for repairing the lawn mower—talents that many of his linguistically oriented classmates did not share.

Multiple Intelligences Theory: Key Corollaries. Multiple intelligences theory has several important implications (Armstrong, 1994). Consider the following:

1. *Each person possesses all eight intelligences.* We must not attempt to label students based on intelligences. Although some intelligences are more developed in some people, most people can develop all eight intelligences to a reasonable level. This means that we should structure opportunities for development of all intelligences.
2. *Although we describe the intelligences separately, they interact with one another.* For example, when we cook a meal, we read a recipe (drawing on linguistic intelligence), decide whether to double or halve the recipe depending on how many are eating (logical–mathematical), modify the recipe for the likes and dislikes of family members (interpersonal), and actually cook the food (bodily–kinesthetic—and perhaps interpersonal, if we are cooking with a partner or two).
3. *There is no one correct way to express any intelligence at a high level.* For example, a student who cannot read may be an amazing storyteller or speaker. Conversely, a person may be an avid reader and writer, yet fumble when asked to communicate orally.

Understanding the Multiple Intelligences of Students. An understanding of multiple intelligences helps us recognize and build on students' strengths. We will often be amazed at positive attributes of students previously unnoticed. For example, when we use drama and movement to teach concepts, we will note students who excel. When we ask students to express mathematical concepts through music or art, we will have other opportunities to identify student strengths.

We can understand our students' intelligences in other ways as well. One of the most interesting is to identify how a student *misbehaves* in class. Often such "behavioral problems" are expressions of the student's need to use a particular channel of learning, or intelligence, that is being stifled. For example, highly spatial students often doodle instead of taking notes. Musically intelligent students may hum constantly or daydream, listening to the music and rhythms in their minds. Kinesthetically intelligent students may move constantly, leave their seats, or tap the desk. (Often these children quickly get identified as having ADD, or attention deficit disorder, when they may in actuality be demonstrating an intelligence that is not very welcome in the classroom.) These behavioral clues can help us identify strengths while giving us strong signals that we need to allow more intelligences into our classroom.

Other good indicators of student intelligences are the ways they spend their free time. When students have total choice regarding learning activities, what do they choose? Do they read books, draw, talk with other students, move around the room from place to place, sit in the study carrel listening to music, or roam the Internet? A journal in which we keep running observations and notes about our students helps identify needs. If such a journal is too time-consuming, we can focus on the few students who pose the greatest challenges.

A final useful strategy can be a simple checklist of sample activities that helps us think about students' intelligences (Armstrong, 1994). A word of caution is needed here, however. Traditional intelligence tests, which measure linguistic and logical–mathematical intelligences, have been used to identify *deficits* of students. Multiple intelligences theory, in contrast, gives us a powerful way of identifying *strengths* of students. We must be careful about labeling students in a new way—as the "art smart kids" or the "deep thinkers," for example. Intelligences are dynamic, and they can change.

Teaching Students about Multiple Intelligences. Teaching students about multiple intelligences helps them better understand their own strengths and abilities (a form of intrapersonal intelligence). Ask specific questions that draw out the diverse abilities of the room: "How many people excel at speaking? How many love to write?" (linguistic). "How many of you love math? How many people enjoy science experiments?" (logical–mathematical).

Teaching with Awareness of Multiple Intelligences. Multiple intelligences theory provides one lens to help teachers design instruction that will reach students' diverse abilities. The concept of multiple intelligences also is a natural fit with interdisciplinary instruction. That is, from one perspective the multiple intelligences correspond to many disciplines in the school—language arts, math, science, social studies. In fact, the whole push towards interdisciplinary studies is based on a recognition that students learn better when different ways of approaching a subject are linked together.

Learning in any subject area can be strengthened when students draw upon multiple intelligences. Similarly, any particular intelligence can be strengthened through the others. This is particularly important when we have students who are struggling in a particular arena.

Let's look at an example. We are working in a high school as part of an interdisciplinary team involving social studies, language arts, and art to help students understand their own culture (intrapersonal intelligence) and learn how to interact respectfully with people of other cultures (interpersonal intelligence). We engage students in gathering information about and reading literature of cultures (linguistic intelligence), have multicultural events at which different customs and food are represented (bodily–kinesthetic, spatial, & musical intelligences), and dramatically act out a key event in the history of an ethnic group (bodily–kinesthetic intelligence).

A useful tool is the multiple intelligences planning grid matrix; a sample matrix, filled in, is shown in Figure 6.7. We recommend the following steps:

1. Identify your theme and the learning goals and objectives.
2. Brainstorm ideas that will actively engage students and that will help them demonstrate what they know and understand. Don't try yet to connect these

Figure 6.7

Multiple Intelligences Planning Matrix

Theme: Human and Legal Rights

Learning Goals and Objectives for Unit: Understand the relationship between the Bill of Rights and the human rights it is designed to protect. Understand and describe specific examples of legal and advocacy strategies groups use to address human rights protected by the Bill of Rights.

LEARNING ACTIVITIES	LING.	LOG.–MTH.	SPAT.	BOD.–KIN.	MUS.	INTER.	INTRA.	NAT.
Read the Bill of Rights as a group.	X					X		
Write and act out play regarding civil rights.	X		x	X		X		
Personal reflections: writing, tape, etc. Some students do individually, some in cooperative group based on choice.	X					x	X	
Create song or drawing to illustrate one of the rights. Present to the class.	x		X		X	x	x	
Conduct study regarding rights violations in a community—legal costs, economics, numbers of complaints lost and won.	x	X				x		x
Write a short story, play, or poem reflecting on the importance of one of the rights.	x		x	X	X		X	

X = primary intelligence associated with activity; x = secondary intelligence associated with activity

ideas with the multiple intelligences. When you have several ideas for good learning activities, write these on the planning form in the Learning Activities column.

3. Use the matrix to indicate which of the multiple intelligences is strongly used in a particular activity. Then analyze the degree to which all the intelligences are utilized and make changes as needed.

4. Finalize your plans, adding more details for how each activity will be implemented in your class or with other teachers.

5. Use your awareness of multiple intelligences to devise alternative evaluation strategies for understanding what students have learned.

In the example in Figure 6.7, the teacher wanted to help students learn about the Bill of Rights. She created many good ideas for how to engage her students. As you can see, in this example the intelligences are often interactive, and both learning activities and demonstrations involve several intelligences at once.

Multiple Intelligences and Students with Special Needs. The multiple intelligences approach is strength-based; as such, it removes pressure from whatever area a student is having difficulty with, identifies and builds on strengths, and uses the other intelligences to "surround" any weak area. Let's look at an example.

One student had a great deal of difficulty writing. He had to concentrate so much on controlling the pen or pencil that he was extremely slow. The teacher, in consultation with the student's parents, built on his strength—oral communication. She did not require him to write at all and had him read text only periodically for fun. The pressure to read and write, to struggle with areas in which he was having problems, was taken away. The student listened, participated in class assignments, and used cassette recordings of text. Over time he gradually learned to use a computer for papers (a different form of writing production) and began reading to his infant sister. Ultimately, he began to read text that was closer to grade level; simultaneously, he was doing complex projects on the computer involving both mathematics and graphics (Smith, O., 1997).

When we talk with teachers about multiple intelligences, they often say, "Don't you want children to read?" Of course we do. However, what we are learning is that it is counterproductive to pressure students to try harder on strategies that are already not working. Recall our discussion on brain-based learning and the importance of "relaxed alertness." When we push students to perform in areas in which they feel like failures, they will not learn. In the example of the student with writing difficulties, the teacher and parents were able to work together to create a condition of relaxed alertness and to provide multiple avenues toward learning course content. The strategy worked.

Learning Styles

By recognizing diverse learning styles, we can create the conditions that are most conducive for diverse student's learning. An understanding of learning styles provides us with another way to build on students' strengths and to design instruction to respond to varied needs. To put it another way, when we watch our students carefully and understand the conditions and situations in which they learn best, we can design our instruction to capitalize on our observations. In addition, we can teach

Schools to Visit

An Urban School for All

Dailey Elementary School
3135 N. Harrison
Fresno, CA 93710
Phone: 559-248-7060
Principal: Steve Gettman
**fresno.k12.ca.us/schools/S011/
   SCH011HP.HTM**

Dailey Elementary is a K–6 school in Fresno Unified School District, an urban district in the agricultural heart of California. The city ranks sixth in the nation in childhood poverty, and students speak 101 languages. Seventy-nine percent of the approximately 630 students qualify for the free/reduced lunch program. The population is culturally diverse; of students 49 percent are Hispanic, 32 percent white, 9 percent Asian, and 8 percent African American. Just over 20 percent have been identified as learners of English as a second language.

The school district is now working to have all children with special needs included in general education classes. Beginning in the 2000–01 school year, students with special needs in self-contained classes returned to Dailey fully included in general education classrooms. Since that time the school has included children with autism, Tourette syndrome, Down syndrome, cerebral palsy, developmental delays, hearing impairment, emotional/behavioral problems, and learning disabilities.

In fourteen of twenty-eight classrooms, in a mix of multiage and regular graded classes, a resource specialist and special day class teacher serve approximately forty children identified with special needs. The school has one full-time and two part-time paraprofessionals as well as a half-day assistant for a student with autism. We have weekly support from an adaptive PE teacher, an occupational therapist, a speech therapist, and a school psychologist. One day a week an inclusion specialist observes children and helps us brainstorm solutions.

Although the teachers have concerns, they are working hard to differentiate instruction to accommodate all the children. Teachers use scaffolding, differentiated instruction, and multiple ways of knowing as a matter of course in many of the classrooms. Supported reading, choral reading, read alouds, interactive writing, reading and writing conferences, individualized spelling work, minilessons, and whole class discussions are all part of the picture. Some children use portable keyboards for writing. Others work on clipboards or use dry erase boards. Visual schedules, break cards, and individualized stories are used to help children who have difficulty staying on task or communicating with students or teachers.

Building community is important to the teachers at Dailey. Even before inclusion, several teachers insisted that I, a special education teacher, work with students with special needs in their classes. Because many teachers follow a workshop or inquiry model, I am able to work with individuals or small groups as needed. Instruction is more easily adapted to the needs of the students.

Our school's vision of inclusion continues to evolve as the general and special education teachers become comfortable with this new challenge, and as our student population ebbs and flows. There have been many positive experiences for the staff, parents, and students; and we continue to learn better ways to make everyone full members of the school community.

By Nancy Barth, Inclusion Teacher;
branwellzamborska@mediaone.net.

students to *understand their own learning styles*. When we engage students in active processing of their own abilities, we give them yet another tool for understanding themselves and becoming partners in designing instruction that meets their needs.

At first glance, the concepts of learning styles and multiple intelligences might seem the same. Although there is certainly a relationship, they are actually quite different. Multiple intelligences theory describes the ways in which people are smart and demonstrate ability and competence. Learning styles, in contrast, have to do with how people are most comfortable learning and most receptive to learning. People's intelligences and learning styles certainly can be—and often do seem to be—related. For example, it would not surprise us if someone who had spatial intelligence and demonstrated this through wonderful drawings also turned out to learn through visual means more than others. However, the connection does not always apply.

Learning styles can involve many specific variables, and many different approaches have been developed. Many are familiar with Grinder's (1991) description of visual, auditory, and kinesthetic learners. Jacobson (2002) has focused on the more sequential, analytic "left brain" versus the more global, intuitive "right brain."

Jensen (1995) synthesized these and other conceptualizations of learning styles into an overall framework composed of four parts: (1) context, (2) input, (3) processing, and (4) response filters. Let's discuss Jensen's parts briefly. By *context* we mean the physical environment for learning. Different people have different preferences for learning conditions, such as being warm or cool, having water, or lying down; and paying careful attention to these is beneficial.

We all take in information and experiences through one or more sensory *input* channels—sight, touch, smell, movement, sound, taste. Some input modalities are more effective for some people than others. For example, one friend of ours has difficulty remembering someone's name unless he sees it written down. Often, as he is introduced, he visualizes the name in writing to help him remember.

We handle the *processing* of information differently as well. Some of us are more global, seeing the big picture (but perhaps missing details); others are analytical. Other processing differences include concrete or abstract thinking, multitask or single-task approaches, and right-brain or left-brain processing.

Once we process information, our minds respond in different ways to determine a course of action, as influenced by our own *response filters*. These filters have to do with our reactions to factors such as time and risk involved or internal versus external referencing. Some of us take many risks. Others take few. Some are more influenced by what others think (external referencing), whereas others make choices based more on internal values. From another perspective, some of us look for patterns of consistency and continuity; others look for "mismatches," differences, and problems.

Rita and Ken Dunn (1987; Dunn, 1996) have developed a useful comprehensive framework that incorporates detailed considerations of context (Figure 6.8). We will use their model to illustrate how we can incorporate awareness of learning styles into our efforts to design instruction for diversity. We can use the framework presented here to structure our classroom so as to give students opportunities to respond to their own learning styles.

Environmental stimuli: We can enable students to vary sound, light, temperature, and the formality of the learning situation in our class. For example, we provide head-

Figure 6.8

STIMULI	ELEMENTS			
Environmental	Sound: Amount of sound. Music and talking for some; silence for others.	Light: Bright versus dim light.	Temperature: Warm versus cool.	Design: Formal versus informal. Sitting in chairs or lying on the floor with pillows.
Emotional	Motivation: High versus low motivation. What tasks or situations create?	Persistence: Ongoing attention to task versus need for frequent breaks.	Responsibility: Conforming versus needing choices and creativity.	Structure: Need for structured guidelines or only for general direction.
Sociological	Responses to being with people while learning. Desire to work alone, with colleagues in a group or team, or with one other person in a pair. Preferences for working with an authority such as a teacher. Or preference for varied work relationships.			
Physical	Perceptual: Preferred sensory input. Auditory: listening and verbal. Visual: print, art, shapes. Tactile/kinesthetic: touch and movement.	Intake: Eating, drinking, chewing to help concentration.	Time: Energy and alertness levels at times of day, as in "morning person," "night person." When do peaks occur?	Mobility: Staying still versus needing to move.
Psychological	Analytic–global: Sequential, step-by-step versus global, intuitive. Left brain versus right brain.	Locus of control: External needs for approval versus internal goal setting.	Reflective–impulsive: Thinking deeply but not volunteering answers versus reacting immediately.	

Sources: Adapted from Dunn & Dunn (1987) and Dunn (1996). For more information, see **www.learningstyles.net/**.

phones so that some students can listen to music while engaging in learning. Earmuffs are available to let some students shut out noise; other students work best in learning groups in which talk is encouraged. Similarly, various types of lighting are available in the classroom and in other areas, such as study carrels with dimmer illumination. To vary the temperature we allow students to wear less or more clothing and have portable heaters or fans available. Finally, parts of our classroom are informal—a couch, pillows on the floor, and so on—whereas in other parts we have formal chairs at tables.

Emotional stimuli: We can design our teaching for varied emotional styles. Seeing lower levels of motivation as a strength is particularly difficult for us. However, if we accept this trait in students and seek ways to connect with those students' interests and needs, they will feel accepted and ultimately will perform more effectively. Similarly, we can provide opportunities for some students to work intensively on some projects while allowing others to take frequent breaks, perhaps shifting from topic to topic. To do this we structure our classroom time so that there are ongoing blocks of time for individual and small group work on assignments. For some students we provide highly structured assignments; we give others more global directions and provide support as they need it.

Sociological stimuli: As we design our classes for diversity, we will want to provide students with a range of opportunities for working alone or with other people. In the learning process some students desire and actually need to work individually. Others will seek opportunities to work with a buddy, with an adult (this could be a teacher, a volunteer, or someone at home or in the community), with a group of students who work as a team, or even with students from another class. Allowing time for both types of activities is important.

Physical stimuli: A diverse classroom will also attend to opportunities for visual, auditory, or kinesthetic learning experiences. Students should be allowed to snack or drink while working on projects. Teachers report that when they begin to allow such intake in their classrooms, they set a few basic rules. Initially almost all the students will bring food or drink. After the novelty wears off, however, they settle into their personal style patterns, and only the few who really need this continue. Some teachers actually have small refrigerators in their classrooms where students can keep food and drink they bring to school. We can also help students understand their own best learning times and how to structure their class time and projects based on this knowledge. Finally, we devise ways to allow students to move about the room. Here again, teachers report that they set some basic ground rules. Within these simple guidelines students can move from place to place, stand while reading, or walk around the room thinking about a project.

Psychological stimuli: Psychological aspects of learning styles require teachers to recognize and appreciate the variations in the way students' minds function and to respond to them accordingly. With students who are analytical, we draw on their strengths to help them sequentially develop work tasks. Yet we may also pair them with globally oriented students who teach them to look at whole concepts, to be less rigid, and to see relationships. We can similarly recognize each student's individual locus of control and build on the natural strengths inherent in this trait, helping students expand their repertoire. Students who have external locus of control will be very sensitive, for example, to the opinions and perceptions of other people and may help those with internal locus of control to hear what people are saying. By the same token, those who tend to act impulsively may demonstrate responsiveness and a sense of action, encouraging more reflective students to speak out. These latter students can, on the other hand, help impulsive students to think through issues more carefully.

How do we identify the learning styles of students? We find that the best and most efficient way is simply to watch our students carefully—a process we call "kid watching." We made a similar recommendation when we discussed multiple intelligences earlier. Kid watching simply means that we pay close attention to what happens with our students. We keep logs or journals and make notes about different students, particularly those about whom we are most concerned; we also keep an ongoing portfolio of illustrative student work. As we teach and watch our students, we will constantly be asking questions about how they learn and about the arenas in which they are most accomplished. Notes help us remember and organize that information. When students puzzle us, we will review our notes, study their work samples, and reflect on our teaching strategies, interactions, and relationships with them. By paying attention in this way, we can learn a lot; we can better understand our students and constantly improve our teaching practice.

Stretching Our Teaching

In this chapter we've explored four foundations to inclusive teaching. We know that first and foremost, we will intentionally teach at *multiple levels*. At the same time, using the ideas of *scaffolding* and the *zone of proximal development,* we will challenge children at their own levels; we will provide support from teachers, support personnel, other children, and parents to help children move to the next level through interesting tasks that are not too hard, not too easy, but "just right." To help us do this, we draw on the natural strengths of the child, understanding *multiple intelligences* and giving students multiple strategies by which to take in information and demonstrate their learning. Finally, awareness of *learning styles* helps us structure the learning environment so that children can learn more easily and effectively. Together, these form four powerful building blocks for teaching all children, together, effectively. Eric Jensen calls these building blocks, and other related strategies tools for *"super teaching"* (Jensen, 1995).

Stepping Stones

To Inclusive Teaching

1. Outline a thematic unit based on the four building blocks of inclusive teaching, using the following steps:
   - Sketch your learning goals and the learning activities you want to use. Think creatively about active learning.
   - Look at the activities and think how students can work at multiple levels. If this becomes too hard and complex, look again at the tasks to see how you can make them more easily incorporate multiple levels.
   - Decide how you may scaffold student learning. Write these ideas down.
   - Use the multiple intelligences grid (Figure 6.9) to check your activities against the in-

   telligences. If there's not a good balance, revise and check again.
   - Use the information on learning styles (Figure 6.8) to look at your classroom and the activities you've designed. See if your outline includes ways that different learning styles can be accommodated. If not make revisions.

2. Analyze your typical teaching strategies from the perspective of the four building blocks. How much are you using these strategies without knowing it already? How might you improve and strengthen your teaching? Identify three ways you will do this.

The challenge before us brings us back to the beginning of our quest. We're on a journey to turn schools into places of joy, excitement, achievement, and care. As we learn to teach this way, brain-based learning strategies that we use with our students can apply to our own learning as teachers as well. We can (1) create with one another ways to be challenged and supported, (2) plunge ahead into the complexities of seeking new ways of teaching, ideally with support from colleagues and other professionals, and (3) create for ourselves places to dialogue, debate, and discuss what we are learning. We too can be "included" as we grow, learn, and develop, having fun and being relaxed in the process.

  ## Key Points

- Traditional teaching practices ensure failure among many students. Their emphasis on narrow skills and worksheets causes many students to get bored and lose interest in learning. In addition, "one-level" instruction is far below the level of many students, offering them no challenge; for many others, it is too high-level and frustrating.

- Both research and the research-based judgment of national professional organizations call for moving away from such traditional practices to more engaging, hands-on, collaborative ways of learning.

- Four key building blocks provide complementary strategies for moving toward best practices for inclusive teaching: multilevel instruction, scaffolding, multiple intelligences, and learning styles.

- Multilevel instruction allows students to learn and be challenged at their own level of ability while working with others at different levels: materials at differing levels, open-ended projects, and group work in which students take differing roles are some of many strategies.

- Scaffolding helps us support students in moving to their next level of challenge in learning.

- Multiple intelligences theory helps us design instruction based on eight ways in which students can be smart, thus building on student strengths.

- Learning styles challenge us to attend to the conditions and situations in which students learn best.

 ## Learning Expeditions

Following are some ideas that may extend your learning.

1. Observe in a classroom of a school that puts great emphasis on being on "grade level" and utilizes one set of grade-level materials for all students. What problems and issues do you observe? How do you interpret your observations?

2. Observe in a classroom where teachers allow students to function at their own level of abilities and have materials and resources at var-

ious levels. How does teaching occur in this classroom? What problems or advantages do you see? Compare this class to the class in observation 1 (above). What does this comparison tell you?

3. Work with a small group to develop a lesson that can be taught at multiple levels without ability grouping; that is, a lesson in which students of differing abilities work together. What do you like about the lesson you developed? What questions did this process raise?

What was hard, what easy about developing this lesson?

4. Develop a rubric for the four building blocks of inclusive teaching. Use this rubric to assess your own teaching or that of another teacher. What did you learn out of this process? What questions arose?

5. Consider your own "intelligences." What are your strongest areas of performance and learning? If you were to design a perfect school just for you, what would it look like? What would students do? How would teachers teach? What are the implications for your own teaching practice?

6. Observe in a classroom and make arrangements with a teacher to work with one student or a small group of students. Have them identify their strongest intelligences, and give examples from their own lives. Ask them to come up with ideas about how teaching might help them learn better. Record these and show them to the teacher. What did you learn about how this class might be taught better for this particular group of students?

7. Consider your own learning style. What situations are you most comfortable in? What do you do when you are studying? If you were to design a perfect school just for you, what variables would be available? How would students sit, how would they dress, or when would they eat? What are the implications for your own teaching practice?

8. Observe in a classroom and talk with students about how they learn best. Referring to the learning styles chart in Figure 6.8. What recommendations might you make to the teacher of this class?

CHAPTER OBJECTIVES

1. Consider the impact of labels on students with special needs.

2. Understand effective strategies for teaching students considered gifted and talented in heterogeneous, inclusive classes.

3. Identify needs and instructional approaches for second-language learners and students with learning disabilities.

4. Develop effective teaching approaches for use with students with mental retardation and brain injury.

5. Reflect on controversies about the education of students with varied academic abilities.

Students with Differing Academic Abilities 7

Best Practices for Meeting Student Needs in Heterogeneous Classes

When we enter Carol Summers's grade 7 language arts class, students are writing at desks, writing on the floor, or sitting at the back table working on editing with their peers. Kendrick is a student labeled trainable mentally retarded, Carol explains; he reads at a second-grade level, and the physical act of writing is difficult for him. However, he is writing many words. Although they are hard to read (many misspellings and letters run together), he is very busy. "What are you writing about?" Carol asks. Kendrick reads what he has written, and she quickly jots his thoughts down on the facing pages of the journal. "Kendrick, that's an interesting story. You have written a lot!"

Sitting next to him is Patrick, an extremely bright child who qualified for the gifted and talented program but wanted to stay with his friends. He is working on writing gripping beginnings and picturesque details. His language is amazingly sophisticated, with images and story lines that could have been created by a college student. As Patrick works, he periodically encourages Kendrick and spells words for him. Carol explains that they are good friends.

At the opposite side of the room, Amanda, a student classified as learning disabled, struggles with reading and writing and has difficulty focusing. She works hard to make her writing understandable. She is alternating between talking and staring at her paper, having written only two lines. "Amanda, why don't you work in your writing chair," Carol says gently, placing dots at the ends of six lines. Amanda goes to a secluded area and shortly comes back with six lines of writing. "Amanda, that's great!" says Carol. "Remember to indent for paragraphs." "Oh yeah!" Amanda exclaims—and returns to her seat smiling.

At break we ask Carol, "How do you manage with such diverse academic abilities?" "The key is learning how to teach to *individuals,* not groups," she replies. "I learn the strengths of each student and where they need to be pushed. The teaching activities I use allow students to work at different levels. I constantly ask myself, 'What is the best next step for this student?' instead of the traditional 'What should a seventh grader be able to do?' For example, look at Kendrick's writing," she says, pulling out his writing workshop folder. "He is writing simple ideas, spelling basic words, adding periods, and spacing letters. These are huge steps for him." She goes on to discuss Amanda. "She needs confidence boosters. The six dots gives her an attainable goal. When she has written as far as the first dot, she is encouraged and given another dot."

She then shares how her students have learned to complement each other's strengths and needs. "They spell words for each other, listen for content, and edit each other's papers. When Amanda gets frustrated, her friend Christine listens and gets her past a tough spot. When Kendrick is staring at a blank page, Patrick asks what he is writing and gets him started. Patrick enjoys helping Kendrick. Sometimes Patrick even asks Kendrick for ideas to write about. These kids learn each other's goals, and they work to make sure that their friends are learning. I could not manage without them."

"Aren't there days you would rather teach children all on the same level?" we ask. She shakes her head, laughing. "Life would be too boring!" As we leave, we think about the concerns some people have that students with "special needs" will hinder other students' learning. That doesn't happen in Carol's class. In fact, the different abilities in her classroom community seem to propel each student forward.

Traveling Notes

We hear often about "disorders," "syndromes," and "deficits" that students have. More are created all the time. As we necessarily discuss labels that we will hear applied to children in our classes, we enter an arena of controversy, an arena that focuses on deficits rather than strengths of children.

1. What are your images regarding a student with learning disabilities, mental retardation, or traumatic brain injury?

2. How do these images differ from your image of students labeled gifted?

3. Carol Summers pretty well ignored these labels and watched carefully how her children responded. She had students involved helping each other, tasks that allowed for challenge at multiple levels. What do you think about Carol's class?

4. We know that some teachers are better at dealing with learning challenges than others. What do they do?

5. We know that some teachers think that if the problem is *in the kid,* there's not much they can do. What is your reaction to this?

6. Where do learning challenges come from? What makes a good teacher of children with learning challenges?

7. How do such students fare in classes that use exemplary instruction?

In this chapter and in Chapters 10 and 13 we discuss students in terms of the issues that bring them to our attention: academic, social–emotional, and sensory–physical needs. In this chapter we explore differences in academic ability—learning disabilities, mental retardation, special talents and abilities, and limitations in the ability to speak English. As we discuss needs of students with academic differences, we want to consider carefully how strategies to assist them and overall best instructional practices relate to one another.

Label Jars, Not People
Seeing Children as People First

In exploring issues related to academic differences, we will encounter many labels given to children (see Chapter 1). Too often we forget that labels are attached to *people*. We hear students called "retards," "POHIs," LD students, or "the gifted." Yet the starting point for labeling children is often the question, "What is wrong with this student?"—a *deficit-driven* approach—or its cousin, "Is this student smarter than others?"—a potentially *elitist* perspective. Both questions reflect the same underlying philosophy, the idea that inherent differences in children set them apart. This philosophy can lead to harmful attitudes. Students with presumed deficits may feel stupid and not worthy. Those with advanced skills can become isolated, compensating through attitudes of superiority. Students then *become* their labels. However a student with mental retardation is mostly a child—happy, moody, fond of singing songs. A gifted high school senior is mostly an adolescent with dreams and fears like other teenagers. Using *people-first language*—speaking of a student *with* mental retardation rather than referring to a mentally retarded student, for example—helps us keep these truths in mind. We must be careful to see students with labels as children first.

The "Best and the Brightest"
Students People Call "Gifted and Talented"

Parents of children with high abilities have been very concerned regarding the education of their children. In 1988 Congress passed the Jacob K. Javits Gifted and Talented Students Education Act to provide federal support to schools aimed at improving the education of gifted and talented students. In the 1994 reauthorization of PL 103-398, Title XIV:

> The term "gifted and talented" . . . means students . . . who give evidence of high performance capability in areas such as intellectual, creative, artistic, or leadership capacity, or in specific academic fields, and who require services or activities not normally provided by the school in order to fully develop such capabilities. (p. 388)

Two points are noteworthy about this definition. First, a student can be "gifted" and also possess another label—such as "learning disabled" or "second language learner." Second, this definition describes regular classrooms as being unable to challenge these students adequately. This description, however, is more an assumption and is based on traditional, one-level teaching practice.

What does research say about highly able students in inclusive classes? The debate appears to hinge on two major issues: (1) values—evaluations of the benefits versus the costs of segregated or ability-grouped education; and (2) assessment of the capacity and willingness of teachers to use best practices, a theme we see related to all students with special needs. Oakes (1985) and Wheelock (1992) comprehensively reviewed research on the issue. They concluded that special programs, clustering across classes, and ability grouping have only mild and periodic academic benefits to high-ability students—but that these practices have negative impacts on average- to low-ability students, because the removal of high-achieving classmates to separate programs takes away students who provide role models and whose higher-level work may engage and strengthen learning opportunities. Further, highly able students often feel isolated and cut off from their friends and the larger school community. Sapon-Shevin (1994b) found that separate gifted programs often promote elitism, a sense that some people are better than others, and break a sense of community

> IT'S AMAZING HOW WELL YOU HAVE ADJUSTED YOUR TEACHING NOW THAT STUDENTS WITH SEVERE DISABILITIES ARE IN YOUR CLASS.

> WELL, I JUST KEEP REMINDING MYSELF THAT MY STUDENTS WERE EACH DIFFERENT BEFORE "INCLUSIVE EDUCATION"; THAT HASN'T CHANGED, JUST EXPANDED.

© 1999 MICHAEL F. GIANGRECO. ILLUSTRATION BY KEVIN RUELLE PEYTRAL PUBLICATIONS, INC. 612-949-8707

MRS. KING SPORTS HER WORN SOFTBALL CAP AS A REMINDER THAT INDIVIDUALIZING TO MEET UNIQUE STUDENT NEEDS IS OLD HAT TO GOOD TEACHERS.

among students, teachers, and parents. Other researchers, such as Gentry & Owen (1999) and Sheppard and Kanevsky (1999), focus more exclusively on academic benefits and argue that the achievement increases of ability grouping are worth other costs and can be beneficial. The degree to which typical teachers can and will use instructional approaches that challenge high-ability students is highly debatable; yet, most agree that if teachers used multilevel, differentiated instruction founded on multiple intelligences and effective scaffolding, segregated programs would either be unnecessary or have limited usefulness (Clark, 1997; Cline, 1999; Kennedy, 1995; Sapon-Shevin, 1994; Willis, 1995).

How can highly gifted students and students with severe mental retardation or learning disabilities learn successfully together? The answer is that we can use techniques from gifted education to benefit all students. Strategies that use multiple intelligences and differentiated instruction can create classes aimed at the highest levels, in which the brightest students bring others along, yet structured so that students can begin where they are, however low or high their abilities. In addition, we must be concerned about the emotional well-being of highly gifted students. Do they feel set apart? When we build a strong community (Chapter 11) while providing opportunities for students to engage in learning at their own level, highly gifted students can be supported emotionally as well as academically. Let's explore how this works.

Classroom Leadership, Problem Solving, and Advanced Learning

We would expect able students to play leadership roles in class discussions, sharing their learning and extending issues to higher levels of complexity. As this happens, these students raise the level of understanding of all students. For example, a teacher might ask the following question: "As we have discussed in this class, people often have trouble getting over their differences—personality, race, culture, wealth, disability. Many people also think kids should all be working at the same level in school. Yet we know you are all at many different levels. How can we make learning work for everyone?" Building an inclusive classroom involves many complex issues, and we can engage our most able children in looking at their experiences with students of different abilities and use these discussions as opportunities to explore a wide range of technical and social issues. This is but one of many examples that suggest how the classroom and school itself can become a learning laboratory for very able students.

Multilevel Teaching Strategies for Higher-Level Learning

Teaching strategies that support gifted and talented students are expansions of multilevel teaching, introduced in Chapter 6. Useful strategies include the following (Cline, 1999; Kronberg, 1999; Tomlinson, 1999):

- *Curriculum compacting:* Preassess students to avoid teaching what they already know, and allow advanced students to pursue enrichment activities or explore units in additional breadth or depth.

■ *Tiered lessons:* Structure lessons that allow students to move ahead as they are able and interested. Provide a range of activities students may select from at various levels of difficulty. Allow and teach students to choose their own activities at their own level.

■ *Open-ended assignments:* Give assignments in which students can explore complexity, assignments that have open-ended rather than finite responses. Instead of saying, "Read this and answer the multiple-choice questions," we would say, "Read and write about how Columbus came to America."

Scaffolding for High-Ability Students

Students who are gifted need scaffolds (see Chapter 6)—technology, resources, and human help—to push and support them as they move to the next level. Some inclusive strategies include the following:

■ *Build scaffolding into all instruction,* including teacher–student interactions and pairings and groupings of students (Graves & Graves, 1994).

■ *Use computers,* and particularly use the Internet as an information source and exploration tool (Cline, 1999).

■ *Obtain materials* at extremely different levels (Cline, 1999; Tomlinson, 1999).

■ *Bring in experts* who can share with the whole class. Identify mentors with whom high-ability level students can communicate (Cline, 1999; Tomlinson, 1999).

■ *Provide complex and challenging experiences.* Social action projects or community-based experiences involving students with different abilities are powerful sources of learning (Dewey, 1916).

Mixed Ability Groups and Higher Learning

Mixed ability groups can be structured as microcosms of the total class, mixing students of different ability levels, genders, and social, cultural, and ethnic backgrounds. We should aim to have at least two students with higher abilities in such groups. Some useful group learning approaches include:

■ *Social action research projects* in which students investigate an area of concern in their community and take action (Cline, 1999; Sapon-Shevin, 1994a, 1999; Willis, 1995).

■ *Literacy circles* structured as cross-ability groups. A student with mental retardation listens to the book on tape while a gifted student reads the book and other resource information to enrich the discussion. The gifted student may help the student with mental retardation draw from his or her own perspective to interpret the story, a process that can increase interpersonal and leadership skills (Daniels, 1994).

■ *Multiage grouping:* Multiage classes offer reciprocal benefits, as when an experienced ten-year-old with learning disabilities stimulates a bright eight-year-old. Also, mixing classes across age groups can be valuable, as in projects involving elementary and high school students or reading buddy programs mixing upper and lower elementary students (Banks, 1995; Hindley, 1996; Schiller, 1998).

- *Flexible groupings:* If we group kids flexibly and have students move in and out of groups, some short-term ability grouping can work in ways that do not undermine classroom community. However, we must be careful. Such groups should not last more than one day; also, different students should be in such groups around different subjects so that we don't have certain students clustered consistently in either high or low groups (Clark, 1997; Cline, 1999; Kennedy, 1995; Peterson, Tamor, Feen, & Silagy, 2002).
- *Collaborative pairing:* Students work together in pairs. We teach students to work together collaboratively, helping them understand how their differences can be interesting and powerful sources of learning (Cohen, A., 1994; Putnam, 1993; Tarrant, 1999a,b).

Some fear that teachers will be tempted to say to gifted students, "Jennifer, tutor John"—and go off to grade their papers. Instead, we can, with the very same activity, say to our gifted student, "Jennifer, you know that John has difficulties learning to read. This is a very big issue in helping people to learn and grow. I think John could benefit from your help. However, you may want to learn more about the controversies surrounding reading strategies as you work with him. Would you be interested?" Jennifer may spend extra time with John, reading to him, helping him develop webs, and working on collaborative projects that use language, all the time learning through other investigations about what researchers say about learning to read. Of course, collaborative cross-ability learning does not necessarily focus on the nature of difference. Almost any topic allows for expanding a knowledge base to help others.

Expanding Opportunities

All students should have opportunities for accelerating learning and extending learning beyond our classrooms. Some strategies include:

- *Grade acceleration:* Some students skip grades. In highly grade-structured schools, this can be a problem socially for students. In a school with multiage instruction or a secondary school that uses interdisciplinary teaching, however, such "acceleration" fits naturally (Clark, 1997; Cline, 1999).
- *Community experiences:* Opportunities can include cooperative learning, service learning, summer work experiences, community mentorships, and other related activities.
- *Enrichment for all:* Some schools structure enrichment classes a certain portion of the day. At Horton elementary school, for example, students select from a wide range of enrichment activities across grade levels three days a week (Peterson, Tamor, Feen, & Silagy, 2002).
- *Integrated honors programs:* Some honors programs contract with students, using tiered assignments. Enriched work is documented and credited toward honors achievement on students' transcripts, allowing formal credit for more extensive work (Peterson, Tamor, Feen, & Silagy, 2002).

These strategies provide a beginning. We would encourage you to seek more information regarding teaching for gifted students and to use these very strategies to help you structure multilevel, engaging lessons for all students.

Two elementary children use math manipulatives as a teacher listens to understand how the children are thinking about solving the problem. Such hands-on learning materials improve learning for all students, including children with special needs.

"They Can't Speak English"
Students with Language and Cultural Differences

A growing number of students whose primary language is not English and who are limited in their abilities to use oral or written English are attending our schools. Many schools have scores of languages represented (Peterson, Tamor, Feen, & Silagy, 2002). Faltis (1997) suggests the term *second-language learner* to help us focus positively on students. In addition, some students may speak English but use a dialect at home. Black English, or ebonics, has been much discussed, but numerous other nonstandard dialects exist—such as those spoken by whites in the Appalachian region or influenced by other ethnic groups (Polish, Italian, German, etc.). We should not tell students that their home language is "incorrect," an action that can damage self-esteem and create barriers between home and school. Rather, children need to learn the differences between formal and informal modes of speaking and writing. We explain that we use language for different purposes in different places and that standard English is used in school, business, and many other settings. This approach helps us respect students' cultures while helping them learn what Delpit (1995) called the "language of power."

People disagree regarding whether students whose native language is not English should be taught in pull-out bilingual classes (either full time or using a resource room model) or should learn in the general education class with a bilingual specialist providing collaborative support. Many different models have been developed. Once again, we will see that good practices for second-language learners are based on good practices for all students, and that second-language learners enrich our class (Faltis, 1997; Miller-Lachmann & Taylor, 1995; Moore, 1999).

Second-language learners need opportunities for interactions with the teacher, other students, and community members. As we build community (Chapter 11) and arrange the physical space to encourage this (Chapter 14), we are designing a classroom to facilitate second language learning. According to Faltis (1997, p. 1) we must implement five learning conditions:

- High incidence of two-way communicative exchanges between teacher and students and among students, regardless of English-language proficiency;
- Social integration of second-language students with native English-speaking students in all learning activities;
- Thoughtful integration of second-language acquisition principles with content instruction so that as . . . students experience and practice new subject matter knowledge, they develop language as well;
- Involvement and participation of second-language students' home community in classroom and school activities;
- The promotion of critical consciousness . . . to oppose social stratification and promote equity.

Faltis (1997) described four types of oral and written language we can use to give students occasions for language learning:

- *Recounts:* Students retell information known to both teacher and student: "What happened today when we visited the zoo, Juanita?"
- *Accounts:* Student shares new information—a special event, weekend activities.
- *Eventcasts:* Students talk about an event in process; for example, they might explain how to do an activity while it is being demonstrated.
- *Stories:* Students read and write fictional accounts.

We must be aware of potential cultural mismatches having to do with language use in the school and the home. In some families, for example, children are expected to listen and are not allowed to talk with adults. When such children are asked to talk with adults in school, they may have difficulty. Similarly, some cultures emphasize cooperation and group work over individual achievement. Students from such families may have problems performing individually. In classes in which children have frequent daily opportunities to use language, cultural mismatches become less problematic than in situations in which teachers do most of the talking (Faltis, 1997; Moore, 1999).

Whatever their skill level in their home languages, second-language learners have gifts to share—experiences in other countries, different languages, cultural differences. We can draw from the experiences of students. In addition, students may reflect on, write about, explore, or celebrate their own life (Faltis, 1997; Miller-Lachmann & Taylor, 1995; Moore, 1999).

The involvement of their parents is particularly important to bolster second-language learners' sense of belonging—and can enrich the entire class. Parents may read to the class in their home language, perhaps having their child interpret, teaching the class some of their language. Children who speak English in various dialects might ask their parents to share about their background experiences. With sensitivity, we can ensure that the presence of students who speak other languages in our class can work and strengthen our classroom community (Faltis, 1997).

Smart but Not Learning
Students with "Learning Disabilities"

Many students are intelligent yet have trouble with reading, writing, math, or related subjects. According to the National Center for Education Statistics, before 1963 the term **learning disabilities** did not exist; yet between 1977 and 1989, the number of students identified as learning disabled increased 150 percent, growth that continues (Sternberg & Grigorenko, 1999; Office of Special Education Programs, 2000).

What Are Learning Disabilities?

What are learning disabilities, and what causes them? Researchers have three perspectives on causes of learning disabilities: (1) intrinsic, (2) extrinsic, and (3) interactive. These perspectives offer useful insights into other disabilities as well, particularly ADHD and emotional disturbance. Here, let's consider these perspectives as they relate to learning disabilities.

In the Mind of the Student: Intrinsic Explanations.

Historically, learning disabilities have been seen as caused by biological and/or neuropsychological deficits in the child. However, Coles (1987, 2000) and Spear-Swerling and Sternberg (1998) have conducted thorough analyses of the research and have concluded that the evidence does not support this view. As Spear-Swerling and Sternberg (1998, p. 29) state, "the history of LD . . . is more the story of a powerful social and political movement than one about the triumph of scientific progress." Nevertheless, researchers continue to search for biological markers of learning disabilities. Coles (1987, 2000) describes a cycle in which a study seems to validate biological causation only to be followed by additional research that calls into question the validity of these claims. This cycle has repeated itself several times since the early 1980s.

Initially, a *medical* viewpoint predominated in investigations of what would later be called learning disabilities, leading to the use of such terms as *brain injured, minimal brain damage,* and even *cripple-brained* (Spear-Swerling & Sternberg, 1998). The *perceptual–neuropsychological* perspective, popular in the 1960s, stated that underlying abilities—visual–perceptual, auditory–perceptual, memory, and motor abilities—support academic achievement. Although research has largely discounted this perspective, diagnostic tests based on the approach are still used in testing for learning disabilities (Spear-Swerling & Sternberg, 1998).

In the 1970s, the *direct instruction* approach emerged, and direct instruction has remained the leading force as an approach to teaching students identified as having learning disabilities. Direct instruction, as applied to reading, involves task analysis of reading skills: Reading skills are broken down into a series of minute decoding tasks, which are taught by means of behavioral strategies. During the 1980s, holistic approaches (*whole language* and others) were developed, and research began to show evidence of their usefulness in teaching students with learning problems. (Spear-Swerling & Sternberg, 1998).

In 1963 psychologist Samuel Kirk proposed the use of the term *learning disabilities* at a meeting of parents where participants formed the Association of Children with Learning Disabilities (ACLD), launching a movement to seek specialized services in schools. Spear-Swerling and Sternberg (1998) stated that the movement was fueled by middle-class parents, for whom the phrase *with learning disabilities* was highly preferable to other terms—brain-injured, mentally retarded, emotionally disturbed—and who were sophisticated enough to garner political support. As funds for special education grew, schools had incentives to identify students with learning disabilities. Further, the intrinsic view of learning disabilities absolved parents and schools of responsibility.

Definitions of Learning Disabilities: Intrinsic Views Made Official. Since 1963, the definition of *learning disabilities* has changed little, as reflected in the current text of the Individuals with Disabilities Education Act:

> "Specific Learning Disability" means a disorder in one or more of the basic psychological processes involved in understanding or in using language, spoken or written, that may manifest itself in an imperfect ability to listen, think, speak, read, write, spell, or to do mathematical calculations. The term includes such conditions as perceptual disabilities, brain injury, minimal brain dysfunction, dyslexia, and developmental aphasia. The term does not apply to children who have learning problems which are primarily the result of visual, hearing, or motor disabilities, of mental retardation, of emotional disturbance, or of environmental, cultural, or economic disadvantage. (Individuals with Disabilities Education Improvement Act [IDEA], 2004, p. 118)

Until 2004, the IDEA required that students have a severe discrepancy between achievement and intellectual abilities in at least one of seven areas: basic reading skill; reading comprehension; listening comprehension; oral expression; written expression; mathematics calculation; or mathematics reasoning. This approach was a "wait to fail" model since it required that students get more behind before they could be declared eligible for services to provide needed help and support.

PL 108-446 *allowed* school districts to eliminate this requirement. Congress also recommended that schools use a "response to intervention" model in which student responses to high quality, research-based instruction are considered as part of the process of diagnosing students with disabilities. From another perspective, the response to the intervention model provides an approach to early intervening services. States are currently developing strategies for implementing this model. All involve several tiers of assistance that begin with identifying student needs and then use a range of instructional strategies that may provide assistance to students. These strategies are consistent with those outlined below and in chapters 6, 8, and 9.

Spear-Swerling and Sternberg (1998) and Coles (1987, 2000) state that evidence is not clear that a biological difference exists between students with learning disabilities and other poor readers. Further, when children (or adults) are told something is wrong with their brain, they may think, "Why try?" thus negatively affecting their own learning potential (North et al., 1995; Spear-Swerling & Sternberg, 1998).

When describing the characteristics of students with learning disabilities, professionals list many learning problems (see Figure 7.1) Often these statements are so general it is difficult to know what they mean. In addition, such characterizations treat student differences as deficits, often ignoring significant student strengths. Englert and colleagues (1995, 1998), Tarrant (1999a), and Spear-Swerling and Sternberg (1998) suggest that it is more effective to describe students in terms of their abilities to engage in learning tasks—such as their ability to frame questions while reading, trouble converting written print to words and sentences, difficulty understanding words that are "read," or difficulty in understanding mathematical

Figure 7.1

Typical Characteristics Attributed to Individuals Labeled as Having Learning Disabilities

General characteristics include:
- Short attention span
- Hyperactivity or hypoactivity
- Distractibility
- Poor impulse control
- Poor self-concept
- Perceptual processing deficits
- Disorganization
- Difficulty following directions
- Inconsistent behavior
- Difficulty generalizing to new situations
- Left/right confusion
- Difficulty with social skills and peer relationships
- Passive learning style
- Inconsistent academic achievement

In *reading*, difficulties may include:
- Confusing words and letters
- Repeating words
- Losing place
- Disfluency
- Comprehension difficulty

In *writing*, may have difficulty:
- Staying on the line
- Keeping work neat
- Copying with accuracy
- Producing age-appropriate written expression
- Completing work promptly

In *math*, may have difficulty:
- Associating numbers with symbols
- Remembering math facts
- Organizing columns and spacing
- Solving story problems
- Understanding concepts

Source: North et al. (1995).

calculations. An understanding of the functional challenges *and* strengths of each student is more useful than a general label.

Impacts of School, Home, and Community: Extrinsic Views. Other educators look to the impacts of home, school, and community on children—an *extrinsic* view of learning disabilities. Skrtic (1994) and Allington (1994), for example, focus on the types of instruction that are provided to children, suggesting that inadequate instruction may cause students to be identified unnecessarily as having learning disabilities. For these analysts a key solution is to teach differently. Other educators, such as Comer (1997), are concerned about the dissolution of community and family supports.

In some cases, families may not read to children, limiting mediated learning experiences between adult and child (Feuerstein, 1979). According to studies by Kronick (1976), some parents feel incompetent and need their children to be seen as incompetent as well—to confirm their own unworthiness or prevent the child from overshadowing the parent's abilities. Thus, continuation of the child's learning problems may be important in sustaining unhealthy family patterns, and improvement is strongly resisted (Coles, 1987; Miller & Westerman, 1995; Weaver, 1994a,b).

However, it is also true that many families experience stress and may have little social support in raising children. Women, the prime nurturers of children, often work full time. In addition, women have the greatest responsibility for housework and are often isolated from other adults. Fathers often work long hours in an economy in which real (inflation-adjusted) wages for the working and middle classes are falling. Additionally, given that jobs are not available for all who desire them, no strong social pressure exists for all learners to succeed (Coles, 1987, 1998).

Schools also may play critical roles in creating learning difficulties. Erdmann (1994) describes it this way:

The instructional programs in our schools create educational disabilities by: . . .

Teaching children in ways they can't learn:

Marching them through prescribed sets of curriculum objectives as though the sequence were sacred.
Ability grouping kids, forcing low groups to see themselves as non-readers and non-writers.
Denying access to real books until they can "read."
Putting six-year-old children into a position to fail.
Expecting kids to learn language from sitting all day without talking.
Asking questions that call for only one right answer.
Reprimanding children for wrong answers so that they avoid risk-taking in learning.

And then:

Referring children to resource rooms.
Subjecting them to testing that further convinces them they know little.
Stigmatizing them with a pathological diagnosis. (p. 503)

The Person and the Environment: Interactive Views. Other researchers view learning disabilities as functions of interactions between the biological makeup of the child and the school, family, and community environment (Coles, 1987, 1998; Weaver, 1994b). According to this argument, children interact with their families, community, and school in complex ways that may contribute to learning problems. An interactive approach helps us look at children holistically and support them in learning.

A divorced mother has recently lost her job and is angry at her daughter, Theresa, who didn't study for a test. "You are just stupid!" she yells in anger. Later she regrets what she said, but what she doesn't know is that a group of Theresa's friends called her stupid on the playground today. "Maybe I am stupid," thinks Theresa. This begins a cycle that Theresa will figure out only many years later. Unfortunately, she has a structured, rigid teacher who makes this downward cycle worse.

Another example: Andrea struggled mostly in math. She just didn't seem to get it. "I recall trying year after year to complete worksheets that always seemed so difficult for me," she says with a twinge of sadness. "Instead of my teachers trying to figure out ways to help me, my papers were often returned with red marks or sad faces, encouraging me to 'try harder.' " Finally, however, an algebra teacher spent time with her after school. "He kept me from flunking that semester," she says. Only as a young adult in college did Andrea figure out her learning differences and begin to learn successful strategies (Tarrant, A., 1999).

Learning Disability or Difference? From a multiple intelligences perspective, every individual possesses a profile of varied abilities. However, we focus only on selected areas as worthy of serious attention. For example, if a child is tone deaf and has difficulty succeeding in music, this is often noted but not treated as an issue of great concern. We certainly don't refer such a student for special education for learning disabilities in music. However, we could. If we think about it this way, almost everyone has some sort of "learning disability" (Armstrong, 1994; Gardner, 1993). In schools, where the primary intelligences used are linguistic and logico-mathematical, it is telling that these are the arenas of difficulty for students labeled learning disabled; it is also telling that such students often have substantive abilities in other intelligences.

Inclusive Education for Students with Learning Disabilities. Inclusive education for students with learning disabilities has been controversial. This, perhaps, should not be surprising, in view of the fact that the learning disabilities movement developed as an effort to obtain identifiable support services for children who were struggling in school. The Learning Disabilities Association (1993) stated that inclusion should be considered on a "case-by-case" basis; the association expressed grave concern about whether students would receive the instruction and supports they need in general education classes.

Some studies have concluded that, indeed, many students in regular classrooms did not receive the assistance they needed to be successful (Baker & Zigmond, 1995; Jenkins, Jewell, Leicester, Jenkins, & Troutner, 1991). Other studies, however, have demonstrated practices that created success in inclusive classes. Students with learning disabilities have been found to improve academically and socially when the following conditions are in place:

- General and special education teachers collaborate well as equal partners (Tarrant, 1999a,b).
- An engaging literacy curriculum combines authentic involvement in literacy with skills instruction in context (Englert, Mariage, Garmon, & Tarrant, 1998; Fuchs, Fuchs, Hamlett, Phillips, & Karns, 1995; Sexton, Harris, & Graham 1998; Tarrant, 1999a,b; Troia, Graham, & Harris, 1999).
- A sense of community is created in the classroom (Rogers, 1993; Tarrant, 1999a,b).
- Teachers continue to learn and to improve their skills in designing curriculum for diverse learners and in making adaptations.

Typical but Ineffective Instruction. In traditional schools, students with learning disabilities go to a resource room for special help. The resource room may serve as these students' primary classroom, and children may leave only to be **mainstreamed** in art, music, physical education, lunch, and recess; or students may be assigned to the room for a period of time each week or day. The theory is that students will get more intensive help from a teacher with a smaller caseload.

However, resource rooms have many problems, and research has not validated these intended outcomes. First, such classes often stigmatize students. Students widely think of resource rooms as the "dummy room," no matter what positive spin schools try to put on the name. Secondly, students with many different kinds of problems are lumped together—students with reading and writing challenges, needs for assistance in math, problems that center in lack of understanding of English (Diener & Dweck, 1978; Spear-Swerling & Sternberg, 1998). Instruction is most often a simplified version of the regular academic curriculum, not individualized to meet the students' varied needs. Third, instruction typically focuses on isolated skills, rather than engaging students through holistic learning approaches. Fourth, in a resource room students are put in a situation that makes bonding difficult, given that students come from many classes; this tactic ignores the social nature of learning. Finally, when students are pulled out of the general education class, they miss ongoing classroom instruction. At worst, resource rooms are chaotic settings, where students with behavior problems are lumped together, become convinced they cannot learn, and eventually drop out of school (Allington, 1991, 1994; Moody, Vaughn, & Hughes, 2000; Schulte, Osborne, & McKinney, 1990; Vaughn, Moody, & Schumm, 1998).

Most instruction for students with learning disabilities has centered on teaching behaviorally defined skills, in isolation from their authentic use, through direct instruction (Allington, 1991, 1993, 1994; Coles, 1998; Sternberg & Grigorenko, 1999). Connie Weaver indicates that "these learners are typically dosed with more of the skills work that has been difficult for them to do" (Weaver, 1994a, p. 488). Coles (1998, 2000) reviewed current research promoting skills instruction, such as instruction in phonemic awareness and phonics, and found the claims for the superiority of such approaches not substantiated by careful analysis. According to comprehensive reviews of research conducted by Rhodes and Dudley-Marling (1996) and Weaver (1994a), holistic approaches, as described in best practices (see Chapter 8), are effective for all students, including students with special needs. In such approaches, skills, including phonics and phonemic awareness, are taught in the context of a balanced program that emphasizes authentic engagement in literacy and other subjects.

Creative Teaching for Different Learners

What specific practices are helpful to students with learning disabilities? We want to engage students with learning disabilities in authentic activities in which they can see meaning and the connection of school with home and community. We want to help them develop skills and strategies to address difficulties they are having. Let's review some of these creative strategies.

Positive Expectations for "Creative Learners." Perhaps most important is that we believe students with learning disabilities can and will learn, knowing also that students learn differently, at different rates, and with different intelligences and that we simply cannot predict where students will go.

Authentic Learning That Builds on Strengths and Interests. Students with learning disabilities often have important strengths in other intelligences. Such students may be excellent artists, good with building, talented with motors, or engaging in social interactions.

- *Activity-based learning:* Students often benefit from open-ended assignments; project-based learning; or activities such as running a class store, bank, or stock exchange to apply math concepts (Lewis & Doorlag, 1999; Sternberg & Grigorenko, 1999).

■ *Multiple intelligences:* Students with learning disabilities often excel when using sensory and other learning modalities as opposed to verbal and mathematical approaches—music, physical movement, computers (see Chapter 6; Armstrong, 1994; Gardner, 1993).

■ *Authentic literacy strategies:* These strategies involve students in reading and writing through teaching skills in context (see Chapter 8), paired reading, literacy circles, read alouds, guided reading, independent reading, choral reading, drama, storytelling, writers' workshops, journals, and learning logs (Englert et al., 1995; Englert, Mariage, Garmon, & Tarrant, 1998; Rhodes & Dudley-Marling, 1996; Strickland, 1995; Weaver, 1994a).

Relieving Stress by Providing Alternative Modes of Input and Demonstration of Learning. Rather than increasing pressure on students in areas of difficulty, we can try to bypass problem areas, build on strengths, and seek different pathways for learning. We can provide students with space to regroup while giving them engaging alternative activities that challenge them and have the potential for reconnecting them with reading and writing through a different channel. For example, we can:

■ *Reduce pressure in areas of difficulty.* If a student is having difficulty with worksheets, quit giving them. If a student feels stress with reading, find alternative ways he or she can be involved in literacy (Caine & Caine, 1991; Smith, O., 1997). We might give a student smaller assignments and use other methods of structuring tasks so as to build on the student's present functioning levels.

■ *Identify the strengths* of the student, design work to capitalize on these strengths, and ensure genuine recognition or visibility of the student's accomplishments in these areas (Englert et al., 1995, 1998; Rhodes & Dudley-Marling, 1996; Strickland, 1995; Weaver, 1994b).

■ *Use multiple intelligences* as routes back into areas of difficulty—most often into reading, writing, or math. Examples of possible activities: literacy circles in which students work to make a play based on the story in a book; storytelling through picture drawing; hands-on projects; manipulatives in math; physical acting out of mathematical concepts (Armstrong, 1994; Gardner, 1993).

■ *Provide scaffolding* to help the student participate with support. Scaffolding support can come from the teacher (read alouds, writing dictated stories), from other students (buddy reading, group reading), and/or from technology (books on tape, talking software, computer-assisted learning) (Englert et al., 1995; Graves & Graves, 1994; Lee, 1999; Tarrant, 1999a,b).

Here's an illustrative example. Vaughn was in the fifth grade and still had not learned to read. He had difficulty writing and was becoming so frustrated that he lashed out in class or played the clown. Together the teacher and his parents developed a plan that ultimately made a real difference:

■ Assignments typed on the computer

- No handwriting (it was very difficult for Vaughn, and the concentration required made him hate to write)
- Obtaining information aurally through taped books, oral reading in the class, and paired buddy reading
- Reading for fun only when he wanted to
- Assistance by the teacher and parents in organizing his materials
- Time set aside each day in which his parents read with Vaughn and helped him with schoolwork
- Participation in Little League and after-school activities

This plan worked for Vaughn. He was less frustrated, began to enjoy going to school, and gradually acquired excellent computer skills. He and his group developed reports about different animals, which they presented using computer graphics. Slowly Vaughn began to develop greater self-confidence, and within a couple of years he began to pick up books and rapidly improved his reading abilities (Smith, O., 1997).

We should not underestimate the power of simple supports. For example, in 1977 Karl, a high school senior, wrote a paper titled: "Give Me My Crutches and Watch Me Run." He had struggled all through school, had been sent to a special class, and had had lots of "perceptual–motor" training, all to no avail. He had worked hard and gradually learned. In his last year of school, however, he made a miraculous discovery. A counselor suggested that Karl use a tape recorder rather than take notes. This simple strategy made an amazing difference. Nevertheless, Karl was angry. Why had no one thought to make such a simple suggestion throughout all those years of school?

Help in Organizing and Looking Ahead. Students with learning challenges often have difficulty organizing themselves. Here are a few helpful strategies (Sternberg & Grigorenko, 1999; Vaughn, Bos, & Schumm, 1997):

- Teach students to use calendars and organizers, make lists of "to do" projects, and track their performance.
- Teach (and model) filing strategies as minilessons in the context of activities and projects that matter.
- Provide student assignments ahead of time (perhaps on Friday) and send them home to parents so they and the student can prepare for the coming week.
- Provide students with books they can take home.
- Rather than short, isolated skill sessions, provide blocks of time for learning—readers' and writers' workshops and thematic units, for example.
- Teach students to use organizers: SQ3R (survey, question, read, recite, review) for reading, plus story mapping, webbing, and other visual organizers.

Specific, Supportive Feedback on Learning and Progress. All students need ongoing feedback from us regarding learning. We should also teach students to monitor and evaluate themselves and to obtain feedback from their peers (Graves & Graves, 1994; Sternberg & Grigorenko, 1999; Vaughn, Bos, & Schumm, 1997).

Two fourth-grade students read a book together in a reading corner in Mishael Hittie's class. Pairing students provides support from one student to another, making reading a fun activity and increasing student motivation. Allowing students to read where they want—on the floor, at desks, in the hall—strengthens learning.

Social–Emotional Support. Students with learning challenges often become very frustrated in traditional classes when it becomes clear that they are not "keeping up." Teachers' negative messages to parents add to the pressure on these students. If we teach in engaging ways at multiple levels, using alternative methods of accessing information and demonstrating learning, we reduce anxiety. When students have difficulty, we respectfully pull them aside, find out what is happening, and coach them regarding behavior and ways to get their needs met. We will talk more in Chapters 10 through 12 regarding ways to help students with emotional and behavioral issues (Kloomok & Cosden, 1994).

From "Christmas in Purgatory" to Community Membership
Students with Mental Retardation

In an inclusive school, we will teach many students with mental retardation. Whereas students with learning disabilities and students at risk have normal overall intelligence, students with mental retardation have below-average overall intellectual abilities. However, people with mental retardation also show talents and abilities. Students with mental retardation have produced interesting artwork, engaged in drama, and shown strong interpersonal skills. Let's explore the official concept of mental retardation, realities of real people, and ways of teaching students who carry the label of mental retardation.

What Is Mental Retardation?

Over the years the definition of mental retardation has been controversial; in fact, the concept is considered by some to be a social construct conferred on a group of people who do not meet standards established by society. Critics point to the fact that members of minority groups have always been identified as mentally retarded at a higher rate than other people (Office of Special Education Programs, 2000). Until the mid-1980s, in schools throughout the Southwest, for example, Mexican American students were labeled mentally retarded at a very high rate—because students who spoke largely Spanish were given intelligence tests in English. Many students are "six-hour retarded," functioning normally at home and in the community, but at a mentally retarded level in school. Often questions used in intelligence tests have had highly culturally laden content. Definitions and diagnostic procedures have tried to correct these problems, as indicated in the current definition of **mental retardation** (American Association on Mental Retardation [AAMR], 1992, p. 5):

> Mental retardation refers to substantial limitations in present functioning. It is characterized by significantly sub-average intellectual function (IQ of 70–75 or below), existing concurrently with related limitations in two or more of the following applicable adaptive skills areas: communication, self-care, home living, social skills, community use, self-direction, health and safety, functional academics, leisure and work. Mental retardation manifests itself before age 18 . . . with appropriate supports over a sustained period.

IDEA uses similar language:

> "Mental retardation" means significantly sub-average general intellectual functioning existing concurrently with deficits in adaptive behavior and manifested during the developmental period that adversely affects a child's educational performance. (Individuals with Disabilities Education Improvement Act [IDEA], 2004, section 300.7)

Both of these definitions incorporate three key components: (1) intellectual abilities that are significantly below average, (2) deficits in "adaptive behavior," and (3) occurrence before age eighteen or during the "developmental period." The AAMR definition also includes a new, important concept we will discuss below—*support*. These definitions, of course, don't tell us much about people with mental retardation themselves. So let's look from a more personal viewpoint.

People with Mental Retardation in Schools and Communities

Overall the impacts of mental retardation can be described simply. People with mental retardation have less capacity for learning and learn at a slower rate. Below-average intellectual abilities affect all areas of life—a person's ability to use language, work skills, social skills. Yet we really do not know the limits of the capabilities that combinations of support, opportunity, and good instruction create. What we do know is that opportunities for people with mental retardation have been severely limited. The inclusive education movement has facilitated the inclusion of many students with mental retardation, and the results have been positive—in students' academics, social skills, and relationships. Freeman and Alkin (2000) found in their comprehensive research review that the more integrated students with mental retardation were, the higher their achievement.

Levels of Mental Retardation. The most typical measure for diagnosing mental retardation is the individual intelligence test. Historically, IQ scores falling within certain ranges have defined the following levels of mental retardation: borderline (IQs of 70–85), mild or *educable* (55–70), moderate or *trainable* (40–55), severe (25–40), and profound (below 25).

Meeting Two People. Let's meet two people to give you an idea of the different levels at which people with mental retardation function.

Martha is sixteen years old. She is classified as severely mentally retarded. The truth is that we don't know what goes on in Martha's mind. Like most people with severe to profound mental retardation, Martha has other serious physical disabilities. She has seizures periodically (down to about once a month with new medication), difficulties with her heart, and malformations of her mouth that make chewing sometimes difficult. She doesn't speak but makes grunting noises to express pleasure or disapproval. She needs assistance in toileting, in eating, and in moving from place to place in her wheelchair. She is able to use a communication board to signal yes or no. Two years ago Martha, having been in a special education school until age thirteen, began attending a regular high school. She has a circle of friends initiated by a school service club. She checks in each morning at a resource center, where she meets peer buddies who take her to and from classes where students and instructors help support her. In art class, for example, her peer buddy involves her in making decisions about the project—choices of colors, the type of drawing to be done—by asking her yes-and-no questions. Jeanine, her mother, says that this experience has been wonderful for Martha, and students say that she has made a difference in the way they view life.

Kendrick, whom we met in Carol Summers's class at the beginning of this chapter, is classified as having moderate mental retardation. When you see Kendrick in Carol's class, however, he looks like any other student. He has no obvious physical disabilities. The primary difference with Kendrick is that he reads and does math at a much lower level than most students. However, Kendrick also happens to be an artist. In his art class he has made some award-winning collages involving fabric, acrylic paint, and objects glued to the canvas. His teachers provide opportunities at his level. In biology, for example, Kendrick has difficulty with the technical names of animals, so his teachers made flash cards with pictures that he can use as an alternative identification tool. It took some very hard work on his part, but he has actually learned how to dissect frogs with a buddy partner. Kendrick is quiet but well liked.

Mental retardation is often, as in Martha's case, concurrent with other disabilities or syndromes. Down syndrome is a common cause of mental retardation based on a chromosomal abnormality. Such individuals have characteristic facial features and often have heart difficulties and other physical problems that may shorten their life span. Seizures, cerebral palsy, hydrocephalus, and other conditions are sometimes associated with mental retardation. In addition, because social skills also involve cognitive perceptions and the ability to communicate, people with mental retardation may need additional time and effort to understand social cues, to learn how to protect themselves from harm, and to learn how to make friends (Drew & Hardman, 2000; Hickson, Blackman, & Reis, 1995).

Support, Opportunity, Abilities, and Dreams.   Although we do not know the ultimate potential of persons with mental retardation, it is clear that their potential for being contributing community members is much higher as they are given opportunities to participate. Inclusive schooling is a critical component of such opportunities.

Traditionally, students with mental retardation are among the most segregated and isolated of children. Despite the impact of the inclusive schooling movement, children with mental retardation most often attend segregated schools or, at best, separate classes in regular schools. Such schools sometimes involve students in learning "functional" skills—cooking, sewing, work skills. Some school districts have established separate vocational training schools. The best of such programs provide instruction and opportunities for participation in the community and at job sites (Falvey, 1989; Rusch & Mithaug, 1980; Wilcox & Bellamy, 1987). However, these programs still separate students from the larger community and from regular school experiences (Ryndak & Alper, 1996).

Adults with mental retardation are often segregated throughout their lifetimes, living either with their parents or, as explained in Chapter 1, in *group homes* (Braddock, Hemp, Bachelder, & Fujiura, 1995; Hill & Lakin, 1984). They often work in *sheltered workshops* (Murphy & Rogan, 1995; Weiner-Zivolich, 1995).

In recent years parents and people with mental retardation have rejected these limited options, demanding that youngsters be included in general education and that adults be given support so they can live in their own homes, work in real jobs, marry, and participate in the community. Remember Jim from Chapter 1? He is now an integral part of his community, living in his own house with a roommate. Stories of community support and enriched lives for people with mental retardation are growing in research reports and in books and other forms of documentaries (Heal, Haney, & Amado, 1988; Jupp, 1994; Kingsley & Levitz, 1994; Nisbet, 1992; O'Brien, O'Brien, & Jacob, 1998; Schaefer, 1997; Schleien, Ray, & Green, 1997). We are seeing leadership and talent in people with mental retardation. Chris Burke, a person with Down syndrome, starred in the television show *Life Goes On.* People with mental retardation are being supported in advocacy organizations called People First and speaking at regional and national conferences.

The story of Katie (C. Basford, personal communication, April 2000; Ohio Developmental Disabilities Council, 1999) demonstrates how people with mental retardation are gently breaking out of roles assigned to them. Katie graduated from high school in 1998, having been included in general education throughout her school career and having worked part time since age fourteen. She wanted to go to college and started at a local community college, taking courses in basic math, drama, and biology. Candee, her mother, describes the support she is getting:

There is no "program." We have again discovered . . . that there are folks out there willing to give it a go, willing to live with uncertainty, willing to

figure things out. . . . The "modifications" for biology include support from a
tutor, extended time on tests, and taking tests with a reader. . . . She gets advice and
support from her biology teacher, her friends, adult staff on campus (in particular
Connie, who works in the cafeteria and plays a mean game of ping-pong), Lisa who
is a student receptionist. Other students help her with homework in the lounge. Of
course there's always her family. (C. Basford, personal communication, April 2000)

Katie and numerous other people with mental retardation are blazing new trails in schools and community life and are illustrating new possibilities and the importance of the intersection of opportunity and *support*. The AAMR (1992) has included this concept as a central feature of the newest definition of mental retardation. Figure 7.2 describes levels of support, which may vary according to the life area in which they are applied (school, health, home, work).

What might supports look like? Here are a few examples (O'Brien & O'Brien, 1996; Perske & Perske, 1988; President's Committee on Mental Retardation, 1998):

- A circle of friends meets every couple of months. They start with a life dream for the person and develop ideas to help the person reach that dream.
- A friend gives advice and listens to concerns.
- In a sixth-grade classroom a buddy and a student with mental retardation share a project together and help each other.
- A paraprofessional comes in to help Jeremy with medical needs each night in his home.

Teaching for All Abilities

One of the most delightful things about teaching students with mental retardation, when we use good teaching strategies, is seeing how much they can learn. We see example after example of such students' accomplishing more than anyone thought

Figure 7.2

Definitions and Examples of Intensities of Support

Intermittent: Supports on "as needed" basis. Intermittent supports may be high or low intensity when provided.

Limited: An intensity of supports characterized by consistency over time; may be time-limited but are not intermittent.

Extensive: Supports that are characterized by regular involvement (e.g., daily) in at least some environments (e.g., school, home, work) and are not time-limited (long-term support).

Pervasive: Supports characterized by their constancy and high intensity; may be provided across environments and be life-sustaining in nature. Pervasive supports typically involve more staff members and intrusiveness.

Source: Adapted from American Association of Mental Retardation (1992, p. 26).

Artwork reprinted by permission of Martha Perske from *Perske: Pencil Portraits 1971–1990* (Nashville: Abingdon Press, 1998).

possible. As we include and teach students with mental retardation, some key principles will help us avoid some common mistakes—principles effective with other students as well.

Age-appropriate participation: Students are involved in activities at their own level, based on their *chronological age,* not on the supposed "mental age" determined by an IQ test (AAMR, 1992; Ryndak & Alper, 1996).

Natural proportions: People with special needs are not clustered together but are distributed in a school or community. For example, in a school that has twenty classes and ten students with mental retardation, we would not expect to see more than one such student in a class (AAMR, 1992; Ryndak & Alper, 1996).

Supports based on need, not formula: When we have a student with mental retardation in our class, we look at that student's needs and develop a plan that makes sense, using both informal and formal supports. We *do not* automatically assign a paraprofessional to a class for every person with mental retardation, though we expect to arrange for such assistance if it makes sense.

Respect, not benevolence: As we include these students, we move beyond exclusion and beyond treating them as "forever children." We expect them to learn, we treat them with respect, and we challenge them at their current ability level while providing support.

Holistic learning, not behaviorism: Much instructional theory in the field of mental retardation is based on behavior modification, minute task analysis, and highly controlled instructional procedures. Consequently, there is a bias that students with mental retardation need to be taught by means of behavioral rather than holistic approaches. Behavioral techniques have worked, based on the objectives they set; that is, to teach particular skills in particular settings under highly controlled situations. However, these strategies assume that one person is in control and uses reinforcers or aversive consequences to control and shape the behavior of another human being, contributing to a potential sense of disrespect (Charles, 1999; Janney & Snell, 2000b; Reavis & Andrews, 1999). Consequently, when used as the primary learning strategy, these strategies have not led to meaningful improvements in students' quality of life and self-determination.

As students have experience with best practices, the limited research to date is promising (Beloin, 1997; Freeman & Alkin, 2000; Hunt, Staub, Alwell, & Goetz, 1994; Kozleski & Jackson, 1993; Logan, Bakeman, & Keefe, 1997; McDonnell, Hardman, Hightower, & Kiefer-O'Donnell, 1997; Ryndak, Morrison, & Sommerstein, 1999). There is no evidence indicating that people with mental retardation learn differently than other people. They simply learn more slowly and need more support.

Making the Commitment. To be successful with students with mental retardation, we must commit to them as *our students.* The idea of teaching students with mental retardation in our classrooms may seem difficult to us at first. Their skill levels, appearance, and general demeanor may make us afraid of doing something wrong.

First, understand why inclusive schooling is so important for people with mental retardation. People with mental retardation have often lived highly controlled and regulated lives, most often segregated from the rest of society. Kendrick is in his school because his principal was aghast at the notion that one of her students would be sent to the local special program to sit in his seat and color all day. Martha is in high school because her mother discovered that she was being abused at the local separate school. Katie had opportunities from the beginning because her parents insisted she be in a regular school.

The second suggestion is pretty simple. We have to give ourselves space—and forgiveness if we fail. What's amazing is how having these students in our class helps us grow as teachers and human beings. For if we can allow ourselves to not know everything, to admit we don't know but to try anyway, we are likely to be much more supportive of our students. We join them as colearners. We connect with these students and their parents as *people.* We relax, listen, and see.

Self-Determination and Self-Management of Learning. One of the most important things we can do is to help students with mental retardation expand their horizons, make choices, and learn skills for managing their own lives and learning. In 1990 the U.S. Department of Education began a national initiative to help students with disabilities develop "self-determination" skills to direct their own lives (Field,

Martin, Miller, Ward, & Wehmeyer, 1998; Hughes & Agran, 1998). Our classes are among the best places for such skills to be learned. Here are some useful strategies.

- *Develop a MAP* (Chapter 4) for a student with a circle of friends (Chapter 11).
- *Broaden horizons:* More students all the time live in families who are involving them in multiple community experiences. Many students with mental retardation, however, still have lives that are restricted.
- *Build on interests and choices:* We help students cultivate their own interests. If their experiences have been limited, students with mental retardation may not have interests they can express. We can give simple choices—at first (Which color? Which book?) and later move to more complex choices.
- *Teach self-management and learning skills:* The organizing skills we described in the discussion of students with learning disabilities are applicable here as well.

Multilevel Teaching. Students with mental retardation give us experience in improving our teaching for all students. Many will have differences that are almost immediately obvious. Students like Martha won't be able to talk and will have other physical difficulties. Other students, like Kendrick, will show their differences in their academic skills. At younger ages the difference between their abilities and those of other students will be less pronounced, but as they grow, ability differences will widen.

Multilevel teaching is a key strategy in working with students with mental retardation. Like gifted students, these students give us the opportunity to experiment with multilevel approaches. Throughout this book we've suggested multilevel teaching strategies. Some additional examples include the following:

- Use picture cues for multiple purposes: daily schedules (clock faces with simple pictures of activities), use of stick-figure drawings to tell stories as a basic writing strategy.
- Provide books at multiple levels of difficulty with good graphics and illustrations.
- Break complex activities into smaller, simpler parts (task analysis). However, take care not to overdo this.
- Partner students with buddies and have students with mental retardation participate in the elements of an activity that they can do.
- Promote connections of skills across home and school. For example, use similar labeling schemes for certain objects both at home and in school, or have books read at home that reinforce information at school.

Authentic Learning Connected to Life Goals. We can provide opportunities for students to connect with their communities and home life as they learn. Some researchers have developed specialized curricula and catalogues of "life skills" and "community activities" that may give students and families some ideas. These include "life-centered career education" (Brolin, 1993) and the "activities catalogue" (Wilcox & Bellamy, 1987). Following are some suggestions that deal with needs of many such students:

- *Challenge to think and apply skills:* We challenge them to think, scaffolding their learning. We avoid making assumptions about what students can and can't learn and let their learning unfold as it will.

Schools to Visit

Multilevel Learning, Support, and Leadership for Change

Hillside Elementary School
36801 West 11 Mile Road
Farmington Hills, MI 48335
Phone: 248-489-3773
Principal: Kathy Obrizak

Hillside Elementary School is located in the upper-middle-class community of Farmington Hills, Michigan, a near suburb of Detroit. The school has only 3 percent on free and reduced lunch, but the children are racially and ethnically diverse, with some thirty languages represented.

Hillside has been working toward becoming an inclusive school for some ten years and represents many exemplary practices. As of the 2001–02 school year, Hillside included students with autism, learning disabilities, emotional impairment, visual impairment, and severe and multiple disabilities in their classes. A range of *supports* are provided to teachers. *Collaborative consultation* provides teachers with formal opportunities to get input from other staff regarding strategies for children. Two *special education teachers* coteach and collaborate with teachers in planning and instruction. *Other specialists* include bilingual and gifted education teachers and a school psychologist who develops collaborative lessons related to social and emotional learning. An *early intervention team* composed of a teacher and several paraprofessionals come to grades K–2 three times a week for forty-five minutes to focus on literacy instruction. General education teachers have substantial expertise in designing multilevel instruction and in building community in their classrooms. They have received training in areas such as multiple intelligences, learning styles, differentiated instructional strategies, and thematic instruction, which has helped them build their skills.

Over the years inclusion has been presented to and discussed by staff, and ongoing opportunities for dialogue and decision making have been provided, resulting in a clear direction owned by staff. In 2000, for example, an outside consultant questioned the clustering of students with disabilities, bilingual students, and gifted students in specific classes across grade levels. The staff decided, after substantial discussion, to group children heterogeneously. The school has had two special education classes. In 2000 the staff began to include these children in general education classes for increasing portions of the day, and they plan to move ahead toward full inclusion of these students. At each step of the way, time has been provided for thoughtful dialogues to discuss progress, issues, needs, and next steps.

Hillside staff have modeled an exemplary change process and provided leadership for other schools. The previous principal, Dr. Jan Colliton, now assistant superintendent for instruction of the district, cochaired a ten-year strategic planning committee that committed all elementary schools to becoming inclusive schools. In the spring of 2001, Hillside staff, as part of their involvement with the Whole Schooling Consortium, invited some twelve schools to form the Michigan Network for Inclusive Schooling to help one another improve and to promote the expansion of inclusive education in Michigan.

- *Make learning fun, natural, hands-on:* Engaged learning in groups, hands-on activities, and action-oriented learning are particularly helpful.
- *Connect learning to community, home:* All people have difficulty learning an abstract "skill" and then applying it in a real situation. People with mental

retardation have even greater difficulty with such "generalizing." We seek ways for learning to be connected to real community and home living tasks.

Support for Teachers and Students. As we build peer support structures in our class, we will find that these provide much of the support we need. For students with complex needs, such as Martha, we will often need assistance related to medical issues, toileting, and eating from support staff and paraprofessionals. For students themselves, the most important thing we can do is to help them build a network of relationships and friendships. Circles of support and other formal mechanisms can be useful.

How does this look when it all comes together? In the Voices feature Barb McKenzie tells of her daughter Erin's experience in middle school and of the total impact on the school; this description gives us one picture. As we witness what is possible through the experiences and successes of people like Erin, Martha, Kendrick, and Katie, and as we compare their lives to the lives of the people with mental retardation we meet in segregated schools, sheltered workshops, and group homes, we will likely be outraged at the differences. This outrage will go a long way toward giving us both courage and hope as we teach students with mental retardation.

Coming Back
Students with Traumatic Brain Injury (TBI)

When Silas was home from college during the summer, he met the most beautiful girl he had ever seen. Amber was smart, had a terrific personality, and was a lot of fun. She wanted to be a lawyer. They went on a date and had a great time. Just three weeks later Silas got a call from Amber's mother. She had been in a terrible accident and was in the hospital. He went to visit her and kept up with her until he had to return to college. Her body was not badly hurt. However, her head was hit hard: She had **traumatic brain injury (TBI).** Over the next few weeks, Amber gradually recovered physically and began the hard road back to being able to use her mind. At first she could not talk clearly at all, because the part of her brain that was injured dealt with language. She was having to learn many basic skills all over again.

In the fall, Amber was able to go back to school, but it was hard. She looked the same, but clearly something was different. She was able to talk but had trouble getting the words out. Walking was also difficult. She was able to read and write but not nearly at her previous performance level. She knew she was different. She remembered what she was able to do before and was very frustrated; sometimes she would lash out in anger and despair.

Amber's story illustrates one way students acquire a traumatic brain injury and points out several areas of their struggle to recover. In many ways, learning

Voices

Reflections on This Year's Journey toward the Vision for Erin

Erin has been in a general education class since she began school. Barb McKenzie, her mother, reflected on Erin's progress toward her visions for her life (Barb McKenzie, personal communication, April 2001).

Vision: To have a life in a community that values diversity and accentuates strengths and to contribute to that community. *What has happened:*

- Erin's excitement about sitting with friends at lunch and on the bus, and her wanting to share that and other events that happen with friends in our talks each day after school.
- Being a "Dancing Tree" in the English class Mythology Play.
- "Her interest and enthusiasm in the classroom are a stimulus for other students who see Erin taking her classroom activities so seriously"—ecology teacher.
- I am learning so much from Erin. I believe I am the lucky one to have her in my class. After twenty-two years of teaching, sometimes it takes a wonderful student like Erin to make me realize why I chose teaching as a profession"—English teacher.

Vision: To have reciprocal relationships with friends. To communicate and to advocate for herself. *What has happened:*

- The independent creation of her "commercial" for ecology—"Don't smoke! Yucky, Gross, Ugly! So there!"—which became the basis for her science group's commercial.
- Reading "scary stories" around the pretend campfire in English.
- Choir! Choir! Singing in choir! Practicing for Choir! Erin's private singing lessons, which she loves too.
- Ushering at plays—and then getting to watch them too.
- Learning about prejudice in the story *To Kill A Mockingbird.*

Vision: To have the same opportunities to learn and participate in typical classroom, extracurricular, and community activities. To graduate from high school in 2004 with her class and move on to post-secondary options such as college and a career she is interested in. *What has happened:*

- Going to New York with the Heritage group, which included some South students, and seeing Erin's new favorite play/CD, *Phantom of the Opera.*
- Erin turned on the bathroom fan/light and came running out to tell about the air going out of our house, like she had learned in ecology that day.
- Learning the term "recycling" and connecting it to what we have always done with our newspapers, etc.
- Walking past the TV show that her dad was watching about the Aztecs and Tenochtitlan and saying, "Oh, that's world history! The capital."
- Erin easily maneuvering computer tools on a measuring program in math. Seeing her work comfortably with charts and other computer programs.

challenges faced by individuals with TBI are similar to those faced by individuals with learning disabilities and mental retardation. A major difference, however, is that these challenges are brought on suddenly. Thus, the emotional aspect involved is of great concern.

In terms of official definitions, IDEA states that

"Traumatic brain injury" means an acquired injury to the brain caused by an external physical force, resulting in total or partial functional disability or psychosocial impairment, or both, that adversely affects a child's educational performance. Traumatic brain injury applies to open or closed head injuries resulting in mild, moderate, or severe impairments in one or more areas, such as cognition; language; memory; attention; reasoning; abstract thinking; judgment; problem solving; sensory, perceptual and motor abilities; psychosocial behavior; physical functions; information processing; and speech. Traumatic brain injury does not include brain injuries that are congenital or degenerative, or brain injuries induced by brain trauma. (Individuals with Disabilities Education Improvement Act, 2004, 300.7)

Traumatic brain injuries can be caused by any blow to the head. Frequent causes include traffic injuries, sports accidents, and gunshot wounds. The context of such injuries is very important. Auto accidents are frequently associated with alcohol consumption; gunshots with aggression, robberies, and gang wars; and blows to the head with child abuse (North et al., 1995). Students with TBI may have had serious problems in their lives prior to their injury that affect how they adjust.

Students who have a traumatic brain injury may also acquire other disabilities. Dalton, for example, is an eighteen-year-old student who has difficulty walking and uses a wheelchair. He talks haltingly with much effort. He has very limited reading and writing ability and functions very much like a person with severe mental retardation. Dalton was injured when he was seven when his father hit him in the head with a golf club. Perhaps even more than students with mental retardation or learning disabilities, students like Amber and Dalton are disturbing to us, in part because we see how easily we could be similarly disabled. A natural tendency is to flee from a sense of danger. In this case, of course, fleeing typically means excluding such students from our classes. We likely will need to struggle through our own feelings of discomfort and fear.

Because the brain controls so many functions, the impacts of traumatic brain injury can vary greatly. Some students will be able, with effort, to regain significant abilities. Others will not. As with both Amber and Dalton, emotional stability is affected because of trauma, the reality of loss of function, and the fact that brain injuries may affect parts of the brain that control emotional responses. The impacts listed in Figure 7.3 *may* be demonstrated by a student with TBI. Associated physical disabilities, impaired learning, and personality changes are common.

Students with traumatic brain injury have in the past most often been served in separate programs. In an inclusive school, however, we welcome these students into our class. When students have an accident, they will necessarily go through a medical recovery period before they return to school. However, such students seldom return to full functioning and often seem to be very different. They need both support and respect. They will also likely be receiving ongoing medical attention, sometimes necessitating their missing school (Begali, 1992; Bell, 1994; North et al., 1995).

Figure 7.3

Possible Impacts of Traumatic Brain Injury

PHYSICAL IMPAIRMENTS	COGNITIVE IMPAIRMENTS	BEHAVIORAL/EMOTIONAL CHANGES
■ Speech loss	■ Reading skills	■ Fatigue
■ Hearing loss	■ Writing skills	■ Excessive emotions
■ Paralysis	■ Concentration	■ Self-centeredness
■ Vision loss	■ Short-term memory	■ Anxiety
■ Lack of coordination	■ Attention	■ Depression
■ Seizure disorder	■ Long-term memory	■ Difficulty coping
■ Sexual dysfunction	■ Perception	■ Low self-esteem
	■ Judgment	■ Agitation and mood
	■ Planning ability	swings
	■ Sequencing	■ Restlessness
	■ Communication	■ Lack of motivation
	■ Orientation	

We want to help him or her get a sense of what has been going on in school and find the place to reenter our curriculum. We pay close attention to how the student is feeling and to responses from other students. A *circle of support* can be a powerful and helpful forum for organizing ongoing support. At first, students' stamina may be limited and they may attend school a shorter day. We can help by having a place in the school or even in our class, if possible, where the student with TBI can rest. Because specific impacts can be so variable and may not be clear until students are in school, we pay close attention to academic performance and emotional responses. The Tools for the Trek feature summarizes key strategies.

Given the devastation of loss, students with TBI particularly need to capitalize on their strengths; similarly, we need to use these strengths as avenues to reach areas of weakness (Blosser & DePompei, 1989; Cohen, 1991; Gerring & Carney, 1992).

Along the Way
Our Journey with Differently Abled Students

In this chapter, we've viewed our classrooms from the eyes of students who have dramatic academic differences. We've explored instructional strategies and issues of which we need to be particularly mindful. We hope that you continue to see how the overall perspective of building a classroom designed for diversity applies to these students. Inclusive teaching is very different from teaching separately for each student, an impossible task even with a small number of students. Rather, we design classroom structures to incorporate ways of dealing with diverse abilities. A suggestion: If you find yourself feeling a bit overwhelmed, stop a minute. Take a deep breath. Try to capture for yourself a picture of a classroom that can incorporate diverse students. Don't feel that you need to have all the details worked out. If you have a philosophy, understand patterns, and have some beginning specifics, you can use this book and references to make it work. And it will!

Tools *for the* Trek

Useful Strategies for Students with Traumatic Brain Injury

INSTRUCTION
- Place emphasis on the process of learning.
- Help identify best learning approaches.
- Use knowledge of multiple intelligences to identify and build on these strengths.
- Enable students to provide information and demonstrate knowledge using different intelligences.
- Provide verbal and written instructions.
- Minimize expectations of rote memory.
- Question students to be sure information is clear.
- Use materials and class structures through which students can get clarification or repetition of information or directions as needed.
- Use examples (pictures, written, verbal).
- Allow time for processing.
- Accompany homework assignments with written instructions.
- Use advance organizers and help students see logical organization of assignments and work through such tools as mapping or outlines.
- Keep a running journal record of student activities and progress.

ADAPTATIONS
- Permit the use of tape recorders, calculators, typewriters, computers.

- Modify and individualize assignments and tests.
- Give students ample time to work on assignments. Keep assignments reasonable—simple at first, then more complex.
- Help students develop a system for maintaining organization.

BUILDING COMMUNITY AND DEALING WITH BEHAVIORAL CHALLENGES
- Be sensitive to emotional state and help discuss needs and problems.
- Organize small groups in which the student can work.
- Select a classroom buddy to assist students with note taking, keeping on track, staying organized, getting to classes.
- From circle of support.
- Encourage discussion of problems.
- Be sensitive to overload (visual, auditory, etc.) Schedule time for emotional release and rest.
- Be consistent.
- Encourage students to engage in extracurricular activities.

LEARNING ENVIRONMENT
- Designate a place for students to check in and/or out each day.
- Identify places in class where students can rest or reduce stimuli as needed.

Source: Adapted from North et al. (1995).

Stepping Stones

To Inclusive Teaching

1. Seek out and get to know one student who is classified with each of the labels in this chapter—gifted, second-language learner, learning disabled, mentally retarded, brain injured. What are your reactions to this student? List some ideas for how you would include this student in your class.

2. Find another teacher who is teaching students from two or more of these categories in class together. Observe. What is working and what is not? Why?

3. Actively recruit a student with learning disabilities, mental retardation, or traumatic brain injury into your class. Keep notes as you work with the student. What are you learning? What is hard? What is easy? What is a surprise?

4. Go to a conference on including students with different academic abilities learning together. What ideas do you get that you will use?

  ## Key Points

- Best instructional practices provide an environment that helps address the unique needs of students with different types of special needs. We look beyond the label to the child.

- As we use multilevel instruction, gifted students provide leadership, explore difficult topics, help other students, and assist in solving classroom problems, and in so doing have many opportunities to develop their own potential.

- Second-language learners can learn much, with support, and can make real contributions to the life of the class.

- Students with learning disabilities need encouragement and support, opportunities for meaningful reading and learning at their level, and engaging learning based on multiple intelligences that pulls from their strengths.

- Students with mental retardation often function well below grade level but benefit from the modeling of other students in our classroom, from opportunities to work with others on projects and learning activities at their own level, and from the development of long-term relationships.

- Students coming back to school after injuries resulting in traumatic brain injury will need much emotional support as well as our use of multilevel teaching, multiple intelligences strategies, and other approaches to build on their residual strengths, helping them to feel welcomed and gain confidence step by step.

  ## Learning Expeditions

Following are some activities that may extend your learning.

1. Interview an individual considered gifted who was in a special program and another who

was integrated in a general education class. Ask them to describe their school experiences. What happened? How did they feel about the value of their learning and their experiences?

2. Do the same types of interviews with people from other groups discussed in this chapter—second-language learners, and people with learning disabilities, mental retardation, and traumatic brain injury.

3. Observe in a resource room and a special education classroom for students with mental retardation. Describe what you see happening. How does this compare with best practices?

4. Investigate what happens with people with mental retardation in your community. Where do they go to school, work, live? What type of support is available to help them take part in community life?

5. Visit an inclusive school. Observe students with the differences discussed in this chapter in class. What type of instructional approaches are used, and how do these compare with best practices? What happens with these students? Talk with teachers. What do they do differently with these students, and how do they feel about having such students in their classes?

6. Interview parents of students with any of the labels in this chapter. What opinions do the parents have about what occurs in school? What is working and what is not for their child, and why?

CHAPTER GOAL

Explore six exemplary instructional practices that apply the four building blocks of inclusive teaching across subjects.

CHAPTER OBJECTIVES

1. Recognize six exemplary instructional practices for inclusive teaching.

2. Utilize strategies for teaching skills systematically in the context of meaningful learning activities.

3. Understand use of the following best practice strategies in teaching students with wide ranges of abilities well together: thematic learning, classroom workshops, authentic learning experiences, small group activities, representing to learn, and reflective assessment.

4. Know issues and approaches related to standardized testing.

5. Critique the incorporation of best practice strategies in school subjects.

Academic Learning in Inclusive Classes

8

Applying the Four Building Blocks in Best Instructional Practices

$\mathcal{L}$et's visit two high schools to see how their efforts toward inclusive teaching are going. In a history class at Garland Heights High School, we watch twenty-eight students laughing and jostling; yet three others are asleep. The teacher is reviewing a lesson about Vietnam for an exam. He has given a handout of facts he expects the students to know, taken from the information required for the high school graduation test. He reads each question from the handout and has a student read the answer. "Any questions?" he asks after each one. Only about a third of the class is paying attention. "Frank! Turn around," he says as one student playfully smacks another on the leg. The special education teacher goes around to the eight students with disabilities in the class. The students obviously like her. "These students are having a hard time," she comments. "James has low reading abilities," she says about a student whose head is down on his desk.

Finally, the teacher hands out a fifty-item multiple-choice test. We hear groans and yawns and shuffling of feet as students start to work.

Next day, in a social studies class at Highlander High School, we find students all over the room in small groups. The general and special education teachers go from group to group answering questions, talking, challenging, making suggestions. Students occasionally laugh and play around but are very intent on their work. The students explain that they are role-playing the passage of the Indian Removal Bill that led to the forced march of the Cherokee Indians from their native lands in Georgia to territory in what later became Oklahoma. Each group represents a different constituency—the Cherokee Indians, the U.S. government under President Andrew Jackson, plantation owners and farmers, missionaries and northern reformers, and Black Seminoles, a tribe in Florida. Each group is studying its own position, preparing a presentation for Congress, and trying to gain allies from other groups. The students are engaged, discussing very complex ideas (adapted from Bigelow, 1995).

After a while we locate the students with disabilities in the class. Mary, who has cerebral palsy and mild mental retardation, is with the Cherokee Indians group. She does not read well and uses a computer with key guards to type papers. Mary is helping the group understand the rejection felt by the Cherokees based on her experiences with her disability. Juan, a bilingual student with learning disabilities, is part of the plantation owners group. He is a good sketch artist and is making posters that dramatically document his group's perspective. Jonathan, a student with severe mental retardation, is part of the missionaries group. Though he has difficulty communicating more than a yes or no, as the group discusses strategies, they periodically turn to Jonathan and ask questions about what he thinks.

Traveling Notes

Major debates regarding effective teaching practice are under way. On the one hand are those who advocate increased use of standardized curriculum and tests and a focus on skills instruction, from phonemic awareness lessons with young children to direct instruction with older students. On the other hand, many educators suggest that we must start first with *meaning* and have students involved in *authentic* community and social issues and activities.

1. What is your philosophy of instruction? What do you believe is the best way to stimulate real student learning, and why?

2. What is the potential impact of each of these two philosophies on inclusion of students with diverse academic, social–emotional, and sensory–physical abilities learning together?

3. What should teachers and others do in response to these issues?

Best Practices for Teaching and Learning
Applying the Building Blocks of Inclusive Teaching

In this chapter we will build on the foundation of the four building blocks presented in Chapter 6, exploring six key instructional practices that provide an environment in which students with significant differences can learn well together (see Figure 8.1). We'll start with a discussion regarding how *skills* are best learned, then explore the six best practice teaching strategies. We'll conclude by investigating best practices in each of the core subject areas.

Learning Skills in Meaningful Contexts
Strategies for Including All

We often encounter a consistent thesis related to many different types of students with special needs, whether they are learning disabled, mentally retarded, at risk, low income, or members of minorities. The reasoning goes something like this:

- These students are different and they learn differently.
- For them, we must break learning down into small component parts and teach these skills in isolation *before* the students attempt to use them.
- Most often, this requires that the student be taught in a special place.
- They need a specialist trained in their particular condition.

Thus, while many students are engaged in rich, active learning, students with special needs are often engaged in rote drills of isolated skills and facts. These students lose sight of the very purpose of learning—to enjoy, to learn from one another, and do activities that have value for them. The thesis says that these students need to learn *skills* so badly that educators cannot afford to engage them in meaningful, authentic learning. The evidence suggests, however, that best practices are *particularly* important for these students. We do need teaching strategies to help students learn skills, but we need to teach them in the context of authentic learning.

Meaning First, Then Skills and Conventions

According to one exemplary teacher of literacy and social studies, "Meaning and voice come *first*, then the conventions of spelling and grammar, not vice versa. Teaching grammar in isolation is a waste of valuable time," she said one day as we talked with her about her years of experience in the classroom. "We must create time to read and write and put time into what produces results. We teach grammar in the context of writing" (Schiller, 1998).

She described one of her students. He was a very poor writer; however, he started a story about playing football to share with his family. The story meant a lot to him. As he wrote, he worked harder and harder to learn grammatical conventions. He

Figure 8.1

Best Teaching Practices

1. *Integrative, thematic units:* Interdisciplinary instruction over longer time blocks centers around real issues, problems, and concerns in the lives of students and the community.
2. *Classroom workshop:* Classrooms function as laboratories, studios, workshops where students explore and create understanding and products of learning.
3. *Authentic learning experiences:* Learning is connected to reality—in lives of students, families, and the community.
4. *Small group activities:* Students work in small groups to engage in learning.
5. *Representing to learn:* Students use expression and representation to crystallize learning through a variety of media—arts, language, drama, physical movement.
6. *Reflective assessment:* Students and teachers assess learning and growth as an integral part of instruction; assessment uses authentic methods in which students apply skills and demonstrate learning in real contexts.

Source: Daniels & Bizar (1998).

wanted to learn because he had a reason. "If students read and write about what they care about, in time they will care that it is right," the teacher explained, echoing enormous amounts of research and the experience of a host of other teachers.

Minilessons and Explicit Instruction

Many times students learn skills in the context of revising and completing authentic learning assignments. There are also times, however, when students need explicit instruction. Teachers have learned to teach short minilessons to the whole class and also to identify students who have similar needs and periodically to group these students for short minilessons. Teachers are careful that these groups involve different students at different times and that the same students are not "tracked" into special lessons. Teachers call a group together during workshop time when the rest of the class is busy with projects. Sometimes the teacher announces that they are going to conduct a minilesson on a skill and invites all students who want help to attend. The teacher may quietly ask others to join, mentioning that she noticed they have been struggling in this area and would find the minilesson helpful for completing what they are working on. When the teacher can show a specific place in important work where a skill is needed, children are usually interested in learning, and they learn the valuable skill of assessing their own work. Often there will be more students than anticipated at the meeting. The minilesson can address anything from choosing books that are too hard to borrowing in subtraction (Calkins, 1994; Fisher, 1995; Kohn, 1999; Schiller, 1998). Tools include:

- Strategy lessons: We may use students' materials to focus on specific skills; for example, spelling sound combinations, editing skills, or other content area skills.
- Group reflections and dialogue.
- Learning logs: Students keep "process journals" describing how they have approached an inquiry.

At the end they review their journals, considering skills they have learned and need to learn. Of course, we don't expect one minilesson to provide all the learning students need. They use skills in their ongoing lessons. Teachers may regroup students later to work on various aspects of skills. Using minilessons, however, we can provide systematic, explicit instruction without stable, ability-based groups.

Students as Experts

We can identify the skills of our students and encourage them to help one another, thus greatly expanding learning resources. Such student-to-student teaching occurs with teacher guidance and observation. For example, Lisa was writing a story but not using needed quotation marks. The teacher said to her, "Writers use quotation marks." She then asked Lisa to look for examples in books. "You've got it!" she said when Lisa shared what she had done. "Will you be willing to help others now?" Lisa said that she would. Later, when another student asked for help with quotation marks, the teacher said, "John, Lisa is good at quotation marks. Ask her for help." As John learned about quotation marks, the teacher asked him if he too would help other students. For the rest of the year, John and Lisa were the teachers for quotation marks.

Another teacher facilitated this process by developing a "yellow pages" that listed student skills. Students were asked to identify two or three skills in which they excelled and write an advertisement for themselves. These were compiled into a class yellow pages book. Students often consulted this book when they needed help on topics. This project gave every child the opportunity to be the teacher, including students with special needs (Fisher, 1995; Kent, 1997; Schiller, 1998).

Copy Search and Share

Copy search is a tool to teach conventions in any subject. When students are having difficulty with any particular part of their work (e.g., how to start a paragraph or how to employ the scientific method), teachers have students look for models in resources. For example, if students are having trouble creating strong story leads, we would then ask them to work in groups to find examples of leads that grab their interest. "See what you notice. Share at your table." Such sharing helps to structure language in the minds of students. The class might then compile a list of types of leads or of books with good examples to be referenced later. This approach allows all students to contribute (Schiller, 1998).

Thematic, Interdisciplinary Instruction
Organizing Instruction around Authentic, Meaningful Topics

A very useful way of organizing teaching is around themes—key topics or issues that are important or of interest in the lives of students and teachers. We might identify such a theme by brainstorming topics of interest and selecting one or more for study. Members of one eight-grade social studies class, for example, identified themes in which they were interested—race relations, poverty, and the impact of technology.

Artwork reprinted by
permission of Martha
Perske from *Perske: Pen-
cil Portraits 1971–1990*
(Nashville: Abingdon
Press, 1998).

The teacher then matched the district goals and state core curriculum with the topics
the students wanted to learn about.

Alternatively, we can start from state and district curriculum guides and look for
ways to cluster discrete skills around thematic and subject areas of interest. We can
also involve students in looking at these mandated topics and brainstorming themes
and ways of organizing our study in the class. This process engages students in critical
thinking while simultaneously linking our teaching to their interests. When an entire
school selects a schoolwide theme, it engages the whole community while providing
an organizer across subject areas and grade levels. As teachers we have so much information to cover that linking topics provides a realistic way of meeting those goals
(Drake, 1993; Jacobs, 1989).

One useful tool is a **curriculum web.** Figure 8.2 illustrates a web organized
around a schoolwide theme—"Going to the Extremes," a study of how human beings fare and adapt in outer space and the depths of the ocean (Hittie, 1999a). The
curriculum web allows us to identify multiple issues, topics, and information around
a particular theme. From these we can select learning goals and activities (Drake,
1993; Jacobs, 1989; Kovalik, 1994; Young, 1994).

Many secondary schools are developing interdisciplinary teams of teachers who
link language arts, social studies, science, math, and the arts in longer time blocks. For
example, at Brentwood Middle School and Shapton High School, two middle school
and two high school teachers collaborated on a project called "Social Issues Research."

Figure 8.2

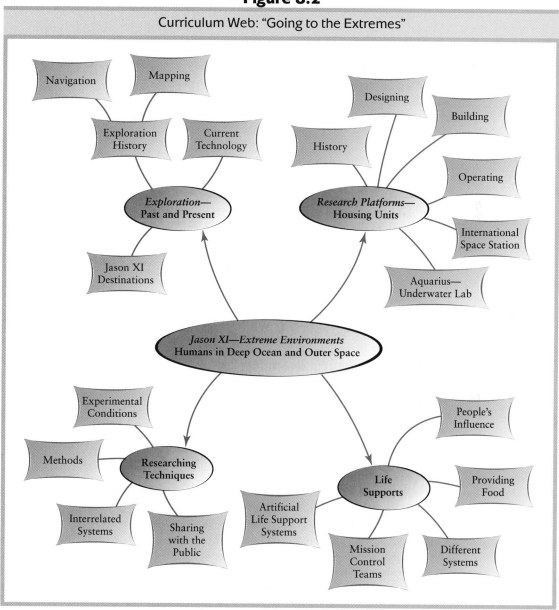

Curriculum Web: "Going to the Extremes"

The classes met four times at the high school, and sixth-grade and twelfth-grade students were paired. In the meetings:

1. Students first brainstormed possible topics. Students read short pieces of fiction including Eve Bunting's *Fly Away Home* (about homelessness) and Maya Angelou's writings. Students free-wrote and then brainstormed topics.

2. In the next two meetings students gathered materials and researched their topic.
3. They then conducted peer conferences on their reports of their findings.

Once the research was done, the teachers said: "Now that you have learned about this topic, how will you make a difference?" The kids decided to raise money to buy an acre of rain forest in Brazil and to collect clothes for a program called Sanctuary for abused children and moms (Schiller, 1998).

Thematic units provide opportunities to structure multilevel teaching in which students engage in challenging but supported learning at their own levels. If we decide to study environmental hazards in our community, for example, some students may conduct complex measurements of chemical levels in water; other students may assist in carrying and setting up equipment and make their own observations at their level of sophistication. Others might pair up to interview people in the community about the environment, one recording notes, another taking photographs. All the students are learning together and sharing what they learn with their peers, no matter what their ability level. (Fisher, Sax, & Pumpian, 1999; Jorgenson, 1998; Sage, 1997).

Classroom Workshop

The **classroom as workshop** is a powerful image for learning; that is, students are engaged in *creating products* that require the use of information, skills, and knowledge. Workshops most often link traditional subjects around themes. In a class we might see some students using a computer to locate information on the Internet and create a PowerPoint presentation. Other students might be recording in their journals, reading novels, or discussing books they are reading in groups. Students at any level can stretch their abilities and thinking. Let's look at a few specific approaches to the classroom as workshop.

Reading Workshop

In *reading workshop* students select books to read at their own level of challenge. During this time they may read alone, in pairs, or in a small group. Students record the books they have read and write in journals regarding their books. The teacher conducts conferences with students to talk about their reading plan, discuss how to think about a book, assess comprehension, or share reading strategies. The teacher may also draw students together for a minilesson based on a specific reading strategy.

An effective inclusive teacher will have a host of reading materials at a wide range of levels—trade books, picture books, reference books, and so on. We help students learn to select reading materials that are easy, just right, and challenging. Most of the time we want students reading **just right books.** At other times, however, reading easy materials is relaxing and enjoyable; and periodically students may want to challenge themselves, particularly in a subject of high interest (Cunningham & Allington, 1999; Duffey-Hester, 1999; Logan & Malone, 1998; Rhodes & Dudley-Marling, 1996; Routman, 1996; Ryndak, Morrison, & Sommerstein, 1999; Tarrant, 1999a, 1999b).

Mishael Hittie helps one of her fourth-grade students select a "just right" book for him in reading workshop. Note the classroom library filled with books on different subjects, of different genres, at differing levels of ability.

Writing Workshop

In *writing workshop* students again select their own topics, often linked to their reading, a science project, or a social studies lesson. We engage students in different genres—poetry, short stories, historical fiction, expository writing. Students keep journals regarding their writing process—ideas to write about, their feelings about the process, or a record of their activities. They write at their own level. The teacher helps them separate *drafting* from *editing* through such strategies as freewriting, in which students write whatever comes to mind with no concern about grammar or spelling. The mechanics come later. Students give feedback and assist one another in editing. Teachers are involved in final editing for *publication* only (Calkins, 1994; Cunningham & Allington, 1999; Graves, 1983; Holdaway, 1979; Routman, 1996).

Individualized spelling lists may be selected from student writing, as illustrated in Figure 8.3. The teacher selects these lists as he or she grades the students' writing, choosing words that are incorrect but close. Students will give each other spelling tests under teacher supervision. (Notice the different levels of complexity in the words in the figure.) Such an approach allows students to be successful, pulling words from

Figure 8.3

Individualized Spelling Lists from Weather Journals

Cathy: probably, travels, autumn, evaporation, equator, movement, video, crystal, glacier, until

Norman: today, cloudy, explode, December, icy, windy, muddy, heat, earth, weather

Kami: revolves, half, certain, autumn, probably, glacier

Jordan: rain, snow, cloud, wet, year, make, some, black, sack, pack

Sean: eight, partly, temperature, degrees, which, blizzard, changes, climate, report, video their own writing. As teachers combine this approach with minilessons and whole group instruction that helps students see regular letter patterns (e.g., *man, can, pan*), spelling proficiency develops effectively.

Math Workshop

In math workshop students explore how math is used and develop a deeper understanding of the meaning of mathematics. For example, teachers can use math manipulatives such as base tens, pattern blocks, and geo-boards to help students shift from knowing "how to do" a numerical operation (such as addition of three-digit numbers) to understanding "why it is done."

Further, teachers can use multiple strategies to help students visualize mathematical operations. Students work together in pairs or small groups, thinking about math and creating, for example, their own methods for adding and subtracting. Curiously, Davis and Maher (1996) indicate that "the present evidence suggests that it is *easier* to invent one's own methods than it is to memorize methods conveyed by other people " (p. 71). Thus, students with learning challenges can excel as they are engaged in thinking with other students. Learning through hands-on activities is particularly helpful for students with special learning needs, as these activities make abstract concepts tangible (Romberg, 1995).

Inquiry Learning

Inquiry learning involves students in developing questions, seeking answers to those questions, and developing products that demonstrate learning. Short, Harste, and Burke (1996) described the "inquiry and authoring cycle," by which we can organize active, student-centered learning, building on the interests and abilities of all students and obtaining authentic opportunities to provide explicit skills instruction. Inquiry learning allows students with special needs to work on projects at their own level of ability, yet to get help and support as needed. Let's explore the inquiry and authoring approach in practice.

Connect to Life Experiences. We help students reflect on their own lives and their interests, developing questions to ask. Strategies to get students started include:

- Students break into pairs, interview each other, and publish the interviews as part of a class newspaper.
- Students interview their families and write "family stories" to share with the class.
- Students create a scrapbook of their lives to introduce themselves to others.

Students can engage at multiple ability levels. In a high school social studies class, for example, a student with mental retardation interviewed his father and recorded the interview on tape. He listened carefully to the tape and used "picture writing" to develop a story. A classmate later transcribed the story in conventional text.

Develop Questions. We can help students formulate questions in which they are interested. Students can use a spiral writing notebook in which they write down ideas about what matters to them, about things they want to know.

Plan Approach. We provide students with guidance in planning how to proceed. If students are to produce poetry or a short story, for example, we have them use a list, web, or sketch sequence to plan and organize important points. If they are to be involved in a collaborative project on a community issue, their plan may involve various methods of gathering and displaying information.

Gather Information. We help students gather, synthesize, and interpret information. Students will implement this step at very differing levels of sophistication. In studying erosion of the soil, for example, some students will make simple drawings of rain taking away soil. Other students may engage in complex mathematical analysis and present charts of erosion under differing conditions. Each student, however, may be putting forth equal effort and learning equal amounts of new information.

Teachers ask focused questions that prompt students to think about where they might find information. We can design guides for conducting interviews and practice interviewing in class, give information on using particular resource tools, and bring materials and people into the class. We establish supports at the level of the student. For example, a student who has difficulty reading and writing is planning to gather information through interviews and collect artifacts from local people. Perhaps the student and a buddy can work together, one of them asking questions and the other writing down the answers. We can help them work out mutual responsibilities.

Draft. As students are ready, they draft their product—a poem, a story, a reflection, a report, an artistic rendition of an event, a play. The type of product being produced depends on the field of study and the student's ability level.

Explore Meaning. Students share with others to gain new perspectives and explore the meaning of their work. Several strategies are useful:

- Sharing circles, in which students share work and solicit comments, ideas, and reactions from others.
- Conferences—individual meetings with the teacher or another student to review work and obtain feedback.
- Student presentations to the entire class regarding their work; classmates may ask questions, give feedback, and so on.

In **peer conferences** students work with one another in groups or pairs to exchange feedback on drafts. Schiller (1998, p. 54) suggests that students comment using prompts such as the following: "This seems to be about . . . ," "What if . . . ," "I thought, . . . ," "I wondered. . . ." We ask students to keep records of their conferences in work folders. To get peer conferences started, we model the process for the class. Teachers can also select students to work with one another. For example, one teacher often linked students with higher and lower abilities to conference together. This raises the level of learning for both students, as one sees higher thinking modeled and the other learns at a deeper level by explaining material. Conference records provide an ongoing assessment record of the students work.

Revise and Edit. Students will revise the product and subsequently obtain assistance for final editing for publication or presentation. This may occur several ways; for example, students may meet at an "editors' table" to edit one another's work, or they may work with the teacher on final review and editing.

Publish and Share Work. Finally, students publish and share their work. There are many ways of doing this in order to recognize and celebrate every student's achievement.

- Incorporate sharing of student products in student-led parent conferences.
- Compile products (poems, stories) around a theme and have a "book signing" at a local bookstore.
- Pair the students' writings with pictures of the students, compile them in a binder, and add to the binder blank sheets that say "We welcome your comments." The teacher may then send the book home, first to those parents the teacher knows will write something to encourage others to contribute.
- These student books are added to the classroom library and enjoyed by others during quiet reading time.

Plan New Inquiries. Finally, we help students understand that inquiry is not just for school but is a tool for life. Students keep "idea folders" that can be used as a start to begin the cycle again.

Authentic Learning
Linking School to the Community

Authentic instruction engages students in tasks connected to real life—to family, community, or larger society; to real-life problems they are likely to encounter outside of the classroom. Newmann and Wehlage (1993) stated that authentic learning:

- Promotes higher-order thinking
- Seeks depth of knowledge (fewer topics are engaged in greater depth)
- Engages students in connecting to the world beyond the classroom
- Encourages student construction of knowledge

What *is* real? What is authentic? Two key aspects of authentic instruction are most important: (1) the topic of focus and (2) the method of engaging students. Topics are authentic when they connect directly to the lives of students and the local community in which they live. This does not mean that we ignore state, national, or global issues, but it does mean that we use the lives of students as the starting place. Sometimes such topics simply involve students in studying real places, events, or people in the community. Frequently topics center on concerns or issues for individuals or the community. A few examples might be useful:

- A student interviews individuals he considers "heroes" and learns about their lives, developing written materials, a poster, a video, or some other depiction.
- Students study a forest at the edge of the school grounds, inventorying the types of animal life they see, writing stories as if they lived in the forest.

- In order to learn to write letters, the class writes a letter to the newspaper regarding an issue. When their letter is published in the paper, they get 600 responses!
- A student's grandparents visit a country that is in the midst of war. The class studies the country and class members write letters welcoming the grandparents to the United States.
- A local industry has just closed, and many people have been laid off. At the same time a new shopping mall is opening and a high-tech industry is being built in a nearby town. A high school class studies why this is happening.

Then there's the question of teaching strategies. At best authentic learning engages students in activities that are meaningful, that are intended to make an impact on the environment or the social life of the community. Students don't do "practice" letters; they write real letters to real people about real issues for real purposes. Students read books for enjoyment, not materials programmed according to certain letter sound combinations. Students gather information regarding real issues. If we want to study a far distant land, we use the Internet and make connections via e-mail with people in that country. We find local people from that country and bring them to class or visit their home or workplace. Authentic learning, then, is not about *preparing* for life. Rather, authentic learning is about *living* life. Through such living experiences students learn at a deep level (Dewey, 1943). We will find that many different levels of ability can be naturally incorporated.

Students with Disabilities and Authentic Learning

Authentic learning that focuses on real-world activities and the real lives of students is particularly important for students with disabilities. Given the well-documented poor outcomes of traditional segregated schooling for students with disabilities, special educators focused for many years on teaching **functional skills,** skills that students are considered to need for daily living and for employment as adults in the community (Brolin, 1993; Falvey, 1989). Some analysts have seen the need for functional skills as contradictory to the move toward inclusive education (Brown et al., 1991; Clark, 1994). The key is to focus authentic learning on the needs and functioning levels of the students involved. The curriculum matrix tool (see Chapter 4, Figure 4.8), for example, can be used to identify needed functional skills of a student and then used to find places in the school curriculum that can promote learning of these skills. The more authentic our curriculum, the more such functional living skills become a natural part of learning. Some very interesting approaches have been developed for authentic learning; let's survey them now.

Microsocieties

In **microsociety** schools, teachers and students operate a miniature civilization that includes a legislature, courts, banks, post office, newspaper, businesses, and an internal revenue service. In the morning students typically attend subject classes, which are taught with a focus on real-world applications. For example, in the English class the emphasis may be on writing and publishing; in mathematics, on personal and social economics;

in social studies, on government. In the afternoon students go to their "jobs" in student-run businesses, government agencies, newspapers, and so forth. A miniature marketplace, currency, and legal system are established and utilized during the school year. *All* students have jobs that they can accomplish at their level of learning (Sommerfield, 1992).

Process Drama

Process drama is a powerful teaching technique that uses theater techniques to engage students and teachers in living through experiences that engage emotions, mind, and body. Begun by Dorothy Heathcote in England in the 1960s, this approach has gained adherents throughout the world (Manley & O'Neill, 1997). Let's observe one class involving two teachers, Randi and Josh.

The story is the Great Fire of 1805, when Detroit burned to the ground. "We are here in 1805. Look around you. What do you see? What was life like in 1805?" says Randi, one of the teachers. The children respond. With guidance Randi and Josh help the students to "see" in their imagination the world of 1805 all around them. There are a few preselected roles for students—farmers, the mayor, mothers. "What does a farmer do?" The teachers illustrate a simple routine that symbolizes planting. "How many people want to be farmers?" they ask. Students raise their hands. "Can you practice being a farmer?" They all act out the role. So it goes, with the drama leading up to the actual event of the fire. All the children have roles in case of fire—carrying ladders, joining the bucket brigade. Josh, with the children's help, makes up simple songs about what is happening. The fire destroys the town. "Here we are looking over at our destroyed city," says Randi, evoking an imaginary scene. "Look!" Half of the students are asked to create a tableau that demonstrates their dismay and horror at the loss of their homes. As they do, Randi says, "Freeze!" The other half of the students discuss the frozen picture they see. "What do they feel? What are they thinking?" Randi asks. The students respond: "Scared. Depressed. Angry." "Why?" inquires Randi. They make thoughtful responses. They are living and feeling a bit of history.

We can incorporate process drama into our daily teaching in many ways. In these dramatic sessions teachers' problems with students virtually disappear. Many students who have trouble with writing and reading shine in dramatic learning (Burke-Hengen & Gillespie, 1995; Rohd, 1998; Wilhelm, 1995; Young, 1994). Some might use these experiences as a springboard to develop their own play. Others might write a story from the perspective of a character and read it to the class or draw pictures of the event (Douglas, 1997; Manley & O'Neill, 1997).

Problem-Based Learning

In **problem-based learning,** students engage in research to solve problems. For example, one class sought to understand health risks posed by low-level nuclear

ANSWERING QUESTIONS
WITH QUESTIONS

wastes. They visited a site where wastes were buried, surveyed the community, conducted experiments, and presented findings and proposed solutions to officials and community activists. One student with challenging needs in this classroom not only assisted in the experiments but also worked on some of his other IEP goals, such as street crossing, orienting to the community, and walking on uneven terrain (Stepien & Gallagher, 1993). The Center for Problem-Based Learning at the Illinois Mathematics and Science Academy has a series of courses and projects in problem-based learning that include short-term projects, which the center dubs "postholes." For example, one "posthole" simulation asks students to respond to a letter from the Nazi Ministry of Propaganda requesting them to review their collections and discard "degenerate" artwork. The teacher asks "What must we know?" to respond to this situation, and students develop solutions (Yager, 1987).

Community-Based Learning

Several strategies can be used to reach out to the community as a tool and place of learning. **Service learning** experiences include assisting in hospitals, museums, community agencies, schools, and other settings via internships and mentorships. One fifteen-year-old student worked mentoring elementary school children he thought might be headed for trouble (Richardson, 1994). Students may participate in cooperative learning with individuals in the community. In one high school students complete a community experience in at least 50 percent of their classes and receive academic credit for each learning experience. For example, several students obtained English credit by working at the local newspaper, a local television station, a nonprofit organization newsletter, and a local book publishing company (Peterson, LeRoy, Field, & Wood, 1992).

Expeditionary Learning

Expeditionary learning programs involve students in community learning organized around themes. An elementary school class, for example, focused on transportation and space exploration; activities included a demonstration of a hot-air balloon, a helicopter landing at the school, and a visit to an air show. In LaCrosse, Wisconsin, a school district developed a School on the River program in which students learn how to canoe, fish, and sample the ecosystem of the Mississippi River (Pitsch, 1994).

Small Group Activities
Heterogeneous Groups Collaborating for Learning

In best practice teaching, we provide multiple opportunities for students to work together. Collaboration requires thought and preparation, however; for students do not automatically know how to share ideas, divide responsibilities, and work peacefully with others. These are skills that must be taught. When it is done well, group work provides a unique opportunity for students across ability levels to learn to work together and assist one another in the learning process. Here are some strategies.

Partner Reading

In **partner reading** we pair students to read together. They sit side by side, reading the same book, taking turns reading and discussing the events of the story. Students of different ability levels can be paired together (Englert et al., 1995).

Literature Circles

As a natural extension of partner reading, **literature circles** bring several children together to read and discuss a book. The students set up their own schedule and decide how they will share. Teachers often also assign simple jobs that rotate, such as finding a moving passage to get the conversation started. Literature circles take conversation to a new level, as students use their personal viewpoints as a springboard to analyze the text. Every child has a viewpoint to share (Daniels, 1994).

Experimenting

Experiments should be ongoing in every classroom. For example, students may be studying light. Some students might set up an experiment in which plants of the same type get exposure to differing amounts and types of light and record the plants' growth. Other students might collect information regarding weather patterns of various regions of the world based on their proximity to the sun. Experimenting is best done in groups of two to four, often with each student playing a different role—observer, recorder, setup person, reporter, and so on. These roles allow children to interact at multiple levels (American Association for the Advancement of Science, 1989).

Editing Groups

In a writing workshop students share ideas, get feedback, and edit one another's work, meeting on a regular basis so that they learn strategies for helping one another and develop trust. This kind of collaboration increases the number of helpers from one—the teacher—to many (Calkins, 1994).

Researching

Organizing students into groups enables them to work together to find information and delve more deeply into a subject. The whole class may discuss a topic and divide it into smaller pieces. In "jigsaw" cooperative learning, different groups study different aspects of the material but are responsible for teaching their particular information to the rest of the class (Johnson & Johnson, 1989b).

Sharing Strategies That Keep All Students Involved

We can involve all students in sharing their ideas about what they read in a variety of ways. Strategies for involving everyone might include (Schiller, 1998):

- *Wraparound:* The teacher poses a question that needs a short answer and asks each student, "What would you put?" All have an opportunity to respond.
- *Book pass:* The teacher pulls several books for each student, using trade books at all reading levels from grade 1 to college. Students then read four minutes (great for students with LD and ADHD); write the title, author, and what they noticed; pass the book to the person on their right; and repeat the pattern.
- *Museum:* Students wander around looking at displays of classmates' writings and favorite objects from home, and write quick Post-it notes to give feedback— "I noticed, felt, wondered," and so on. Students are asked to respond to as many items as they can in a fifteen-minute period. The creators of the displays put the Post-it notes in their writer's notebook and free-write in response.

All of these strategies can be successful in many different classrooms, but they require a strong sense of community that we deliberately nurture. When group activities become part of the everyday routine, our students will surprise us by working together and learning in ways that exceed our expectations. In many classrooms we have seen students of all ages running their own meetings or moving purposefully around the room. This clearly shows that children at all levels can learn to be responsible for their own learning.

Representing to Learn
Creating as Learning

In workshops and authentic learning, students *create products* as they learn. Rather than having students learn first and then show us what they learned, they learn while demonstrating. For example, if students are learning to write short stories, they don't read about writing and then write. They learn by writing, receiving critiques, rewriting, and editing (Daniels & Bizar, 1998). As students develop products, or representations of learning, they engage mind, emotion, and body, strengthening learning. Similarly, while students are learning, teachers are constantly assessing understanding and changing their lesson plans to address what students need to know. Thus, representing to learn helps teachers to better meet the needs of all their children. According to Daniels and Bizar (1998, p. 189), "There are two main types of representing to learn: one especially useful for constructing meaning, and the other for sharing it." Let's explore these.

Constructing Meaning

Many educators recognize that students play an active role in learning and making sense of new information. They construct meaning based on what they already know and expect. One way to help students construct meaning is to have them maintain written journals in which they record their thoughts, reactions, questions, and feelings about a subject. The writing is short, can be a combination of sketches or words, and is often used as a springboard for discussions. Journals can take many forms, as shown in Figure 8.4. Journals are a useful tool to help students organize and retrieve thoughts and ideas. Students, for example, may write in a journal after a science lesson to record key facts or after a social studies lesson to review a concept discussed. They might use a math journal to describe how they understood a problem. Or students might record their feelings about an event in their daily life and use this account later as an idea for a project.

Figure 8.4

Types of Journaling	
Freewriting	Students write as much as they can in a given time span on a given topic.
K-W-L	In three columns students write what they know, what they want to know, and later what they learned.
Dialogue journals	Written conversation about a topic goes back and forth between teacher and student or between student and student.
Learning logs	Continuous writing about what was learned that day, in an academic subject or a given topic. A student's learning log is a place to hold sketches, K-W-Ls, etc.
Book journal	Thoughts, predictions, likes/dislikes, or feelings about a story read.
Double entries	Journal pages divided into columns, where on one side problems can be worked out and on the other side the rationale is explained.

Another way to help students construct meaning is to use comprehension aids and writing/thinking organizers, which assist students in focusing on key elements of either fiction or expository text. By combining words, pictures, and color in story maps and webs, children remember important information in an easily accessible manner. These tools are particularly helpful for students with reading difficulties and can be applied across curriculum areas (Rhodes & Dudley-Marling, 1996; Strickland, 1995; Tomlinson, 1999). Schools are increasingly using software such as Inspiration, which allow easy construction of such tools using computers (Genesis Technologies, 2001).

Sharing Meaning

When students share learning, they may use media such as art, video, music, computer technology, projects, plays, or poetry. For example, they may create a mural to depict what they have learned in a book, write a poem about the differences between two countries, or create a multimedia presentation on the ocean. If students are learning about economics, have them make holiday cards, then market and sell them. One multiage teacher states, "In my class, I have seen students who could not memorize facts about the unit they were studying, but when given the freedom to create, they made creations that took my breath away and illustrated a depth of understanding that surprised me" (S. Huellmantel, personal communication, September 2001).

Stretching Our Comfort Zone

As we begin using these different methods of demonstrating learning, we may not feel confident in our abilities in some arenas. We might, for example, feel comfortable teaching various genres of writing but less comfortable teaching art, music, or computer graphics. We have heard teachers say, "I can't draw. How am I supposed to teach my students to draw?" However, this strategy is not about what *we* can do but about allowing students options to create. In addition, it can be very helpful if we confess our own limitations to students. In doing so we provide a powerful model for students' supporting one another and taking risks.

Reflective Assessment
Meaningful Demonstrations of Learning

Reflective assessment involves a process by which teachers and students understand what a student has learned and how that student learns best. We use the term *reflective* to emphasize the importance of thinking deeply. As our teaching becomes more authentic, so will the assessment practices that we use: We will move from traditional paper-and-pencil tests to methods by which students demonstrate their learning.

When teaching students with diverse abilities, we may be confused about assessment and grading. Will grades be adjusted to accommodate for individual students' disabilities? Will these adjustments be indicated on report cards? Will all students be graded on the same activities? These questions fit into the broader issues concerning best practices for evaluation and grading.

As teaching practices shift from lecture and worksheet to best practices, evaluation of students changes as well. Assessment should be aligned with instruction. For example, if students have been writing stories by choosing their own topics and conferencing with peers, we do not then grade them by supplying a topic that they have to complete on their own. Assessment becomes embedded in classroom instruction. When we use good teaching practices, students will research ideas, solve problems, create projects, and write stories—all of which we will use to assess their learning. We are interested in knowing how students can *use* skills they have learned to create or do something meaningful, not merely whether they can fill out a worksheet of math problems correctly. This approach to assessment helps schoolwork make sense to students with learning difficulties and deepens learning.

Good assessment involves children in writing, discussing, personally reflecting, and sharing their growth and learning with people outside the immediate classroom. Projects involve teamwork so that each student has a stake in everyone doing well. Evaluation focuses on what students have *learned* and how we can push each individual child to the next level of understanding, as opposed to whether children meet abstract standards. It celebrates the differing achievement levels of individual students.

Another function of assessment is to help us create a picture of each child's learning, and **process evaluation** is a method of seeing how students learn as well as what they are able to do. The math standards of the National Council of Teachers of Mathematics (NCTM), for example, state that one of the most important tools is to *listen* to students talk as they learn (1987, 1991).

In thinking about evaluation in new ways, we should also be prepared to relinquish some of our exclusive control on grading. To effectively evaluate growth and learning, we need lots of people involved. Students evaluate themselves and one another. Support teachers and parents provide input as well. Next we discuss some exemplary assessment strategies.

Student-Led Conferences

In student-led conferences students themselves show and explain their work and learning to parents. With teacher guidance, students decide which pieces of their work they want to save for their portfolios. The examples may be chosen because they demonstrate individual growth and progress, show exemplary work overall, or represent the individual student's interests and talents. These chosen examples are placed in the child's portfolio. Parents, siblings, grandparents, and mentors are then invited to portfolio night, and on portfolio night each student conducts his or her own conference with their family. The student goes through the portfolio, discussing each piece of work chosen. Multiple student-led portfolio conferences are conducted at the same time. The teacher greets each family and hands each student his or her portfolio. Thus, the classroom teacher serves as a greeter and facilitator during conference night. In addition to conducting portfolio reviews, the students have an opportunity to show their families around the classroom; they can demonstrate some daily routines, introduce classmates, and show parents classroom resources such as computer programs, curriculum, equipment, and classroom libraries. Classrooms often choose to set up math activities, experiments, or other key activities in the card-marking period to do with the parents. One urban school had a previous attendance rate for parent–teacher conferences of about 20 percent; with student-led conferences attendance increased to 90 percent. Student-led portfolio conferences thus provide opportunities for students to be positively involved in bridging the home–school communications between families and school personnel (Kent, 1997; Wolf, 1989).

Portfolios

Portfolios are collections of students' work that demonstrate growth and learning. Students choose examples of their best work in each subject, as well as work that shows improvement. They also complete an information sheet that describes what they learned and what they could have done better. In one high school class, for example, students included an early piece of work, a later piece of work, a description of their learning, and a reflective essay. Two copies of each portfolio were made, and one was sent home with a cover letter and photos of the student and the class (Kent, 1997; Wolf, 1989).

Conferences

When students are working, they are expected to confer with the teacher to share what they have learned and discuss what they'll do next to improve. **Conferences**

Middle school students study a world atlas as they work on a class project. Collaborative learning can provide opportunities for differing roles so that students can contribute and be challenged at their own levels of ability.

can be one-on-one or in a small group and can focus on developing reading strategies, testing comprehension, sharing a new writing skill, editing a paper, or sharing a finished piece. They can be structured so that other children are working individually or in small groups while the teacher is conducting conferences (Calkins, 1994; Daniels & Bizar, 1998).

Anecdotal Records

Anecdotal records are simple narrative records of what we see and hear as we observe students. It is amazing the insights that we can gain by observing what a child does and how the child reacts over the course of a day. One teacher carries a clipboard and jots notes about five students each day so that by the end of the week she has captured observational information on all twenty-five students in her class. Another makes notes on Post-its and places them in a notebook that has a section for each child. Such observations help us gather information without being restricted by narrow categories, thus deepening our understanding (Calkins, 1994). Figure 8.5 illustrates one fifth-grade teacher's notes regarding her students' reading. The teacher took these notes when reading individually with students during reading workshop, the first time she read aloud with them. The reading levels of books range from grade 1 to grade 7. Although some students are reading at a lower level, they still receive good grades because they are working hard and reading and comprehending well at their level.

Rubrics

As teachers are conferencing, observing students' work in progress, or viewing a final project, they may use a **rubric** or checklist of specific skills or behaviors. For example, a teacher may use a checklist of key reading and verbal expression skills.

Figure 8.5

	Teacher Observation Notes on Students' Reading Performance

GRADE	NOTES
C	Roger: *Shiloh* p. 27. Cases—got second time. Sounded out families. Sack = snack. Wheat = what. Reads kind of rough. Missing basic words like A and there that I know he knows. Bottles = boatels. Deposit = disposal. Totally missed aluminum.
A	Cathey: *A Wrinkle in Time* p. 79. Great flow. Not sure Cheshire—used magic E rule with prompt to figure out. Want = what.
A	Bryant: *Spiders.* It's = it is. Smooth flow—halted over few words not sure. Is = can. Halted over purring and fourth.
B	Joey: *Chang's Paper Pony* p. 48. Pete = pat. Galloped = growled. Dust = treasure. Spread = sprout. We worked on getting meaning from sentence.
A	Aaron: *Soccer Stars* p. 90. Reads nice flow. Corrected that to though. Needs more expression. While = we'll. Corrects most words but pauses to think.

She checks a skill with a date when she sees that skill mastered within authentic classroom work. When a teacher assigns a project, she gives a rubric for the project so that the students are aware of expectations. This tool can be particularly valuable when children are engaged in thinking about what makes a quality example of the work they are trying to achieve and create their own rubrics.

Classroom Tests

Classroom pencil-and-paper tests can be useful, although they should be used sparingly. Often teachers divide the curriculum so that different groups of students study different parts of the same topic and then are expected to share. In this jigsaw approach, if pencil-and-paper tests are used, different groups take different tests. Classroom test questions can also be open-ended and can encourage a variety of answers. One teacher we know allowed her sixth-grade students to use any resource in the classroom to find answers they did not know. This required them both to know information and to possess research skills for finding answers.

Performance Assessment

Finally, we use **performance assessment,** in which we evaluate products or performances of students—a story, a play depicting an episode in history, a science experiment, research on a social issue. We can assess skills involved as well as quality of the product and effort. One teacher had students write and illustrate stories. A middle school teacher had students create artwork with captions in response to a novel they read. A high school football player brought in a shoe box and told a story with action figures. The teacher wrote everything down the student said and handed him the text, saying: "You are a writer" (Herman, Aschbacher, & Winters, 1992).

Grading

Although much research indicates that grading is counterproductive to learning (Kohn, 1999), most schools continue to use some version of the traditional A–E grading system. A typical problem in grading practices is that some students may work very hard and yet get low grades while other students do little and get all A's. One valuable approach in grading is to base grades on three key factors:

1. Effort
2. Growth and improvement
3. Goals reached

Such a scheme is more fair than the typical method of assigning grades based on absolute criteria or on the percentage correct on a test. It also allows us to make good use of best practice assessment strategies described above.

We can ask students to set goals for themselves in our classes. A goal might be expressed as a number of books to be read; as a set of skills on which a student would like to improve; or as a product, such as a short story, play, or artistic depiction, that the student would like to develop. Once students set goals, we can provide simple forms on which they can record progress toward such goals.

One useful strategy is to involve students in evaluating themselves and making grade proposals and justifications. At the end of the card-marking period, some teachers ask students to propose the grade they should receive and to provide evidence that justifies this request. We can also ask students to write reflective journals regarding what they have learned over a particular period. These strategies help involve students in thinking about their progress, thus increasing the meaning of the grades they receive.

Laura Schiller, a sixth-grade teacher, explains how she uses this process: "I have a range of kids in my class," she says, and "some talented and gifted kids have gotten E's because they did not push themselves and take risks." If students typically receive A's, their parents may be concerned about failing grades. However, students have been asked to keep self-evaluations; so when parents inquire, the teacher simply explains her grading process and asks students to show their parents the papers in their folder. Lower-functioning students may get good grades if they are pushing themselves and working hard (Schiller, 1998).

Best Practices and Academic Subjects
Multilevel Instruction Applied

How do these best practices play out in the different subject areas? How do we relate principles of best practice to the mandates of local and state curriculum guides? In this section we'll look at these issues.

Standardized Tests

Standardized tests play a powerful role in today's classrooms. Student scores on these tests often drive community opinions of schools, administrators, and teachers. The tests themselves also may drive what (and often how) we teach. Although standardized tests have always been used in schools, in recent years their use has expanded dramatically, and most schools are under great pressure to produce high test scores.

This increased emphasis on standardized test scores grew out of concern for the nation's education, as articulated in the 1983 report *A Nation at Risk* (National Commission on Excellence in Education, 1983). Education initiatives were launched by the federal government to increase student achievement by (1) defining standards for what students should know, (2) improving teaching and learning, and (3) developing standardized tests (Popham, 2001).

Many policymakers see standards and standardized tests as procedures by which schools can be held accountable for producing effective learning (Popham, 2001). Others see this movement as harming effective learning and increasing racial and socioeconomic divisions across communities. These analysts argue that tests may focus mostly on memorization of facts rather than on deep understanding (Kohn, 1999; Ohanian, 1999) and lead teachers to feel pressured to produce high test scores, even if this means a shift away from best teaching practices. Many schools are spending an increasing amount of instructional time in explicit preparation for the examinations (Hilliard, 2000; Kaiser, 2000; Kohn, 1999, 2000). It also is increasingly common to use test scores to determine students' promotion from one grade to another or even to allow students to graduate from high school, a purpose for which experts agree such tests were not designed (Heubert & Hauser, 1999; Popham, 2001; Townsend, 2000). Finally, national analyses of scores in many states indicates that test results themselves depend much more on the socioeconomic status of students' parents than on schooling practices (Heubert & Hauser, 1999; Hilliard, 2000).

Advocates and educators have hoped that the increased focus on standards for all, combined with IDEA's requirement that students with disabilities have access to the general education curriculum and be given opportunities to participate in state assessments, would assist students with disabilities in being more included and better educated in general education classes (Office of Special Education Programs, 2000a). Others, however, are concerned that increasing numbers of students will be referred to segregated special education classes when they are not able to "keep up" with the increasingly standardized curriculum; in some systems teachers and administrators hope to exempt students with learning differences from the tests (Heubert & Hauser, 1999) or seek not to count these students' test scores so as to increase schools' average scores (Heubert & Hauser, 1999; Peterson, Tamor, Feen, & Silagy, 2002; Thurlow, 2000).

What are best practices in relation to standardized testing? First, we can keep the tests in perspective. We can use the state standards and curriculum guidelines to help us focus on topics—but we can resist any implication that we should organize our whole teaching around the test. We understand that the best hope for the learning of our students, and even for higher test scores, is to use best instructional practices.

Second, we can help students prepare for taking the test using best teaching practices. We teach students to approach the test as a special genre of literature. This is more than having students practice traditional test-taking skills. We teach them to break apart the test and think about what the test is really asking. We involve them in brainstorming strategies. Students write their own questions and share their efforts, using "wraparounds" to explore ideas. We teach students that skilled test takers are those who can move easily from the text to the questions and back. The students spend time learning to write and think in the formal English that test writers use. They learn not to expect the test to be interesting. We would recommend an excellent, readable book by Calkins, Montgomery, Santman, and Falk (1998) that provides best practice strategies for teaching students these skills.

Third, we can follow the letter as well as the spirit of the law related to students with disabilities. IDEA states that students with disabilities must have the same opportunity as other students to take state standardized tests. The Americans with Disabilities Act and Section 504 of the Rehabilitation Act of 1973 require accommodations in the testing process. (We discuss these in Chapter 9.) To access such accommodations, however, a student needs to have either a 504 plan or an Individualized Education Plan (IEP) (see Chapter 4). In addition, for students with moderate to severe disabilities, for whom the regular state test is deemed inappropriate, each state is required by law to develop an **alternative assessment** (Individuals with Disabilities Education Improvement Act [IDEA], 2004).

Fourth, we can provide information to parents and others regarding how the tests work, and we can explain to parents their rights regarding exemptions for their children. In some states taking the standardized test is mandatory. In other states, however, parents have the right to exempt their children.

Finally, we can take action to support effective policies related to standardized testing. A national movement to challenge standardized tests is growing. We can educate ourselves regarding the impact of standardized tests, develop our own opinion, and become part of the effort to influence policymakers to create the conditions most effective for learning. See Kohn (1999) and Ohanian (1999), and see the FairTest website (**www.fairtest.org**) for comprehensive critiques of standardized testing and information on effective models of assessment.

Literacy

We walk into Joanne Butler's first-grade class and see students all over the room, some on the floor, some at their desks, a few in groups of two or three. She welcomes us and explains that this is "reading workshop" time. All the children are reading—most in picture books with a few words, but a couple in chapter books. Joanne helps her students select books in which they are interested. "Earlier this week," she says, "we all got down on the floor and picked out books. They helped each other. I asked them to get one book that was easy, one that was just right, and one that they liked but was challenging." Some students are reading silently alone. Others are reading in pairs. Students meet together to talk about their books and ask questions. This helps all the children have experiences with different books and learn to ask questions. Joanne reads some of the harder books aloud to the class as a group. Curious, we ask, "How are they learning their basic phonics?" She replies that she observes the students reading and writing and talks with them, figuring out what problems they are having. "I might cluster students for a minilesson, say on the different ways to say the letter *g*. As I figure out who is good at particular skills, I have students learn to come to one another for help so that I am actually ending up with twenty-four teachers in this room rather than just myself," Joanne laughs (Peterson, Tamor, Feen, & Silagy, 2002; Schiller, 1998).

Best practice literacy instruction helps children understand and communicate meaning through authentic activities. Students learn to read and write by doing just that—reading and writing. Figure 8.6 illustrates some exemplary literacy strategies used across age groups. Students listen to reading, practice with family and friends, and are taught skills within the context of their own written work and reading books. Teaching literacy this way allows each child to learn at their own pace and own level (Daniels, 1994; Goodman, 1986; Holdaway, 1979; Smith, F., 1997, 1998).

Mathematics

Children are very often intimidated by math. Let's visit a classroom in which students are working on a worksheet of algebra problems.

Figure 8.6

Selected Exemplary Literacy Strategies for Inclusive Classrooms

STRATEGY	DESCRIPTION	SCAFFOLDS AND MULTILEVEL TEACHING
Thematic unit	Teachers use a topic of study to focus literacy activities and link to other subjects. Students use reading/writing to investigate and explore the topic.	Students with higher abilities investigate in greater depth.
Choral reading	Sstudents read poems, predictable books, class stories, and student-authored texts together out loud.	Students participate at the level of which they are capable.
Read alouds	Teacher reads books aloud and dramatically and engages students in predicting, analyzing, and summarizing texts.	All students listen or read along at their level of ability.
Reading workshop	Students read along with another student, an adult or peer, or listen to a story on tape at a listening center. They share what they have read with a partner and write responses in a journal.	Students read materials of their own choosing at their own level.
Partner reading/ writing	Students read or write with a buddy or small group. Students may listen to stories with a partner, respond in writing to text, complete story maps, develop a play from a story.	Students of differing abilities are paired or grouped together.
Sharing chair	Students share with the whole class or a small group—literature, poems, their own writing, a picture representing part of a story. Students ask and answer questions.	Students share at their level of ability. As needed, they are given assistance in asking and answering questions. Teacher models respect.
Comprehension aids—story maps, webs, etc.	Students use these aids to help them organize their predictions and reading results, using different variables. They can write or draw pictures.	Students use aids at their ability level. May work with buddy or teacher who provides assistance in thinking through questions.
Journal writing	Students keep readers' and writers' journals, responding to reading and describing their writing process.	Students write at their ability level, sketch pictures, or use a tape recorder.

(continued)

Figure 8.6

Continued

STRATEGY	DESCRIPTION	SCAFFOLDS AND MULTILEVEL TEACHING
Dramatic play of reading and writing	Students work in pairs or small groups to develop a dramatic enactment of a poem, story, or expository text.	Students take different roles in this process at their ability level.
Writing workshop	Students work with one another to draft, revise, edit, and publish. Students peer conference to assist and provide feedback. The teacher reviews final drafts and helps students edit and publish.	Students produce writing at their ability level.
Minilessons	Teacher provides instruction in specific skills—to whole class or to small groups of students with similar skill needs. Students identified as "class experts" help other students.	Teacher provides minilessons aimed at ability levels and skill development needs of students.
Publishing student work	Teachers find multiple ways to "publish" students' work—displays of poetry, summaries and illustrations of stories in read alouds, collections of edited student work in binders, etc.	All students have work published at their own level of ability with support.

Source: Adapted from Tarrant (1999a,b).

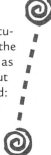

We see examples on the board as the teacher walks around helping. Several students are finished and look very bored. Most are struggling. One student in the back of the room is simply staring at his paper, his head down, his eyes sad as he attempts to decipher the exercise. A buddy leans over and explains again, but he shakes his head, saying, "I can't do it." Later, the teacher too shakes his head: "Angus tries hard but simply cannot do basic algebra." We leave feeling sad that both Angus and the teacher have given up on his math abilities.

What is it about math that intrigues some and makes others incredibly frustrated? What do we do about students like Angus? Fortunately, important changes are happening in the way we teach math. Let's visit another classroom at math time.

Linda asks the students to gather at the front of the room. They are learning about place value, and two numbers are on the board. "Which one is the larger number?" she asks. She continues to ask questions as the students get more descriptive explaining their thinking. Everyone gets a chance to share, no matter how sophisticated or simple their thoughts. After the discussion Linda asks the students to write what they think in their journals. They then play a game that teaches about place value. "Several students have had a lot of problems in math in previous classes," Linda says. "However, in here, although they are learning slowly, they love math and ask to play math games in their free time."

Math educators (National Council of Teachers of Mathematics, 1987) have restructured mathematics teaching greatly in recent years. Rather than seeing math as the memorization of numerical algorithms, the new approach to mathematics seeks to create *mathematical power*—the capacity to use mathematics as a tool for daily life as well as in the specialized applications of science, technology, economics, and so forth. This shift dramatically increases our capability to teach to multiple levels and to involve special needs students. The standards issued by the National Council of Teachers of Mathematics (1987) stress the following:

- More time for children to explore and invent alternative strategies for computing mentally
- Increased focus on concrete experience, using objects rather than symbols
- Focus on mathematics as a way of thinking; emphasis on teacher's listening to and understanding how students are thinking
- Discussion among students regarding approaches to solving mathematics problems
- Emphasis on taking students' thinking seriously—listening, coaching, reflecting, and challenging as students construct approaches to mathematical problems

Science

Champagne, Newell, and Goodnough (1996) describe the excitement of Ms. Carrese, a high school science teacher, on her return from a conference at which she learned new approaches to teaching science. She decided to put these new ideas to work in a project she called "The Archeazoan Project." She set the stage for her students. "The town of Archeazo has no electricity," she explained. "The town board will hire several consulting firms representing solar, nuclear, chemical, hydro, and wind energy to develop proposals. The class will divide into groups forming consulting firms to advise citizens." She further explained that they were to prepare and present their proposals to include the following elements: "pros and cons, how your form of energy is converted to electricity, why yours is most beneficial, and hazards." "It was great. It was so much fun . . . and . . . I didn't have to stand there and say, 'This is solar energy'" (Champagne, Newell, & Goodnough,

1996, p. 24). She talked about how helpful this project was to several students with disabilities. One student with ADHD seldom finished homework assignments. However, he became engaged with the hands-on Archeazoan activities and worked very hard. He was in charge of making the display that illustrated complex information in an interesting way. His parents were delighted that he was excited about learning.

Reforms in science education have been founded on two interactive goals, which Anderson and Fetters (1996) summarized as (1) meaningful understanding and (2) science for all. We involve students in learning through hands-on activities to which they can relate, drawing together multiple disciplines—science, math, literacy, social studies—and the scientific disciplines themselves. These activities focus on major concepts and involve in-depth investigation of a limited number of topics. Learning involves students in active *inquiry* about problems and issues rather than stressing memorization of isolated facts. Technology, the community, and peers together provide social, technical, and intellectual resources to support student learning. In Ms. Carrese's class, for example, students contacted experts in the community, used the library and the Internet, and called resource organizations to gather information (Champagne, Newell, & Goodnough, 1996).

The goals of science education have also shifted. Rather than seeing science as only for scientific specialists, students learn how science is an integral part of everyday life. Studies suggest that these trends in science education have the potential to assist students with disabilities, as well as other students, achieve at a higher level. Several major projects have sought to develop curricula to assist teachers and to include and support students with a wide range of abilities (American Association for the Advancement of Science, 1989):

- *Science, Technology, and Society (STS)* seeks to promote acceptance and celebration of diverse student contributions (Yager, 1990).
- The *Jason Project* links students through the Internet and teleconferencing to investigations of recognized scientists. Some schools have organized schoolwide themes based on the yearly changing focus of the Jason Project.
- The *Voyager Project* involves students in a wide range of hands-on activities by which they can construct their own understanding and investigate subjects.

Social Studies

Social studies educators take two general approaches. In one approach, social studies instruction aims to preserve existing values and structures. In the second approach, teachers help students critique social practices with the goal of encouraging social change (Hursch & Ross, 2000). Some teachers mix these two approaches. Given these complexities and the many subfields of social studies (history, psychology, sociology, and more), it is not surprising that the efforts of this discipline to develop both content and teaching/learning standards has been riddled with conflict (Gibson, 1999; Zemelman, Daniels, & Hyde, 1998).

Do we want to engage students so that they think for themselves, gaining tools and skills to analyze communities, issues, and tools for change? Some teachers involve students in exciting and often important projects; these projects help students to value and understand resources in local communities while at the same time learning to ask important questions, to critique their social situation, and to promote change. Social studies can come to life as teachers take the risk of engaging students in real learning. Given the typical exclusion of students with disabilities, and given issues related to differences in ability, race, gender, sexual orientation, and/or socioeconomic status, a class of diverse students is often a microcosm of society. The dynamics of the class then become an opportunity for learning (Bigelow, Christensen, Karp, Miner, & Peterson, 1994; Burke-Hengen & Gillespie, 1995; Isaac, 1992; Young, 1994).

The Arts and Music

In elementary schools, music, art, and gym are traditionally thought of as the "specials" and are taught as separate subjects. Increasingly, however, the interdependence of the arts and academic education are being recognized. For teachers and schools for whom teaching diverse learners using brain-based learning, addressing multiple intelligences, and respecting various learning styles are serious endeavors, the arts are integrated throughout the curriculum. Rather than having only the "art class," such teachers and schools view visual arts, drama, and music as integral tools to support the learning of any academic subject. This view encourages the production of art as a way of life for all, not merely for for the specialized few. In best teaching practices, then, the arts become a part of the total school and teachers of the arts become total school resource staff. They support academic teachers by incorporating academic themes into art and music classes, and they develop collaborative programs with academic teachers around schoolwide or multiclass themes. Given that many students who struggle with traditional academic subjects excel in the arts, this approach gives such students new opportunities for success and recognition. In other words, the visual arts and music provide further modes of expression of learning. We also see therapists, such as art therapists and occupational therapists, working collaboratively with art teachers on arts projects that will enhance therapeutic goals for students (Cole, 1995; Johnson, 1997; Kovalik, 1994; Short, Harste, & Burke, 1996; Young, 1994; Zemelman, Daniels, & Hyde, 1998).

Physical Education

Physical education courses are full of opportunities for instructors to allow students to function at multiple levels of ability. In a school that is seeking to use effective learning principles, physical movement, well-being, and skill can be integrated into and supportive of the total school curriculum rather than being an isolated subject. We might see elementary teachers incorporating dance and games into their thematic study about ancient Greece or a country in Africa. We might see math teachers using physical movements of the class as a way to demonstrate mathematical functions. Relatedly, we might see physical therapists or adapted physical education teachers (teachers with specialized training in working with students with disabilities) collaborating with general physical education teachers helping to integrate a

▰▰●▰▰●●▰● **Stepping Stones** ▰●▰▰●●▰●●▰●

To Inclusive Teaching

1. Conduct a self-assessment of your own teaching. Compare your teaching approaches with those listed in the principles (Figure 8.1) and the six best practices (Figure 8.2). What does this comparison tell you? Would you be willing to strengthen your use of best practices? Why or why not?

2. Over the school year, use one of the six best practices in your class. Incorporate the four building blocks as you do so. Keep notes regarding how your brightest and most struggling students respond. What did you learn? Can you move your teaching more toward using these practices? How?

3. Identify the student in your class who is having the most difficulty. Try to understand this student and to design a few lessons for the whole class that use one or more of the six best practices but would specifically be helpful for this student. What did you learn? How did this student and the total class respond?

4. Visit a class with a teacher whom you know to be very skilled in using best teaching practices. How do students with lower and higher abilities fare? What specific strategies or ways of thinking did you notice that could help you deal with students with academic differences?

student with cerebral palsy who is in a wheelchair into the overall program (Block & Zeman, 1996; LaMaster, Gall, Kinchin, & Siedentop, 1998; Reeves & Stein, 1999; Schilling & Coles, 1997; Villa & Thousand, 1996).

Unified Sports is a program that combines equal numbers of athletes with and without mental retardation and other disabilities, of similar age and ability, on teams that compete against other Unified Sports teams. Unified Sports was launched throughout the United States in 1989, with basketball, bowling, distance running and walking, soccer, softball, volleyball, and cycling; other sports are on the way (North Carolina Special Olympics, 2001). A manual for coaches is available, and most states now have coordinators who can give physical education teachers information on how to begin (Connecticut Interscholastic Athletic Conference, 2001).

Making Schools Work for All Students: The Beginning and End of the Journey

We talked not long ago with a group of teachers in a school that is seeking to become an inclusive school. A student with a very severe disability, Denise, is in the sixth grade with support by a paraprofessional. Several students with autism are also in general education classes full time. One day we watched as Denise's whole class was energetically engaged in discussing questions they would e-mail to a man who was making a movie in the northern part of the state. The students called out all sorts of good ideas; a student recorder wrote them down. I thought, "This is a terrific authentic writing project." Afterward the teacher explained to us that the man making the movie is Denise's father, to whom she is very close. Partly because he'll be out on the movie set for the next few months, Denise has been very down and depressed. The teacher came up with this authentic activity, connected to their ongoing class objectives, to help Denise feel better. "Denise," she said to this student, whose eyes sparkle and connect as the teacher talks but who has no verbal language, "we are going to ask these questions to your dad and he's going to write us back!" Denise laughed.

We held a focus group discussion with teachers regarding their progress toward inclusive teaching and listened carefully as Denise's teacher talked. "What we have to realize," she said, "is that we don't ask ourselves, 'How do I include this one kid?' We ask ourselves, 'How do I help create a culture and way of teaching in my class that welcomes all, where all students can work to their own potential?'" We agree with Denise's teacher. In this chapter we've reviewed some best practices in teaching. We've suggested that these practices offer us many strategies to help students learn at multiple levels. Our challenge and opportunity is to teach and to build a classroom culture in ways that really do support students in learning together. As we think about it, the sun shines a bit more brightly in our mind's eye. We see schools full of teaching and learning and laughter and interest, beyond the dark and dismal images of learning that lie behind us on this road we are traveling.

Key Points

- Six key, complementary, interactive instructional strategies provide opportunities to implement the four building blocks effectively, particularly allowing students to learn at their own level of ability and challenge.

- Discrete skills, from phonemic awareness to use of grammar to computational skills in mathematics, are best learned in the context of authentic, meaningful learning activities.

- We can use activities such as minilessons, child-to-child sharing of expertise, and searches for examples of skills in context to help students learn skills effectively without ability grouping or segregated pull-out instruction.

- *Thematic units* on meaningful and interesting topics provide an effective way to organize instruction around a web of interrelated ideas and issues.

- *Classroom workshops* allow students to learn by engaging in productive work that links themes and subjects.

- *Authentic learning* connects instruction to activities that have real meaning in the life of our students.

- *Small group activities* allow students to work in heterogeneous groups on meaningful projects.

- In *representing to learn*, creating products becomes learning in and of itself as students crystallize information and knowledge through varied media.

- *Reflective assessment* moves away from multiple-choice, fill-in-the-blank, or standardized tests and allows students to demonstrate learning in multiple and interesting ways—journals, portfolios, products, student-led conferences.

Learning Expeditions

Following are some activities that may extend your learning.

1. Visit a school that is reported to be doing a good job of inclusive education. Observe

classes; talk with teachers about the teaching strategies they use and about how they deal with students who have ability differences. What conclusions might you draw?

2. Develop a multilevel thematic unit of study based on using best practices presented in this chapter.

3. Observe a student with a disability and interview him or her about interests, hobbies, and hopes. Make some recommendations, based on ideas in this chapter, about how teaching could be improved for all students in ways that might help this student learn more.

4. Observe a class taught by a teacher who has students with diverse ability levels and who is known to be a good teacher. What teaching techniques are used? How does the teacher incorporate students with multiple ability levels? How stressful is this teaching situation for the teacher, and how does he or she feel about it?

5. Review this chapter, keeping a journal as you read and record your feelings, thoughts, questions, and ideas. What do you want to do as a teacher? How do you feel about teaching using what we've called best practices? How do you feel about engaging learners at multiple ability levels? Why? What are the roots in your own experiences in the past?

Understand the theory and practice of adapting curriculum and instruction to enable students to participate successfully in inclusive classes.

CHAPTER OBJECTIVES

1. Comprehend a framework that can clarify the match of student to environment and guide instructional adaptations.

2. Utilize a systematic process for understanding student needs and developing adaptations and modifications.

3. Understand and implement practical adaptations of academic instruction.

4. Visualize how adaptations work holistically to support individual students.

Adapting 9 Academic Instruction

Strategies for Meeting Special Needs

How goes it for John? His teacher, Mari-Jane Medenwaldt, has worked hard with him all year. She talks about her challenging student (Medenwaldt, 2000, pp. 3–4):

> It is May, and John is beginning to reach his "limit" in terms of output, attention, and ability to stay focused. However, unlike the students whose language abilities gave them the freedom to communicate their feelings, John's fatigue and frustration is beginning to manifest itself as roaming through the hallways on endless visits to the water fountain, bothering other working students, and, on the worst days, tossed desks and slow-motion punching gestures. In an attempt to respond to his frustration during writing periods, I decided to adapt and modify some of his activities and formatted a "schedule" with different choices.
> *Hurray for me . . .*
> The notion of negotiation becomes very clear as later John presents me with an "organizer" he has created outlining his choices for activities during our morning writing period.
> *Hurray for John . . .*
> As I reflect back on my hasty efforts to adapt and curb his behavior by "scheduling" his activities, I realize I neglected to *ask him* for suggestions. The process had become external to

him, yet it was *for him*. Underlying my quick decision was also a sense of mistrust and inability to consider that, given choices, John would choose educationally sound learning activities. His self-generated schedule is an extremely power-ful communication; it is a negotiation document, telling me to relinquish some of the curriculum power that I hold, yet also, by adapting the format and layout of the schedule I had given him, a collaborative gesture show-ing me what I needed to do to support his learning. John used his orga-nizer, which changed and mutated a few more times, until the end of the school year.

   Hurray for us!

In Mari-Jane's story, we see how *adaptations,* the subject of this chapter, can move from impersonal, technical strategies to ways to connect with chil-dren as human beings. Mari-Jane describes how community, care, academics, and supportive interactions with students all roll into one as we seek to make adaptations so students can succeed.
Mari-Jane reflects

   . . . To move from this place of accommodation towards true inclusion or care is to begin speaking honestly from our experience. For inclusion to truly exist, we need to think and talk about receptivity, which is the heart of inclusion, and evolve our practice outwards from that philosophical cen-ter. This includes *our* ability to receive the care of others, and to risk sur-rendering the control we exercise. It involves re-negotiating the classroom space with resource teachers, teaching assistants, and parents to engage in a truly collaborative process. As my students and I have learned, caring is laughter, belonging, support, strength, membership, and success. (Meden-waldt, 2000, p. 7)

Recently we asked a group of teachers what adaptations they had observed in schools. They responded with numerous stories of students who were having diffi-culties and of simple adaptations that had helped. In one class a student was given fewer spelling words. In another a student whose parents were getting divorced was very upset; the teacher talked with him, let him know she cared, and looked for ways to help him gain control. In another the teacher used reading materials and a com-puter program with many illustrations and photographs to help a student under-stand information.

   We also asked if they knew at least one poor teacher. When everyone said yes, we asked them to describe this teacher. Among the responses: "Teaches the lesson without attending to whether students are learning," "is rigid, allowing students few opportunities for choices," and "humiliates students who are having difficulties."

   As these comments indicate, adapting curriculum is *not* something done only for special needs students. Good teachers adapt all the time. Good teachers know their subjects and are masters at designing strategies by which students learn facts, ideas, theories, and skills. When teaching does not address learners' needs, good teachers change. When teachers consciously understand strategies for adapting instruction for students with special needs, they are more effective with all their students. We are always amazed at what teachers already know, and teachers often surprise them-selves as well.

A high school marching band includes a student in a wheelchair who plays the xylophone that she holds on her lap, a simple adaptation that allows her to be a full member of the band.

Traveling Notes

Mari-Jane and the group of teachers cited in the text here offer vivid and humane examples of "adapting" teaching. Making adaptations is not a mere technical process but involves the meeting of a teacher with the essence of what is happening with a student. As we consider the strategies in this chapter let's think about these stories and keep in mind the following questions:

1. How can we adapt instruction for students who don't seem to be learning or whose abilities don't match the way we are teaching?

2. Should we have to adapt teaching? Shouldn't all students be able to keep up or go to another class? What do you think, and why?

3. Federal law requires that adaptations and accommodations be made for persons with disabilities. Is this fair? Does this create a level of dependence? Or is this a way of promoting equity?

4. How might adaptations we develop for students with special needs be useful to us as we work with all our students?

"Reasonable accommodations" is one of the most important provisions for people with disabilities in school, the workplace, and the community included in Section 504 of the Rehabilitation Act of 1973 and the Americans with Disabilities Act (see Chapter 1). In addition, the Individuals with Disabilities Education Act (IDEA) requires that students be educated in the least restrictive environment with needed related services and accommodations in the general education curriculum. Strategies described in this chapter give us tools to meet these legal requirements.

An Ecological Foundation for Adapting Instruction
Matching Students and Instruction

Learning to adapt our teaching, to constantly assess student abilities, and to provide supports, scaffolds, and engaging instruction to help students move ahead—all of these are at the heart of good teaching. The **ecological model of adaptations,** graphically represented in Figure 9.1, helps us think systematically about the relationship of an individual with an environment, whether the environment is a school class, a community setting, or a future job (Lofkuist & Dawes, 1980).

Let's explore how this model can help us think about adaptations in the classroom. First, if the needs of a person match the resources provided by an environment, the person is "satisfied" and will *prefer* to stay in that setting. Relatedly, if the abilities of the individual meet the minimum "requirements," the person is considered "satisfactory" and is *allowed* to stay in the position. For a person to fit well into a particular setting, both conditions must be in place: Others must consider the individual to be satisfactory, and the person must be reasonably satisfied.

Let's consider two school situations as examples:

The assignment is to read a book and write a play based on the book. My student can't do this. I am teaching in a seventh-grade language arts class. However, one of our students does not read or write well enough to complete this assignment. What do I do?

A student who can't play an instrument is in the band. I am a band instructor in high school. Because we are making efforts toward inclusion, a student with a severe physical disability comes to my class. She has very little motor control in her upper arms, is in a wheelchair, and has little language. She certainly cannot play a typical instrument or read music. Yet she is excited about being in my class, the other students think it is neat that she is there, and I would like to make her involvement meaningful for us all. What do I do?

In each situation the student's abilities do not meet the typical expectations of the classroom. The student would most often be thought of as not satisfactory and be asked to leave. What do we do when this occurs? Traditionally, two strategies are used: (1) Try to change the skills of the person so that they meet typical expectations of the setting; (2) if this does not work, remove the person from the situation. In the first example, the teacher might try several strategies to improve the student's writing skills; if the student did not improve, traditionally the teacher would initiate ef-

Figure 9.1

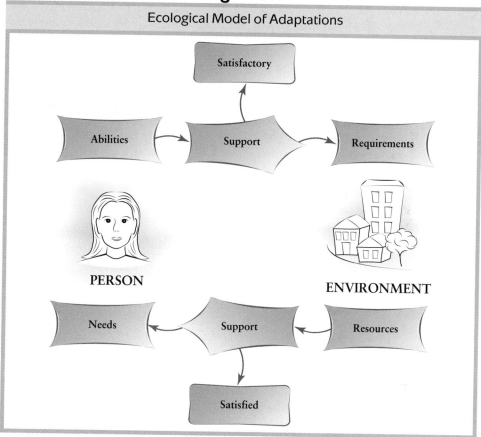

Ecological Model of Adaptations

forts to refer the student to special education. In the second example, given the very small likelihood of the student's learning to play a typical instrument and read music, the student would traditionally not have entered the class in the first place.

Yet let us look again at the person (needs and abilities) and the environment (requirements and resources). What could change to improve the person–environment match? True, we can try to change the person—but we can also change the *environment*. We can *adapt* the expectations in various ways; we can make adjustments in what is to be done, how a task is to be performed, or the level of performance expected. We can also adjust the resources an environment provides. Perhaps our class is very competitive and this environment causes many students difficulty. We can work to change our classroom atmosphere to focus more on cooperation and caring. The model helps us focus on how environments should be designed for people as opposed to people being designed to fit environments. Although initially we may be instituting change in our class to meet the needs of a specific student—*adapting*— we will eventually incorporate these new ideas into how we run our class—*designing for diversity* (Peterson, 1994, 2000).

However, there is another major strategy. Looking at Figure 9.2, you will see that we have added a mediating component between the person and the environment: *support*. What does this mean? In general, if a person's skills do not match expectations, various types of help or support may help bridge the gap. We discussed support in depth in Chapter 5 and scaffolding in Chapter 6. If I need to read aloud in a class and have difficulty, a "reading buddy" can be helpful. If I can't climb the stairs because I am in a wheelchair, someone can help navigate my wheelchair up the stairs. (Of course, an elevator or ramp ought to be available.) We hope this figure establishes a fundamental concept in your mind: If people don't "fit" in our classes, we can adapt and provide support. This is not about changing people to fit our classrooms, though our goal is certainly to help students learn, develop, and grow. It is about how we design, adapt, and provide supports to include everyone. Using this model, how might we deal with these situations? Let's look at possibilities.

The assignment is to read a book and write a play based on the book. My student can't do this. We change our requirement that the student write a play based on reading. Instead, we ask the student to "read" a book on tape (following along) and then to "create" a play, recording it in the way that is best for that student—drawing pictures, recording on the tape recorder, and so on. We involve the student in developing these strategies.

A student who can't play an instrument is in the band. Again, we want to involve the student and probably the rest of the class in figuring out some ideas. Maybe one of the drummers and this student can work together; he could hold her hand and together they could carry the bass percussion with a simple but powerful rhythm. Maybe several students can trade off. If the student can use a head-directed signaling device, maybe she could direct a computerized music synthesizer.

Figure 9.2 provides us with yet another example of a learning activity that a student will have trouble performing and possible solutions. In this case, a high school

Figure 9.2

Developing Adaptations: Problems and Solutions

LEARNING ACTIVITY	PROBLEM IN PARTICIPATION AND PERFORMANCE	SOLUTION
High school history class is to read about the U.S. Constitution and complete a worksheet of questions and answers for comprehension.	Student reads at third-grade level and can't read the text. She also has difficulty writing answers and understanding complex material.	■ Student is given simplified material about the Constitution at her reading level. ■ A peer buddy summarizes key points and explains them. ■ The student works with a group illustrating some key points.

Figure 9.3

Steps for Developing Adaptations

1. *Understand student needs*—abilities, interests, fears, resources, supports.
2. *Analyze our classroom and school environment*—expectations, norms, resources, supports, culture.
3. *Determine discrepancies* or mismatches between the person and the environment. State the problem. Whose problem is it? The child's? The school's? The family's? All of the above?
4. *Develop solutions to needs*—manageable strategies to help the student participate meaningfully, learning at his or her own level.

history class is studying the U.S. Constitution and answering questions. However, one student reads only at a third-grade level. What to do? The three-part form can help us organize our thoughts as we consider adaptations.

What did we do in each of the scenarios above? We adapted: We revised our narrow expectations and still reached an appropriate outcome—developing a simple play (in the first example) and performing in the band (in the second example). Both scenarios offer options for support that are meaningful for all parties involved. In each, we attend not only to the skill–requirement match but also to the match of personal needs and environmental resources.

Building on the ecological model we discussed above, we can systematically develop curriculum adaptations, using the four steps outlined in Figure 9.3. When we are learning how to do adaptations, we may use these steps sequentially, overtly, and consciously. As with learning to ride a bicycle, however, these strategies will become much more intuitive as they become an integral part of our teaching practice. Let's discuss each step.

Step 1: Understand Student Needs
Student Profiles for Planning

As we work with students, we are constantly learning and constantly asking the question, "*Why* does this student act and perform in these particular ways?" We also are careful to understand that when children have difficulties, there is a complex interaction between the way they are and the world around them. Some problems and challenges appear to be inherent in students. However, if we ask, "What is the student doing? Why? How can I help?" we will be much more likely to make a difference than if we ask, "What is wrong with this child?"

We've seen teachers work in groups to develop adaptations. Typically, teachers quickly identify numerous creative solutions. What we have come to believe out of these experiences is that *good teachers already know how to adapt lessons for students with even the most severe disabilities.*

Notice how we frame the issue. We do not identify a problem as "not keeping up with grade 3 or grade 8 work." Rather, we ask, "How do we help the student participate and learn at his or her own level?" This is a very big difference. It moves us away from the one-size-fits-all curriculum, away from the mandate to have all students "at grade level." If we seek to engage all together in valuable learning activities, it will be much easier to manage than we might imagine—and more fun, too, because we won't feel guilty about sending students from our classes.

Step 2: Analyze Our Classroom Environment
Just How Do We Teach?

When we see students having difficulty, it is good to step back and take a new look at our class and school. We sometimes take our class so much for granted that we cannot see realities. What do we expect of students? What are the rules? What flexibility is there? How does the total culture of our class function? How supportive is it? These are important questions.

The form shown in Figure 9.4 illustrates a class profile and can provide one useful tool for self-analysis of our teaching style (Ford, Fitzgerald, Glodoski, & Waterbury, 1997). Given that this form identifies a range of possibilities in different areas of classroom functioning, it can also be useful as a menu of strategies, a listing of ideas that we might try. For example, under "General Approach to Curriculum" we might note that our tenth-grade biology class is largely textbook driven, with some hands-on activities as part of the labs. We can think about students' responses to this instruction and consider other options listed. Similarly, we should look at our classroom expectations, our way of teaching, the culture among students and staff, and the supports provided for students and teachers.

Step 3: Determine Discrepancy between Student and Our Classroom Environment
What Is the Real Problem?

What are the academic challenges of students in our classes? What is the discrepancy between what is expected and the abilities and needs of any given student? Do we expect more ability than that student demonstrates? Does the student have needs that are unmet in our class? These discrepancies will often be experienced as *problems*. We have some key questions to ask in this context. Who experiences this discrepancy as a problem? What are the differences among the problems people perceive? Why do we see discrepancies as a problem?

Using the class profile in Figure 9.4, we can develop a form to compare our class assessment with student characteristics and to target discrepancies for adaptations. Sometimes such detailed classroom and student assessment and planning can be useful. Many teachers find, however, that written records and forms are much less important than the thinking and analysis on which they are based—looking carefully at what we are doing in our class, assessing student characteristics and needs, and developing responsive plans for adaptations and supports. Such tools are extensions of ideas that we discussed for planning purposes in Chapter 4. They can be useful in developing and documenting IEPs and Section 504 plans.

Figure 9.4

Class Profile

GENERAL APPROACH TO CURRICULUM

- ☐ Interdisciplinary
- ☐ Hands-on
- ☐ Community projects–oriented
- ☐ Project-based
- ☐ Student-directed
- ☐ Textbook-driven

CURRICULUM MATERIALS

For planning	For student use
☐ _____	☐ _____
☐ _____	☐ _____
☐ _____	☐ _____
☐ _____	☐ _____

ADVANCE PLANNING MEANS . . .

- ☐ Weeks ahead of time.
- ☐ One or two days in advance.
- ☐ As I enter the room.

CONTENT

- ☐ Tend to cover it all.
- ☐ Decide what's essential and add/subtract based on individual needs.
- ☐ Readily depart to follow students' interests.
- ☐ Tend to have single-concept lessons.
- ☐ Anchor it to a major project.

PHYSICAL ENVIRONMENT/SEATING

- ☐ Desks are clustered to promote peer-to-peer interaction.
- ☐ There are small group spaces.
- ☐ Computer stations are available.
- ☐ Bulletin boards are used for:

  _____
- ☐ Students have assigned seats.

STUDENT PARTICIPATION

Peer to peer
- ☐ Mutual helping by students
- ☐ Cooperative groups
- ☐ Peer partners
- ☐ Peer tutors

Self-management
- ☐ Schedule reminders
- ☐ Assignment booklets
- ☐ Study guides
- ☐ Contracts and self-checklists
- ☐ Organizers
- ☐ Frequent self-evaluation

TEACHER PRESENTATION/FACILITATION

- ☐ Moves around a lot
- ☐ Fairly structured
- ☐ Uses questioning techniques
- ☐ Involves all students
- ☐ Gives specific feedback and guidance
- ☐ Gives lots of praise
- ☐ Tolerates low levels of noise
- ☐ Lectures a lot
- ☐ Leads lots of large group discussions
- ☐ Demonstrates and models
- ☐ Uses video, film, audio

TESTS, ASSIGNMENTS, AND EVALUATION

- ☐ Portfolios are used.
- ☐ Grading tends to be based on: ___ curve ___ mastery criteria ___ IEP ___ individual student progress ___ contracts ___ multiple grading (effort and achievement)
- ☐ Maintenance of journal/class notebook
- ☐ Homework given: ___ daily ___ 2–3 times per week
- ☐ Usually takes: ___ 15 ___ 30 ___ 60 minutes
- ☐ Students demonstrate what they learn through: ___ projects ___ written/oral tests ___ written/oral reports.

(continued)

Figure 9.4

Continued

CLASSROOM CLIMATE AND MANAGEMENT

- ☐ Students must raise hand to talk.
- ☐ Students move around a lot.
- ☐ Students have assigned jobs.
- ☐ Students routinely conference with teacher.
- ☐ Students select their own work to display.
- ☐ Rewards include: ___ praise ___ special privileges such as _____
- ☐ Corrective strategies include: ___ time out ___ loss of privilege ___ ignoring ___ staying after school ___ peer mediation

HOME–SCHOOL COMMUNICATION

- ☐ Class newsletter
- ☐ Assignment notebook
- ☐ Special rules
- ☐ Regularly scheduled phone calls
- ☐ Homework hotline
- ☐ Daily journals

Step 4: Adapt Instruction to Solve Problem
Strategies for Learning

In Step 4 we build on the analysis we did in Steps 1 through 3 and develop solutions to address the mismatch between the individual student and our class. As we are planning adaptations to instruction, we will be driven by two primary considerations: (1) how to adapt instruction to meet the student's needs, and (2) how to help the student increase his or her learning in a struggling area.

Principles for Effective Adaptations

There are many strategies that teachers can use to adapt academic instruction for students. When do we use what strategies? Let's look at a few helpful guidelines.

Meeting Needs. The most obvious guideline is to select the strategies that will most directly meet the needs of the student. If a student is having trouble organizing work, we use strategies that help the student develop organizational skills. If the work is too complex, we look for tasks that can be simplified. If a student cannot read the textbook, we search for reading materials related to the subject that the student is able to read. If a student needs emotional support, we try to arrange this.

Least Intrusive and Most Inclusive. We use adaptations that keep students connected rather than drawing them off into separate corners. For example, although we could adapt the curriculum by having a paraprofessional and a student work on a related but different activity at the back of the class, this would separate the student from the total classroom community. We want adaptations that are barely noticeable and the least time intensive possible. For example, a student might read simplified material next to other students in the class who are reading more complex material.

Challenging at Zone of Proximal Development. One of the most frequent mistakes teachers make is simply to "make the work less difficult." We obviously don't want students struggling to work at levels above their capacity so that they fail and quit trying. However, we also don't want to make the work so simplistic that learning no longer occurs. If we know our students, we provide support and scaffolding to challenge them at their *zone of proximal development* (Vygotsky, 1978) (see Chapter 6).

Impact on Instruction. We also want to pick adaptations that help us experiment with new teaching strategies. For example, a boy is having difficulty learning to read but is very physically active and shows signs of athletic abilities. For this student we consider ways to incorporate more movement into reading lessons. Rather than writing in journals, perhaps he and other students could create and act out a play. Perhaps the whole class could line up to spell words outside on the playground. Perhaps simply allowing the student to stand and move while reading, with the book on a podium, might be helpful. We may decide we like some of these ideas and want to use them in the future for other students.

Let's now explore different tools and strategies for adapting academic learning.

Planning Tools for Adaptations

Several tools help us plan and track our use of adaptations. We can use several formats to compare what typically goes on in class; a student's capabilities and characteristics; needed adaptations; and support staff, if appropriate, to provide assistance. Figure 4.9 in Chapter 4 provides one format and example. Figure 9.5 illustrates an overall semester planning format, showing possible adaptations for each subject and the responsibilities, as these are applicable, of support staff.

Figure 9.6 on pages 267–268 summarizes adaptation strategies. In the subsections that follow, we will look more closely at the ideas outlined in this figure.

Presentation of Information and Learning Activities

First, we consider our overall teaching process. Are we designing our instruction for diverse learners? Do we allow room for students to work at multiple levels? Do we respond to different intelligences, consider different learning styles, and use best practices in instruction? As we develop adaptations for individual students, we always reassess classroom instruction as a whole and the ways in which it will be affected positively or negatively. For example, Mark, a fifth-grade teacher, realized that he had students who would benefit from guided reading. He selected children to read a book that would interest them at their own level together. As the other students in the class read individually on Thursday mornings, Mark read with this group and focused on specific reading skills and strategies. He liked this so well that he decided to do such groups once a week with all the students in the class.

As we identify student needs, we also come up with alternative ways of presenting information or different types of learning experiences. We can make changes in the total class setup and watch the responses of specific students who are having

Figure 9.5

Individual Student Adaptations and Support in School Subjects

STUDENT: *Shane French, Grade 9*	ADAPTATIONS	STAFF SUPPORT (if needed)	EVALUATION NOTES
Literacy: Reading and writing workshop. Guided reading. Read alouds. *Adele Smith, teacher*	Books on same topic at grade 3 level. Focus on periods. Sit next to Christopher to model/ ask questions.	Visits Student Support Center during study hall to read orally and edit stories.	Keep daily log on progress toward goals.
Social studies: Group projects related to poverty in community. *Russell Lee, teacher*	Group asks him questions to draw into discussion. Shane draws picture to illustrate issue.	Supply Support Room with reading about topics so can support if needed.	Ask oral questions to test knowledge of issues. Make up rubric for group project.
Math: Manipulatives, interest groups based on curriculum goals. *Sydney Blanning, teacher*	Working on addition using real-life questions. Use calculator to subtract and multiply.	Works with whole class, checking in daily. Plans block with teacher.	Mark date on checklist when goals are achieved.
Music: Choral production of *Fiddler on the Roof.* *Connie Bueller, teacher*	Listens to songs on tape to memorize. Practices with partner.		Participation in class.
Art: Study impressionist paintings. Do own nature paintings. Self-portraits. *Marjorie Sanchez, teacher*	Shares work with buddies in other classes. Receives help on art he is doing for social studies.		Keep log of strengths seen. Positive aspects to boost moral. Self-evaluate progress.
Physical education: Daily calisthenics, volleyball, team running races. *Harvey Stott, teacher*	Gross motor development worked into curriculum. Cooperative, not individual, work stressed.	Therapist plans with teacher to incorporate goals. Works in class twice a week to assist.	Log of progress kept by teacher. Add notes from therapist in planning. Self-evaluate progress.

difficulties. Any of the methods presented in Chapters 6 and 8 will help us rethink our instructional approaches. For example, one teacher lectured to his whole biology class about cellular structure. Students were expected to have read the textbook, to take notes, and then to respond to questions on a worksheet in preparation for an exam. However, two of the students could not read well enough to read the textbook and took terrible notes. What could the teacher do?

Figure 9.6

Curriculum Adaptation Strategies

TEACHING STRATEGIES

Presentation of information and learning activities	Lecture with media: Chalkboard, transparencies, computer graphics, videos, interviews of informants
	Reading: Expository, fiction, poetry, websites
	Teaching strategies: Speakers, field trips, community-based experiences, role plays, simulations, board games, plays, artistic and musical presentations
	Accommodate individual learning styles or intelligences.
Expectations	Difficulty: Same content but less complex
	Amount: Vary the amount of work required (e.g., number of pages of writing or reading; number of spelling words; length of a speech or presentation; numbers of projects).
	Time allotted: Vary amount of time allotted to an activity (e.g., give some students more time, others less time).
	Degree of participation: Vary the degree to which a student engages in a particular activity. (E.g., if the class is reading *Tales of a Fourth Grade Nothing* and creating a play to perform, one student might read a simpler version or be involved in the performance only.)
	Adjust performance standards *and evaluation criteria*.
Instructional materials	Same content but variation in size, number, or format
	Additional or different materials at ability level or interest area
	Materials that allow for different mode of input and/or output
	Materials that reduce the level of abstraction of information
Student methods of obtaining information	Location in the class (at front if difficulty seeing)
	Sign language, braille, talking computer or calculator, reader, note takers, tape recorder
Instructional formats	Small group, cooperative learning, peer buddies, individual assignments at own level
Methods of performing tasks	Alternative and augmentative communications: Typing or word processing, writers, communication boards, assistive computer technology
	Sign language for communication

(continued)

Figure 9.6

Continued	
SUPPORT AND SCAFFOLDING	
Peer support	Peer buddies assist in completing tasks, understanding, etc.
	Cooperative work groups; heterogeneous ability levels
Information and materials available	Advance notice of assignments
	Books at home
	Home learning activities with parents (optional)
Teacher scaffolding	Arrange for reading with a fellow student; do one-on-one questioning; provide cognitive organizers of reading.
In-class support	One-on-one tutoring and assistance by specialist—special education teacher, occupational therapist, speech therapist, etc.
METHODS OF EVALUATION AND ASSESSMENT	
Methods of demonstrating learning	Tests: Narrative, multiple-choice, short-answer
	Portfolios of best work
	Plays, posters, artistic and musical renditions
Adjusted grading	Effort, improvement, achievement of identified criteria for grade levels, adaptations set by IEP

Faced with this concern, we start by asking ourselves the question, "Is this the best way to teach this material?" In fact, if we follow the best practice strategies summarized in Chapters 6 and 8, we find that it is not. Instead, what if we have students work in small groups? First, students could plan their work by using a **K-W-L strategy** to brainstorm what they know and what they want to know. Subsequently, the teacher could help them organize ways to research information, with different members of the group engaging in different research activities.

As usually happens, when the biology teacher applied these strategies, the two students who had difficulty reading did much better. First, they participated as part of a group, engaging in tasks that required less sophisticated reading. Then one of the two students interviewed a parent who is a biologist to learn answers to some questions. The other student was the artist of the group. In addition, as the group reported back and discussed what they were finding, all the students learned through this oral communication more readily. One very gifted boy decided that he would like to include complex pictorial descriptions in his projects and began to do so.

Multiple Intelligences. A multiple intelligences–based approach takes a comprehensive view of the skills and needs of students and lends itself to strategies for adaptations. Figure 9.7 illustrates how we might use multiple intelligences for this purpose.

Figure 9.7

Levels of Ability and Multiple Intelligences: Sample Adaptations

INTELLIGENCE	POTENTIAL PROBLEMS	SOME SOLUTIONS
Linguistic	Verbal and written language abilities either higher or lower than those of the majority of the class	Reading materials at multiple levels Buddies and partners who assist the student Study guides
Logical–Mathematical	Difficulty in thinking in logical sequences Difficulty in understanding mathematic concepts	Thinking organizers Task analysis Hands-on activities
Spatial	Visual disability Difficulty with spatial relationships (gets lost in the high school halls) Inability to draw or represent graphically	Using touch in place of sight—feeling objects, sculpting rather than drawing Orientation to the layout of the school by an orientation and mobility specialist Stick-figure drawing Supporting effort at own level
Bodily–Kinesthetic	Physical disabilities—uses wheelchair, weakened by physical condition Poor physical coordination Tactile-defensive	Modified rules of games to allow participation Unified Sports Play supporting role in sports—leading fan, etc
Musical	Tone deaf Difficulty with rhythms	Allow to participate at own level (if tone deaf, sing but moderate volume)
Interpersonal	High needs for attention Frequently angry and acting out Withdraws from other students	Listen, understand what student is feeling Connect with supportive students Circle of support
Intrapersonal	Fear of being alone Difficulty understanding own feelings	Develop opportunities for student to work with others in class projects Provide lessons to all students about how to identify emotions and healthy ways to respond
Naturalist	Difficulty synthesizing and seeing the how small pieces fit into the whole; gets lost in details	Work with others who can explain the relationship of the part to the "big ideas" of a lesson

Figure 9.8

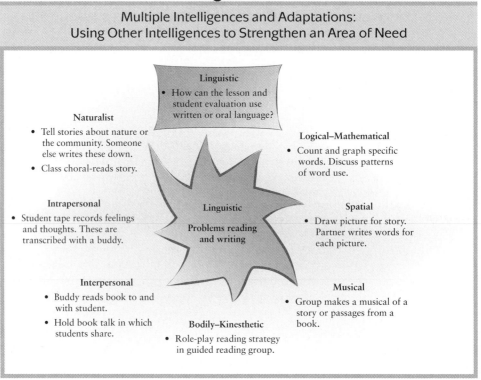

Multiple Intelligences and Adaptations: Using Other Intelligences to Strengthen an Area of Need

We can use all the other intelligences to provide alternate routes to help strengthen a particular area of need. Figure 9.8 illustrates this strategy in relation to literacy difficulties—problems with linguistic intelligence. If, as in this example, a student is having difficulty reading and writing, we consider multiple intelligences and provide opportunities for learning through other modalities and abilities: spatial, musical, bodily–kinesthetic, interpersonal, intrapersonal, and naturalist. This does not mean that we give up on reading and writing. We simply provide strategies that approach reading from a different perspective, lifting some pressure from the student.

Learning Styles. We can modify the environment, learning situation, and input styles by addressing various *learning styles* as described in Chapter 6. Here are two examples:

- *Comfortable learning setting:* Give students the opportunity to have drink or food accessible as they study; allow them options for where they work—sitting at a desk or on the floor with a pillow, standing at a high table, and so on.
- *Music:* Allow students to use a Walkman while working, or to work in the hall or in a corner with earmuffs so the noise of the class does not bother them.

Best Teaching Practices. We can apply the techniques presented in Chapter 8 to adaptations for individual students as well. Here are a few more examples.

- *Community-based project:* A student engages in a community-based project instead of a research paper. For example, the student might learn about the problems of the local public transportation system, develop a poster on it, and bring in a resource speaker to talk with the class.
- *Internet research:* A student obtains information about a topic using the Internet (with assistance and support if needed) and develops a presentation, using software such as PowerPoint to organize materials.

In one math class, for example, a boy with learning disabilities participated in a group working on a project studying the local economy. The project linked science, math, and social studies. In math the students used several algebraic equations to help develop solutions. The student with learning disabilities took charge of the manipulatives that helped the team visualize the situation, which helped him understand what the algebraic equations meant.

Expectations

We also consider modifying our expectations or learning goals—changing the amount or difficulty of work or selecting alternative learning goals that a student can accomplish within the class. Following are interrelated strategies.

Difficulty of Work. First, we can vary the difficulty of assignments. We "adapt the skill level, problem type, or the rules regarding how a learner may approach the work" (Deschenes, Ebeling, & Sprague, 1994). Examples include:

- Allow calculator use in math.
- Have a student draw quick sequential sketches to record journal responses to a story read by the teacher or books on tape.
- Change the standard by which we evaluate the product a student produces (e.g., give credit for a simpler product).
- If the class is reading a Shakespeare play, have one student read a simpler version.
- Simplify directions by limiting words or number of steps.

Amount of Work. We can also alter the amount of work required of different students, either increasing or decreasing based on student needs (Deschenes, Ebeling, & Sprague, 1994). For example, we might adjust:

- Number of pages of writing or reading
- Number of spelling words
- Length of a speech or presentation
- Number of projects
- Number or length of homework assignments

Time Available. We can also simply provide students opportunities to take additional time with the material. Three general strategies are useful (Deschenes, Ebeling, & Sprague, 1994).

■ *Additional guided practice:* We gather students for miniskills lessons; peer buddies provide in-class or out-of-class review and tutoring; we arrange occasions such as science nights when families engage in fun learning together.

■ *Changes in the pace of instruction and performance:* We slow or increase the rate at which students are asked to obtain information and perform tasks. For some students, we provide additional time (often for fewer responses or performance tasks). For other students, we require more rapid performance on certain tasks.

■ *Extra time:* We allow extra time within or outside of class for students to complete their work. If we give other students an hour to finish a project, we might give a particular child two hours. Of course, this also means that we may have to exempt the child from other work that some students complete.

Degree of Participation. Students also engage in learning activities at different degrees of participation (Deschenes, Ebeling, & Sprague, 1994). As we use this strategy, however, it is important to ensure that the student participates as fully as possible. The danger is that the student can become only a spectator. Some examples of modified degrees of participation:

■ A student participates in a science lab speaking into a recorder.

■ A student group is conducting research on a country using the Internet, the globe, and written materials. A student with special needs helps another student search

Artwork reprinted by permission of Martha Perske from *Perske: Pencil Portraits 1971–1990* (Nashville: Abingdon Press, 1998).

PERSKE

the Internet by clicking specific sites with the peer student's guidance. He also holds the globe as a group of students investigate neighboring countries.

- A student listens to research reports of other students and draws a picture of one thing she learned.
- A student chooses which of three topics a group will study.

Linda, an eighth grader, is in an English class that is studying Shakespeare. Groups are putting together performances of selected scenes from *A Midsummer Nights' Dream* and writing reflective journals. Linda can't read above a third-grade level. However, she loves to hear Shakespeare read aloud. Linda is participating in the play, speaking a few lines on which the other students are coaching her. She is "reading" the scenes on cassette tape, which she enjoys; is using "stick-figure writing" to summarize key elements in the play; and has created drawings to express her feelings about the scenes. Her group has decided to enlarge these and use them as part of the visual props when they perform on open house night at the school.

Alternative Learning Goals. Some students engage in learning activities with learning goals different from those of other students in the class (Deschenes, Ebeling, & Sprague, 1994). These can vary across ability levels. For example, as a class is studying the history of exploration in outer space, a learning goal for a student with highly developed linguistic abilities might be to "understand the outer space exploration programs of the United States and the Soviet Union and their social impact on education in each country." This student might develop a multimedia presentation for the total class. On the other hand, a learning goal for a student with limited abilities in the same class might be to "learn to work cooperatively with other students." The student would then engage in group activities, possibly even aiding the other student with the multimedia presentation.

We also look at alternative goals for the student's total school program. Curricula have been developed in special education that focus on "functional life goals" such as obtaining employment, developing relationships, and engaging in community activities. Brolin's (1993) Life-Centered Career Education (LCCE) curriculum, and the Activities Catalogue Curriculum (Wilcox & Bellamy, 1987) provide a valuable source of alternative learning goals that can be incorporated into IEPs to provide a direction for the engagement of these students in classroom activities and learning.

Instructional Materials

We also adapt instructional materials. Again, this is much easier if our instructional resources involve a wide range of authentic materials. In reading, if we use trade books at a range of ability levels, such adapting is already built into the way we teach. In science, if we have a range of instructional materials—books, photographs, internet sites, audiotapes, videos, plants, microscopes, and models—we will need

There Are *So* Many Ways to Adapt

In an online discussion group, a mother of a child with Down Syndrome, who is fully included in general education, shared with us about adaptations from her experience.

The main thing is to be creative. You need to remember *who* you are working with . . . what their goals, interests, and abilities are . . . and fit it into their life. For example, with history he can be working on spelling the state name or simply recognizing the letters and pointing it out on the map. . . . With regular spelling the child can circle the correct word on the spelling list, match a card with the same word, trace the letters spelling the word, many things.

At the beginning of the year my second grader fit into the lowest reading group and could "track" with the class. When it was time for them to do the reading words *he* would get the cards and give them to the teacher. He was able to answer a few of the comprehension questions at the end of a story. By the middle of the year they were beyond him. So his aide took the stories and made new questions that dealt with categorizing and sequencing but still having to do with the story that the group was reading. When they got to the questions, the teacher would ask his questions. . . . With math he followed along with the class and worked on the overhead, and she would always have a problem he could solve, but when they worked on regrouping, he worked on number recognition . . . and one-on-one correspondence. The main thing is that he was working on what *they* were working on, just at his level. He had to finish his work before he could go to centers. One of the centers was a game center, and lots of the games were games we had made that the class could play with him.

I am not saying that it always worked out, but it can be done . . . and is fun for everyone when it is working.

(W. Michdock, personal communication, February 1999).

fewer adaptations than if we are relying on a textbook as the primary teaching material. In math, similarly, the use of manipulatives and other hands-on materials creates the same advantage. As we gather our instructional materials over time, we will work toward having materials at different levels that help us hook various interests of students and that respond to different individual modalities, learning styles, and intelligences.

Adapting Existing Materials. We can adapt existing materials using the following strategies (Price, Mayfield, McFadden, & Marsh, 1998):

- *Highlight* the important information in written materials. This can be done with a yellow highlighter by the teacher or aide, or by peer helpers.
- *Summarize* key points and information from texts and materials.

- Have materials *recorded* on a tape recorder, in braille, or in large print. Tape-recorded material is particularly useful not only for students with visual disabilities but also for students who have difficulty reading material. Computer programs and hardware are available that can convert text to speech, convert text to braille, and enlarge text.
- For a particular activity, provide *picture booklets* showing step-by-step instructions. These could be developed by a support person or student. Making such booklets could even be part of a group activity and would help all the students better understand the procedure.

Adding Information and Supplementary Materials. We can also provide assistance with additional information and materials. These include (Wood, J., 1994, 1998):

- *Study guides and topical course outlines:* Provide specific information regarding learning objectives, topics to be covered, and suggested study strategies. Study guides and outlines constitute a resource to which students can refer.
- *Advance notice of assignments:* Particularly for students who work more slowly and need more assistance in becoming organized, giving advance notice of assignments (for example, sending information home on Friday about topics and assignments for the following week) can allow a student to get a "head start" on a topic.
- *Books and course materials at home:* Allowing students to have copies of course materials at home is an obvious form of help and support. Parents can then provide direct assistance to a student as they are able.
- *Optional home learning activities with parents:* Send home optional supplementary (and fun) learning exercises that reinforce lessons in school.

Supplementary instructional materials may also be useful. We can identify materials that summarize key information at a lower reading level. We might, for example, be able to obtain abridged versions of textbooks or study guides. Even comic book versions of literature can be useful, as well as readable and interesting trade books and magazines (Price, Mayfield, McFadden, & Marsh, 1998). For students with higher abilities, we should have available articles, websites, or books that go into a topic in greater detail or from a more analytical viewpoint. We will want to supplement print materials with other resources. These might include:

- Videos that can be checked out or used with a small group in class.
- Books of photographs around particular themes.
- Literature and stories that focus on expository material.
- Computer-assisted instruction. We would caution, however, against the use of computers as fancy worksheets. Some excellent, hypertext-linked programs are available and can provide instruction to students, linking them to resources both on CDs and on the Internet. Computer-based reference materials such as encyclopedias, are excellent examples, as they have text as well as video clips and graphics that foster a multisensory learning process.
- Websites, particularly those that use photographs, articles, even video clips.

- Local community resources. Among these are places to visit related to a topic as well as people who are knowledgeable and willing to talk to students.

Methods of Obtaining Information, Communicating, and Performing Tasks

In some cases students need to use special tools to help them gain information. We will explore these in depth in Chapter 15. Here we will provide a brief summary.

Alternative communication systems: A range of alternative methods exist for both reception (input) and expression (output) of ideas, information, emotions, and concepts (Kameenui & Carnine, 1998; Wood, J., 1998).

Alternative written symbols: In some cases, alternative written communication systems, such as bliss bymbols and "stick figure writing," can be helpful.

Technology-based communication systems: A variety of technologically based systems are available to help persons who have various types of communication limitations. These systems can facilitate communication output, input, or both. Here are some examples (see Chapter 15 for more information):

- *Speech synthesizers*
- *Assistive listening devices*

- *Computers* can convert speech into text for students who have difficulty writing physically. Other devices can convert text to spoken speech or braille.
- *Augmentative communication devices*

Communication support services: In addition, we may assist students in obtaining information by providing helpers such as the following (Hiibner & Fracassi, 1999):

- Note takers
- Lab assistants
- Readers
- Writers
- Interpreters—of sign language or of languages other than English

Instructional Formats

Adaptations of instructional formats can be used for our overall teaching as well as for individual students or groups of students. Some of the primary ways we cluster students in learning include the following (Janney & Snell, 2000a):

- Individualized, one-on-one instruction
- Small group
- Large group
- Individualized learning stations
- Learning centers
- Cooperative group

As we discussed in Chapter 8, best practice instruction provides many opportunities for students to work in groups. Group work allows students to draw from one another's strengths and encourages students to assist one another in their work.

Support and Scaffolding

We can vary the amount of support provided—give much/little support to a student who is performing an activity, have students work individually, expect one student to lead another student. We will also provide ongoing and multiple scaffolding strategies to assist students in performing tasks that they could not otherwise do (Vygotsky, 1978).

Peer Support. We will talk in detail about strategies of peer support in Chapters 11 and 12. Student-to-student help is a critical part of building an inclusive and effective classroom.

Teacher Scaffolding. In one sense, scaffolding is not an adaptation at all but a central teaching strategy that we employ on an ongoing basis. From another perspective, however, scaffolding is one of the ways in which we adapt constantly. Here are a few illustrative examples teachers have used:

Schools to Visit

Effective Adaptation of Curriculum

Powell Valley Elementary School
4825 E. Powell Valley Rd.
Gresham, Oregon 97080-1951
Phone: 503-661-151
Principal: Gary Paxton
Gary_Paxton@gbsd.gresham.k12.or.us

Powell Valley Elementary School has 518 children in grades K through 5. Powell Valley's beliefs speak to the success of the school. Effective curriculum adaptation is a product of teamwork and a belief in children. When you believe all children learn best when they are actively involved in their learning and when they use real-life situations for problem solving, every child has the opportunity to learn within his or her own learning style. When you practice the belief that all children can and want to learn, all children are welcomed and valued for what they as individuals bring to the classroom community. When you build a caring school community based on the belief that all children need to feel a strong sense of community and collaboration, all children are involved not only in their own learning but in the learning of others.

Curriculum adaptation is at the heart of the success of inclusive schooling at Powell Valley. When teachers look at upcoming activities and consider how they will optimize every child's learning, they collaborate with other teachers, assistants, and the Supported Education Team. Collaboration and teaming become the way to meet the students' needs with the best of ideas while saving time.

Together the teachers have learned that adaptations begin with the same work the whole class is doing. As the team works on the lesson, some adapations are on the spot, such as a fold in the paper or the highlighting of some problems. Other ideas take a little more time and planning, but ideas always expand beyond one child, often being used to enhance the learning of many students. Teachers have discovered that when they begin their adaptation with the work everyone in the class is doing, they set up a natural opportunity for students to work together. If an "adaptation" is something totally different from what the class is doing, peers can't help one another, because it isn't always clear what the work is about or how it ties to the current lesson. Consistently, teachers have discovered that when they look at another way to teach the general lesson to fit a certain child, they improve their own teaching and reach more children.

For example, in one class, as students study the Oregon Trail, they write about how they would prepare for the journey and what supplies they would bring. A student who is unable to read or write verbally describes the supplies they would bring, using a paper wagon and pictures of supplies, thus providing the same opportunity to plan and participate. As classmates join in and use the "adapted" version of the lesson, the visuals assist in their processing and their writing becomes more expanded and clear. Another student has begun independently to use visuals for routines and schedules because the whole class is using them and he doesn't feel different. In another class a student was frustrated because writing her name on her paper took her the whole lesson. The teacher and assistant came up with the idea that while the rest of the class practiced their handwriting, this student would write her name on a page of labels that she could peel and stick on each assignment. She was then able to participate in lessons rather than spending all her time writing.

Although there are lots of simple ideas for adapting curriculum, the staff at Powell Valley has discovered that the keys to adapting curriculum are a team approach, a focus on the child, and a belief that through the adaptations we make, learning is enhanced for every child.

By Patti McVay, Outreach Center for Inclusive Education; **patti_mcvay@mesd.k12.or.us.**

- A student is stuck on a math problem. We prompt him with questions to help him figure it out. He begins. We show him the next step and ask why. He explains. We leave him to go the next step and ask another student to work with him.
- One student is in a group and we ask a question whose answer we know she knows. However, she gives an answer that doesn't make sense. Rather than going on, we stop and ask the student to explain. We discover that her thoughts were, in fact, quite logical. We explain this to other students and she beams.

These are two simple examples in which we provided scaffolding—helped students deal with situations—and also ensured that *their voice was heard*. This is a critical part. Often students who are struggling in our classes will either withdraw or act out. Either way, they tend to be silenced. As we support students in doing *tasks,* we will also support them in thinking and *expressing themselves* by showing that their contributions are valued. We will find that when we ensure that our students with greatest challenges have a voice, this will have a tremendous impact, not only on these students, but on the total culture of our class.

In-Class Support. In Chapter 5 we discussed various professional resources for in-class support of students—special education teachers, speech therapists, and others. These individuals can assist us in making adaptations.

Study Skills and Tools. Often students simply don't know how to study and need explicit assistance in developing such skills. Such efforts can be organized many ways. Some teachers incorporate teaching study skills into their ongoing lessons. Sometimes (particularly at middle and high school levels) specific study skill classes are taught in student learning centers in the school library or in a special drop-in class. As with any skill that is taught in a decontextualized way, however, instruction in study and organizational skills can be very boring to students. We recommend that these skills be taught as students need them, in the context of what they are trying to do (Roth, Bartlinski, & Courson, 1994).

Moreover, we should not assume that our "bright" students automatically develop good study and organizational skills and that our "slower" students are the ones that need help. One parent of a high school student shared her realization that her son was not deliberately choosing not to do his best in school; he simply did not automatically know how to organize his tasks and study. Here are some key study skills and tools that many students need help with and suggestions for incorporating them into ongoing instruction.

- *Strategic learning:* Much learning is based on the use of specific strategies that can be taught—the use of webs to organize complex concepts; outlining strategies to break down plot, characters, themes in a piece of literature; brainstorming and freewriting to get the brain considering various options.
- *Calendars and assignments:* In the early grades we should help students learn how to use calendars and to track projects due and break larger projects into steps.
- *Scheduling tools:* We should help students understand scheduling tools—particularly Gantt charts, in which students list tasks down the side of the chart and

Young children work in teams to solve multiplication problems at Patrick O'Hearn Elementary School. Such collaborative learning allows children to learn from one another, contributing at their own level.

calendar dates across the top, drawing lines that show how the beginning and end of each task is scheduled. We can help students summarize tasks, use calendars to identify due dates, and develop a work schedule.

- *Setting personal goals and designing activities to achieve goals:* We should help students establish personal goals for themselves.
- *Studying for exams:* We can help students learn how to make summaries, review their notes, and use strategies designed to imprint learning beyond short-term memory.
- *Personal organizing:* We can help students organize major topics, courses, projects, and their own files. A variety of methods will help them remember important items—color coding, Post-it notes, and reminder systems.

If we can help students learn these skills as tools to help them achieve what *they* want to do rather than as irrelevant school requirements, we will increase the likelihood that students will use such skills effectively. We model the use of planning notebooks, ask students to have planning notebooks in our classes, and teach them how to use them. We help them organize outside projects based on their own initiative and interests. When students are having difficulty, we suggest (but not demand) that they use a particular tool, and we demonstrate how the tool may be helpful to them.

Methods of Evaluation and Assessment

Finally, we can adapt evaluation, assessment, and grading procedures—the ways that a student demonstrates learning.

Methods of Demonstrating Learning. We can provide a wide range of means by which students may complete assignments, develop products, and demonstrate their learning. First, to assist students in preparing for assessments, we can provide several types of assistance. These might include (Deschenes, Ebeling, & Sprague, 1994; Wood, J., 1994; 1998) providing study guides with key concepts and vocabulary and suggesting exam study strategies to students—relaxation techniques, key concepts, summarizing notes, and so on.

If we are relying primarily on multiple-choice or true/false tests, we should consider providing different options for all of our students. However, we can adapt even these forms of exams. Some strategies include (Deschenes, Ebeling, & Sprague, 1994; Wood, J., 1998):

- Reducing the number of test items or simplifying concepts
- Allowing all students to retake tests
- Having a student respond to the test orally and tape-recording the exam or having it recorded by a writer
- Allowing the use of helping devices on exams—computers and calculators
- Allowing time extensions
- Providing alternative test formats—short-answer, multiple-choice, oral, or essay questions
- Splitting administration of an exam over more than one session

In Chapter 8 we discussed options for effective evaluation of student learning that allow a wide variety of modalities. If we are using such approaches, we will more easily find ways to accommodate students with special needs. Even if we are not, we may decide to use one or more of these alternative performance strategies as an individualized adaptation (Siegel-Causey & Allinder, 1998). These include:

- Portfolios of best work
- Plays, posters, artistic or musical renditions
- Projects completed as alternatives to exams and tests

Grading. In some cases no modification of grading is required. This occurs when the learning objectives are the same for all students, even though some additional specialized objectives may be included. Grades may be based on IEP goals rather than on the typical expectations of the classroom. We will most often track achievement of individualized education plan goals and objectives on a special form, rating scale, or task analysis list. In such tracking, depending on the nature of the goal, we may report numbers of responses, compute the percentage of a goal/objective completed, produce a qualitative narrative evaluation or rating, or simply complete a checklist that indicates satisfactory performance of various skills.

This type of individualized grading should be consistent with what we use for all of our students. At best we will establish individual learning goals for each student that we negotiate with them—and if we do so, this is very similar to what we will do with evaluating learning objectives established in IEPs. Adaptations for grading include (Christiansen & Vogel, 1998; Janney & Snell, 2000a; Price, Mayfield, McFadden, & Marsh, 1998):

- Grading based on the accomplishment of learning goals established on the IEP or our own individualized agreement with a student.
- Grading based on (1) improvement and (2) effort—standards of grading that some teachers prefer for all their students.
- Providing additional projects for students to bring up grades.

How grades are *recorded* on a report card varies. Some schools indicate on the report card that the grade reflects an "adjusted" grading system. Other educators argue that grades are subjective in all cases and simply cannot reflect a uniform measure of student achievement. These educators do not indicate adaptations or "adjustments" in the grading system.

In considering grading for students with special needs, we need to be aware of the research on grading in general. The research is clear: The more we emphasize grades (or any type of test performance, for that matter), the more students lose interest in learning, focusing primarily on how they did rather than on the substance of what they are learning (Christiansen & Vogel, 1998; Kohn, 1999). If we are nevertheless required to give grades, as is the case in most schools, then we must strive to grade in a way that encourages and rewards students when they put forth effort and demonstrate an interest in learning. Using the three strategies described above helps us move toward accomplishing this goal (Janney & Snell, 2000a).

State Standardized Tests. **Accommodations** can be used with standardized examinations. The provisions of both the Americans with Disabilities Act and Section 504 of the Rehabilitation Act of 1973 require that appropriate accommodations or **modifications** be provided for students who have been identified through special education or who are considered as having a disability under either one of these acts. These accommodations may be documented as part of an IEP, or may be part of a Section 504 plan for a student with a disability who is not eligible through special education, such as a student with ADHD. Such adaptations include:

- Reading the questions to the student
- Having someone write the responses the student dictates
- Providing visual aids to enlarge the examination
- Presenting the exam in alternative formats—braille, the native language of the student, and so on
- Administering the exam in a location that is quiet
- Allowing for breaks and an extended time period

The Individuals with Disabilities Education Act (IDEA) requires that students with disabilities be eligible to take all local or state standardized exams. However, many states have provisions that allow students to be exempted from such exams. The IDEA requirement was intended to prevent schools from unilaterally exempting all special education students so that these students' scores would not depress the average scores of the school as a whole.

Stepping Stones
To Inclusive Teaching

1. Identify two students—one with high and one with low academic abilities. Use the strategies in this chapter to develop and try out some curriculum adaptations for these two students. How did this work?
2. Keep an "adaptations journal" for a week; in it, jot down adaptations you make daily on the fly. What does this exercise tell you about areas in which you could improve? About good strategies you are using of which you weren't even aware?
3. Take the list of adaptations discussed in this chapter (see Figure 9.8). Put a check beside those that you use. How might the strategies you don't use be beneficial in your work with some of your students? Identify two approaches you'd like to use in the coming weeks. Try these out and evaluate how they worked.
4. Design a way to teach students themselves about adaptations as tools that can help them learn. Design a strategy by which you could incorporate these tools into mini-lessons and into all your instruction throughout the year.

We think the decision as to whether a child with learning difficulties should take standardized exams must be made with consideration of the impact on the student. Many parents exempt their children from these examinations. Many teachers, too, are concerned about the negative impact of failing these exams on students' self-concept (Peterson, Tamor, Feen, & Silagy, 2002). In this context, recommending that a student with special needs not take these tests may make sense.

Adaptations for a Fifth Grader: Seeing the Whole Picture

Let's explore a plan for an actual student in the fifth grade whom we will call Kent. Kent has been classified as "trainable mentally retarded." Kent is a very quiet student most of the time. Periodically, however, he gets frustrated and strikes out at other students. Both his parents are supportive, though they are divorcing and there has been much stress in the home in the last two years. Kent reads at about a first-grade level and began to write discernible sentences only last year. The adaptations and supports being used with Kent are summarized in Figure 9.9. Note how strategies related to academics, social–emotional needs, and physical-sensory needs are intermixed and interactive.

When we observe Kent in the classroom, it's not at all obvious that he is a student classified as having special needs. As we watch him work, it's clear he is functioning at a lower level than many students in the class. However, he participates in the full curriculum—most of which is designed in the first place to allow students to work at different levels. In many ways, the "adaptations" for Kent simply fit within the teaching used in the class. In other ways, adaptations actually grow out of the teaching process. Michelle, his teacher, laughs as she tells us what happened yesterday in class. It's obvious that she likes and enjoys Kent.

Figure 9.9

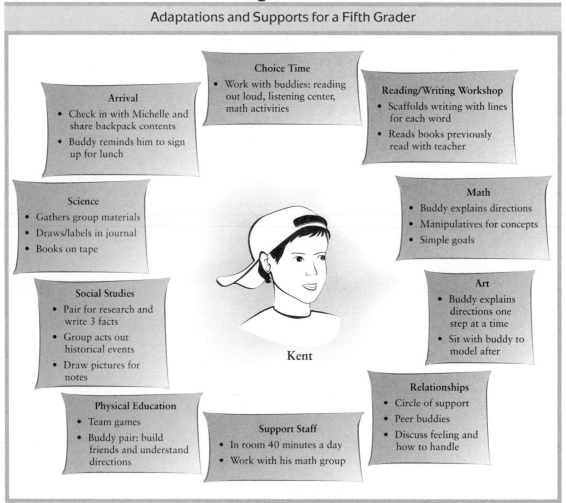

Adaptations and Supports for a Fifth Grader

Choice Time
- Work with buddies: reading out loud, listening center, math activities

Arrival
- Check in with Michelle and share backpack contents
- Buddy reminds him to sign up for lunch

Reading/Writing Workshop
- Scaffolds writing with lines for each word
- Reads books previously read with teacher

Science
- Gathers group materials
- Draws/labels in journal
- Books on tape

Math
- Buddy explains directions
- Manipulatives for concepts
- Simple goals

Social Studies
- Pair for research and write 3 facts
- Group acts out historical events
- Draw pictures for notes

Art
- Buddy explains directions one step at a time
- Sit with buddy to model after

Kent

Physical Education
- Team games
- Buddy pair: build friends and understand directions

Support Staff
- In room 40 minutes a day
- Work with his math group

Relationships
- Circle of support
- Peer buddies
- Discuss feeling and how to handle

It was wonderful. We were doing multiplication or column addition, depending on their working level, to find distance on a map. The students needed 640 times 4. I knew Kent would have problems even adding 640 four times, so I gave him a different strategy to use. I asked him to add 640 plus 640. He was able to do this fine. Then I had him add the resulting sum together again. I pulled all the students together and we talked about the different strategies they used to solve this problem. His peer buddy for this activity, Pedro, explained what they had done as Kent wrote it on the board. The other students loved this strategy. They decided to call it "Kent's invention"!

In many ways, Michelle's thinking about adaptations for Kent is not all that different from her thinking about adaptations for any of her students.

"They all are different," she says. "My job is to know where my students are socially, in academics, and in their lives, and to design lessons and adjust as we go to help them grow and develop." She does have assistance and support from Sarah, a special education teacher, who comes in for forty-five minutes a day. Sarah does not work only with Kent, however, but provides support when the class does centers for math or reading and writing workshop. Sarah has been helpful in coming up with hands-on ways to teach subjects. It's interesting, we think, to see the degree to which adaptations and support have become an integral part of the culture of this class.

Learning to Adapt

We've looked at a plethora of adaptations that can help students succeed academically in our classes—and at strategies that can help us manage the process of adapting. How do we start? We think the key is to understand that all of our teaching involves adaptations all the time, and that when "special" adaptations are needed, this most often happens because we're encountering students who need adaptations and supports we're less accustomed to using. The more that we teach all students together, the more making needed adaptations will become intuitive and hardly noticeable. If we think this way, rather than putting "adaptations" in a special place in our mind, we'll be surprised at how many new and creative ideas begin to pop up daily. Like the teacher portrayed in the vignette at the beginning of this chapter, if we spend our time thinking not about *whether* our class can include a student but about *how*, we free up all sorts of creativity and energy.

Key Points

- When we design our classes for diversity based on best practices (Chapters 6 and 8), we'll be successful with many more students. When difficulties persist, however, we may need to adapt our instruction.

- An ecological framework helps us compare an environment's requirements and resources to the abilities and needs of the person. When mismatches occur, this framework helps us think systematically about developing supports and adaptations.

- When student problems occur, we look carefully at how we teach and structure our classroom, and we compare our findings to the characteristics of the student. We can change how we teach or provide support.

- Many strategies are available for adapting teaching. For example, we can change our expectations about difficulty of work, amount of work, and time to be allowed; use different materials; allow students differing ways to perform tasks or demonstrate learning; and/or use different criteria for evaluation and grading.

Learning Expeditions

Following are some ideas and activities that may extend your learning.

1. Observe in a class a student with a significant mental or physical disability. Use the ecological adaptation framework in Figure 9.1 and conduct an analysis of the match of student skills to class expectations, the situation's reinforcers (resources) and the needs of the student, and the types of supports and adaptations available. How useful is this framework in helping you think how to work with a student? What are your recommendations for this student based on your analysis?

2. Use the class profile form in Figure 9.4 to complete a profile of a particular class. Observe in the class and interview the teacher. As you observe students with special needs, what ideas does this profiling process give you for helpful changes?

3. Interview a teacher and ask her to describe to you the differing kinds of abilities in the class, using as a guide the eight "intelligences" of multiple intelligences theory. What are some of the adaptations the teacher is using related to these abilities?

4. Interview a special education support teacher regarding the types of adaptations that he or she sees being used for students with special needs. Critique these. Are changes in overall teaching approaches considered? If so, how? What types of adaptations are used? How effective do these appear to be? Why?

5. Interview a parent of a child with special needs. What is the parent's perception of the quality of education the child is receiving? What types of adaptations does the parent think are being used in the classroom? What types of adaptations and strategies does the parent use at home?

6. Review information about a student who went to a hearing or filed a lawsuit because of a lack of needed accommodations and adaptations. Critique the issue and describe what you think the teacher or school should have done.

CHAPTER GOAL

Identify and explore special needs of students with behavioral and emotional challenges, and examine methods of responding that maintain and strengthen the classroom community.

CHAPTER OBJECTIVES

1. Review and understand ADHD and strategies for effective instruction and support of students with this condition.

2. Explore issues and information associated with the use of Ritalin and related drugs.

3. Know the different conditions associated with emotional disturbance and practices for supporting such students.

4. Understand instructional approaches that are effective with students with autism.

5. Reflect on and recognize the connection between the needs of students with behavioral and emotional challenges and best practices for teaching and learning.

Students with Behavioral and Emotional Challenges 10

Reaching Out to Maintain and Strengthen an Inclusive Classroom Community

Maria tells us about her middle school–aged son. "Matt has driven me crazy since I got divorced and he began this new school. The doctor says he has ADHD. That Ritalin has sure helped! Matt is calmer now but I worry. His sparkle seems gone, and he is depressed a lot." Donald, a high school science teacher, describes James, a similar student in another school who was "just wild in that last school." "He is very smart, but needs to be moving and needs a listening ear. We've done OK; he's worked with other kids, and I've encouraged creative and active ways to learn. I don't believe that these kids should be put on Ritalin so much. They have potential to be our leaders, and we will quash that if we make obedient zombies of them."

Jerrod, a sixth-grade teacher, tells us about one of his students: "Dylan has had a rough time in his short life. He says his dad died because he drank too much. This year his family

287

was evicted. He gets angry at other students a lot and became very defensive after they moved into the shelter. He reacts if kids touch him or get close. He is labeled as emotionally disturbed, learning disabled, and ADHD. When Dylan first began school, within a week the teacher had him at the back of the class with his desk facing the wall. Fortunately, we pulled together a team and have developed a plan that is working—team teaching, integration of social skills instruction in the daily routine, academic adaptations, supports for organization and frustration, and a behavior support plan" (adapted from Meadows, 1996).

Doria, a fifth-grade student who has autism, stands in the doorway as if she is paralyzed. The children say hello as she enters the room, but her face is frozen in a blank panicked stare, her hands twitching in response to the class noise. The teacher, Maureen, watches as another student comes over and looks directly at Doria, not touching, and asks if she wants to sit down. She goes to her special place in the corner and sits on the cushions. She reads a book for the first ten minutes of class. Some other kids come over and ask her to join them in working on a project. She does.

Donna Williams is a person with autism who has written several books about her experience in learning to develop relationships and cope with her disability. She describes conversations with friends who were also caught in the world of autism and managed to break out and communicate:

> "My world was beautiful," said Susan. "It was full of colors and sounds. There were no people in it," she said matter-of-factly. "One day I made a friend. That's how I lost my world . . . when I was five I became interested in the way my friend did things and more and more I stopped visiting my world and I lost it." (Williams, 1994, p. 200)

> Suddenly, [Ian] stopped and crouched in the middle of the road, his long arms wrapped around his knees. "It hurts," he said, "it hurts so much." "It's emotions," I said pausing, "they can't hurt you." "I'd do anything to get rid of this," said Ian shaking violently. . . . "Would you want to feel dead like before?" I asked. "No!" said Ian. . . . "It hurts to have a self," I said. (Williams, 1994, p. 226)

Working with students with emotional and behavioral issues may challenge our commitment to being inclusive teachers more deeply than anything else. When students cause disruptions based on emotional needs that they don't know how to handle, challenging our abilities to respond positively, we may feel insecure in our own abilities. We may be concerned for the safety of other students or may worry that our own responses might exacerbate the problem. Yet unless we commit to bringing these students into our community, they are likely to be segregated and set on a path that most often leads to greater problems in later life. How do we respond?

Dealing with deviant behaviors was once a community responsibility, often resulting in cruel treatment—public floggings, expulsion, and more. Beginning in the late nineteenth century people with problem behaviors became the responsibility of specialists working in institutions whose purpose was to control and reform behavior—special schools, asylums, juvenile facilities, mental hospitals, prisons. In recent years behavioral problems have often been viewed as biological and neurological, requiring medication as a prime mode of treatment. Social conditions—poverty, family dynamics, schooling—are given little attention. The following statements summarize a view that has gained influence (Kauffman, 1997; McKnight, 1995; Skrtic, 1994):

- The emotional and behavioral problems of children are caused by biology.
- We must diagnose and label children to provide treatment.
- Medications can counter the effects of these biological, neurological conditions.
- Specialists trained in dealing with specific problem conditions are necessary.
- Often children with emotional and behavioral problems need to live and to go to school in separate places.

However, it is clear that efforts based on this view are not helping to reduce problems and return people to communities as was once hoped. Rather, the numbers of incarcerated, institutionalized, and medicated children continues to grow at a dramatic rate (Diller, 1998; McKnight, 1995). We think a different way is possible and needed, and once again schools are key. Many schools and teachers are building caring communities that promote inclusion of these students. In this chapter we will discuss three conditions often diagnosed in children who demonstrate behavioral and emotional challenges in schools: (1) *ADHD*, (2) *emotional disturbance*, and (3) *autism*. As we consider these children and their needs, can we see ourselves including them? Can we see them as *children* rather than as "disorders" or "conditions"? We will find that the key element needed by these children, *community*, is also needed for all our children—a topic we will take up in Chapter 11.

𝒯raveling 𝒩otes

In recent years increasing numbers of schools have established zero tolerance policies, leading to suspension and expulsion of increasing numbers of students for increasingly trivial problems. This trend is but one indicator of a growing concern about behavioral challenges. Fortunately, teachers and other educators are responding by listening to and connecting with these challenging students.

1. Many teachers think we need to "control" children with punishments, rewards, or drugs. What is your opinion? How would you treat Matt, Dylan, or Doria?

2. We're using more and more drugs with children. We'll discuss Ritalin in this chapter. What do you think about the use of drugs to control behavior?

3. We're also seeing many more students with autism in our classes, as the incidence has shot upward in recent years. Articulate people with autism like Donna Williams and Temple Grandin, whom we'll meet later, show us a picture of need and a terror of connecting with other people. How can we help?

4. Do we see children with emotional and behavioral difficulties as "ours"? How might we bring these students into our classrooms? What strategies are successful teachers and schools using?

Perhaps no other set of students need us more or are rejected more often by schools and teachers. Let's think deeply about our commitment to all children, raising issues and seeking strategies as we journey forward.

"The Wildest Colts Make the Best Horses"*
Attention Deficit/Hyperactivity Disorder

In recent decades a literal explosion has occurred in the number of students who are labeled as having **attention deficit/hyperactivity disorder** (**ADHD**) (Breggin, P., 2000; Diller, 1998). We can be assured we will have at least one such student in almost any class. What are the behaviors that call attention to these students? Here are examples.

By kindergarten, Ricky had developed a reputation. He was avoided because he would pull hair, push, or annoy classmates. He spent much time in time-out during kindergarten. Academically, Ricky knew the answers, constantly blurting them out. However, he rarely wrote. In first and second grade, behaviors grew worse, and he was removed from the classroom periodically "in order that the other students could have an opportunity to learn" (adapted from Bender, 1997, p. 191).

Ms. Lee, a third-grade teacher, was concerned that Sam was fidgety and frequently out of his seat during reading. Other students were disrupted by Sam's behavior every time he was out of his seat (adapted from Bender, 1997, p. 163).

Melanie was a high school senior. For the last few years she had been turned off by school and had skipped classes a great deal. During a typical day she would either daydream or sleep in the back of the class. She turned in hardly any homework. However, the teacher just ignored her (adapted from Davis, 1996).

The typical process for identifying ADHD looks only at behaviors of the child. However, several other questions seem important; "*Why* is this child doing this?" "What is going on in the family and in class?" In a class based on best practices, children are engaged in collaborative interactions much of the time, so "blurting out answers" is much less of a problem. In such a class hardly *any* kids would be in their seats during reading workshop, so "out-of-seat behavior" would not be such an issue. So what is this all about? These are the kinds of questions that we encounter in the literature on ADHD. Some see the problem as based on biological deficits in the child and as treatable largely with medication. Others see the causes of ADHD as largely environmental, based on social pressures in a fast-moving world combined with unstimulating classroom instruction. (Parents often report that the problems their children have are limited to school; in the summer they can completely take them off their medications.) Still others see an interactive mix of biological tendencies and environment.

*Title of book by John Breeding (1996).

A teacher talks with a girl who is upset with a class-mate, helping her put her feelings into words and try-ing to understand why she is angry.

What Is ADHD?

How did we get here? During the late twentieth century, researchers identified the characteristics now packaged as **attention deficit/hyperactivity disorder (ADHD)**. They first focused on hyperactivity as a component of minimum brain damage (MBD) and by the 1970s identified a unique "hyperactive child syndrome." In 1972 researcher Virginia Douglas presented a seminal paper regarding children whose problems centered on "deficits in sustaining attention and controlling impulses" (Diller, 1998, p. 53). A new name—attention deficit disorder, or ADD—was soon created and was included in the *Diagnostic and Statistical Manual of Mental Disorders* (DSM) in 1980.

The term used in the most recent version, the **DSM IV–TR** (American Psychiatric Association, 2000), is ADHD (attention deficit/hyperactivity disorder). Several subtypes are identified: (1) *inattentive* (previously thought of as "ADD" without hyperactivity; (2) *impulsive and hyperactive;* and (3) *combined type*—exhibiting all three behaviors of concern. The diagnostic criteria for ADHD are listed in Figure 10.1.

For a child to be diagnosed as ADHD, he or she must exhibit at least six of the nine symptoms of inattention or hyperactivity–impulsivity. These must be seen before age seven in at least two situations—for example, at school and at home; must cause significant problems in functioning; and must be unable to be better explained by another diagnosis. Many more boys are identified than girls, particularly as hyperactive or impulsive. Although many claim that the ADHD diagnosis is objective, others disagree. Diller (1998) claims that physicians often simply check off criteria based on an interview with parents without observing the child or delving adequately into the child's life. The criteria describe conflict with adults that could easily be occasioned by stress, family dynamics, lack of time with teachers and parents, or simply boring instruction. However, these factors are seldom adequately considered (Breggin & Ross-Breggin, 1994; Diller, 1998).

Figure 10.1

DSM IV-TR Criteria for ADHD

INATTENTION

- Often fails to give close attention to details or makes careless mistakes in schoolwork, work, or other activities.
- Often has difficulty sustaining attention in tasks or play activities.
- Often does not seem to listen when spoken to directly.
- Often does not follow through on instructions and fails to finish schoolwork, chores, or duties in the workplace (not due to oppositional behavior or failure to understand instructions).
- Often has difficulty organizing tasks and activities.
- Often avoids, dislikes, or is reluctant to engage in tasks that require sustained mental effort (such as schoolwork or homework).
- Often loses things necessary for tasks or activities (e.g., toys, school assignments, pencils, books, or tools).
- Is often easily distracted by extraneous stimuli.
- Is often forgetful in daily activities.

HYPERACTIVITY

- Often fidgets with hands or feet or squirms in seat.
- Often leaves seat in classroom or in other situations in which it is inappropriate (in adolescents or adults, may be limited to subjective feelings of restlessness).
- Often has difficulty playing or engaging in leisure activities quietly.
- Is often "on the go" or often acts as if "driven by a motor."
- Often talks excessively.

IMPULSIVITY

- Often blurts out answers before questions have been completed.
- Often has difficulty waiting turn.
- Often interrupts or intrudes on others (e.g., butts into conversations).

Source: Reprinted with permission from the *Diagnostic and Statistical Manual of Mental Disorders,* Fourth Edition, Text Revision. Washington, DC, American Psychiatric Association, 2000.

Researchers have sought a biological cause for ADHD. Many writings report such biological causation as an established fact. Others admit a lack of evidence but presume biological causes have yet to be identified (Kauffman, 1997). Coles (1987, 1998) conducted an exhaustive analysis of the research and concluded that there is no basis in fact for claims of a biological origin.

At a minimum, this debate suggests that a biological cause cannot be assumed and that we must pay attention to how the environment affects children in our classrooms.

Estimates of the incidence of ADHD vary widely. For some, the whole disorder is simply a hoax and does not exist at all (Goodman & Poillion, 1992). DuPaul and Stoner (1994) indicate that up to 5 percent of the population may be classified as ADHD; Biederman (1996) put that figure at 10 percent, and Shaywitz and Shaywitz (1988) at 23 percent. The National Institute of Mental Health (2001) estimates that 3 to 5 percent of school-age children will be diagnosed with ADHD and that it occurs three times more often in boys than in girls.

Inattention. People are normally able to engage and disengage attention as needed; but in ADHD, Nelson (1996, 1998) suggests, people shift between inattention and distractibility and bursts of "hyperfocusing." She describes three states or types of inattention: hypofocus, mixed focus, and hyperfocus:

Type 1: Hypofocus: Some students are not able to focus or attend well and are prone to impulsiveness and physical hyperactivity They struggle to engage their cognitive processes and sustain concentration. They are kinesthetic learners who learn best in situations involving movement. They seek stimulation through physical activity and intense experience.

Type 2: Hyperfocus: These students focus intensely on the subject at hand, blocking out other sources of input. Their minds race with ideas, and they are often physically overactive and impulsive. They may become so overstimulated they "shut down and withdraw to escape overload" (Nelson, 1998, p. 1), have difficulty attending, and need help to focus *less* so that they can also attend to other stimuli. Such students may amaze teachers with their creativity and energy. However, these same students are extremely frustrating when they can't seem to stop working on one project and switch to another.

Type 3: Mixed Focus: These children shift back and forth between underfocusing and hyperfocusing—they're inattentive one hour, overattentive the next, often mixing inattention with physical underactivity. When underfocusing a student may seem "spacey," prone to too much thinking and too little action. The student may have trouble finishing activities and may need help both in focusing and in disengaging from an activity.

Hartmann (1996) similarly describes people with ADHD as attending to everything, particularly what is *interesting*. Hartmann points out that ADHD characteristics such as constant attention to multiple stimuli, impulsivity, and hyperactivity were valuable when human beings relied on hunting for survival. Hunters must constantly scan the environment, attend simultaneously to multiple inputs, and make snap judgments. "In a classroom, the child . . . is the one who notices the janitor mowing the lawn outside the window, when he should be listening to the teacher's lecture on long division. The bug crawling across the ceiling, or the class bully preparing to throw a spit wad, are infinitely more fascinating than the teacher's analysis of Columbus's place in history" (Hartmann, 1996, p. 23).

Impulsivity. As students with ADHD behaviors constantly scan the environment, making mental connections between ideas, they jump from one idea to another. When a thought comes to mind, they speak it out loud, despite what others are saying. Such a student may hear something and run to the window (Bender, 1997). "Lines. I am incapable of waiting in lines. . . . Impulse leads to action . . . that's why I . . . lack tact"—which is "entirely dependent on the ability to consider one's words before uttering them (Hallowell, 1996, p. 5). Yet impulsivity can be very valuable. Rather than hesitating, these students "act on instant decisions" with the "willingness to explore new and untested areas" (Hartmann, 1996, p. 24) and may be highly creative and stimulate lively discussion. Students need help in channeling this energy.

We may give such students responsibilities for helping to lead a class discussion or ask them to organize an activity with a small group of students.

Hyperactivity. Some students are full of energy and movement. According to the National Institute of Mental Health,

> people who are hyperactive always seem to be in motion. They can't sit still; they may dash around or talk incessantly. Sitting still through a lesson can be an impossible task. They may roam around the room, squirm in their seats, wiggle their feet, touch everything, or noisily tap a pencil. They may also feel intensely restless. (2001, p. 1)

Ritalin: Issues for Teachers

Use of drugs to control ADHD behavior is growing dramatically. In 1970 only 150,000 patients used the drug Ritalin; in 1990, 900,000; and in 2000, an estimated 5 to 8 million (Breggin, 1998; Diller, 1998). Some suggest that at least 10 million children need to be taking Ritalin. The key question is—what role do teachers play in decisions about medicating with Ritalin? Nancy Creech (personal communication, June 21, 2000) a multiage teacher, talked about her experiences.

> In the thirteen years I have been teaching, I have never had a girl on Ritalin. Before and after lunch, when the line forms in our building for medication, there are two girls out of some thirty kids. Ten percent of our building is on medications. Ninety percent of these boys come from single-parent homes. The two girls are among the most artistic in the building. They have no problem attending when they draw. In my opinion our teachers just haven't attended to a different learning style.
>
> I had a little boy come in this year from kindergarten on Ritalin. He never smiled. His mom took him off in November, and he didn't stop smiling until June. Did he behave better? No. Did he attend better? No. But he wasn't any worse either.
>
> I don't have answers, just questions based on observations that appall me. We say we don't have the time or the money to give these kids what they need, so we encourage them to take a drug because it is easy. But when I see all those boys lined up, my stomach gets in knots and I wonder what we are doing to our children.

Strong social forces drive the use of Ritalin and other medications to help control the behavior of children. Many adults with ADHD feel Ritalin is useful and necessary, like taking medicine for the flu (Hartmann & Bowman, 1996). Schools pressure parents to have their kids diagnosed and medicated (Diller, 1998) If parents refuse to do so, a small but growing number of schools have reported parents to Protective Services, charging them with child neglect and abuse (Karlin, 2000). Psychiatrists report that many parents come specifically to obtain prescriptions, and "Ritalin mills" have sprung up (Diller, 1998).

A growing number of researchers and practitioners, however, are asking critical questions and building a countermovement. Numerous writers and researchers are questioning drug use, analyzing both impact and side effects, and suggesting alternatives for both parents and teachers (Armstrong, 1997; Breeding, 1996; Breggin, 1998; Diller, 1998; Stein, 1999).

Ritalin's Effects. We can summarize what we know about **Ritalin** in a few sentences. First, Ritalin (which paradoxically is a stimulant) does work with ADHD, in the sense that it helps children and adults focus for a short time, reduces emotional responses, and helps to moderate impulsivity. Research has established that Ritalin has similar effects on those who are and are not considered to have ADHD, discounting an early myth that its impact affects only kids with ADHD (Diller, 1998).

Ritalin has several potential side effects. Some are common, others more rare (Figure 10.2), many of which are very serious despite assurances about the drug's safety. Long-term effects are not known, as most follow-up studies do not go beyond three months. Breggin and Ross-Breggin (1994), and Diller (1998) have expressed concern about Ritalin's potential impact on the developing brain. Most obvious is the drug's tendency to sap children of their spirit, creating a "zombie" demeanor. As a stimulant, the drug can actually worsen the conditions it was designed to prevent—agitation, restlessness, insomnia (Breggin, 1998). In addition, the *rebound effect*, typical withdrawal responses that can last up to ten days after ingestion, may make a child's behavior worse than it was before use. These reactions often convince people that the drug is needed *and* that increased dosages may be necessary.

Finally, critics are also concerned about psychological effects. Breggin and Ross-Breggin (1994) state that the drug shields children (and adults) from the need to work through conflicts and removes the need for adults to critique their own behavior. In addition, two studies report that children on Ritalin tend to see their success as based on a drug rather than as attributable to their own work and effort (Breggin & Cohen, 1999). Finally, many believe that for some children a combination

Figure 10.2

Adverse Side Effects of Ritalin	
Cardiovascular	Palpitations, tachycardia (abnormally increased heart rate), increased blood pressure
Central nervous system (CNS)	Excessive CNS stimulation (can cause convulsions), psychosis (toxic or organic), depression or sadness, dizziness (vertigo), headache, insomnia, nervousness, irritability, attacks of Tourette's or other tic syndromes
Gastrointestinal	Anorexia (loss of appetite), nausea, vomiting, stomach pain, dry mouth
Endocrine/metabolic	Weight loss, growth suppression
Other	Blurred vision, leukopenia (low white blood cell count), hypersensitivity reaction, anemia

Sources: Breggin (1998) and Drug Enforcement Administration (1995).

of social supports, effective instruction, and reasonable drug use can be effective (Comfort, 1994; Diller, 1998; Weaver, 1994). With good teaching practice we should expect substantial reductions in the present use of Ritalin and related drugs.

Teachers and Ritalin. What do we do as inclusive teachers? Many teachers recommend that parents get their children evaluated and put on Ritalin. In fact, such pressure has become so widespread that states have begun to pass laws prohibiting teachers from making such recommendations. Most teachers using best practices will work out more positive ways of supporting students.

What do we do when students are already on Ritalin? This question is harder, because parents may have come to rely on the drug. Although teachers do not have the training to recommend dosage, we can nevertheless support any parents who wish to reduce the levels of medication their children are taking: We can express an openness to reducing dosage amount if the parents want to explore this with their physician. We may be surprised by the trust that this generates with parents. We will likely have colleagues who tend to pressure parents to get their children on Ritalin, and we will need to be able to explain our position and raise questions while resisting any efforts to get us to respond likewise.

Teaching Students with ADHD Behaviors

Students with ADHD behaviors challenge us to emphasize three important areas: balancing creativity and engagement with individual options, help with organizational skills and structure, and providing emotional support.

ADHD and Special Services. Most students with ADHD remain in the general education classroom (Bender, 1997). Although ADHD is not a special education category, students with ADHD can qualify under the category of "other health impaired" if they need special education services (Office of Special Education and Rehabilitative Services, 1991). Many students labeled ADHD also are considered learning disabled. Even if they do not receive special education services, they are covered under Section 504 and schools must provide reasonable accommodations.

Teaching with Creativity and Engaging Activities. Students with ADHD need stimulating activities to engage their attention (Nelson, 1996, 1998). John Weaver, a student diagnosed with ADHD in high school, stated that "we find it next to impossible to do whatever seems boring" (Weaver, 1994, p. 48). For John, approaching assignments creatively was very important. For example, "I gave my report under the guise of a ghost. For a costume, my mother allowed me to mutilate a bed sheet" (p. 47). John and three friends also asked to do a book report in which each wrote a short story about a figure in *Huckleberry Finn*.

Too often teachers try merely to reduce distractions and control students. Many a creative, holistic teacher has been told that "your class is too active and unstructured for these kids." However, students with ADHD *need* both active learning and structure. John Weaver said it this way: "What happened when the assignments didn't allow for creativity? . . . I froze up on regular paper and pencil tests; oral reports were even worse. . . . In front of a class . . . I was paralyzed. . . . Could creativity have helped? Yes. Could the teacher have done something more to help me with my situation? Yes" (Weaver, 1994, pp. 47–48).

The strategies discussed in Chapters 6 and 8 provide numerous ways to create engaging learning opportunities that will help students with ADHD behaviors. Here are a few.

- Allow students to propose alternative approaches to assignments.
- Use multiple intelligences.
- Give work that asks students to "take time to think and to problem-solve rather than allowing them to supply ready answers impulsively" (Comfort, 1994, p. 68).
- Use workshops; authentic learning; and activity-based learning involving story, pictures, manipulatives, and games.
- Offer choices and opportunities for creativity.

Providing Options That Respond to Individual Needs. What does it take for a student with ADHD to engage and focus? For some, class noise makes concentration difficult. Others *need* background noise. We can help these students monitor fatigue, create transitions from mental to physical activity, take breaks to release energy and tension. We can provide environmental options such as:

- Social interactions while working—tables, gathering places with pillows, a small sofa
- Places where students can be alone and where it is quieter—desks or pillows in the hall, study carrels (with headphones and tape players with soft music)
- Spaces for individual work—desks, floor work areas with pillows
- Varied lighting—different types of lamps and study areas next to windows

Helping Students Organize and Structure Their Work. Students may have difficulties organizing their work. They need tools, reinforcement of their worthiness, and the opportunity to direct themselves. We must carefully balance help and opportunities for self-direction. Following are useful strategies:

- Help students set goals, plan, break goals into short-term steps, and monitor their progress.
- Provide tools for planning, scheduling, and tracking assignments—a calendar, project task analysis, daily and weekly schedules, journaling. In secondary school, learning resource centers can assist all students in these areas.
- Help students organize work with student notebooks (three-ring binders, notebooks for each subject); filing systems (alphabetic, topical); and computer organization, including the use of computer "folders."

We can teach these skills as minilessons. The following ideas also help provide "flexible structure":

- Give written as well as oral instructions and ask students to verify their understanding of what has been said (Comfort, 1994).
- Establish due dates or ask students to develop a timeline for assignments.

- Pair students or organize work groups in which students report to and support one another.
- Provide timely and frequent feedback—daily quizzes (Weaver, 1994), student-to-student progress reports.
- Keep accessible copies of parent letters, work expectations, and assignments.

Providing Emotional Support and Understanding. Students with ADHD behaviors have likely been criticized much. Teachers often become frustrated when students don't complete assignments, are active in the class, or can't concentrate. Often a negative cycle begins: Teachers try to control and punish students, and students' behavior gets worse. We should not act as if something is "wrong" with them. When they are inattentive, impulsive, or hyperactive, we seek to be patient and to use these occurrences as opportunities for learning (Comfort, 1994). Related ideas:

- Pay attention to students' emotions and build on strengths.
- Develop community structures for emotional support (Chapter 11)—listening to students' voices through circles of support, peer partnerships, class meetings.
- Help students understand their own actions and consequences. Get them to think about what they need. Have them journal about their actions and feelings.
- Provide positive outlets for student energy—opportunities for movement, creative expression.
- Form a personal relationship with the student.

How Students with ADHD Can Improve Our Class. Students with ADHD have the potential to bring creativity and energy to our class. They need both opportunities to be stimulated and express themselves *and* structure that allows them to focus

Artwork reprinted by permission of Martha Perske from *Perske: Pencil Portraits 1971–1990* (Nashville: Abingdon Press, 1998).

PERSKE

their energies. Because they need both, they challenge us to learn how to create this balance. As we do so, other students will benefit from our deepened skills.

A Good Kid but Troubling Sometimes
Serious Emotional Disturbance

Pamela's first-grade class is on the first floor of a school in a working-class neighborhood. Lately Mahmed has had trouble, frequently running out of the room. This happened last week. When Pamela tried to get someone to help, no one was available, and Mahmed wandered the halls till the end of the day. When we visit the class, we see Mahmed and some classmates putting block models together for a project. "He's doing OK," says Pamela, "but he can get upset easily." She has tried various systems of rewards and punishments, such as separating him from other children. None has worked. "Pamela, why is he doing this?" we ask. She doesn't know. This question has never been discussed, even though the principal, mother, and teachers had a long meeting last week. Later we talk with the principal, Carl, who says briskly, "We are sending Mahmed to our special school for children with emotional problems. They have specialists who can watch him and control his behaviors." Carl didn't want to help Mahmed remain at the school.

Mahmed's situation is one example of what occurs with children labeled "emotionally disturbed." Emotional difficulties involve high degrees of interaction between the characteristics of the child and the environment. Too often, as in Mahmed's case, family, community, and school all fail these children. We often see poverty, lack of emotional support, abuse, high levels of stress, disengagement of parents, and controlling and punishing schools in the lives of children with emotional difficulties. Unfortunately, however, the problem is usually defined as the child's and is described as a "disorder" (Breggin, P., 2000; Breggin & Ross-Breggin, 1994; Cullinan, Epstein, & Sabornie, 1992; Marder, 1992; Wagner, 1995). As we look at clinical descriptions of problematic behaviors of children, we may understandably find ourselves feeling uncomfortable. What difference might we make with such students in a caring, engaging learning environment with reasonable support?

What Is Emotional Disturbance? Problems, Terminology, and Definitions

Definitions of emotional disorders have been much debated. Many use the term *emotional*, emphasizing the common importance of emotions as driving forces behind problems. Others employ the word *behavioral*, focusing on observable actions. Increasingly, these terms have been linked, as in the phrase *emotional and behavioral disorders.* Many problems are clustered under the umbrella phrase of *emotional disturbance,* however. The Individuals with Disabilities Education Act (IDEA) defines "serious emotional disturbance' as

> a condition exhibiting one or more of the following characteristics over a long period of time and to a marked degree that adversely affects a child's educational performance:
>
> (A) An inability to learn that cannot be explained by intellectual, sensory, or health factors.
> (B) An inability to build or maintain satisfactory interpersonal relationships with peers and teachers.
> (C) Inappropriate types of behavior or feelings under normal circumstances.
> (D) A general pervasive mood of unhappiness or depression.
> (E) A tendency to develop physical symptoms or fears associated with personal or school problems.

The term includes schizophrenia. The term does not apply to children who are socially maladjusted, unless it is determined that they have an emotional disturbance. (Individuals with Disabilities Education Improvement Act [IDEA], 2004)

This last phrase, commonly called the "exclusionary clause," is particularly significant. In our schools we will see many students who have great emotional and behavioral difficulties. However, if their problems are considered to be "socially maladjusted", then they will not be deemed eligible for special education services. This distinction has been quite controversial.

Figure 10.3 identifies common emotional and behavioral difficulties, which we now briefly describe. In the DSM IV–TR (American Psychiatric Association, 2000), three "externalizing" conditions are described as **disruptive behavior disorders**—ADHD, oppositional defiance disorder, and conduct disorder (see Figure 10.3). However, researchers state that it is difficult to differentiate among these conditions (Cohen, M. K., 1994; Nelson, 1992; Skiba & Grizzle, 1992). Students with **oppositional defiance disorder** (ODD) exhibit negative, hostile behavior lasting at least six months in which they frequently do four of the following: lose temper; argue with adults; defy or refuse to comply with adults' requests; deliberately annoy people; blame others; and/or act touchy, angry, resentful, and spiteful.

Conduct disorder ups the ante and involves persistent rule breaking and aggressive behavior such as defiance, fighting, bullying, disruptiveness, and problematic relationships with both peers and adults (Cohen, M. K., 1994; Forness, Kavale, & Lopez, 1993). Students labeled as having conduct disorders are frequently diagnosed

Figure 10.3

Emotional and Behavioral Disorders

EXTERNALIZING DISORDERS
- Attention deficit/hyperactivity disorder (ADHD)
- Oppositional defiance disorder (ODD)
- Conduct disorder
- Pervasive developmental disorders (PDD)

INTERNALIZING DISORDERS
- Substance abuse
- Feeding and eating disorders
- Anxiety and social withdrawal
- Depression
- Schizophrenia and psychosis

with ADHD, learning disabilities, anxiety disorders, and depression (Clarizio, 1992; Zoccolillo, 1992). These students are the largest single group in separate day schools and residential treatment centers (Doucette, 1997; Forness, Kavale, King, & Kasari, 1994; Sinclair & Alexson, 1992).

The fourth category of externalizing conditions (Figure 10.3), pervasive developmental disorders, will be discussed later in this chapter. We turn now to the "internalizing" disorders, in which emotional upsets direct their impact inward:

Substance abuse: Many students with other emotional disorders are also substance abusers (Capaldi & Dishion, 1993; Leone, 1991) and engage in illegal acts that bring them into contact with the juvenile justice system (Leone, 1991).

Feeding and eating disorders: Students with *anorexia nervosa* are terrified of gaining weight and typically starve themselves. *Bulimia* is a related condition in which students starve themselves, then go on eating binges followed by self-induced vomiting to prevent weight gain. Such students typically act depressed, withdrawn, and irritable. These problems can lead to other serious medical conditions (American Psychiatric Association, 2000).

Anxiety and social withdrawal: Some students have difficulty with situations that promote anxiety. They may complain about physical problems, worry, and need much reassurance (American Psychiatric Association, 2000).

Depression: Depression among young people has been recognized as a growing problem. Some signs typically include sad, lonely, or apathetic behavior; avoidance of social contacts; chronic problems with sleeping, eating, or elimination; fear of being with others in public places; and talk of suicide. Students who are depressed may also turn outward on occasion, becoming angry, irritable, and upset and seeking an emotional outlet for their pain (American Psychiatric Association, 2000; Karp, 1996; Vaughn, Bos, & Schumm, 1997).

Schizophrenia and psychosis: Schizophrenia is diagnosed when two or more of the following symptoms are present: delusions, hallucinations, disorganized speech, disorganized or catatonic behavior, and problems in the ability to think logically or make decisions (American Psychiatric Association, 2000).

What would happen if we put any of these behaviors in a social context? If we looked at the lives of children with emotional disturbances, might we typically find meaning and purpose in behaviors that otherwise seem purposeless, out of control, or bizarre? Some argue that behaviors always have social meaning.

The Demographics of Emotional Disturbance

As we look at who is labeled emotionally disturbed and consider the treatment these students receive, we discover troubling patterns. We are failing to support children whose lives are very difficult.

Who Are They? Who is most likely to be labeled emotionally disturbed? The answers call into question the practice of focusing only on student behavior without understanding the students' social situation. Nationally, approximately 0.9 percent of the student population is identified as emotionally disturbed (Oswald &

Coutinho, 1995). Some observers, however, believe that a more accurate figure would be 3 to 6 percent of the student population (Kauffman, 1997). States vary enormously in their identification rate—from Mississippi at 0.01 percent to Minnesota at 2 percent of students. Published research (Cullinan, Epstein, & Sabornie, 1992; Office of Special Education Programs, 1999; Wagner, 1995) indicates that students labeled emotionally disturbed are disproportionately likely to be:

1. Male
2. African American
3. Economically disadvantaged
4. In secondary school (in 1996 3.5 percent of students with disabilities were labeled as emotionally disturbed at age six to seven, but 13 percent at sixteen to seventeen)
5. Living with one parent, in foster care, or in another alternative living arrangement (Office of Special Education Programs, 1999)

It should be noted that boys are more likely to be aggressive or to act in ways that disrupt the classroom, and teachers are more likely to identify students who are disruptive (Boggiano & Barrett, 1992; Gresham, MacMillan, & Bocian, 1996). Young women are more likely to exhibit internalizing behaviors that do not directly affect teachers or other students (Zahn-Waxler, 1993). Also, some teachers expect black students to be problematic, thus running the risk of creating a self-fulfilling prophecy (Horowitz, Bility, Plichta, Leaf, & Haynes, 1998; Metz, 1994).

What Causes Emotional and Behavioral Problems?　Researchers have explored both biological and environmental factors in seeking to understand the causes of emotional and behavioral difficulties. Despite substantial research, however, no direct biological causes have been established. At best, some individuals appear to have greater predisposition or risk of having emotional disturbance. Even in such cases, however, the effects of family, school, and community experiences may either protect and build resilience or contribute to emotional crisis. In his synthesis of relevant research, Kauffman (1997) concluded that "social learning is nearly always far more important than genetics. Little or no evidence supports the suggestion that specific behaviors are genetically transmitted" (p. 195).

All of the following life stresses have been found to be significantly associated with emotional disturbance: poverty, malnutrition, homelessness, family conflict, divorce, inconsistent child-rearing practices, and child and sexual abuse (Eber, Nelson, & Miles, 1997; Kauffman, 1997). Brooks (1985) found that 62 percent of a sample of thirteen- to eighteen-year-old females with emotional disorders were sexually abused before the age of sixteen (Brooks, 1985).

Kauffman (1997) uses social learning theory to explain violence and aggression. That is, children learn by observing individuals who model aggressive behavior—family, peers, community members, people in the media. Children are encouraged when they act aggressively and receive no aversive consequences or are rewarded by "overcoming their victims" (p. 340). This reaction is particularly common when children have been ridiculed or abused. Even punishment may strengthen aggression "when it causes pain, when there are no positive alternatives to the punished response . . . or when punishment provides a model of aggressive behavior" (p. 341). These dynamics play out in many schools where children, mostly low-income males, are not given support and modeling for new behaviors but are punished for aggression. Sometimes boys literally learn from teachers how to be aggressive and violent (Kauffman, 1997).

Finally, some forms of emotional disturbance, particularly schizophrenia, are considered in mainstream psychiatry to have neurobiological causes. This conclusion is hotly contested by many, however. Opponents suggest that even bizarre behaviors often represent reasonable responses to high degrees of stress and abuse. Modrow (1996), for example, describes how the collusion of family, school, and psychiatry led one child to hallucinations, antisocial actions, and delusions of grandeur, all as ways of coping with a difficult emotional situation.

How Well Do They Do? Some 55 percent of students labeled emotionally disturbed drop out of school (Wagner, 1995). Black males from poor families are the most likely to be segregated and the least likely to receive counseling and graduate from high school (Osher & Osher, 1996). On leaving school, 73 percent of dropouts and 58 percent of graduates are arrested within five years (Wagner, 1995; Wagner, Blackorby, Cameto, Hebbeler, & Newman, 1993). These figures sketch a picture of poor treatment and outcomes for children with many problems in their lives.

Inclusion in School

Although many students with emotional disturbance are included in general education classes and schools, supports for these students have been inadequate. More than 50 percent of students labeled emotionally disturbed are placed in segregated schools, classes, or private or public psychiatric institutions.

The degrees to which students with emotional disturbance are included and supported in general education varies dramatically from state to state. In 1994–95, for example, in Iowa and Vermont 80 percent and 78 percent of these students, respectively, went to regular schools; fewer than 20 percent did so in other states. Nationwide, between 1984–85 and 1995–96 the percentage in general education rose from 12 percent to 23 percent (Office of Special Education Programs, 1998).

Treatment of students with emotional disturbances sometimes seems designed to exacerbate their problems. These students particularly need emotional support. As Breggin puts it, "an 'out-of-control child' needs more security, more trust, more love—not medication and isolation" (Breggin & Ross-Breggin, 1994, p. 192). However, what such students most often get is (1) separation from other students and the larger community, (2) isolation and punishment, and (3) medications (Lewis, Chard, & Scott, 1994). Support services are often fragmented or insufficient (McLaughlin, Leone, Warren, & Schofield, 1994). Schools may actually reinforce problematic behavior (Shores, Gunter, & Jack, 1993), focus on controlling students instead of building on student strengths (Knitzer, Steinberg, & Fleisch, 1990), and shift students frequently from place to place (Kortering & Blackorby, 1992; Mayer, 1995; Osher & Hanley, 1996). As extreme aggression is motivated by "futility and self-hatred—inspired ultimately by feelings of worthlessness and humiliation" (Breggin

& Ross-Breggin, 1994, p. 189), it's not surprising that these students' difficulties are often strengthened by schools and organizations whose intended purpose is to help.

Inclusive Teaching and Schoolwide Support for Students with Emotional Disturbance

Some schools have made proactive efforts to include students with emotional and behavioral disturbance in general education classes. The key is to develop collaborative and flexible supports through a partnership of professionals from agencies, friends, family, and community. In 1994 the U.S. Department of Education commissioned a group to develop a "national agenda" (Center for Effective Collaboration and Practice, 1994) to improve services for these students. The key points of the *National Agenda for Achieving Better Results for Children and Youth with Serious Emotional Disturbance* include:

- Expand positive learning opportunities and results.
- Strengthen school and community capacity.
- Value and address diversity.
- Collaborate with families.
- Promote assessment of services.
- Provide ongoing skill development and support.
- Create comprehensive and collaborative systems.

In addition, the national agenda states that collaborative efforts must extend to initiatives that *prevent* emotional and behavioral problems from developing or escalating; services must be provided in a *culturally sensitive* and respectful manner; and services must empower all stakeholders and maintain a *climate of possibility and accountability.*

Our role as teachers is very important. When we build community in our classroom, use engaging teaching practices, and collaborate with and support families, we play our part in bringing this agenda to life. At best, we will be part of a school and community team implementing what Cheney and Muscott (1996) call *responsible inclusion.* The school, they say, must commit to including students and have support systems in place *before* inclusion occurs. Schools that have been successful in supporting students with substantive emotional and behavioral challenges have common characteristics, and many of the strategies for students with learning disabilities and ADHD are directly applicable to students with emotional disturbance. Let's explore these.

Schoolwide Planning. Effective schools involve all in developing a culture in which staff share a common child-centered orientation, seeing every student as theirs and focusing on individual strengths and needs (Cheney & Muscott, 1996; Quinn, Osher, Hoffman, & Hanley, 1998).

Problem Solving. Effective schools use a problem-solving approach, rejecting punitive strategies. Rather than expelling or suspending students, effective schools work to keep all their students successfully engaged, in what some have called a "zero reject" policy (Johns & Keenan, 1997; Quinn, Osher, Hoffman, & Hanley, 1998).

MR. MOODY TRIES A NEW TECHNIQUE
AFTER GETTING LOST AT A NATIONAL
EDUCATION CONFERENCE AND SPENDING
A WEEK AT A USED CAR SALES SEMINAR.

Clear Expectations and Proactive Schoolwide Discipline Plan. Effective schools state simple, understandable expectations in positive terms rather than creating a list of prohibited actions and punishments (Cheney & Muscott, 1996). For example, one school promulgated three key desired behaviors—respect, responsibility, and trustworthiness. Schools communicate these expectations in friendly ways. In one school, students role-played positive and negative behaviors in a class play at the beginning of the year. Students may create colorful posters illustrating positive behaviors (Reavis & Andrews, 1999).

Social Support Structures and Options. Support structures can be developed to provide assistance to students, teachers, and parents. Particularly important are *support teams* (see Chapter 5) that can develop behavior intervention and support plans for students with extremely problematic behaviors (Meadows, 1996; Quinn, Osher, Hoffman, & Hanley, 1998; Westerly Public Schools, 1999; Zionts, 1997) or for students with emotional and behavioral disorders who may be transitioning from segregated programs to inclusive classrooms. Such students need flexible options such as partial day programs as they work to reenter the school and cope with emotional difficulties (Cartledge & Johnson, 1996, p. 56).

Schools often develop a supported place where students can go to regroup. For example, schools may use planning centers, where any student can go who is in need of emotional support, cooling-off time, academic assistance, or just a quiet place to problem-solve with an adult or a peer. Such centers contain educational equipment such as computers and carpeted areas with rocking chairs or other soothing materials, and are staffed by a teacher trained in behavior management (Westerly Public Schools, 1999; Quinn, Osher, Hoffman, & Hanley, 1998).

We can use this same idea in our own classrooms, designating a protected space. For elementary children that space might be under our desk; or it might be a desk outside our room or even a special location in the classroom. We can offer these places for a student to go if they need to cool off, think, or just have time alone to settle down if something traumatic has occurred. If a student is in conflict with us, we can ask them to go to a cooling-off spot, rethink their position, and return with an alternative. If a staffed center is available to us, the teacher there will dialogue with the student and send a note when the child is ready to return to class (Center for Effective Collaboration and Practice, 1999).

Positive Learning Opportunities. It is not by chance that involving students with emotional disturbance in active, student-centered, engaging instruction is the first strategic target named in the *National Agenda*. Such instruction provides an opportunity for students to build on their strengths. These students often have difficulty with self-esteem and have been in many environments that were structured and boring at best and violent and abusive at worst. Our classroom, as a place of fun and interesting activities, can provide the base for growth and development (Cessna & Skiba, 1996; Knoff, 1995, 1999; Quinn, Osher, Hoffman, & Hanley, 1998).

Trust and Safety: Building Community and Providing Emotional Support. Some students come from environments where they have felt unsafe and unprotected, physically and emotionally. Such students may test us. A key strategy will be to use positive behavioral support strategies (discussed in detail in Chapter 12), standing strong while treating the student with respect and attempting to meet their needs (Cartledge & Johnson, 1996; Quinn, Osher, Hoffman, & Hanley, 1998).

Some students may deal with stress and emotional problems by turning inward, withdrawing from interactions with others, becoming depressed, taking drugs, acting irritable. They may have difficulty maintaining relationships with others. Teachers seek ways to establish a trusting relationship, letting students know we are available to help. We want to encourage participation and involvement in group activities to strengthen their social connections. However, we allow them to work alone if they want (Cartledge & Johnson, 1996; Harrell, Doelling, & Sasso, 1997). Our classroom should allow students to deal with their emotions in different ways:

- "Quiet time" in a corner, in the hall, or under a desk or other furniture
- Group work and sharing with other students
- Individual work
- Time in a carrel equipped with headphones for a tape recorder or to use with the computer—to aid students in focusing and in withdrawing, when necessary

As we have opportunity, we help students reflect on and share their experiences and feelings as part of the class. We should also be aware that sometimes students communicate feelings through art, writing, or actions that may be disturbing. If we understand that students are seeking to communicate what is inside them, this understanding can validate them as individuals, build on their strengths, and provide rich, deep learning for other classmates. For example, in literacy or social studies, we may ask students to journal about emotional experiences and write a story or develop a play. In so doing, we give students tools to understand their own feelings and communicate needs as part of academic work. Of course, we need to be sensitive, giving students opportunities for self-expression but not making this mandatory. If students do share feelings with us, we will want to be aware when to call on others for help—for example, if we are concerned that students may have the potential for violence to themselves or others.

We will also do our best to help students develop and strengthen relationships and friendships. Strategies might include (Cartledge & Johnson, 1996; Harrell, Doelling, & Sasso, 1997; Meadows, 1996):

- Cooperative learning
- Having students write about their desires for relationship, the friends they have, their fears, or other personal matters and share these as part of author's chair or writing teams
- Rope course and other outdoor adventure activities
- Peer buddies—pairing students together to engage in collaborative class work and encouraging students to do things together
- Circles of support—developing a formal circle for a particular student
- Providing guidance to other students who may be willing to help

In our classes we will not only guide students and teach them specific skills but also give them choices that will allow them to help structure their lives in the classroom—choices of activities in lessons, of partners, of ways to structure assignments, of methods of dealing with interpersonal conflicts so that their needs are met. Such choices will enable them to have more control.

Should we be concerned about giving students who act aggressively tools to express power and control over their lives? These students often feel powerless and so overwhelmed that they perceive only two ways—to withdraw or to strike out. When we give students tools by which they can influence their situation, they often become calmer. As one example, many students with aggression problems take classes in kung fu, a highly disciplined martial arts training. These students often report that they gain a sense of power from their ability to protect themselves and so do not need to actually use the skills they have (R. Gibson, personal communication, September 12, 1999). We can look for other ways to empower students in our classes and schools. We can provide opportunities for students to help us create lessons, give them valued jobs, explore interesting learning opportunities.

Skill Development: Academic and Social Skills. We must first help students feel emotional support before they can learn academic skills effectively in our classes (Hitzing, 1994). As we start a school year, we work to build community in our class, make our class fun and interesting, and set a positive tone. We use academic projects that involve group work, sharing, and collaboration to build community while facilitating learning. In addition, as needed, we focus intentionally on community building through class meetings, peer-to-peer sharing, or even circles of support.

Whether we teach algebra in high school or a K–2 multiage elementary class, dealing with emotional and behavioral needs and helping students develop social skills is a critical part of our job.

We identify areas in which students' social skills and abilities need improvement, and we provide learning opportunities as an integral part of the regular curriculum. In addition, some students may need more intensive social skills training, and we may find that we can valuably incorporate explicit social skills training into our class. Several curricula have been developed that can help us teach students social skills by modeling desired behaviors and having students act out such behaviors in simulations. School psychologists and social workers often work with teachers in providing such social skills instruction (Cartledge & Kleefeld, 1994; Goldstein, 1988; McGinnis & Goldstein, 1984).

Four children work together to solve a problem one student is having. When teachers
model and help students learn human relations skills, they can be of great assistance to
one another and provide support for students who have difficulty managing emotions
and social interactions.

Positive Behavioral Supports. When students are having difficulties, we want to understand what is happening from their point of view. We should always take behaviors of the student seriously and reach out, seeking to establish a personal connection.
We should listen to what the student is saying, attempt to state aloud what we are hearing, and respond to the needs we see underlying the behavior. Our frequent instinct, of
course, is to react—either by becoming aggressive ourselves or by withdrawing. Both
can lead to problems. If students are depressed, we might see if they want to talk or
write about their feelings. If students are angry and have difficulty controlling their feelings, we can help them verbalize or write what they are feeling, share in peer buddy dialogue sessions, or talk with us one-on-one (Cheney & Muscott, 1996; March &
Sprague, 1999; Reavis & Andrews, 1999; University of Oregon, 1999; Zionts, 1997).

Professional Support. A variety of more traditional services provided by various
professionals can be very important and helpful in giving students emotional support and someone to talk to. Such services may be provided by school or agency staff
either at our school or off-site. These services should be offered to a student but not
mandatory. They include (Quinn, Osher, Hoffman, & Hanley, 1998; Zionts, 1997):

- Individual counseling
- Counseling groups

- Support groups in the school for special problems (e.g., for students with divorcing parents)
- Tutoring

Collaboration with and Support for Families. Many families have substantial problems that have an impact on the total family life. Wraparound services connect interagency teams, local informal community resources, neighbors, and friends, who come together to provide intensive supports to families. Processes such as MAPS (Chapter 4) help us identify the strengths of the family as well as the family's needs for services and resources across agency lines. As teachers we will be important participants in a wraparound team, participating in meetings to develop a plan with a family and communicating with different team members as we work together. This team will provide important support for us as well.

Partnerships with families are particularly critical with students with emotional disturbance. We invite parents to our class so that they can help but also so that they can learn how to interact more positively with their child (Knoff, 1995, 1999). Often, parents of children with emotional disturbance have received very negative reports from schools. They may not trust us at first until we build a solid relationship. When parents see positive aspects of their children through engaging in some fun activity with them, they often see their children in a different light.

Effective schools provide a range of supports for families with which we can coordinate our efforts. In some cases we may want to be directly involved in such supports. Among them:

- In-home parent training to help parents learn how to teach and reinforce positive behaviors, support academic learning (University of Oregon, 1999)
- Support groups (Cheney & Muscott, 1996)
- In-school parent centers (Knoff, 1995, 1999) to encourage parent participation in school activities and give parents access to training and learning materials
- Integrated social services in the school (Westerly Public Schools, 1999)

Supporting Ourselves: Networking for Teachers. If we are fortunate enough to be working in an effective inclusive school, we will have lots of help from others. Support for teachers may include behavioral consultation by specialists, a school support team, in-class collaboration with special education teachers, and in-service training (Kane & Boltax, 1999; Keenan, 1997; Meadows, 1996; Quinn, Osher, Hoffman, & Hanley, 1998; Reavis & Andrews, 1999; Zionts, 1997).

If we do not have that good fortune, we must develop a support system ourselves. This is important in all our teaching. However, we particularly need a support network as we teach students with emotional disturbance, given the emotions that dealing with such students may bring. Here are some suggestions:

- Identify teachers who are especially effective at dealing with emotional and behavioral needs of students. Get to know them and ask for help if needs arise.
- Collaborate with in-class support teachers, or consult with a trusted counselor or school psychologist (Quinn, Osher, Hoffman, & Hanley, 1998).
- Identify and attend professional conferences or training sessions; these gatherings can give you strategies and help connect you with others.

Schools to Visit

Starting Inclusion with Students Labeled Emotionally Disturbed

Emily Dickinson School
725 West End Avenue
New York, New York 10025
Phone: 212-866-5400
Principal: Bob O'Brien
www.nycenet.edu/csd3/ps75m/

The Emily Dickinson School (P.S. 75) on the Upper West Side of Manhattan has more than 700 students in kindergarten through fifth grade. The school's population reflects the full diversity of the United States, including students of many races, ethnicities, home languages, and with a large range of achievement (with no special gifted and talented program). Since 1997, led by a new principal—Bob O'Brien—the school has become a leader in quality and inclusive education. Parents have also played a key role in advocating for and supporting inclusive classrooms.

Initially, the staff of P.S. 75 decided to focus their inclusive efforts on students from a nearby special education school who were labeled severely emotionally disturbed. The teachers thought that these students, who had average academic skills, would be the best ones to start with as the Emily Dickinson School began working to integrate all its students from self-contained settings into their home-zoned school. P.S. 75 has subsequently supported students with diverse labels, including autism, multiple disabilities, and severe cognitive disabilities.

Working closely with Philip Santise, the principal of the self-contained special education school, Mr. O'Brien asked teachers to volunteer for the inclusion program—which was initially supported by the New York Statewide Systems Change Project. That first year, two third-grade teachers successfully included one student in each classroom. In 2002, approximately 100 children

with IEPs who required special education teacher support were fully included in fifteen different general education classrooms at every grade level, including seven students in dual language classrooms (Spanish/English).

The principal and the teachers were relieved to find that as more and more students with disabilities were fully included, schoolwide test scores increased, particularly for children without IEPs who were considered "at risk" and had lower test scores. This outcome can be understood in part as a function of the way P. S. 75 has distributed throughout the school the special education teachers from formerly self-contained classrooms. There are currently six special education teachers who spend their days in two or three classrooms each, supporting not only the 100 children with IEPs but the general education students as well. These "Methods and Resource" teachers provide what New York City now calls Special Education Teacher Support Services, including team teaching, small group instruction, curriculum adaptations and modifications, and some pull-out services for groups of children. These pull-outs are for specific skills instruction, and membership in the groups is flexible, depending on who needs extra help; all the pull-out groups include general education students as well as those with IEPs.

In New York City, the school district has organized separate special education districts throughout the city; this makes the work of including students labeled emotionally disturbed challenging and complex. In spite of these barriers, the teachers at P. S. 75 have benefited from the expertise of the special education teachers and administrators, particularly in regard to positive behavior support plans and ways to work with children in emotional crisis. The administrators from the two schools blended resources to provide joint professional development resources and ongoing in-class supports.

As we obtain support from others, of course, we must be careful to maintain confidentiality. We never share information in such a way that students or families can be personally identified.

How Students with Emotional Disturbance Can Help Improve Our Class. Students with emotional and behavioral problems bring into sharp focus the importance of building community and honing our skills for proactive and positive behavioral supports. We will see ever so clearly how punishment and lack of attention to the needs of children damage them. We will also see how community and proactive responses can have dramatic positive impacts on their lives. In addition, working with students with intense emotional challenges will provide the rest of our students with concrete, authentic experience in developing their own emotional and social skills—learning experiences that will be invaluable throughout their lives.

Rainman and Beyond
People with Autism

In the 1988 movie *Rainman,* Dustin Hoffman portrays a man with autism. His character is fixated on structure, repeats words often, has trouble communicating, and cannot handle stressful situations. This portrait, however, represents just one of many possible patterns of behavior associated with autism (Koegel & Koegel, 1995). The word *autism* was originally coined by Leo Kanner in 1943, when Kanner was studying people who were slow learners but did not fit the pattern of emotionally disturbed children. The word *autism* was used at the time to mean "escape from reality." Hans Asperger identified a similar disorder, of individuals who had substantial problems in social interaction but did not show cognitive or language delays. Until recently some 3 or 4 in every 2,000 children had autism, but the numbers have risen dramatically in recent years (Bertrand, Mars, Boyle, Bove, Yeargin-Allsopp, & Decoufle, 2001; Koegel & Koegel, 1995; Varin, 1998). IDEA defines **autism** as

> a developmental disability significantly affecting verbal and nonverbal communication and social interaction, generally evident before age 3, that adversely affects a child's educational performance. Other characteristics often associated with autism are engagement in repetitive activities and stereotyped movements, resistance to environmental change or change in daily routines, and unusual responses to sensory experiences. Autism does not apply if a child's educational performance is adversely affected primarily because the child has a serious emotional disturbance. (Individuals with Disabilities Education Improvement Act [IDEA], 2004, section 300.8)

Young children who have symptoms similar to those of autism are often classified as having **pervasive developmental disorders (PDD).** Children may be aggressive or withdrawn and may say strange things, repeat words over and over, and engage in unusual behaviors such as nail biting, rocking, or head knocking (American Psychiatric Association, 2000; Kauffman, 1997).

Impacts of Autism

Autism is a neurological disorder that interferes with the development of reasoning, social interaction, and communication. Children and adults with autism have substantial problems in the area of communication. Some are nonverbal. Others use language very concretely with a limited ability to understand or express abstract ideas. People with autism may not attach appropriate meanings to words or understand the multiple meanings of some words. **Echolalia,** the repetition of memorized words or phrases, is common. Autism is a lifelong disability that impairs learning and can lead to serious behavior problems. Autism has no known cause or specific underlying impairment. As recently as the 1960s, the cause was thought to be lack of parental warmth or an inadequate emotional bond between the parents and child (Bettelheim, 1967). Now, however, this disorder is considered to be organic in origin, linked to biological, neurological, biochemical, or genetic factors (Koegel & Koegel, 1995; Varin, 1998). Five behaviors are common in many persons with autism, all related to these individuals' difficulty understanding and relating to social interactions (Koegel & Koegel, 1995; Wagner, 1999):

1. *Lack of language development:* At one point 50 percent of people with autism did not develop language; today, however, most learn to communicate via language or other tools such as communication boards. This process has led to a reduction in behavioral problems.
2. *Self-stimulation:* Repetitive behaviors such as hand flapping, twirling of objects, body rocking, or staring at lights can be subtle or obvious.
3. *Self-injurious or aggressive behaviors.*
4. *Preoccupation with certain objects or a routine:* Individuals may become very upset if a routine is changed.
5. *Lack of social/communicative gestures and utterances:* Individuals with autism may be unable to make eye contact, acknowledge smiles, or return handshakes. They often use language only to obtain things, not for social interaction.

Two therapeutic programs have been predominantly used with people with autism, each built on a very different philosophy. Lovaas (1987) developed an intense program involving intensive behavior modification techniques to eliminate unwanted behaviors, the teaching of new skills, and the reinforcement of desired behaviors, a program sometimes known as **applied behavior analysis (ABA).** This controversial, expensive treatment takes place over three years and continues some forty hours per week, 365 days per year. Some researchers have questioned the validity of claimed results; they have further expressed the concern that the program virtually demands a segregated setting (Gresham & MacMillan, 1997).

Another program is called **TEACCH,** Treatment and Education of Autistic and Related Communication-Handicapped Children, and seeks to develop an individual program based on a child's skills, interests, and needs. Teachers organize the physical environment, create schedules, use visual materials, and make expectations very clear. This program seeks to foster independence by encouraging the development of skills to the point where the child can use them without adult prompting. Parents involved in this program have been very enthusiastic, and 96 percent of adults with autism who have been involved in this program are living in their local communities. Before TEACCH, 39 to 74 percent of adults with autism lived in residential settings away from their homes (Varin, 1998).

Donna Williams (1996), a woman with autism, described how difficult communication is for people with autism. Often people with autism do not understand their own feelings, as if their inner self is trapped behind fear and they are able to respond only by mimicking learned behaviors, such as motions or phrases they have been taught or seen on TV. Breaking out of this cage by communicating what they feel is a traumatic, intense experience. Basic things that are automatic processes for many people, such as knowing what food we like, holding someone's hand, or talking to new people, are extremely difficult for people with autism. In the Voices feature here Temple Grandin, now a university professor, tells of her experience with autism.

Inclusive schooling is critical in helping students with autism develop social skills and become part of their communities. Early intervention and support of young children experiencing pervasive developmental disorders is particularly important. Once developed, friendships help increase communication and reduce the fear of changes experienced by children with autism. By sheer repetition of appropriate modeling, direction, and practice, children's social responses become more comfortable and their ability to think through a problem becomes more easily accessed. It is also less likely that further mental health problems will occur later in life (Wagner, 1999). In a website posting Ginger Kwan (1999), a parent of a child with autism, describes the impact on her son Mickle:

> Mickle was diagnosed with autism [and] is almost 4 and a half years old now. Mickle goes to Meredith Hill Elementary. . . . In this classroom there are 16 children, 11 typical developing children integrated with 5 children with disabilities. Mickle is the only child with autism and has the most profound needs. . . . Mickle is . . . still very much nonverbal. He uses a picture exchange system to communicate both at home and school. Since Mickle started this inclusive preschool about 2 months ago, we have seen him become more sociable. At home he plays with his sisters more often and also plays with some toys in which he showed no interest before. His eye contacts have increased. At school, he is able to sit in circle time longer and participate in activities. He has more appropriate interaction with people now. . . .

Teaching Students with Autism

We may feel that teaching students with autism will be hard. However, the approaches that are best for children with autism are only variations on good teaching for all children. Sometimes a paraprofessional is assigned to provide support for a child with autism. However, such assistance is not always needed. The first thing to understand is that just as some children need help with math or reading, these children need help with social skills. We provide such extra help just as we would in any subject. We begin by finding ways to integrate social skills instruction into daily class routines (Koegel, 1995; Wagner, 1999). Many children will benefit from this instruction. We might choose one particular skill a week—a ten-minute lesson on

Voices

Temple Grandin: An Inside View of Autism

I am a 54-year-old autistic woman who has a successful international career designing livestock equipment. I completed my Ph.D. in animal science at the University of Illinois in Urbana, and I am now an assistant professor of animal science at Colorado State University. Early intervention at age 2½ helped me overcome my handicap. . . .

Many people ask me, "How did you manage to recover?" I was extremely lucky to have the right people working with me at the right time. At age 2, I had all the typical autistic symptoms. . . . I was referred to a speech therapist who ran a special nursery school in her home. The speech therapist was the most important professional in my life. At age 3, . . . my day consisted of structured activities such as skating, swinging, and painting. The activities were structured, but I was given limited opportunities for choice. For example, on one day I could choose between building a snowman or sledding. She actually participated in all the activities. She also conducted musical activities, and we marched around the piano with toy drums. . . .

I went to a normal elementary school with older, experienced teachers and small classes. Mother . . . worked very closely with the school. She used techniques that are used today in the most successful mainstreaming programs to integrate me into the classroom. The day before I went to school,

she and the teacher explained to the other children that they needed to help me. . . .

In high school and college, the people that helped me the most were the creative, unconventional thinkers. The more traditional professionals . . . were actually harmful. . . . Later when I became interested in meat-packing plants . . . the manager of the local meat-packing plant took an interest in me. For three years I visited his plant once a week and learned the industry. My very first design job was in his plant. I want to emphasize the importance of a gradual transition from the world of school to the world of work. . . . People with autism need to be gradually introduced to a job before they graduate. . . .

. . . It is my opinion that effective programs for young children have certain common denominators. . . . Early, intense intervention improves the prognosis. Passive approaches don't work. . . . Good programs do a variety of activities and use more than one approach. A good little children's program should include flexible behavior modification, speech therapy, exercise, sensory treatment (activities that stimulate the vestibular system and tactile desensitization), musical activities, contact with normal children, and lots of love. . . .

Source: Grandin, 2000. Used with permission.

Monday to which we refer often throughout the week and about which we hold a ten-minute discussion on Friday. An extension of the circle of support approach, discussed in Chapters 1 and 11, is beneficial for children with autism. However, an adult will need to teach the other children how to encourage social skills and interactions. Some helpful ideas are listed in the Tools for the Trek feature following.

Tools *for the* Trek
Strategies for Teaching Students with Autism

- *Social stories:* Describe social situations and provide opportunities to understand social cues and responses (see Chapter 12).
- *Picture exchange system (PECS):* In an alternative communication system for young students with autism, children exchange a picture for something they need. PECS provides a concrete way for a child to communicate and moves away from social rewards, to which children with autism often cannot relate.
- *Redirect:* Teach other students to redirect the attention of a chlid with autism when the child is doing something inappropriate. They might point at something, show an object, or take the child's hand.
- *Hurt feelings:* When a child with autism says no, meaning they do not want to play or do an activity with a classmate, the refusal is not something that classmates should take personally. Explain that the child fears the activity or does not understand why playing with someone else is fun. They should redirect and try again.
- *Eye contact:* Eye contact is important, as people with autism are very visual learners. Say, "Look at me." Get in the child's line of vision.
- *Smiling and laughing:* Make a point to smile and laugh so as to communicate that playing and working with others is fun.
- *Vocalizing:* Teach classmates of a child with autism to say what they are doing as they do it, as in "Look how I can slide like this" or "Watch how I can help Eric fix his spelling."

- *Lunch bunch:* Having a time for the circle of support to eat together with a teacher present can be an excellent way to encourage social interactions as well as providing a venue for discussion of issues. The group may meet once a week in a private setting. They can talk about issues related to the student with autism, exchange ideas on something they are learning about, or play a fun game.
- *Class jobs:* Students with autism can be responsible, as are other children, for a job in the class that requires some type of social interaction. The teacher can ask them to pass out papers (thus requiring them to know peoples' names and interact with them), deliver messages with a peer, ask students if they are eating hot or cold lunch, do roll call, or work with another student to file papers.
- *Calming-down time:* Teach children with autism to use a self-regulated calming-down time when they are upset. Explain that it is OK to feel upset, and talk about acceptable responses. Write down useful strategies and create a visual signal that means: "Stop activity; I sense you are becoming upset. Use coping skills." Coping skills can be anything from taking a walk to sitting in the hall, reading a book, or playing with a particular object. It is important to have a time limit for calming down, however, so that this does not become an all-day escape.

Although students with autism can sometimes behave in ways that are confusing and even frightening, it is important to remember that such behavior rarely happens out of the blue. Too often adults have tended to focus on how to stop the behavior. We would again ask the question, "Why is this student responding this way?" Take a look at what happened just before the incident. Typically, we will realize that the student was trying to *escape* a particular demand, activity, or situation that he or she found uncomfortable; to make a *demand* for an object, activity, or routine; to get someone's *attention;* or to engage in *self-stimulation* because it is fun (Koegel, 1995; Wagner, 1999; Williams, 1996). Because people with autism depend on routine in their lives, it is important that we provide this in our classrooms. Changes are scary for these students, and being involved in unfamiliar situations can cause them to freeze in fear. They cannot handle the situation and thus must draw on previously learned behaviors. If there are no appropriate prior responses to draw on, children with autism will react in whatever way they have previously memorized. Their way may not fit what is socially acceptable or comfortable.

Thus, when unfamiliar social situations arise an important strategy to prevent a frightened reaction from students with autism is to have *rehearsal time* (Koegel, 1995; Wagner, 1999). With someone they trust, students can practice behaviors and words required for the new activity. First we tell them what is going to occur and then talk about how they may feel and what they can do in response. Then they actually do the motions or verbalize what is needed for the new situation; for example, the student talks to a person and shakes the person's hand or practices walking to the auditorium. When the time comes, the student can draw on these rehearsed responses and will be less likely to panic. **Social stories** provide a related strategy for rehearsal (Gray, 1994).

Simple things can be very important to people with autism. They are very visual learners. This need for visual order can exhibit itself in many ways; for example, a student with autism may arrange things in a desk in a precisely symmetrical fashion, hang a coat so that it folds the exact same way each day, eat at the same time each day, or line up boots in the hallway. Some ways to respond to this need for structure without being stifling are:

1. Post a schedule of the day, pointing out any noticeable changes.
2. Do certain things, like reading workshop or math, at the same time every day.
3. Provide the student with a particular place to hang or store things.
4. Allow time after an activity for the student to reorder his or her desk.
5. Put the student in charge of routine jobs—taking the attendance after lunch or straightening books.

Teaching children with autism can be very rewarding. A generation ago, 90 percent of these children were in institutions. Now many live in communities and attend regular school. The key to working with children with autism is prevention and understanding. Children with autism have strong visual skills, excellent ability to recognize details, and an amazing memory. These can become the basis for a successful life and can add to a classroom community.

Challenging Students and Teaching

Perhaps the worst fear of teachers is having "the class from hell." So talking about including kids with identified emotional and behavioral challenges can feel particularly scary. We hope this chapter has provided helpful perspectives on these stu-

⌒⌒⌒⌒⌒⌒● **Stepping Stones** ●⌒⌒●⌒⌒●⌒

To Inclusive Teaching

1. Make a commitment to working with one child who is having emotional struggles. Find out about that child's life. What do your findings tell you? What strategies might you try?

2. Find a teacher who seems particularly good at dealing with students labeled as having emotional and behavioral challenges. What does this teacher do that is so effective?

3. Visit a separate school for children labeled emotionally disturbed or autistic. Then visit a class where such children are supported in a regular school. What did you learn?

4. Journal regarding your own feelings about children with emotional and social problems. How do your own experiences and hurts in the past (or present) affect your responses? Describe to yourself how you would *like* to be with such children. What are your strengths, your needs? What type of support do you need in working with such children? Talk with someone at your school about these needs and about ways they might be met so as to help you include these children.

5. Do an assessment of your school and your class. Do you have in place strategies that can help support children with emotional and behavioral challenges? If not, what would you like to see in place? How might you and other teachers in your school get started?

dents. Ultimately, it is critical that we work to make schools places that promote healing, inclusion, support, and care; schools should help build the base for productive citizenship rather than serving as a quick route to prison, life on the street, or a mental institution. When we are successful, we learn much from these students about how to create real communities of learners.

 Key Points

- Students with behavioral and emotional needs challenge us to commit to caring about all our students and building a strong community.

- Students labeled ADHD have many skills and abilities along with their energy, restlessness, and difficulty focusing. They need help in being organized; at the same time, they need activities that are engaging and fun, and that involve active learning. These students will be least responsive to traditional worksheet teaching.

- Ritalin and related drugs are very controversial even though their use has grown dramatically in recent years. Many feel that these drugs are grossly overused. Teachers are often called on to pressure parents to get physicians to prescribe medication for their children. Many inclusive teachers work to teach in a way that reduces the need and call for medications.

- Students labeled emotionally disturbed may have many different types of conditions, from externalizing disorders (in which emotional upset is projected outward, as with oppositional defiance disorder) to internalizing disorders (in which emotions impact inward, as with eating disorders or depression). Often these students experience much disorder in their lives.

- Inclusive teaching may be effective for students with serious emotional disturbance when a strong school and classroom community exists, teachers are committed to helping children learn to cope with emotional and social needs, teachers collaborate with families, and positive behavioral supports are used.

■ Students with autism have difficulty interpreting social situations and may experience emotional upset and panic when they don't under-

stand. Unfamiliar situations and many kinds of sensory stimuli may be upsetting.

■ Many students with autism can learn and be successful if they are given systematic, explicit guidance in understanding social situations (as with social stories) but are also allowed choices, and if a strong community exists in which students and teachers reach out but provide needed space.

 Learning Expeditions

Following are some ideas and activities that may extend your learning.

1. Observe students labeled as ADHD, emotionally disturbed, and autistic in a school and interview them. Where are they going to school? What is happening in their lives? How do they act in class and in the interview? What do they feel and think about their lives and their school?

2. Go to meetings related to ADHD and Ritalin. These might include a meeting of a local chapter of CHADD (Children with Attention Deficit Disorder) or an in-service for a school. What view of ADHD and Ritalin use was promoted? What questions does this bring up?

3. Interview two teachers—one in a setting where Ritalin is used much and the other where it is not. What are their different perspectives? How do these teachers view ADHD and the use of Ritalin?

4. Sign on to a listserv of adults with ADHD. "Listen" to the conversations. What are some common themes in what people say and share? How do these relate to school issues?

5. Collect some data on the number of kids identified locally as ADHD, emotionally disturbed,

and autistic. What questions do the data raise? What conclusions might you draw?

6. Observe in a class with a student labeled emotionally disturbed. Talk with the student and the teacher. What are the key problem areas? How are these being addressed? How does the school effort compare to the *National Agenda* recommendations and the guidelines in this chapter?

7. Visit a segregated school or class for students with emotional disturbance. Who is there, and what types of problems do they have? What is the program, and how does it relate to their needs? What are your opinions regarding having these students in a segregated program? Why?

8. Interview a student and an adult with autism and a parent of a child with autism. Ask them to tell their story. What type of schooling is involved? What seems to be working? What are the challenges, and how are these being dealt with?

9. Go to a meeting of a local chapter of the Autism Society of American. What are people saying? How much do they focus on inclusive education? Why?

Visualize and understand how to create an inclusive community of learners in the school and classroom.

CHAPTER OBJECTIVES

1. Consider the relationships between meeting social and emotional needs and academic learning.

2. Learn strategies for strengthening community in the school as a whole.

3. Explore and utilize methods of building community in the classroom.

4. Understand how to explicitly and openly recognize and value differences among students in the classroom.

Building Community 11 and Supporting Prosocial Behavior

Strategies for Strengthening Mutual Care, Support, and Celebration

We're all sitting in the living room talking—a group of teachers who get together periodically. It's been a long day. Tonight we talk about our own experiences as students. What was good? What was bad? What influenced us? "I had one teacher who was absolutely cruel," says Jan. "He belittled students, called us stupid. Controlling the class was the most important thing to him, and he sent many to the office. I had fun causing trouble without getting caught!" She smiles, and everyone laughs, setting off a round of similar stories.

"But what was good?" Silence surrounds us as we are lost in thought. "I remember Miss Annie, my sixth-grade teacher," Rich says. "In many ways she was an old-style teacher. We diagrammed sentences, and more than once I got in trouble in her class. But one thing you knew about Miss Annie—she cared deeply for every one of us." After a pause Rich continues. "We had what we would today call a learning community. She taught us by example about caring and helped us create that with one another. Many of us continue to go by Miss Annie's house," he said, "even though she's been retired many years." One by one, all of us recall stories about teachers who made a deep difference in our lives—by being who they were as much as by the academic skills they taught us.

Our evening discussion highlights the importance of emotions, care, and a sense of community in our classrooms. We first remember people for whom we cared and who cared about us in school. Parents ask first, "How does this teacher treat my child?" and "Does this teacher really care about my child?" Our students do the same.

Let's visit classrooms and think about this.

Darcie Holland's sixth-grade social studies classes are always interesting. Darcie has a dynamic personality and engages students in lessons of discovery. We particularly want to observe how she includes Duane, a student with a severe disability who uses an electric wheelchair, has limited control of his arms and legs, and doesn't speak. As the students read from their social studies book and engage in discussion, a cluster of two boys and one girl stand or sit around Duane. One holds the book for him and points to the passage; he is a member of the class. Every now and then Darcie directs the conversation to Duane. His eyes glisten and he smiles. Later Darcie directs the students to get into groups of two or three and read with one another, talking and answering questions. Two children wheel Duane to a table in the corner of the class under which his wheelchair can fit, and the three of them work together.

We then talk with Martha, a third-grade teacher, as we watch her learners in their reading workshop. "I am teaching third grade this year after having 'looped' last year from fourth grade," she explains. "So I have a new group of kids. One of these is Kevin, a student who has been labeled 'trainable mentally retarded.' He's a nice kid but he functions far below most students in my class. However, it's important to me that Kevin is welcomed and can work at his own level. I build community in my class, and the students help one another. Community has provided a basis for Kevin's learning and growth this year." As we walk around the class, Martha talks about the multiple ways she builds community in the classroom and how these interact with academic instruction. She uses cooperative learning groups, students helping one another as "experts," classroom meetings, and heterogeneous grouping of students with students who can help and learn from one another. "You should have seen Kevin showing his parents what he has been learning in his student-led conference," Martha says. "For Kevin, writing just a short sentence now is a lot, but he *likes* to write and read. It was terrific to watch him with his parents, who were a bit amazed."

We would hope that all teachers and all schools would seek to build community in classrooms and schools—to create safe havens for children, who are under increasing stress across the socioeconomic spectrum. Unfortunately, this is not the case. We've been in schools where we have seen teachers scream at children, where such teacher behavior has become an expected part of the school culture. We've seen some schools struggle mightily to develop a sense of community and care in their buildings, trying particularly to help children whose lives are traumatic; and we've seen other schools where tension, pressure, and anger are the rule of the day, where children with high emotional needs are criticized bitterly by school staff. We have choices to make: Do we seek to build community for all children, or do we react with power and punishment when children don't do what is expected, building a culture of competition and isolation? That's the core issue that this chapter addresses.

Traveling Notes

1. How can teachers build community in their classes, even in schools that are punitive? What impact does community have on children with challenges in their lives?

2. Is it our responsibility as teachers to take care of the emotional and social needs of children? Can we afford not to?

3. How do emotional well-being and academic learning relate to each other? How might we build a classroom where children have a safe haven and a place of healing in a sometimes hurtful life?

Let's think deeply about these questions in our journey, for they are likely to be among the most important we ask.

What Is Community?
Individual Growth Thriving with Care and Support

Students come to us with many strengths and abilities. They may also come to us with pain and hurt in their lives. Our challenge is to create in our classrooms a culture that helps students build on their strengths and heals their hurts so that learning can occur. Rather than focusing on the deficits of students, we attempt to build a caring community of learners in which they have emotional support and a safe place to deal with their concerns and needs (Developmental Studies Center, 1994; Flurkey & Meyer, 1994; Noddings, 1992; Sapon-Shevin, 1999; Sergiovanni, 1994).

What is **community**? Community occurs when diverse people develop relationships and work together so that each person is supported by the group in growing,

In Mishael Hittie's fourth-grade class the students dance in the middle of the room as part of the daily greeting. "One, two, three, four! Come on, Carmen, hit the floor. We're so glad you're here today. Hooray! Hooray! Hooray!" Daily greetings communicate that each individual is special and welcomed, strengthening the classroom community.

learning, and coping with challenges; when the group works together to accomplish common goals in an atmosphere of mutual respect and care; and when a flexible balance of emotional support and productivity occurs (Shaffer and Anundsen, 1993). The qualities required of members of real communities are commitment to one another, trust, honesty, compassion, and respect.

Solving problems through **community building** is as old as humanity. Over the last century or so, however, many social trends have contributed to increased isolation of individuals from one another and the weakening of community (McKnight, 1995), with attendant consequences of increased loneliness, drug abuse, child abuse, crime, and other social pathologies. In recent decades a growing host of writers and social activists have been calling for efforts to build and strengthen community (Bellah, Madsen, Sullivan, Swidler, & Tipton, 1985; Gardner, 1989; Kretzmann & McKnight, 1993; Schwartz, 1992, 1997), and community building is growing into an international movement. Scott Peck (1987), for example, developed a process for community building, gathering groups of people for three-day sessions of intense social interactions. In low-income neighborhoods, foundations have sponsored initiatives to help residents identify strengths and resources and work together to strengthen their community. Representatives from different cities formed the National Community Building Network (1995) to link individuals and organizations seeking to support comprehensive community building in low-income communities. Businesses talk about community building in the workplace, and educators discuss creating communities of learners (Sergiovanni, 1994). Let's look at key components of a good community and implications for teaching (Peck, 1987; Sarasson, 1974; Warren, 1988).

Belonging: A good community exists when people have a **sense of belonging** and feel valued as members of the group. The opposite of community is isolation and aloneness. As we seek to help all students belong, we become aware of the ways in which students are sometimes rejected and seek to counter these patterns. We explicitly deal with differences and conflicts that hinder relationships, connections, and acceptance and use numerous strategies to ensure that all members are part of the class. We are particularly observant of students whose characteristics may make them more susceptible to both feeling and being isolated—students with disabilities, students from minority cultural and ethnic groups, even the more able students (Amado, 1993; Developmental Studies Center, 1994; Gibbs, 1998; Kunc, 1992; Sapon-Shevin, 1999).

Inclusion: A good community is *inclusive* when membership is open and we make intentional efforts to accommodate and value diversity (Joseph, 1995; Kretzmann & McKnight, 1993; Schwartz, 1997). **Segregated communities** have historically been the norm, with people clustering together according to ethnic and cultural backgrounds or socioeconomic status. Gradually, however, new models of building inclusive communities are coming into being, and we have the opportunity to pave the way in our classrooms (Beaumont, 1999; Cohen, E., 1994; Sapon-Shevin, 1999).

Support and care: In a community members receive the support, assistance, mentoring, and caring that they need if they are to cope with the problems of their lives (Sarasson, 1974). Those with "special needs" are not separated from the community and put into "special places" (Condeluci, 1991; O'Brien & O'Brien, 1992). In the classroom we help students learn about one another's needs and help one another (Fitzgerald, Henning, & Feltz, 1997; Sapon-Shevin, 1999). For example, Nathan, a student with autism, has difficulty coping with the noise level as the high school drama class readies for the presentation of their play; he screams loudly. A classmate simply helps him refocus. No one is distracted—they know their friend Nathan, and they go on.

Contributions and responsibility of all members: All members have both the opportunity and the responsibility to contribute to the good of the whole (Etzioni, 1993; Gardner, 1989). In inclusive classes all students, whatever their ability, contribute. No one is considered helpless. By providing support good communities enable

I DON'T GET IT. WHAT DOES KEITH SEE IN JOEY? HE CAN'T WALK OR TALK, HE NEEDS HELP WITH EVERYTHING, YET THEY'RE INSEPARABLE.

MAYBE PART OF BEING FRIENDS IS LIKING A PERSON FOR WHO THEY ARE - NOT JUST WHAT THEY CAN DO.

© 1998 MICHAEL F. GIANGRECO. ILLUSTRATION BY KEVIN RUELLE. PEYTRAL PUBLICATIONS, INC. 612-949-8707

MYSTERIES OF FRIENDSHIP.

each person to operate as an individual while caring about others in the group and about the dynamics and health of the community as a whole. Consequently, individualism and community are not contradictory but are complementary (Kohn, 1996, 1999; Peck, 1987; Sapon-Shevin, 1999). A student who is beginning to learn English may love bugs and poems and share with the class a poem she has written about a bug. A middle school student with diabetes may be encouraged and assisted in monitoring his blood sugar and may share with fellow students his excitement about a new monitoring device he has received from his doctor.

Democratic problem solving: In any group of people, conflicts regarding priorities or personal relationships are inevitable. In a community we engage members in dialogue to make decisions and deal with conflict. Many teachers, for example, begin their day with a morning meeting in which the class helps decide what will be accomplished during the day and in what order. When conflicts occur among students, a classroom meeting may be held in which students help develop solutions. We communicate directly and respectfully. Each person "speaks their own truth" when they are "moved to speak," in Scott Peck's words (1987). Each person has the responsibility of listening and understanding as well as the right to articulate their own perspective (Elias et al., 1997; Peterson, 1992; Sapon-Shevin, 1999).

Reaching out: Finally, a community *reaches out to and connects with* the larger world, making partnerships with other communities and groups (Gardner, 1989). In a school we seek to connect with parents, the community, other classes within our school, students in other schools. Parents are invited into class; students visit a local nursing home, developing relationships with the older people there; a high school English class comes to a third-grade elementary class once a week to read with them and work on joint projects.

When we walk into a school or class, we frequently sense almost immediately whether the culture fosters community or promotes exclusion and competition. Figure 11.1 describes what we might see in each type of culture; the tone and the impact on children of each type are unmistakable. When community is in place in a class, we are struck by the many connections, the movement from place to place, the ongoing discussions, and the way in which power is shared among students and the teacher. It's a class that feels like a place we would like to be.

Why Build Community in Schools?
Emotions, Relationships, and Learning

Community makes sense at one level. Yet in our society many powerful trends work to destroy community. People feel increasingly unsafe and limit relationships with others. Work demands reduce time available for community interactions, and financial pressures drive multiple family members into the workforce, making the balance of home, family, and community life difficult. With increased mobility people frequently move away from family and friends and are constantly challenged to develop new relationships. Despite ongoing assaults, however, community sur-

Figure 11.1

Seeing Community in a Classroom

WHEN A CLASSROOM FUNCTIONS AS A COMMUNITY, WE SEE . . .	WHEN A CLASSROOM IS *NOT* A COMMUNITY, WE SEE . . .
■ Students constantly work with and help one another.	■ Some students are ridiculed; others are isolated; cliques abound.
■ Students of vastly different ability levels, cultures, ethnic groups work together. You hear them talking about their differences and what each person needs or likes.	■ Students with learning differences are sent to special programs.
■ When conflicts occur, students have strategies to work through them (peer mediation, etc.).	■ Students act out—either through direct aggressive verbal or physical acts or in passive-aggressive ways.
■ Circles of friends operate with some students who want and need them.	■ Teachers yell at students, frustrated that students will not "behave."
■ Teachers and students frequently interact in classroom meetings to set rules and deal with problems.	■ A lot of time and energy is put into controlling students.
	■ Conflicts erupt in fights and arguments.

vives as a basic human need. Community contributes powerfully to solving numerous human problems. Real community can (Shaffer & Anundsen, 1993):

■ Improve people's health. When people are in relationships and receive emotional support, they have reduced incidence of stress-related illnesses; cancer patients live longer, and birth problems are reduced.
■ Help prevent addictions and assist people in recovering from addictions.
■ Help people weather terrible crises in their lives.
■ Promote learning and growth by providing a "safe place to grow."

Teachers make critical contributions to building a better society not only by teaching students academic skills in their classes, but also by giving students a chance to experience community. In this sense a very quiet revolution is occurring in which schools provide models for embracing, rather than destroying, diversity. Thus, inclusive teaching and community building are allied. Given the challenges to community, it's important that community be solidly grounded in our schools. Numerous educational researchers and writers provide a theoretical and practical foundation for community building in schools.

Community and Five Needs of Human Beings

William Glasser (1992) developed a model of schooling that he calls the **quality school,** which is being used in more than 1,000 schools. The quality school is a school in which the "bosses" of the school—teachers—-interact with students in a noncoercive way. According to Glasser, "lead management is the basic reform we need" in schools (1992, p. 31). "Lead management" means talking with students and helping them think through better choices rather than dictating, directing, or controlling. According to Glasser, there are **five needs of human beings,** and as teachers, we provide students with opportunities to meet their five basic needs:

1. *Survival:* We help students survive, physically and emotionally, by creating safe places.
2. *Love and belonging:* Many of our students come to us having been rejected in one way or another in their lives. However, when we facilitate the connection of learners with one another, provide opportunities for collaboration, and ensure that each student is treated with respect, we provide the foundation out of which a sense of love and belonging may emerge.
3. *Power:* Helping students experience power is probably the most challenging. We are told in many ways that a key job of the teacher is to keep students under control. Yet creating community means giving students power along with responsibility. When we engage students in dialogue about the class—about how it will operate and how they will be evaluated—and when we listen to and act on what they say, we are sharing power with students. When we give students real opportunities to make decisions in small groups as they work on a project, we are giving power.
4. *Fun:* In a quality school, instruction is engaging and related to students' lives and, consequently, fun rather than boring.
5. *Freedom:* In such a school students have many opportunities for choices and can move around the classroom and school as they do their work, thus experiencing freedom.

Community and Maslow's Hierarchy of Needs

Maslow (1970) also identified five needs of individuals that occur in a hierarchy, beginning with lower-order and moving to higher-order needs:

1. Physiological needs: food, shelter, sexual gratification
2. Safety/security: physical and emotional survival and safety
3. Belonging/love/affiliation: being part of a community and experiencing caring relationships
4. Self-esteem: a positive sense of self, often attained through personal achievement
5. Self-actualization: the realization of the inner self's full potential in the world

According to Maslow (1970), we can't effectively move toward meeting higher-order needs such as self-actualization until lower-order needs are met. First, the basic *physiological needs* must be met; if they are not, it is very difficult to move to the following levels. This is why it's so hard for students who are homeless or hungry to function well at school. Given the necessities for survival, people seek to ensure their *safety and security*—both physical and emotional. Once safety is in place, needs for *belonging, love,* and *connection,* or affiliation, with others become paramount. Our experience of community, according to Maslow, is a prerequisite for achieving *self-esteem* and personal achievement. As people develop self-esteem, they often are restless to pursue their unique gifts and talents, seeking to express the essence of who they are, a final need that Maslow called *self-actualization.*

Kunc (1992) argued that schools often ensure that students with disabilities do *not* have their needs met by expecting students to achieve self-esteem (and academic mastery) as a *prerequisite* to being able to join the school community. For example, students who have been abused may have behavioral difficulties. We expect these students to "behave" before we allow them to be part of the community. We expect students who have significant learning problems to meet "seventh-grade standards" *before* they are allowed to be part of the general education classroom. Maslow's theory and decades of accompanying research demonstrate that this is exactly the wrong order. If students are to achieve and build a sense of self-esteem, these attainments must be built on the foundation of support and care in the community, not the other way around. We include students who have been abused to help them learn social skills. We include students with learning challenges with others in an engaging classroom environment so they can learn more effectively.

Connections between Academic Learning, the Emotions, and Community

In schools we often act as if we must choose between helping students with "academics" *or* with social–emotional needs. However, scientists are learning that the two are inextricably linked. In 1995 Daniel Goleman described the breakthrough research of Joseph LeDoux showing that emotional and academic learning are linked in the hard wiring of the brain, and emotional responses set the stage for academic and cognitive growth. According to Goleman (1995) **emotional intelligence,** or the ability to handle emotions well—interpersonal relationships, anger, feelings of sadness, and sense of self-worth—accounts for at least 50 percent of success in life. However, schools too often put little emphasis on emotional growth and development. This mismatch calls for a rethinking of the role of emotional learning in schools.

Building Resilience

Many researchers have become interested in **resilience,** the ability of some people to survive and become emotionally healthy when they are abused and mistreated or experience devastating circumstances, whereas others do not. We may have many children in our classes with whom we may feel helpless in light of their life circumstances. However, research has identified several characteristics of those who are able to weather traumatic circumstances to become healthy adults and has identified strategies that promote resiliency. These strategies give us hope. The strategies are twofold: (1) *Reduce* factors that increase the risk of harm, and (2) *increase* protective factors such as positive relationships, particularly with caring adults (see Figure 11.2) (Elias et al., 1997; Geller & Hunt, 1995; Noddings, 1992; Rutter, 1977).

Behavior Management, Care, and Community: Beyond Punishments and Rewards

Perhaps no arena causes more concern for teachers than student behavior problems. Alfie Kohn (1996) tells of his frustration when he visited the classes of teachers who

Figure 11.2

Characteristics of Resilient Children and Protective Factors

CHARACTERISTICS OF RESILIENT CHILDREN	PROTECTIVE FACTORS THAT BUILD RESILIENT CHILDREN
Social competence ■ Good communication skills ■ Sense of humor ■ Caring attitude ■ Ability to see different sides ■ Adaptability ■ Positive relations with others **Problem-solving skills** ■ Ability to think abstractly and flexibly ■ Abililty to try different solutions **Autonomy** ■ Self-control, self-discipline ■ Clear sense of separate identity ■ Independence ■ Self-esteem ■ Exertion of control over environment **Sense of future and purpose** ■ Goal orientation ■ Persistence ■ Achievement and education orientation ■ Hope for bright future ■ Sense of faith ■ Healthy expectations	Warm and close adult relationships Positive relationships with other children High expectations for success Variety of opportunities (music, art, etc.) Youth participation and involvement Ability to contribute meaningfully Acceptance and fulfillment of responsibilities AbIlity to make decisions that affect them A safe and predictable environment Clear norms regarding tobacco, alcohol, and other drugs

Source: Adapted from Geller & Hunt (1995).

had reputations for dealing effectively with discipline. In Kohn's visits misbehavior seldom happened, so he did not get the opportunity to see how the teachers handled it. After a while, he says, "it dawned on me that this pattern couldn't be explained just by my timing. These classrooms were characterized by a chronic absence of problems." After concluding that these teachers were not simply "getting the good kids," he looked more carefully. He discovered that these teachers did *not* concentrate on being good disciplinarians; nor did their teaching stress worksheets and students' working alone at desks. Rather, what he saw were engaged classes working on interesting projects and classrooms in which community and care were actively and intentionally promoted.

Kohn (1996) reviewed so-called **behavior management** programs and concluded that most are antithetical to good teaching. Relying on coercion through various forms of rewards and punishments, such programs reinforce an *external locus of control,* in which motivation is influenced primarily by others, rather than the more desired *internal locus of control,* in which drive and effort come from the internal interests and initiative of the person. Teachers often become frustrated at students' lack of inner motivation, their "not doing anything unless they are told," when that is what typical behavior management programs actually promote.

Kohn (1992, 1993, 1996, 1999) and others (Goleman, 1995; Noddings, 1992; Sapon-Shevin, 1999) recommend that we assist students in taking control of their own learning; work to build community, respect, and responsibility in our classrooms; and move beyond competition to building cooperative learning and interactions (Johnson & Johnson, 1989a; 1994). When we do this, our behavior problems decrease.

Students with Differing Abilities in a Community of Learners

In a traditional competitive class, the self-esteem of students who don't do as well as others is always on the line as the class sorts itself into groups of nerds, jocks, and dummies. In an inclusive school, we may have a student with rudimentary verbal language skills in classes with a budding novelist, a gifted artist working alongside others whose artistic abilities are very limited, a talented athlete teaming up with an individual who has cerebral palsy and gets around in a wheelchair. Our goal, however, is for students to see differences yet learn to appreciate and value one another, working against the social sorting that breaks community. Rather than pretending that everyone is the same, students in effective inclusive schools recognize these differences and make a place for all as the school and classroom community goes about its individual and corporate work. For students with obvious ability differences, a caring community provides a context in which they can build on their strengths, learning at their own level and developing self-esteem in the process (Grigal, 1998; Haring, Breen, Pitts-Conway, Lee, & Gaylord-Ross, 1998; Hughes et al., 1999; Johnson & Johnson, 1989a).

Building a Culture of Community in the School
Adults Collaborating and Caring

Nancy Creech (personal communication, June 21, 2000), a multiage teacher, says, "The key is that I teach *children.*" Not English, not the sixth grade, not math, but children. We have choices. On the one hand, we can work to build community and support prosocial behavior. On the other hand, we can seek first and foremost to control children and punish them when we can't.

As we work to create community in our school and class, we can expect this process to occur in stages. Community doesn't just happen. It is created through hard work and perseverance. Peck (1987) described a series of stages through which a group of people go as they build community:

1. The process starts with **pseudocommunity,** a state in which people act as if they are community and are "nice" but do not connect.

2. Next, when people begin to speak the truth to communicate authentically, *chaos* ensues. Conflict occurs, and some people try to convince others that their position is correct. It is at this stage that people often give up. For example, staff may be angry at one another; students may get upset and withdraw sullenly.

3. If the group continues without falling apart, they next settle into *emptiness:* a time of waiting, listening, confusion. We may literally not know what to do, but we are there listening.

4. Eventually, people begin to communicate and listen to one another, reach out, and build an actual *community*—a state that is both felt and objectively real. This often starts with some genuine sharing on the part of one or two people. Gradually, their risk taking gives others courage, and others share too.

5. *Maintaining* community, of course, is an ongoing process as well. Oftentimes a group will recycle through earlier stages.

How does all this look with children and staff in a school? Sandy is a first-grade teacher and Michael a ninth-grade English teacher. Both seek to build community in their classes, and both describe some experiences that are similar each year. Both begin their year helping students get to know one another. They set up times to discuss how the classroom community is operating—each day for Sandy, once a week for Michael. Every year, they see Peck's cycle operate. At first, everyone is very friendly, chattering away. "I think they are actually hiding how nervous they are," explains Michael; Sandy nods her head in agreement. Then the conflicts begin. Each teacher facilitates discussions, but they allow students to air their feelings. "They really get angry!" says Sandy. She often has to resist jumping in too quickly. Watching such conflicts, the group will settle into silence. Then a student will say, "You hurt my feelings." Another might say, "My mom got her feelings hurt last night." Suddenly the real sharing begins, the basis of community.

If we understand these stages, we can more clearly appreciate the difficulties and the richness of the project as we work toward community in our teaching. We will know that "niceness" and "pleasantness" are not real community. We'll also know that conflict and chaos are inevitable as we and our students actually open up to one another and build authentic relationships. We'll know that community is born out of a struggle to listen, share, and communicate honestly and authentically with respect—and that this struggle is an ongoing process that is never complete.

The Foundations of School Community

Let's now explore specific strategies for building community. First, three basic foundation stones are important both schoolwide and within our classrooms (see Figure 11.3):

Democratic and Collaborative Decision Making. The first building block is democratic and collaborative decision making. For example: In a traditional school, the principal makes major decisions and tells teachers what to do; teachers in turn tell students. In an effective inclusive school, the principal allows teachers and other staff to work together to consider issues related to the whole school. At best, all

Figure 11.3

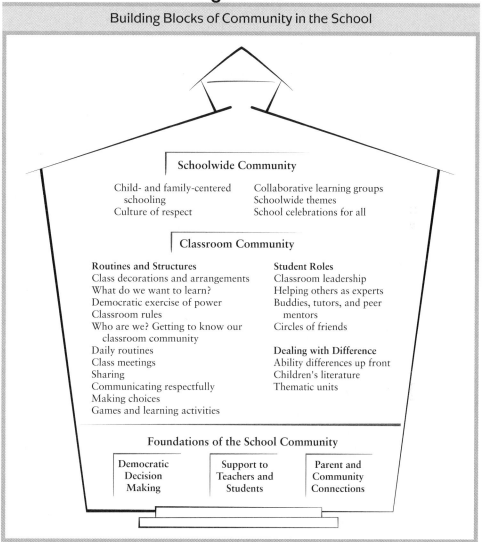

Building Blocks of Community in the School

Schoolwide Community

Child- and family-centered schooling
Culture of respect

Collaborative learning groups
Schoolwide themes
School celebrations for all

Classroom Community

Routines and Structures
Class decorations and arrangements
What do we want to learn?
Democratic exercise of power
Classroom rules
Who are we? Getting to know our classroom community
Daily routines
Class meetings
Sharing
Communicating respectfully
Making choices
Games and learning activities

Student Roles
Classroom leadership
Helping others as experts
Buddies, tutors, and peer mentors
Circles of friends

Dealing with Difference
Ability differences up front
Children's literature
Thematic units

Foundations of the School Community

| Democratic Decision Making | Support to Teachers and Students | Parent and Community Connections |

school staff participate, including the secretary, the janitor, the teachers, the speech therapist, the lunch aides.

Democracy, of course, means that we can use our own influence, in collaboration with others, to make decisions and set directions—that is, to exercise power. In democracy we decide that our voice will be heard even, or perhaps especially, when those above us do not want to hear it. In standing for what we believe, we can model empowerment for students. We can create new energy and engage the support of others who are emboldened by our courage. This prevents the energy-draining disempowerment when we feel helpless (Apple, 1995; Banks, 1990; Skrtic, 1994).

Support for Teachers and Students. The second schoolwide foundation stone is the development of support for teachers, students, and others. In Chapter 5 we explored many support strategies and structures. As we collaborate, we form relationships and develop trust that mirrors the support and caring we give students in classrooms. It is very difficult to build community with our students if we do not have a supportive community among school staff. For example, as Fran, the art teacher, Cathy, the social studies teacher, and Randall, a special education teacher, work together to develop a multicultural unit on freedom, linking the experience of the Underground Railroad and the fight for freedom in South Africa, they develop a personal bond and enjoy one another. The students sense this, and it transforms the whole experience; and through the students' final assembly performance, the effects of the teachers' mutual support have an impact on the whole school.

Parent and Community Connections. The third foundation stone is involvement and connection with parents and the larger community. In Chapter 3 we explored ways to build these relationships and connections. Here we point out that these connections are a critical part of building community in the school as we bring many people into the lives of our students.

Key Schoolwide Practices
That Promote Community

We can walk into any school and within a very few minutes get a feel for its culture. We may be treated rudely or ignored by a secretary, hear teachers yelling at students, see the principal acting tense. Or we may see friendly people who ask if they can help us in an open way. Students and parents feel the climate of a school as well, and respond.

Creating a Child- and Family-Centered Vision. First and foremost, we create a common vision of our school that is centered on children and families. If we see the school as driven by the goal of achieving higher test scores, we act differently than if our purpose is to create a supportive community where all grow and learn together. If we have a courageous and creative principal who supports child- and family-centered learning, we are fortunate. If we do not, we still can work toward this end and seek partners among other like-minded teachers and parents (Kohn, 1999; Schwartz & Pollishuke, 1990).

Building a Culture of Respect

A clear indicator of school culture is the way teachers talk to and about children and parents, particularly those with whom they are having difficulty. I walk into Sharon Watson's class and I see her talking with her first graders in highly respectful tones. "Class, let me introduce you to our visitor," she says. She asks students questions, gets their opinions, listens to them. She is concerned about one child with whom she has not yet been able to develop a good relationship.

Where respect flourishes, staff and students interact openly and spontaneously. Laughter and smiles are frequent. In other schools, however, tension fills the air; people talk hesitantly, with restraint, with forced smiles and with laughter that does not feel genuine. It is essential that we work to respect others, communicate in caring ways, and model honesty and directness.

Collaborative Learning Circles. How do we constantly renew ourselves, learn new teaching strategies, and build community with our coworkers? Increasingly, teachers gather, often supported by university faculty or staff development specialists, to share, talk, and explore innovative teaching. For example, at Barnard Elementary School, teachers meet every month after school as part of a "literacy circle." Teachers have taken the leadership in this group—deciding on scheduling, letting people know of meetings, setting the agenda. Learning circles are powerful, engaging, fun ways for teachers to grow that parallel best practices in our classrooms.

Schoolwide or Multiclass Themes for Learning. Several teachers, or the whole school, may adopt a common theme to organize learning. A high school, for example, might focus on "working for justice" to link subjects throughout the building. Or several teachers might develop a collaborative theme. For example, teachers in first, third, and fifth grades might decide to involve their students in the theme of animals in captivity. They could link subjects around this theme and develop collaborative activities across grade levels (Manning, Manning, & Long, 1994; Nesbitt, 1991; Zemelman, Daniels, & Hyde, 1998).

School Celebrations for All. We can promote community through schoolwide celebrations and assemblies, where we set a tone and demonstrate what we value. With the increased emphasis on raising standardized test scores, for example, many schools have assemblies honoring students who passed the test. Such awards ceremonies divide students who passed from those who did not.

In an inclusive school, celebrations recognize multiple talents and the gifts of all. We may have awards for the most improved or the funniest; for hard workers; for caring and compassion; for creativity. Our assemblies are fun, involving students, parents, community members, and teachers. We might sing songs; share stories; and break into small groups to act out a simple story involving teachers, students, and parents together. We look for ways to strengthen and celebrate our bonds with one another (Developmental Studies Center, 1994; Kohn, 1993).

Building a Community of Learners in Our Class
Valuing Our Differences and Helping One Another

When we use best teaching practices, we find multiple opportunities to build community. At the same time, as we have seen, community building supports academic learning. Let's now turn our attention to yearlong strategies and structures that help create community in our classroom.

Routines and Structures for Building Community: Getting Started and Building throughout the Year

Community starts and ends with daily classroom routines, building through small, ever present interactions and procedures. At the beginning of the year, we remember that first impressions, for adults as well as children, can endure; we seek from the beginning to set a tone and build a culture of mutual support. "What about the subjects—biology or spelling or math?" we are often asked. "Shouldn't we get into those right away?" Effective inclusive teachers take time for community-building activities. Teachers who intentionally work to build a community consistently believe this time to be well spent, establishing a foundation on which they build throughout the year (Denton & Kriete, 2000; Gibbs, 1998).

What Do We Want to Learn? We involve our students early on in talking about what they want to learn. Linda, an eleventh-grade English teacher, for example, has students brainstorm ideas about the course, recording the suggestions on sheets of paper so all can see. The class then groups these ideas into workable themes. Linda has discovered that students often choose many ideas that she herself had and that are in the school curriculum. However, by helping to shape the class, students gain the feeling that it belongs to them and they are not just visiting (Manning, Manning, & Long, 1994).

Promoting Student Ownership through Democratic Exercise of Power. Students need to understand that the classroom belongs to everyone, not just the teacher. This understanding must be fostered through careful thought and consideration. Students need opportunities to help create the rules that will govern their lives in the classroom. Creating classroom rules together—a process in which everyone's ideas are listed, then grouped into a few rules that are easy to remember—is essential. We must be willing to give up the feeling of total control and to replace it with a feeling of pride in teaching students how to control themselves. Once the group agrees to the rules, we post them and refer to them often. We might say, "Lorinzo, that breaks the agreement you made to abide by rule number four." This system puts the responsibility for actions on the students and reminds students of agreements made together (Manning, Manning, & Long, 1994; Peterson, 1992; Sapon-Shevin, 1999).

"You Can't Say You Can't Play": Classroom Rules That Promote Community. Any group of people can develop rules of conduct that encourage care and support or that create conflict, exclusion, and isolation. Students often reject one another, create cliques, or are cruel, reflecting the society around them. However, we will challenge students to promote rather than destroy community. When we see students creating divisive rules or acting out assumptions and prejudice, we ask them to think through these issues. Vivian Paley (1992) tells of her experience with a new rule she suggested to her kindergartners: "You can't say you can't play." She describes how her children sought to make this rule real and the dialogues that occurred as they presented their experience to older students. The rule helped children become more aware of ways in which they rejected one another and helped some isolated students join the classroom community.

Who Are We? Getting to Know our Classroom Community. Early on we help students know each other, discovering commonalties and differences. During the first two weeks of the school year we may engage in fun community activities, playing games that encourage interactions. We ask students to bring pictures from home, make art projects together, read fun books, and share ideas.

Daily Routines. We either make or break community in daily routines. In elementary schools, going to the bathroom is one of the most important. For example: We enter Lowe Elementary School and see a class lined up. The teacher admonishes the children to stay quiet while trying to rush them to the bathroom. The noise of laughter and scuffling is heard through the bathroom door. In about twenty minutes, the teacher gets the class back to work. In another class Bob explains that children go as they need, waving a bathroom pass to ask permission without interrupting; he nods yes and checks the clock to make sure they are not gone too long. This process teaches children responsibility while not wasting learning time.

We must help students take on responsibilities and provide supportive structures to enable them to do so. Each basic daily routine can be fun while teaching dependability. Here are strategies to build community and responsibility in daily routines:

- *Getting class attention:* Clap hands in a rhythm and have students imitate; ring a bell or other musical instrument; hold up a silent hand and count down while children join in; quietly ask each group to put their eyes on you. Involve students in selecting attention-getting strategies.
- *Transitions between areas or activities:* Begin singing a song all know; ask students to fill in blanks in a funny story; start reading a poem; begin a riddle.
- *Bathroom:* Have a signal to ask permission silently; use a bathroom pass; provide consequences for misuse.
- *Lining up:* Have children lead with teacher following, stopping at key areas.
- *Lunch count:* Use a magnetic board with two columns for hot and cold lunches. Have students move their magnetic ticket to hot or cold lunch, and charge one student with the job of pulling tickets and sending information to the office.
- *Dismissal:* Set a routine for leaving room; assign jobs for straightening up.
- *Attendance:* Have students take attendance on a sheet, passing it around.

Class Meetings. Classroom meetings are important tools for engaging students in decision making regarding needs and problems. Many effective teachers meet frequently, whether about teasing, staying on task, turning in homework, or celebrating an accomplishment. Meetings vary in length; some may be only ten minutes, others longer. Classroom meeting topics are chosen by both students and the teacher. Students or the teacher can anonymously write issue topics and put them in a box, allowing those not comfortable with sharing aloud to have their needs addressed.

Classroom meetings are run by children, not by the teacher—a difficult shift for some teachers. Students take turns in the roles of note taker and moderator. The class establishes basic rules that allow students to speak one at a time, often using a designated object (a "talking stick," for example) to pass to the person who has the floor to speak. Students are not required to speak and may pass if they want.

Artwork reprinted by permission of Martha Perske from *Perske: Pencil Portraits 1971–1990* (Nashville: Abingdon Press, 1998).

Most importantly, when the class makes a decision, action occurs (Gibbs, 1998; Sapon-Shevin, 1999).

Sharing: Celebration, Joys, Challenges, Grief, and Pain. If our class is a community, it must be first and foremost a place of sharing—sharing of hopes, dreams, joys, fears, challenges, and sometimes hurt, grief, and pain. As teachers we model by taking risks, sharing our own lives with students. This will encourage students similarly to share with one another. In an elementary classroom students might write daily in journals about events in their lives and share them in "morning news," which we can record on chart paper and edit. This information could go into our weekly class newsletter. We can use a similar time in a high school class. The more trust we create, the more students will share during this time (Gibbs, 1998; Peterson, 1992; Sapon-Shevin, 1999).

Along with daily sharing, we also need routines for special times. Celebrating special events creates a feeling of community. We are alert for events in our students' lives—achievements, family events (weddings, graduations, etc.). We look for opportunities to tell students that we appreciate their work, help in class, or caring acts.

Sometimes, when a student is having a hard time, the total class may help the student. Perhaps a student's father has died and she is crying. We might ask if she would like to talk. If she wanted to talk, we might ask her to share what happened and tell the class about her father. Students could offer sympathy and practical ways to help.

Communicating Respectfully. "When you are done writing, please match eyes with me so I'll know we can go on. Renae ready?" said Shawna. This is an example of a respectful strategy for interacting with students to move from topic to topic. Through respectful communication we promote acceptance in the class and do not embarrass students or put them on the spot. For example, anytime students don't want to talk, they just say "pass." They will be more likely to respond later. If they pass all the time, we talk with them individually. We invite students to participate but do not demand participation. As we make transitions, we say: "Would you bring your writing/conversation to a close, please?" Waiting respectfully, we say "Thank you" to those who do stop (Schiller, 1998). However, we do *not* compare students to one another: "I really like the way Renae stopped when I asked her to." Students recognize this as a manipulative ploy rather than true appreciation.

We communicate respect (or lack of it) as we respond to our most difficult students. In a fourth-grade class, Jennifer was arguing insistently with the teacher. Although the teacher tried to stay calm, she finally began yelling at Jennifer. Another student muttered, "Great! Now she'll be mad at all of us." When the teacher treats all students with respect, despite their behavior, they are more comfortable taking risks and sharing. When they feel intimidated or worried, however, the community bond is broken.

Making Choices. Children need both help from adults in the form of structure and freedom to make choices. We can establish many ways to give students reasonable choices. Often we can present options to the entire group and allow students to make selections through discussion (Apple, 1995; Etzioni, 1993; Geller & Hunt, 1995; Glasser, 1992; Kohn, 1993). Some examples include:

- *What to learn:* At the beginning of the year or of each unit, we find out what students would like to learn and incorporate their ideas.
- *What order:* Students choose order of work activities. Should they learn the new lesson or go over homework first? Do reading or writing workshop first?
- *Choice time:* We structure time, whether it is a certain time every day or the beginning twenty minutes of the hour every Friday, for students to choose from several activities, such as literacy, physics experiments, or algebra.
- *What to read/write:* Students select books to read or stories to write. Even if teachers pick the genre, students select the content.
- *Day-to-day goals:* Students identify daily or weekly goals related to academics or behaviors. Teachers suggest, but do not demand, goals, chosen reflectively, that need improvement.
- *Seating arrangement:* Although students may have assigned seats for collaborative group work, a student rarely needs to sit in an assigned seat at other times.

Students may sit in a preferred location as long as they are working. Teachers help students to understand that the total room belongs to them all, no matter whose things are at a given seat. This provides many student options and facilitates more effective use of available space.

Games and Learning Activities That Build Community. Whether in the first five minutes of an hour class or during recess time, we can take time to play games that encourage community. Most games can be used, with adaptations, at all ages. Community-building games involve everyone in the class and are cooperative, as opposed to competitive: Students learn that for them to win, others do not have to lose. Rather, they learn that for one to win, all must cooperate and win together. Community games also teach conflict resolution and demonstrate commonalities and understanding of one another. Figure 11.4 summarizes some fun community building games based on the work of Mara Sapon-Shevin (1999), many of which can be played in ten or fifteen minutes.

Multilevel Cooperative Learning. Working together helps students accomplish tasks they could not do alone. Students can work together on any subject, whether reading a chapter book together or teaming up as editing partners or math homework partners. We can create projects that require that students work together, but at different jobs requiring types and levels of expertise. For a science experiment, for example, differing students might have the following job roles: obtain materials, set up the experiment, read directions, record results, share with the class, and draw a picture of what happened. Every student has a job at their own level on which others depend. Students learn that each person has different strengths to contribute (Cohen, E., 1994; Johnson & Johnson, 1989a, 1994).

Cross-Grade-Level Interactions. Interactions across grade levels can also strengthen community. Older students might pair with younger partners to read once a week. Classes might do research or art projects together, take field trips, write a story together, share completed work (Nesbitt, 1991; Sapon-Shevin, 1999).

Clock Partners. From kindergarten through high school, a good way to pair students for activities is the **clock partners** technique. Each student has a large clock drawn on a sheet of paper with a line at each hour. Students sign each other's clocks at the same time. For instance, Jeremy and Amy both decide to be two-o'clock partners together. Students go around the room till they have a partner for each hour. They cannot have the same partner twice. Also, if someone asks, the student cannot say no. For an activity, we ask students to get their clocks and join up with, for example, their ten-o'clock partner. This simple strategy removes the aggravations often associated with pairing students—no more hurt feelings or efforts to separate students who always work together.

Sharing Work. Sharing completed work gives students a sense of pride in their own accomplishments and appreciation for others, building self-esteem and community simultaneously. When a writing project is completed, we can have share time, have

Figure 11.4

Games That Promote Community Building

GAME AND DESCRIPTION

1. *Cooperative musical chairs:* Children try to make sure that every person is on a chair, whether there are two people on a chair or six. This involves helping instead of pushing the slower and weaker ones out.

2. *Children write facts and fictions about themselves,* and class has to decide which is which. Or students write clues about themselves and class guesses who they are.

3. *Stand up/sit down* in categories or move to different walls. This shows students how they are alike and different.

4. *"Make a group":* Call out something, like a kind of breakfast food, and students who fit that category make groups of three or more. Change categories constantly so students are moving around a lot.

5. *Mimic others' actions:* For example, pretend to toss different objects while the other person catches them, or pass faces or sounds around a circle.

6. *Riddle concentration:* Each student has a card with either question or answer. Play like child's game Memory to find matches. Students can get help from classmates sitting on either side. Put matches in middle and cheer when all win.

7. *Get in groups by birthday month:* Each group makes rhyming chant about its month, then presents it.

8. *Hug tag:* Put in groups of two or three. One or more children are given a red flag or sock, which they try to give to other children. Children are "safe" if they are in a group that is hugging one another. When the teacher says "switch" the groups disband and regroup while the "huggit" tries to give the flag away.

9. *Tug of peace:* Stand in circle with rope, hold out with two hands; all pull together, leaning back, to pull everyone up at same time; Cheer; try to sit down without falling.

10. *Hula hoop pass:* In circle children hold hands and try to pass hula hoop from one person to next without letting go of the others' hands. Do with one then two together.

11. *Cooperative stories:* Retell aloud a story about a certain subject or chain of events. Each person adds line to story so it makes sense.

12. *Nonverbal lineups* on different topics. Students line up in order based on chosen topic. They must communicate without talking.

13. *Cooperative word sentences:* Put words on cards. One student has verbs, another adjectives, another with nouns, and so on. In groups of four to six, make different kinds of sentences—longest, funniest, and so on. Must use word from each person's set, and each person must be able to say the word to get credit, thus the peer tutoring aspect.

14. *Cooperative 20,000 pyramid:* In groups students generate clues to get people to guess items in a certain category—for example, among citrus fruits, to guess orange, lemon, and so on. Make sure clues are not misleading. Then play. Students need to use lots of skills to generate good clues. Can change skill level by selection of categories or by timing the game. Each team discusses as they hear each clue and decides whether to answer or ask for another clue.

Source: Adapted from Sapon-Shevin (1999).

a book signing to which adults are invited, or read stories to other classes. At the end of a unit, we can have a celebration for which children prepare activities and set up projects, skits, and written work showing their learning; we invite other classes or parents (Schiller, 1998).

Student Roles in the Learning Community

We develop opportunities and structures within which students can help and support one another. In addition, we explicitly teach students *how* to do this.

Student Classroom Leadership. When students exercise leadership, they increase their understanding, sense of responsibility, and self-esteem. In the class community every student has a job and takes responsibility for it without constant reminders. We recently observed a classroom in which all twenty-five students had meaningful and needed jobs—watering the plants, straightening books, passing out materials, helping on computers (Peterson, 1992; Sapon-Shevin, 1999).

As students make choices, leadership roles often evolve naturally. We may rely on some students to serve as peer mediators (see Chapter 12), to be members of circles of support, to give comfort, or to lead and facilitate discussions. Students may help design the way we approach the curriculum or may give input as to how to help students who are having difficulty learning (Peterson, 1992).

Helping Others as Experts. Students need experience teaching others. To teach someone about something, a child must have a deeper understanding of that subject. By having children explain their thought processes to others, we can teach a much needed skill and demonstrate that everyone can be an expert. Our class becomes transformed into a place where there are many people to ask for help, not merely one teacher who cannot be everywhere at once (Fuchs, Fuchs, Kazdan, & Allen, 1999). We also help students understand the difference between helping and doing the work for a peer.

Students may even lead lessons they have seen taught several times. Maybe the physics class always starts out with an example problem that is discussed. We rotate students who choose the homework problem and lead the discussion. This strategy gives students a learning opportunity that is both powerful and fun; it also provides an excellent window into their thinking.

We can ask students to help others after finishing their work. Alternatively, we may ask one student to teach a few other students a new skill that the whole class needs to learn and then send others to this expert group for help. This is an excellent way for students who normally finish last to have experience being a leader.

Students can be experts on any subject—spelling, adding, dividing, proving theorems, capital letters, the Internet, quotation marks, making a cursive *m*, even quantum physics. The key is to teach the students to share knowledge—and to accept information from others (Au, Mason, & Scheu, 1995; Girard & Willing, 1996).

Buddies, Tutors, and Peer Mentors. Sometimes we formalize ways for learners to help one another. We might, for example, pair students on an ongoing basis as **study**

Schools to Visit

Building Community to Support Student Learning

West Orient Middle School
29805 SE Orient Drive
Gresham, OR 97080-8816
Phone: 503-663-3323
Principal: John Koch
John_Koch@gbsd.gresham.k12.or.us

West Orient Middle School, with 430 students in grades 5 through 8, has a long history of being a school that builds community. Several years ago, as the school construction committee worked on plans to remodel the old building set amidst farm-land and tree nurseries, they invited students to join the planning committee. The students' first thought was: If the library was to be at a lower level, how would their friend Shawn get there? They were used to bumping his wheelchair across the rough playground and around the old school, but it was time to consider everyone's needs. Their question was not disability focused but friend fo-cused. These students were key in reminding the adults that with the library at a lower level, there would need to be an elevator.

Today West Orient is a school that includes both students and parents in the development of school goals and in decision making. Partnering with families is another area where West Orient shines. This partnership has significant influence on the results demonstrated by students and is viewed as essential to the school's future success. With concern about school safety on the minds of all parents, West Orient was a leader in making it a priority that all students feel safe and respected. This explicit goal is being accomplished through a focus on building relationships between teachers and students and student to student.

At West Orient community means that every student, even those with significant disabilities, is a valued integral member of the school. It's not unusual to see the principal or the vice-principal sitting in the cafeteria with a group of students, helping a student with significant disabilities eat lunch. This isn't seen as a job and relegated to an assistant or a teacher, but is a time for adminis-trators to connect with students and enjoy the lunchroom commotion.

The students themselves know what commu-nity is about—not because it's a rule or they are supposed to be nice, but because they live it each day and watch their teachers value every child. Students see one another's value beyond what adults often see. When students look at Nick or Sarah or another friend who has a disability and see the enthusiasm that these friends bring to the class or recall that they are allowed to protest when they are upset or that they keep the most private of secrets, they see the depth of their friends. The students say things like "I hate it when Nick is sick, because he's the one who pipes up when things are getting boring. Sarah reminds the teacher to call on all of us—even when we're the quiet ones." Students are also quick to re-mind adults that teenagers need both time alone and time with their friends—not always with adults.

At West Orient it's the students who often lead the way in demonstrating that when we reach out to one another and build relationships, we build communities that are strong and support-ive. It doesn't matter whether you have a disabil-ity, or are a fifth grader among eighth graders, or can't talk or read or write, or are the most athletic or musical; what matters is that you belong to the community at West Orient because you came through the door.

By Patti McVay, Outreach Center for Inclusive Educa-tion; **patti_mcvay@mesd.k12.or.us.**

buddies. (For older students, we'd call it something else, obviously—class partners, for example.) Or we could shift such pairings more frequently; across subjects we might pair certain students in reading and others in math, or we might change pairings from week to week (Girard & Willing, 1996; Sapon-Shevin, 1999).

More and more schools are utilizing **cross-age buddies and tutors:** older students who serve as tutors, reading buddies, and mentors for younger children. It is not unusual to walk into an elementary school and see a high school student reading with an eight-year-old or helping a fifth grader with his/her math assignment (Nesbitt, 1991). Students with special challenges themselves can also very effectively serve as tutors, mentors, and helpers for other students. For example, a sixth-grade student struggling to read sixth-grade material can fluently read a story to a first-grade student.

Some schools operate formal peer tutoring programs in which students receive training, provide tutoring, and receive credit. In one high school, students considered at risk because of academic and behavioral problems mentored students with mental retardation. The students with mental retardation developed friends and were able to negotiate the school environment. The self-esteem and academic performance of the at-risk students increased dramatically as they were successful in a highly responsible role (Fitzgerald, Henning, & Feltz, 1997; Murray-Seegert, 1989).

Circles of Support. A **circle of support** (sometimes called circle of friends) is a powerful way to help when students need more intentional, intensive support. The idea is simple: We ask peers, friends, and family of a student to come together to provide support (see Chapter 4). Although circles were born to help students with disabilities, they are powerful tools for anyone. A student coming into our class having just immigrated to the United States may not speak our language well. A student with autism may have difficulty relating to others. A student with an abusive father may be doing poorly in school.

To get started we ask students if they would like to have a circle of support. An adult acts as a facilitator for the group. A social worker or psychologist may meet with students during the day after school or on the weekend to facilitate a circle meeting. Some teachers have met with circles on their lunch hour or during their planning period (Peterson, Tamor, Feen, & Silagy, 2002). In other situations teachers have taught students about circles and students conducted circles during the school day. Most school circles meet at the school building. Circles, however, may choose to meet at home or in a community setting.

Students themselves decide whom to invite to their circle. A student may also, with our help, open the invitation to all students within a class. In other situations, when a student is new to our room and does not know anyone, we may ask for class volunteers.

Once the group is selected and a meeting time and place established, the group meets. Most circles have found it helpful to use some form of person-centered planning, like the MAPS process described in Chapter 4, to focus. In a MAP, the "focus person" and the group explore the dreams and fears of the student and develop an action plan, including assistance from circle members. One teacher used a very simple version of this process, asking a student what help he wanted. The circle then identified ways they could help (Peterson, Tamor, Feen, & Silagy, 2002).

High school friends who serve as a circle of support for one another share their feelings of care. Circles of support can be powerful tools in helping any student experiencing difficulties.

Circles have been very powerful. In Chapter 1 we described Judith Snow's experience with the first formalized circle of support. In schools circles have helped students with challenges by helping with many issues—homework, problems with relationships, the blues. In Kitchener, Ontario, we visited with the circle of friends of May, an eighth grader with Down syndrome. This group of young people had greatly helped May to be part of their class. They decried the "life skills class," where, they said, May "was not learning anything." What was particularly interesting, however, was the critical thinking and problem solving going on among these students (Falvey, Forest, Pearpoint, & Rosenberg, 1998; O'Brien & O'Brien, 1992).

When we spoke with Martha, early in this chapter, about Kevin, she also spoke of a circle of support. She talked with Kevin and his mother, asked him to suggest five children he wanted to be involved, and then she asked the children one-on-one. Even though these third graders gave up one recess a week and knew it was a working commitment, not one of them said no. "It says something about the community we have built," said Martha. "Children can meet very high expectations." The children began by deciding who would help Kevin with reading and other needs he expressed. We were struck by the fact that the children wanted to help Kevin with subjects in which they needed improvement also.

We can get more information through Inclusion Press (see **www.inclusion.com**). The developers of MAPS and circle of support concepts strongly urge that we invite friends and family to our own circle and MAPS session before facilitating a circle for someone else. You'll be surprised how valuable and fun this is (Falvey, Forest, Pearpoint, & Rosenberg, 1998; O'Brien & O'Brien, 1992).

Celebrating Differences

We help students learn to understand and value one another. Simultaneously, we work to (1) understand common needs of all as human beings across our differences; and (2) explore ways in which human beings are different and ways in which these differences contribute to the total community. We seek to build an inclusive community in which students notice, value, and celebrate differences that include:

- Race and ethnicity
- Culture
- Ability
- Age
- Socioeconomic status
- Gender
- Sexual orientation

These differences provide a rich tapestry for learning and exploration that can cross subject areas. We help our students experience and understand different perspectives, the influences of life experiences, and the contribution that each person can make to the whole, enhancing learning and community building simultaneously.

Intentionally Promoting Inclusion and Relationships. Daily we work to support students in developing positive, caring relationships. If Jorge seems isolated, we look for opportunities to pair him with supportive classmates. If Anthony has a difficult time handling his emotions, we may ask some students if they could help Anthony out or group him with socially skilled, emotionally stable peers. If students seem afraid of Mary, a girl with severe cerebral palsy who must struggle to speak and is sometimes loud in the process, we ponder ways we can help classmates understand and support her. For it is certain that if some students do not have friendships and supportive relationships, these students are feeling isolated, fearful, sometimes angry, and our classroom community is weakened.

Fisher (2001) developed a helpful framework for understanding the social place of any child within the class (see Figure 11.5). If a child is at risk for being marginalized, this framework helps us consider our options. In ways, it is a more detailed breakdown of the journey from benevolence to community that we described in Chapter 1. As we think about children, how do they interact? Is there one child who has no "regular friends" or "friends forever" but has many "helpers"? Is one child actually ignored by almost everyone (a "ghost/guest")? What might we do to change that? One teacher brought a situation like this to the attention of students, who subsequently invited the child to their house on the weekend. Do all children get to be helped? Perhaps Lisa, who is labeled gifted, is always helping other students but not receiving help herself. Might we suggest that a student with cerebral palsy help Lisa in an area in which he is strong?

Ability Differences Up Front. It is important to help students understand and accept that we all have different abilities and that these differences do not make us better or worse. Teaching students about multiple intelligences can be constructive. This helps

Figure 11.5

Frames of Relationship

FRAME	SAMPLE WORDS	SAMPLE ACTIONS
Ghost/guest	"Nothing to do with us!"	Being invisible, ignored, excluded
Inclusion kid/different friend	"He is weird." "She is cute." "It's not nice to tease special students!"	Differential treatment by everyone Affection Politeness
Kid who needs help	"Can I push him to science?" "It's my turn to help her."	Helping
Just another kid	"It's no big deal." "Like everyone else."	Typical reciprocal interactions
One of my friends	"He's just my friend." "He's got my back."	Hanging Affection Invitations to parties Having fun together
Best friends forever	"Part of my life." "Best friend." "Trust with anything."	Hanging Having fun together

Source: Adapted from Fisher (2001).

students who function lower in some areas look at their strengths in other areas. We also help students understand that different students will be working at different levels.

As we do this we are providing enormous learning that will benefit students in later life. Students learn to value and look for one another's abilities. They learn how to work effectively with people having very different abilities.

The example we set as we interact with students with obvious ability differences is most important. If we are frustrated with and belittle a student for lack of understanding, if we ignore or isolate such a student, we will promote these responses in other students as well. In contrast, we can model respect and teach students practical strategies for supporting one another (Sapon-Shevin, 1999; Tomlinson, 1999).

Children's Literature. Literature is a powerful tool for engaging students in understanding differences and experiencing the human condition from different perspectives. Many children's books deal explicitly with issues that confront children. We've listed just a few excellent resources in Figure 11.6. We can read and discuss such books aloud; or students may read and discuss them in literacy circles, write their own stories and compare their experiences with characters in the story, and/or act out parts, playing different roles and reflecting on the life of the person portrayed (Sapon-Shevin, 1999).

Figure 11.6

Children's Literature Examples

Don't Feel Sorry for Paul. Wolf, 1974. Lippincott. I	Paul was born with incompletely formed hands and feet but is first and foremost a child—riding his bike, going to school, at a birthday party.
Rachel. Fanshawe, 1977. Bradbury. P	Picture book for young children that illustrates how Rachel navigates her life in a wheelchair—swimming, being part of a Brownie troop, going on vacations.
I Have a Sister—My Sister Is Deaf. Peterson, 1977. Harper. P	A sensitive book in which a girl tells about her sister and how she handles being deaf.
My Friend Jacob. Clifton, 1980. Dutton. P	Fiction; two high school students, one of whom has abilities far below typical for his age, are friends.
The Balancing Girl. Rabe, 1981. Dutton. P	Story of two students—one, in a wheelchair, can line up dominoes and then make them all fall down together; the other feels the need to knock down the dominoes. They work through this conflict.
Jamaica Tag-Along. Havill, 1989. Houghton Mifflin. P	An African American girl is rejected by her brother and does the same to a younger child. After she realizes that she's doing the same thing, they build a sand castle together, and finally her brother joins her as well.
Living in Two Worlds. Rosenberg, 1986. Lee & Shepard. I	Photo essay about biracial children that describes segregation and prejudice in housing, culture, and religion and conveys the pain of being teased.
Come Sit by Me. Merrifield, 1990. Women's Press. P	A young boy in a day care center has AIDS, and some children won't play with him—but Karen does.
The Big Orange Splot. Pinkwater, 1977. Scholastic. P	Mr Plumbean lives on a "neat street." He decides to paint his house to illustrate his dreams. At first the neighbors are upset, but by the end the street has all sorts of new designs!
Fly Away Home. Bunting, 1991. Clarion. P	A homeless boy scrounges for food and shelter at the airport where he lives with his father. He is given hope when a bird escapes from the terminal.
White Socks Only. Coleman, 1996. Albert Whitman. I	A young African American girl takes off her shoes and steps to the "Whites Only" water fountain in her white socks. A controversy ensues, ending with the removal of the sign on the fountain forever.
The Number on My Grandfather's Arm. Adler, 1987. UAHC Press. P	A little girl's grandfather tells her the story of the concentration camp in Hitler's Germany after she notices a number on his arm.
Sweet Clara and the Freedom Quilt. Hopkinson, 1993. Knopf. P	Twelve-year-old Clara, a seamstress slave, escapes on the Underground Railroad, leaving behind a quilt that shows the directions to the North for others.

P = Primary; I = Intermediate; A = Advanced

Source: Adapted from Sapon-Shevin (1999).

Stepping Stones
To Inclusive Teaching

1. Does a sense of community and care exist in your school and your classroom? Why? Why not? Use the ideas in this chapter to develop two strategies to strengthen community.
2. Talk with a few teachers. See who would be interested in meeting to talk about community and the social and behavioral needs of both children and staff in your school. Meet and develop a plan to try two new strategies.
3. What conditions exist in the administration of your school that help support building community and/or that weaken community? How do teachers and parents now respond to these conditions? What might be done?
4. Identify teachers in your school who are using different community-building strategies. Approach these teachers and talk with them about what they do. Ask to visit their class; write down notes of what you see, take pictures of what they do, and organize these into a booklet that you can pass out to all staff.
5. Have a party and ask each teacher to talk about one positive happening with a child who is having difficulty in the class. Celebrate these achievements!

Thematic Units. We can study human differences as a **thematic unit.** We might even use the categories of difference listed previously. For example, one thematic unit could be: How do people differ in intellectual abilities? This question could lead into an exploration using multiple intelligences as a framework and include a study of IQ tests. Or we could explore the history of people who are deaf or differing ethnic groups. One teacher did an extended study project, for example, on "Coming to America." Students read books, researched ways groups came to America, interviewed family members, and wrote the stories of their families, which were then read in class by parents. Another group of students investigated civil rights of persons with disabilities. They interviewed local people, invited presenters, and enacted a drama of the takeover of the president's office at Berkeley in California in 1972 (Manning, Manning, & Long, 1994; Zemelman, Daniels, & Hyde, 1998).

In the End
The Growing Circles of Community

At first building community of third graders, eighth graders, or high school seniors may seem a bit far-fetched. After all, most of us have experienced schools where feelings were not considered important. Many of us probably long for deeper community—yet many of us have been hurt so often by interactions with others that the idea of a caring community seems questionable.

We would do well to look at ourselves and explore how our own needs for belonging, love, power, freedom, and fun are being met. What is our experience of community? What do we understand? Have we had positive experiences that lead us to understand community, or will we need to feel our way carefully from scratch?

The fact is that the hunger for an unmet need for community is strong for many people, underlining the potentially powerful impact of community in our class. This fact also makes the challenge greater as we learn. Yet it seems reasonable to hope that we can be community-building leaders in our schools. Teachers all over the world are building a literature of practices that far extend the beginnings we've sketched in this chapter. The community-building movement in neighborhoods, churches, businesses, and whole municipalities is similarly growing, and there is much from which to learn. We have to be wise in the process, of course. What Peck (1987) calls pseudocommunity—everyone smiling and being nice—is not real. Community building is a journey that's full of both excitement and many false paths, but we'll find that it's key to teaching.

We may also find that the community we build with students contributes to a richness in our own lives that we wouldn't have thought possible. When we are greeted enthusiastically by students in the grocery store, when a college student we had in the fourth grade drops by to introduce us to his fiancee, when the whole student body throws us a farewell party as we move to another school, we'll reflect on community and the circling impacts of genuine care and support.

 # Key Points

- For students to learn, they must feel safe and emotionally secure. Otherwise they become tense and it is very difficult for them to take in new information. For this reason building a caring community is critical for learning.

- Community helps all students feel that they are welcome and that they belong. Caring classroom communities go far to help *prevent* many social and behavioral challenges and provide a setting in which *problem solving* among the community can occur when difficulties do occur.

- Building community throughout the school is critical—a welcoming atmosphere, friendly staff, and assemblies that honor many and celebrate the community are helpful.

- Building community in classrooms is enjoyable. We have many strategies—such as giving stu-

dents involvement in the decoration of the room, providing jobs that make students actually responsible for much of the functioning of the class, holding class meetings, promoting peer learning, and establishing circles of support.

- We particularly are attentive to helping potentially marginalized students be connected in our class, creating interactive opportunities, problem solving with students, creating structures through which students can develop real friendships as well as be helped.

- We explicitly help children learn about and appreciate differences among themselves, teaching them strategies to tap into classmates' strengths and to help one another.

Learning Expeditions

The following activities may be helpful in extending your learning.

1. Make a checklist of the community-building practices we have described in this book. Visit a class in a local school. Observe and talk a bit with the teachers. Check community-building practices you do and do not see being used. What is the impact on the behaviors and learning of students?

2. Think about community in your own life. Write about the influence of relationships and about your experience of being part of a caring, supportive group.

3. Interview a parent of a child who has been having "behavioral problems" in a local school. What has been occurring in the classroom? How is community built in the classroom and how has the teacher responded to the problems? What conclusions might you draw?

4. Locate a school that uses peer buddies and mentors. Observe and interview students involved in this process. What do they think? How does the system help them learn? How do they feel about the process?

5. Locate a school that uses circles of friends. Observe a meeting and interview the students involved. How do they feel about this responsibility? How has it enriched their own lives? How has it changed the life of the student they are helping?

6. Find out what children are included in a local school district. Where do the children go who do not attend regular classrooms? Visit one of these rooms. Interview the students to find out how they feel about their school setting. What does this say about community?

7. Complete a MAP on yourself by inviting a circle of trusted friends and family and using a process facilitator and graphics recorder.

CHAPTER GOAL

Develop knowledge and skills to build an understanding how challenging behavior communicates needs of students; learn about proactive strategies for responding to social and behavioral problems.

CHAPTER OBJECTIVES

1. Evaluate and understand research on the effects of traditional practices utilizing rewards and punishments.

2. Visualize types of challenging behaviors and needs these behaviors may communicate.

3. Understand how imposing control rather than meeting needs strengthens problematic behaviors.

4. Explore and utilize proactive strategies for meeting student needs.

5. Understand legal requirements and procedures for developing Behavioral Intervention Plans.

Responding Proactively to Social and Behavioral Challenges

Positive Strategies for Difficult Situations

"These kids are driving me crazy! I don't know what to do!" How do we respond to social and behavioral challenges? We've seen that the first strategy is to *prevent* problems by designing engaging instruction and by building a classroom community. Yet, despite our best efforts, we will experience problems with some students. In the Voices feature here, teachers discuss their students' behavior. They list behavioral problems and helpful and hurtful responses. We are surprised by what they say does *not* work—rewards punishments, bribes and threats, rejection and expulsion. What *does* work, they think, is building respect for students, teaching well, giving choices, providing support, and developing relationships. These teachers' findings agree substantially with the research literature. "This is the only way that kids know someone really cares for them," said Sheila, a high school science teacher.

Voices

Teachers on Dealing with Problem Behaviors: What Works and What Does Not

Some Common Problems in Classrooms
- Student is off task.
- Talks during instruction.
- Won't sit still.
- Attracts others' attention and gets them off task.
- Is unprepared for class.
- Makes excuses to leave class.
- Hits other students or the teacher.
- Insults other students.
- Acts belligerent.
- Withdraws and does not want to participate.

What Works?
- Give students attention.
- Encourage cooperative learning and play groups.
- Teach in fun and engaging ways.
- Study culture or "difference" of the week in the room to promote understanding and acceptance of differences.
- Have students help make rules and structure learning activities in the classroom.
- Have students help other students—use peer mediation, peer buddies, circles of friends.
- Institute sharing time to talk about events in life.
- Show concern and care.
- Stop till student gets under control.
- Emphasize group work. Ask "Do you need to . . . ?" Give options.

What Does Not!
- Boring, unengaging teaching.
- Extra assignments.
- Yelling.
- Lack of respect—lashing out rudely, nagging, pleading, begging.
- Intimidation—misuse of power.
- Punishment.
- Detention.

One of the other teachers was aghast, however. "Are you people crazy? There is no way this will work!" (Peterson, 1998). This reaction reflects the debate regarding behavioral challenges in schools. Do we try to control students through rewards and punishments? Do we label them as disturbed and get them out of our classes and into special education? Or do work to build relationships, care, and respect? Do we seek to understand and respond to student needs? How can we meet our own needs also?

Quincy: A Student out of Control

We are talking with a young teacher who has developed a reputation for success with challenging students. William teaches grades 4 and 5 and has been "looping" in a school serving a racially diverse, low-income area. We were immediately impressed by the student work that literally covers the walls, ceilings, and windows of William's classroom.

"I want to tell you about Quincy," William says.

"I can't do anything with him. He hits other students all the time." Quincy has quite a reputation, and several teachers think he should be in a class for students with emotional disorders. "I met Quincy my first year, when I took over his fourth-grade classroom," William continues. "I was the third teacher that year, and the class was in chaos." "What did you do?" we ask, thinking of stories about new teachers thrown into challenging classes.

"First, I made the classroom fun and inviting. Some friends helped me transform the room from drab to colorful. I wanted students to know this was going to be better and fun. However, Quincy hated everything, fought, and sometimes lashed out in a violent rage. He frequently turned over desks and jumped from tables. The only way I could get him to cooperate was to give him a choice of spending his time in class or in the office."

"He's afraid and angry at home, treated with disrespect at school." We expect William to tell us he tried to get Quincy in the special education class. Instead he says, "I really wanted Quincy to be successful." His eyes flicker in anger. "I was incensed when I saw how the previous teacher had treated Quincy. She placed masking tape on the floor around his desk, creating an invisible jail. If I had been Quincy, I would have rebelled too!"

"Confused by what was making him act this way, I soon learned that Quincy was living in a small apartment with his mother and grandmother. His mother's boyfriend regularly beat her and did not like Quincy. The grandmother was threatening to kick Quincy and his mother out. I began to understand. Quincy was angry and scared. He did not feel safe or know if he would have a place to live!"

"The other teachers wanted to get rid of Quincy. Not my student!" William tells us that almost daily, teachers asked when Quincy would be sent to the center for children with emotional disturbance. Their answer was to get rid of him. Yet William persevered and began to experiment.

"I built on his interests and gave him choices." Quincy kept playing in the coat closet, swinging from the doors. "Rather than restrict him, I made him the coat closet monitor. This worked. He now had a reason to be there and was proud of his job. I also gave Quincy choices involving hands-on activities and work partners. I moved students who liked to help others to his table, and I got another student to read with him every day. During computer time I let him catch up on his work. He surprised me by working hard during this time."

"Quincy's behavior began to change. He knew I cared." William smiles again. "Quincy gradually improved. I remember the first day without having a real confrontation. I hugged him and congratulated him like he had just won the lottery! He began to listen to me when I asked him to sit down instead of fighting. One day he told me that a child was bothering him. I was so excited that he was *thinking* rather than just reacting. Another day, Quincy saw Karee's daily progress report, which listed things like 'Did you do all your work?' 'Did you follow the teacher's directions?' and 'Did you help the teacher?' He asked me if he could have a daily progress report. He was evaluating his own behavior. He also began to do nice things for me, such as putting away materials."

William responded to Quincy as a person, not by using M&M's or praise as manipulative tools. He gave feedback about personal growth and strengths. Quincy began to see him as a friend and ally, not as a controlling authority. William explains, "I think two things were responsible for Quincy's gradual change. First, my class was fun and he did not want to miss it. He had choices, and he could move around. No worksheets or invisible jail in my class. Second, he realized I cared about him and he responded.

"He began to do his academic work, and to learn. A few simple adaptations went a long way." As Quincy's behaviors began to improve, so did his academic work. "I became convinced that Quincy was afraid he could not do work and was refusing in order to save face. So I worked to make him feel comfortable and successful. He would read aloud with me or with a partner, not in front of the whole class. In spelling I allowed him to pick five words instead of ten. Although I expected less written work, my expectations continued to grow as he did more and more. On one report card he had A's, B's, and one C. When he saw his grades, he was shocked. 'Those are A's . . . and B's!' he exclaimed. I will never forget the proud look on his face."

"I invited Quincy home. We had fun and strengthened our relationship." William also reached out to Quincy beyond the school day. "This was the turning point. A couple of other teachers took selected students with high needs to their houses and encouraged me to do the same, despite negative teachers who warned me of lawsuits. The first time we had pizza. Quincy ran around the back yard wearing out my dog. It was terrific to see him playing and laughing. Over the next year I periodically had him for dinner, games, or swimming."

The most improved award for Quincy: "By the end of the year, Quincy was a different kid. He still had periodic problems. However, when a conflict arose, he would stop and think. At the honors assembly I was proud to give Quincy the Most Improved award. He wants to get on the academic honor roll next time."

In this vignette, we should recognize what William did *not* do. Yes, he ensured that Quincy did not hurt other students by keeping careful watch, helping Quincy think about his behavior, and getting other students to help Quincy. However, William did *not* spend most of his time focusing on Quincy's problems; nor did he refer him for special education or suggest medication. William knew his job was to meet Quincy's needs and to *help him learn how to interact in positive ways,* not to forcibly control his behavior. Quincy's story illustrates what is possible and highlights themes we will see throughout this chapter (Peterson & Hittie, 2000).

𝒯raveling 𝒩otes

Our group of teachers had some wonderful ideas about helping students deal with behavioral issues. Yet some teachers would respond to that story with "too perfect, unrealistic, wouldn't happen in my school." "Students have to be controlled; you can't let them get away with things."

1. What do you think?

2. Mostly schools try to punish or provide rewards. Do these work? Or do they merely encourage students to be dependent upon external influences?

3. Do we control students or seek to meet their needs?

4. Do we expect children to be respectful to us only? Or do we model being respectful to them?

5. Are we the only person "in charge" in a classroom, or do we seek to engage our community (our children) in dealing with difficulties that occur?

These are critical questions. What is your philosophy?

Creating a Positive, Student–Centered Approach

Educators are increasingly concerned about behavioral challenges and violence in schools. To deal with these problems, three general approaches are used:

1. Punishment
2. Rewards (technically, "reinforcers")
3. Meeting student needs and promoting growth and relationships

Many discipline programs promote use of power by adults, in the form of combinations of approaches 1 and 2, to control the behavior of children. Rather than helping children make choices based on their own internal values, interests, and motivation, an **internal locus of control,** most seek to control students' behavior through external rewards, incentives, or punishments, an **external locus of control.** Yet research clearly shows that both punishment and rewards often create more problems than they fix. Let's look briefly at these two very widely used strategies.

Rewards and Punishment to Control Behavior: Typical Strategies That Deepen Problems

First, let's distinguish between the popular conception of rewards and punishment and the technical definitions used in behavioral psychology. In the popular parlance, **rewards** are perceived positive consequences or incentives bestowed by a person or persons with power in order to promote desired behavior. Such rewards may be social (a smile, praise, congratulations); sensory (a touch, a kiss, a pat on the back); fiscal (money, a gift certificate); or physical (food, books, a car).

A **reinforcer,** on the other hand, is an action associated with a behavior that *increases* the occurrence of the behavior. The point is that a reward is in the eye of the giver. A reinforcer, however, is defined by its impact on behavior. Reinforcers are of two types: (1) Positive reinforcement involves *providing* a stimulus to promote a behavior; (2) negative reinforcement involves *removing* something, typically something undesirable, when the desired behavior occurs. For example, if a student is promised time on the computer, for good behavior, that is positive reinforcement. When a student is isolated in the classroom, allowed only to return to the group when his behavior improves, that is negative reinforcement. Either way, to be called a reinforcer, an action must result in the increase of a behavior. In any case, we generally use the more popular term *reward* when describing efforts by those in authority to provide reinforcing consequences to obtain behavioral responses they desire (Charles, 1999; Janney & Snell, 2000b.; Reavis & Andrews, 1999).

Similarly, **punishment** is popularly understood as an undesired consequence one person uses to *decrease* the behavior of another—taking away recess privileges, grounding a child, drawing frowny faces on a chart, requiring extra work. In the technical behavioral definition, however, a *punisher* is an aversive stimulus resulting in the reduction of a behavior. The other behavioral strategy for reducing behaviors is *extinction*, the withholding of stimuli that reinforce a behavior (Charles, 1999; Janney & Snell, 2000; Kohn, 1993, 1996; Reavis & Andrews, 1999).

How effective is punishment? Here is what research indicates:

- We can eliminate behaviors through punishment in the short run. However, this outcome occurs only if the punishment is sufficiently strong—and lasts only while punishment remains in effect (Beach Center on Families and Disability, 1994; Koegel, Koegel, & Dunlap, 1996; Martin & Pear, 1996).
- Punishment does not address underlying needs, and new behavioral challenges often emerge (Carr et al., 1994; Hitzing 1994; Janney & Snell, 2000b.).
- A focus only on behavior prevents us from really understanding the person. We often distance ourselves from the "problem" student and depersonalize our reactions, thus setting the stage for additional future problems (Hitzing 1994; Marin, Gilpin, Goodman, & Moses, 1996)
- Punishment reduces or eliminates guilt, ensuring that any change in behavior is caused by external force rather than internalized decisions (Cragg, 1992; Gilligan, 1996). As a result, "the more harshly we punish . . . the more violent they become; the punishment increases their feelings of shame and simultaneously decreases their capacities for feelings of love . . . and of guilt." (Gilligan, 1996, p. 110)

Many suggest that combined with consequences (punishments), we should provide rewards to reinforce positive behaviors. Most behavior management programs use this strategy (Kohn, 1992). At first glance this might seem rational and humane. However, Kohn (1993, 1999) conducted a comprehensive review of research and found that rewards

- Punish—because (1) they are a form of control and (2) not everyone gets a reward. Someone is always left out.
- Rupture relationships—a person in power metes out rewards, and competition for rewards breaks a sense of community.
- Ignore the reasons for behaviors.
- Discourage risk taking—people do "exactly what is necessary to get [a reward] and no more" (Kohn, 1998, p. 63).
- Undermine intrinsic interest and motivation.
- Encourage mediocrity. Students who focus on rewards (grades, scholarships, praise) rather than on intrinsic interests are less likely to do well over time.
- Must be desired strongly enough to make an impact.
- Are effective only in the short run, as long as they "keep coming."

The impacts of rewards on interest and motivation, and their consequent effects on learning and achievement, are particularly serious. In a comprehensive review, Lepper and Henderlong (2000) found that the motivation of students in public schools declines as they grow older, that the use of rewards reduces interest and motivation in a task, and that performance declines as a result. Aware of this, many of the best teachers we know say that they work hard *not* to reward students externally but to help them become intrinsically motivated by pursuing their own interests.

We ask teachers, "If you want students to improve their own behaviors, what works? How do people learn?" Teachers suggest that students need both positive role models and positive relationships that bring out their best. Yet what often happens to students causing behavioral problems? Students are often placed (1) in an "alternative school" or (2) in special education classes for students with emotional disturbance (Kauffman, 1997). To put it another way, a student having tremendous emotional and behavioral problems is often put full time with other students having similar difficulties—in a setting where positive role models are not available and where students learn poor behaviors from one another. It is not surprising that outcomes of such programs are poor (see Chapter 10).

Meeting Student Needs: Promoting Growth and Relationships

Another approach is available: positive behavioral support. In this approach we seek to understand what behaviors communicate about needs and to help students meet their needs in a socially acceptable way. If a student curses in class, we want to know why that student is doing so. We'll be thinking about the student's needs and welfare as much as we are about prohibiting negative behavior. As other students understand that we care, we'll also be surprised how this helps to strengthen our classroom community. In effect, we are modeling how we'd like to see students help and support one another.

This does not mean that we condone disrespectful or problematic behavior. Quite the opposite. For example, if Lawrence enters our class cursing and calling us names, we pull him aside and ask him what is happening; we make it clear that his behavior is not acceptable but that we know something is bothering him. (In effective classes students know the class routines and will continue to work together, allowing the teacher time to talk with the student.) In doing so, we are helping Lawrence think about his behavior and showing we care about him, not just keeping him in line. Further, we gain the respect of students by being strong enough to attend to them as individuals rather than merely using our authority to demand compliance.

One way of contrasting the traditional and positive behavioral support approaches is pictured in Figure 12.1 (Albin, Horner, & O'Neill, 1994; Evans & Meyer, 1985; Faber, Mazlish, Nyberg, & Templeton, 1995; Hitzing, 1994; Kohn, 1996). As the figure indicates, traditional behavior management focuses on controlling a student's behavior from the perspective of others in the environment, particularly adults. Positive behavioral support, however, seeks to respond to the needs of the student and to help the student learn respectful and proactive ways of having needs met. In the first approach, other people decide when the problem is resolved; in the second, the problem is not resolved until the students sees his or her needs being met.

Creating a Student-Centered School. Throughout the world, schools are increasingly developing schoolwide approaches to challenging behaviors. Some schools rely heavily on efforts to control students, using what Kunc (1998) calls the "habits of exclusion"—**time-out, detention,** hall monitors directing the physical movement of students. In other schools control is maintained through rewards. Students are expected to learn the rules and create plays about them; teachers give daily tokens that

Figure 12.1

Traditional Behavior Management versus Positive Behavioral Support

	TRADITIONAL BEHAVIOR MANAGEMENT	POSITIVE BEHAVIORAL SUPPORT
Problem	Behavior is causing us or others trouble, so we want to eliminate it.	Behavior, which is learned, is *communicating* something important.
Assessment	Specify the problem behavior and determine frequency, strength, duration.	Conduct "functional analysis" to determine *reasons for* the behavior.
Goal	Eliminate problem behavior.	Help student learn better ways of communicating needs.
Intervention	Reduce reinforcement of behavior ("extinguish" by ignoring) or punish when target behavior occurs.	Develop a sense of safety and trust between teacher and student. Make the class fun and interesting so there is a "pay off" for positive participation. Provide support from another person; reduce frustration in the setting. Teach alternative ways to communicate. Teach how to tolerate school conditions.
Success	The behavior is eliminated and people in power view the situation as better.	The person's problem is solved from *his or her point of view.*

Source: Adapted from Hitzing (1994).

can be turned in at the school store. Yet the focus is still more on controlling behaviors than on promoting real human growth.

What do schools look like that use a **student-centered** approach, one focused on student needs? Numerous schools are moving in this direction. Westside Elementary School provides one example. The school operates with only five rules: (1) Try, (2) be safe, (3) be kind, (4) work hard, and (5) be respectful. These are positive rules indicating what is *desired* rather than what is prohibited. Throughout the school, there is no punishment. When there is a conflict, staff assume that behavior signals an unmet need. For example, instead of missing recess or lunch, the class clown might be given five minutes a day to do a stand-up comedy routine. A bully "might become a tutor to the younger children he earlier terrorized. The clown needed attention and the bully needed to be admired by younger children" (Berg, 1989, p. 10B).

The school principal reports that such proactive strategies resolve more than 90 percent of discipline problems. When additional measures are needed, a child is expected to develop a plan, essentially a contract, in which the problem is defined and the student indicates what steps he or she will take to resolve it. The school seeks to help students learn new ways of responding. Building on William Glasser's **reality therapy,** staff lead students through a series of questions designed to help them think: "What did you want to happen? What did you accomplish? What are the pros and cons of your behavior? What do you want to do now? What do you need to do to get what you want?" (Glasser, 2000). Teachers use **cooperative learning** in the classroom, and the school holds periodic open meetings where children can "speak their minds without fear of reprisal from staff or peers" (Berg, 1989, p. 10B).

In another school, staff were concerned about their many behavior problems. The new principal said, "We won't look at students as being a problem but as *having* a problem." With this view in mind, he removed the school's "behavior room" and approached Helen—the warmest, most caring teacher—and asked her to work as a **mediator** with students and teachers. Whenever problems occurred, the student and teacher went to Helen's room and she helped them work out solutions. This became an opportunity for *learning* rather than punishment. After a while Helen said in a staff meeting, "I am glad you send students to me. However, at this point, if you have a conflict with a student, call me down and I will cover your class while you work out the problem yourself." She gradually began to spend most of her time providing such support for teachers (Kunc, 1998).

Comprehensive programs using a student-centered philosophy, at their best, incorporate the following components (Garbarino, Dubrow, Kostelny, & Pardo, 1992; Kay, 1999; Lantieri & Patti, 1996; McLane, Burnette, & Orkwis, 1997):

- Building community in the school (see Chapter 11)
- Peer mediation and conflict resolution
- Teaching students how to support one another through peer buddies and circles of support (see Chapter 11)
- Professional support—individual and group counseling, support groups
- Mentors through such programs as Big Brothers and Big Sisters
- A building support team (see Chapter 5)
- Interagency support and intervention for families

Teacher Roles and Perspectives. We watch our students as they arrive in the morning. George, whose parents were divorced a month ago, looks better today. Nicole is laughing, but she's abused at home and children's teasing sometimes sets her off in a violent fit. Keith is withdrawn. Classified as "mentally retarded," he's been working really hard lately, learning to read a book he enjoys. There's Patricia. Thank goodness for children whose home lives are together. She's a leader and has been particularly helpful with Keith and Nicole.

What are some of the strategies that successful teachers use to deal with challenging students? To help George cope with his parents' divorce, we seat him with very nurturing students at his table, and a special friend talks with him about anything he needs to talk about for the first ten minutes of class. The teacher has organized **informal peer supports,** connecting George with other students who make sure he has someone to play with at recess. Because he loves to draw, he is helping the art teacher make the backdrop for the school musical. This keeps him busy, which always helps when people are hurting.

Nicole needs a lot of support. She has a circle of friends that meet once a week who help her with her homework and are teaching her to be a good friend by example. They are patient with her. When she gets really upset, they sing with her.

Keith is growing by leaps and bounds, thanks to his mother and his special group. They read with him in the mornings, sit with him in the group area to help keep him focused, remind the teacher to write down instructions for him, and play with him at recess. He does not read or write at the same level, but the whole class works on individualized materials, so he does not stand out. The students are aware of his limits and congratulate him when he tries hard.

As we look at the many needs of our students, we also come face to face with ourselves. There is no other arena in which students' responses will raise more personal issues—issues about our own lives, relationships, and abilities to handle emotions. As we seek to understand students, we must do the same for ourselves. Why do we respond the way we do? What do our responses mean, and how can we grow? How were we raised? What was and is our relationship with our parents? Were we abused? How did teachers and others in authority treat us? How do we feel about ourselves? Were we provided models of joy, hope, and support? Do we know how to have fun while working hard? We are challenged to understand ourselves but not to lay blame. The fact is, if we can't and don't do this with ourselves, neither will we be able to do it with our students. The good news is that our seeking to work positively with students can simultaneously help both us and our students.

Challenging Behaviors
A Call for Understanding

As we respond to behavioral challenges, we find many complexities. Let's look at some common social and behavioral problems that face teachers in schools. Then we'll explore the meaning of these behaviors.

How Do Challenging Behaviors Look?

We see five general categories of social and behavioral problems in school: (1) underacheiving, (2) isolating, (3) distracting, (4) disruptive, and (5) dangerous (Albert, 1996; Janney & Snell, 2000b.).

Underachieving. Most teachers become concerned about students who don't complete assigned academic work. Such students lose assignments and don't work in class or turn in materials. They do almost anything, it seems, other than class work.

Isolating. Students may withdraw or be rejected by others and thus feel alone and lonely. Although these students often don't actually cause *us* problems, their withdrawal is frequently an indication of conflicts within, which may erupt in more overt problems. One student diagnosed with ADHD tells of literally sleeping in classes throughout her high school career. Other students may have few interactions or relationships. Often considered "shy," such isolated students often have low self-esteem and fear of failure, and often have difficulty making friends.

Mishael Hittie facilitates a conversation in her fourth-grade class to deal with a difficult problem. "I was disappointed in you today," she explains. "What should I do about this and what should you do next time?" Such conversation models "I" statements for students and involves them in prob-lem solving, an authentic but systematic way to teach social skills.

Distracting. Students may be distracting to the point of frustration. These are the students who tap pencils, pull one another's hair, tumble or fall on the floor laugh-ing. Evans and Meyer (1985) include various self-stimulating behaviors in this cat-egory, behaviors stereotypically associated with persons with autism. Such students play with sources of light, twirl pencils or other objects, rock, or flip coins over and over (Janney & Snell, 2000b). These types of behaviors often occur when a student is feeling frustrated, bored, or disconnected.

Disruptive. When a student is disruptive, he or she actively intrudes on the flow of the class or on work with other people. Students can do this in many ways: being constantly negative, complaining, being verbally abusive, throwing tantrums, en-gaging in angry outbursts, physically fighting, taking the work of another student, destroying classroom materials, and more (Janney & Snell, 2000b).

Dangerous. On rare occasions students are dangerous either to themselves or to others. Dangerous behaviors are the most difficult and may include self-injury (from constantly scratching to suicide attempts); bullying; threats and intimidation; or physical violence—hitting or the use of knives, guns, chains, or other weapons. Such violent behavior is growing (Garbarino, Dubrow, Kostelny, & Pardo, 1992; Gilli-gan, 1996; Lantieri & Patti, 1996).

What Do Problem Behaviors Mean?

If we see behaviors as controlled only by external stimuli, we will seek to control students through reinforcers or punishments. If we believe behaviors are based on moral choices, we will exhort students to choose correctly and chastise them when they don't. *A more effective and accurate view is to see behaviors as efforts by which people communicate about their own needs.* If we adhere to this view, we deal with problem behaviors by trying to help students learn positive ways to meet their needs. Let's use Glasser's (1992, 2000) five needs of human beings, introduced in Chapter 11, to think about common needs communicated by problem behaviors.

Survival. People need to survive and to have resources to stay alive—food, water, clothing, shelter, and medicine. Survival responses can take many forms—concerns about personal safety, emotional anxiety, hunger. Our students may react in surprising ways out of a fear for their survival. Jan, an elementary teacher, tells this story:

Lynette spilt a pop all over us and we had to remove our shoes. Julian, a student with autism, became quite agitated. He said over and over, "No fire alarm today!" As soon as we put our shoes back on, he calmed down. We figured out that he was worried that a fire would break out and we would be in the school when the alarm rang. He knew the rule—must have shoes on to go outside. The panic that Julian must have felt when he believed we might perish in a fire! (A. Jones, personal communication, January 15, 2000)

Survival does not necessarily have to be objectively threatened. The threat to survival is what is *experienced* by the student and may be physical or emotional.

Love and Belonging. We have a powerful need to be loved, to belong with a group of people, to feel needed, wanted, and appreciated. For many students, however, this need is not met. In both high- and low-income families, students often do not receive adequate attention through personal time spent with parents, eating family dinners and discussing the day or reading books together. Some parents are so busy providing food and clothing that there is no time or energy left over. Other parents are involved with work or social commitments. Many students have no close adult relationships and have limited experience of nurturing relationships.

When students do not feel a sense of love and belonging, they often react in many problematic ways—acting the class clown, breaking rules, making loud jokes or obscene gestures, constantly putting themselves at center stage (Albert, 1996; Gilligan, 1996; Paley, 1990). Other students join gangs involved in dangerous and illegal activities (Garbarino, Dubrow, Kostelny, & Pardo, 1992). Yet others withdraw. Underlying these actions are desperate needs for connection and care and feelings of unworthiness and low self-esteem.

Power. All people need some control over time, space, activities, or situations and chances to feel skilled or competent. For many reasons, however, students often feel overwhelmed, alone, restrained, and powerless. Parents may not give their children opportunities for choices. Schools make matters worse with structured and rigid classes. Students with special needs often have been in small, highly controlled special education classes. Some students come from homes in which they have been abused and where alcohol and drug abuse make their lives unstable, where they feel they cannot control even small parts of their lives. Students who are poor may feel that they are powerless in a nation of wealth.

When students feel a lack of power and competence, they may react in many negative ways. Some seek *revenge* for real or imagined hurts. Gilligan (1996) found that abused murderers committed their crimes seeking to achieve a sense of *justice*, "an eye for an eye." Others seek *avoidance of failure*. Believing that they can't be successful, they compensate by withdrawing and appearing inadequate, hoping that people will not remind them of their unworthiness. A teacher told this illustrative story:

One day I had the kids make a French calendar. They were to write the name of the month and days of the week. Vernon kept saying, "This is stupid Mrs. Kwoslo, this is stupid, stupid. . . ." Then he looked up at me and said, "This is hard, Mrs. Kwoslo." (B. Quinlan, personal communication, March 16, 2000)

Most disconcerting are occasions when students refuse to respond to our requests, most often called **noncompliance.** Kunc (1998) says we should think of this *no* as the tip of an iceberg. What might *no* mean? There are numerous possibilities: "Ask me later"; "I am afraid of failure"; "Not with you!"; "I am embarrassed."

Fun. We all need activities that are enjoyable and invigorating, simply fun. When students are bored, they will do almost anything to change that. Students daydream and escape in other ways—playing games, making faces, throwing spitballs. They may also become frustrated, get into conflicts, or tell us in many other ways, "I don't want to be here." The following story is illustrative.

Ruben was entering Margaret's third-grade class from a school where he had been in a special education class. He had terrible problems there and would tantrum, scream, and toilet on himself daily when he came to the classroom door. In the special class he had to "sit straight and practice writing his name over and over before he could do anything else." Margaret's eyes glisten as she tells what happened on the first day in her third-grade class:

On his way into class he started to become upset at the doorway, but I caught him casting a mildly interested eye at the fish tank. Before I was introduced to him or his parents, I handed him the fish food and asked him to feed the fish. End of a big problem with a long history. He walked right in happily. This great kid and the fish are flourishing. (M. Alkari, personal communication, September 12, 2000)

This child, with limited verbal communication abilities, had been saying by his behavior, "I hate this class. It is boring, repressive. I don't want to go." He fought with all his might. Several years of "behavior programs" based on behavior modification had done nothing; but the simple, attentive response of this teacher made a difference. Of course, Margaret built on this initial response, building an accepting, engaging community for Ruben.

Freedom. Freedom means both a lack of restraint and the ability to choose, to make decisions. If any single human need is the most widely ignored in schools, it is probably this one. In talking with groups of teachers about this topic, we frequently ask about the ways they got into trouble in school. Everyone laughs. "Why is this funny?" I ask. The reason it is funny is that one of the main causes of the trouble was always that the teacher was rigid and controlling; the problem behaviors defied an authoritarian regime in which rules were more important than people. We see over and over that teachers who provide students choices and freedom to move around and talk while they work have fewer problems in their classes. Such teachers do, however, spend a lot of time helping students learn how to handle their freedom.

Vicious Cycles

What happens when a student's needs are not met? According to Hitzing (1994) a vicious cycle often develops, in which negative behaviors and distrust spiral downward. Figure 12.2 demonstrates how this works. For example, suppose a student feels emotion based on an unmet need and reacts with unacceptable behavior. When he acts out or withdraws, he gets more of his needs met, though in a negative way. If the student wants greater control, he gets it; if attention, he gets this. In other words, rather than understanding needs and looking for positive ways to meet these, we often respond in ways that exacerbate the original problem. We may restrict the student, become angry, hold the student out of interesting activities. Consequently, problematic behaviors continue with increased intensity.

Students with social and emotional challenges often are struggling in very difficult situations. On the one hand, students *need* someone to care for and listen to them; they need attention, help in learning how to get what they need in positive ways, and someone to reach out to them. However, what they frequently *get* is punishment, anger, rejection, and segregation—responses that ensure that they feel more anger, hurt, and loneliness (see Figure 12.3).

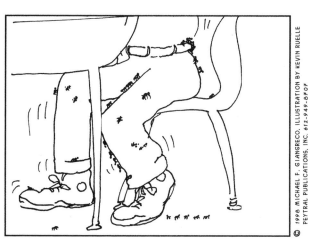

AFTER A HASTY SPECIAL EDUCATION PLACEMENT FOR BEHAVIOR PROBLEMS, SCHOOL OFFICIALS WERE EMBARRASSED TO LEARN THAT MARTY REALLY DID HAVE ANTS IN HIS PANTS.

© 1998 MICHAEL F. GIANGRECO. ILLUSTRATION BY KEVIN RUELLE PEYTRAL PUBLICATIONS, INC. 612-949-8707

Figure 12.2

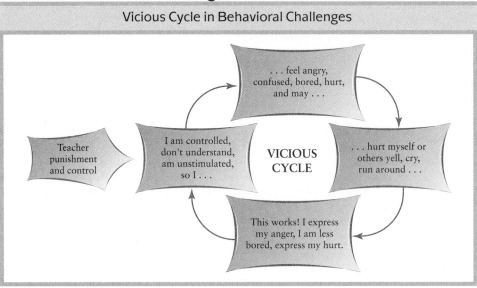

Vicious Cycle in Behavioral Challenges

Source: Adapted from Hitzing (1994).

Proactive Responses to Social and Behavioral Challenges:
From Punishment and Control to Choice and Care

There is good news, however. Surprising as it may seem, when we respond proactively to students based on the principles we outline in this chapter, students often

Figure 12.3

Needs of Students and Typical Responses

WHAT STUDENTS NEED	WHAT THEY OFTEN GET
Care and love	Rejection
Sense of belonging	Segregation (special education class, alternative school)
Support	
Attention	Anger
Respect	Punishment
Help with learning positive ways to get needs and desires met	Humiliation
Encouragement	

will move toward prosocial, responsible behavior. It's the difference between being kept in a jail by hated taskmasters and joining a family that has fun together. Responding proactively is not easy, of course, though on occasion we'll be surprised as a serious problem seems simply to vanish. Perhaps hardest for us will be learning how to shift from teacher-centered to student-centered teaching. Let's look at some key strategies that promote positive interactions and prevent vicious cycles.

Meeting Student Needs

When we see puzzling and troubling student behavior, we ask "What need is not being met for this child?" Every action communicates a message. When we work to meet student needs we do so in two ways: (1) preventive and (2) responsive (Janney & Snell, 2000b). For each need we constantly seek to provide opportunities that *prevent* problems from occurring. We work to create a class that is fun, safe, and emotionally secure. In other words, if we want students to act respectfully, our class must be a place they enjoy, where they feel physically and emotionally safe, where they know we care about them. Anything short of this and we become one of the factors creating behavioral problems (Albert, 1996; Hitzing, 1994; Kohn, 1996, 1999).

We also see a student always as a *person*. As students cause us trouble, we can too easily focus only on their problem behavior. We get angry or upset and often distance ourselves, depersonalize our actions. By doing this we may actually exacerbate problems. Treating our students with respect as people is a simple but powerful approach. We talk with respect, no matter what students have done (Glasser, 1992, 2000; Kameenui & Darch, 1995; Lovett, 1996; Maag, 1997; Paley 1990).

We also seek to *respond* effectively, understanding that challenging behaviors demonstrate unmet needs. We help students find ways to meet their needs in positive ways. To explore proactive strategies, let's again use Glasser's (1992, 2000) model of human needs.

Survival. Many children come to school with their basic needs insufficiently met. We cannot change their home environments, but we need to be aware of their intense feelings. To help, we can keep some basic food supplies from the cafeteria in the room for students who are hungry, allow water bottles, and find people with whom students can talk. We can also be aware of how children respond emotionally, sometimes feeling a sense of panic and fear. Some children with autism, for example, respond with panic to loud noises. For such students we can reduce noises and provide extra support through social stories and other strategies.

Love. Many children do not feel loved and accepted. One way to combat this is to create times and places where socializing is part of classroom activities. When students need approval, we can ask them to take a message to a group, send them to talk to another student who is upset, or simply get very excited over an assignment they have done well. Of course, preventing students from being segregated into special classes is a key strategy in helping reduce isolation and create a sense of belonging. In addition, teaching that utilizes cooperative learning and peer buddies provides opportunities for the growth of relationships (Amado, 1993; Hughes et al., 1999). When students cause problems, we figure ways to meet the situation positively. A seventh-grade teacher told about Erma, a student who frequently left her desk to go talk to friends when she was supposed to be completing her work. The teacher decided to incorporate more social time, not less, into Erma's daily schedule.

Power. Students who have been denied power can be the most challenging. When students act out, our instinct is often to want to *reduce* their efforts to achieve power. Therefore, when we intentionally develop strategies to give these students *more* power, it can feel very risky. Yet we can find ways to do so that will make a difference (Kunc, 1998; Smull & Harrison, 1992; Walker & Walker, 1991). Examples:

- A student stands up in the middle of class and tells us this lesson is crap. We ask to meet with him at the end of the class. We ask him if he would work with us to redesign how we teach the lesson. Surprised, he agrees.
- Jay is always bullying younger students. We tell him that we can't let that happen. We ask him what would he like to do to make amends. We give him some choices—tutoring children after school (under supervision), taking a child on a field trip with a group, volunteering to help at a local circus.
- Create classroom jobs for all so that each student has control in a specific situation.
- Have each student be an "expert" in something he or she can share with others.
- Involve students in making decisions—choosing topics on which to focus, solving problems in the classroom, selecting order of activities for the day.

Fun. Making our class fun is an ongoing process. We use students' interests to get them into learning. If a student is interested in cars, for example, we can take a physics concept and revolve it around cars; in language arts we can provide reading materials and research information for a project on types of transportation. We can use many other strategies too:

- Incorporating multiple intelligences—music, dance, art, drama
- Playing games, particularly cooperative games
- Laughing a lot, telling funny jokes, using humor
- Sharing aspects of our lives and using these as the basis for curriculum activities

When students react in ways that tell us they are not having fun, rather than punishing and making our class even more grim, we look for ways to respond. If Jalessa interrupts the class by making funny faces, we give her the job of telling a joke to the class once a week. Or suppose students at the back of our high school algebra class, who have been having trouble with the class work, are constantly laughing together. We ask them to lead the class in a discussion regarding how to make algebra fun. They surprise us by making a play out of a homework assignment.

Freedom. If we have a class in which there is little chance of choice and freedom, students will create their own choices. How can we provide freedom for students in our class when we are supposed to be "in charge" as the teacher? Here are some examples:

- Provide choice time, a time when students may choose from any of several different activity options related to the study topic.
- Allow students to sit where they want.
- Have water or snacks that can be taken when needed.
- Have students choose books to read and write stories on subjects they select.

Figure 12.4

Balancing Information and Power in Relationships

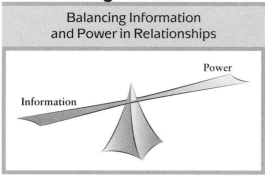

Source: Kunc (1998).

Providing Information for Learning: Moving beyond Constant Power Struggles

To communicate respectfully with students, we need the strength to communicate clearly to them our expectations along with the warmth through which we show we care. Too often we vacillate between being overly warm and being too strong. The more information we can give students—feedback, strategies, ways to think, and more—the less we have to use power to control their behavior (Figure 12.4) (Kunc, 1998). Let's look at specific strategies for giving students information in respectful ways.

Communicating to Promote Learning. Figure 12.5 summarizes contrasting approaches of control versus respect (Kunc, 1998; Faber, Mazlish, Nyberg, & Templeton, 1995). The feature illustrates some helpful strategies—and some practices to avoid or minimize. Let's explore these strategies and practices a bit. A student is running down the hall screaming. Rather than *assuming* we know what is going on ("That Brad is screwing around again, just showing off"), we can express *curiosity:* "Wow, what is going on? What's up?" This response prompts us to attend to the student in a different way.

In the same situation, one teacher might yell, "Don't run in the hall! You know the rules!"—an obvious demand that calls on authority. Another teacher seeing the same student might say, "Walk please," a request. One response *demands* obedience, whereas the other respectfully *requests* compliance. A demand gives a student no choice; a request conveys the power to choose.

As we work through conflicts, we explore multiple ways to solve problems. Rather than assuming we know *the* way, we can work out solutions. Relatedly, as we interact with students we can help them *understand the rationale* for our requests as opposed to using our *authority* and the implied force behind it.

We also seek to use clear **I-statements.** Rather than saying, "You must not leave campus to go to lunch," we say, "I want you to be safe. This rule was made to help keep you safe. I hope you will follow it because I care about you." The difference is tremendous. Once again, we become a person and they are given choices.

Often we hear that we should maintain a professional distance from

Figure 12.5

Communication Based on Respect or Control: Philosophies at War in Practice

RESPECT	CONTROL
Curiosity	Assumption of intent
Request	Demand
Third alternative	One right way
Rationale/explanation	Authority
Clear I-statements	"You should" statements
Sharing/disclosure	Professional distance
Listening/support	Domination/coercion
Negotiation	Rewards/punishments

Source: Adapted from Kunc (1998).

Artwork reprinted by permission of Martha Perske from *Perske: Pencil Portraits 1971–1990* (Nashville: Abingdon Press, 1998).

our students and not get involved personally. Distancing ourselves from our students and their families supposedly enhances our authority. In fact, however, our real impact comes from the relationships with our students and the care they feel from us. Therefore, we *share about our life,* our feelings, our thoughts. We help students see us processing what to do, share our own insecurities. We may fear that this will promote a sense of weakness, but the opposite actually occurs. As William reached out to Quincy earlier in this chapter, so we can connect with our students on a personal level. We can move to being a person rather than only an authority figure.

We also *listen* to students. Stephen Covey (1989) stated that a characteristic of effective people is that they seek "first to understand, and then to be understood." Further, we use good facilitation skills to *reflect back to them* what we hear them saying and the underlying thoughts or feelings that are coming through. "Morice, you seem tense. I know you've been under a lot of stress lately." "Jean, you're telling me that you're exhausted because you were sick all night. That must make you feel a lot of pressure right now." This approach contrasts dramatically with discipline by domination and coercion: "Morice, get in your seat right now." "Jean, I don't care what happened last night, you know your responsibilities."

We *negotiate* with students to help them meet their needs. We try constantly to understand students; we are neither a pushover nor a dictator but set expectations, communicate these, and work out arrangements so the needs of all can be met.

We help students understand themselves, too, and help them *set their own goals and evaluate their behavior.* Reality therapy, as mentioned earlier, is one useful approach for this purpose. In reality therapy a teacher might approach a student and pose a series of questions that go something like this: "You are doing this. What do you think the result of this action will be? Is this what you want? If not, what do you want? What do you need to do to get what you want?"

Social Skills Instruction. Students often come to school not knowing how to make friends, talk about problems, or interact pleasantly with people they don't like. **Social skills instruction** is an unwritten school curriculum that every teacher at every grade level must address daily. We can use many strategies for helping students learn social skills. However, the most effective and manageable strategy is to incorporate these skills into the daily fabric of our teaching. Many curricula for teaching social skills have been developed and may be useful (Amish, Gesten, Smith, & Clark, 1988; Elias et al, 1997; Kusche & Greenberg, 1994; L'Abate & Milan, 1989; McGinnis & Goldstein, 1984).

Rehearsal approaches can be particularly powerful, giving students opportunities to practice how they could react. For this purpose Gray (1994) developed *social stories,* which depict situations of concern to children. Each social story describes a social interaction in the first person, telling where the situation occurs, who is involved, what is happening, and why. Stories may also describe the feelings of the individual. Students apply these stories to daily interactions as part of a learning process; the approach has been found effective with students with autism and with others who have difficulty learning social skills (Kuttler, Myles, & Carlson, 1998; Swaggart et al., 1995). Some educators have added music and other multimedia strategies when using social stories (Brownell, 2000).

Some teachers or support staff use social skills curricula in classes or groups on dealing with emotions, feelings, coping with loss, dealing with anger, and so on. However, we can also use these guides to infuse social skills instruction into our classroom in the form of "social minilessons." For example, when discussing negotiations between two countries regarding trade agreements, we might help the class focus on negotiation as a skill; we could provide some short information about listening and coming to win–win agreements, then have students practice in groups. Also, when a real conflict arises, we can use this confrontation to help the students learn to solve problems, drawing on resource materials.

A Time for Power and Control. On occasion, we will need to use our power to control a situation that is out of hand (Kunc, 1998). In order to understand when to respond this way, however, we can think through our *"nonnegotiables"*—conduct that is simply intolerable. What is nonnegotiable and why? Too often we create difficulties when we define reasonably minor items as nonnegotiables. Do we seek greater control and compliance than is useful or necessary? In some situations, what is considered nonnegotiable may actually not be that important—rules about raising one's hand to talk, being quiet, and staying seated unless permission is asked. Other situations, however, are dangerous; for example, a student may be hitting other students, kicking, or throwing chairs. When students do cross the line, we may have to use our power and control. When we need to assert direct authority, it will be easier if we have a history of positive relationships. It is also important to exert control in a respectful manner:

1. Use a caring tone of voice and gestures.
2. Provide a reason why something is nonnegotiable.
3. Be respectful. "I know this is important to you, but . . ." (Kunc, 1998).

Engaging the Classroom Community in Problem Solving

In typical classrooms, when behavioral problems occur, the teacher takes charge of the situation and metes out rewards and punishments. In a more effective class, however, the classroom community is involved. As teachers, we do have responsibility for our class. To fulfill this responsibility effectively, however, we support students in their efforts both to master the curriculum and to grapple with social and behavioral issues. For this support to work, our classroom community must have mechanisms and forums by which conflicts and problems are solved.

Class Meetings. Class meetings are an effective way to solve daily problems. These can be scheduled or created on the spur of the moment. In these meetings the teacher is a participant, not a leader, in a problem-solving discussion. Students discuss, create, and implement solutions (Developmental Studies Center, 1994; Glasser, 1992; Elias et al., 1997). Let's observe such a meeting.

Stephanie is a high school English teacher. As we enter her class, she is in the corner of the room in an intense conversation with two boys. The two students clearly were in a conflict with each other and the teacher earlier in the class. The tension among the three of them is strong.

As we sit down, Stephanie is describing her feelings to Mark and Nathan regarding their rude actions. She explains why their behavior was not helpful. She clearly is upset, but she speaks calmly, with no judgment in her inflections. After talking a while, Stephanie and the boys join the rest of the class, who gather at the front of the room. She asks Mark and Nathan to explain their reactions. Classmates then share how they felt. They are encouraged to use I-statements, such as "I felt mad when you said that to me" but are not permitted to interrupt, yell, or accuse. Following their discussion, the class creates a plan for what to do the next time. The boys reluctantly suggest they read a funny skit tomorrow and decide to write in a special journal that Stephanie will keep available when they have something vital to tell her.

Later in the day, in contrast to this, the teacher down the hall has the same two students. When they act out, she first tries sarcasm, then yells at them. Finally they are sent to the office, where they receive two days' suspension. Unfortunately, there is no plan in place for the next time, and they certainly do not feel that this teacher cares about them.

Circles of Friends. As we discussed in Chapter 11, circles of friends can be a powerful tool both to prevent problems and to deal with challenges. Any student who needs support can have such a group, and many children benefit by participating in one.

Peer and Conflict Mediation. Many schools are establishing school- and district-wide "peacemaker programs" to train volunteer students in **conflict resolution** and **peer mediation** (Fisher & Ury, 1991; Fletcher, 1986; Johnson & Johnson, 1995; Lane & McWhiter, 1992; Porro, 1996). However, we can do this in our own class

Two peer mediators in Mishael Hittie's fourth-grade class work as a team to help two students work through a disagreement. Students can provide powerful assistance to one another when they have training and support of the teacher.

as well (Paley, 1992). Conflict resolution programs give opportunities for certain children to volunteer to be "peacemakers" or peer mediators. It is important that volunteers represent a mix of the class—that they come from different ability levels, genders, and ethnic groups, for example. Students receive training in helping other students. Here's how it works in the peacemaker program. If two or more children are having a problem, they approach a child designated as a peacemaker, who asks each student: "Do you want to solve a problem?" Each child then gets a turn to tell his or her story. When one speaks, the other listens. When each understands the other, the peacemaker facilitates a discussion regarding solutions. In several schools teachers report that peacemaking has become an integral part of teaching and problem solving at their school. Children begin using language like "I feel" and "I need" and begin listening to others' points of view. One urban school reported that parents were even learning such skills from their children (Baer, 1994; Fine, 1994).

Peer Supports. Students can help one another in many ways. We can create structures such as "peer buddy" programs, in which students work together on certain assigned topics or help a newcomer become accustomed to the school. When a community has been built, however, students also will naturally help each other in unpredictable ways. They will read together, help with classwork, talk to a hurting student, or calm down an angry friend. When we expect learners to help and teach them how, they do so in ways that are invaluable in encouraging those with behavior struggles. No matter what the problem—whether it is about the loss of a boyfriend, a bad grade, or calling names, and whether the children are very young or in high school—students can help each other through problems. Indeed, students often accept the help of a peer when they will not talk openly to an adult (Farmer, Pearl, & Van Acker, 1996; Hughes et al., 1999; Rosenberg, McKeon, & Dinero, 1999).

Restorative Justice in the Classroom. Beginning in classrooms and ending in the courtroom, our idea of "justice" is centered typically in punishment. Someone breaks a rule and there are consequences imposed by those in authority. Research has conclusively proven, however, that such an approach does not help change undesirable behavior. It further weakens the community, too, because the people who were injured and the person who created the problem are separated. There is no attempt at reparation or opportunity for healing (Janney & Snell, 2000b; Koegel, Koegel, & Dunlap, 1996; Kohn, 1993, 1996). A new approach called **restorative justice** is now being used (Consedine, 1995; Gerard, 1997; Young, 1995). Gerard (1997) explains that

> restoration, or healing, becomes the goal of the justice process. A restorative approach seeks to repair the damage of crime. . . . It is commonly equated with giving victims a voice in the justice process through some form of mediation; holding offenders directly accountable for their behavior; and giving offenders "a way back" into the community through meaningful sanctions of benefit to the people who have been adversely affected. In essence, restorative justice is concerned less with fixing blame or meting punishment than with "making things right." (p. 1)

The restorative justice model gives us a powerful way to think about how to help students learn responsibility without using punishment—while simultaneously strengthening our learning community. Rather than punishing, we can ask a student who has done wrong to another to make amends. In a class meeting, we might talk about what happened, ask the class and the student for ideas about how to repair the damage and heal hurt feelings, and negotiate ways to welcome the student back into the community. Students may have similar dialogues with individual classmates, with peer mediators, or in circles of support. Through these processes students with social and behavioral challenges can simultaneously learn truly responsible behavior and experience community and care (Fletcher, 1986; Cragg, 1992).

Giving Students and Ourselves a Break

Sometimes teachers and students simply need a break from one another. Typically, teachers send students to the office as a punishment. We would suggest that this and similar tactics be used less as punishments than as ways of giving us and students a break. It may even be helpful to explain this idea to the student and suggest that we both might use the time to think and then get together to talk. We can also make arrangements with colleagues to allow the student to come to their classroom, or ask the school social worker or psychologist to assist us when things get to be too much.

Better yet, we can create places for breaks for students to get away on their own initiative. These could be locations in or near our classroom—under our desk, in the reading corner, in the hall. Some high schools have established open student support rooms where students can come at any time for help or to study, talk, or just hang out. Similarly, one elementary school established a quiet, pleasant location next to the principal's office where students could come when they needed to get away. All these strategies are helpful in giving a student a place to be alone to process emotions.

Taking a break allows us to break the cycle of conflict and to regather our thoughts and emotions. This approach is also a sharp contrast to forced "time outs" for students, which require that students sit out their lunchtime or recess in the school office, and to in-school suspension, in which students are required to go to a special room supervised by a counselor or teacher.

Utilizing Professional and Community Supports

A range of professional supports can be useful when you are working with social and behavioral difficulties. Here are a few of the most widely available types of services; many additional variations have been developed based on unique resources in local communities (Garbarino, Dubrow, Kostelny, & Pardo, 1992; McLane, Burnette, & Orkwis, 1997):

1. **Support groups** for students with special problems and needs—divorcing parents, death in the family, drug abuse, pregnancy, and so on
2. Consultation support concerning student needs, provided to teachers by a psychologist, social worker, or counselor
3. Individual counseling
4. Group counseling; most effective when students participate voluntarily rather than being referred for "behavior problems"

Although these professional services can be helpful, they are not sufficient to help students solve serious behavioral problems. Counseling and support groups can help students begin to understand themselves—to identify, label, and think about their feelings. However, students need daily practice and learning through modeling and gentle instruction. Our class is a key place where this can occur.

Engaging Parents in Partnership

Engaging parents is very critical. We want to reach out to parents as partners. We walk a fine line here, however, for a parent may be an important contributor to the social or behavioral problem a child is having. We have to reach out, communicate, and listen carefully. On the other hand, we have to be careful not to make unwarranted assumptions (Garbarino, Dubrow, Kostelny, & Pardo, 1992; Koegel, Koegel, Kellgrew, & Mullen, 1996). Several strategies may be particularly useful when we are dealing with families in relation to behavioral concerns:

- Be aware of the history of the family, of the challenges the family faces, and of how these have affected the child. Ask the parents about their lives.
- Tell parents the problems that are showing up in school and ask whether they see similar things at home. Ask their opinion as to what to do.
- Although families of children with behavioral problems often have many problems themselves, look at the strengths of the family. Focus and build on these.
- Communicate with the family about positive attributes of the child and about the child's growth and successes as well as about his or her problems.
- With some students, consider sending home frequent "behavior reports."
- Also be aware, however, of the dynamics in the family. In some situations in which children are being abused, negative reports from the school can set off additional abuse.

Nonviolent Crisis Intervention

The strategies we've outlined will be sufficient to deal with most social and behavioral problems. Sometimes, however, crises erupt after building over a long period of time. At these moments, we need strategies for nonviolent crisis intervention.

Tools *for the* Trek

Crisis Cycle

STAGES OF CRISIS DEVELOPMENT	COUNTERPRODUCTIVE RESPONSES	HELPFUL RESPONSES
Anxiety demonstrated by . . . 　Noncompliance 　Disruption 　Unusual actions	*Issue Directive:* "Do this!" *Set limits:* "You can't do that." *Establish consequences:* "If you do this, I will . . ." *Label the student:* "You're . . . a problem, an angry child . . ."	*Listen and reflect:* "Mary, you seem upset today." *Express curiosity:* "What's going on?" *Be supportive:* "I'm here if you want to talk." *Partner:* "Let's work together on this." *Express healthy expectations:* "It will be OK."
Trigger: Action sets crisis in motion . . . 　Questioning—"Why do we have to?" 　Refusal 　Emotional outburst *Crisis:* A serious crisis develops. We see . . . 　Intimidation 　Threat 　Violence	*Demand compliance:* "Sit down!" *Apply consequences:* "You will get an F for this course." *Make threat/intimidate:* "Stop or I will call your mother" *Show anger:* "Back off!" With loud voice and flushed face. *Move in:* Move toward screaming student to stop him. *Retaliate/expel:* "Go to the office now!" *Punish:* "You lose your privileges for the week!"	*Cool off:* Take some deep breaths, acknowledge feelings. *Agree to work it out:* Show willingness to solve problem and let person know you are ready to discuss issues. *Give personal point of view:* Give your point of view using I-statements. *Solve the problem:* Brainstorm win–win solutions.
Recovery: Student settles down and feels . . . 　Embarrassment 　Guilt 　Shame *Resolution* 　Calm	*Blame:* "You always act this way." *Use instruction to retaliate:* "I've told you, walk out when you feel upset. What is wrong with you?" *Remind of crisis:* "You were out of control earlier, you know." *Avoid:* Teacher won't look at student. *Expect recurrence:* "He's going to go off again if they don't get him out of my class."	*Listen:* "You look like you are sad." *Support:* "How can I help?" *Normalize crisis:* "All of us have times when we lose it." *Make personal disclosure:* "I did this when I was your age." *Collaborate:* "How can we work together to help you?" *Analyze:* "What happened? What would have helped you?" *Problem-solve:* "What would be better next time you have these feelings? How can we help you deal with the issues facing you?"

Source: Adapted from Kunc (1995) and Lantieri & Patti (1996).

Fisher and Ury (1991) describe three types of negotiating styles used in crisis situations: (1) soft, (2) hard, and (3) principled. **Soft negotiators** tend to focus on the relationship and may even fear conflict more than the problem itself. Such individuals often try to ignore issues rather than deal with them. **Hard negotiators,** on the other hand, seek to win no matter what the costs. **Principled negotiators** avoid both of these extremes. Separating the person from the problem, they seek a situation where all have their needs met and are treated with respect.

In some cases problems may escalate into a crisis in which a student loses control and may become dangerous. The Tools for the Trek feature here illustrates five typical stages of crisis and a range of both helpful and counterproductive responses. At any point in time during a crisis, the problem may escalate to a higher or lower level of threat depending on how those involved respond.

Often the development of a crisis begins with an individual who is experiencing unusual *anxiety*. This anxiety may show itself in several forms—noncompliance, disruption, extreme withdrawal. If we can listen, be supportive, be curious, and expect positive results, students are likely to settle down. However, if we act in authoritarian ways—directing students to act, setting limits, or labeling them or their behaviors—we often push them to the next level.

At the next level, some action may spark a response. Often this **trigger** will be trivial—a dirty look, a nasty comment, one person's stepping on another's shoes; but such triggers often set off feelings of rejection, unworthiness, and consequent shame (Gilligan, 1996). In this stage we see student challenges escalate—questioning, refusals to comply, emotional outbursts of anger or crying. Nonhelpful but too typical responses involve demands for compliance, threats, and punishment. The person does not feel heard, and the anxiety he or she felt in the first place goes up.

Depending on the person and the situation, the highest levels of *crisis* can take many forms, ranging from intimidation and threats to serious violence to property or people. Those using a paradigm of control will simply match the force of the person with force of their own—moving in, showing anger, and threatening either in words or in actions to retaliate and punish.

Lantieri and Patti (1996) outlined options in this stage: (1) avoid; (2) diffuse; or (3) confront, either *(a)* violently or *(b)* nonviolently. Soft negotiators tend to avoid the conflict, although this is often problematic. Hard negotiators tend to move toward the use of violence to "take down" students. However, those involved in **non-violent crisis intervention** use other strategies, as shown in the Tools for the Trek feature. These negotiators suggest that we take steps to cool off, share our view of what is occurring while agreeing to work out a solution, and brainstorm solutions. In the most desperate of situations, such actions often help calm the person and allow us to find alternatives that prevent violence and actually promote learning and growth.

What might this kind of intervention look like? Consider this scenario.

Darius came in looking very glum this morning. Carmen, his teacher, knew he'd been having a tough time lately. Before she knew it, however, things escalated. Darius was at the back of the room, screaming and holding a knife on Mitchell. Terrified, Carmen nevertheless stopped, breathed deeply and said, "Darius,

you're really making us afraid. We know you've had a hard time lately and we all want
to help you. We can do that. Would you please give me the knife." She stopped and
waited, watching him and making eye contact. It seemed an eternity. However, he slumped
just a bit, handed the knife to her, and sat down at the back of the class with his arms over
his head.

The subsequent phases following the crisis provide an opportunity to help students think about their reactions. This is not a time for blame but a time for listening, sharing, and reflecting. It is a time for all involved to help students think through their needs and explore ways to get those needs met. Helping students find ways to make amends in interaction with the classroom community can be particularly effective and powerful.

IDEA and Behavioral Challenges
What the Law Says

The Individuals with Disabilities Education Improvement Act of 2004 maintained the procedures related to behavioral challenges of students with disabilities that became part of the law for the first time in 1997. Concerns with student discipline continued to spark substantial debate in Congress during the reauthorization process. The IDEA provisions include the following:

1. *Suspension and expulsion.* Schools frequently suspend and expel students who cause behavioral problems. However, as an assistant principal recently said, "We send students home for three days. They come back to school and cause more problems. We suspend them again. We are not doing anything." Schools using **suspension and expulsion** seldom have a strategy for helping students learn new ways of behaving. In response to this reality, the law stipulates that students with disabilities can be expelled or suspended for problem behaviors only if the behaviors are shown *not to be directly related to the disability* of the student. However, a student may be removed from the school for up to ten days, even over the parents' objection, if such procedures are consistent with the treatment of students without disabilities. A student who brings a weapon to school or uses or sells illegal drugs may be removed from the school for up to forty-five school days. During this time school personnel work with the student and parents to develop a Behavioral Intervention Plan (Janney & Snell, 2000b.; Koegel, Koegel & Dunlap, 1996).

2. *Manifestation determination review.* A team must meet to determine if problematic behaviors are directly related to a student's disability. The team conducts a review of student information within no more than ten days after a student is suspended or removed from the classroom for behavioral problems. If there is a direct relationship between the student's disability and his or her behavior, the school must develop a Behavioral Intervention Plan (BIP).

3. *Behavioral Intervention Plan (BIP).* A plan to address behavioral concerns must be developed by a team as part of the IEP when the "behavior impedes his or her

Schools to Visit

School as Inclusive Community

Camden Elementary School
208 Washington Ave.
Camden, TN 38320
Phone: 731-584-4918
Principal: Lori Cantrell

Camden Elementary, a small school in rural Benton County in Tennessee, is a partner school of the Restructuring for Inclusive School Environments (RISE) project at the University of Memphis. RISE is one of two technical assistance projects in the state working with schools as they move to have students with special needs in less restrictive settings.

Inclusion began at Camden in 1985 when two children with developmental disabilities were included in a general education classroom for one hour a day with an assistant. Before 1985 all students with special needs were in pull-out programs; some never leaving these special settings, even for lunch or PE. A special education teacher began inviting general education teachers and their students to her room, where they would serve ice cream or cookies and have informal parties. A few teachers agreed to have her students in their classrooms. From this humble start the school progressed to the present: Today all school staff have ownership of, and responsibility for, all students.

An inclusionary program can thrive only if administration shares the vision. When the inclusion program began, the supervisor of special education for Benton County gave support, and soon after became principal of Camden Elementary and was able to infect all faculty with her spirit and vision. This leader developed a set of guidelines as the foundation of the program: *(a)* Provide staff development for all teachers; *(b)* provide material incentives for teachers who embrace the vision; *(c)* understand that diverse functioning levels already exist in the regular classroom and that no mystical cure exists within the special education room; *(d)* develop a strong team approach, focusing on students' personal goals; *(e)* set up time for effective collaboration among teachers, support staff, and parents; *(f)* develop strong paraprofessional support; *(g)* seek assistance from outside service agencies (through RISE); *(h)* introduce the teachers to creative instructional strategies such as cooperative learning groups and center approaches for focused learning; *(i)* include a proactive behavior model with the principal following up with each teacher every day; *(j)* ensure that staff live out the school's mission of reaching all students; *(k)* use technology to enhance the classroom setting for learners at diverse levels.

One proactive behavioral support used at the school is video self-modeling (VSM), in which students simulate and role-play positive ways to deal with situations in which they are having difficulties. Students are videotaped while performing the correct behavior. Staff edit tapes to ensure that they represent only positive behavior. Students then view the tapes at their leisure, seeing themselves performing well—a process termed *feedforward* (as opposed to feedback). Students enjoy the process of making the videos and viewing themselves on TV. More importantly, implanting this positive image of themselves seems to be a strong tool to alter behavior without more intrusive interventions.

Camden is providing a model for child-centered change and growth for rural communities in Tennessee, a process that continues and changes daily.

By Rita Parrish, Michele Cervetti, & Tom Buggey; **tjbuggey@memphis.edu.**

learning or that of others, and must consider, when appropriate, strategies, including positive behavioral interventions, and supports" (Individuals with Disabilities Education Improvement Act, 2004). At best, a BIP will be developed when behavioral challenges are evident, rather than after a crisis has occurred. A BIP can be developed for any student with a disability, not only for those classified as emotionally disturbed.

   4. *Functional assessment.* A **functional assessment** is required whenever a school removes a child from his or her current educational placement. The intent of such an assessment will be to assist the school in developing a Behavioral Intervention Plan for the student.

   Educators who utilize the positive approaches outlined in this chapter (and in recommended references) will be fulfilling both the spirit and the letter of the law. Sometimes, however, students' behavioral problems are so puzzling and challenging that we need to develop a formal Behavioral Intervention Plan for a student. This may be part of a student's IEP, Section 504 plan, or part of a plan desired by the school staff or parents. Although the student's problem may be complex, the BIP steps are simple (see Albin, Horner, & O'Neill, 1994; Hitzing, 1994; Janney & Snell, 2000b.; Koegel, Koegel, & Dunlap, 1996).

Step 1: Identify Social and Behavioral Problem(s).
We first identify clearly the behaviors about which we are concerned, explaining in clear terms exactly what a student does. Rather than saying, "Justine is angry all the time," we describe what exactly Justine does, how she shows her anger. "Many times when boys in the class talk with Justine, she will grimace at them and tell them loudly to go away. She argues with friends during lunch and sits at the back of the class and sulks." This paints a clearer picture. We may find it helpful to keep a running record in which we describe students' academic, social, and behavioral actions. This helps us see interconnections between instruction and the behaviors.

Step 2: Develop a Student-Centered Theory.
Recently we talked with a teacher who was having a lot of trouble with a student. She was desperate to figure out a strategy that would "control this student's behavior." However, when we asked, "*Why* is this student acting this way?" she did not know. The question had not been asked by anyone. When we go through a systematic process of looking at a student's behavior to determine its strength and the underlying causes or situations that trigger the problem, we are doing a version of a functional assessment (O'Neill, Horner, Albin, Storey, & Sprague, 1996). Rather than responding only to the behavior itself (most often merely symptomatic of the real issue), we seek to understand what is going on and to develop a theory that will give us a sound basis for devising strategies to help the student. Rather than asking, "How can I control this kid?" we then ask questions like the following (Albin, Horner, & O'Neill, 1994; Evans & Meyer, 1985; Hitzing, 1994; Janney & Snell, 2000b.):

■ What is the quality of life for the student?
■ Why is this behavior occurring? What is the person trying to communicate through this behavior? What legitimate human need is being signaled?
■ To what people, places, choices, and activities is the student connected?
■ What is going on at home or in the community that might affect the student?
■ From what resources can the student draw emotional strength and support?
■ How well does the student communicate? Through what modalities most effectively?
■ Why does this behavior concern me? Is it really important, or is the problem more about my need for control?
■ How can I help the student not feel the need to react this way?

With these questions in mind we gather information. We can talk with students, have them write about their homes and lives as part of classroom literacy activities, observe them in the school, talk with parents and others who know the students, and make home visits. The key here is to focus on understanding the student but not to be rigid about how we gather information. We want to understand the *student's story* as it is now and as it has unfolded in the past.

Often we will find it helpful to think carefully about what was going on before and around the time that a behavioral incident occurred—what behaviorists call "antecedent information." This information may signal a specific need or something the person is trying to communicate. Useful questions may include (Janney & Snell, 2000b):

- *Who* is present? How many people? Is someone coming or going?
- *What* is going on when the behavior occurs? Is there a pattern? What is happening when the behavior *never* occurs? In what type of task is the student involved—reading, math, gym? Is the task too hard or too easy? Is the student waiting a turn?
- *When* does the behavior occur? Is there a pattern? Before lunch? Just before the end of the day?
- *Where* does the behavior occur? On the playground? In class, in the office, at home, at the movies, at the grocery store? In a large open space or a closed space?

As we look at the *behavior itself*, we may find it valuable to count and record the time of day, duration, and strength of the behavior. Recording forms exist for this purpose, and we can use them to graph behaviors. Behavioral interventionists often use such charts to track the impact of strategies on behaviors. Such information can help us think more clearly about the problem.

We also want to pay attention to the *consequences* of the behavior. What occurred after the behavior? Did the person obtain desired outcomes? We also look for clues in the student's total life, bringing together what we know about the student's story, life, behaviors, and expressions of thoughts and feelings as we listen for *patterns* (Evans & Meyer, 1985; Hitzing, 1994; Janney & Snell, 2000b).

As we proceed, we develop a theory about what is happening. This theory will guide our subsequent efforts to develop strategies to meet the students' needs. Out of this process we should be able to articulate a coherent, if tentative, view regarding (1) why the behaviors are occurring, the (2) underlying needs of the student, and (3) strategies to help the student meet his or her needs in a more positive way.

We will involve the student in all parts of this process. It should come as no surprise to the student that we are targeting certain behaviors. We want to know what students think of their own behavior and whether they think it needs to change. We will engage families and students in gathering information, in helping us all to understand what is going on. Most important, we will communicate with students about their needs and desires and explore better ways to meet these. What is important in the whole process is that we seek to be a partner with students and families rather than sitting back as the "professional authority."

Step 3: Develop and Implement a Plan. When students exhibit serious behavioral problems, we may develop a written plan that can be part of the IEP or Section 504 plan (see chapter 4) for a student. Whether we develop a formal written plan or an informal working strategy, we need the same information (Albin, Horner, & O'Neill, 1994; Hitzing, 1994).

- Behaviors of concern
- Planned responses to behaviors or strategies to prevent and respond to behavioral problems
- Roles of teachers, support staff, parents, and others
- Method of evaluating the success of the plan
- A mechanism for reviewing the outcome and making necessary revisions.

Many different formats are used for documentation. We will particularly want to have forms for recording strategies that include space for (1) prevention, (2) teaching new social and behavioral skills, and (3) responding to crisis situations (Janney & Snell, 2000b).

Step 4: Evaluate Outcomes Together. A key difference between control strategies and student-centered approaches lies in the question, "How do we know when an approach that aims to deal with a behavioral problem actually works?" Under a control philosophy, authority figures identify the problem. A strategy is deemed successful when the problem behavior disappears or when desired behaviors occur: The student quits fighting, or he reads when he is told.

Stepping Stones
To Inclusive Teaching

1. With one or two other teachers, identify the two or three children in your school who are having the worst behavior problems. Bring together a group to brainstorm ideas to help these students and provide teacher support. For each student:
   - Identify the behavior.
   - Seek to understand *why* the behavior is occurring. What *need* is being communicated?
   - Develop some ideas that focus on helping the student meet his or her needs in a more positive way while ensuring that other students and the teacher have their needs met as well.
   - Think together about how this student's situation relates to community—or to a lack of community—in the school.
   - Meet together periodically to assess what is happening, and use this assessment process as an opportunity to learn.

2. Keep a journal regarding how you deal with students in your class who have challenging behaviors. What do you do? Are you punitive, angry, and controlling, or are you seeking to meet the students' needs? Are you treating the students with respect or using power exclusively? If change is needed, what two strategies might you employ to try to shift what is happening?

3. Has there been a student in your school who has been sent to a separate school for students with emotional disturbance or to an alternative school? If so, visit the child in this new school. What do you think about what you see?

4. Review the strategies outlined in this chapter and develop a plan regarding how you could make these part of your teaching practice this year. How will you get support for doing this? Share your ideas and plan with another teacher.

However, a student-centered approach turns this around. Although the perspective of others in the setting will be important, we are *most* interested in the viewpoint of the student. For if behaviors are related to a range of individual needs, it will not be possible to eliminate or create behaviors without addressing the key needs of the person. In this view, the problem is solved when the needs of the person are met according to the *student's* viewpoint (Hitzing, 1994; Lovett, 1996).

Moving On to Respect

Dealing with social and emotional challenges is an important part of our journey. Students belong in caring classroom communities in which peers can help them work out their problems. They should always be treated with respect and deserve to have help in achieving their own goals and meeting their needs. With this attitude and some solid strategies, we will find ourselves reaching more difficult students than we ever thought possible. Few experiences can compare to the feeling of creating bonds with difficult students that allow them to feel safe enough to change their defensive behaviors. It is the reason we continue to work toward a community that includes all children.

 Key Points

- Traditional behavior management emphasizes controlling rather than meeting the needs of students. Some control strategies involve punishment; others, reinforcement and rewards; many combine these tools. However, the focus is still control.

- Research on outcomes of punishment shows that in general it is effective only briefly, and then only if strong enough.

- Rewards tend to destroy internal motivation and interest in learning, ultimately creating a reliance on more and more rewards.

- Students' challenging behaviors in classrooms range from those that are simply distracting to those that are dangerous. All such behaviors, however, communicate powerful messages about needs that are not being met.

- Glasser's five needs of human beings are: (1) survival, (2) love and belonging, (3) power, (4) fun, and (5) freedom. When students act in

ways that are problematic, we can use these needs to analyze behavior and develop strategies designed to help them meet their needs in more positive ways.

- We are most successful with students when we reach out to develop a caring relationship, even in the midst of challenges; when we move away from power struggles; and when we seek to provide information, helping students learn how to manage their own behavior rather than using our power and authority.

- We can use many positive strategies to help students; these include obtaining help through problem solving in class meetings, peer supports, circles of support, and professional help.

- If students with disabilities have a Behavioral Intervention Plan, it should be part of their IEP. A BIP is required if a student is in danger of being suspended from school.

Learning Expeditions

Following are some activities to extend your learning and thinking about dealing with students who have behavioral challenges.

1. Find a teacher who is having problems with a child or children in his or her class. (This should not be hard.) Visit the class. Using the ideas in this chapter, explore the following questions: Who in the class is having problems, and of what kind? What needs are being communicated through behaviors? How is the teacher meeting or not meeting student needs, helping or hurting?

2. Locate a teacher who has a reputation for dealing with difficult children very well. Talk with the teacher and find out how he or she thinks about students. What are this teacher's ideas about dealing with challenging behaviors?

3. Visit a class that is including a student with challenging behaviors that are affected by a disability. What does the student do, and how do the teacher and the rest of the class respond? What is the student trying to communicate with the problematic behavior? What would you recommend, and why?

4. Interview a parent of a child who has had behavioral problems in school. What do you think about what has happened, and why? Would you recommend changes? If so, what changes and why?

5. Observe a student with autism who is included in a general education class and has a history of behavior problems. Review the student's past history and the existing plans for responding to the challenging behavior. What is the student doing, and what do you think the behaviors might communicate? What recommendations do you have?

6. Read some additional articles or information in the references list and visit some websites that deal with behavioral issues. The website for *Inclusive Teaching* can help you get started. What do you make of the wide range of opinions about students with behavioral challenges? What makes the most sense to you, and why?

CHAPTER GOAL

Understand needs and strategies for inclusive teaching with students who have communication difficulties and other physical and sensory disabilities.

CHAPTER OBJECTIVES

1. Learn the types of communication disorders and strategies for helping children with these challenges.

2. Understand inclusion of students with severe and multiple disabilities.

3. Develop strategies for teaching students who are deaf or blind and collaborating with specialists who support them.

4. Recognize a wide range of orthopedic disabilities and other health impairments and consider instruction and support strategies.

5. See the connection between inclusion and support of students with physical and sensory disabilities and best practices for teaching and learning.

Students with Differing Communication, Physical, and Sensory Abilities

13

Understanding Student Needs and Effective Strategies

Steve Wright (1999) tells this story: "There is a member of my community, Mick, who is thirty and has severe scoliosis. He is also a dancer, despite the fact that his mobility is restricted. He is part of an incredible dance company called Company Chaos, a 'mixed-ability' dance troupe that includes people labeled with various mental and physical disabilities. As the dancers all came on stage at a performance, I found myself wondering, 'Mmmm . . . I wonder if I can spot the "disabled" ones.' The dance troupe had made a unique and precious virtue out of the 'disabilities' present. The choreography incorporated and built upon the personality and abilities of each person so that each 'disability' was highlighted and suddenly it wasn't a disability at all. It was an amazing dance performance where each person rejoiced in their talent and dis-ability and asked us to rejoice too. It was a humbling experience. Mick, who spends more

383

time in a wheelchair these days, enjoys the expressions on people's faces when asked 'what he does.' He replies, 'I'm a dancer.' "

This story of a dance company powerfully illustrates how people with disabilities can be part of our community. Yet in a culture in which physical traits (such as beauty, skin color, physical prowess) carry much weight in our attitudes, people with physical disabilities often struggle for acceptance. What people with physical disabilities do, perhaps, is bring all of us face to face with mortality and real humanity. Across the ages people with physical disabilities have been viewed in curious ways—as demons sent from hell, as the blessed of God, as superheroes overcoming the ravages of disability. Too seldom have they been seen simply as *people.*

Although many see disability as a tragedy, growing numbers of people view the experience of disability as providing a unique and valuable perspective on the human condition. Many people who are deaf, for example, reject recently developed surgical procedures that would make them able to hear, preferring their own deaf community to the hearing world. Norm Kunc, an activist and speaker who has cerebral palsy, said that "if I found out tomorrow that my cerebral palsy could be corrected, I would not do so. Why? Because my disability is not something separate from who I am. It is part of what makes me me. It gives me insights on oppression and connections with others" (Kunc, 2000).

Other people, however, continue to hold the view that disability is a great tragedy and that a person with a disability is a tragic mistake. Disability often reflects our worst fears—the loss of sight, the loss of our ability to walk. Not surprisingly, we hear language about people who are "afflicted" or who are "confined to" a wheelchair (as opposed to being a "wheelchair user" or even being "liberated by using a wheelchair"). The ideas underlying this language are powerful. Those who view disability in largely negative terms also tend to believe that people with disabilities should be separated from others.

We are again faced with the question of the type of community we want. Who belongs in our school and class? Why? Janice Fialka (1999) wrote the poem in the Voices feature for the parent of a child with a severe disability. "It Matters" says much, we think, about inclusive schooling.

In this chapter we will discuss different major types of sensory and physical disabilities, seeking to understand students with these disabilities and exploring ways to include and support them in our classes. We will review assistive technology tools valuable for many students in Chapter 15. We begin with the largest category we encounter in school—communication disorders.

Traveling Notes

There is much technical information to know about successfully teaching students with physical disabilities. Mostly, however, we need to simply approach them as people and learn after that.

It Matters (For a Mother in Iowa)

By Janice Fialka

They say my two year old
  can't see
  can't hear
  can't think

So why
  send her to preschool?

I say
  because
    just because.

They say
  children like her
  never go to school

  They need
    oxygen,
    tubes,
    hospital beds,
    special care

So WHY
  send her to preschool?

I say
  just because.

They say . . .
  and on and on
  and on, they say.

I'm persistent.
  I say
    because
    because

Then one day
  my lioness
    "BECAUSE"
    wins.

My deaf, blind,
  fragile daughter
    goes to school.

She has
  a teacher
  a desk
  a book.

At recess
  butterscotch sunrays
  warm her cheeks
  and children's giggles
  find paths to her heart.

For six glorious days,
  she is finally
    a student.
  And I am finally a mother.

Nothing can take that from
    her
  not even her
    premature death
    six days later.

She was and will always
  be
  my preschooler
      just because.

Reprinted by permission of the author. Janice Fialka is a national speaker, social worker, and mother of two children, one of whom has developmental disabilities. This poem is published in a collection of her writings called *It Matters: Lessons from My Son.* To obtain a copy of the book or to receive information on her other publications or her workshops on parent–professional partnerships, go to www.danceofpartnership.com.

1. As you think about teaching students with physical and sensory disabilities, what do you *feel?* What is your reaction to these students as people?

2. What are your experiences around people with physical disabilities? Do you or your family have personal relationships?

3. What are the questions that come to your mind about teaching such students? What are the feelings? (You might want to keep notes separate for these as we travel; that is, for different students, make notes about the questions you have, and separately note your feelings. It may help to differentiate these two responses.)

Communication Disorders
Talk Matters

Georgia Larson has three children with communication problems in her grades 4–6 multiage class. Each student receives individual help from a speech therapist twice a week. Each student's communication is affected in different ways:

- Shardae can most often be understood, though she has trouble pronouncing the *r* sound and other consonants. She says her teacher's name as "Mrs. Lawson."

- Carl talks like a much younger child. Although he's in fourth grade, his voice is unusually high-pitched; he mispronounces and skips words and rushes what he says, often speaking under his breath. When asked to repeat himself, he may refuse. Carl's friends don't always understand him.

- Ricky is in sixth grade. He has an amazing capacity to remember what he reads. However, he stutters, and if students tease him, he may explode in anger. He has perfected a tough-guy routine to cover up his difficulties. He gets frustrated when he is stuck on a word.

Each of these students has a *communication disorder,* defined in IDEA as "stuttering, impaired articulation, a language impairment, or a voice impairment, that adversely affects a child's educational performance." (Individuals with Disabilities Education Improvement Act [IDEA], 2004, Section 300.7)

People depend on being able to communicate with others—to express their needs, to convey ideas, to share simple human companionship—and children can become very frustrated and humiliated when they have difficulty communicating. These reactions can then create additional problems in learning, relationships, and emotional well-being. Although dialects of speech vary dramatically, a problem with speech is considered a disorder *only* when it interferes with communication and creates discomfort. People with **communication disorders** may have difficulty both understanding others and expressing themselves. Some 7 to 10 percent of school-age children receive speech services. Although these children represent 20 percent of students serviced by special education, only about 2 percent of students in special education have a *primary* disability in communication. The vast majority of students with communication disorders also have another disability that is considered more significant (McCormick, Loeb, and Schiefelbusch, 1997).

Types of Communication Disorders. One of the two types of communication disorders is a **language disorder:** difficulty using *oral and written symbols*. Students may use words inappropriately, may have difficulty learning grammatical patterns and distinguishing speech sounds, and may have trouble comprehending others. Because children develop communication skills gradually, we become concerned only when children lag in typical development. For example, we might expect a student to make grammatical errors and skip words in preschool. By the fourth grade, however, such errors cause concern.

Students with a **speech disorder,** the second type, have trouble with the *physical act* of expressing thoughts orally—articulating sounds, maintaining fluent speech rhythms, and controlling their voice. Often children with speech disorders are identified in the early grades (McCormick, Loeb, & Schiefelbusch, 1997). A speech disorder can reveal itself in several ways:

- *Articulation:* A child has trouble saying certain sounds and may try to compensate in several ways—*substituting* an easier sound, *omitting* a difficult sound altogether, *adding* sounds to words that are difficult, or *distorting* a sound while trying to pronounce it, creating a lisp.
- *Delayed speech:* A child's speech develops later than that of peers, and the child may communicate mainly through gestures rather than words.
- *Disfluency:* Speech is too fast or too slow, resulting in poor voice quality.
- *Stuttering:* The speaker gets stuck on the first sounds of words.

Causes of Communication Disorders. Speech is a complex process involving the lungs, larynx, mouth, ears, and brain. Conditions that affect breathing, such as emphysema or other chronic lung problems, also cause speech problems. Vibrations in the larynx turn breath into voice. Cancer, other problems with the larynx, or surgical removal of the larynx can cause loss of voice. Articulation takes place in the mouth. Difficulties involving the teeth, gums, tongue, or palate can affect a student's speech. A problem in hearing can result in delayed speech or can cause the voice to deteriorate (McCormick, Loeb, & Schiefelbusch, 1997).

Conditions that affect the brain can also affect speech. Because speech is learned and requires use of the brain's motor areas to control movements, stroke, brain injury, autism, mental retardation, or cerebral palsy are often associated with communication problems. The loss of speech due to brain injury is referred to as **aphasia** (Smith, D., 1998; McCormick, Loeb, & Schiefelbusch, 1997).

The physical malformation involved in cleft palate and cleft lip also cause difficulties. *Cleft palate* is an incomplete fusion of the roof of the mouth that leaves an opening from the mouth to the nose. *Cleft lips* similarly involve an incomplete fusion of the lips. Both can usually be corrected surgically. These conditions are usually caused by genetic factors, but can also result from injury to the embryo. Depending on when surgery occurs, the child may or may not have normal speech when he or she starts school.

Specialists and Treatment. If a child with communication problems is born with a cleft palate or another surgically correctable condition, doctors and nurses will be the main specialists involved. For other students, professionals may be involved—general education teachers, special education teachers, speech therapists, and language specialists. However, *speech therapists* (also called "speech pathologists") are the professionals primarily involved with students with communication disorders. Augmentative and alternative communication (AAC) specialists (Chapter 15) are typically trained as speech therapists (McCormick, Loeb, & Schiefelbusch, 1997).

Strategies for Inclusive Teaching. To encourage and support a student's communication, we will collaborate with the student's speech therapist regarding strategies to incorporate into our teaching. We should also be aware of the impact of speech and language difficulties on children's self-esteem and their formation of friendships. These approaches build naturally on best teaching practices. Here are a few helpful strategies.

- Be patient and allow the child to communicate even if it is clear what the student wants. This can be encouraging and motivating.
- Give students classroom jobs that require communication on a small scale. Examples include directing students to seats, indicating food choices in the cafeteria, conducting a survey, transmitting a message to another teacher.
- Provide choices and ask students to verbalize their choice.
- Play barrier games in free time as part of the curriculum: Place a barrier between two students so that they cannot see each other's work. The lead person works and describes to the other player what he or she is doing. The second student can ask clarifying questions. Then the second student tries to duplicate the work. When both are done, remove the barrier, compare, and then switch.
- Get to know students and ask questions about their interests.
- Have a student practice difficult sounds with a classmate by writing and/or reading passages that include that sound.
- Play word games: Show a card with a word or picture on it. Have students tell a partner a word that rhymes or has the same sound or number of syllables; have them come up with antonyms, synonyms, homonyms, different meanings of the same word, or examples of other words with the same suffix or prefix.
- Encourage peer interactions.

Students with communication difficulties often have low self-esteem because of being teased about "baby talk" or because their teachers cannot understand them. The ideas about community in Chapter 11 provide a foundation for addressing these self-esteem problems, on which the following suggestions build (McCormick, Loeb, & Schiefelbusch, 1997; Vaughn, Bos, & Schumm, 1997):

- Attend to *what* students say, focusing on meaning, not on how they are saying it. Other students will follow the teacher's example.
- In whole group discussions, try to ensure that the full class is attending so that the need for the student to repeat words is minimized.
- Don't interrupt children to correct or criticize their speech. After they are finished, model correct speech by rephrasing or using different words.
- Allow classmates to ask questions about the student's difficulties, and provide simulations to allow them to experience how the student feels. Do not allow teasing, however; discuss the reasons why teasing must not happen.
- If a student struggles with an oral assignment, make changes that reduce the problem. For example, allow the student to sing, read/speak in unison with another student, whisper, speak in a monotone, or use a higher or lower pitch.
- Allow for *wait time* when students are stuttering or their speech is slow and labored. Do not finish their thoughts.
- Students need to connect spoken language with familiar activities and objects, hearing language used in context. We can describe what we are doing or thinking as we do it (self-talk) or describe what someone else is doing (parallel talk).

A teacher reads a picture book while an interpreter signs for a student who is deaf in an inclusive first-grade class.

Inclusive Schooling and Students with Communication Disorders. In 1998–1999 95 percent of students with communication disorders were educated in general education classrooms. However, students with communication disorders traditionally have left the regular classroom several times a week to receive individual or small group help from speech therapists. In the field of speech therapy, there is a growing movement toward "naturalistic" classroom- and community-based services that support inclusive teaching (Office of Special Education Programs, 2001).

The reason for this trend is that problems with pull-out speech therapy have been identified. Many students, particularly those with severe disabilities, have trouble applying skills learned in one-on-one therapy in the classroom or community. In addition, students miss instruction when they leave the classroom, often experience a sense of humiliation as they walk down the hall to therapy sessions, and are frequently seen negatively by other students. Finally, research shows that individual therapy is no more effective than naturalistic approaches (McCormick, Loeb, & Schiefelbusch, 1997). Thus, speech therapy is moving in new directions that include:

- Working with students and small groups in natural environments, such as their regular classroom or their homes
- Moving away from standardized testing and toward observing language in naturalistic environments
- A focus on spoken language and the clues it offers about literacy development
- A focus on cultural diversity and its impact on speech

In speech therapy, as in other disciplines, change is slow and traditional models die hard. Consequently, the majority of speech therapists continue to use a pull-out model. As teachers we can, however, request that they provide in-class services and work collaboratively with us. At best, we can work together with therapists to plan lessons and instruction involving language and speech development. In McNichols Elementary School, for example, the speech therapist works intensively with teachers in the lower elementary grades to incorporate fun games and learning activities into the curriculum. These activities engage groups of children in using good oral communication skills and let them practice oral communication in context.

Severe and Multiple Disabilities
Yes, There Is Someone There

Adam, sixteen, has cerebral palsy and severe mental retardation. Throughout elementary school Adam went to a special school for students with severe and multiple disabilities. Last year his parents decided they wanted him to attend the regular middle school. This was a new experience for everyone. However, a group of students agreed to help Adam be a part of the school as his circle of friends. Adam gets around in an electric wheelchair, which he has learned to direct. He communicates through facial gestures and through a computerized communication board. He likes music. His IEP goals include improving his sitting position, developing basic interaction skills using the communication board, and responding to simple requests.

Like Adam, some children have disabilities that impact many areas—academic and physical abilities, adaptive skills, cognitive functioning. These students require substantial support. TASH defines persons with severe disabilities as

> individuals of all ages who require extensive ongoing support in more than one major life activity in order to participate in integrated community settings and to enjoy a quality of life that is available to citizens with fewer disabilities. Support may be required for life activities such as mobility, communication, self-care, and learning. (Meyer, Peck, & Brown, 1991, p. 19)

These students typically have more than one significant disability. Most have severe to profound mental retardation; other conditions may include epilepsy, respiratory problems, cerebral palsy, heart disease, or other difficulties. The bodies—arms, legs, face, trunk—of many of these students are shaped very differently from those of other children, resulting in an appearance that seems disfigured to many people.

Given their multiple and pervasive disabilities and the degree of ongoing and intensive support that they need, many ask: "Do these students belong in general education classes? What might they obtain there?" In dealing with students with severe and multiple disabilities, we are confronted directly with the strength or weakness of our belief that students should learn together. Traditionally these students are placed in separate schools or classes along with students with other severe disabilities. At first this makes sense, in light of their intense and specialized needs. Then we visit such classes and note what we see.

Melanie, a thirteen-year-old student, has severe mental retardation but is able to communicate yes or no via a communication device. She uses a wheelchair, although she finds it difficult to sit up straight. As we enter Melanie's special education class we see eight other students, all with a range of severe and multiple disabilities. None can talk. A key part of Melanie's IEP is to communicate with others. We watch as a paraprofessional engages Melanie in "functional communication": "Do you want a snack? Tell me yes or no." Melanie presses her communication device, which speaks the word *yes*. Six other students are sitting waiting for their turn. Later we return and find Melanie waiting herself. It seems that unless one of the two adults in the room is speaking directly with Melanie, no communication is going on.

Twice a week a middle school student takes Melanie to art class. As we enter the class, Rob and Katie say, "Melanie! It is good to see you!" and shake her hand. Melanie beams and hits her communication device, which says, "Hello, I am glad to see you." The class is abuzz with talk as Mr. Florio gives directions. Jill and Melanie join a group that is working on a large papier-maché statue of a wolf, the team mascot for the school's football team,. Periodically a student asks Melanie. "Which color should we use? Red? Blue? Green?" and Melanie responds yes or no to each choice. We are amazed at how much more Melanie's IEP is being met in this class—and the teacher is not doing anything special. In the special education class, in contrast, two people were working hard, but students sat doing nothing much of the time.

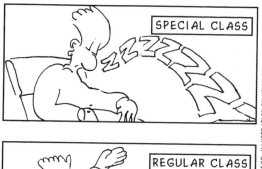

AFTER RULING OUT A MEDICAL REASON, BOBBY SUE'S PARENTS COME TO THE CONCLUSION THAT THERE'S JUST A LOT MORE TO BE AWAKE FOR IN REGULAR CLASS.

© 1998 MICHAEL F. GIANGRECO, ILLUSTRATION BY KEVIN RUELLE PEYTRAL PUBLICATIONS, INC. 612-949-8707

Perhaps, instead of questioning whether these students should be in our classes, we might ask, "Why don't people want these students in classes?" We think it boils down to two issues. First, people are simply uncomfortable and frightened. These students often look so different that we don't know how to respond. Second, our opinions are often fortified by input from professionals who have largely spent their lives in segregated special education classrooms and schools. They have had little experience in general education; perhaps they are even frightened of us and our classes!

Yet the positive impact of inclusion for these students has been demonstrated in many studies (see Berrigan, 1994; Cole & Meyer, 1991; Hunt, Farron-Davis, Beckstead,

Curtis, & Goetz, 1994; Janney & Snell, 1997; Meyer, Peck, & Brown, 1991; Smith, D., 1998). When students with severe disabilities come into the general education classroom, they enter a world of stimulation and interaction that addresses their most significant need: learning to communicate. In separate special education rooms with peers who do not talk, even with teachers working hard, these students often sit with no interaction, waiting, for significant lengths of time every day. Inclusive classrooms offer these students the equivalent of twenty-four teachers (McDonnell, Hardman, Hightower, & Kiefer-O'Donnell, 1997; York, Vandercook, MacDonald, Heise-Neff, & Caughey, 1992).

So what do we do? Over and over again, when we see teachers get beyond their fears, wonderful things happen. Our students can help us develop ideas about how to include a student with severe disabilities. We may be surprised at the positive impact the inclusion of such a student can have on our class. It's hard not to find ourselves thinking, "Wow. If we can do well with this student in our class, the minor differences of some of our other students look pretty easy."

Deafness and Hearing Impairment
Beyond Isolation and Silence

Sixteen-year-old Theresa, who comes from a close-knit inner-city Latino family, is totally deaf. Theresa is very smart and knows American Sign Language. Her mother wants her to go to the school for the deaf, but Theresa does not want to. She has insisted on going to a regular high school. Theresa is interested in marketing and wants to take vocational courses in that field and later to go to the university.

Navaz's family is originally from India; no English is spoken in her home. Navaz is seven years old and has a moderate hearing loss that requires her to use a hearing aid to understand speech. Even with the hearing aid, she must look directly at a person to understand what the person is saying. She is in second grade and receives help from the speech teacher twice a week. She reads well and enjoys school, even though she has some trouble making friends.

What Are Deafness and Hearing Impairment?

Both of these children have hearing loss; one is totally deaf, whereas the other has a hearing disability. IDEA defines these two conditions in the following way.

"Deafness" means a hearing impairment that is so severe that the child is impaired in processing linguistic information through hearing, with or without amplification, and that adversely affects a child's educational performance.

"Hearing impairment" means an impairment in hearing, whether permanent or fluctuating, that adversely affects a child's educational performance but that is not included under the definition of deafness in this section. (Individuals with Disabilities Education Improvement Act [IDEA], 2004, section 300.7)

Of all the mental and physical losses, hearing loss may initially seem to be the least intrusive. However, hearing is very important. Even before babies learn to speak, they orient their world by the sound of familiar voices and begin to communicate. Hearing gives us a foundation for learning spoken language—which, in turn, helps us learn to read and write. Hearing loss can create obstacles in personal, social, and academic development.

Types of Hearing Loss. Students who are **deaf** cannot use their hearing to understand speech, even with amplification. Students who are *hard of hearing* have a loss that requires some special adaptations, but through these adaptations they can often understand speech. The categories of hearing loss are based on the part of the ear that sustained the loss. A **conductive hearing loss** occurs when there is interference in the movement of sound from the ear canal to the inner ear—blockage by an object, wax, or damage to a membrane. A **sensorineural hearing loss** occurs when the inner ear or auditory nerve is damaged. A *mixed hearing loss* involves both.

The two main dimensions by which we classify sound are intensity and frequency. The *intensity,* or loudness, of a sound is measured in decibels (dB). Normal hearing ranges from 0 to 130 decibels. Anything louder than 130 dB is painful to the ears, and anything less than 0 dB cannot be detected. The degree to which a person is considered hearing impaired is based on measures of hearing acuity (Gething, 1992; Hardman, Drew, & Egan, 1996):

1. *Slight:* Loss of 27–40 decibels. Difficulty hearing faint or distant speech.
2. *Mild:* Loss of 41–55 decibels of sound. Difficulty with conversation unless face to face or within three to five feet.
3. *Moderate:* Loss of 56–70 decibels of sound. Difficulty with conversation unless loud. Serious difficulties with language development.
4. *Severe:* Loss of 71–90 decibels of sound. Ability to hear only loud voices right near ear. Serious problems hearing speech, even with amplification.
5. *Profound:* Loss of 91 or more decibels. Ability to hear only occasional very loud sounds; perception of sounds usually limited to vibrations. Dependence on vision for communication.

The other dimension of sound is *frequency.* Frequency is measured in cycles of sound per second, or hertz (Hz). The more rapid the frequency, the higher the pitch of the sound that we hear. The human ear responds to a wide range, from a low of 20 Hz to a high of around 20,000 Hz. Additional sounds occur at frequencies above and below this range and cannot be heard by human beings. For example, dog whistles emit a sound that dogs can hear but humans cannot.

Hearing impairment sometimes affects the ability to perceive particular frequencies of sound. Various areas of the ear respond to different frequencies, and an area that responds to certain frequencies may be damaged while other areas remain intact. Loss of the ability to hear speech, which occurs in the range of 500–2,000 Hz, profoundly influences social interactions (Hardman, Drew, & Egan, 1996; Smith, D., 1998; Vaughn, Bos, & Schumm, 1997).

Causes of Hearing Loss. Hearing loss can be caused by either genetic or environmental factors. In *genetic* cases, parents pass a hearing loss on to their child, by passing a recessive gene either (in cases in which the parents are both hearing but carry the gene) or (in cases in which both parents are hearing impaired and pass the gene along). More than 200 forms of genetically based deafness have been identified. Most often genetically based deafness involves a sensorineural loss. In a few cases the bones in the middle ear are malformed, causing a conductive loss.

Numerous environmental factors also may influence hearing. These include:

- Premature birth.
- Viral infections, such as German measles.
- Incompatibility of the blood of the mother and the child.
- Otitis media, an infection that occurs in many children as fluid builds up and the eustachian tube is blocked.
- Concussions.
- Birth complications.
- Otosclerosis, a disease of the bones of the middle ear.
- Environmental impacts—loud workplaces, concerts, certain military occupations, stereos, sports events, air bags, and even hair dryers and children's toys are increasingly damaging hearing. As a result approximately 15 percent of children ages six to nineteen show signs of some hearing loss (Lewis & Doorlag, 1999; Smith, D., 1998; Turnbull, Turnbull, Shank, Smith, & Leal, 2002).

Specialists and Treatment. Several types of professionals specialize in dealing with individuals who are deaf or have a hearing impairment:

- *Audiologists* are professionals trained to assess hearing loss and to prescribe tools to improve hearing, such as hearing aids.
- *Sign language interpreters* listen to what is being said orally and translate this into sign language. As the deaf person signs back, the interpreter speaks the signed words to other parties.
- *Augmentative hearing specialists* work in the development and prescription of augmentative devices such as hearing aids and speech augmentation tools.
- *Special education teachers* are specifically certified in working with students who are deaf or hard of hearing.

Inclusive Teaching with Students Who Are Deaf and Hearing Impaired

Students who are deaf or hard of hearing will need assistance in being part of the class and in overcoming the isolation that can occur because of problems in receiving information. In addition, students who are deaf often struggle to develop academic language skills—both oral and written. Our challenge, then, is to include students in our class, providing multiple opportunities to use language. Let's look at a few specific strategies, starting with strategies for facilitating communication.

Communicating with Students Who Are Deaf. Students who are deaf or hearing impaired have challenges both in *expressing* themselves and in *receiving* information.

Strategies will vary depending on the extent and type of hearing loss. We will work carefully with specialists to develop a plan for our classroom. For students considered deaf, two key strategies are used in oral communication: sign language and speechreading.

Sign Language. Sign language is a visual language using hand gestures. Many types of sign languages are used. *Signed English* exactly replicates grammatically "correct" speech. That is, in signed English signs are produced for each word, and the system uses standard English syntax. Although this parallels standard English, it is also cumbersome to use efficiently. Children who are deaf learn sign language as their first language and use this as the basis for learning English as a second language.

American Sign Language (ASL) uses its own syntax. Signs may abbreviate or contain multiple words in ways that allow more efficient and fast communication. For many deaf adults this is the preferred mode of speaking. Once prohibited in state schools for the deaf, ASL has grown and is extensively used by deaf adults. It is the fourth most used language in the United States. Different dialects of sign language exist; for example, sign language in New York will not look the same as sign language in Australia. Further, signing systems also use **finger spelling,** in which people spell out names or words using finger signs for each letter, when there is no direct sign available (Beukelman & Mirenda, 1992).

When sign language is used in the classroom, an interpreter is often available full or part time. These individuals are trained and certified through either a university or a community college program. Interpreters translate all words to the student with hearing loss. Such interpreters are very expensive, so this has been a controversial support service contested in several court cases. Schools, however, are increasingly providing interpreters in general education classes.

Many teachers decide to take an introductory sign language course to learn basic signing skills. In addition, in many schools an interpreter may teach the whole class basic signs. Some high schools provide classes in sign language for a foreign language credit. The physical activity involved in sign language adds a richness to classroom communication and is often helpful to students with ADHD behaviors and students with learning disabilities. At Woodward Elementary School a note was sent home offering students the opportunity to join an after-school sign language club. Ninety students in the school wanted to participate. Later in the year several classes presented a musical production and simultaneously signed most of the songs while moving in rhythm and dance—all prompted by a third grader who was deaf.

Speechreading. We know speechreading by its familiar name of "lipreading," in which a deaf person learns to understand by watching another person speak. Speechreading is an extremely difficult skill, however, and only a small percentage of people who are deaf can read lips. In addition, only about 30 to 40 percent of spoken language can be understood by visual cues alone, and the person must constantly look directly at the speaker. To make speechreading more workable, **cued speech** has been developed. Cued speech is a visual communication system that, in English, uses eight hand shapes in four locations ("cues") in combination with the natural mouth movements of speech to make all the sounds of spoken language look different. As in finger spelling, it is based on phonetic spelling of words. Many hearing parents of children who are deaf have found this to be the most valuable technique for communication and learning with their children.

Speech and Students Who Are Deaf. Given our reliance on hearing for developing spoken language, students who are deaf before developing spoken language may have difficulty speaking. However, this is not always the case. The speech patterns of students who are deaf typically have a unique quality that may sound more nasal and have fewer inflections than typical. We should, however, provide opportunities in all our teaching for students who are deaf to speak in our class.

Communicating with Students Who Are Hearing Impaired. Students who are hearing impaired often can hear with assistance. Most often, we can use one of several devices to adjust the volume and frequency of sound so that it is more intelligible to a student with a hearing impairment.

A **hearing aid** is a small box that fits the inside of the ear and increases the intensity of sound that the student perceives. Hearing aids can help students with mild hearing losses. However, the hearing aid amplifies all sounds, not just speech, making sounds louder but not necessarily clearer. Some newer types of hearing aids, although very expensive, can increase speech sounds only. Others can be fitted into the frame of glasses or are worn behind the ear. We should encourage a student with hearing loss to use his or her device, check to ensure it is working, and keep an extra battery at the school, notifying the parents when it is used.

An **FM unit** is a device designed to get around the problems of hearing aids in noisy situations. The classroom teacher wears a wireless microphone around the neck, and the student wears a wireless receiver. Many receivers look like a Walkman and are worn around the neck; other versions are worn behind the ear and look like hearing aids. The FM unit amplifies the teacher's voice 12 to 15 decibels over the rest of the classroom noise.

Sound field amplification is similar in that the teacher uses a wireless microphone. With this system, however, the sound comes out of speakers placed around the room. This may benefit not only the child with the hearing impairment but many other students as well. Schools are increasingly using such units to provide comfortable ways for teachers to be heard.

A *cochlear implant* is a small device, surgically implanted inside the ear, that picks up sounds from a microphone and electrically stimulates the auditory nerve. This device bypasses parts of the ear to transmit sounds directly in the inner ear (Gething, 1992; Hardman, Drew, & Egan, 1996).

Visual Communications for All Students. Using visual tools and strategies can be particularly helpful to deaf and hearing-impaired students. In addition, we will find these tools helpful to all our students. Here are some ideas that may be useful (Banks, 1994; Vaughn, Bos, & Schumm, 1997).

- Post a schedule or list of activities at the front of the room.
- Create word walls.
- Put up displays of student work.
- Display assignment summaries on a transparency or post them on the wall.
- Use graphics and pictures for basic communication.
- Use an overhead projector to write directions.
- Employ visual cues to indicate different directions or concepts being taught or to signal which student is currently speaking.

- Face students when speaking directly to them.
- Use captioned films and TV whenever possible. Often captions are available for tapes used regularly in the classroom.
- If a student is not understanding speech, rephrase rather than repeat words.

When communicating with students who are deaf or hearing impaired, the key is to be natural and to focus on the student as a person, seeking meaning and relationship. This may seem obvious, but strange things are sometimes done. What we *don't* want to do is yell or talk very loudly. This typically distorts our voice. Nor do we want to exaggerate our facial gestures. Again, this makes us hard to understand. If students with hearing loss are difficult to understand at first, we will gradually become accustomed to their speech patterns.

Hearing and the Learning Environment. We want our classroom to help students who are hearing impaired use their hearing most effectively. Adding rugs, carpets, corkboard, felt boards, and curtains to classrooms can do much to minimize unnecessary noise. This allows all our students to focus better. We should also avoid placing the student next to a noisy area.

Promoting Belonging and Relationship. One of the most devastating problems of deafness is isolation and disconnection. Students who are deaf may *physically* be present, but unless there is some way for them to exchange ideas and feelings, they will feel—and be—isolated. It is largely for this reason that some adults who are deaf are opposed to inclusive education. They have lived lives in which the primary relationships they had were with other deaf people. In many schools today students who are deaf and hard of hearing are breaking through this isolation. However, we must be intentional about helping this to happen. Here are some beginning strategies that build on the foundation in Chapter 11:

- Constantly look for ways to engage students in communicating and receiving ideas and feelings. We can use words, art, gestures and expressions, strategies that address multiple intelligences.
- Mobilize circles of support, peer buddies and partners, and other social connecting strategies.
- Be aware of the feelings and relationships of students with hearing loss. When isolation occurs, step in to help provide new opportunities.
- Call class meetings. The class as a whole can be made aware of the isolation a student may experience and can help develop solutions. Students can lay the groundwork by thinking through what might help.

Academic Learning. Although children with hearing impairments are often very intelligent, they may have particular difficulty with language skills—reading and writing and the multiple areas of learning that are connected with these skills. Some specific academic instructional strategies may include the following (Banks, 1994; Vaughn, Bos, & Schumm, 1997):

- *Multiple intelligences and activity-based learning:* Provide learning opportunities that utilize different media and active learning: cooperative learning, experiments, learning projects, and other active approaches can allow students with hearing impairments to shine in areas other than language skills.

■ *Multiple access points to language:* Provide access to the written word in multiple ways—through books, magazines, written directions, lecture notes, and letters.

■ *Pretutoring* a student on a subject, or assigning the subject for reading homework before teaching it in class, can be very useful in enabling the student to contribute to the discussion.

■ *Provide copies of notes* taken by another student.

■ *Student expression:* Give students with hearing loss as many opportunities to speak as other children.

Providing Support and Encouragement. Relying on vision for all communication can be very tiring. Children who are hearing impaired are constantly watching and trying to process, understanding only part and trying to figure out the rest. It is important to be alert for signs of fatigue. If the child is too tired to comprehend, we can change the activity to give them a break.

Inclusive Schooling and Students Who are Deaf or Hard of Hearing. Fewer than 1 in 100 children have a severe hearing impairment. Many challenges exist for these students. In 1999 only 69 percent of hearing-impaired children received a high school diploma, and more than 14 percent dropped out of school before graduation (Office of Special Education Programs, 2001).

In addition, students who are deaf are among the most segregated of students with disabilities. In 1999 more than 42 percent of hearing-impaired children were taught in separate classrooms, schools, or residential facilities greater than 60 percent of the time. Special schools were developed for students who were deaf early in the twentieth century, and many adults who are deaf spent their childhood years in these residential schools. These individuals, along with professionals who teach in separate schools, have been concerned about the movement toward inclusive education (Cohen, O., 1994). They argue that the group support that exists among deaf students will not be available in a typical school and students will be isolated. On the other hand, many hearing parents of children who are deaf are insisting that they be educated in typical schools with support (Enabling Education Network, 1999). In many cases, these parents are reporting that their children are integrating well into the school community.

Some schools are moving to include students who are deaf. John H. Kinzie School in Chicago, Illinois, successfully merged a separate hearing-impaired program with the regular K–6 students that attended school there (Banks, 1994). Bloomfield Hills–Lahser High School in Michigan has for many years run a "center" program for students who are deaf within the framework of a general high school. Students who are deaf are integrated in academic and technical classes throughout the school (Peterson, 2000).

Children who are integrated with hearing students at a preschool age and are given extensive language help are less likely to feel socially isolated as they get older. Teachers and classmates can play a dramatic role in how students feel about interacting in the hearing world. Do they feel needed or wanted? Do they contribute as viable members of their community? Are adequate supports, such as sign language, offered? How we answer these questions will influence our success in including students with hearing impairments.

Blindness and Visual Impairment
Seeing a Community

We live in a society in which vision is central. Some have estimated that 85 percent of typical schooling requires the use of vision. This centrality of vision makes it difficult for many of us to imagine how we might function were we blind—a difficulty that often translates into fear of people who have visual impairments as well as a sense of panic regarding how we might include such a student in our classes. Let's explore the nature of visual impairment and ways to include these students in our classes.

What Are Blindness and Visual Impairment?

The definition of **visual impairment** in IDEA is pretty simple and straightforward:

> Visual impairment including blindness means an impairment in vision that, even with correction, adversely affects a child's educational performance. The term includes both partial sight and blindness. (Individuals with Disabilities Education Improvement Act [IDEA], 2004, section 300.7)

Some 75 percent of people with visual impairments have some functional vision, in which case the terms *partially sighted, low vision,* or simply *visually impaired* are often used. Visual problems are defined in relation to two factors: (1) visual acuity and (2) field of vision, or visual field.

Visual acuity, or sharpness of vision, is measured based on the distance from which an object can be recognized. In our country, perfect acuity is described as 20/20 vision. This means simply that an individual can see an object clearly (often a letter on a chart) at 20 feet. However, if an individual is able to read at 20 feet only what a person with 20/20 vision could read at 200 feet, we would describe that person's visual acuity as 20/200.

The term **visual field,** refers to the angles from which the eye receives sensory input. People with normal sight have a visual field of 170 degrees: 85 degrees from center for each eye. Some individuals have narrow visual fields or *tunnel vision,* as low as 10 degrees. Others have limited vision in the center of the visual field but have *peripheral vision.* This means they can't see straight ahead but can see a small area to either side (Gething, 1992).

The word **blindness** means to most people the inability to see at all in any functional way. However, many people considered blind still perceive some light or shapes. People who have **low vision** or who are **partially sighted** are considered *legally blind* (one of the most important impacts of which is the legal inability to drive a car) when their visual acuity is better than 20/200 but not better than 20/70 in the best eye after correction with lenses, or when their visual field is less than 20 degrees (Vaughn, Bos, & Schumm, 1997). Actual ability to use vision varies with individuals. It is helpful to simply ask a person how well they can see—in terms of light, shapes, acuity, and visual field.

Causes of Visual Impairment. Visual impairment has many causes, among them diseases, injury, and occasionally genetics. In the 1960s an epidemic of rubella resulted in thousands of children's being born blind and deaf–blind (Hardman, Drew, & Egan, 1996). Although some 20 percent of the U.S. population has some sort of visual problem, most defects are corrected adequately with eyeglasses or surgery. Nelson and Dimitrova (1993) estimate that 1.5 percent of school-age children have vision loss significant enough to require special assistance. However, the vast majority of people with visual impairments are older adults, as eyes degenerate with age.

Types of Visual Impairments. Visual impairments are of three types: (1) *refractive problems* involving the lens of the eye; (2) *muscle disorders* that affect the ability to focus; and (3) *receptive problems* associated with degeneration or damage to the retina and/or optic nerve. We are most familiar with *refractive problems* such as farsightedness (hyperopia) and nearsightedness (myopia); in these conditions, respectively, an individual sees well at distances but not at close range or well at close range but not at a distance. Other refractive problems include *astigmatism,* which results in lack of clarity and distortion of visual images, and *cataracts,* in which the lens becomes opaque. Cataracts are likely to develop with age and can often be corrected with surgery.

Muscle disorders include *nystagmus* (uncontrolled rapid eye movement), strabismus (crossed eyes), and *amblyopia* (an eye that appears normal but does not properly function) (Hardman, Drew, & Egan, 1996).

Numerous *receptive disorders* exist. *Optic atrophy* involves degeneration of the nerve fibers that connect the retina to the brain. *Retinitis pigmentosa* is a hereditary dsorder; it begins with night blindness and progresses to total blindness as the retina degenerates. *Retinal detachment* causes total blindness. Finally, *retinopathy of prematurity* (previously known as retrolental fibroplasia), damage to the retina caused by the administration of excessive oxygen to premature infants, has largely ceased but once was a significant cause of blindness in young children.

Specialists and Treatment. Several professional specialties provide assistance to people who are blind or visually impaired:

- **Ophthamologists** are physicians who specialize in diseases, treatment, and functioning of the eye.
- **Optometrists** prescribe corrective lenses for visual difficulties. However, many of these individuals do not have training related to various *low-vision aids* for individuals with more significant sight loss.
- **Low-vision specialists** often work in special centers.
- *Rehabilitation teachers* help persons with blindness learn how to function at school, at home, and in the community using adaptive methods. They teach everything from braille to how to obtain taped books, how to cook safely, and how to organize school materials.
- **Assistive technology specialists** may also be trained as low-vision specialists or rehabilitation teachers.
- *Orientation and mobility specialists* help people who are blind to get around the community safely. They teach people how to use canes, sighted guides, and guide dogs. They orient a person to a new area—school grounds, a work site.
- *Special education teachers* certified to teach students who are blind and visually impaired.

We should expect assistance from specialists when blind or visually impaired students come to our class. Special education consultants and orientation and mobility specialists are often employed in countywide cooperative school districts. In addition, most states have at least one center where both children and adults receive assistance from orientation and mobility specialists, rehabilitation teachers, and low-vision or assistive technology specialists.

Strategies for Teaching Students Who Are Blind or Visually Impaired

Including students with blindness and visual impairments takes practice. However, what we do is by and large applied common sense. We use two primary strategies. First, we help students access information through sound and touch to compensate for lack of visual information. Second, we ensure that these students are an integral part of our classroom community in all activities. At best, we have the assistance of a specialist with whom we can work out an accommodations plan.

Caroline provides an example of teaching strategies with a student who is blind.

Caroline is in the third grade. She is totally blind. Over the last two summers she has gone to a rehabilitation center to learn how to use a cane. A rehabilitation teacher is available on an itinerant basis to help Caroline begin to learn skills in braille and the use of adaptive equipment. In class she has learned to get around. She is using recorded books, books in braille, and peer buddies who read aloud to her on a rotating basis. She also uses talking software and is learning how to type with the other students at the school's media center.

Kinesthetic and Activity-Based Teaching. Students who are blind or visually impaired need learning opportunities that allow them to rely on other intelligences and on senses other than sight. When we use teaching strategies that involve groups' working together, hands-on projects, and learning by doing, we give students with visual disabilities opportunities for obtaining input via touch, sound, even smell in ways that deepen and strengthen their learning (Smith, D., 1998).

Orientation and Mobility. One obvious impact of a visual disability is that difficulty in seeing makes it harder to get around in the physical environment. Orientation and mobility services are an important part of supporting learning for students with visual impairments and have recently been required for consideration in IEPs for these students.

The first thing for us to do is to learn how to be a good **sighted guide** and to help our students learn this as well. Our first instinct, taking the person by the hand and leading them around, is *not* helpful. Instead, we stand beside the person and have the person put a hand on the back of our elbow or arm. With young children, we can put our arm straight down and have them hold our arm. This allows a greater sense of independence. As we go through a narrow space, we walk first, putting our arm behind us so that the person can hang on, walking behind us. If there are overhanging obstacles, such as a low-hanging tree limb, we warn the person. When we come to stairs, we stop and say, "Stairs," then proceed up or down at a smooth pace. This becomes natural and intuitive after a very short time.

We will orient a child to our room. The student may ask us questions. The key is to walk around indicating parts of the room; then we can do likewise throughout the school. As we show different parts of our room, we want to give students with visual impairments opportunities to feel with their hands—to touch the table, the globe, and so forth. We can use directions to help in this process; for example, "Your pencil is right in front of you, about one foot." When students understand angle degrees, we can say things like "The globe is at 45 degrees left." (Think, by the way, how this helps teach basic geometry.) We might also use the numbering system on a clock face, as in "Your mashed potatoes are at twelve o'clock on your plate, and your steak is at nine." Also, if we change the layout of the room during the year, we will apprise visually impaired students of these changes so they won't be confused.

Having said this, students who are blind have several tools that can be used to aid them in their moving from place to place. An orientation and mobility specialist will provide training in these as part of the school day, after school, or during the summer:

- **Canes** can help students move safely from place to place once they have a general understanding of an area. Students learn to walk swinging the cane in front of them from side to side to feel obstacles or drop-offs. Barriers above waist level, however, cannot be detected. If you see a student about to walk into an overhanging barrier, you should warn the person gently.
- Many training programs with **guide dogs** are available throughout the country. The person and the dog learn to work as a team; however, the person is in charge and guides the general direction of the dog. Note that when a guide dog is with a person, we should not pet the dog: It is working and should not be distracted. If we have a guide dog in our room, we will need to help our students learn this as well.
- Technological aids for mobility are interesting, although still not widely used.

Reading. What we do in schools is largely based on reading. Obviously, blind students can't see the text. So what do we do? Several options are available that use two general avenues—touch and sound.

Braille. Braille uses touch: different arrangements of raised dots on a six-dot pattern that represent different letters. Reading braille is much slower than visual reading. Braille is difficult to learn and is used by a small percentage of people who are blind. Nevertheless, braille is a very effective tool for some. We can get books brailled through the Library of Congress and through local groups. In addition to **braillers** (braille typewriters), braille printers for computers are available. We work with specialists to consider how a particular student will be instructed in the use of braille. This may occur on a pull-out basis during literacy time—or, at best, we can incorporate the services of a specialist into the context of our total class. Many students also attend specialized summer training programs in rehabilitation centers where they learn braille.

Optacon. An optacon scans text and converts the letters into vibrating tactile replicas.

Auditory Strategies. Strategies based on hearing can be used with any student who is blind but who can hear. Auditory tools include:

- *Talking computer:* In Chapter 15 we review software and hardware combinations by which any text on the computer can be spoken.
- *Kurzweil scanner:* This machine scans text and converts it to synthesized speech.
- *Tape-recorded text:* We can tape-record information. Tapes are available for many books. Many blind people use variable-speed tape recorders that allow them to listen to text at different paces to increase their "reading speed."
- *Sighted readers:* Readers often work with people who are blind. Sometimes special education or vocational rehabilitation funds are available to provide readers. We also can make arrangements for peers to assist the student, perhaps alternating this across students in the class. Additionally, reading services could be provided by a teacher or a paraprofessional.

Large Print for Partially Sighted Students. For students who are not blind but partially sighted, we also can use approaches based on enlarged print. These include:

- *Large-print books.*
- *Low-vision aids:* Magnifiers include hand-held magnifiers, desktop units, and devices designed to be used with computers.
- *Computer software and enlarged printouts:* Software is available that will increase the size of text and graphics on the monitor screen and will print enlarged text.
- *Closed-circuit television (CCTV):* A camera is pointed at printed text and magnifies it on a television screen.

Writing. Several workable alternatives to handwriting exist for students with visual impairments:

- *Tape recorder:* Students can tape-record their work. However, listening to taped material takes much more time for teachers than would reading written material.
- *Typing:* Work can be typed on a typewriter or word processor.
- *Sighted writer:* A sighted person takes dictation, then transcribes the material for the individual who is blind.
- *Computer software:* Sortware allows an individual to dictate responses, which are recorded in a word processer and can then be printed.

Organizing and Accessing Materials. Students with visual disabilities may need assistance in learning how to organize and access materials. Useful tactics include:

- Brailled tabs or other tactile tabs on materials so they can be identified via touch.
- Efficient organizing of materials where they are kept in routine locations.

Participation in Class Activities. So much of typical teaching relies heavily on vision that we need to be constantly aware of the need to ensure the full participation of a student with blindness or visual impairment. Some considerations include:

  Class discussions, lectures, and presentations: We want to watch for visual information that other students are receiving but that the student with a visual impairment is not. Sometimes we can give tactile (touch) alternatives. Often we will need to explain in words what is going on. We should involve both the student and the class in helping to figure this out.

Schools to Visit

Peer Tutoring at an Inclusive High School

Santana High School
9915 Magnolia Avenue
Santee, CA 92071
Phone: 619-448-5500
www.guhsd.net

Santana High School is located in Santee, in Southern California. Approximately 1,800 students attend the school. Diversity in the classrooms exists not so much in racial differences as in ability levels, as students receiving special education services in the "moderate–severe handicapped" program are enrolled in general education classes. At Santana all students with significant disabilities attend classes according to their grade level, not according to their disability, and have done so since the early 1990s.

This high school provides a variety of supports to students with disabilities. The most essential is peer tutoring. Santana offers a peer tutoring course as an elective toward graduation credit. In the course students from grades 9 through 12 are paired with and assist students with moderate to severe disabilities in general education courses. Peer tutors attend the general education classes in which the student with a disability is enrolled; their sole responsibility is to support the student with the disability, both academically and socially.

In addition to receiving ongoing training and support provided by special educators, peer tutors participate in five formal trainings throughout the eighteen-week term. These trainings focus on in-formation pertaining to inclusion, curriculum modification, support strategies, the use of people-first language (e.g., "a person with a disability," not "a disabled person"), forms of communication, and a variety of learning disabilities. Major emphases of training are on respect and on empowering the student being supported. Students learn to strive for social justice for people with disabilities and to celebrate human diversity.

The trainings encourage peer tutors to develop an understanding of people with disabilities, and this understanding results in better support for students. The response from the peer tutors during group discussions is phenomenal. They truly recognize that the students they are assisting are individuals just like themselves and their peers. Trainings are specifically designed to encourage and guide the peer tutors to come to this realization on their own.

Although the objective of the peer tutoring course is to provide support to students with disabilities who are included in general education courses, many other benefits also have evolved. The general school population experiences increased opportunities to interact with people with a variety of ability levels. General education students discover the commonalities they share with people with disabilities. Peer tutors also increase their own knowledge of the subject matter of classes as they provide tutoring. Friendships are developed; academics are effectively taught; and, most importantly, individual needs are being met in a supportive, inclusive environment.

By Rebecca Bond and Liz Castagnera.

Videos and films: We can have a student interpret what is visually being shown on the screen. If we are stopping the video periodically to discuss what is going on, we can briefly describe what is being discussed.

Measurement devices: Many measuring devices are available that have either tactile markers or synthesized speech.

Peer supports: We want students with visual disabilities to give as much assistance as they receive so that relationships are reciprocal. For example, students can be peer buddies, serve as members of circles of support, and/or do cross-age tutoring.

Class membership and emotional well-being. One of the most difficult problems for people who are blind or visually impaired is the rejection they experience. We work to welcome students with visual impairments as class members. We also will guard against pitying them. Class meetings, small group discussions, and peer mediation can be helpful.

Inclusive Schooling and Children with Blindness or Visual Impairment. Residential schools for blind children were developed in the early twentieth century and often located in the state capital. Many blind children grew up in such residential schools. Other special services for people who are blind were established early. For example, sheltered industries where 75 percent of the workforce had, by law, to be people with visual disabilities were established early in the twentieth century (Javits-Wagner-O'Day Act as Amended, 1994). At present a national network of programs employs blind people in segregated work settings. Such workplaces receive preferences in bidding on contracts with the federal government. In addition, numerous regulations and statutes give special support to people who are blind, including tax deductions and social security disability insurance benefits.

Until 1950 blind children in special schools outnumbered those in typical public schools by a ratio of 10 to 1 (Hardman, Drew, & Egan, 1996). Since 1980, however, the population of schools for children who are blind has dropped dramatically. Many such schools now house only a small number of children with the most severe disabilities. In 1993 a coalition of eight professional organizations drafted a statement in which they opposed full inclusion of students with visual impairments as the primary educational option for such students. Others, however, are pushing for full inclusion of students with visual disabilities.

Orthopedic Impairment
Beauty Is in the Eye of the Beholder

Many states have grouped students with orthopedic and other health impairments under a category they label "physical and other health impairments (POHI)" in their special education services. This section will discuss common orthopedic disabilities. IDEA defines orthopedic handicaps in the following way:

"Orthopedic impairment" means a severe orthopedic impairment that adversely affects a child's educational performance. The term includes impairments caused by congenital anomaly (e.g., clubfoot, absence of some member, etc.), impairments caused by disease (e.g., poliomyelitis, bone tuberculosis, etc.), and impairments from other causes (e.g., cerebral palsy, amputations, and fractures or burns that cause contractures). (Individuals with Disabilities Education Improvement Act [IDEA], 2004, section 300.7)

Cerebral Palsy

One condition we will likely see is **cerebral palsy,** a neurological condition that affects the portions of the brain that control motor movements. The condition has multiple causes that include genetics, prenatal infections of various sorts, trauma during pregnancy, and problems in the birthing process itself. Given that cerebral palsy is a result of damage to a portion of the brain, it is not surprising that people with cerebral palsy often have other disabilities as well. These may include mental retardation, seizure disorders, and visual and/or hearing impairment (Gething, 1992).

Many people with cerebral palsy have normal or very high intelligence and have distinguished themselves in their social contributions. Bob Williams, a recognized poet, leader in disability rights, and director of the Administration on Developmental Disabilities under the Clinton administration, has severe cerebral palsy that makes his speech difficult to understand and requires that he use a wheelchair. Norm Kunc (2000), an individual with mild cerebral palsy, is an internationally known consultant on social justice and a disability rights activist and is known for his ability to engage people in his speeches.

Phoebe has very severe cerebral palsy. She uses a small wheelchair and can push herself along slowly with her feet, though she cannot propel herself well and has to be pushed for going longer distances. She has a cheerful personality and is very interested in learning. She also is very interested in reading and writing. She reads all the time. Her speech is very difficult to understand. She uses the computer along with a key guard to do most of her papers; sometimes she will dictate to another student. Often people have to ask her to repeat what she has said. Her parents are caring and supportive people, though their resources are limited. She has developed some friends in the last two years.

Specialists and Treatment. Medical treatment of cerebral palsy aims to prevent further physical deformities and to improve individuals' ability to use muscles, ensure alignment of joints, and maximize good posture. Frequently orthopedic surgery will be conducted to lengthen heel cords, hamstrings, or tendons to reduce deformity and improve function (Hardman, Drew, & Egan, 1996; Stolov & Clowers, 1981). Given the multifaceted problems many people with cerebral palsy have, an interdisciplinary team of specialists is often involved. These specialists may include physical therapists, who help to improve muscle use and mobility; occupational therapists, who assist in accommodations at home, school, and work; and assistive technology specialists, who aid in the selection and use of augmentative communication and other assistive devices (Bigge, 1991; Gething, 1992; Orelove & Sobsey, 1987).

Strategies for Inclusive Teaching. Our approach to including students with cerebral palsy in our classes will vary somewhat depending on the severity and specific type of impact of each student's disability. However, some guidelines are useful.

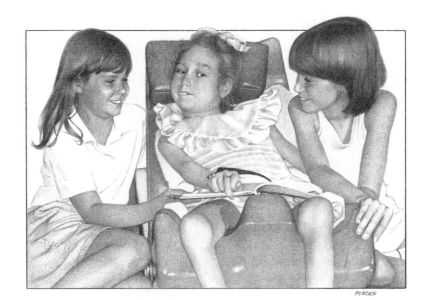

Artwork reprinted by permission of Martha Perske from *Perske: Pencil Portraits 1971–1990* (Nashville: Abingdon Press, 1998).

Communication, Listening, and Classroom Community. Students with cerebral palsy often struggle to speak. We may have difficulty understanding, and they may be embarrassed. However, just as all parents learn—with practice—to understand the barely decipherable speech of young children, so will we. Our key is to relax and listen and, when necessary, to ask the student to repeat what he or she said. If we don't understand, we can often ask the class, "Did someone understand what Sam said?" The children will often begin to understand more quickly than we will.

As we do this, several things happen at once. We are showing respect, a message not lost on our students. Our class is learning and practicing listening skills. We are also helping the self-esteem and sense of belonging of the student with cerebral palsy, thus heightening the likelihood that classmates will interact with the student on a one-on-one basis or include the student in groups (Gething, 1992; Orelove & Sobsey, 1987).

Assistive Technology. Students with severe communication problems may benefit from various augmentative communication devices and may need adaptive equipment to be able to use computers effectively, such as keyboard guards (Orelove & Sobsey, 1987).

Mobility and Movement. Some students who are only mildly affected by cerebral palsy are able to walk, though with some difficulty. Some may use crutches or braces to assist them in walking. Other students may be in wheelchairs, often motorized units that can be controlled with various types of switches. For students in wheelchairs we will want to have tables at a slightly raised height so that the wheelchair can fit under the table. These students may have difficulty grasping pencils or reaching for books, as well. The low-tech strategies discussed in Chapter 15 are helpful—

nonslip pads, shelving that allows easy access to materials. We should expect assistance from an occupational therapist in identifying useful adaptations and assistive technology (Gething, 1992; Orelove & Sobsey, 1987).

Rest Room and Feeding Assistance. Some students with cerebral palsy may need assistance in going to the rest room or in eating. Arrangements for a student can be made ahead of time as part of the student's IEP or general plan. Often a paraprofessional can assist. However, we should allow and encourage other students to assist if both parties are interested and willing. This kind of helping can be valuable if approached carefully, but we want to take care that it does not generate a relationship only of "helping" and get in the way of more reciprocal interactions. Another strategy would be to involve older students in providing this and other types of assistance in the class as part of service learning one period a day. Such a program would need to be carefully developed; it would need to include training for the students and collaboration with the families involved.

This type of assistance by students in the class can be an area of growth and learning for all. For, despite all the emphasis on physical appearance in our society, we are very hesitant to deal openly with normal bodily functions. This hesitancy is a cultural creation not shared in many parts of the world. The experiences of helping a classmate can give students an opportunity to learn how to care for another person—clearly an experience they will have later if we, their parents, live to an old age and need assistance. This experience in itself can become an important part of sharing and reflection via journals or discussion in the class.

Life Goals and Our Class. Even bright and able people with cerebral palsy have difficulty obtaining employment in a competitive economy that provides little accommodation and support in the workplace. A critical part of our role as teachers is to constantly help all our students envision their future roles in work and community. This area is particularly important for students with significant challenges. While this same theme is applicable to all students with disabilities, we can hone our skills in addressing this issue with students with cerebral palsy. We can have students explore, as part of other assignments, the types of job roles people have. Perhaps the student with cerebral palsy, and a group in the class, could study how the student might perform different jobs of interest with appropriate supports and accommodations. Or the group might interview employed people with cerebral palsy in the community.

Inclusive Schooling and Cerebral Palsy. United Cerebral Palsy (1993), a largely parent-based advocacy organization, has been one of the leading organizations promoting inclusive education in recent years. Their board of directors adopted a policy on full inclusion in 1993 that called on leaders to "invest our collective time and resources for a more inclusive society that recognizes and embraces the talents of all Americans" and, where necessary, to provide supports in the interactive arenas of assistive technology, transportation, architectural barriers, and personal assistance.

Other Orthopedic Disabilities

Numerous other orthopedic disabilities exist, although they are more infrequently encountered. Many of the guidelines for students with cerebral palsy will apply.

Spinal Cord Injuries. **Spinal cord injuries** occur when the spinal cord is damaged or severed. In very young children spinal cord injuries are most often caused by auto accidents or child abuse. With older children and adults, frequent causes include auto accidents, falls, gunshot wounds, and diving accidents. About 85 to 90 percent of people who have spinal cord injuries are males aged sixteen to thirty, largely highly active people. Some 8,000 to 10,000 spinal cord injuries occur each year (Gutierrez, Vulpe, & Young, 1994).

The effects of spinal cord injuries vary dramatically depending on the location of the injury. Essentially, the higher on the spinal cord the injury, the more disabling the effects. In addition, spinal cord injuries most often occur together with damage to other body parts. These may include traumatic brain injury (15 percent of the time), fractures (20 percent), and serious injuries to the chest (Gutierrez, Vulpe, & Young, 1994). Unless there has been a brain injury, however, the intellectual functioning of people with spinal cord injuries is not affected. Three general terms are used for individuals with different types and levels of injury:

- *Paraplegic:* The person's legs are immobilized but there is full use of the upper body and arms.
- *Quadriplegic:* Both legs and arms, as well as the upper body, are affected. The specific impacts vary with the level of the injury.
- *Hemiplegic:* The arm and leg on one side of the person's body are paralyzed.

Spinal cord injuries are traumatic events. Typically, young, active, athletic people must learn a new life. In the hospital physicians work to stabilize the spine, often with patients held in a special device that rotates them periodically. In the rehabilitation process individuals must learn new ways of managing their lives, using adaptive equipment and wheelchairs and moving from the wheelchair to a bed or couch.

Most students with spinal cord injury will not require a great deal of assistance or modification. Key needs will be desks or tables that are high enough for the wheelchair to fit underneath. In addition, we will need to help students arrange materials so that they can reach them easily. We may also need to arrange the classroom so that there is ample room for the wheelchair to traverse the room. As with students with cerebral palsy, sometimes these students will need assistance going to the rest room.

Spina Bifida. In **spina bifida** an abnormal opening in the spinal column occurs at birth. Severe spina bifida often results in weakness or paralysis in the legs and lower body and an inability to control the bladder or bowel. A very mild form of spina bifida (spina bifida occulta) is present in an estimated one-third of the population of the United States (Rowlye-Kelly & Regel, 1993). The most serious form, spina bifida myelomeningocele, often involves other orthopedic difficulties, such as club feet or dislocated hips. About 90 percent of children with severe spina bidifa also develop hydrocephalus, an excessive accumulation of cerebral fluid in the brain. Untreated, hydrocephalus will result in mental retardation. However, physicians perform surgery to install a shunt, in which a tube is inserted between the ventricles of the brain and distributes fluids to an absorption site in the child's abdomen. Although students with spina bifida have little if any control over bowel or bladder, medical professionals assist them in learning to use a catheter to manage this process (Bigge, 1991). Spina bifida does not affect intellectual abilities, and most students have traditionally been in general education classes. We need to provide access in our

Students make buildings with blocks as Ricky, a second grader with a disability, is assisted by a physical therapist.

classroom for wheelchairs; provide time, if needed, for students to deal with bowel and bladder management; and simply ensure that these students are included in our class and the school, including field trips and extracurricular activities.

Muscular Dystrophy.   The muscles of people with **muscular dystrophy** will gradually degenerate, and these individuals slowly lose their ability to walk and or to use their arms and hands effectively. With this condition, which affects only males and is caused by a complex genetic aberration, fatty tissue actually replaces muscle tissue over time. By age twenty individuals with muscular dystrophy use a wheelchair for mobility; they typically die in their twenties or thirties. About 1 in every 3,000 males is affected. Medicine has no cure, so the primary treatment consists of aiding the individual in maintaining functioning as long as possible, then providing supportive devices such as walkers, braces, and surgical corsets.

Dealing with Death

Death is a reality of life, and we can be assured that students with terminal conditions such as MD are well aware of the short time they have to live. To the degree that we can help them process and deal with their fears and their anger about their condition, we can make our class a better place for all our students. Journal writing; exploration of themes of coping and dealing with death in literature; having the student talk to the group, if he wants, about his experience of this disability and his feelings about his shortened life span—these approaches may provide important opportunities for the student to deal openly with his own life situation, and can facilitate learning for all.

Other Health Impairments
From Hospital to Community

Children have many health-related disabilities that IDEA calls "other health impairments," which mean

> having limited strength, vitality or alertness, including a heightened alertness to environmental stimuli, that results in limited alertness with respect to the educational environment; that is due to chronic or acute health problems such as asthma, attention deficit disorder or attention deficit hyperactivity disorder, diabetes, epilepsy, a heart condition, hemophilia, lead poisoning, leukemia, nephritis, rheumatic fever, and sickle-cell anemia; and adversely affects a child's educational performance. (Individuals with Disabilities Education Improvement Act [IDEA], 2004, section 300.7)

Not too many years ago, children died of serious diseases that physicians today can treat if not cure. Also not so long ago, these students would stay at home, visited weekly by a special teacher for the "homebound," then later go to a separate school. That still happens in many school systems. However, many students with other health impairments are now returning to their school community, so we will periodically have children in our classes who have a wide range of chronic medical conditions. Figure 13.1 provides a brief summary of the more common conditions.

Seizure Disorders (Epilepsy)

About 1 out of every 100 students will have some sort of seizure disorder. Although seizure disorders may occur alone, they also are frequently associated with other disabilities such as mental retardation. The terms **epilepsy** and **seizure disorder** both denote a range of disorders in which abnormal neurochemical activity in the brain produces the unusual physical and mental responses that we typically call seizures. Some have likened seizures to electrical storms in the brain. However disconcerting seizures are, they do not directly affect the person's cognitive abilities or emotional well-being. About half of individuals with seizure disorders experience an "aura," a physical sensation that a seizure may soon occur—numbness, dizziness, or slight abdominal discomfort. Seizures follow several patterns:

■ **Tonic–clonic seizures** (once known as *grand mal* seizures) cause a loss of conscious awareness, as the body goes rigid and convulsively jerks. If the person is standing, he or she will likely fall. Seizures typically do not last more than a few seconds. Once a seizure is over, the person will be tired and sometimes confused. Although the condition is not dangerous in itself, an individual may get hurt when falling or hitting desks or sharp objects with flailing hands. When a seizure occurs, or if the person has an aura, we *should* do the following (Gething, 1992; Hardman, Drew, & Egan, 1996; Stolov & Clowers, 1981):

Part II: Inclusive Teaching   www.ablongman.com/petersoninclusive

Figure 13.1

Common Chronic Health Impairments

Asthma: A common condition affecting some 3 million children. Children with asthma will have episodes of coughing, shortness of breath, and wheezing. Irritations are caused by allergies or other causes (viral infections, pollutants) but can be treated with medications and sometimes with inhalers. In some cases changes may have to be made in classrooms to rid them of allergy-causing irritants. Teachers can help students to remember to take medications, allow students to rest if an attack does occur, work with the student and parent in developing a plan, and involve other students in understanding how to respond (American Lung Association, 2000).

Cystic fibrosis: Children with cystic fibrosis have secretion glands which produce an abnormal amount of mucus, sweat, and saliva. The mucus fills the lungs, hindering their proper functioning and gradually destroying them with repeated infections. As this occurs, problems with the heart and pancreas ensue. Treatment of cystic fibrosis has vastly improved, and over half of these children now live beyond their twenties. Medical treatment focuses on the prevention of infections and management of respiratory infections. Children with cystic fibrosis often have significant psychological and social problems—their chronic coughing and small stature often tend to isolate them from other children (Walker, Durie, Hamilton, Walker-Smith, & Watkins, 1991).

Diabetes: This condition results from an inadequate supply of insulin, a hormone that is needed to help the body utilize glucose (blood sugar). Buildup of glucose in the blood can cause loss of consciousness. Immediate problems can be controlled with insulin injections and monitoring of blood sugar. However, juvenile diabetes can have serious consequences that include blindness, heart attacks, and kidney problems. 10 out of 100,000 children have diabetes (Ross, Bernstein, & Rifkin, 1983; Turnbull, Turnbull, Shank, Smith, & Leal, 2002).

Pediatric cancer: Cancer occurs in fewer than 1 in 600 children, and length of life of pediatric cancer patients is slowly climbing. However, children with cancer often die very young. Treatment involves chemotherapy, radiation, and surgery and can have many negative side effects—nausea, vomiting, diarrhea, hair loss, fatigue, and more. Students may miss school frequently and may need assistance in keeping up. They particularly need emotional support and the engagement of the teacher and students in the class (American Cancer Society, 2000).

Lead poisoning: Up to 40 percent of children in some urban low-income areas have been exposed to lead in paint and in the general environment, and studies have shown impacts on intellectual functioning and school performance (Dyer, 1993; McMichael, et al, 1988; Needleman, Schell, Bellinger, Leviton, & Allred, 1990).

Sickle-cell anemia: An inherited disorder among African Americans (1 in 600), sickle-cell anemia involves a distortion of the shape of the red blood cells. People experience extreme weakness and severe pain in the arms and legs; the condition may affect the physical growth and development of children. Most children and adults are able to lead normal lives, though periodic health crises may occur (Ezekowitz & First, 1994; Rudolph & Kamei, 1994).

■ Ease the student to the floor, preventing the student from falling and clearing an area to prevent banging against harmful objects. Put a pillow or jacket under the student's head and loosen tight-fitting clothes at the neck.

- Turn the student on his or her stomach with the head to the side so that any excess saliva can drain out.
- When the seizure has stopped, cover the student with a coat or blanket and let him or her rest.
- If the seizure lasts more than ten minutes, contact a health professional. However, this is very rare.

It is important that we help all students in the class know what to do. One or two classmates will help us support the student while the others continue their work. Likewise, we will return to our work after the seizure, periodically checking on the student. However, we *should not* place anything in the student's mouth. This can result in the student's choking, cracking teeth, or even injuring us, as their biting movements are very powerful during the seizure. (Despite popular myths, it is not possible for people to swallow their tongue!)

- **Absence seizures** (previously known as *petit mal* seizures) occur almost exclusively in young children, and students often outgrow them as they move into secondary school. In these seizures students very briefly lose consciousness. Absence seizures may appear as "staring spells" with slow rhythmic blinking of the eyes; or, more infrequently, a child might slump to the floor, returning to a state of awareness every few seconds. Such seizures may be difficult to notice at first. However, if students are "blanking out" many times an hour, they will have difficulty attending to the flow of learning. Some 40 percent of children with this seizure pattern later develop tonic–clonic seizures. If we see these patterns occurring, talk with the school nurse and parents to facilitate a medical examination.
- **Psychomotor seizures** (or *temporal lobe* seizures) are so called because a part of the brain that controls physical activity is activated. A person may stare blankly, pick at clothes, smack lips, or display more complex patterns of activity—wandering aimlessly, washing a dish over and over. In general it is best to keep an eye on the person and then let him or her rest following the seizure. Psychomotor seizures are rare in children, though almost 50 percent of adults with seizures have these types (Stolov & Clowers, 1981).
- **Focal and Jacksonian seizures** occur in only one part of the body, producing, for example, difficulty in speaking for a period of time. The Jacksonian seizure is a specific type of focal seizure in which one part of the face, arm, or leg begins to jerk (Stolov & Clowers, 1981).

The pattern for seizures varies for each student. We will want to talk openly with the student and parents and get information from them about what happens and how best to respond. Questions might include:

- How often do your seizures typically occur? How long do they last?
- Are there stimuli that help set off the seizures? (Heat, stress, and light patterns can all have this effect.)
- How do you act when you have a seizure? What is best for us to do?
- Do you need or want to rest after seizures? For how long?
- What else should we know?

We can also plan together regarding how we might share information with the class and others. We want to involve the whole class in supporting the student with seizures in a respectful way. If having seizures can become just another difference, then we will do much to support the emotional health and self-esteem of these students. We engage the class in planning ahead for seizures and promote discussion in a calm manner. However, we want classmates to be able to share their feelings about the seizures in supportive ways. Sharing helps students with seizures feel accepted for who they are and helps other students obtain complete information.

Seizures can be caused by a variety of circumstances—trauma, brain injury, infections, fevers, poison (such as lead poisoning or high use of alcohol), and more. In some cases, however, the cause is not known. Students with other conditions, such as mental retardation or cerebral palsy, may have seizures as well. Seizure disorders appear at different times throughout the life span. Some 30 percent begin at birth to age five; another 34 percent in elementary school; 13 percent in secondary school; and a final 23 percent in the adult years (Gething, 1992).

Seizures are controlled through drug use in some 80 percent of people (Cornelius, 1980). However, medication can have some side effects—drowsiness, skin problems, or interactions with other drugs such as alcohol. In some people, too, drugs are able only partially to control seizures. A physician, usually a neurologist, will prescribe medications for the student.

Historically, the reactions of others are the biggest problem of people with epilepsy. People often draw back, fear that the condition is contagious, and stigmatize those who have seizures. Consequently, people with epilepsy may struggle with employment, relationships, and feelings of low self-worth. In a class that builds community and in which we promote open acceptance of students, we will do much to enhance the quality of life of a student with epilepsy.

Acquired Immune Deficiency Syndrome (AIDS)

In recent decades perhaps no health condition has caused so much concern as has **acquired immune deficiency syndrome (AIDS).** Throughout the world the number of cases is growing dramatically; in certain countries of Africa, the incidence of the disease has reached overwhelming epidemic proportions. AIDS results when the human immunodeficiency virus (HIV) attacks the body's immune system, leaving the person vulnerable to infections or cancers.

The Centers for Disease Control (2001) has estimated that in the United States some 2 percent of children under the age of thirteen and 4 percent of children aged thirteen to nineteen have the HIV virus. Although young children represent only 2 percent of recognized cases of AIDS, it is expected that the numbers of children infected will continue to grow. In young children HIV is transmitted largely prenatally or during birth. However, only 30 percent of mothers infected with the HIV virus pass it on to their children. Adolescents acquire the virus largely through sexual contact or by using contaminated needles to inject drugs.

HIV/AIDS involves several stages over a number of years. For many years there may be no sign of the disease at all. At some point, however, the immune system will begin to break down and the person will be susceptible to infections and illnesses. Eventually the immune system collapses and the person dies of infections or tumors.

Reasonable precautions can ensure safety. The disease cannot be transmitted via casual contact; it is most often transmitted via sexual contact or other intense forms of contact with blood and/or body fluids. The following summary guidelines were developed to prevent transmission of *any* contagious disease (Centers for Disease Control, 1988; Gross, 1999):

- Handle blood only with latex or other nonpermeable disposable gloves.
- Ensure that bloody material and gloves are disposed of in a tightly sealed, child-proof container.
- Wash hands and any contaminated body areas immediately with soap and water.
- Clean surfaces and solid objects that may be contaminated and use dustpan and broom, tweezers, and so on to pick up sharp objects that may be contaminated.
- Hand washing without the use of gloves is sufficient for contact with feces, nasal secretions, sputum, sweat, saliva, tears, urine, and vomit unless tinged with blood.
- Seek medical attention for any significant exposure to blood of a person.

Based on highly visible court actions, most schools have established policies for inclusion of students with HIV. In general, information about a student's HIV status does not have to be disclosed. It is important that we maintain confidentiality regarding a student. Depending on their status and the stage of the disease, students with HIV/AIDS may be absent because of illness and medical problems. Their energy level may be low, and we may need to make adaptations by reducing their workload or finding other ways to reduce stress. These students may have difficulty with feelings of depression and be concerned about death. Our efforts to support them if they are willing to involve our total class will be important.

Stepping Stones

To Inclusive Teaching

1. Journal about your experiences with and feelings toward people who have physical or sensory disabilities. What feelings do you have? Fear, embarrassment? Admiration? How do these feelings affect your behavior toward students with such disabilities?

2. Do students with severe physical disabilities go to your school? If so, what do you feel you most need to learn to help teach such students better? Make a plan that identifies two learning goals for this year.

3. If students with physical disabilities are not in your school, find out where they go. Visit that school. Make it known that you are interested in including a student with a severe physical disability in your classroom. Let people know of your concerns and interest. Develop a plan and keep a journal as you learn with this student.

4. Seek out adults who have one or more physical disabilities. Talk with them about their school experiences and get their ideas about how to start off teaching such students. You might have them share with your students on career day or come to read to the class so that students can see role models who have disabilities.

Embracing Students Who Look Different

So many different types of students, with so many different problems in their lives. The truth is that even if all students with sensory and physical disabilities were included, we wouldn't see students with all of these types of conditions, even over several years. Ultimately, however, over the course of a teaching career, we will have many of these students in our class. Obviously, this chapter has provided only a short introduction. However, we hope that you see the connection between a foundation of good teaching practices and the inclusion of these students—who need schools in which to grow and develop, gain friendships, and become who they can be.

 Key Points

- An inclusive class will, over time, have students with many different types of communication problems and/or other physical and sensory disabilities. This chapter has provided some basic information. As we have students in our classes we'll learn more about their specific disabilities and needs.

- Students may have many different types of difficulties in communicating—in effectively creating speech sounds and in communicating and understanding meaning—difficulties that often affect their self-esteem.

- Speech therapists work with students with communication disorders. They can provide support for language development and even work on articulation issues in small groups in our class.

- Students with severe and multiple disabilities will benefit greatly from being part of our classroom community. By using multilevel teaching and engaging our class in problem solving, we can find a valuable place for these students in the class.

- Students who are hearing impaired often feel isolated because of their difficulties in communicating. Sign language interpreters can help such students. They can also help us and our other students learn some sign language.

- Students who are blind will need the most help accessing written information and understanding other visual information; they will also need assistance in becoming oriented to our classroom and the school. Helpful strategies range from assistive technology, including talking computers and text scanners, to human helpers such as readers or sighted guides.

- We may have students with orthopedic impairments or many other different types of physical disabilities or health impairments in our classes. Their needs vary depending on their conditions. We'll need to obtain additional information from family and medical personnel.

 Learning Expeditions

Following are some activities that may extend your learning and thinking about working with students who have physical and sensory challenges.

1. Seek out a school and classroom that has one or more students with the kind of disabilities described in this chapter. Observe how the students are being included. Talk with the teacher. What are the students and their classmates doing? What challenges are apparent? With what are you particularly impressed or concerned?

2. Visit your state's school for the deaf or blind. Observe classes there. Ask the staff what they think about inclusive education. Then visit a school that has deaf or blind students included. What are the issues? What do you think should happen?

3. Go to a local children's hospital that deals with various types of chronic disorders—heart disease, cancer, epilepsy. Obtain permission to observe an interdisciplinary team conducting an evaluation of a child. How does what you see inform your thinking about teaching these students?

4. Interview an adult who is blind and an adult who is deaf. As them about their school life, their life as an adult, their opinions about the move toward inclusive education. What do you learn that might help you as an inclusive teacher? What are the issues?

5. Visit a group meeting of parents of children with special needs—children in any of the categories in this chapter. What do people discuss? What attitudes and what needs do you hear expressed? What did you learn about being an inclusive teacher of these children?

CHAPTER OBJECTIVES

1. Understand universal design and the principles of healthy learning environments.

2. Recognize schoolwide methods of using and designing space.

3. Explore and identify classroom approaches to using space, technology, and resources to respond to students' learning styles and abilities.

4. Examine strategies for community-based learning experiences.

Developing an 14 Inclusive Learning Environment

Using Space and Physical Resources to Support All Students

The first of the year is always hard and exciting all at once. We come into our classroom and look around at the bare walls and the boxes and boxes of materials. "How will the year go?" we wonder. We imagine the room filled with students. How do we arrange the physical environment of our classroom to promote effective teaching of diverse students? That's what this chapter is about. Let's first visit two schools that are working hard to develop positive learning environments.

A high school for learning: We are impressed by the attractiveness of Santa Fe High School. Walking through the entrance, we see bright banners proclaiming WE ARE A LEARNING COMMUNITY in the commons area, a large open area at the building entrance next to the principal's office. Part of this commons area is the cafeteria, which has movable tables that can be folded away as needed for community and extracurricular events. As we visit classrooms, we discover that many rooms are connected to encourage interdisciplinary teaching. Students are working at tables in groups; others are working at computers using software that converts text to spoken language. Another student, who does not read or write well, is working with a partner on a story, dictating it into a computer that converts speech to text. Teachers are organized in interdisciplinary teams—each team including science, social studies, language arts, art, and special education. Students are also divided: into "colleges" of some 200 students each, with whom the same team of teachers will work for all three years. There are no special education rooms in the school. A learning resource center is staffed by a teacher and a counselor and is available for any students at any time during the day. This is a fun room where students can study, get special help, take adapted tests, or just hang out.

This school seems like home. We are struck by how warm Edwardo Elementary School feels. The office feels open and comfortable; secretaries welcome all who come in with a genuine smile, and the principal chats with children, teachers, and parents. We are particularly interested in the book projects displayed throughout the entrance hall, with students' artistic renderings or other representations of parts of books they have read. Classrooms, too, are filled with student work—not only on the walls but also hanging from ceilings. We also see all sorts of children—one in a wheelchair, another with a sign language interpreter. The student in the wheelchair has a communication device that speaks for her. Her friends are learning to use this device. Again, there are no special education classes in this school; special education teachers and paraprofessionals spend most of their time teaming with general education teachers in the classroom. We want to come visit again.

Traveling Notes

1. What makes you feel comfortable in a school? What reactions did you have as we visited these two schools? What lessons are there regarding how we might build environments for learning, care, and growth?

2. Some buildings are difficult for anyone to get around, especially someone who uses a wheelchair or who has limited strength. Some schools are so crowded and noisy that there's no place to be alone at all. What do we do if we work in such a school?

3. How can we use the resources we have to make our learning environment supportive of learning for all children?

Environments have a big impact on our lives, and we put a lot of time and energy into arranging them. Yet so much of our teaching environment often feels given, unchangeable—a large, older high school building, a dreary classroom, inaccessible steps. Even so, we can always shape our environment as well as be shaped by it. Our goal is to structure the learning environment, to the degree possible, to support best practices in teaching and learning. What will make an environment most conducive to teaching diverse learners well together? What will enable us to use best practices in teaching and learning? What specific tools can we use to create effective inclusive learning environments? We will address these questions in this chapter.

The Learning Environment
A Tool for Learning and Growth

What is our learning environment? As teachers, we may automatically answer, "Our classroom, of course!" We suggest that our learning environment is much more. At minimum, our "extended classroom" encompasses (1) the school building and grounds, (2) the classroom, and (3) the community surrounding the school. If we think of our learning environment in this way, we will find numerous ways to use these many places and spaces to structure learning. This chapter will discuss each of these learning environments in order. First, however, let's think in a more general way about what is needed for students of diverse abilities to learn together. Two interactive frameworks are helpful: (1) universal design and (2) guidelines for healthy environments. Let's discuss each of these.

Universal Design

Architects and other design professionals are using a new concept to inform the shaping and organization of space and resources—*universal design*. Like the concept of designing teaching for diversity, on which this book is based, universal design involves a conceptual revolution. In the past, environments and products have most often been designed to fit the physical characteristics of average human beings. In contrast, universal designers seek to develop "products and environments to be usable by all people, to the greatest extent possible, without the need for adaptation or specialized design" (Steinfeld, 1994). Here are a few examples:

- Ramps and automatic doors are helpful not only to people in wheelchairs but also to many other people who must struggle with stairs or heavy doors—shoppers with packages, parents pushing strollers, older people with canes.
- Talking software, originally developed for people with visual impairments, is being marketed for all people. In some technical devices the talking computer interfaces have increased productivity by some 25 percent.
- Recorded books, long used by blind people, are now commercially marketed for travelers; people who enjoy listening to books read aloud; and people with limited reading challenges, such as individuals with learning disabilities.

The Center for Universal Design (Connell et al., 1997) developed seven principles for designing environments and products to take into account the full diversity of human abilities (Figure 14.1). These principles constitute a powerful set of statements that can help us evaluate our present teaching practices and the way that the learning environment either contributes to or detracts from inclusive teaching.

Universal design is being applied to some degree in the architectural design of schools, particularly with the explosion of technology. We can involve our students

Figure 14.1

The Principles of Universal Design

PRINCIPLE 1: EQUITABLE USE

The design is useful and marketable to people with diverse abilities.
1a. Provide the same means of use for all users: identical whenever possible, equivalent when not.
1b. Avoid segregating or stigmatizing any users.
1c. Provisions for privacy, security, and safety should be equally available to all users.
1d. Make the design appealing to all users.

PRINCIPLE 2: FLEXIBILITY IN USE

The design accommodates a wide range of individual preferences and abilities.
2a. Provide choice in methods of use.
2b. Accommodate right- or left-handed use.
2c. Facilitate the user's accuracy and precision.
2d. Provide adaptability to the user's pace.

PRINCIPLE 3: SIMPLE AND INTUITIVE USE

Use of the design is easy to understand, regardless of the user's experience, knowledge, language skills, or current concentration level.
3a. Eliminate unnecessary complexity.
3b. Make use consistent with user expectations and intuition.
3c. Accommodate a wide range of literacy and language skills.
3d. Arrange information consistent with importance.
3e. Provide effective prompting and feedback during and after task completion.

PRINCIPLE 4: PERCEPTIBLE INFORMATION

The design communicates necessary information effectively to the user, regardless of ambient conditions or the user's sensory abilities.
4a. Use different modes (pictorial, verbal, tactile) to provide redundant presentation of essential information.
4b. Provide adequate contrast between essential information and its surroundings.
4c. Maximize "legibility" of essential information.
4d. Differentiate elements in ways that can be described (i.e., make it easy to give instructions or directions).
4e. Provide compatibility with a variety of techniques or devices used by people with sensory limitations.

PRINCIPLE 5: TOLERANCE FOR ERROR

The design minimizes hazards and the adverse consequences of accidental or unintended actions.
5a. Arrange elements to minimize hazards and errors: Most used elements should be most accessible; hazardous elements should be eliminated, isolated, or shielded.
5b. Provide warnings of hazards and errors.
5c. Provide fail-safe features.
5d. Discourage unconscious action in tasks that require vigilance.

PRINCIPLE 6: LOW PHYSICAL EFFORT

The design can be used efficiently and comfortably and with a minimum of fatigue.
6a. Allow user to maintain neutral body position.
6b. Use reasonable operating forces.
6c. Minimize repetitive actions.
6d. Minimize sustained physical effort.

PRINCIPLE 7: SIZE AND SPACE FOR APPROACH AND USE

Appropriate size and space is provided for approach, reach, manipulation, and use, regardless of user's body size, posture, or mobility.
7a. Provide a clear line of sight to important elements for any seated or standing user.
7b. Make reach to all components comfortable for any seated or standing user.
7c. Accommodate variations in hand and grip size.
7d. Provide adequate space for the use of assistive devices or personal assistance.

Source: Connell et al. (1997).

Figure 14.2

Toward Universal Design of Learning Environments

	SCHOOL	CLASSROOM	COMMUNITY
Academic	■ Student work all over the building ■ Total school staff who see themselves as supporting student learning ■ Effective library and media center that is accessible to students and offers materials at many different levels ■ Computers in the media center that have talking software, speech to text, scanners, etc.	■ Books and other resources for different ability levels ■ Talking computer software ■ Multiple tools to use to express learning—speech-to-text software, graphics, audiotapes ■ Sound amplification devices; FM receivers available as needed ■ Visual magnification devices available; large-print display and software for computers ■ Sign language offered as a foreign language class	■ Mentors who come into the school and read or do investigations with students ■ Community organizations that host student learning activities ■ Accessible playgrounds and museums
Social–emotional	■ Welcoming place—student and staff greeters ■ Parent and community volunteers ■ Supportive and caring culture ■ Cheerful building with work of students highlighted throughout	■ Places to work together, or alone in privacy ■ Peer buddies ■ Circles of support ■ Student participation in organizing and decorating of room ■ Classrooms filled with student work	■ Local places where businesspeople and community members welcome students ■ After-school mentors and circles ■ After-school programs involving community members and parents
Sensory–physical	■ Wheelchair access ■ Clear signs using both words and pictures ■ Displays of student work that encourage looking, touching	■ Talking software and input devices ■ Braille printout from computers ■ Places for movement in the class ■ Allowance for drink and food ■ Clear labels for materials in the class with picture cues ■ Spaces for wheelchair access	■ Accessible playground equipment ■ Accessible public buildings and businesses

in answering the basic question: "How do we arrange our physical environment in ways that meet our needs and promote learning among students of different abilities, races, and cultures?"

Figure 14.2 provides some ideas for using the principles of universal design to shape environments so that they are accessible and encouraging to all students, limiting the need for individual accommodations. Notice that the chart uses the three environments of school, classroom, and community in interaction with the three key areas around which we have structured this book—(1) academic learning, (2) social–emotional needs, and (3) physical–sensory abilities. This chart offers ideas to get you started as you plan your class at the beginning of the year.

Healthy Learning Environments

Architects say that "form follows function." In other words, if our environment is to be effective, it should be structured based on the functions that we want it to perform (Greenman, 1988; Meek, 1995). If we see our classroom as a place of control, the environment will be structured to control. If we see our classroom as a place of joy, fun, choice, and learning, the room will come bit by bit to look this way. If we seek to design inclusive learning environments, we also ensure that our environment promotes health and well-being; stimulates optimum intellectual, emotional, and physical functioning; and aids us in implementing best practices for teaching and learning. Figure 14.3 lists some guidelines drawn from literature on universal design, healthy environments, and school design. Let's look briefly at each guideline.

Stimulate Positive Awareness of Ourselves and Our Students. At best our school and class are tools through which students can become more aware of who they are—places of student self-expression where young people can better understand themselves. On any given day, students see their own products. When we visited Mitchell Elementary School to observe student-led conferences, one fourth grader spent an hour showing her work—literally walking through the classroom, showing her work located on tables, walls, and the ceiling. This student clearly felt ownership of this classroom and saw expressions of her inner self all over the room.

Figure 14.3

Guidelines for Healthy Learning Environments

1. Stimulate positive awareness of ourselves and our students.
2. Enhance our connections with nature, culture, and people.
3. Do us no physical harm.
4. Be beautiful and inviting.
5. Provide for meaningful, varying stimuli.
6. Encourage times of relaxation and privacy.
7. Balance constancy and flexibility.
8. Use resources flexibly for multiple purposes.

Enhance Our Connections with Nature, Culture, and People. Our learning environment helps us develop multiple connections—with varied peoples, with cultural expressions, with nature. Our school is filled with the art, music, and literature of varied cultures—particularly those in our local area.

In an inclusive school, our students connect with classmates from various cultural and socioeconomic backgrounds as well as with youngsters with disabilities.

Do Us No Physical Harm. It might seem almost too obvious to state, but we don't want our environment to hurt us. Unfortunately, this requirement is sometimes not met. In many older schools, buildings still contain lead or asbestos that can have negative effects on the well-being of children. Similarly, the neighborhoods in which some children live are physically unhealthy. If we work in such situations, we will face many challenges and will need to work hard in our own classroom and to interact with local community people to deal with these issues. In any classroom, however, it is our responsibility to organize our space so it is as safe as possible.

Be Beautiful and Inviting. Carol Venolia (1988, p. 15) stated that "the creation and experience of beauty is immediate, whole, and healing. It enlivens our senses, warms our hearts, relaxes us, and puts us at one with the entire surroundings." A beautiful environment can help stimulate students and help promote a sense of safety and security (Greenman, 1988; Mann, 1997; Meek, 1995).

Provide for Meaningful, Varying Stimuli. We allow for multiple ways for students to be grouped and move about the classroom and school and draw on multiple intelligences to ensure that students have many ways to obtain information, express themselves, and learn. We establish locations where students can talk, be alone, read quietly, make noise, sit, run, and jump. We have a working space for projects involving the integration of literacy, art, music, dance, and drama.

Encourage Times of Relaxation and Privacy. Teachers and students need space and time for periodic relaxation and privacy, allowing students to regroup, to let their minds settle. Although this guideline may seem very difficult to implement in a crowded school, we can find ways if we are creative. Students need places to be alone—to think, read, or even cry.

Balance Constancy and Flexibility. The brain-based need for "relaxed alertness" (see Chapter 6) means that there is ongoing interaction between involvement in challenging activities and the ability to move away. In physical terms, it also means that we periodically change the environment—displaying new student work, shifting tables for a special project—but also maintain stability and predictability. The brain needs both novelty and security for learning—and our skill in providing both opportunities for stimulation and stability will help establish conditions for the linkages of academic learning, emotional calm, and community building.

Use Resources Flexibly for Multiple Purposes. Space and physical resources are often categorized as fulfilling one function, for example copy room and hall. However, if we are designing healthy environments, we realize that any space can be effectively used in multiple ways. Because resources are limited, such flexible and creative use of space has the effect of expanding our capacity. For example, some teachers assign each desk to one student.

Two students read together under the teacher's desk. Using all the space in the classroom in creative ways makes learning fun and more effective.

The School
Creating a Welcoming Place for All

Trends in school design reflect our evolving images of school. In the early twentieth century, the idea that bigger is better—and more efficient—was dominant. That period was the time of the growth of large industries. It also was the time when many elementary schools were built to house more than 1,000 children and when high schools were designed to dominate local neighborhoods. In these buildings desks were arranged in precise rows, often bolted to the floor (Meek, 1995). Today, however, our understanding of the connection between social interactions and learning has greatly shifted our thinking about how to design space. Let's survey the elements of a welcoming school.

A Welcoming Place to Be. We want to promote a spirit of community and common ownership rather than seeing the school as belonging only to the power structure. This spirit is communicated in the smallest matters. We display student work prominently on walls and in display cases. Artwork, essays, photographs of a class play or of community projects, and student work reflect the cultural and ethnic diversity of the area. Colors are attractive and bright rather than institutional green. We post signs of welcome and encouragement throughout the building, many made by students. Our school office has comfortable chairs and an open, inviting atmosphere (Greenman, 1988; Meek, 1995).

Commons. A **commons area** may be located in a central area of the building with park benches, water fountains, and other amenities to encourage conversation and interaction. A commons gives students a place to gather before and after school and at lunch, and serves as a gathering point for groups. Schools often intentionally locate their commons next to the school administration office to convey a sense of openness, and administrators often interact informally with students and parents (Greenman, 1988; Meek, 1995).

School within a School. A smaller school size, optimally 100 to 200 students, can make a big difference in students' sense of community (Meek, 1995). Large high schools were designed to provide adequate numbers for many programs; increasingly, however, smaller schools are being built, or schools are being designed to allow the student body to be broken into smaller groups. Schools often seek to arrange space where these teachers can work together in flexible ways—linking classrooms in older buildings by doors or cutaways, placing offices between classrooms where teachers can work together, or fitting rooms with movable walls that allow teachers to combine their classes or work separately.

Parent and Community Center. It is very helpful to have a designated space where parents and community members can work, study, or just be while in the school. This space can be a separate room, or it can be part of an area such as the media center (library) or support staff offices.

Media Center/Library. In many ways, the media center is the heart of the school. In many schools media specialists run programs to help students learn the basics of word processing, using the Internet, and accessing information. Media specialists can also be a fount of useful information on ways to integrate computer use into the classrooms; on teacher- and child-friendly Internet sites to explore; and on books to use for any purpose, from a read aloud on a certain subject to literature circles.

Space and Inclusive Classes. Schools can send powerful messages about who belongs and who does not. The "special education class" or "resource room" is often down at the end of the hall. Students cycle in and out the speech therapist's office. Talk to almost any student who has been in these special places and they can tell you of the fear, dread, and embarrassment they feel.

Jordan, a student who was placed in a special education room when he was in the fifth grade, was terribly ashamed and simply would not stay in the room. He wandered the halls to prevent his former classmates from seeing him in the special education room and making fun of him. He was eventually kicked out of several schools and sent to a special education center—where his fondest dream was to go to a "regular" high school.

In an inclusive school we do not have special classes for students with labels. Rather, students are heterogeneously mixed in general education classes. Figure 14.4 contrasts uses of space in inclusive and segregated schools, classrooms, and communities.

Figure 14.4

Segregated and Inclusive Uses of Space

INCLUSIVE	SEGREGATED
SCHOOL	
■ There are no special education, bilingual, or Title I classrooms. Specialists are housed as teams in offices. ■ Technology and "specials" are integrated into ongoing classroom instruction, and special and general education classroom teachers work together to integrate instruction.	■ The school has special classes for special education, bilingual, and Title I classes that are most often at the end of the hall. ■ Specialists' offices are separate from those of the rest of the school staff.
CLASSROOM	
■ Students work in groups at tables or clusters of desks; there is a hum of activity. ■ Groups of students include diverse ability levels, ethnic and cultural groups, genders. ■ Students' work covers the walls, hangs from the ceiling, is displayed outside the room. ■ Students are seen in many places—at desks and tables, sitting on the floor and on bean bags, out in the halls working in pairs. ■ Speech therapists, special education teachers, and other support staff come into the class and help with students. However, you can't tell who they are there to work with.	■ Desks are arranged in rows; some desks are at edge of room. ■ Students are grouped by ability levels as they engage in activities. ■ Students of color are most often in the lower-level ability groups. ■ Teacher-made bulletin boards abound with rules and lists of consequences for infractions. ■ Students sit at desks. The teacher attempts to ensure that they are quiet, in their seats, and working independently. ■ Some students leave periodically for special help, causing a good deal of coming and going. ■ Students with disabilities are not allowed to mix with other students, even at recess or lunch.
COMMUNITY	
■ Students frequently go on short or longer study trips into the community. ■ Local community organizations and individuals come into the school. ■ The school has an active community and parent center where local people organize their work in classrooms and student engagement in the community. ■ Students in the school are actively involved in studying local community issues.	■ Students stay in the school building all day, except when they go to the playground. There is little connection with the local community. ■ When students with disabilities finish school, they go to sheltered workshops and group homes.

When educators begin to learn about inclusive schooling, a frequent question is: "How much does it depend on money? Can only rich districts do this?" In schools that serve low-income people, particularly in cities, this question gets turned into one of space. "We already have thirty-five kids in a class," said the principal of a very segregated middle school. "If we put kids with disabilities in these classes, we would have classes much too large." However, when you begin to look at numbers, this doesn't hold true.

Let's look at Georgetown High School as an example. The school is located in a poor but very racially diverse area. Some 30 percent of the students are African American, 30 percent Latino, and the rest an even mix of whites from the Appalachian region and Asian Americans. In this school 40 teachers serve about 1,000 students. Of the teachers, 18 are "general education" teachers, each of whom has 35 students. The other 22 faculty members teach in segregated classrooms; they include 9 special education teachers, 9 bilingual teachers, and 4 teachers of at-risk students, each of whom has 10 to 15 students. All these teachers know that their students would rather be in general education classes. Now let's do a bit of math. If all teachers took all students, the teacher-to-student ratio would be 1:20, an amazing figure in this district. Although teachers would need new training to address student needs, this could work.

Let's consider another option. If 30 teachers were general education teachers and the other 10 were support teachers, the student teacher ratio would be 1:33—high, but still less than the present ratio. Each of the 10 support teachers could work with 3 general education teachers; in other words, each general education teacher would have the equivalent of a support specialist working with the class one-third of the time. It becomes clear that many options are available if we decide to look for them.

Effective Use of Limited Space

Having inclusive classes also helps schools use space most effectively. In the Georgetown example above, shifting to inclusive education would free up space in a very crowded school. Belle Elementary School provides another example of possibilities. As in other schools in this district, the school library had virtually disappeared, a fact that was of great concern to teachers and the principal. The room that had been the school library was being used for a special education class. The special education teacher convinced her principal to let her students attend general education classes, thereby allowing her room to be used as a library and teacher workroom.

Spaces for Specialists. In an inclusive school, specialists seldom use offices for pull-out services. Because such specialists spend most of their time in the classroom, they often have designated work space there. Some classrooms may have two desks, one for the general education teacher and the other for a specialist or support teacher. In other classrooms specialists and the teacher might share one desk. Often these professionals will be housed together in an office, freeing up some space where teachers can counsel individual students and parents or work with small of groups of students in activities. Housing a small group of specialists together also has potential to increase day-by-day communication regarding issues, needs, and strategies being implemented with specific students.

Lunch and Recess. Given their relative lack of structure, lunchtime, recess, and extracurricular activities present both opportunities and potential problems. How schools structure and foster community, responsibility, and inclusion during these times is particularly important. Teachers are usually on their break, and there are easily 200 to 300 students in one area at a time. At lunch students must all be able to eat and get back to classes on time and in an orderly fashion. If a student is not accepted, it is at this time that he or she is most likely alone, rejected, even ridiculed. Similarly, if there are racial tensions, they are most likely to be come evident during lunchtime. On the other hand, it is during this time that students have a chance to really talk, play, and engage one another as people, and relationships can flourish.

A typical reaction to lunchtime tumult is to ask students to sit quietly without talking at assigned tables. However, this is one of the few times in the day when students can chat with friends and interact without interrupting someone's learning. Students need this break. Instead of trying to control their actions, we should devise ways to teach them to make responsible choices during unstructured periods.

What might make students comfortable, keep their interest, and encourage positive interaction during lunch, recess, and in extracurricular activities? Effective elementary and secondary schools establish a selection of interesting activities students may engage in during their free time with the help of teachers, aides, and community volunteers. Students rotate between activities, changing who gets first choice every day. This idea works well at all ages. Some of the ideas schools have organized include:

- Computer time
- Outside organized games
- Art areas
- Board games
- Literacy rooms, where kids are led in group activities like poetry and singing
- Tutoring room
- Gym time with games and exercise classes

Torland City High School, for example, runs such a program with community volunteers. A student with autism at the school has made friends with some other students in the weight-lifting program. This has reduced his sense of isolation, which was a great concern for all.

In addition, many schools assign older students jobs during lunchtime. In some schools teachers choose to eat lunch with their students. Other teachers meet several times a week with different student groups, eat lunch, discuss ways to help one another, and do fun things together.

Using Materials for All Students. In inclusive schools, materials bought through different programs benefit all students. In other words, materials purchased with Title I, special education, or gifted and talented funds are not locked in closets when the special teacher isn't using them with a labeled population of children; instead, these materials are used throughout the school.

Getting Places. Some students with disabilities have special needs for transportation that are difficult to meet on conventional school buses. Consequently, special education programs often purchase small buses that can transport children who use wheelchairs or have other special transportation needs. However, the "handicapped bus," like a special education classroom on wheels, separates students with disabilities. What to do? First, many students with disabilities can be transported on a typical school bus. Increasingly, buses are being designed with lifts and space and locks designed for wheelchairs. Older buses can be retrofitted: Taking out some seats provides a place for the wheelchair. It is also possible, although this is a less desirable solution, to arrange routes so that some students without disabilities ride in the special bus with wheelchair access. Students who have needs other than wheelchairs can be paired with other students in their area and ride the regular bus, or an aide may ride the bus to provide assistance. In addition, many students come to school through car pools, and parents can work out arrangements with one another. Whatever the solution, a team of general and special educators working together can help put inclusive transportation into action.

Inclusive Playgrounds. One physical location that is important to all children is the school playground. Nationally and internationally, people are beginning to use the principles of universal design to develop **inclusive playgrounds.** As part of this movement, an organization called Boundless Playgrounds was created in 1997 as a grassroots movement inspired by Amy and Peter Barzach of West Hartford, Connecticut.

> In the summer of 1994, [Amy and Peter] observed a beautiful little girl in a wheelchair watching bravely with quiet tears while other children enjoyed a playground that this child was not able to use. Five months later, the couple's nine-month-old son, Jonathan, died from spinal muscular atrophy. To work through their grief, a bereavement counselor encouraged them to do something in his memory. The couple recruited and mobilized an army of 1,200 volunteers to create a playground where children of *all* abilities could play together—including children like the little girl they had seen at the park. Research, creativity, hard work, and community support combined to form an extraordinary and universally accessible 25,000-square-foot playground, "Jonathan's Dream." Opened in 1996, it is the first Boundless Playgrounds children's park. (Boundless Playgrounds, 2001)

When an article appeared in *Time* magazine, Amy and Peter Barzach received hundreds of requests for assistance from around the world. In 1997 Boundless Playgrounds was formed, and by 2001 the organization was operating twenty-four projects in disadvantaged communities.

The National Center on Accessibility (2000) developed guidelines for parks based on the Americans with Disabilities Act that can be helpful to schools. An interesting project for students would be to investigate how to make play accessible for all children using these guidelines. To meet the guidelines, at least one of each type of *ground-level play* components on a playground, such as spring rockers, swings, and stand-alone climbers, must be accessible. Although not all *elevated play* structures will be accessible, access to ground-level play structures is used to offset this. For example, if a play area has ten elevated play components, at least five must be accessible. In addition, at least three accessible ground-level components are required, each of a different type. At least half of elevated play areas must be accessible by ramp or by transfer via a special platform. *Soft contained play structures*—such as ball pools, slides, climbing nets, and crawl tubes—are enclosed and made of pliable materials such as plastic, netting and fabric. These devices must provide access to the entry points of each structure and should be accessible via ramp, transfer system, or platform lift.

In addition, designers of play components should consider:

- Space for wheelchair maneuvering to and from the play component
- Wheelchair space
- Height and clearances of play tables
- Height of entry points or seats
- Provision of transfer supports (such as a grippable edge or some other means of support)
- Surfaces soft enough to limit injury from falls but also firm and stable enough for wheelchair maneuvering

Once we begin to understand and think about how space is or is not accessible to all children, we don't take it for granted that some children have to be excluded. We realize that we can work to change the environment.

The Classroom
Designing an Inclusive Learning Community

Our own classroom, of course, is the space most important to us. How do we design an inclusive classroom? How do we improve our teaching and learning environment over time? Several key guidelines to consider:

1. Establish a comfortable, homelike atmosphere.
2. Allow for different learning styles, providing tools and resources that give students alternative points of access to information.
3. Design multiple ways for students to obtain information and express their learning.
4. Ensure sensory and physical access.
5. Use space in the school and class to support inclusive teaching.

We seek to design our class so it includes all, provides emotional support, and allows us to teach effectively. We want people to walk in and know this is a place where real learning is happening for very diverse learners.

Classroom Design for Best Practices

Our use of space is one important way we move toward or away from best practices. Traditional teaching is organized hierarchically: Students are involved in individual, rather than collaborative, work and are focused on minute skill development rather than on authentic and meaningful tasks; classes are dominated by teacher lecture rather than by student-initiated work (Goodlad, 1984; Haberman, 1998; Kohn, 1999). It is not surprising that in traditional classrooms the arrangement of physical space is designed to reinforce this approach. Traditional images die hard. Like lecturing at the chalkboard, moment-by-moment teacher domination of the learning process is still preeminent—and so are the traditional rows of desks.

Artwork reprinted by permission of Martha Perske from *Perske: Pencil Portraits 1971–1990* (Nashville: Abingdon Press, 1998).

If we seek to implement best practices for diverse students, however, we will use space and physical resources differently. If we are to build community in our class, we must organize space to encourage student interactions, cooperative work, and collaboration. If we are to teach authentically, our class will begin to look like a workshop.

Making a Home in Our Class

Students of all grade levels learn best in classrooms that are inviting, warm, and cozy rather than formal and stress-inducing. The more we can create relaxed and secure classrooms, the more students will take risks, and the more they will learn. To start, we assess our classroom. Where are the windows, outlets, doors, tables, cabinets, computers, the sink? What arrangement of areas will make the room work practically and make it stimulating? Many effective elementary teachers put quiet areas, like reading, writing, or listening centers, on one side of the room and louder areas, like science, math, and art, on the other. We can use windows to create a science area that includes growing plants or birds at a feeder, and we might put the aquarium or art center by the sink. Plants and lamps add to the appeal of these areas and create a comfortable atmosphere. An area does not have to be large to be effective. A poetry area could simply be a bucket full of poetry books. (Fisher, 1995; Zutes, personal communication, March 17, 2000).

In a middle or high school class, we can use similar strategies. We may have activity areas for centers that focus on different activities, group work, and small group discussions; a video center with tapes, videotapes, and CD-ROMs; a place for art and design work. Computers may be either in one part of the room or spread around. Plants and animals can be valuable in a secondary class as well. In all, we seek to provide a sense of home and comfort, areas and resources that work for different learning styles, and tools to facilitate different modalities of information access and expression.

Classroom Decor and Ownership

We talked to Mark about how he decorates his eighth-grade classroom. "When I began teaching," he said, "I made a conscious decision not to use commercial posters or materials on bulletin boards. I put up bright fadeless paper with colorful borders, and a few things such as a calendar and some titles as to what might go on the boards. When the students arrive, they see a brightly colored classroom that has only begun to evolve." He went on to explain that he involves students the first day in discussing how bulletin boards might be used and how they would fill them with student work throughout the year.

Part of building a learning community is creating an environment both students and teachers enjoy. This is important for secondary as well as elementary students. The walls can be a collage of interesting materials to explore and from which to draw ideas. These will include student work, book covers, artwork, artifacts from places being studied, information on famous people, multiple posters, a calendar, maps, interactive bulletin boards to do in spare time, pictures, and anything else that will pique students' interest. We involve students in deciding what types of work and artifacts should be displayed. We might even take a hint from some restaurants, which cover the tables with white paper and give out crayons.

The Teacher's Desk. In a traditional classroom the teacher's desk is the focus of the room, and a few students' desks are often placed "close to the teacher." In best practice teaching, however, we are constantly moving: assessing, reviewing, helping, and encouraging students, engaging in experiments, creating projects based on research, and writing. With this change in teaching style, the room also shifts its focus. The teacher's desk is off to one side or in a corner. In some classrooms teachers have a small area on a table or counter—or carry their main supplies in a large bucket and have no desk at all. One teacher laughingly said, "My desk is basically a place to stack materials I need that day and for students' work. By the end of the day, it usually resembles a small tornado!" In another room the students used the desk more than the teacher, as she allowed them to sit at it and work (Fisher, 1995; Zutes, personal communication, March 30, 2000).

Student Seating. We learn a lot about a teacher by observing his or her class. If students are expected to stay in their individual seats and not interact with others, we can be sure that the teacher spends a lot of time and effort trying to control students. Students do not want to stay by themselves for six hours a day, so they will inevitably push their limits. In such a situation, students who have different learning styles or need the help of peers will become problems. Control-oriented teachers respond by removing such students, often alienating others through fear.

In an effective inclusive class, in contrast, students sit in groups in which we encourage social interaction. Yet we also structure places where students can be alone, and for this purpose we find that using tables instead of individual desks is most helpful. However, many districts are unable to spend the money to replace their individual desks. In these schools we can push desks together to form clusters where students can work together as teams.

Creating ways to let students move throughout the day allows students who are stimulated through kinesthetic movement to learn more effectively. However, for some students this will not be enough; flexibility in seating is also important. We can allow kids choices about whom to sit with. One tenth-grade computer lab teacher says, "You may sit anywhere, as long as you are working!" What is important is not that students are sitting in their seats but that they are learning and having fun. We find that given choices, students will end up in many varied seating arrangements. Having places where kids can sit in chairs is only one option. Other approaches:

1. Provide pillows and carpet squares to sit and work on.
2. Demarcate standing stations at cabinets, podiums, or counters for when students need to work but are tired of sitting.
3. Furnish old easy chairs or rockers to be comfortable on.
4. Plan areas that are under, behind, or beside things where students can feel private.
5. Allow students to sit on tables and cabinets.
6. Let students work in the hallway at an extra desk or table or on the floor.
7. Clearly state that students can sit at anyone's seat as long as they respect the person's possessions.

Encouraging daily interactions by teaming students makes sense on several levels. Young people need to feel that they belong to a team and that their ideas are valuable. Seating students in groups also helps us foster community by providing ongoing, natural opportunities for interaction and sharing.

We are careful, however, not to cluster students by ability (see discussions of ability grouping in Chapters 5 and 8). Rather, we intentionally structure heterogeneous groups based on multiple variables—racial backgrounds, abilities of various sorts, personalities, genders. Erasing ability lines does not mean putting students together at tables in any haphazard way.

1. What personalities will complement each other?
2. What students are unable to interact well together?
3. What are the academic strengths and weaknesses of each student?
4. Do certain students need friends they have connected with nearby?
5. Are certain areas better equipped for certain students—for example, for students who daydream, need to move a lot, need to be alone, or need to be social?

ISLAND IN THE MAINSTREAM

MRS. JONES AND MRS. COOPER ARE STILL TRYING TO FIGURE OUT WHY FRED DOESN'T FEEL LIKE PART OF THE CLASS.

Finally, we also organize space so that there is room between tables or clusters of desks. Open space is essential for students who use wheelchairs or who have difficulty walking, such as students with cerebral palsy. Providing open space further allows students to work easily in different places—on the floor, at other students' desks, under desks, or in the group area.

Group Area. Every classroom needs an area where the class can meet to conduct whole class activities. Whether the teacher is reading or explaining an experiment, the group is working on a math problem, or a class meeting is being run, gathering students together increases the feeling of community that is vital to helping students grow. The area should be defined so that it is recognized as a separate place. There may be a rug, individual carpet squares to sit on, or a chair. Whether there is a carpet or a rocking chair by the open space, this area becomes the focal point of the room (Fisher, 1995).

Individual Space. In an environment in which we expect students to interact peacefully together for a long period of time, we specifically design ways for students to find private time and work individually. We can do this in many different ways. For example, in rooms where there are movable cabinets or bookshelves, we can often turn these to extend out from the wall, automatically creating dividers that children can sit around and behind. We can place tables or pillows in the hall. Separate desks can be designated for students who choose to sit by themselves. While we may be concerned that we cannot see all our students, we can learn to listen well. One sixth-grade teacher said to her class, "I can tell that some people have gotten off task, because the noise no longer sounds like working noise but playing noise. I would ask some of you to make different choices." She then proceeded to walk around and talk to several students (Fisher, 1995).

Learning Centers. In a well-structured environment, we plan ahead for students who finish early. Some of these students fulfill their need for social interaction by helping others with their work. Others will want different choices. Having *learning centers* with which students are familiar encourages them to engage in meaningful activities without taking our time away from students who still need help. Learning centers can be used for all ages of students. They should be easily recognizable, and the students should be taught how to use them ahead of time. Directions should be left by the area, and supplies should be easily accessible. This arrangement gives students shared responsibility for continuing learning and maintaining order in the area, stimulates independence, and adds to the homey feeling of school. Some examples include (Fisher, 1995; Jensen, 1995):

1. Opportunities to create plays and develop songs, using music synthesizers on the computer, to illustrate the class topic
2. Microscope setup with slides provided
3. Class museum on current topic
4. Activities that involve maps: map hunts, map puzzles, maps to create own trip plans
5. Theme-related books
6. Listening center with books on tape (even for older students)
7. Math puzzlers: problem stumpers on current topic
8. Writing center where students can find a story starter, write poems, write letters to friends, make cards, or "publish" books
9. Spelling games: word hunts, games that use letters, crossword puzzles, magnetic letters to practice spelling

Hallways as Learning Places.   In an inclusive school, space is used in creative ways for learning. In many such schools students work in the hallways—alone, in pairs, or in small groups of three or four. When you ask students why they are there, it's never because they were misbehaving. Many like the novelty of working in the hallway; for others it is a quieter place to concentrate.

Many teachers devise creative spaces in or near the classroom for one-on-one or small group work. In these spaces teachers bring students together for multiple purposes, to receive assistance from a volunteer, or to work together on a collaborative project such as writing and rehearsing a play. One elementary school teacher took a large cardboard box that had housed a new refrigerator and, together with the students, cut and decorated it so that it looked like a castle. She placed it right outside the entrance to her room. Students use it as a reading corner or a place for two peers to talk or work on a project together. Other teachers obtain similar results by using a small tent, either in the classroom or just outside the classroom.

Movement, Food, and Drink.   We can also give students opportunities for movement—over and above walking down the hall with a pass to the bathroom. In one fifth-grade class, as the students finished work, they joined a "parade around the classroom" in which students quietly walked, making gestures as in a parade. Another teacher put on loud music chosen by the students to which they danced individually or in a simple line dance as a five-minute transition activity. Other teachers have five-minute aerobic exercises or activities that involve sharing information, such as searching for clock partners throughout the class for a few minutes.

Some students also need food and drink to function at their best. If we think about ourselves, how often are we munching on a snack or drinking coffee or water as we work? Provision for eating and drinking can look different ways in different classrooms. Many high schools have drink and snack machines in the commons area; one of the best ways to gather people together is to provide food, so this draws

In this second-grade class, students read together in a "reading tent." Such special environments help children have a place that feels secure, more private, and more like an adventure, all while reading.

students together as a community. Similarly, teachers can allow snacks or water bottles in the classroom. We can establish simple structures for keeping the mess picked up and avoiding accidents. Engaging students in this process increases their independence and responsibility.

Multiple Strategies to Support Access to Information and Expression of Learning

In an inclusive classroom we also need materials, tools, and media to help all students obtain information, develop products that demonstrate learning, and deal with their limitations—whether these limitations are in reading ability or in ability to walk or hear or see. The more resources we have for all students, the easier inclusive teaching becomes. What are strategies we can use?

Multiple Intelligences and Learning Styles. Over time we work to collect a wide range of learning materials at differing levels of ability for different student interests, topics of study, and sensory input modalities. These will include (1) books; (2) alternative print access resources (scanners that can be used with talking software, books on tape, braille, sign language books on video); (3) computers;

(4) media—video, CD-ROMs, tape recorders; (5) contacts for experiences in the community; (6) materials for hands-on activities—simulations and authentic experiences. We can use our knowledge of multiple intelligences as a framework to help us think about providing avenues for both input of information and expression of learning (Jensen, 1995).

Disability as a Tool for Designing Our Class for All Learners. In an inclusive school, we want learning environments to include all students without necessitating special adaptations. That's the goal. A simple way to start is to analyze our school and classroom from the perspective of individuals with different types of limitations. We could even go farther and ask different people with disabilities to come to our class and help us think through how we use space, materials, computers, and other learning resources. We can also involve students in thinking from this perspective. It's a terrific way to help them learn about disability in a framework that is positive and proactive rather than focused on deficits. Maybe we could borrow a child-sized wheelchair and have a student use it for a couple of days and make recommendations. We could do the same for hearing: All of us could wear earplugs and then identify ways to make the class better. Same for vision: Perhaps several students could wear blindfolds, and we could teach other students how to be sighted guides and help them go from place to place. We could all think together about how to make the class better for these students.

Also, when we know that a student with a particular limitation will be in our room, we can think about the design of our room with this specific student in mind. We can contact the family and arrange for the student to walk through and become familiar with the environment before school begins.

Students with ADHD often need more access to private areas where they can concentrate than do some other students. A student who is easily distracted can have problems in areas that would not bother another person. The buzzing of the overhead, people talking in the hall, or the chatter of birds can all distract certain youngsters but have no effect on others. Having areas to which students can retreat (and feel that it is perfectly acceptable) can break up the distractions of a large room. Finding out who works best in what situation is important, as long as it is understood that every student is part of the community and that where he or she works best is somewhere in this room (Zutes, personal communication, March 30, 2000).

In the Tools for the Trek feature here, we've sketched some examples of how you might start this kind of "disability analysis" and chart out what you find. Take the simple matter of talking software. Initially many teachers acquire this for students with visual impairments and students who have difficulty reading—but discover that when their most able readers use the software on occasion, interest and comprehension rise dramatically for those students as well.

Books and Print Resources. Whether we teach high school math or physics, fifth grade, or kindergarten, we need a multitude of books available at multiple levels. In specific subject classes, the books may revolve around one topic, but we will want a choice of genres, from fiction and nonfiction to poetry; from chapter books to references. Materials about any subject can be found in almost any genre (Fisher, 1995).

Tools *for the* Trek

Disability Analysis for Learning

DISABILITY	ISSUE	STRATEGIES	BENEFIT TO OTHER STUDENTS
ADHD	Trouble sitting still; need for movement and places to be alone periodically	Movement around the class within certain guidelines as part of the daily routine Places in the class for privacy and being alone	Many other students also may need to move and be alone at different times.
Mental retardation	Limited reading ability Trouble understanding complex directions	Print materials with a wide range of ability levels and pictures Scanner and talking software Picture cues for tasks—teacher or student designed Peer buddies Cooperative groups	Students with limited reading ability benefit, as does any student who likes to hear a story. Other students can see different ways of communicating; strategies give them ways of synthesizing the key elements of a task.
Blindness	Inability to see print (reading books, directions) Inability to see videos	Books on tape Peer buddy for reading Adult volunteers Books on disk or CD with talking software Peer buddies to explain pictures Descriptions of key elements of pictures by teacher	Students with limited reading ability benefit, as does any student who likes to hear a story. Peer buddies focus on video content. Teacher's descriptions help students focus on key elements in video.
Deafness	Inability to hear teacher instructions Inability to hear videos	Interpreter Sign language instruction for classmates and teacher Closed-captioned films	Students learn another language; those with needs to move can do this as they talk. Comprehension increases for all. Students can talk while watching the video!
Epilepsy	Seizures	Carpeted areas; move furniture to prevent harm	Students learn sensitivity and are taught about preventing injuries.
Need to use wheelchair	Need for space to get around and access to materials	Books and resources at lower level Tables and spaces organized to allow for wheelchair access	All students have easy access. There is space for movement, creating a greater sense of openness in the room.

To teach students to care for books, we must have and model a system. We need our books organized so students can easily find and replace materials. Some teachers organize books by author's last name, title, subject, or genre. Some group them in rectangular plastic bins, with the cover facing out; other teachers place books on bookshelves with the spines facing out. Or we can remove the doors from a conventional storage cabinet to make it accessible to students as special shelving for books about the current subject being studied. Or books on a current topic can be placed on a designated bookshelf or laid on a table to capture the interest of students as they walk by.

Computers and Technology. As computers and related learning technology have increasingly become part of school life, the question of space to house them has become an issue. Many schools initially set aside a special room as the "computer lab" and cycled whole classrooms of students through it. More recently there has been a move to incorporate computers as part of the school media center and classrooms. The uses of computers in the classroom, too, have gone through phases. In some early applications, software was used essentially as computerized worksheets that could track student responses.

We now understand, however, that technology can help us embrace the principles of universal design, expanding our capacity to teach students with vastly differing abilities well together. Computers, rather than being taught as a a separate subject, can function as ongoing tools, much like a blackboard, in the classroom. Rather than using computers only to fill out electronic worksheets, students are learning to use word-processing programs, spreadsheets, databases, graphics software, and other electronic tools to obtain information in a variety of formats and to produce learning products. Computers can enable students to generate text, graphics, animation, video, and sound, and even to control robots.

For example, suppose we want students to obtain information about the Civil War. Traditionally they would read information in the textbook, which might have a few illustrations and photographs. With a computer, however, students could:

1. Have the text read aloud via a speech synthesizer while they follow along in the book or simply listen.
2. Access a multimedia encyclopedia in which text could be read aloud and illustrated by graphics, pictorial illustrations, and even video clips demonstrating concepts or enactments of events of the era.
3. Access information at varying degrees of difficulty or complexity.
4. Use speech-to-text software to dictate a report rather than writing.
5. Create a presentation combining words and pictures to display knowledge.
6. Use bulletin boards, chatrooms, and online journals.
7. Create multimedia lessons and interesting projects for other students.
8. Develop electronic portfolios to demonstrate learning.

For teachers and parents computers offer other potentially valuable capabilities. Many teachers increasingly communicate with parents via e-mail. Teachers may set up electronic bulletin boards for working groups of students and for open communication with parents. Student work may be demonstrated on a website or bulletin board, providing another way to facilitate interaction between school, home, and even the community.

Schools to Visit

Committing to All Children

Ausable Primary School
306 Plum Street
Grayling, MI 49738
Phone: 517-348-7641
Principal: Barbara Mick
BMICK@casdk12.net

Ausable Primary is a K–2 school located in the rural community of Grayling, Michigan. Grayling is a resort town known for canoeing and snow-mobiling; however, the prevalence of poverty is high, and some 56 percent of Ausable's 430 students receive free or reduced-cost lunch. The incidence of significant disabilities is also high—in a county with the highest infant mortality rate in the state.

The design of Ausable Primary, a relatively new school, was shaped by the dreams of a principal, staff, and community members who wished for a school that would meet the developmental needs of young children. From the beginning the school has been fully inclusive, reaching out to children and their families and seeking to keep all children in general classes. In 2001 the school included in general education classes children with autism, mental retardation, cerebral palsy, learning disabilities, and emotional disturbance.

What's particularly amazing about Ausable is the degree to which all staff genuinely have adopted inclusion as a value. They struggle with students, but the commitment they share is clear. The principal, Barbara Mick, has been a leader in

developing this philosophy, carefully selecting new staff and gathering all staff in yearly retreats.

The school has been a pilot for use of the Michigan Literacy Progress Profile (MLPP), an exemplary assessment tool based on best literacy practice. The MLPP also provides a framework for literacy instruction that effectively incorporates skills instruction within a context of authentic literacy learning. Classes rely heavily on the use of small group learning led by teachers, paraprofessionals, and support staff—special education teacher, speech therapist, occupational therapist.

Ausable has developed a particularly strong support system for inclusive education. The special education teacher, speech therapist, counselor, and occupational therapist share an office in the center of the school and coordinate support services in collaboration with general education teachers. Once a month each teacher in the school has a Wednesday afternoon planning session with the specialist team. All specialists provide in-class collaborative teaching and support. In addition, almost every classroom has a full-time paraprofessional to assist with students with special needs. Support staff and general education teachers have learned to work as a family team. Every adult takes responsibility for all children in the school, and all constantly share information and ideas, particularly in informal lunchtime discussions when specialists and teachers eat together in the office. Finally, school staff are active in accessing community agencies to provide support to families and children.

Hearing and Learning. In active classrooms noise can be a problem. Teachers may be tempted to talk loudly or may spend a lot of time trying to get students quiet so they can be heard. In one research study, however, Barnett (1982) found that the hum of engaged learning in a busy classroom actually helps students to screen noises and concentrate.

One important tool used in many schools is voice amplification. As we explain in Chapter 13, a microphone can be used to raise the loudness of the teacher's voice just a few decibels. This can allow the voice of the teacher—or of a student who might use the device—to be slightly above the classroom noise so that a normal tone of voice can be easily heard. Amplification makes it unnecessary for teachers to raise their voices in pitch and thus makes the whole environment more pleasant.

The Local Community
Local Resources for Learning

The local neighborhood and community is potentially an important learning environment as well. Although some schools divorce themselves from their neighborhood, others see their surroundings as a key learning resource—whether the area is filled with broken glass and a landfill or the school sits next to the city library and art museum.

If we look carefully at the instructional strategies described in Chapters 6 and 8, we will see what Kovalik and Olsaen (1997) call a hierarchy of preferred learning. The Tools for the Trek feature here, too, indicates that some practices are clearly more effective than others. In brief, rich immersion in complex experience is critical for learning, and the most powerful learning strategies immerse students in hands-on experiences and real-world events. This means that the local community can be the most valuable teaching resource that we have.

However, schools traditionally don't connect well with neighborhoods. The reality remains that schools are often physically separated from local community resources. Although it might seem natural and obvious, for example, to cluster schools and other community resources—local businesses, libraries, art museums, social service organizations—we seldom see this. Consequently, we always have logistical difficulties in connecting with local communities. The most traditional procedure is

---

Tools *for the* Trek
Guidelines for Creating an Enriched Environment

- Immerse students in reality; use firsthand sources.
- After all firsthand resources have been exhausted, use secondhand experiences that allow for hands-on interactions with real items (not plastic replicas).
- Use books and other print materials, video, and pictures as supplementary extensions of firsthand experiences and resources.

- Provide each class with a broad-based reference library, trade books, encyclopedias, CD-ROMs, and videodiscs.
- Make the environment body-compatible.
- Eliminate clutter, avoid distraction and overstimulation.
- Change bulletin boards, displays, and materials frequently.
- Don't purchase textbooks; instead, spend money on real materials for students.

the infrequent field trip, an event in which a busload of students is driven somewhere and then returned to the school. Yet this kind of experience is very limited. Given our constraints, how might we routinely see the local community as a learning environment? In Chapter 3 we explored some ideas taken largely from the work of Kretzmann and McKnight (1993). Here are a few others.

Almost all schools are located in areas with local resources. Residences, businesses, community institutions, even open fields can offer a wealth of learning opportunities. We have to think and look. We might start with questions about the area that students could explore. For example, if our school is in a neighborhood of houses, we might ask:

1. Who lives here? Where do they come from? Why do people live here?
2. What are the relationships among people in the local area? What types of problems exist? What do people think ought to be done about them?

We might gather information from the Internet, ask community members to talk to our class, conduct door-to-door interviews, walk through the neighborhood. We will likely find that as we follow leads and connect with area people, we will find opportunities to link literally everything in our curriculum to local resources.

In a movement called **place-based education,** a growing number of educational writers and reformers, including the leaders of the Annenberg Rural Challenge initiative, are calling for schools to center their study in the local community. Given the interdependence of communities throughout the world, this is not a return to a parochial view of the world. Rather, it is a way of connecting the larger influences, ideas, and needs in the world to the experience of students and their families.

As teachers we may have particular concerns about this approach if our school is located in a low-income neighborhood that many consider dangerous. Yet this is where our students live. This is their neighborhood. The fact that few teachers live in the area in such schools makes a place-based approach the more needed and powerful. We may begin to see new resources to strengthen learning in ways that we have not imagined; and we will likely gain important understanding and appreciation of the lives of our students, their parents, and the area.

One school we know well, for example, is located in a low-income area in a large city. Across from the entrance of the school are a series of houses, one of which burned to the ground and seriously damaged some of the other houses. The school has been broken into several times, and computers have been stolen. Behind the school is an empty lot; across the lot are a pipe-threading shop and large outside storage areas for metal structures. The school has no playground. About two blocks from this school are two major streets and two large churches, both very old.

What might this area offer for study? We could start with the questions we asked above. Who lives here and why? Likely there are some very interesting people across the street who would appreciate the opportunity to share their experiences and ideas. What about the vacant lot? How big is it? Who owns it, and why is it vacant? What plants, insects, and animals live in this lot? The businesses across the lot—what do they make and for whom? What connections do their products have with other countries? Who works there, and where do they live?

Graves, Graves, Schauber, and Beasley (1999) and Russell (1998) have developed guides to help teachers devise lessons based on neighborhood studies and use of the school grounds and local areas for learning investigations; we recommend such guides to expand these ideas.

Students can be involved in important, real neighborhood projects that connect with others who are trying to improve the community. Lewis (1998a, 1998b) developed useful teacher guides for student involvement in social action and service projects, and Graves and Graves (1997) have described an interdisciplinary process by which students can engage in community planning. Other guides from the Center for the Understanding of the Built Environment (CUBE), too, can be very helpful to teachers. The potential for engaging inquiries that would involve literacy, math, science, social studies, art, and physical exercise is substantial. Such inquiries engage students in real experience, offering opportunities for children at multiple levels of ability to work together in pairs, small groups, and even large groups.

Toward Inclusive Learning Places

In this chapter we've thought about applying the principles of universal design to our schools, classrooms, and communities to support the learning of all students. This is both a complex and an exciting challenge. We know that what we've outlined here only gets us started. Yet we can build over time. Together with Chapters 8 and 11, this chapter begins to give us a picture of how we might design academic instruction for

Stepping Stones

To Inclusive Teaching

1. Conduct an assessment to determine how well your school is designed to promote community, engage children in learning, and be inclusive. This would be a great thematic study for children in your class. What does the school do well? What might be improved? How?

2. Using Figure 14.3 do the same for your classroom. How well does your physical space allow students with different abilities, disabilities, and intelligences to obtain and express ideas and information? What are three simple ideas presented in this chapter that would improve how your class is structured?

3. Teach your students about the idea of universal design. Engage the students in a unit in which they think about and design different types of environments that are responsive to the needs and characteristics of all people. (A great science project!)

4. Use the chart in the Tools for the Trek feature on page 439. With other teachers or with your students, do a "disability analysis" of your classroom. Talk about different disabilities and problems they present. Have students themselves identify practical ways that your classroom could be structured to accommodate each disability. Have them also talk about how such accommodations might help (or hurt) other students. What do you and they learn?

all learners, build community that supports students emotionally, and design the physical learning environment to include all students learning together and to support best practices in teaching and learning. Over time, as we expand and hone our thinking, gather materials, and seek to use these ideas, we'll have some of the most exciting, creative, fun classrooms around—classrooms in which many students naturally thrive.

 Key Points

■ *Universal design* is a concept and practice that helps us design environments and tools to take into account the full range of human variability. This concept is parallel to our *designing for diversity* strategy and can help us think about our school and classroom.

■ Schools and classes need to be based on guidelines for healthy environments: They should stimulate, enhance connections, do no harm, be beautiful and inviting, provide varied stimuli, encourage relaxation and privacy, balance constancy and flexibility, and use resources flexibly for multiple purposes.

■ Schools can work to use the ideas of universal design in schoolwide design through a range of strategies. Among the most important concepts are the following:
  ✓ A sense of welcome
  ✓ A commons area
  ✓ Small schools and schools within a school
  ✓ Parent and community center

  ✓ Using all space inclusively; no segregated classrooms
  ✓ Inclusive transportation to school—no special buses

■ In our own classroom we can use space and resources to respond to our students' differing learning abilities, intelligences, and physical capabilities. Some strategies include:
  ✓ Multiple places to work and be—teacher's desk, space in the hall, floors, comfortable chairs, tables
  ✓ Varied books and print resources
  ✓ Use of technology to access information
  ✓ Space that is organized to provide access and movement for all

■ We can use the local neighborhood and community as extensions of our classroom; learning expeditions can start right on the grounds of the school.

 Learning Expeditions

Following are some learning activities that may extend your understanding of ideas and strategies discussed in this chapter.

1. Locate a builder in your area who is designing houses using the principles of universal design. Visit one of these homes. What are the implications for the design of schools and of your own classroom?

2. Visit a school that is designing curriculum to address multiple intelligences. How does this approach influence the way that the school and its teachers organize space? What tools and materials do faculty have in their rooms that recognize multiple intelligences?

3. Visit a traditional classroom that is organized with desks in rows and uses a textbook- and worksheet-driven curriculum. With the

teacher's help, identify one student in the class who is having difficulty. During a class, watch what goes on. What are the needs of this student, based on what you see and know from the teacher? How are the uses of space, teaching resources, and learning tools helping or hindering the student's learning? What might be done to improve learning for this student? What might be the impact on other students if these changes were made?

4. Visit a school where at least one student with a sensory or physical disability is included in a general education class. Spend a morning or afternoon with this student. Describe how he or she is interacting with the environment. What do you see that helps this student? What gets in the way? What might be done to help the student be more successful in the class? Where might you find the answer?

5. Think about a place you love to be, where you are comfortable and feel that you could be your best in learning new things. Identify this place, describe the setting, and explain what about it makes it a good learning place for you. What are implications for your classroom and teaching? How might these implications relate to students with "special needs"?

6. Conduct a "disability analysis" of a classroom. What in the classroom and in the curriculum might cause some students difficulty? How might these problems be solved? How might these solutions be integrated into the ongoing design of the class? How would other students benefit?

Making
Environmental 15
Accommodations
and Using
Assistive
Technology

*Tools That Extend
Human Capacity and
Promote Learning*

Cedric is a fifth-grade student at Glenwood Elementary School. We really don't know what goes on in his mind or how much he understands. From one perspective, Cedric has several difficulties. His peripheral vision is poor. He is considered "mentally retarded," has no verbal language, and has difficulty walking, sometimes getting tired in the afternoon and using his wheelchair. He is, however, very social, and he communicates his likes and dislikes in many ways. He's an interesting guy.

We visit Cedric's class to see how technology is being used to assist him. On his desk he has a simple communication device—a rectangular plastic device about four by twelve inches that has two large buttons. The green button has the word *yes* printed on it; the red one, *no*. Cedric can use this device to respond to questions. When he presses a button, an electronic voice says the word aloud.

As we enter the room, Cedric is using a computer program that matches sounds to pictures with the help of a paraprofessional. After a few minutes, Pat Squires, the teacher, calls the kids to the rug area at the front of the room. She says, "Tell me something good." Cedric's peer buddy encourages Cedric to raise his hand. When Pat calls on Cedric he presses a button on a device which announces, "I went to the new library." "You did?" says Pat. "The new one downtown?" Cedric signs "Yes" with his hand. Later, when all go to centers, Cedric uses a tape recorder with headphones to listen to directions for the activity or a story being read.

"I was nervous at the first of the year," recalls Pat. "I have never had a student with disabilities as severe as Cedric's. Yet he has done fine. He likes my class. His buddies are learning a lot about helping other people. We all are learning how technology can be used to help Cedric communicate." Although Pat was also anxious about these new technological gadgets, she has become more comfortable with experience. "For Cedric," she says, "learning how to *use* these tools is an important part of his learning." She compared this use of assistive technology to other students' proficiency with computers.

Shannon is a senior at Longview High School and is planning to be a lawyer. She is also blind. As we talk, she says, "The school has really been great! A specialist came to the high school when we moved here, and together we thought about what help I would need." An orientation and mobility specialist familiarized Shannon with the layout of the school. She traverses the campus quite easily with the help of her cane. She describes how she uses assistive technology:

- Student buddies read books aloud and help her in other ways.
- Shannon accesses books on tape, using a tape recorder.
- She can read books on CD by using talking software.
- She writes her papers on a word processor, and her words can be read back to her thanks to talking software.
- She also has dictation software, but she likes to use the keyboard now that she has learned to type.

"It's interesting," Terrance, her guidance counselor, says, "how other kids responded to the technology designed to help Shannon. Several are now using the text-to-speech software, and teachers say it is helping them."

We follow Shannon to her American history class, which is studying the civil rights movement. The teacher has broken the students into groups representing different parts of the community in Little Rock, Arkansas, in 1954. Shannon has used a scanning program at the school to put the text from the book on a disk, which she has read at home using speech synthesis software. The groups are developing presentations to be moderated in a "town meeting." Shannon takes notes on a laptop.

Cedric and Shannon represent important examples of how technology can support inclusive teaching. *Technology* is an important tool for adapting the environment and providing support.

How do we utilize assistive technology in our class? On the one hand, we can accept and encourage use of adaptive tools *and* learn how to help students master assistive technology. On the other hand, students with disabilities and the technology they bring provide important learning opportunities for all our students. Assistive technology can give all of us a fresh perspective regarding how technology can interact with human beings—an interdisciplinary lesson in science, social studies, psychology, and literacy, which we receive just by interacting with a student with special needs and technology. Throughout the year we could involve students in exploring questions like the following: How is technology being used to help people with their limitations? What is being developed now? What might we like to see? The many positive outcomes can include:

- Increased self-motivation
- Increased independence
- Greater participation
- More accountability
- Expanded learning and life experiences
- New opportunities for interactions and communication
- Changed visions of a child's potential on the part of adults, peers, and the child (Sheets & Wirkus, 1997)

Traveling Notes

Technology makes a difference in all of our lives. From one perspective, we are all disabled, and technology helps us do things we could never accomplish otherwise. Cedric and Shannon give us a glimpse of what technology can do to help people we think of as having disabilities. Such technology is likely to be new to us. As we proceed in this chapter, we'll see lots of examples of tools that may have many uses in our classes.

1. What is your own reaction to technology? Do you love figuring out all the new software and video and audio devices? Or do they scare you? How will your responses affect your use of assistive technology needed by students with disabilities?

2. Jot down notes regarding tools of particular interest. Can you see how these might be integrated into your total class and used for all your students?

An Introduction to Assistive Technology
Technology Expands the Capabilities of All

First, comments about language. The phrases *assistive technology, adaptive technology, and enabling technology* are used interchangeably (Cook & Hussey, 1995). Each term refers to technology that helps a person with special needs to learn or perform a task they could not otherwise do. The term **rehabilitation engineering** refers to similarly the skills of an engineer to develop technological adaptations to assist in people's rehabilitation or to enhance ability to function at work, at home, in school, or in the community. When we speak of the modification of physical places, we talk about environmental "accessibility," "modifications," or "accommodations." The Technology-Related Assistance Act of 1988 (PL 100-407) and IDEA define assistive technology as including "any item, piece of equipment, or product system . . . that is used to increase, maintain, or improve functional capabilities of individuals with disabilities" (Individuals with Disabilities Education Improvement Act, section 602)—capabilities such as " speaking, writing, listening, seeing, eating, drinking, moving around one's home or community, using the telephone or computer, opening and closing doors, turning lights on and off" (King, 1999, p. 13).

Is assistive technology only for individuals with "special needs"? Truthfully, all of us use technology to compensate for our limitations or expand our capacities. No human being, for example, can run at forty miles an hour, even though some animals do. Compared to those other species, we have a physical disability. By the same token, compared to cats, we have a visual disability: Our capacity to see in the dark is much more limited.

Because human beings have limitations, technology has been a powerful force in human history. As human beings developed tools for plowing and cultivating land, for example, they could survive in one location rather than constantly moving to hunt for prey. The rapid development of technology in the nineteenth century produced what we now call the Industrial Revolution. Most people in the United States rely on an adaptive technology device called an automobile, communication devices called telephones, and adaptive writing devices called computers. These are all tools to compensate for human inadequacies.

Once we begin to think about technology in this way, tools used to aid people who have specific types of limitations don't look so different. Given that all of us use technology to help us accomplish valued tasks, adaptations originally designed to compensate for limitations in people with disabilities are often useful to others as well. The rise of the field of universal design, discussed in Chapter 14, recognizes this fact.

Categories of Assistive Technology

We can view assistive technology through many lenses. Categories help us organize information and ways of thinking about how we use technology in our classroom.

First, many find it helpful to distinguish between low and high technology. **Low-tech** solutions are often simple manual adaptations that require little cost or

A third-grade boy with a disability writes a story with the assistance of a computer while a paraprofessional provides assistance.

sophistication—though they often reflect great creativity (Cook & Hussey, 1995). Examples include:

- A rubber pad on a desk to help materials adhere more easily, for students with limitations in their control of their arm and hand movements (such as children with cerebral palsy)
- Large pencils or foam blankets for pens to make these implements easier to grasp
- Communication boards that have pictures or simple words to which a student can point to communicate

High-tech devices, on the other hand, involve more sophisticated engineering (Beukelman & Mirenda, 1992; Brett & Provenzo, 1995). Obvious examples include:

- Computers, including scanners and systems that run talking software
- Electronic alternative communication devices with which students use eye gaze or head bands to focus on words or pictures, causing the device to say words aloud in digital speech
- Electric wheelchairs that are guided by a joystick or by "puff-and-sip" commands activated by the person's mouth

This distinction between high and low technology is useful in that it helps us think broadly about the term *technology*—meaning the use of any tool or device that can help a person perform a task or learn.

Software and *hardware* are two other useful categories. When we are talking about computers, *software* refers to the programs that perform the work—word processors, spreadsheets, databases, statistical analysis programs. *Hardware,* on the other hand, is the actual physical structure of the computer—monitor, disk drives, central processing unit (CPU), and so forth. In assistive technology, the actual devices are hardware. However, the information and skills people need to possess in order to use the devices, or the manuals in which information is contained, are the software. The ways in which people can be of assistance, as in reading aloud for people who are blind, also can be thought of as software (Brett & Provenzo, 1995).

We can further categorize assistive technology based on what it helps a person *do.* Assistive technology fills various functional needs of individuals. For each of these functional activities, many different types of devices can be used. Organizing assistive technology based on functional needs is helpful; for example:

1. Numerous devices help people with *communication;* these range from simple devices that record one to three spoken messages to complex communication aids.
2. Other devices such as wheelchairs, adapted automobiles, or leader guide dogs aid people in *mobility,* or getting from one place to another.
3. Some devices may assist primarily in *written communication*—scanners and talking software, books on tape, dictation software.
4. Other technology may help with *hearing or interpretation of sounds*—hearing aids, software that converts recordings to text, sign language interpreters (Cook & Hussey, 1995; King, 1999).

At other times we develop categories of *types* of assistive devices. Examples include: wheelchair, computer, interface between technology and the person (e.g., computer keyboard, touch screen, on–off switch, control panel), automobile, optical magnifying lenses, and augmentative and alternative communication device (AAC). In some cases there is an obvious correspondence between type of device and function; for example, a wheelchair is used for mobility. In other cases, however, a device will be used for multiple purposes. A computer, for example, can be used to access print, to communicate, to control other devices at home or in the school classroom. Similarly, an on–off switch can be used to activate any number of messages, other devices, lights, and so on (Cook & Hussey, 1995; King, 1999).

Adaptive Technology Information and Services

With the growing importance of adaptive technology, numerous efforts are under way to make these available. The cost of developing and producing devices presents a serious hurdle, particularly when the target group is small. Consequently, assistive technology is both funded by governmental programs and marketed for profit by companies that specialize in assistive technologies. As universal design principles become more widely used, separate assistive technology devices for persons with special needs may be needed less and less and costs will go down dramatically (Orkwis & McLane, 1998; Steinfeld, 1994).

Every state in the United States has resources for assistive technology. In some states these form a comprehensive network and work effectively. In others, resources are more scarce and uncoordinated. Most states have established at least one resource center for assistive technology and are members of the **Alliance for Technology Access.** The federal government provides funds to assist states in developing coordinated assistive technology systems. In some cases centers associate with rehabilitation hospitals that work with injured adults or with hospitals for children with special health care needs. In other cases centers operate as freestanding organizations. In such centers specialists assess individuals and help select wheelchairs, seating devices, and other low- and high-tech solutions to the daily life needs of the individual (Flippo, Inge, & Barcus, 1995; Kelker & Holt, 2000).

Assistive, or adaptive, technology is required under IDEA for students with disabilities and can be written into a student's IEP (Kelker & Holt, 2000). Given this requirement, most state variations on intermediate school districts provide support for assistive technology for students with special needs. Large school districts may have their own staff and center established for this purpose.

In addition, national organizations provide ongoing research and development and information—publications, reviews of hardware and software, and other relevant resources. The *Center for Applied Special Technology (CAST)* has developed a model of universal curriculum design and has produced tools designed to move in this direction. **Closing the Gap** provides both an online and a hard-copy catalogue of hardware and software. A network of "rehabilitation engineering centers" have also been funded to conduct research and development on various types of adaptive technology for both children and adults with disabilities. These organizations often develop new solutions to problems that may then be marketed through private companies.

Many companies produce and sell assistive technology for profit. As with any product, it can be difficult to judge which product is the best or whether a given device really meets a need.

In addition, assistive technology is gradually developing as a professional field in its own right. Assistive technology crosses many traditional fields but is not dominant in any—engineering, occupational therapy, physical therapy, speech therapy, special education. Some university programs, however, now offer courses or even degree programs in assistive technology. Although training and expertise is not as widely available as needed, many people are working in this field, and the number is constantly growing (Cook & Hussey, 1995; King, 1999).

Professionals from different fields tend to specialize in specific types of assistive technology, though this is not a hard-and-fast practice. For example, speech therapists tend to be most knowledgeable about augmentative and alternative communication (AAC) devices. Engineers often work with adaptive use of computers, mobility, and workstation design. Occupational therapists use many low-tech devices to aid individuals in activities such as reaching and using a pen—all functions of the upper extremities, the area of focus for occupational therapists (Cook & Hussey, 1995; King, 1999).

For teachers, of course, learning to use technology is part of ongoing professional development. Technology is changing rapidly, and new tools are constantly being developed. We would particularly recommend use of the websites of Closing the Gap (**www.closingthegap.com/**) and the Center for Applied Special Technology (**www.cast.org/**).

Selecting Assistive Technology

With any technological device, we seek to match the person with the most helpful tool. We can do this informally or more systematically. Two models in everyday life serve for comparison—shopping for a car and buying glasses. In the first model, we don't tend to go to experts for a "car–person assessment." Rather, we take it upon ourselves to review car ads, test-drive cars, study consumer data about different cars. This is true despite the fact that automobile purchases are very expensive. Many people also adhere to this model in obtaining assistive technology. One way to identify helpful tools for our class is to follow a similar strategy. Assistive technology centers often allow people to "test-drive" various technological tools. Similarly, vendors of assistive technology help people select materials of interest and try them out (Kelker & Holt, 2000).

However, a growing service, available in both for-profit companies and government funded agencies, involves a more systematic process. In this approach an assistive technology specialist obtains detailed information about the functioning capacity of the person through interviews, observations, or performance testing. The specialist also obtains information about desired uses of technology and may visit the locations in which technology will be used—the home, a classroom, a job site—and conduct a detailed "environmental analysis" of these environments. Specialists then use this information to recommend different technological tools (Cook & Hussey, 1995).

IEPs for students such as Cedric and Shannon cover assistive technology and specify that the students receive assistance from one or more assistive technology specialists. As teachers we may receive assistance from our intermediate school district (or our state's equivalent structure). However, we can decide to use a local or state assistive technology center that is not directly connected with our school system (Flippo, Inge, & Barcus, 1995; Kelker & Holt, 2000; Ryndak & Alper, 1996).

Selecting technology that works for a person turns out to be very complex. Some assistive technology research indicates that almost one-third of devices obtained—at the cost of much time and money—are not used. This occurs for many reasons. Sometimes the devices don't work well or break down. Sometimes, however, a device is hard to learn to use or may be an embarrassment to the individual. Technology specialists refer to these latter issues as "human factors" (King, 1999).

As in Cedric and Shannon's cases, our role as teacher is critical, even when (or maybe especially when) we are new to the technology our students are using. A law for technology use has been developed that can be stated rather simply: Motivation is the key to using technology. Said more fully, when time and physical, cognitive, and linguistic effort required for use of a technology exceed the motivation to learn, the technology will be discarded. The implications are clear. If, even unintentionally, we make a student uncomfortable in using an assistive tool, then we contribute to a failure in learning and growth that the technology could have helped mitigate. However, if we welcome and support the student (thus making effort lower), then we help make the student's chances of success much, much higher (King, 1999).

Modifications to the School and Classroom Environment
Creating Access

When designing or retrofitting a school for all learners, we seek to develop an environment that both allows and invites all students to be active participants. We do this with care, for it is certainly possible to make extensive modifications for a specific student in ways that isolate the child from other classmates, even in the same room. Following are key areas for consideration (Sheets & Wirkus, 1997).

Building Access

School buildings and classrooms should provide access for students with different types of limitations. The school must provide ramps with smooth access to the building; doors should be easy to open or be motor assisted so that they open with a gentle push. When the school is an older building, this will necessarily require retrofitting—creating ramps, installing elevators to higher floors. Grab rails throughout the building support students with poor balance or general weakness.

Similarly, *bathrooms* should provide access for students with poor balance or limited strength. For young children, "training" commode chairs may be needed. A light switch extension allows a student in a wheelchair to turn lights on and off; a motion sensor automatically turns water on and off (Sheets & Wirkus, 1997).

We should also consider access of students with physical disabilities to the *playground* or other recreational facilities. In one school, for example, a student was physically challenged and could not hold onto the swing chains. Another student could not use the slide because he couldn't get himself in a safe position. The school purchased an adapted swing and placed rails at the top of the slide that allowed children to stabilize themselves. They also attractively paved the sidewalk through the play area to allow easier access by a student in a wheelchair (Sheets & Wirkus, 1997).

Classroom Modifications

Classrooms also may need modifications. We ensure adequate *floor space* for a student in a wheelchair by organizing students in clusters of tables rather than individual desks, creating pathways in and through the classroom, and organizing spaces for centers. This allows physical access for students with mobility limitations; it also breaks up the space into smaller units, providing a sense of security and focus for distractible students, and establishes a known pathway for students who are visually impaired. We arrange *shelves* so students who cannot stand can access materials on lower levels. Again, grab rails serve as balance supports for students with many kinds of weaknesses.

A *couch* can support a student unable to sit independently on a regular chair because of neurological, muscular, or sensory motor impairments. A couch also

LABORATORY RETRIEVER

© 2000 MICHAEL F. GIANGRECO. ILLUSTRATION BY KEVIN RUELLE PEYTRAL PUBLICATIONS, INC. 952-949-8707

encourages cooperative play, because two or three children often sit on it at a time. *Chairs with arms* such as captain's chairs or substitute chairs such as cube chairs or beanbags also offer more support for students with poor posture control, weak sensory orientation, or a very short attention span. Nonslip surfaces for tables and chairs also can provide greater stability (Sheets & Wirkus, 1997).

For students who have difficulties reaching and grasping, *desks* can be difficult. Students may have trouble leaning over to see materials on their desk and may constantly knock pencils, paper, or other materials off. A variety of simple items can help solve this problem. For example (Ryndak & Alper, 1996; Sheets & Wirkus, 1997):

- Paper or object stabilizers include double-sided tape, Post-it tape, clamps, or magnets (if the desk is metal). Also, rubberized pads mounted on a desk help materials move less easily.
- Various-sized drawing utensils include large and regular crayons, magic markers, and sponge brushes.
- Modified grippers attach to the hand and clamp to a pen; pens with enlarged bodies or covers can be easier to hold.
- Adapted scissors include loop-handled scissors and large-handled scissors or regular scissors.
- A portable slant tabletop made to fit an entire table can allow eight children to work at one time. This allows students to see work more easily, reduce fatigue, and help students with poor visual skills get closer to the work.
- Desks and tables can be made adjustable.
- One adapted desk is designed so the top functions like a lazy Susan and students can rotate it to access different objects (Cook & Hussey, 1995).

Functional Applications of Assistive Technology
Using Technology to Live and Learn

In addition to focusing on general environmental adaptations, technology has many specific functional applications. Let's consider the key areas in which assistive technology can aid both children and adults.

Aids to Assist in Understanding and Remembering

A variety of aids are created to help students understand or remember. We already use helpful low-tech tools. For example, on our classroom walls we often have a list of the daily schedule, assignments and due dates, word walls, or lists of technical terms. Similar individualized tools can be created for students (Weisgerber, Dahl, & Appleby, 1980):

- A daily pictorial schedule that shows a clock with a time, a picture of an activity, and the words that represent this activity can be made for one student, several, or posted for the whole class.
- Tape-recorded instructions for an activity can indicate steps to be carried out.
- Checklists (with pictures if needed) enumerate steps for a particular activity.

Manipulating and Controlling the Environment

We rely on technology in our home—we use lights, oven, air conditioner, radio, TV, VCR. The same goes for the classroom, where we depend on, lights, timers, computers, VCR, transparency projector. Children and adults with significant disabilities, however, have difficulty using typical controls—difficulty reaching, turning, moving around the room. A wide variety of low- and high-tech tools for manipulating and controlling the environment can provide assistance (Cook & Hussey, 1995; King, 1999).

Low-Tech Aids for Manipulation. Low-tech aids are designed as *general purpose* tools for numerous functions or activities. In contrast, *special purpose* devices are specifically designed for one particular function. In addition, some are designed to *augment* a person's ability to perform a task in a standard way; others use *alternative* means of accomplishing a task. Let's look at ways that devices can help.

Mouthsticks and head pointers are two general purpose aids frequently used for direct manipulation of objects by people who cannot use their hands and fingers well. They are used to turn the pages of books; to write (with a ballpoint pen attached to the end); to pick up objects (by means of a pincher attachment opened and closed by tongue action); and to grip objects (with a suction cup attached). They can also help people dial a telephone, type, and turn lights on and off.

Reachers help a person reach and grasp objects and are useful for a person who cannot stand (or for any of us when an object is on a high shelf). A handle grip is on one end of a pole that has grasping jaws, often covered with rubber or another nonslip material. With this mechanism a person can pick up and move many objects—cans, packages, books, paper, tapes, CDs, and so forth.

Special purpose aids most often involve specialized handles on tools designed for specific purposes. These might include, for example, a brush with an extended handle, a pen or pencil with an enlarged grip, a key holder with a large grip, a spoon with a bent handle for scooping or with a swivel handle. Electronic aids include page turners and feeders; feeders help people with limited use of arms or hands to eat more independently (Cook & Hussey, 1995).

Switches and Environmental Control Units. A wide range of adapted switches can control numerous devices. Switches fall into the following categories: (1) direct selection, (2) scanning, and (3) coded access.

Direct selection occurs when the individual directly selects the item—by hand and finger movement, by use of a mouthstick, or even via an electronic pointer mounted on the person's head. Such switches may be flip switches (like a typical light switch), buttons, or turn knobs.

Scanning involves an electronic device in which choices are provided and a cursor or light moves from one to the other. The switch is activated by the person when the correct choice is indicated.

Finally, *coded access* typically involves the use of Morse code to send signals to units to activate switches. For any switch, selection may include a simple on–off function (called "latching"); variability (as with varied intensity of lighting); or "momentary" function, meaning that the switch is on as long as it is being pressed and off when released. This brief introduction to switches illustrates the potential complexity of what most of us take for granted (Cook & Hussey, 1995).

An interesting application of switches is the development of *environmental control units*. A single environmental control unit, which looks like a small box with multiple switches or controls, can control multiple functions—light switches, oven, tape recorder, VCR. Although these are used mostly in homes, such a unit could be used in a school to give a student with limited mobility the opportunity to control some operations within the classroom (Cook & Hussey, 1995).

How might an environmental control unit work in a classroom? One high school used three units with infrared remote capability that controlled multiple appliances and office machinery. Using these devices, several students with severe disabilities were able to engage actively in classes by turning on the following types of equipment:

- Overhead projector
- Tape player or stereo—to dance, exercise, or hang out
- Book light
- Tape recorder with test questions/answers and books on tape
- Kitchen appliance for class cooking activity
- Office machines such as paper shredder, stapler, or letter opener for a cooperative work task

This helped the students be a real part of the class. Other students were interested in the control units, which helped to prompt positive social interaction (Wise, 1999).

Seating and Positioning

For any of us to work for a length of time, we must have comfortable seating and posture. For students with disabilities affecting body structure, balance, and/or muscle strength, this is sometimes difficult in typical seating. We should pay attention to students' positions on the floor, at a desk or table, or in their wheelchair, as well as to their posture during other daily activities—in the bathroom, at the pool, on the playground, or on the school bus (King, 1999).

Physical therapists can help us select and design adaptive seating for students with severe disabilities and can provide consultation regarding ways to support a student in our class. Working with a team, often in a special clinic, physical therapists conduct a careful assessment of the physical capacities and needs of the person, try various approaches to seating, and help a family obtain needed devices.

In addition to comfort, two major areas of focus are important when we consider seating and positioning: (1) postural control and deformity management and (2) pressure control (Cook & Hussey, 1995). Let's discuss these briefly and explore implications for the classroom.

Posture Control. Some individuals have muscle weakness and uncoordinated movements that make it difficult for them to sit upright in a wheelchair or other seating. If not dealt with, these difficulties can, over time, cause general health problems and skeletal deformities that worsen the disability. Students with cerebral palsy most often have this difficulty, as do those with muscular dystrophy and multiple sclerosis. Treadwell and Roxborough (1991) described three levels of postural control ability for which different types of assistance are needed:

- Hands-free sitter: The person can sit without using hands for support. Seating is designed to provide mobility and a stable, comfortable base of support.
- Hands-dependent sitter: Hands are used to maintain support. Seating helps provide pelvic or trunk support to free the person's hands for activities.
- Propped sitter: The person lacks any ability to support himself or herself. Seating provides total body support.

Here are a few examples of types of seating support:

- A seat raised on the outer side to prevent the person from sliding forward
- A seat belt, lap belt, or bar to assist the student in maintaining position and to offer pelvis stabilization
- Foot supports so that feet don't hang too low
- Adjustable supports on the sides of a wheelchair to help a person with severe scoliosis maintain a more erect posture
- Head supports on a wheelchair to help stabilize the neck
- Seat with custom contours specially designed to fit the body structure of the student

What is both tricky and important about developing and using supported seating is that it is vital, on the one hand, to help students maintain good posture to prevent worsening of their disability, and, on the other hand, to provide flexibility so that they can engage in activities—reaching, writing, drawing, reading.

We work with the parents, the physical therapist, and the student in thinking about the physical structure of the class and the various ways the student can participate—sitting at the desk, sitting on beanbag cushions on the floor, moving the wheelchair throughout the room. Start by thinking about a typical classroom day and the many movements of students as they engage in active learning; then enlist the advice and assistance of the physical therapist. Other students also can learn how to help the person navigate the classroom and sit properly.

Pressure Control. Students with spinal cord injuries have the greatest difficulties related to pressure. Because they have limited feeling, they may develop sores from pressure at particular points (technically, *decubitus ulcers*), which can be dangerous.

Two key strategies are used to assist with this problem. First, good posture is maintained as discussed above. Second, various types of cushions are used. Finally, individuals engage in pressure relief activities—namely, a routine of shifting the weight of the body in different directions or of sitting in a way that relieves pressure, lying down, lying back in a wheelchair, and so on. With some children with significant disabilities, we may periodically help them shift their weight to aid in both pressure and posture control. A physical therapist will help us understand when and how to do this.

Augmentative and Alternative Communication (AAC)

Many students with more severe disabilities have difficulties talking. In some cases, as with cerebral palsy, individuals have deficits in muscular control; they are able to speak but do so slowly and may be difficult to understand. For students who speak at some level, tools may *augment* or improve their communication abilities. For students who are not able to talk to any meaningful extent, we use *alternative* communication strategies. The **augmentative and alternative communication (AAC)** approaches we use sometimes rely on tools and technology ("aided" communication) and sometimes on use of the body or expression ("unaided" communication) (Beukelman & Mirenda, 1992; Chedd, 1995). The Voices feature here tells the story of one child who uses an AAC device to aid in play during recess.

Physical Movement and Gestures. Some approaches are not technological but build on typical alternative communication tools. We all use our bodies to communicate in a variety of ways—through facial expressions, gestures, nodding our head, pointing, or touching (Cook & Hussey, 1995). We all use such methods as ways to augment what we say in words. Many students with severe disabilities who cannot talk otherwise communicate much in these ways. *Sign language* is valuable not only for individuals with significant hearing losses but also for students who are unable to talk (see Chapter 13).

Facilitated Communication. **Facilitated communication** is a process in which a facilitator works with an individual, often at a computer, helping to stabilize the person's hands as he or she types messages and information on a computer. Developed by Australian educator Rosemary Crossley, facilitated communication has been heralded by some as a way of giving voice to many individuals with severe disabilities, particularly those with cerebral palsy and autism, who have not communicated effectively before (Crossley, 1994). Biklen (1990, 1992) brought the technique to the United States, where it has spread rapidly throughout the country. The approach has been controversial, however, with many doubting that the communications are the product of the person rather than the facilitator (American Speech and Hearing Association, 1994; Jacobson & Mulick, 1992; Levine & Wharton, 1995; Shane, 1994). Research to date has demonstrated cause for cautious optimism that this strategy may be able to open up a new life for some individuals (Biklen, 1990, 1992). On the one hand, individuals on both sides of the controversy acknowledge that facilitators can and do influence what is said. On the other hand, studies have demon-

Voices

Second-Grade Recess and Assistive Technology

Manuel is a second grader in Sonya Chases's class. He is a very pleasant boy, but he has some significant disabilities. Manuel contracted a serious illness when he was two weeks old and now is considered quadriplegic (he can move his arms a bit but can't use his hands of fingers to grasp well, and he can't walk) and nonverbal (though he can say yes and no). Manuel needs assistance with self-help skills, which an aide (sometimes with help from another student) provides. He uses a power wheelchair and a Light Talker, an augmentative communication device in which a light beam scans visual icons; when selected, the icons "talk" with synthesized speech.

We arrive for a visit as the class is heading out to the playground for recess. "Manuel has asked Eugene to be his buddy today at recess," Sonya says; "several of the boys have really become friends with Manuel." We watch Eugene wrap his arm around Manuel as he walks beside the buzzing, slightly meandering wheelchair. Manuel and Eugene join a group of children, and we hear Manuel's Light Talker say for him, "I like you Eugene." Eugene beams. Then, "Let's play ball." We're a bit surprised to see the children include Manuel in their softball game. One of his classmates hits for him, and he "runs" in his power wheelchair. He makes it to first base!

strated that this technique has been effective in allowing people previously thought to have minimal intellectual abilities to communicate deep and complex ideas, feelings, and thoughts. The websites of the Facilitated Communication Institute (2001) at Syracuse University and of Rosemary Crossley's Australian center (2001), DEAL, offer further information, including links to critics.

Communication Boards ("No Tech"). Technological aids vary dramatically in their degrees of technological sophistication. At the lowest-tech level are locally or commercially produced **communication boards** of various sorts. The simplest type of communication board might consist of pictures with words that express a meaning placed on a piece of cardboard. The student would point to the desired message—"Go to the bathroom," "I am hungry," "Yes," "No."

Simple Electronic Communication Aids ("Low Tech"). Other communication aids use technology to a limited degree. For example, Versascan is a simple aid that uses a few picture icons arranged in a circular pattern on a square board. A light shines behind each picture in turn. When the light arrives at the desired picture, the individual hits a simple switch and the message is spoken aloud in synthesized speech. A frequently used, simple communication device is the BIGmack, shaped like a large hamburger made of plastic. On this device one message may be recorded at a time and is then activated when the individual presses the top of the apparatus (Cook & Hussey, 1995; Sheets & Wirkus, 1997).

Sophisticated Electronic Communication Devices ("High Tech"). **Voice output communication aids (VOCA)** are portable speech output mechanisms, many of which are very sophisticated. VOCA appliances can be thought of as computerized electronic communication boards. Typically the size and shape of a laptop computer, they are often mounted on wheelchairs. Most are divided into rows and columns of squares on which icons for messages are located. In some cases the VOCA instrument is multilevel, which means that more than one message may be stored under each key. Some produce synthesized speech output—the "robot" sound. Many use digital speech, which sounds like a human voice, either male or female. A range of message selection systems are available: In *scanning* a light or cursor moves from selection to selection and the user activates messages using a switch; in *direct selection* the person may use touch, a mouse, a joystick, or a head-mounted pointing device. Some mechanisms support *eye gaze* as a way of selecting choices as well (Cook & Hussey, 1995).

Dynavox (made by Sentient Systems), for example, uses an icon display and is accessed via touch, single- or dual-switch scanning, joystick, or mouse. The Pathfinder (Prentke Romich) provides high-quality speech synthesis with different age and gender options. It also can be used as an alternate keyboard to most computers and operates a variety of environmental controls. The Touch Talker (Prentke Romich) has 128 touch-sensitive keys that can be custom programmed and use additional overlays. The instrument can be hooked to a printer and used as an input device to a computer. A much less expensive, commonly used system is the Wolf (AdamLab). The least sophisticated version of the Wolf looks like a child's portable tape recorder and has four programmable squares for icons and words. It can be turned on via touch or adapted for scanning (Beukelman & Mirenda, 1992; Closing the Gap, 2000; Sensory Access Foundation, 2000).

Let's look at a couple of examples of how communication aids are used. In an elementary school Latisha, a minimally verbal student, was having difficulty participating in story time. The teachers could not tell if she was understanding or if she was even involved in the story. When they asked Latisha questions, she would point vaguely and make sounds they could not understand. Another student, Aaron, who had physical disabilities was in a specially designed seat and also was not always involved. To deal with this problem, they used a range of strategies. They put beanbag and cube chairs on the reading carpet where the children sat on the floor in a semicircle around the teacher. These allowed extra support for both Latisha and Aaron. A grab rail mounted near the teacher allowed Aaron to pull himself up to participate, using felt or Velcro boards. They also used a range of augmentative communication and interactive story extensions that included gestures, animated facial expressions, sign language, communication boards, puppets, and Velcro boards. An easily programmable, augmentative communication device allowed both children to comment on the story or to ask or answer questions. They found that verbal students, too, often used the augmentative communication devices as well as talking. In addition, many shy children or those lacking confidence participated more often, using a voice output device that eventually gave them enough confidence to begin speaking more often (Sheets & Wirkus, 1997).

In a high school, students with severe disabilities were able to make meaningful contributions by using some simple communication aids—the Speakeasy, BIGmack, and Step-by-Step75 (all produced by AbleNet, **www.ablenetinc.com/**). These programmable devices allowed students to do the following (and more) (Wise, 1999):

- Greet classmates
- Introduce self/classmates/coworkers
- Respond to attendance call
- Give directions for activity/assignment/work task
- Give an individual/group report, with classmates recording student's portion
- Share joke, riddle, or quote of the day
- Share weekend activities, with classmates transcribing in journal
- Answer comprehension question
- Make announcements over public address system
- Join in choral reading activity or recite lines of a skit
- Request assistance in holding/using materials
- Share the day's events with family, with message(s) recorded by peer

Adapted Computer Access

Computers are important tools for accessing information and producing work; according to Sheets and Wirkus (1997), various adapted computer formats can help to level the playing field for people with disabilities. Typically, to use a computer effectively, a person must be able to see a monitor screen, read what is on the screen, and type to input information. However, many students, including those with disabilities, have difficulty with one or more of these processes. Assistive technology identifies ways to help with these limitations. One example is to modify the placement of the monitor. Beyond monitor placement and access, three additional considerations are important:

- Computer interface—the way the individual provides input to the computer
- Output—how the person receives useful output from the computer
- Software—programs that are based on best practices and encourage learning at students' own ability levels

Computer Interface. Some students need alternative methods of providing input to the computer beyond the standard keyboard. The first type of adaptation uses a standard keyboard but alternative methods of typing, rather than hands. For example, a mouthstick or head stick allows head motions to press keys. A similar device attached to the hand with a splint allows hand, rather than finger, movements to press keys.

Adaptations to the Standard Keyboard. For some people with disabilities, the standard keyboard causes various problems for which there are software solutions. For example, a student with cerebral palsy might have difficulty pressing a letter in such a way that it does not repeat itself over and over. Both Windows and Macintosh have available software that delays the amount of time required before a letter is repeated (Alliance for Technology Access, 1996; Cook & Hussey, 1995).

This young boy in a wheelchair uses a computerized communication device.

Alternative Keyboards. Special keyboards are useful for some individuals with limited ability to move fingers. These alternatives include (1) TouchWindow, a program that puts a keyboard on the screen which can be activated through touch; (2) Big Keys, a large-lettered, bright-colored keyboard on which the keys are arranged in alphabetical order; and (3) IntelliKeys, which allows for a single-switch adaptation (Sheets & Wirkus, 1997).

Communication Devices as Alternative Inputs. Some of the communication devices discussed earlier can provide input into the computer, thus requiring the person to learn commands for only one device. However, the device must be physically connected to the computer. In addition, there are sometimes technical problems; communication between some devices and the computer can require manual programming, thus complicating this option (Alliance for Technology Access, 1996; Cook & Hussey, 1995). Examples include:

■ *Scanning and switch-controlled keyboard:* When an individual cannot use any type of keyboard because of physical limitations, then scanning or Morse code is used. Scanners provide on-screen choices to the individual, either a line at a time or with rows and columns that cover half of the screen (Cook & Hussey, 1995). The individual can employ control switches select items scanned on the screen, using a "sequentially stepping selection cursor" (King, 1999, p. 18).

■ *Morse code:* Software is available that allows "sequenced pulses from special switches to operate the computer" (King, 1999, p. 18) in Morse code. Use of Morse code allows more flexibility; however, it also requires the individual to memorize complicated sequences. Additionally, some required commands, such as "space," are not easily conveyed via Morse code (Cook & Hussey, 1995).

■ *Voice recognition:* Dictation software allows individuals to speak to the computer to control functions and engage the different commands of different software programs (Cook & Hussey, 1995).

Computer Output. We are familiar with typical computer output—words and images on a screen and/or printed materials. However, a variety of other outputs are available.

Text to Speech. For both Windows and Macintosh operating systems, software is available that converts text to speech on personal computers. Some text-to-speech programs are specifically designed to assist in promoting literacy development with elementary-age students. According to the Sensory Access Foundation (2000), both a voice synthesis card and screen review software are required. Newer computers come with voice synthesis built into the operating systems for both Windows machines and Macintosh; older computers may require a separate voice synthesis card. In addition, external voice synthesizers may be used.

Two types of speech output are used with computers and other devices based on the use of microchips: digitized and synthesized speech. *Digitized speech* has been recorded onto some medium such as a magnetic tape, hard drive, or a read-only-memory (ROM) chip and produces a natural human sound. *Synthesized speech,* in contrast, uses complex rules to produce sounds based on spelling and syntax and produces a definitely "electronic" sound (Sensory Access Foundation, 2000).

Screen-reading programs work with the synthesizer to convert information on the screen into spoken words. By means of a screen reader, a blind user can read anything on the screen, from a single character to the entire screen display; and the screen review software can even notify the user that something has "popped up" on the monitor. With a single keystroke the user can command the synthesizer to speak out a word, a sentence, a paragraph, or an entire document. The only such program available for the Macintosh is Berkeley Systems' outSPOKEN, which works with the speech synthesizer built into the operating system. Numerous such programs are available for both DOS and Windows-based computers. Additionally, work is under way, though in its infancy, to convert graphics on the screen (graphical user interface, or GUI) to spoken words (Cook & Hussey, 1995; Sensory Access Foundation, 2000).

Magnified Screen Images. For persons with partial sight, enlargement of text on the computer screen can make an important difference. Magnification can be done by means of magnification software or through use of a closed-circuit television (CCTV). Software can be installed that magnifies images on the screen and changes colors and contrast so that materials read more easily. One such program built into the operating system for the Macintosh is Closeview, which magnifies text and graphics two to sixteen times. Similar programs are available for Windows-based computers. This software can also change the color of the text and background. For example, if users are light sensitive but need contrast, they can have the text displayed in bright yellow on a soft gray or powder blue. Many students find this beneficial, particularly students with visual processing disabilities. In addition, optical screen magnifiers placed over monitors or closed-circuit television systems not only magnify printed materials but enlarge information on a computer screen (Alliance for Technology Access, 1996; Cook & Hussey, 1995; Sensory Access Foundation, 2000).

Tactile Output. Also available for computers are appliances that produce tactile output in two formats—letter shapes and braille. The **Optacon** is a device that creates a "tactile facsimile" of print, using pins that vibrate in the shape of each letter. Braille output can be accessed either as an electronic display or as hard-copy printed braille. An electronic braille display converts text on the screen to pins that raise and

Including by Not Excluding in the First Place

Fulton Elementary School
225/228 W. Orange Street
Lancaster, PA 17603
Phone: 717-291-6110
Principal: J. Drue Miles
DMILES@lancaster.k12.pa.us

Fulton Elementary School is home to 472 students in kindergarten through grade 5. Ninety percent of the children come from families with incomes at or below the poverty level; 42 percent are Latino, 33 percent African American, 24 percent white, and 1 percent Asian American.

In a school district that averages 24 percent of students in special education, Fulton Elementary has a special education student body of 4 percent, and that 4 percent is included. Through the use of asset-based community development principles and systems theory thinking, Fulton went in eight years from serving 25 percent to only 4 percent of its student body in special education. "It's a culture," says principal Drue Miles. "Nobody talks special education or thinks in out-of-my-classroom strategies. We simply use a variety of strategies to make learning available to everyone."

The district and school have traditionally used a three-step process to serve students. Tier 1 is a teacher's requesting individual consultation regarding a student. Tier 2 is the formation of a small team for consultation. Tier 3 is a coordinating council that considers a student's potential as a special education student. Mr. Miles, however, suspended tier 3 meetings and expected all students to be served by teacher (peer) consultation and assistance.

The key, according to Mr. Miles, is that teachers as a group identify student problems as student competency issues, not teacher competency issues. Once the vehicle for passing a student to special education ("I'm not able to teach this stu-

dent") was eliminated, the practice of taking what was considered the lower portion of students and recommending special education came to a halt.

Mr. Miles decided that the faculty and professionals in the school had the required talents to keep all children in the classroom. He created a resource bank based on assets-based community development of staff skills, talents, and interests. Today, each time a faculty member approaches Mr. Miles about a student, the principal searches the resource bank for the person with the solution. For example, a common gate to special education, in Mr. Miles's experience, is the practice of labeling a first grader with phonemic awareness deficits. The Fulton Elementary speech therapist has listed as assets both competency regarding phonemic awareness and a skill for teaching teachers. The therapist has further expressed a desire to get out of the speech office. Now Fulton has a speech therapist who enters the classroom, implements strategies for the student, and mentors the teacher—and the student stays in the first grade.

At Fulton Elementary 18 of the 472 students are in special education, and most students and faculty cannot identify them to visitors. Four students are in a segregated classroom and are served by an agency separate from the district. Drue Miles explains his motivation for inclusion: "The existing systems cause children to be classified as 'thought-to-be's' (a term used to denote children not yet labeled as special education students but under observation). I was a special education teacher, and I dealt with the reality of teachers' not wanting children in their classrooms. I wanted to purify special education. Now teachers can do real inclusion, and special education teachers can be a real part of the school community."

By Thomas J. Neuville, Millersville University, Millersville, Pennsylvannia; **tneuville@millersville.edu** lower so they can be felt. The person can use the device to control access to the computer without switching back and forth. Such units, however, are very costly. Also available are braille printers, which, like any printer, vary in speed and quality. Two frequently used printers sell for as low as $500, although higher-quality braille printers can cost thousands of dollars (Alliance for Technology Access, 1996; Cook & Hussey, 1995; Sensory Access Foundation, 2000).

Computer Software: Scaffolding Learning with Technology. Computers and software provide powerful tools for many of our students. What is *not* particularly useful, however, is to use computer programs as automated worksheets. Unfortunately, much educational software, particularly in packages sold to school districts, encourages just this type of use. However, software can provide multiple ways of presenting information to students and multiple ways to allow them to express information, including:

- Text- and graphics-based reference books such as encyclopedias on CDs
- Interactive programs based on best teaching practices
- Speech synthesis software and programs that allow books to be read and accompanied by pictures and graphics
- Games that incorporate skills in literacy, mathematics, science, social studies, and other disciplines (e.g., space exploration programs that require calculations of fuel use, resource use of different colonies, etc.)
- Instructional software that teaches students how to use computer-based production programs—word processors, graphics, and so on. Many instructional programs are designed with graphics and sound to appeal to children.

That's just a start. Computers also offer students wonderful opportunities to produce evidence of learning that draws on different intelligences. Many programs have been developed to appeal to children of different ages with different levels of skill and sophistication. Among them:

- Word processors
- Presentation software (PowerPoint; KidPics is a children's version of such a program)
- Graphics software—for drawing, painting, and so forth
- Spreadsheets
- Databases
- Music writing programs
- Website development software

Such programs allow students to develop products. When used with adaptive input technology, these programs can allow students with a wide range of academic abilities to write, draw, develop songs, assemble slide presentations, or create pictures. These productions can be used as a basis for other activities in the classroom; for example, a group might act out a story written by a student, use computer-generated graphics to design props for a play, organize a class sing-along based on songs written on the computer by a student (or group of students), maintain a database of books in the class library, or create a class book that incorporates students'

Voices

Ninth-Grade Algebra and Assistive Technology

In her ninth-grade algebra class, Jan Larson has several students who have learning disabilities and one student, Brian, who is considered educable mentally retarded. On the day when we visit, Jan has students broken into groups and has given them projects that will involve the use of a range of mathematics skills, including algebraic equations and geometry. Brian is working with a group that is designing the size and structure of a radio tower in a valley. (Jan tells us that she has been collaborating on some of these projects with the art and social studies teachers.) The students are building a scale model of the valley and the tower. We're interested to see how Brian is involved with the group. He pulls out a measuring tape and measures the height of the tower and the mountain. The tape speaks the measurement in synthesized speech! Jan explains that she tries to have Brian work with students on projects like this at his own ability level. "However, the other students are helping him to understand the most basic algebraic equations and what they might be used for." When we ask about other uses of technology, she says that Brian especially likes the interactive math and graphics software she has in the class. "The software has been particularly helpful for Sue," she adds, "who has a learning disability. The software engages the students in using mathematics concepts in applied situations rather than having them simply calculate equations they don't understand."

graphics and research on a current topic of study (Alliance for Technology Access, 1996; Center for Applied Special Technology, 2000). The Voices feature describes one classroom in which access to computers provided assistance to students with disabilities—and to their classmates as well.

Aids for Students with Partial Sight or Total Blindness

Students with visual impairments range greatly in their visual acuity, field of vision, and other characteristics. Individuals with partial sight benefit from a variety of magnification tools that can help them make the most of the vision they have. Individuals who have no useful sight also can access information with the help of a growing range of strategies and tools.

Magnification Devices. Perhaps the most common form of assistive technology, used by a large part of the population, are devices that help us see better. Many people wear glasses or contacts. As people get older, almost everyone uses some sort of "corrective eyewear" or combinations thereof—contacts with reading glasses, prescription sunglasses, sports glasses, and so on. For people with more extreme visual impairments, other optical devices are available. These include various types of optical or electronic magnifiers of all sorts and sizes—from hand-held to desk magnifiers. **Closed-circuit television (CCTV)** can function as an electronic magnifier: A camera focuses on a document or is connected electronically to a computer and sends the image to a tele-

Artwork reprinted by permission of Martha Perske from *Perske: Pencil Portraits 1971–1990* (Nashville: Abingdon Press, 1998).

vision screen that enlarges the image. Different versions are available, including a hand-held camera using an NTS interface that connects to a typical television, other portable cameras that use a table on which documents are placed and are connected to a computer monitor, and stand-alone units (Sensory Access Foundation, 2000).

Recorded Materials. For individuals who have no useful vision, a great variety of devices and tools are available. Although these require training to use, technology increasingly provides blind individuals with access to information. Many books are available through commercial companies that provide books on tape, through the Library of Congress, or through local services that often provide access to newspaper and other materials. Materials available through libraries can also be accessed without charge for students who have learning disabilities or other problems accessing written materials (Sensory Access Foundation, 2000).

Braillers. Braillers operate like small typewriters. Mechanical braillers are as noisy as a manual typewriter; however, more recent versions operate like small laptop computers. Additionally, a person may use a computer to record information in typical text format and then have the computer convert this, if desired, to braille with either hard copy or electronic print (Cook & Hussey, 1995; Sensory Access Foundation, 2000).

Reading Systems. Technological devices give persons who are blind more independence in accessing information. Reading systems allow individuals who are blind or visually impaired to access printed material. They consist of a scanner, a computer to which the scanner is connected, and software to turn the scanned image into text that can be read aloud through speech synthesis and/or displayed in electronic braille format. Stand-alone systems consolidate the computer, software, and scanner into a single unit in which one keystroke engages the scanning and text conversion process.

Software-based systems require more computer skills but have the capability of editing and printing information. Among reading systems are Arkenstone's Open Book and Open Book Unbound, Telesensory Corporation's Oscar, and Xerox Corporation's Reading Edge (Cook & Hussey, 1995; Sensory Access Foundation, 2000).

Adapted Tools and Measuring Devices. A wide range of adapted tools and measuring devices are available. Although designed largely for persons who are blind or visually impaired, they can be useful to our other students as well. They include rulers with raised markings, talking clocks, watches with raised markings, braille labels, light probes (used to determine if lights are turned on), and liquid level indicators that sound a tone when electrodes placed in a container reach a certain level, as in measuring ingredients for cooking (Weisgerber, Dahl, & Appleby, 1980).

Assisted Hearing and Alternatives

Assistive devices to aid people in hearing are among the oldest and most used assistive technologies available. They are used by so many people that we no longer consider them unusual or think of them primarily in connection with people with limitations. For individuals who have partial ability to hear, assistive devices include:

- Hearing aids—electronic aids that are mounted behind the ear, in the ear, or in the ear canal
- Amplified telephones with volume controls
- Headphones that allow students to listen to tapes with increased volume
- Classroom amplification systems in which teachers use microphones and speakers mildly amplify the sound
- **FM units,** in which the speaker uses a microphone and amplified sound is accessed through a receiver carried by the individual with a hearing impairment

For individuals without functional hearing, we need alternative tools. We have discussed sign language. Technological tools are important as well.

Telephone Access. The telephone provides an important challenge. People who are deaf can communicate either with other deaf people or with hearing persons using a **TDD (telecommunications device for the deaf),** a keypad device that acts as a modem. If another deaf person has such a device, when the telephone connects, the two TDD users can type messages and send them back and forth to each other. If a deaf person is calling a hearing individual, the telephone company provides a "relay operator," an individual who reads the message from a TDD and then translates this into speech for the hearing person. (Interestingly, AT&T employs blind people in these jobs; the relay operators receive incoming messages in electronic braille.)

Another option for telephone communication involves use of a computer and speech synthesis software with a touch-tone phone. The computer is connected directly to the telephone. As the person who is hearing impaired types messages, the computer converts the text to spoken language. The TDD used by the person who is deaf can function automatically as a bidirectional TDD, allowing the hearing person on the other end to use the keys of the telephone as a simple text input device.

This technology has allowed widened opportunities, as it requires neither the use of special equipment by the hearing person nor dependence on a relay operator.

A final option, not yet in wide use, is video transmission—which would allow two deaf people to speak to each other using sign language. Given the enormous memory requirements for such transmission, this technology is not yet used over telephone lines. It can be used, however, with local area networks (LAN); video transmissions can link two persons who are deaf or even link a hearing individual, a person who is deaf, and an interpreter together (Cook & Hussey, 1995).

Speech Interpretation Aids. Two types of aids are sometimes used to help people who are deaf interpret oral communications. Lip-reading aids depend on specialized types of glasses. Upton glasses employ a microphone that helps people interpret difficult sounds by means of color codes for different sound categories. This allows people to increase their speech-reading ability (Cook & Hussey, 1995).

Alerting Devices. Many sounds are important in daily life—doorbells, ringing telephones, car horns, smoke alarms, a child's cry. For people with hearing loss, devices are available that detect these sounds and cause either a vibration that can be felt or a flashing light or both. Microphones may be placed in key areas—near the front door, near the telephone—to detect sounds and turn either on a flashing light or a wrist-worn vibrator. For smoke alarms a special frequency can be set to provide a unique signal. Alarm clocks or timers can be tactile (under a pillow, on a wrist, or in a pocket) or can activate a light (Cook & Hussey, 1995).

Aids for Persons Who Are Both Deaf and Blind. People who are both deaf and blind use tactile input to obtain information and communicate. The oldest method is called the Tadoma Method. Both people involved must know sign language (or have an interpreter). The person feels hand signs and finger spelling with his or her hands. An automated version of the Tadoma Method has also been developed, in which the

Voices

Senior English Project and Assistive Technology

In Nan Sheldon's senior English class, students are working on a project for the yearbook, editing stories and incorporating these with photographs that the graphic arts class will use to design the layout and cover. Nan has a series of computers in her class. Jasmine, a student who is deaf, is at one of these. She has had to work hard to learn to write well and is now working with a partner. "We have our computers networked," Nan says as we watch. "Jasmine and the other kids have figured out that the best way for them to work together is to use the computers to send e-mail back and forth. This way Jasmine can read what is said and doesn't need the help of an interpreter." Nan explains that Jasmine sometimes does use a sign language interpreter and that over the year several of the students have gotten pretty good at basic conversation with her. "Also," she says, "some of the kids take notes for her. It's worked out well."

speaker talks into a microphone and a device converts the sound to vibrating pins, as in the Optacon. An interesting piece of equipment currently under development connects a mechanical hand to a computer, which can receive input from a TDD or a speech-to-text speech synthesizer. The hand moves in finger spelling and sign as a real person's hand would (Cook & Hussey, 1995).

Mobility

By mobility, we mean our ability to move around in our immediate environment as well as our capacity to move safely and efficiently from one location to another. Some people with disabilities have many problems of mobility: It may be difficult or impossible for them to turn over in bed; climb stairs; walk; or access automobiles, planes, or buses. Numerous devices are available to help solve these problems.

Mobility for Persons Who Are Blind. A range of strategies are used to help persons who are visually impaired or blind to move around from place to place. The most used approaches are low-tech:

■ Professionals who provide training and assistance to support blind people in mobility are called *orientation and mobility (O&M) specialists.*

■ *Sighted guides* are persons who can see who help people with visual impairments move safely from one place to the other. The person who is blind typically will grasp the arm of the guide. The sighted guide will alert the person for steps, pausing briefly just before descending or ascending, or for objects or barriers. Sighted guides do *not* take the hand of the person who is blind and pull; this takes away a sense of dignity.

■ *Canes* allow blind individuals to independently traverse an area with which they have some familiarity, and *guide dogs* assist individuals in safely moving around and walking.

Electronic travel aids have been developed to overcome limitations of the cane. Each uses some device to sense objects and/or drop-offs and provides feedback to the user in the form of sounds—high- or low-frequency tones or clicks—or vibrations. For example, a **laser cane** extends the range of the standard cane and can detect drop-offs. Three narrow laser beams are emitted, which detect objects and provide different feedback depending on location—a high-pitched tone if the object is upward, a low-pitched tone for a drop-off, and a vibration for an object directly in front of the person (Cook & Hussey, 1995; Sensory Access Foundation, 2000).

Wheelchairs. For someone for whom walking is difficult or impossible, a wheelchair provides a way to move from place to place. The history of the wheelchair itself tells us a lot about changing views of disability. The oldest wheelchairs looked much like large wooden rocking chairs on wheels; they were designed so that it was impossible for an individual to propel themselves.

A wheelchair has several typical parts—a seat, armrests, footrest, and brake. Typically, a sling seat allows the wheelchair to be collapsed for placement in a car or closet (Cook & Hussey, 1995). A person propels a *manual wheelchair* by turning the outer rim of the wheel. In recent years a new breed of wheelchairs has been developed to accommodate individuals involved in sport. *Ultralight* wheelchairs often sport bright colors, do not have armrests, and are made of aluminum alloys, titanium, or similar lightweight materials rather than the steel of the conventional chair. These wheelchairs are often used in wheelchair basketball and in all sorts of sports involving persons with disabilities.

Some children or adults may not have adequate strength or agility to propel themselves adequately in a manual chair. Increasingly, *powered wheelchairs* have become available. The decision to use such a chair must be made carefully, however; as with driving a car, using a powered wheelchair requires training and skill. These wheelchairs have a power unit and may incorporate any of a range of control devices. The most typical control is a *four-way joystick* that controls both speed and direction of movement. Joysticks can be mounted in different locations to be used with the hand, chin, foot, or head. A *puff-and-sip* control is used by an individual who has limited movement of body parts other than the head. Two switches are activated. When both are puffed, the wheelchair moves forward; when both are sipped, it moves backward; and when only one switch is activated, the wheelchair turns. Different settings of speed and rates of braking can be selected for indoor and outdoor use. Oftentimes people who use powered chairs also use other devices that are carried on the wheelchair—a respirator or an augmentative communication device, for example (Cook & Hussey, 1995).

Vehicle Accommodations. Automobiles, vans, and other vehicles can now be modified so that persons with very severe disabilities can drive safely. These accommodations open up opportunities for many individuals with physical disabilities and can be funded through state vocational rehabilitation agencies or insurance companies. The first issue is simple *access* to the vehicle. Transfers to and from a car can be assisted with use of sliding boards, bars to grab, and straps. If a person is not able to transfer independently to a car, a *van with a powered lift* can be used to move the wheelchair from the ground to the floor level of the van. Similar types of lifts are available for school and city buses. Once in the van, a *wheelchair tie-down* should be used to stabilize and ensure the safety of the person. Additionally, an "occupant restraint system"—a seat belt or similar device—will hold the individual in the wheelchair in case of an accident.

The primary driving controls of a vehicle govern steering, acceleration, and braking. *Acceleration and braking controls* can manually augment conventional controls so that they require less pressure; or, in the case of a missing limb, controls can be moved from one location to another. A lever arrangement can be placed next to the steering wheel; the person pushes to brake and pulls to accelerate. Variations include push–twist and crank options. *Steering*, too, may be accomplished through a range of adaptive aids (Cook & Hussey, 1995).

Embracing Assistive Technology

You have to agree: That's a lot of technology. If you are a technology enthusiast and this was new to you, you likely loved it and want to know more. There's much to learn about technology, and it's an exciting part of the journey. If you're not into computers and other technology, however, this discussion may have seemed a bit overwhelming. When the first personal computers came out, many adults were

Stepping Stones

To Inclusive Teaching

1. What technology and tools do you have in your school and classroom to help students compensate for disabilities or to provide additional help? Do an assessment of your classroom and school and identify three or four additional needs that should be addressed. Use the information in this chapter as a guide.

2. Visit a local center for assistive technology and experiment with different tools described in this chapter. Identify several you would like to see in your school and explain how they might bene-

fit all students. Get the specs and submit these to your principal or technology coordinator.

3. Obtain and install talking software and software that allows students to dictate stories. Watch what happens with student learning over several weeks. What do you see?

4. Contact vendors of assistive technology equipment or a local assistive technology center and arrange a hands-on demonstration fair for children, teachers, and parents. Make it a fun event!

scared to death of them. Kids took to them naturally. Now, many of us can't imagine managing our jobs or our personal lives without a computer.

Assistive technology professionals talk about the **transparency of technology,** and the more transparent the better. Technology becomes transparent when it is so much a part of our lives that we literally don't think about it. We don't think of driving a car, calling someone on the telephone, typing a report on a word processor, or cleaning our eyeglasses as unusual.

What makes some of the technology described in this chapter different is that it is new and sometimes not so easy to use. In some instances there are many bugs to work out. Also, most of us have had little experience with some of the people who need to use such technology. Yet if we had grown up with these people as children, had known them as adults, and had become familiar with their new augmentative communication device when we were learning how to use our computer, neither they nor the technology would seem strange. They would be part of our landscape—"transparent," so to speak. That, of course, is what inclusive schooling is all about. One of the goals of inclusive schooling is to make the people and the aids and supports they use part of all of our lives.

What will likely help us to truly embrace both assistive technology and the inclusion of students with severe disabilities in our classes, however, will be the moment when we discover the benefit for all our students as we become comfortable with these students and this special technology. By way of analogy, consider one of the key things we know about literacy—namely, the fact that we can always read a passage more easily when we have *background information.* As we develop experience with even one student, our fund of *background information* skyrockets, and we can build on that fund over time. Perhaps, the most clear signal of our own growth and learning will be the change that will occur when we don't think of this technology as "special" at all. When we teach we will simply incorporate a growing range of technology into the ways we share information with students and into the opportunities we give students to demonstrate their own learning—following the guidelines for universal design of the curriculum that we discussed in Chapter 14.

 Key Points

- As technology does for us all, assistive technology uses both high- and low-tech tools to help extend the capacities of students with special needs.

- Special education funds can be used to purchase needed assistive technology. In addition, every state has centers for assistive technology where people can explore and try out different types of devices. Specialists can often help us understand how to incorporate particular tools into our teaching process.

- Students who use assistive technology can provide interesting opportunities for learning about the interface of human beings and technology for all our students.

- Modifications are often needed to school grounds, buildings, and classrooms to ensure accessibility to students with physical or sensory disabilities.

- Many different types of tools and devices can help students accomplish tasks and extend their abilities. These range from talking computers to devices that convert print to braille and modifications that allow students to use hand controls to drive vehicles.

 Learning Expeditions

Following are some learning activities that will help extend your understanding of the information and ideas in this chapter.

1. Locate and visit an assistive technology center in your area. Talk with staff at the center. Investigate and describe briefly the resources the center has; how the center is used; and how friendly it feels for children, families, and teachers.

2. Visit a classroom in which technology is being used to assist students with mild learning challenges as well as students with more severe disabilities. What do you see happening? Does technology help each student be part of the curriculum and the class? How do the teacher and other students react? How "transparent" is the technology in the class?

3. Interview an individual with a severe physical or sensory disability who uses technology—a wheelchair, talking software, and/or other devices. Talk with the person about his or her life story and the role that assistive technology is playing. What difference has technology made? What are the problems in its use?

4. Gather a panel of professionals who work with assistive technology—a speech–language therapist who specializes in augmentative communication, an occupational therapist, a physical therapist, a rehabilitation engineer. Ask these people to tell your group about what they do, positive developments in their areas, and challenges/problems they encounter. How do they work together to provide support for a person or family? What are problems and issues with such cross-disciplinary work?

5. Visit a school that has a reputation for doing a good job of inclusive schooling with students having a range of disabilities. Talk with staff and observe in classrooms. How does technology in general and assistive technology in particular fit into this school? Who is responsible for what? How well does the support system work? What are problems? How do teachers feel?

CHAPTER OBJECTIVES

1. Reflect on the degree to which schools are inclusive and the challenges and opportunities this presents.

2. Explore lessons about school change.

3. Examine the process by which individual teachers move from being frustrated and alone to working with others for change.

4. Understand and utilize strategies for change toward inclusive teaching and schooling.

5. Ponder what the experiences described in this book can mean to you and your students in the future.

Teacher Leadership for 16 Innovation and Change toward Inclusive Schooling

Creating the Schools All Children Need

We're nearing the end of our journey. We have explored effective teaching of very diverse students and have analyzed exemplary schooling practices that support all students' learning well together. Along the way we've seen how inclusive teaching is connected to major social issues—exclusion, segregation, poverty. In this chapter we think about how teachers can lead the way in *creating* inclusive schools. Figure 16.1 provides another view of our journey—as a pyramid, with our leadership as teachers at the foundation.

Figure 16.1

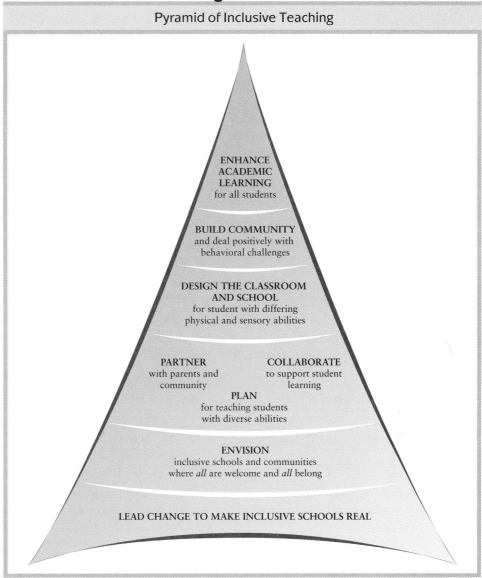

Pyramid of Inclusive Teaching

ENHANCE ACADEMIC LEARNING
for all students

BUILD COMMUNITY
and deal positively with
behavioral challenges

DESIGN THE CLASSROOM AND SCHOOL
for student with differing
physical and sensory abilities

PARTNER
with parents and
community

COLLABORATE
to support student
learning

PLAN
for teaching students
with diverse abilities

ENVISION
inclusive schools and communities
where *all* are welcome and *all* belong

LEAD CHANGE TO MAKE INCLUSIVE SCHOOLS REAL

Many teachers are, in fact, leading. We know all of the following teachers:

- A teacher who made sure that a student with mental retardation was placed in her room.
- A teacher who collaborated with a special education teacher in a very segregated school, arranging to include her special education students.
- A teacher who refused to "just sign the IEP" when she had not been at the meeting; she also refused to refer a student to be classified as emotionally disturbed and put in a special education school.

■ A teacher who taught a student with multiple, very severe disabilities and used this experience to question the existence of three separate special education classrooms in the school.

We will find many opportunities to promote positive change. In this last chapter, we discuss lessons about change that have emerged from school reform, strategies we can employ to move toward inclusive schooling, and specific actions we may take as teachers.

𝒯raveling 𝒩otes

Schools and communities are not what they should be. We know much about making schools better for all children as well as for the adults who work in them.

1. Whose responsibility is it to be part of creating such change? Yours? Someone else's? Or does this responsibility and opportunity belong to us all?

2. Reflect on the ways in which you have been involved in change. As you read the strategies for change in this chapter, ask yourself what you believe regarding how to create schools where all children learn well together.

The Lessons of School Change
Not Easy but Worth the Trip

If there is one thing we've discovered about schools, it is that they are very difficult to change. The factory model of schooling has survived many efforts to reform it (Tyack & Cuban, 1995). Some researchers have also found, however, that when inclusive education becomes part of a school, it becomes the new reality and becomes equally resistant to change. So change is hard; but when good practices become part of the culture of a school, we have hope that they may last (Fisher, Sax, & Grove, 2000). In his book *Change Forces*, Michael Fullan (1997) describes eight key lessons for creating a paradigm of school renewal. Let's discuss each of these, applying them to movement toward inclusive schools.

First, *change cannot be mandated* except in those concrete, specific areas that require little understanding or thought. Important change requires shifts in people's beliefs, skills, and behaviors. We must be about creating conditions that "enable and press people to consider personal and shared visions, and skill development through practice over time" (Fullan, 1997, p. 23). For inclusive teaching we explore our own belief system, see how inclusive teaching fits as part of good instruction, look for opportunities to share, dialogue, raise issues, and ask questions.

Second, *change is not linear*. It is impossible to plan all the steps in a change process. Rather, we begin a journey, take the first steps, and reevaluate. We can't know how to teach inclusively before we start. We can't have an inclusive school *until* we start. We do the best we can and solve problems that occur.

Third, *problems really are our friends*. Inquiry, constant appraisal, analysis, and self-reflection on problems and solutions is critical. We can expect that we will be confused, that conflict will occur. If we immerse ourselves in problems, however, "we can come up with creative solutions" (Fullan, 1997, p. 26).

Fourth, *action and visioning must occur together*. Fullan summarizes it this way: Rather than the traditional "ready, aim, fire," if school change is to be successful, the order is "ready, fire, aim." In other words, it is only through action in a direction that we gain enough experience to create a comprehensive vision; and only through struggle among a group of people can that vision be shared. *"Productive change is very much a process of mobilization and positive contagion"* (Fullan, 1997, p. 31).

Fifth, we *balance individual and collaborative efforts*. These must remain in tension. On the one hand, we want shared vision and values. On the other hand, some of the worst atrocities in history have resulted when whole groups decided to take oppressive courses of action. Individual thought, risk taking, and initiative are always key in challenges to the status quo. Yet building a community is also critical.

Sixth, we can't wait until administrators take action to initiate change. Similarly, administrators can't wait for teachers and parents. Said another way, *top-down and bottom-up strategies must both work together*. In other words, administrators and board members must work together with empowered parents, teachers, and students. This means that each of us can and must initiate change as well as respond to change efforts coming from above—challenging, tweaking, suggesting alternative directions. Teachers can begin efforts for inclusive teaching and can challenge administrations to remove segregating practices and to put resources in our schools and classrooms.

Seventh, our efforts to build better schools must be *connected to issues in our community and society*. We are not islands unto ourselves. Schools support community and social needs. As Fullan (1997, p. 38) explained,

> individual moral purpose must be linked to a larger social good. Teachers still need to focus on making a difference with individual students, but they must also work on schoolwide change to create the working conditions that will be most effective in helping all students learn. Teachers must look for opportunities to join forces with others, and must realize that they are part of a larger movement to develop a learning society through their work with students and parents.

Finally, *every person must be a change agent*. School dynamics are simply too complex for those "in charge" to understand completely. Teachers know this well, because they see politicians and administrators create initiatives that simply don't make sense. As Fullan (1997, p. 39) says, "every teacher has the responsibility to help create an organization capable of individual and collective inquiry and continuous renewal, or it will not happen."

Change Strategies for Moving toward Inclusive Schooling

As the movement toward inclusive education has grown, several strategic patterns or approaches to the change have emerged (Hoskins, 1996; Roach, Ascroft, & Kysilko, 1995; Villa & Thousand, 1996). Let's survey strategies used.

One Student at a Time: Parent Requests. The parent requests route is perhaps the most typical process in districts where segregated classes and schools for students with disabilities are the norm. Rather than taking a schoolwide or districtwide look, parents request, often demand, that their children be included in general education classes. For real change to begin, the number of these requests must increase over time. This pattern puts the onus on parents, who are often reasonably very frustrated.

With proactive efforts the results of parents' efforts can set a model for possibilities. In Halstead Elementary, for example, a parent insisted that a student with severe and multiple disabilities participate in general education even though there were separate classes for students with learning disabilities in the building. This student's success in these classes led staff to begin asking why these separate classes existed.

Forced Change: Legislation and Class Action Suits. Given the least restrictive environment clauses of IDEA, you might think that federal monitoring might force action. To date, however, the federal government has been lax in enforcing this legislation. At most federal monitors write reports pointing out areas in which the law is not being followed; the states then develop "corrective action plans," only to go through another similar procedure several years later. However, parents in some school districts have

A boy with Down syndrome waters seeds while a classmate records plant growth in an inclusive elementary classroom.

A TALE OF TWO SCHOOLS.

filed successful class action suits that forced the districts to look more broadly at their policies.

Teacher-Initiated Inclusion. In many schools, general and special education teachers have taken the initiative to move toward inclusive teaching. In one school, for example, a teacher in a special education classroom made arrangements for some of her students to go to another teacher's class one period per day. Eventually the two teachers worked out an arrangement to team-teach together.

Such teacher-initiated efforts can help get things going and build some new images in a school. The danger is that change will stop there. However, if we continue to build an image of what is most desirable, we can reach out to other teachers, expand partnerships, and gradually expand inclusive strategies across the building and grade levels.

Building-Based Systemic Change. An entire school can work systemically toward inclusive schooling. Teachers may initiate efforts like the one mentioned above, then develop a proposal to the principal and leadership team. In other cases a principal may be the prime initiator. Typically a planning group is formed to collect information, obtain input, and develop a plan—which might include collaboration between general and special education, placement of children, professional development, visits to other inclusive schools, and so on.

Districtwide Systemic Change. Some school districts develop districtwide initiatives to move toward inclusive schooling. Such an initiative sometimes grows out of the impact of a model effort in one school; in other cases it is the result of a court order; in yet other cases it emerges in response to combined pressures from parents and leadership from school administrators. In a districtwide effort a planning committee is often convened and includes teachers, parents, and administrators.

Teacher Leadership and Action
We Really Can Make a Difference, Together

Support for inclusive schooling necessarily occurs at different levels—in our classroom, in our school, in our school district, and in state and national educational policy. As teachers we owe our first allegiance, and the vast bulk of our energy, to what we do in our own classroom. However, we quickly learn that policies can either enhance or seriously undercut our ability to teach children effectively. We must also become effective agents of change to help create conditions for best practices. However, this work is not for the fainthearted. We must have courage and persevere.

The Courage to Teach

Parker Palmer (1998) describes the process by which teachers move from lonely despair to activism for positive change (see Figure 16.2). We begin isolated and disconnected, often feeling beaten down by problems and issues. We may be concerned about how students are treated, particularly those identified as having special needs—but, initially at least, we may feel we are the only one who is concerned. However, as we look for opportunities to make change *and* to build a support network, we soon discover others who feel similarly. This process may begin with another teacher in our building or with someone we talk to in the grocery store. Gradually we get together as a group—as a study forum, an online chat, an issues discussion group. We form what Palmer calls a "community of congruence," a group of people concerned about similar issues. Ultimately, our efforts lead us to create formal structures to support our community—structures that may range from a modest listserv to a collaborative center for teaching and research.

At some point, we discover that our issues and the solutions we suggest have public importance. The group decides on ways to go public—whether through conference presentations, demonstrations, articles in journals or letters to the local paper, creation of a newsletter, initiation of research projects, or other avenues. According to Palmer, this is the critical step in becoming a real movement.

For a movement to prosper, alternative reward systems are critical. Institutions mete out their own rewards, such as money and security—but activism for change can offer rewards of different kinds. At first, we learn more about who we are. Then we experience connection, fellowship, and the support of others. As the effort grows

Figure 16.2

Building a Movement for Quality Inclusive Teaching
Stage 1	*Divided no more:* Isolated people make an inner decision to reclaim their integrity and identity—to take responsibility for making change rather than blaming the "enemy." They often find their "center" outside of the institutions in which they work.
Stage 2	*Communities of congruence:* Individuals begin to discover one another, offering mutual support and finding opportunities to develop a shared vision.
Stage 3	*Going public:* Groups learn to convert their private concerns into public issues.
Stage 4	*Alternative rewards:* New ways of receiving support and encouragement emerge, as well as new mechanisms for pressuring the institutional reward system.

Source: Adapted from Palmer (1998).

and we have some impact, we feel rewarded and encouraged by seeing the fruits of our efforts. In some cases we may even gain employment or fiscal resources. For most people, however, helping to create positive change is a central source of gratification. In the words of Parker Palmer (1998, p. 182),

> I am a teacher at heart, and I am not naturally drawn to the rough-and-tumble of social change. I would sooner teach than spend my energies helping a movement along and taking the hits that come with it. Yet if I care about teaching, I must care not only for my students and my subject, but also for the conditions . . . that bear on the work teachers do.

Beginning in Our Classroom

This brings us to some of the practical things we can do to influence school change. We begin in our own class. We seek to learn daily how better to be an inclusive teacher, and to implement best practices. As we do so, daily journaling will help us continue to reflect on and understand what we are doing and why. We should also know from the beginning, however, that as we teach inclusively we will have a rippling impact in our school and even across schools as people become aware of what we are doing. At best, we'll find ourselves forming partnerships and a support network of teachers with whom to share ideas and support.

Knowing and Communicating the Philosophy of Inclusive Teaching. Most important, we think, is that we keep an image of our inclusive class in our mind—a philosophy of inclusive teaching that we can explain to parents, other teachers, and our administrator. We should know that the inclusive classroom is based on research, law, and best practices. We'll get clearer over time, of course; but even in the early stages, we'll be surprised at what impact we can have with our colleagues.

Teaching Inclusively. We seek to construct our teaching inclusively. Whether or not we have officially labeled students in our class, it is typical for teachers to have ability spreads of four or five grade levels. We can teach in ways that engage all students at their own levels of ability; and we can think ahead about what we might do if the ability range broadened, if we had a "severely gifted" or "severely disabled" student in our class. When the opportunity presents itself (and it will), we will be ready to demonstrate inclusive learning.

Welcoming Special Students. Whether we find ourselves in a school that is trying to be inclusive or in a school where students clearly are in separate classes, we can recruit students with special needs into our class. Here are some actions we might take.

1. Communicate to the principal, other teachers, the special education teacher that we're interested in having very heterogeneous students in our class, including a few gifted kids as well as students with mild to severe disabilities.
2. Put this in writing in various formats—as part of the welcoming letter to parents and students at the start of the year, as an open letter to parents to be distributed at the PTA open house, as a proposal to the principal (see Figure 16.3).

Figure 16.3

Sample Letter from an Inclusive Teacher

Note: Underlined items will change depending on the school, teacher, and class.

To Whom It May Concern:

My name is <u>Laura Johnson.</u> I am a <u>seventh-grade social studies</u> teacher at <u>Burbank Middle School.</u> I am writing this letter to anyone who may be interested to let you know about my desire to have students with "special needs" in my class.

I believe that all students ought to go to school together. That's where they develop friendships that will last them all their lives, where they learn how to deal with others and handle their frustrations and fears. I'd like to have a class with students who have abilities ranging from gifted to severely cognitively impaired.

How will I teach such students? Well, please know that I am learning and that I expect to make mistakes. However, if we can work together, I know this can be a fun and valuable class for all my students. Students who can't yet talk will find a place, as will students who are exploring complex or advanced problems.

Building a community in which students can help and support one another is very important in my class. We have many ways to help that happen—peer buddies, cooperative work groups, and more. My classroom community gives students ways to lean on one another. If your child has some problem behaviors, we'll all be trying to understand what he or she feels and provide support.

I ask a few things. Here they are:

- That if you have a concern, you talk with me about it.
- That you be patient with me. I am learning.
- That students with special needs be the same age as my other students.
- That special education help and be delivered in my classroom and that I have some say in the type and extent of support I receive.
- That I not be sent *all* the students with special needs.

If you are a parent of a child with special needs, you may never have heard of a general education teacher who *wants* your child in her class. Trust me. I do.

If you are a special education teacher, you may feel the same way. I look forward to partnering with you.

If you are a student who they say has "special needs," I look forward to having you in my class.

Sincerely,

Laura Johnson

---

3. Find out if our school automatically sends some students to a special school or class based on their label. Consider getting a copy of your letter to those children's parents through the special education parent group.

In a school where all or some of the students with special needs are sent to separate classes, special education teachers often feel separated from the rest of the school. In some cases their students are not allowed to go on school field trips or to attend schoolwide assemblies. As we genuinely communicate to the special education teachers and parents that we'd like to have their children in our class, they will likely be surprised, grateful, and amazed. As we get to know special education teachers, we can explore ways to collaborate.

However, we'll also want to spell out some commonsense ground rules: some expectations based on best practices and on the reasonable supports available under the law. What might these expectations include?

1. That the student(s) will be the same age as all our other students (not the presumed same "mental ability level")
2. That special education services will be provided in our class and negotiated with us
3. That we will have time to plan collaboratively
4. That natural proportions will be adhered to—that students with special needs will be the same approximate percentage of our class as they are in the general district student population (around 12 percent as of this writing across the United States)

Supporting Change in Our School

Our goal is to help our students learn. However, the school culture in which we work makes an enormous difference. Most inclusive teachers find that they quickly discover ways to promote a culture of inclusion in the school as a whole (Fullan, 1997; Lipsky & Gartner, 1997; Taylor, Coughlin, & Marasco, 1997).

Artwork reprinted by permission of Martha Perske from *Perske: Pencil Portraits 1971–1990* (Nashville: Abingdon Press, 1998).

Modeling for and Supporting Other Teachers. As we begin to welcome students with special needs into our class, our class itself can become something of a model for the school. As we build relationships with other teachers, some will be interested in obtaining support, advice from us. A special note: If we are young, or even if we are an older but "new" teacher, we should not let our inexperience keep us from providing leadership. New teachers often bring perspectives and knowledge that can be valuable in helping to renew a school faculty. It may seem strange, at first, to find ourselves mentoring older teachers; but if we are being true to our journey toward inclusive teaching, we will be learning strategies that other teachers have never even thought about, much less tried.

Questioning Problematic Schoolwide Issues. Pretty quickly, we will begin to notice any number of issues that inhibit good learning for many students, including those with special needs. For example, we might find that . . .

- The special education resource teacher is busy all the time doing pull-out services, so she can't help support a student with learning disabilities in our class.
- There is no behavior support team, and the school has a zero tolerance policy, so students are suspended for minor infractions.
- The speech therapist repeatedly brings completed IEPs and asks us to sign them, rather than having IEP meetings as required by law.
- All special education students attend a segregated class in the building.

In each of these situations, we can question these practices and the rationales - behind them. As we do so, we may become clearer about our own thinking and philosophy.

Gaining Alliances. On the one hand, we want to build a culture of community in the school. On the other hand, in any community differences exist—and we will want to identify who is likely to support authentic, inclusive teaching. As we build relationships, talking and engaging in dialogue will help us gain allies.

Launching Schoolwide Change Efforts. A few of us will go into schools where inclusive teaching is simply how work is done. The schools that have moved successfully to full-fledged inclusion have also been able to build a community of learners that balance group collaboration with individual initiative. In such a school, it will be our role to continue to learn and grow and work with colleagues to improve.

Many of us, however, will find ourselves in settings that are very segregated—schools where students still go largely to separate special education classes or separate schools. Others of us will be in schools that have moved toward inclusive schooling but have stopped short of the goal. We'll see some strange practices. In all these situations, we have an important responsibility and an opportunity to seek ways to help spur continued change.

At best, we will be able to get together with general and special education teachers and with others who may be interested—perhaps parents and a university professor. We can function as a study or planning group. Some schools have such groups as part of ongoing school renewal efforts. If there are other groups in the school, we'll want to connect with them. Inclusive education interacts intimately, as we've discussed in this book, with instruction, parent partnerships, and support structures within the school. Such a group may simultaneously:

- Develop partnerships between general and special education teachers.
- Obtain videos or written materials to learn more about inclusive teaching.
- Visit inclusive schools.
- Gather data about the needs of students, including students with special needs—ranging from gifted students to second-language learners to students with mild to severe disabilities.
- Develop optional plans for rearranging the roles of special education teachers and assigning students to classes.
- Find students with more severe disabilities who would typically attend the school but who may be at a segregated special education school.

The leadership of the principal is critical, and in many cases the principal will actually initiate this process. Of course, inclusive teaching has its foundation in law. If a school is violating both the letter and the spirit of the law, as many do, administrators are usually well aware of this—and of their potential liability in the case of a lawsuit. We may be able to help them avoid lawsuits that would be harmful to all involved. Figure 16.4 reviews a few core targets that must be addressed as a school moves toward inclusion.

Being Part of District Initiatives

As we work to make our school a better place for all children, we will inevitably run up against problems—and opportunities—that are tied to districtwide policies and

Figure 16.4

Key Areas of Focus for Schoolwide Movement toward Inclusive Education

Welcoming all together: Commit to the idea that students of diverse abilities can learn well together. If opportunity presents itself, welcome a student with a severe disability into the school and class. Success with such students can provide a powerful model.

Instruction for all: Analyze methods of instruction. Does the curriculum require certain basal readers and texts that are at only one level? How can teachers teach at multiple levels, differentiating instruction? How might this teaching be improved?

Finding "lost" students: Many schools and districts send students with moderate to severe disabilities to special education programs without ever giving them the real chance to enter a regular school. We can identify these programs in our catchment area and find out who is there. We can offer the parents the opportunity to have their children in our school.

Structuring in-class support: Develop strategies for shifting special services from a "pull-out" to a "push-in" model. Explore ways to assign the caseloads of special education teachers or related services personnel.

Building-based support team: Any school needs multiple support strategies for teachers and students. With a support team that meets regularly, we can ask for assistance and ideas when we are having difficulties with a student.

Community and positive behavioral supports: Both building a culture of community in the school and developing proactive ways of responding to behavioral challenges are particularly important.

practices. If we are willing, we can find small ways and even major ways to confront these issues. We may discover, for example, that:

- The superintendent is pushing the school to raise average test scores on the state test. Many students with disabilities are sent home on test day; also, teachers spend two months focusing on rote learning for the test, gradually moving away from best practices as a result.
- Many students who should be going to our school don't even get the opportunity, because the central special education office sends students with moderate to severe disabilities to a segregated "center" program.
- The only software that can be installed on the computers in our classrooms must be programs approved by the district, so obtaining talking software or other materials is difficult.
- Equipment from the assistive technology center can be used only in the segregated school where the center is located and cannot be taken home.
- Interpreters can be used only in classes where deaf students are clustered.

For districtwide change we can mobilize strategies similar to those we employed in our own building. For example, we might:

- Develop allies and relationships with other teachers and staff members in the district. As we become effective in working with students of difference, we likely will find and be found by others who also are looking for allies.

- Raise questions about practices and offer solutions that will support inclusive teaching.
- Volunteer to serve on district committees—such as curriculum, parent partnerships, and inclusive education committees.
- Invite others to visit our class to demonstrate how we are working to teach inclusively. Offer to do presentations in other schools about how we teach, in collaboration with others.
- Develop relationships with parents and community representatives who would like to see inclusive education expanded, and offer to provide information about what we are doing.
- Consider working with others to intentionally organize; perhaps develop ways to present innovative proposals to the administration.

A high school girl shoots basketball at a youth camp.

As we and other teachers in our school teach inclusively, our school will likely be visited by other educators who are seeking to understand how inclusive schooling can work. This attention and recognition can help to strengthen our school's commitment to inclusive teaching, helping inclusion become part of the culture of the school.

Schools to Visit

Systematic Change for Inclusive Schooling

Rincon Middle School
925 Lehner Avenue
Escondido, California 92026
Phone: 760-432-2491
**www.escusd.k12.ca.us/Schools/rincon/
    index.htm**
Principal: Lou Bailey

It was the fall of 1997 when Rincon Middle School in Escondido, California, started the journey that would lead to the complete revamping of its primarily pull-out and special class model to a team teaching and consultative approach that allowed all students to be fully included in general education classes. How did this happen? What can we learn about the change process from the Rincon experience?

Villa and Thousand (1992) offer a four-phase model for values-based change. Phase one of any change initiative involves *visionizing*. Visionizing includes defining the potential preferred future and helping the community to understand this vision, see its benefits, and embrace it for the future. It was Ginny Sharp, then principal of Rincon, and Lisa Houghtelin, a parent of a child with disabilities and spokeswoman for a growing number of families seeking inclusion, who had the initial vision and the wisdom to assemble a core team. Following Ginny's passionate and tenacious lead, the team visited other inclusive schools, articulated their commitment to inclusive education, and drew in all of the special education faculty to devise a viable model for getting services into, rather than students out of, general education classrooms.

Phase two of the change process involves *introducing* the change, requiring visionaries to create discomfort and a sense of urgency by helping people understand that the old solutions no longer work to achieve equitable learning oppor-

tunities. At Rincon, they did this by having frequent personal dialogues with faculty members and by using outside helpers to redesign options and address faculty questions. For more than six months, the core team regularly and publicly met until they came up with the collaborative approach they believed could be sold. Knowing the importance of creating successful first examples, the principal advocated for and secured time for faculty to plan modifications and extra paraprofessional time that the team had identified as critical to making the plan work. The trust that the faculty had developed over the years, together with the observed support from the "outside" helpers, enabled faculty to overcome their initial fears and take the risk.

The goal of phase three, the *expanding* phase of the change process, is to transform the school culture so that everyone has not only a moral commitment to the new way but also the skills to act on this commitment. At Rincon, skill development was accomplished through daily and weekly in-service and "role release" sessions in regular planning and consultation meetings among teammates in the several "village" teams into which the school was divided. Each village team was made up of four subject-area teachers (i.e., humanities, social studies, mathematics, and science) and at least one special education professional and paraprofessional.

As part of expansion activities, faculty members were recognized in many ways for their risk taking and innovation. Site visits were made by notable national and regional inclusion leaders before and during the first year of implementation. Teachers were given a public forum to voice concerns and to celebrate one another's stories of positive impact. Visitors streamed into the school to look, listen, and learn from the faculty. Finally, the special education faculty solicited and secured outside grants.

(continued)

Schools to Visit

The fourth and final phase of the change process involves *selectively maintaining the change and the change process.* Despite the fact that the school has had three different principals since the inclusive model was conceptualized, the model is as strong as ever. At Rincon inclusive beliefs are key hiring criteria. At Rincon, students with disabilities are "hand scheduled"—these students are considered first, not last, when it is time to match them with classes, teachers, and the supports they need to succeed.

As with marriage, *maintaining* inclusive education requires eternal vigilance, compassion, questioning and active listening, positive storytelling, and a "solution-finding" versus a "problem-admiration" attitude. *Advancing* change and maintaining the change process requires that people understand that change is a journey, an ongoing process in which every member of the community is compelled to engage. There is no static, clear end point at which we all eventually arrive. The authors believe that at Rincon this is well understood and taken seriously.

By Jacqueline Thousand, professor, California State University–San Marcos, **jthousand@csusm.edu,** with Richard Villa, president, Bayridge Consortium; Sherri Zehnder, assistant principal; Lisa Houghtelin, parent; Terri Termath, sixth-grade humanities educator; Carolyn Zeisler, special educator; and Larry Welsch, seventh-grade humanities educator; also Ginny Sharp, former Rincon principal and instructor, and Janet McDaniel, professor, California State University–San Marcos.

Organizing to Influence Policy

Many teachers are coming together with parents and community members to help change educational policies. Some work through professional associations. Others have organized local action groups. We can engage in many types of actions to promote better policies. A few examples:

- Testifying at public policy forums held by legislators
- Making presentations at conferences regarding policy issues
- Writing letters to legislators or state bureaucrats concerning policies
- Working to organize legislative efforts to pass new laws or regulations or to defeat particular policies

Onward Ho!
Toward Creating Good Schools for All

It is time to part now. We've been honored to journey with you, and we've learned a lot. The journey has been hard and exciting and confusing. At its end we have more questions than when we began. Ah, yes—we've heard that happens when learning is at its best. As we rest at the end of our trek, our mind wanders through the mountains and valleys of our journey. We can't wait to make what we've seen in a few schools become a new reality for all students.

So the real journey is about to begin. As we travel these new lands of creating real inclusion in an exclusionary world, we'll continue to discover both the route and the concrete destination as we gather together with other travelers who decide

Stepping Stones

To Inclusive Teaching

There are many practical strategies you can use to be an inclusive teacher and to help build an inclusive school. Here are a few practical suggestions for applying the ideas in this chapter.

1. Talk to people in your school and in your school district. Find out about initiatives, studies, or work groups that have addressed issues of inclusion, least restrictive environment, differentiated instruction, and related topics. Who was involved? Talk to the participants and ask them what happened.

2. Similarly, talk to the principal of your school, the special education director, or other teachers to find out what district-level initiatives or plans, if any, are in process. This will help you understand what support might undergird your efforts to be an inclusive teacher.

3. Know your school. Find out how the different services for students with special needs—students with disabilities, students labeled gifted, at-risk students, bilingual students, and others—are being implemented. If changes are needed, see how people are thinking.

4. At the same time, start in your own class. Work toward figuring out how to teach children together at multiple levels. Do a lesson or two to get started.

5. If students with disabilities are in classes in your school, ask that *all* the neighborhood students who would typically come to the school are invited in. At many schools students with mild disabilities are included, but those with moderate to severe disabilities still go to separate schools. In collaboration with the special education teacher, invite *one* new student into your class.

6. Every state has a group working toward inclusive education. Find that group and go to a meeting. Ask about having a member of the group come to your school and talk about inclusion.

7. Mostly, get clear about your own position. Write it down. Articulate why you believe what you believe. Reflect on this often.

to journey with us. As we face change on our way, our "key to success," in fact, "lies in the creative activity of making new maps" (Stacey, 1992, p. 1). We'll share those maps with other explorers, and gradually we can settle in this new land.

We look forward to visiting you one day in your inclusive school. We anticipate watching you engage students of various races, cultures, and abilities; seeing you in

a discussion with a group of fellow teachers as you ponder over a student problem or rejoice in an amazing turn of learning and growth; listening as you share at a conference with a team of students, parents, and teachers the amazing wonders of growth, pain, laughter, sorrow, and learning in your inclusive classroom. We look forward to learning new lessons from you on that day. We'll smile and greet you, knowing that at the end, courage and comradeship are what really matters.

Till then,

We are Michael and Mishael

 Key Points

- The evidence is pretty clear that inclusive schools would improve the learning of all students, including those with mild to severe disabilities. Yet such schools are a minority. We all have the responsibility to help create good schools and to promote excellence in instruction.

- School change is not easy, but it can be done. Change involves all of us. It must be both top-down and bottom-up. Problems can be helpful; they force us to think in different ways.

- When teachers decide to become leaders for change, we gradually shift from isolated frustration to connection with like-minded others. We can come together to provide support and take action in ways both large and small. Ultimately, we build a movement for change.

- We can use many strategies to move toward inclusive schooling. We've outlined many in

Stepping Stones features throughout this book. First, we must decide to become leaders to promote change. Then we can:

✓ Model inclusive teaching in our classroom, welcoming students with differing abilities and needs into our class and reaching out to a special education teacher to recruit a student with a disability into our class.

✓ Support change in our school and district by networking with other teachers, making suggestions to administration, serving on study committees.

✓ Connect with networks of others to influence state and national policy by writing position statements, interacting with policymakers, and participating in conferences.

 Learning Expeditions

Following are some activities that may deepen your understanding of issues and strategies discussed in this chapter.

1. Visit an inclusive school. Talk with teachers about the roles that they played in helping the school become inclusive. What do they say? What patterns do you discern?

2. Visit a school in which students are sent to separate special programs—gifted, special education, bilingual, and so forth. Ask the general education teachers for their opinions about inclusive teaching. What do they see as their role in helping improve the school as a whole, and what do they think about having students with special needs in their classes? How do you interpret their responses?

3. Ask a panel of inclusive teachers to discuss their classes and their school. Conduct a focus group

discussion with them. What do they think has been their role in advocacy for change in their class, in their school, in the district, and in state/federal policy? What actions have some of them taken? What do their responses mean?

4. Outline a plan for how you would start to move a school toward inclusive teaching. Where might you start, and why? How would you deal with concerns?

5. Interview parents and students in an inclusive school in a small focus group discussion. What has been their experience? What do they feel about the school? What might make the school better? What role did they see teachers playing in making the school inclusive?

6. Write your own letter setting forth your beliefs about teaching and about the inclusion of "students with special needs." Share and discuss this letter with a small group of other teachers.

References

Adam, B. (1978). *The survival of domination: Inferiorization and everyday life.* New York: Elsevier.

Adams, J., Swain, J., & Clark, J. (2000). What's so special? Teacher's models and their realization in practice in segregated schools. *Disability and Society, 15*(2), 233–245.

Affleck, J., Madge, S., Adams, A., & Lowenbraun, S. (1988). Integrated classroom versus resource model: Academic viability and effectiveness. *Exceptional Children, 54,* 339–348.

Agnew, J., Van Cleaf, D., Camblin, A., & Shaffer, M. (1994). Here's how: Successful scheduling for full inclusion. *Principal, 74*(2), 18–22.

Agron, J. (1998). The urban challenge: Meeting unique and diverse facility demands. *American School and University, 70*(11), 18–20.

Ainscow, M. (1999). *Understanding the development of inclusive schools.* London: Falmer Press.

Albert, L. (1996). *Cooperative discipline.* Circle Pines, MN: American Guidance Service.

Albin, R. W., Horner, R. H., & O'Neill, R. E. (1994). *Proactive behavioral support: Structuring and assessing environments.* Eugene, OR: Research and Training Center on Positive Behavioral Support.

Allen, R., & Petr, C. (1995). *Family-centered service delivery: A cross-disciplinary literature review and conceptualization.* Lawrence, KS: Beach Center on Families and Disability.

Alliance for Technology Access. (1996). *Computer resources for people with disabilities: A guide to exploring today's assistive technology.* Alameda, CA: Hunter House.

Allington, R. (1991). Children who find learning to read difficult: School responses to diversity. In E. Hiebert (Ed.), *Literacy for a diverse society: Perspective, practices, and policies.* New York: Teachers College Press.

Allington, R. (1993). The reading instruction provided readers of differing reading abilities. *The Elementary School Journal, 83*(5), 548–559.

Allington, R. (1994). What's so special about special programs for children who find learning to read difficult? *Journal of Reading Behavior, 26*(1), 95–115.

Altman, R., & Lewis, T. J. (1990). Social judgments of integrated and segregated students with mental retardation toward same-age peers. *Education and Training in Mental Retardation, 25,* 107–112.

Amado, A. (1993). *Friendships and community connections between people with and without developmental disabilities.* Baltimore: Paul H. Brookes.

American Association for the Advancement of Science. (1989). *Science for all Americans: Project 2061.* Washington, DC: Author.

American Association on Mental Retardation (AAMR) (1992). *Mental retardation: Definition, classification, and system of supports* (9th ed.). Washington, DC: Author.

American Cancer Society. (2000). Cancer in children. Retrieved July 1, 2002, from www.cancer.org/eprise/main/docroot/CRI/CR1_2x?sitearea=LRN&dt=7.

American Federation of Teachers. (1993). *Resolution on inclusion of students with disabilities.* Washington, DC: Author.

American Lung Association. (2000). Asthma attacks. Retrieved July 1, 2002, from www.lungusa.org/asthma.

American Psychiatric Association (APA). (2000). *Diagnostic and statistical manual of mental disorders. Fourth edition. Text revision.* Washington, DC: Author.

American Speech and Hearing Association. (1994). *Facilitated communication: Technical report.* Rockville, MD: Author.

Americans With Disabilities Act (1990), 42 U.S.C.A. § 12101 *et seq.* (West 1993).

Ammerman, R., Van Hasselt, V., & Hersen, M. (1988). Abuse and neglect in handicapped children: A critical review. *Journal of Family Violence, 3*(2), 53–72.

Amish, P., Gesten, E., Smith, J., & Clark, H. (1988). Social problem-solving training for severely emotionally and behaviorally disturbed children. *Behavioral Disorders, 13,* 175–186.

Anderson, C., & Fetters, M. (1996). Science education trends and special education. In M. Pugach & C. Warger (Eds.), *Curriculum trends, special education, and reform: Refocusing the conversation.* New York: Teachers College Press.

Apple, M. (1995). *Democratic schools.* Alexandria, VA: Association for Supervision and Curriculum Development.

Armstrong, T. (1994). *Multiple intelligences in the classroom.* Alexandria, VA: Association for Supervision and Curriculum Development.

Armstrong, T. (1997). *The myth of the A.D.D child: 50 ways to improve your child's behavior and attention span without drugs, labels, or coercion.* New York: Plume Book.

Arnold, A. (1998, January). *Inclusion: Whole schooling.* Address presented at the University of Wisconsin–Stevens Point, Stevens Point, WI.

Asante, S. (1997). *When spider webs unite*, pp. 75–76. Toronto, ON: Inclusion Press.

Au, K., Mason, J., & Scheu, J., (1995) *Literacy instruction for today.* New York: HarperCollins.

Baer, J. (1994). The web we weave: Creating the fabric of peacemaking. *Primary Voices: K–6, 2*(4), 12–14.

Baines, L., Baines, C., & Masterson, C. (1994). Mainstreaming: One school's reality. *Phi Delta Kappan, 76*(1), 39–40.

Baker, E. T. (1994). *Meta-analytic evidence for non-inclusive educational practices: Does educational research support current practice for special-needs students?* Unpublished doctoral dissertation, Temple University, Philadelphia.

Baker, E. T., Wang, M. C., & Walberg, H. J. (1994). The effects of inclusion on learning. *Educational Leadership, 52*(4), 33–35.

Baker, J., & Zigmond, N. (1995). The meaning and practice of inclusion for students with learning disabilities: Themes and implications from five case studies. *Journal of Special Education, 29*(2), 163–180.

Balboni, M., Giulia, F., & Pedrabissi, L. (2000). Attitudes of Italian teachers and parents toward school inclusion of students with mental retardation: The role of experience. *Education and Training in Mental Retardation and Developmental Disabilities, 35*(2), 148–159.

Ballen, J., & Moles, O. (1994). *Strong families, strong schools.* Washington, DC: U.S. Department of Education.

Banerji, M., & Dailey, R. (1995). A study of the effects of an inclusion model on students with specific learning disabilities. *Journal of Learning Disabilities, 28*, 511–522.

Banks, J. (1990). Citizenship education for a pluralistic democratic society. *The Social Studies, 81*, 210–214.

Banks, J. (1995). *Creating the multi-age classroom.* Edmonds, WA: CATS Publications.

Banks, J. (1994). *All of us together: The story of inclusion at the Kinzie School.* Washington D.C.: Gallaudet University Press.

Barnett, D. (1982). The effects of open-space versus traditional, self-contained classrooms on the auditory selective attending skills of elementary children. *Language, Speech, and Hearing Services in the Schools, 13*, 138–143.

Barnett, D. (1997). *Helping children learn: Comprehensive school-linked services.* Detroit: Skillman Center for Children, Wayne State University.

Bauer, A., & Myree-Brown, G. (2001). *Adolescents and inclusion: Transforming secondary schools.* Baltimore: Paul H. Brookes.

Bauwens, J., & Hourcade, J. (1998). *Cooperative teaching: Rebuilding the schoolhouse for all students.* Austin, TX: Pro-Ed.

Beach Center on Families and Disability. (1994). *Positive behavioral support as a means to enhance successful inclusion of persons with challenging behavior.* Lawrence, KS: Author.

Beaumont, C. (1999). Dilemmas of peer assistance in a bilingual full inclusion classroom. *Elementary School Journal, 99*(3), 233–254.

Becher, R. (1984). *Parent involvement: A review of research and principles of successful practice.* Washington, DC: National Institute of Education.

Begali, V. (1992). *Head injury in children and adolescents: A resource and review for school and allied professionals.* Brandon, VT: Clinical Psychology.

Bell, T. (1994). Understanding students with traumatic brain injury: A guide for teachers and therapists. *School System: Special Interest Section Newsletter, 1*(2), 1–4.

Bellah, R., Madsen, R., Sullivan, W., Swidler, A., & Tipton, S. (1985). *Habits of the heart: Individualism and commitment in American life.* San Francisco: Harper & Row.

Bellamy, G. T., Rhodes, L., Mank, D., & Albin, J. (1988). *Supported employment: A community implementation guide.* Baltimore: Paul H. Brookes.

Beloin, K. (1997). *Using read-alouds for students with intellectual disabilities in general education classrooms: Implications for educators.* Unpublished manuscript, Cardinal Stritch University, College of Education, Milwaukee, WI.

Beloin, K. (1998). Strategies for developing inclusive practices in small, rural schools. *Rural Special Education Quarterly, 17*(1), 12–20.

Bender, W. (1997). *Understanding ADHD: A practical guide for teachers and parents.* Columbus, OH: Merrill.

Benjamin, A. (1981). *A helping interview* (3rd ed.). Boston: Houghton Mifflin.

Berg, P. (1989, May 7). School runs with no punishment, just simple rules. *St. Paul Pioneer Press*, pp. 1b, 10b.

Berk, L., & Winsler, A. (1995). *Scaffolding children's learning: Vygotsky and early childhood education,* Washington, DC: National Association for the Education of Young Children.

Berkowitz, E. (1987). *Disabled policy: America's programs for the handicapped.* Cambridge, UK: Cambridge University Press.

Berres, M., & Knoblock, P. (1987). *Program models for mainstreaming: Integrating students with moderate to severe disabilities.* Rockville, MD: Aspen.

Berrigan, C. (1994). *Schools in Italy: A national policy made actual.* Syracuse, NY: Center on Human Policy, Syracuse University. Retrieved July 1, 2002 from web.syr.edu/~thechp/italy.htm.

Bertrand, J., Mars, A., Boyle, C., Bove, F., Yeargin-Allsopp, M., & Decoufle, P. (2001). Prevalence of autism in a United States population: The Brick Township, New Jersey, investigation. *Pediatrics, 108*(5), 1155–1161.

Bettleheim, B. (1967). *The empty fortress: Infantile autism and the birth of the self.* London: Collier-Macmillan.

Beukelman, D., & Mirenda, P. (1992). *Augmentative and alternative communication: Management of severe communication disorders in children and adults.* Baltimore: Paul H. Brookes.

Biederman, J. (1996). Are stimulants over-prescribed for children with behavioral problems? *Pediatrics News, 3*, 3–4.

Bigelow, B. (1995). Show, don't tell: Roleplays and social imagination. In M. Burke-Hengen & T. Gillespie (Eds.). *Building community: Social studies in the middle years.* Portsmouth, NH: Heinemann.

Bigelow, B., Christensen, L., Karp, S., Miner, B., & Peterson, B., (Eds.). (1994). *Rethinking our classrooms: Teaching for equity and justice.* Milwaukee, WI: Rethinking Schools.

Bigge, J. (1991). *Teaching individuals with physical and multiple disabilities* (3rd ed.). New York: Macmillan.

Biklen, D. (1985). *The complete school: Integrating special and general education.* New York: Teachers College Press.

Biklen, D. (1990). Communication unbound: Autism and praxis. *Harvard Educational Review, 60*(3), 291–314.

Biklen, D. (1992). Typing to talk: Facilitated communication. *American Journal of Speech-Language Pathology, 1*(2), 15–17.

Biklen, D., Corrigan, C., & Quick, D. (1989). Beyond obligation: Students' relation with each other in integrated classes. In D. Lipsky & A. Gartner (Eds.), *Beyond separate education: Quality education for all.* Baltimore: Paul H. Brookes.

Bishop, K., Woll, J., & Arango, P. (1993). *Family/professional collaboration for children with special health needs and their families.* Burlington, VT: Department of Social Work.

Blanksby, D. (1999). Not quite eureka: Perceptions of a trial of cluster grouping as a model for addressing the diverse range of student abilities at a junior secondary school. *Educational Studies, 25*(1), 79–88.

Blatt, B. (1966). *Christmas in purgatory: A photographic essay on mental retardation.* Boston: Allyn & Bacon.

Block, M., & Zeman, R. (1996). Including students with disabilities in regular physical education: Effects on nondisabled children. *Adapted Physical Activity Quarterly, 13,* 38–49.

Bloom, B. S. (Ed.). (1956). Taxonomy of educational objectives: The classification of educational goals: Handbook I. Cognitive domain. New York/Toronto: Longmans, Green.

Blosser, J., & DePompei, R. (1989). The head injured student returns to schools: Recognizing and treating deficits. *Topics in Language Disorders, 9*(2), 67–77.

Blum, J. (1968). *The national experience.* New York: Harcourt, Brace, & World.

Boggiano, A. K., & Barrett, M. (1992). Gender differences in depression in children as a function of motivational orientation. *Sex Roles, 26*(1), 11–17.

Booth, T., & Ainscow, M. (1998). *From them to us: An international study of inclusion in education.* London: Creative Press and Design.

Boudah, D., Schumacher, J., & Deschler, D. (1997). Collaborative instruction: Is it an effective option for inclusion in secondary classrooms? *Learning Disabilities Quarterly, 20,* 293–316.

Boundless Playgrounds. (2001). *Welcome to Boundless Playgrounds.* Retrieved July 1, 2002, from www.boundlessplaygrounds.org/index.html.

Bowen, M., & Glenn, E. (1998). Counseling interventions for students who have mild disabilities. *Professional School Counseling, 2*(1), 1–9.

Bracey, G. (2000). The 10th Bracey report on the condition of public education. *Phi Delta Kappan, 82*(2), 133–144.

Braddock, D., Hemp, R., Fujiura, G., & Bachelder, L. (1995). *The state of the states in developmental disabilities* (4th ed.). Washington, DC: American Association of Mental Retardation.

Bradley, V. (1994). Evolution of a new service paradigm. In V. J. Bradley, J. W. Ashbaugh, & B. Blaney (Eds.), *Creating individual supports for people with developmental disabilities: A mandate for change at many levels.* Baltimore: Paul H. Brookes.

Braithwaite, D., & Thompson, T. (Eds.). (2000). *Handbook of communication and people with disabilities: Research and application.* Mahwah, NJ: Erlbaum.

Brantlinger, E. (1995). *Sterilization of people with mental disabilities: Issues, perspectives, and cases.* Westport, CT: Auburn House.

Bredekamp, S., & Copple, C. (Eds.). (1997). *Developmentally appropriate practice in early childhood programs* (Rev. ed.). Washington, DC: National Association for the Education of Young Children.

Breeding, J. (1996). *The wildest colts make the best horses: What to do when your child is labeled a problem by the schools.* Austin, TX: Bright Books.

Breggin, G. (2000). Ritalin class action suit filed. Center for the Study of Psychiatry and Psychology. Retrieved July 1, 2002, from www.breggin.com/classaction.html.

Breggin, P. (1998). *Talking back to Ritalin: What doctors aren't telling you about stimulants for children.* Monroe, ME: Common Courage Press.

Breggin, P. (2000). *Reclaiming our children: The healing solution for a nation in crisis.* Cambridge, MA: Perseus.

Breggin, P., & Cohen, (1999). *Your drug may be your problem: How and why to stop taking psychiatric medications.* Reading, MA: Perseus Books.

Breggin, P., & Ross-Breggin, G. (1994). *The war against children: How the drugs, programs, and theories of the psychiatric establishment are threatening America's children with a medical "cure" for violence.* New York: St. Martin's.

Brett, A., & Provenzo, E. (1995). *Adaptive technology for special human needs.* Albany, NY: State University of New York Press.

Briggs, H. E. (1996). Creating independent voices: The emergence of statewide family networks. *Journal of Mental Health Administration, 23*(4), 447–457.

Briggs, H. E., Koroloff, N. M., Richards, K., & Friesen, B. J. (1993). *Family advocacy organizations: Advances in support and system reform.* Portland, OR: Research and Training Center on Family Support and Children's Mental Health, Portland State University.

Brinker, R. P., & Thorpe, M. E. (1984). Integration of severely handicapped students and the proportion of IEP objectives achieved. *Exceptional Children 51*(2), 168–175.

Brolin, D. (1993). *Life-centered career education curriculum guide.* Reston, VA: Council for Exceptional Children.

Bronfenbrenner, U. (1979). *The ecology of human development: Experiments by nature and design.* Cambridge, MA: Harvard University Press.

Brooks, G. (1985). The study of maturational timing effects in adolescence. *Journal of Youth and Adolescence, 14*(3), 149–161.

Brown, L., Schwarz, P., Udvari-Solner, A., Kampschroer, E., Johnson, F., Jorgensen, J., & Gruenwald, L. (1991) How much time should students with severe intellectual disabilities spend in regular education classrooms and elsewhere? *Journal of the Association for Persons with Severe Handicaps (JASH), 16*(1), 39–47.

Brown, T. (1998). *Dorothea Dix: New England reformer.* Cambridge, MA: Harvard University Press.

Brownell, M. (2000). *The use of musically adapted social stories to modify behaviors in students with autism: Four case studies.* Lawrence, KS: University of Kansas.

Burke-Hengen, M., & Gillespie, T. (1995). *Building community: Social studies in the middle school years.* Portsmouth, NH: Heinemann.

Butler-Hayes, R. (1995). *A study of high school stakeholders' attitudes about inclusion in the Chicago Public Schools.* Unpublished doctoral dissertation, Roosevelt University, Chicago.

Buysse, V., & Bailey, D. (1993). Behavioral and developmental outcomes in young children with disabilities in integrated and segregated settings: A review of comparative studies. *The Journal of Special Education, 26,* 434–461.

Caine, R. N., & Caine, G. (1991). *Making connections: Teaching and the human brain.* (1997). Alexandria, VA: Association for Supervision and Curriculum Development.

Caine, R. N., & Caine, G. (1995). Reinventing schools through brain-based learning. *Educational Leadership, 52*(2), 43–47.

Califano, J. (1982). *Governing America.* New York: Touchstone.

Calkins, L. (1994). *The art of teaching writing.* Portsmouth, NH: Heinemann.

Calkins, L. M., Montgomery, R., Santman, D., & Falk, B. (1998). *A teacher's guide to standardized reading tests: Knowledge is power.* Portsmouth, NH: Heinemann.

Campbell, L., & Campbell, B. (1999). *Multiple intelligences and student achievement: Success stories from six schools.* Alexandria, VA: Association for Supervision and Curriculum Development.

Capaldi, D., & Dishion, T. (1993). *The relation of conduct problems and depressive symptoms to growth in substance abuse in adolescent boys.* Eugene, OR: Social Learning Center (ERIC document: ED356077).

Carkhuff, R. (2000). *The art of helping in the twenty-first century.* Amherst, MA: Human Resource Development Press.

Carlberg, C., & Kavale, K. (1980). The efficacy of special versus regular class placement for exceptional children: A meta-analysis. *Journal of Special Education, 14,* 295–309.

Carpenter, S., King-Sears, M., & Keys, S. (1998). Counselors + educators + families as a trans-disciplinary team = more effective inclusion for students with disabilities. *Professional School Counseling, 2*(1), 16–25.

Carr, E. G., Levin, L., McConnachie, G., Carlson, J., Kemp, D. C., & Smith, C. E. (1994). *Communication-based intervention for problem behavior: A user's guide for producing positive change.* Baltimore: Paul H. Brookes.

Cartledge, G., & Johnson, C. (1996). Inclusive classrooms for students with emotional and behavioral disorders: Critical variables. *Theory into Practice, 35*(2), 51–57.

Cartledge, G., & Kleefeld, J. (1994). *Working together: Building children's social skills through folk literature.* Circle Pines, MN: American Guidance Service.

Ceifetz, C. (1997). *Inclusive education observation report.* Detroit: Wayne State University.

Center for Applied Special Technology (CAST). (2002). Retrieved July 1, 2002, from www.cast.org/.

Center for Disease Control. (1988). Perspectives in disease prevention and health promotion update: Universal precautions for prevention of transmission of human immunodeficiency virus, hepatitis B virus, and other bloodborne pathogens. *MMWR Weekly, 37*(24), 377–388.

Center for Disease Control. (2001). *HIV/AIDS surveillance report.* Atlanta, GA: Author. www.cdc.gov/hiv/stats/hasr1301/fig5.htm.

Center for Effective Collaboration and Practice. (1994). *National agenda for achieving better results for children and youth with serious emotional disturbance.* Washington, DC: Office of Special Education and Rehabilitative Services, U.S. Department of Education.

Center for Effective Collaboration and Practice. (1999). Think time strategy. Retrieved July 1, 2002, from *Success Stories.* www.air-dc.org/cecp/resources/success/think_time.htm.

Cessna, K., & Skiba, R. (1996). Needs-based services: A responsible approach to inclusion. *Preventing School Failure, 40*(3), 117–123.

Champagne, A., Newell, S., & Goodnough, J. (1996). Trends in science education. In M. Pugach & C. Warger (Eds.), *Curriculum trends, special education, and reform: Refocusing the conversation.* New York: Teachers College Press.

Charles, M. (1999). *Building classroom discipline.* New York: Longman.

Chase, P., & Doan, J. (1994). *Full circle: A new look at multiage education.* Portsmouth, NH: Heineman.

Chedd, N. (May, 1995). Getting started with augmentative communication. *Exceptional Children, 28*(5), 34–39.

Cheney, D., & Harvey, V. (1994). From segregation to inclusion: One district's program changes for students with emotional/behavioral disorders. *Education and Treatment of Children, 17*(3), 332–346.

Cheney, D., & Muscott, H. (1996). Preventing school failure for students with emotional and behavioral disabilities through responsible inclusion. *Preventing School Failure, 40*(2), 109–116.

Christiansen, J., & Vogel, J. (1998). A decision model for grading students with disabilities. *Teaching Exceptional Children, 31*(2), 30–35.

Clarizio, H. F. (1992). Social maladjustment and emotional disturbance: Problems and positions II. *Psychology in the Schools, 29*(2), 331–341.

Clark, B. (1997). *Growing up gifted.* Columbus, OH: Merrill.

Clark, G. (1994) Is a functional curriculum approach compatible with an inclusive education model? *Teaching Exceptional Children, 26*(2), 36–39.

Cline, S. (1999). *Giftedness has many faces.* New York: Foundation for Concepts in Education.

Closing the gap. (2000, February/March). *2000 Resource Directory: Hardware, Software, Producers, Organizations: A Guide to the Selection of the Latest Computer Related Products for Children and Adults with Special Needs, 18*(6).

Cogswell, A. (1984). *When the mind hears: A history of the deaf.* New York: Random House.

Cohen, D. (1990). A look at multiage classrooms. *Education Week, 9*(2), 13–15.

Cohen, E. (Ed.). (1994). *Designing groupwork: Strategies for the heterogenous classroom.* New York: Teachers College Press.

Cohen, M. K. (1994, July). *Children on the boundary: The challenge posed by children with conduct disorders.* Alexandria, VA: Project FORUM, National Association of State Directors of Special Education.

Cohen, O. (1994, April 29). Inclusion should not include deaf students. *Education Week,* pp. 10–13.

Cohen, S. (1991). Adapting educational programs for students with traumatic brain injury. *Journal of Head Injury, 6*(1), 56–63.

Cole, D., & Meyer, L. H. (1991). Social integration and severe disabilities: A longitudinal analysis of child outcomes. *The Journal of Special Education, 19*(4), 483–492.

Cole, R. (Ed.). (1995). *Educating everybody's children: Diverse teaching strategies for diverse learners: What research and practice say about improving achievement.* Alexandria, VA: Association for Supervision and Curriculum Development.

Coleman, J. S. (1994). Family involvement in education. In C. Fagnano & B. Werber (Eds.), *School, family, and community interaction: A view from the firing lines.* San Francisco: Westview Press.

Coles, C. (1987). *The learning mystique: A critical look at "learning disabilities."* New York: Pantheon Books.

Coles, G. (1998). *Reading lessons: The debate over literacy.* New York: Hill & Wang.

Coles, G. (2000). *Misreading reading: The bad science that hurts children.* Portsmouth, NH: Heinemann.

Comer, J. (1987). New Haven's school–community collaboration. *Educational Leadership, 44*(6), 13–16.

Comer, J. (1988, November). Educating poor minority children. *Scientific American,* pp. 42–48.

Comer, J. (1997). *Waiting for a miracle: Why schools can't solve our problems and how we can.* New York: Dutton.

Comfort, R. (1994). Understanding and appreciating the ADHD child in the classroom. In C. Weaver (Ed.), *Success at last: Helping students with AD(H)D achieve their potential.* Portsmouth, NH: Heinemann.

Condeluci, A. (1991). *Interdependence: The route to community.* Orlando, FL: Paul M. Deutsch.

Connecticut Interscholastic Athletic Conference. (2001). *Unified Sports coaches handbook* Cheshire, CT: Author.

Connell, R., Jones, M., Mace, R., Mueller, J., Mullick, A., Ostroff, E., Sanford, J., Steinfeld, E., Story, M., & Vanderheiden, G. (1997). *The principles of universal design.* Center for Universal Design. Retrieved July 1, 2002, from www.design.ncsu.edu/cud/univ_design/principles/udprinciples.htm.

Consedine, J. (1995). *Restorative justice: Healing the effects of crime.* Lyttleton, New Zealand: Plowshares.

Cook, A., & Hussey, S. (1995). *Assistive technologies: Principles and practice.* New York: Mosby.

Cornelius, D. (1980). *Inside out.* Washington, DC: Regional Rehabilitation Institute, George Washington University.

Council for Exceptional Children. (1993). *CEC policy on inclusive schools and community settings.* Reston, VA: Author.

Counseling Services Learning Skills Program. (2001). *Bloom's taxonomy.* Victoria, British Columbia, Canada: University of Victoria.

Covey, S. (1989). *The seven habits of successful people: Restoring the character ethic.* New York: Simon & Schuster.

Cragg, W. (1992). *The practice of punishment: Toward a theory of restorative justice.* New York: Routledge.

Crider, B. (1998, April). *Families and professionals: A needed partnership for inclusion.* Presentation at the College of Education, Wayne State University, Detroit.

Criteria for determining the existence of a specific learning disability, 34 C.F.R. 300.541 (1997).

Crossley, R. (1994). *Facilitated communication training.* New York: Teachers College Press.

Cullinan, D., Epstein, M., & Sabornie, E. (1992). Selected characteristics of a national sample of seriously emotionally disturbed adolescents. *Behavioral Disorders, 17*(4), 273–280.

Cunningham, P., & Allington, R. (1999). *Classrooms that work: They can all read and write.* New York: Longman.

Daniels, H. (1994). *Literature circles: Voice and choice in the student-centered classroom.* York, ME: Stenhouse.

Daniels, H., & Bizar, M. (1998). *Methods that matter: Six structures for best practice classrooms.* York, ME: Stenhouse.

D.F. v. Western School Corp., 23 IDELR 1121 (Ind. 1996).

Dart, J. (1987). *Disability policy.* Address at the annual meeting of the National Association of State Directors of Vocational Rehabilitation, Washington, DC.

Davis, M. (1996). *My experience as a person with ADD.* Presentation at Wayne State University, Detroit.

Davis, R., & Maher, C. (1996). A new view of the goals and means for school mathematics. In M. Pugach & C. Warger (Eds.), *Curriculum trends, special education, and reform: Refocusing the conversation.* New York: Teachers College Press.

DEAL Communications Center (2001). Caulfield, Victoria, Australia. Retrieved July 1, 2002; from home.vicnet.net.au/~dealccinc/.

Delpit, L. (1995). *Other people's children: Cultural conflict in the classroom.* New York: New Press.

Deno, E. (1970). Special education as developmental capital. *Exceptional Children, 37,* 235.

Deno, S., Maruyama, G., Espin, C., & Cohen, C. (1990). Educating students with mild disabilities in general education classrooms: Minnesota alternatives. *Exceptional Children, 57*(2), 150–161.

Denton, P., & Kriete, R. (2000). *The first six weeks of school*. Greenfield, MA: Northeast Foundation for Children.

Deschenes, C., Ebeling, D., & Sprague, J. (1994). *Adapting curriculum and instruction in inclusive classrooms: A teacher's desk reference*. Bloomington, IN: Institute for the Study of Developmental Disabilities, Indiana University.

Developmental Studies Center. (1994). *At home in our schools: A guide to school-wide activities that build community*. Oakland, CA: Author.

Dewey, J. (1916). *Democracy and education*. New York: Macmillan.

Dewey, J. (1938). *Experience and education*. New York: Collier.

Dewey, J. (1943). *The school and society*. Chicago: University of Chicago Press.

Diener, C., & Dweck, C. (1978). An analysis of learned helplessness: Continuous challenges in performance, strategy, and achievement cognitions following failure. *Journal of Personality and Social Psychology, 35*, 451–462.

Diller, L. (1998). *Running on Ritalin: A physician reflects on children, society, and performance in a pill*. New York: Bantam.

Disability Rights Advocates. (1999). *Forgotten Crimes: The Holocaust and people with disabilities*. Retrieved July 1, 2002, from www.dralegal.org/projects/disability/holocaust/.

Doucette, A. (1997, December). *Profiling preliminary results of family-research collaboration: The CMHS evaluation*. Paper presented at the Comprehensive Community Mental Health Services Program for Children with Serious Emotional Disturbances Project Directors' Meeting, New Orleans, LA.

Douglas, R. (1997). Democracy and empowerment: The Nashville student sit-ins of the 1960's. In A. Manley & C. O'Neill (Eds.), *Dreamseekers: Creative approaches to the African-American heritage*. Portsmouth, NH: Heinemann.

Dover, W. (1994). *The inclusion facilitator*. Manhattan, KS: Master Teacher.

Dowson, S., & Salisbury, B. (2000). *Foundations for freedom: International perspectives on self-determination and individualized funding*. Baltimore: The Association for Persons with Severe Handicaps (TASH).

Doyle, M. (1997). *The paraprofessionals guide to the inclusive classroom: Working as a team*. Baltimore: Paul H. Brookes.

Drake, S. (1993). *Planning integrated curriculum: The call to adventure*. Alexandria, VA: Association for Supervision and Curriculum Development.

Drew, C., & Hardman, M. (2000). *Mental retardation: A life cycle approach*. Columbus, OH: Merrill.

Dryfoos, J. (1994). *Full-service schools: A revolution in health and social services for children, youth, and families*. San Francisco: Jossey-Bass.

Drug Enforcement Administration. (1995). *Methylphenidate: A background paper*. Washington, DC: Drug and Chemical Evaluation Section, Office of Diversion Control, D.E.A., U.S. Department of Justice.

Duffey-Hester, A. M. (1999). Teaching struggling readers in elementary school classrooms: A review of classroom reading programs and principles for instruction. *The Reading Teacher, 52*(5), 480–495.

Dunn, L. (1968). Special education for the mildly retarded: Is much of it justifiable? *Exceptional Children, 35*(1), 5–22.

Dunn, R. (1996). *How to implement and supervise a learning style program*. Alexandria, VA: Association for Supervision and Curriculum Development.

Dunst, C. (1987). *Enabling and empowering families: Conceptual and intervention issues*. Morgantown, NC: Western Carolina Center, Family Infant and Preschool Program.

DuPaul, G., & Stoner, G. (1994). *ADHD in the schools: Assessment and intervention strategies*. New York: Gilford Press.

Dybwad, G., Bersani, H., & Williams, B. (1998). *New voices: Self-advocacy by people with disabilities*. Cambridge, MA: Brookline.

Dyer, F. (1993). Clinical presentation of the lead-poisoned child on mental ability tests. *Journal of Clinical Psychology, 49*(2), 94–101.

Eber, L., Nelson, C., & Miles, P. (1997). School-based wraparound for students with emotional and behavioral challenges. *Exceptional Children, 63*(4), 539–555.

Edelsky, C. (Ed.). (1999). *Making justice our project: Teachers working toward critical whole language practice*. Urbana, IL: National Council of Teachers of English.

Elias, M., Zins, J., Weissberg, R., Frey, K., Greenberg, K., Haynes, N., Kessler, R., Schwab-Stone, M., & Shriver, T. (1997). *Promoting social and emotional learning: Guidelines for educators*. Alexandria, VA: Association for Supervision and Curriculum Development.

Enabling Education Network (1999, June 14). *Inclusion and deafness: A report on a seminar*. Manchester, UK: University of Manchester.

Englert, C., Garmon, M., Mariage, T., Rozendal, M., Tarrant, K., & Urba, J. (1995). The early literacy project: Connecting across the literacy curriculum. *Learning Disability Quarterly, 18*(3), 253–276.

Englert, C., Mariage, T., Garmon, M., & Tarrant, K. (1998). Accelerating reading progress in early literacy project classrooms: Three exploratory studies. *Remedial and Special Education, 19*(3), 142–159.

Engstrom, K., & Putnam, K. (1981). *A guide to the individualized planning process for handicapped students in vocational education*. Belmont, MA: CRC Education and Human Development.

Epstein, J. (1994). Theory to practice: School and family partnerships lead to school improvement. In C. Fagnano & B. Werber (Eds.), *School, family, and community interaction: A view from the firing lines*. San Francisco: Westview Press.

Epstein, J., & Salinas, K. (1998). *TIPS: Teachers involve parents in schoolwork: Language arts and science/health: Interactive homework in the middle grades*. Baltimore: Center on Families, Communities, Schools and Children's Learning, Johns Hopkins University.

Erdmann, L. (1994). Teaching "learners with a difference" in a whole language classroom. In Weaver, C., *Reading process and practice: From socio-psycholinguistics to whole language.* Portsmouth, NH: Heinemann.

Etscheidt, S., & Bartlett, L. (1999). The IDEA amendments: A four-step approach for determining supplementary services. *Exceptional Children, 65*(2), 163–174.

Etzioni, A. (1993). *The spirit of community: Rights, responsibilities, and the communitarian agenda.* New York: Crown Publishers.

Evans, I., & Meyer, L. (1985). *An educative approach to behavior problems: A practical decision model for interventions with severely handicapped learners.* Baltimore: Paul H. Brookes.

Ezekowitz, R., & First, L. (1994). Hematology. In M. Avery & L. First (Eds.), *Pediatric medicine* (pp. 53–60). Baltimore: Williams & Wilkins.

Faber, A., Mazlish, E., Nyberg, L., & Templeton, R. (1995). *How to talk so kids can learn—at home and in school.* New York: Fireside.

Facilitated Communication Institute. (2001). Syracuse, NY: Syracuse University. soeweb.syr.edu/thefci/.

Faltis, C. (1997). *Joinfostering: Adapting teaching for the multilingual classroom.* Columbus, OH: Merrill.

Falvey, M. (1989). *Community-based curriculum: Instructional strategies for students with severe disabilities.* Baltimore: Paul H. Brookes.

Falvey, M., Forest, M., Pearpoint, J., & Rosenberg, R. (1998). *All my life's a circle: Using the tools—circles, MAPS, & PATH.* Toronto: Inclusion Press.

Farmer, T., Pearl, R., & Van Acker, R. (1996). Expanding the social skills deficit framework: A developmental synthesis perspective, classroom social networks, and implications for the social growth of students with disabilities. *The Journal of Special Education, 30*(5) 232–256.

Federal Register: Assistance to State for Education of Children with Disabilities and Early Intervention Program for Infants and Toddlers with Disabilities. Federal Register, March 12, 1999, p. 12456.

Featherstone, H. (1980). *A difference in the family: Life with a disabled child.* Washington, DC: Association for the Care of Children's Health.

Feldman, J., & Gray, P. (1999, March). Some educational benefits of freely chosen age mixing among children and adolescents. *Phi Delta Kappan,* pp. 507–512.

Feuerstein, R. (1979). *The dynamic assessment of retarded performers.* Baltimore: University Park Press.

Fialka, J. (1997). *It matters: Lessons from my son.* Huntington Woods, MI: Author.

Fialka, J., & Mikus, K. (1999). *Do you hear what I hear? Parents and professionals working together for children with special needs.* Ann Arbor, MI: Proctor Publications.

Field, S., Martin, J., Miller, R., Ward, M., & Wehmeyer, M. (1998). Self-determination for persons with disabilities: A position statement of the Division of Career Development and Transition. *Career Development for Exceptional Individuals, 21*(2), 113–128.

Fine, E. (1994). Peacemaking as a tool for change. *Primary Voices: K–6, 2*(4), 2–11.

Finkelhor, D., & Hashima, P. (2001). The victimization of children and youth: A comprehensive overview. In S.

White (Ed.) *Handbook of youth and justice.* New York: Plenum.

Fishbaugh, M. S., & Gum, P. (1994). *Inclusive education in Billings, MT: A prototype for rural schools.* (ERIC Document Reproduction Service No. ED369636)

Fisher, B. (1995). *Thinking and learning together: Curriculum and community in an elementary classroom.* Portsmouth, NH: Heinemann.

Fisher, D. (1999). According to their peers: Inclusion as high school students see it. *Mental Retardation, 37,* 458–467.

Fisher, D., Pumpian, I., & Sax, C. (1998). High school students' attitudes about and recommendations for their peers with significant disabilities. *Journal of the Association for Persons with Severe Handicaps, 23,* 272–280.

Fisher, D., Sax, C. & Grove, K. (2000). The resilience of changes promoting inclusiveness in an urban elementary school. *The Elementary School Journal, 100*(3), 213–227.

Fisher, D., Sax, C., Pumpian, I. (1999). *Inclusive high schools: Learning from contemporary classrooms.* Baltimore: Paul H. Brookes.

Fisher, D., Sax, C., Rodifer, K., & Pumpian, I. (1999). Teachers' perspectives of curriculum and climate changes: Benefits of inclusive education. *Journal for a Just and Caring Education, 5,* 256–268.

Fisher, M. (2001). Andre's story: Frames of friendship. In M. Grenot-Scheyer, M. Fisher, & D. Staub (Eds), *At the end of the day: Lessons learned in inclusive education.* Baltimore: Paul H. Brookes.

Fisher, R., & Ury, W. (1991). *Getting to yes: Negotiating agreements without giving in.* New York: Penguin.

Fitzgerald, M., Henning, G., & Feltz, S. (1997). *Youth mentoring youth: Case examples and perspectives of a student support program.* Milwaukee, WI: University of Wisconsin–Milwaukee, Wisconsin Inclusion Project, and Waukesha West High School.

Fletcher, R. (1986). *Teaching peace.* New York: Harper & Row.

Flippo, K., Inge, K., & Barcus, J. (1995). *Assistive technology: A resource for school, work, and community.* Baltimore: Paul H. Brookes.

Flurkey, A., & Meyer, R. (1994). *Under the whole language umbrella: Many cultures, many voices.* Bloomington, IN: National Council of Teachers of English.

Ford, A., Fitzgerald, M. A., Glodoski, J., & Waterbury, K. (1997). *Team planning to accommodate learners with disabilities.* Milwaukee, WI: University of Wisconsin–Milwaukee, Wisconsin Inclusion Project.

Forness, S. R., Kavale, K. A., King, B. H., & Kasari, C. (1994). Simple versus complex conduct disorders: Identification and phenomenology. *Behavioral Disorders, 19*(4), 306–312.

Forness, S. R., Kavale, K. A., & Lopez, M. (1993). Conduct disorders in school: Special education eligibility and comorbidity. *Journal of Emotional and Behavioral Disorders, 1*(1), 101–108.

Fowler, B. (1996). *Bloom's taxonomy and critical thinking: Critical thinking across the curriculum project.* Lee's Summit, MO: Longview Community College. www.kcmetro.cc.mo.us/longview/ctac/blooms.htm

Fraser, A., Clickner, R., Everett, N., & Viet, S. (1991). *Asbestos in schools: Evaluation of the Asbestos Hazard Emergency Response Act (AHERA): A summary report.* Washington, DC: U.S. Environmental Protection Agency.

Freeman, S., & Alkin, M. (2000). Academic and social attainments of children with mental retardation in general education and special education settings. *Remedial and Special Education, 21*(1), 3–18.

Freie, J. (1998). *Counterfeit community: The exploitation of our longings for connectedness.* New York: Roman & Littlefield.

Friend, M., & Bursuck, W. (1999). *Including students with special needs: A practical guide for classroom teachers.* Boston: Allyn & Bacon.

Friend, M., & Cook, L. (1996). *Interactions: Collaboration skills for school professionals.* White Plains, NY: Longman.

Fryxell, D., & Kennedy, C. H. (1995). Placement along the continuum of services and its impact on students' social relationships. *Journal of the Association for Persons with Severe Handicaps, 20*(4), 259–269.

Fuchs, D., & Fuchs, L. (1994). Inclusive schools movement and the radicalization of special education reform. *Exceptional Children, 60*(4), 294–309.

Fuchs, L., Fuchs, D., Hamlett, C., Phillips, N., & Karns, K. (1995). General educators' specialized adaptation for students with learning disabilities. *Exceptional Children, 61*(5), 440–459.

Fuchs, D., Fuchs, L., Mathes, P., & Simmons, D. (1997). Peer assisted learning strategies making classrooms more responsive to diversity. *American Educational Research Journal, 34*(1), 174–206.

Fuchs, L., Fuchs, D., Kazdan, S., & Allen, S. (1999). Effects of peer-assisted learning strategies in reading with and without training in elaborated help giving. *The Elementary School Journal, 99*(3), 201–219.

Fullan, M. (1997). *Change forces: Probing the depths of educational reform.* New York: Falmer Press.

Fullan, M. (1982). *The meaning of educational change.* New York: Teachers College Press.

Garbarino, J., Dubrow, N., Kostelny, K., & Pardo, C. (1992). *Children in danger: Coping with the consequences of community violence.* San Francisco: Jossey-Bass.

Gardner, H. (1993). *Multiple intelligences: The theory in practice.* New York: Basic Books.

Gardner, J. (1989, fall). Building community. *Kettering Review.*

Gartner, A., & Lipsky, D. (1998). Support for inclusion in I.D.E.A. 1997. In *Bulletin of the National Center on Educational Restructuring and Inclusion.* New York: The Graduate School and University Center, City University of New York.

Gaustad, J. (December, 1998). Implementing looping. *ERIC Digest 123.* Portland: University of Oregon.

Geller, S., & Hunt, D. (1995, November). *Resilient children: Making healthy choices.* Presentation at the annual conference of The Association for Persons with Severe Handicaps (TASH), Chicago.

Genesis Technologies. (2001). *Inspiration 6.0.* Austin, TX: Author. www.academic-softwares.com/inspiration.asp.

Gentry, M., & Owen, S. (1999). An investigation of the effects of total school flexible cluster grouping on identification, achievement, and classroom practices. *Gifted Child Quarterly, 43*(4), 224–243.

Gerard, G. (1997). Community-based restorative justice: A capacity-building tool for confronting crime. Retrieved July 1, 2002, from freenet.msp.mn.us/org/ssco/rj/rjpaper.htm.

Gerring, J., & Carney, J. (1992). *Head trauma: Strategies for educational reintegration.* San Diego, CA: Singular Press.

Gething, L. (1992). *Person to person: A guide for professionals working with people with disabilities.* Baltimore: Paul H. Brookes.

Giangreco, M. F. (1997). *Vermont interdependent services team approach: A guide to coordinating educational support services.* Baltimore: Paul H. Brookes.

Giangreco, M. F., Dennis, R., Cloninger, C., Edelman, S., & Schattman, R. (1993). "I've counted Jon": Transformational experiences of teachers educating students with disabilities. *Exceptional Children, 54,* 415–425.

Gibb, G., & Dyches, T. (2000). *Guide to writing quality individualized education programs.* Boston: Allyn & Bacon.

Gibbs, J. (1998). *Guiding your school community to live a culture of care and learning: The process is called Tribes.* Sausalito, CA: Centersource Systems.

Gibson, R. (1999). *Michigan social studies standards: A critical review.* Unpublished manuscript, Rouge Forum, Detroit.

Gilligan, (1996). *Violence: Reflections on a national epidemic.* New York: Vintage.

Girard, S., & Willing, K. (1996). *Partnerships for classroom learning: From reading buddies to pen pals to the community and the world beyond.* Portsmouth, NH: Heinemann.

Glasser, W. (1992). *The quality school: Managing students without coercion.* New York: Harper.

Glasser, W. (2000). *Reality therapy in action.* New York: HarperCollins.

Goldstein, A. P. (1988). *The prepare curriculum: Teaching prosocial competencies.* Champaign, IL: Research Press.

Goleman, D. (1995). *Emotional intelligence.* New York: Bantam.

Goodlad, J. (1984). *A place called school: Prospects for the future.* New York: McGraw Hill.

Goodman, G., & Poillion, M. (1992). ADD: Acronym for any dysfunction or difficulty. *Journal of Special Education, 30,* 691–709.

Goodman, K. (1986). *What's whole in whole language?* Portsmouth, NH: Heinemann.

Gostin, L., & Beyer, H. (1993). *Americans with Disabilities Act: Rights and responsibilities of all Americans.* Baltimore: Paul H. Brookes.

Grabb, E. (1997). *Theories of social inequality: Classical and contemporary perspectives.* New York: Harcourt Brace.

Grandin, T. (2000). *An inside view of autism.* Retrieved July 2, 2002, from www.autism.org/temple/inside.html.

Grant, J. (1996). *The looping handbook: Teachers and students progressing together.* Peterborough, NH: Crystal Springs Books.

Graves, D. H. (1983). *Writing: Teachers and children at work.* Portsmouth, NH: Heinemann.

Graves, D. H., & Graves, G. (1997). *Box city: An interdisciplinary experience in community planning.* Prarie Village, KS: Center for Understanding of the Built Environment (CUBE).

Graves, D. H., Graves, G., Schauber, S., & Beasley, J. (1999). *Walk around the block.* Prarie Village, KS: Center for Understanding of the Built Environment (CUBE).

Graves, M., & Graves, B. (1994). *Scaffolding Reading Experiences: Designs for Student Success.* Norwood, MA: Christopher-Gordon Publishers.

Gray, C. (1994). *The social story kit.* Austin, TX: Future Horizons.

Greenman, J. (1988). *Caring space, learning places: Children's environments that work.* Redmond, WA: Exchange Press.

Gresham, F., & MacMillan, D. (1997). Autistic recovery? An analysis and critique of the empirical evidence on the early intervention project. *Behavioral Disorders, 22,* 185–201.

Gresham, F., MacMillan, D., & Bocian, K. (1996). Behavioral earthquakes: Low frequency, salient behavior events that differentiate students at-risk for behavioral disorders. *Behavioral Disorders, 21*(4), 277–292.

Grigal, M. (1998, July/August). The time–space continuum: Using natural supports in inclusive classrooms. *Teaching Exceptional Children,* pp. 44–51.

Grinder, M. (1991). *Righting the educational conveyer belt.* Portland, OR: Metamorphous Press.

Gross, S. (1999). Educating children and youth to prevent contagious disease. *ERIC Digest.* Washington, DC: ERIC Clearinghouse on Teaching and Teacher Education. (ERIC Document Reproduction Service No. ED437368)

Grubb, D., & Diamantes, T. (1998) Is your school sick? Five threats to healthy schools. *The Clearinghouse, 71,* 202–207.

Gutierrez, P., Vulpe, M., & Young, R. (1994). Spinal cord injury. In J. Stein (Ed.), *Internal medicine.* St. Louis, MO: Mosby.

Haberman, M. (1998). *The pedagogy of poverty versus good teaching.* University of Wisconsin-Milwalkee. Retrieved July 2, 2002, from equity.enc.org/equity/eqtyres/erg/111376/1376.htm.

Hacker, A. (1993). *Two nations: Black and white, separate, hostile, unequal.* New York: Scribners.

Hagner, D., & Dileo, D. (1993). *Working together: Workplace culture, supported employment, and persons with disabilities.* Cambridge, MA: Brookline.

Hale, J., & Franklin, V. (2001). *Learning while black: Creating educational excellence for African-American children.* Baltimore: Johns Hopkins University Press.

Hall, L. J. (1994). A descriptive assessment of social relationships in integrated classrooms. *Journal of the Association for Persons With Severe Handicaps, 19*(4), 302–313.

Hallowell, E. (1996). What's it like to live with ADD? In T. Hartmann & J. Bowman (Eds.), *Think fast! The ADD experience.* Grass Valley, CA: Underwood.

Hampel, M. (2000, November 13). *Teachers partnering with parents of children with special needs: We need you!* Presentation at the College of Education, Wayne State University, Detroit.

Hardman, M., Drew, C., & Egan, M. (1996). *Human exceptionality: Society, school, and family.* Boston: Allyn & Bacon.

Haring, T., Breen, C., Pitts-Conway, V., Lee, M., & Gaylord-Ross, R. (1998). Adolescent peer tutoring and special friend experiences. *Journal of the Association for Persons with Severe Handicaps, 12*(4), 280–286.

Harrell, L., Doelling, J., & Sasso, G. (1997). Recent developments in social interaction interventions to enhance inclusion. In P. Zionts (Ed.), *Inclusion strategies for students with learning and behavior problems: Perspectives, experiences, and best practices* (pp. 273–295). Austin, TX: Pro-Ed.

Harris, K., & Graham, S. (1994). Constructivism: Principles, paradigms, and integration. *The Journal of Special Education, 28*(3), 233–247.

Hartmann, T. (1996). Are you a hunter or a farmer? In T. Hartmann & J. Bowman (Eds.), *Think fast! The ADD experience.* Grass Valley, CA: Underwood.

Hartmann, T., & Bowman, J. (Eds.). (1996). *Think fast! The ADD experience.* Grass Valley, CA: Underwood.

Hayden, M., & Senese, D. (1995). *Self-advocacy groups: 1994–95 Directory for North America.* Minneapolis, MN: Research and Training Center on Residential Services and Community Living, University of Minnesota.

Heal, L., Haney, J., & Amado, A. (1988). *Integration of developmentally disabled individuals into the community.* Baltimore: Paul H. Brookes.

Helmstetter, E., Peck, C. A., & Giangreco, M. F. (1994). Outcomes of interactions with peers with moderate or severe disabilitiies: A statewide survey of high school students. *Journal of the Association for Persons with Severe Handicaps, 19*(4), 263–276.

Henderson, W. (2000). *Inclusion: A catalyst for whole school reform.* Boston: Boston Public Schools. www.coe.wayne.edu/CommunityBuilding/ARTInclCatalyst.html

Heubert, J., & Hauser, R. (1999). *High stakes: Testing for tracking, promotion, and graduation.* Washington, DC: National Academy Press.

Herman, J., Aschbacher, P., & Winters, L. (1992). *A practical guide to alternative assessment.* Alexandria, VA: Association for Supervision and Curriculum Development.

Herold, E. (1998). *Co-teaching in Erin Herold and Pam Gutierrez's class.* Unpublished manuscript provided for SED 705 Mainstreaming Handicapped Students at Wayne State University, Detroit.

Hickson, L., Blackman, L., & Reis, E. (1995). *Mental retardation: Foundations of educational programming.* Boston: Allyn & Bacon.

Hiibner, C., & Fracassi, K. (1999, June). *Three ways to differentiate curriculum.* Presentation at the Whole Schooling Summer Institute, Detroit.

Hill, B., & Lakin, C. (1984). *Classification of residential facilities for mentally retarded people.* Minneapolis, MN:

Center for Residential and Community Services, University of Minnesota, Department of Educational Psychology.

Hilliard, A. G. (2000). Excellence in education versus high-stakes standardized testing. *Journal of Teacher Education 51*(4), 293–304.

Hindley, J. (1996). *In the company of children*. York, ME: Stenhouse.

Hinz, A. (1996). Inclusive education in Germany: The example of Hamburg. *The European Electronic Journal on Inclusive Education in Europe, 1*. Retrieved July 1, 2002, from www.uva.es/inclusion/texts/hinz01.htm.

Hittie, M. (1999a). *Including a child with behavioral challenges*. Unpublished manuscript, Southfield Public Schools, Southfield, MI.

Hittie, M. (1999b). *Jason Project at Macarthur Elementary School*. Unpublished manuscript, Southfield Public Schools, Southfield, MI.

Hitzing, W. (1994). Support and positive teaching strategies. In S. Stainback & W. Stainback (Eds.), *Inclusion: A guide for educators*. Baltimore: Paul H. Brookes.

Holdaway, D. (1979). *The foundations of literacy*. New York: Scholastic.

Hollowood, T. A., Salisbury, C. L. Rainforth, B., & Palombaro, M. M. (1995). Use of instructional time in classrooms serving students with and without severe disabilities. *Exceptional Children, 61*(3), 242–253.

Holly, L. (2000, August 24). Message posted to www.quasar.ualberta.ca/ddc/inclusion/intro.html

Hopfenberg, W., Levin, H., Chase, C., Christensen, S. G., Moore, M., Soler, P., Brunner, I., Keller, B., & Rodriguez, G. (1993). *The Accelerated Schools resource guide*. San Francisco: Jossey-Bass.

Horowitz, S. M., Bility, K. M., Plichta, S. B., Leaf, P. J., & Haynes, N. (1998). Teachers assessments of behavioral disorders. *American Journal of Orthopsychiatry, 24*(3), 29–38.

Hoskins, B. (1996). *Developing inclusive schools: A guide*. Bloomington, IN: Forum on Education.

Hudson v. Bloomfield Hills School District, 23 IDELR 612 (E. D. Mich. 1995).

Hughes, C., & Agran, M. (1998). Self-determination: Signaling a systems change? *Journal of the Association for Persons with Severe Handicaps, 23*(1), 1–4.

Hughes, C., Guth, C., Hall, S., Presley, J., Dye, M., & Byers, C. (1999, May/June). "They are my best friends": Peer buddies promote inclusion in high school. *Teaching Exceptional Children*, pp. 32–37.

Hundert, J., Mahony, B., & Mundy, F. (1998). A descriptive analysis of developmental and social gains of children with severe disabilities in segregated and inclusive preschools in southern Ontario. *Early Childhood Research Quarterly—Special Issue: Inclusion in Early Childhood Settings, 13*(1), 49–65.

Hunt, P., Alwell, M., & Farron-Davis, F. (1996). Creating socially supportive environments for fully included students who experience multiple disabilities. *The Journal of the Association for Persons with Severe Handicaps, 21*, 53–71.

Hunt, P., Farron-Davis, F., Beckstead, S., Curtis, D., & Goetz, L. (1994). Evaluating the effects of placement of students with severe disabilities in general education versus special education. *Journal of the Association for Persons with Severe Handicaps, 19*(3), 200–214.

Hunt, P., Goetz, L., & Anderson, J. (1986). The quality of IEP objectives associated with placement in integrated versus segregated school sites. *Journal of the Association for Persons with Severe Handicaps, 11*(2), 125–130.

Hunt, P., Staub, D., Alwell, M., & Goetz, L. (Winter, 1994). Achievement by all students within the context of cooperative learning groups. *Journal of the Association for Persons with Severe Handicaps 19*(4), 290–301.

Hurch, D., & Ross, W. (2000). *Democratic social education: Social studies for social change*. New York: Falmer Press.

Hyde, K., Burchard, J., & Woodworth, K. (1996). Wrapping services in an urban setting. *Journal of Child and Family Studies, 5*(1), 67–82.

Johnson, L. (1996). Evolving transitions? *Teacher Education and Special Education, 19*(3).

Idol, L., Paolucci-Whitcomb, P., & Nevin, A. (1994). *Collaborative consultation* (2nd ed.). Rockville, MD: Aspen.

Individuals with Disabilities Education Act. (1997). Pub. L. No. 105-17, 20 U.S.C. 1400.

Individuals with Disabilities Education Act (IDEA). (1999, March 12). Education of Children with Disabilities and Early Intervention Program. 34 C.F.R., 300 & 303. Vol. 64, No. 48.

Individuals with Disabilities Education Improvement Act (2004) PL 108-446. 118 STAT. 2647.

Ireland, J., Wray, D., & Flexer, C. (1988). Hearing for success in the classroom. *Teaching exceptional children, 20*(2), 15–17.

Isaac, K. (1992). *Civics for democracy: A journey for teachers and students*. Washington, DC: Essential Books.

Isaac, R., & Armat, V. (1990). *Madness in the streets: How psychiatry and the law abandoned the mentally ill*. New York: Free Press.

Jacob K. Javits Gifted and Talented Students Education Act, Title XIV. (1994). Pub. L. No. 103-398, U.S.C.

Jacobs, H. (1989). *Interdisciplinary curriculum: Design and implementation*. Alexandria, VA: Association for Supervision and Curriculum Development.

Jacobson, J., & Mulick, J. (1992). Speak for yourself, or . . . I can't quite put my finger on it! *Psychology in Mental Retardation and Developmental Disabilities, 17*(3), 5–7.

Jacobson, S. (2002). *Education about education with neuro-linguistic programming*. Lincoln, NE: iUniverse.

Janney, R., & Snell, M. (1997). How teachers include students with moderate and severe disabilities in elementary classes: The means and ends of inclusion. *Journal of the Association for Persons with Severe Handicaps, 22*(3), 159–169.

Janney, R., & Snell, M. (2000a). *Behavioral support: Teacher's guides to inclusive practices*. Baltimore: Paul H. Brookes.

Janney, R., & Snell, M. (2000b). *Modifying schoolwork*. Baltimore: Paul H. Brookes.

Janney, R., Snell, M., Beers, M., & Raynes, M. (1995). Integrating students with moderate to severe disabilities into general education classes. *Exceptional Children, 61*(5), 425–439.

Javits–Wagner–O'Day Act as Amended. 41 U.S.C. 46–48c. (1994).

Jenkins, J., Jewell, M., Leicester, N., Jenkins, L., & Troutner, N. (1991). Development of a school building model for educating students with handicaps and at-risk students in general education classrooms. *Journal of Learning Disabilities, 24*(5), 311–320.

Jenkins, J., Jewell, M., Leicester, N., O'Connor, R. E., Jenkins, L., & Troutner, N. M. (1994). Accommodations for individual differences without classroom ability groups: An experiment in school restructuring. *Exceptional Children, 60* (4), 344–359.

Jensen, E. (1995). *Super teaching: Over 1,000 practical teaching strategies.* San Diego, CA: Brain Store.

Jensen, E. (1998). *Teaching with the brain in mind.* Alexandria, VA: Association for Supervision and Curriculum Development.

Johns, B. H., & Keenan, J. P. (1997). *Techniques for managing a safe school.* Denver, CO: Love.

Johnson, D. W., & Johnson, R. T. (1989a). *Cooperation and competition: Theory and research.* Edina, MN: Interaction.

Johnson, D. W., & Johnson, R. T. (1989b). *Leading the cooperative school.* Edina, MN: Interaction.

Johnson, D. W., & Johnson, R. T. (1994). *The new circles of learning: Cooperation in the classroom and school.* Alexandria, VA: Association for Supervision and Curriculum Development.

Johnson, D. W., & Johnson, R. T. (1995). *Reducing school violence through conflict resolution.* Alexandria, VA: Association for Supervision and Curriculum Development.

Johnson, P. (1997). *Pictures and words together: Children illustrating and writing their own books.* Portsmouth, NH: Heinemann.

Jorgensen, C. (1998). *Restructuring high schools for all students: Taking inclusion to the next level.* Baltimore: Paul H. Brookes.

Joseph, J. (1995). *Remaking America: How the benevolent traditions of many cultures are transforming our national life.* San Francisco: Jossey-Bass.

Jupp, K. (1994). *Living a full life.* London: Souvenir Press.

Kagan, S., & Weissbourd, B. (Eds.). (1994). *Putting families first: America's family support movement and the challenge of change.* San Francisco: Jossey-Bass.

Kaiser, J. S. (2000). Are high-stakes tests taking control? *Schools in the Middles, 9*(7), 18–21.

Kameenui, E. J., & Carnine, D. (1998). *Effective teaching strategies that accommodate diverse learners.* Upper Saddle River, NJ: Prentice-Hall.

Kameenui, E. J., & Darch, C. B. (1995). *Instructional classroom management: A proactive approach to behavior management.* White Plains, NY: Longman.

Kane, D., & Boltax, R. (1999). *Building effective supports for teaching students with behavioral challenges in Vermont (BEST).* Montpelier, VT: Vermont Department of Education.

Karlin, R. (2000, May 7). Ritalin use splits parents, school. *Times Union,* Retrieved July 1, 2002, from www.breggin.com/schools.

Karp, D. (1996). *Speaking of sadness: Depression, disconnection, and the meanings of illness.* New York: Oxford University Press.

Kaskinen-Chapman, A. (1992). Saline area schools and inclusive community CONCEPTS (Collaborative Organization of Networks, Community Educators, Parents, the Workplace, and Students). In R. A. Villa, J. S. Thousand, W. Stainback, and S. Stainback (Eds.), *Restructuring for caring and effective education: An administrative guide to creating heterogeneous schools* (pp. 169–185). Baltimore: Paul H. Brookes.

Katz, L., Evangelou, D., & Hartman, J. (1990). *The case for mixed-age grouping in early education.* Washington, DC: National Association for the Education of Young Children.

Katz, M. (1985). *In the shadow of the poorhouse: A social history of welfare in America.* New York: Basic Books.

Katz, M. (1995). *Improving poor people: The welfare state, the "underclass," and urban schools as history.* Princeton, NJ: Princeton University Press.

Kauffman, J. (1993). How we might achieve the radical reform of special education. *Exceptional Children, 60*(1), 6–16

Kauffman, J. (1997). *Characteristics of emotional and behavioral disorders of children and youth.* Columbus, OH: Merrill.

Kauffman, J., Lloyd, J., & Baker, J. (1995) Inclusion of all students with emotional or behavioral disorders? Let's think again. *Phi Delta Kappan, 76,* 542–546.

Kauffman, J., & Hallahan, D. (Eds.). (1995). *The illusion of full inclusion: A comprehensive critique of a current special educatin bandwagon.* Austin, TX: Pro-Ed.

Kavale, K. (1990). Effectiveness of special education. In T. Gutkin & C. Reynolds (Eds), *The handbook of school psychology* (2nd ed., pp. 868–898). New York: Wiley.

Kay, P. (1999). *Prevention strategies that work.* Burlington, VT: University of Vermont.

Keefe, C. (1996). *Label-free learning: Supporting learners with disabilities.* York, ME: Stenhouse.

Keenan, S. (1997). Program elements that support teachers and students with learning and behavior problems. In P. Zionts (Ed.), *Inclusion strategies for students with learning and behavior problems: Perspectives, experiences, and best practices* (pp. 117–138). Austin, TX: Pro-Ed.

Kelker, K., & Holt, R. (2000). *Family guide to assistive technology.* Cambridge, MA: Brookline.

Kennedy, C., & Fisher, D. (2001). *Inclusive middle schools.* Baltimore: Paul H. Brookes.

Kennedy, C., Shulka, S., & Fryxell, D. (1997). Comparing the effects of educational placement on the social relationships of intermediate school students with severe disabilities. *Exceptional Children, 64*(1), 31–48.

Kennedy, D. (1995). Teaching the gifted in regular classrooms: Plain talk about creating a gifted-friendly classroom. *Roeper Review, 17*(4), 232–234.

Kent, R. (1997). *Room 109: The promise of a portfolio classroom.* Portsmouth, NH: Heinemann.

King, T. (1999). *Assistive technology: Essential human factors.* Boston: Allyn & Bacon.

Kingsley, J., & Levitz, M. (1994). *Count us in: Growing up with Down syndrome.* New York: Harcourt Brace.

Kishi, G. (1989). SAT scores for a school complex: Pre- and post-integration. San Francisco: TASH.

Kloomok, S., & Cosden, M. (1994). Self-concept in children with learning disabilities: The relationship between global self-concept, academic "discounting," nonacademic self-concept, and perceived social support. *Learning Disabilities Quarterly, 17,* 140–153.

Knitzer, J., Steinberg, Z., & Fleisch, B. (1990). *At the schoolhouse door: An examination of programs and policies for children with behavioral and emotional problems.* New York: Bank Street College of Education.

Knoff, H. M. (1999). *Project ACHIEVE: A collaborative, school-based school reform process improving the academic and social progress of at-risk and underachieving students.* Tampa, Florida: Institute for School Reform, Integrated Services, and Child Mental Health and Educational Policy, University of South Florida.

Knoff, H. M., & Batsche, G. M. (1995). Project ACHIEVE: Analyzing a school reform process for at-risk and underachieving students. *School Psychology Review, 24,* 579–603.

Knoll, J. (1994, summer). *Inclusive Communities: The Newsletter of the Developmental Disabilities Institute* (Wayne State University, Detroit), pp. 4–6.

Kohn, A. (1996b). What to look for in a classroom. *Educational Leadership, 54*(1), 54–55.

Knowlton, E. (1998). Considerations in the design of personalized curricular supports for students with developmental disabilities. *Education and Training in Mental Retardation and developmental disabilities, 33*(2), 95–107.

Koegel, L. K., Koegel, R. L., & Dunlap, G. (1996). *Positive behavioral support: Including people with difficult behavior in the community.* Baltimore: Paul H. Brookes.

Koegel, L. K., Koegel, R. L., Kellegrew, D., & Mullen, L. (1996). Parent education for prevention and reduction of severe problem behaviors. In L. K. Koegel, R. L. Koegel, & G. Dunlap (Eds.), *Positive behavioral support: Including people with difficult behavior in the community.* Baltimore: Paul H. Brookes.

Koegel, R. L., & Koegel, L. K. (1995) *Teaching children with autism: Strategies for initiating positive interactions and improving learning opportunities.* Baltimore: Paul H. Brookes.

Kohl, H. (1967). *36 children.* New York: New American Library.

Kohl, H. (1998). *The discipline of hope.* New York: Simon & Schuster.

Kohn, A. (1992). *No contest: The case against competition: Why we lose in our race to win.* New York: Houghton Mifflin.

Kohn, A. (1993). *Punished by rewards: The trouble with gold stars, incentive plans, A's, praise, and other bribes.* Boston: Houghton Mifflin.

Kohn, A. (1996). *Beyond discipline: From compliance to community.* Alexandria, VA: Association for Supervision and Curriculum Development.

Kohn, A. (1998). *What to look for in a classroom . . . and other essays.* San Francisco: Jossey-Bass.

Kohn, A. (1999). *The schools our children deserve: Moving beyond traditional classrooms and "tougher standards."* New York: Houghton Mifflin.

Kohn, A. (2000). *The case against standardized testing: Raising the scores, Ruining our schools.* Portsmouth, NH: Heinemann.

Kortering, L. J., & Blackorby, J. (1992). High school dropouts and students identified with behavioral disorders. *Behavioral Disorders, 18*(1), 24–32.

Kovalik, S. (1994). *Integrated thematic instruction.* Kent, WA: Books for Educators.

Kovalik, S., & Olsaen, K. (1997). *Integrated thematic instruction: The model.* Kent, WA: Books for Educators.

Kozleski, E., & Jackson, L. (1993). Taylor's story: Full inclusion in her neighborhood elementary school. *Exceptionality, 4*(3), 153–175.

Kozol, J. (1991). *Savage inequalities: Children in America's schools.* New York: Crown.

Kretzmann, J. P., & McKnight, J. (1993) *Building communities from the inside out: A path toward finding and mobilizing a community's assets.* Chicago: Northwestern University, Center for Urban Affairs and Policy Research.

Kroll, J., & Bachrach, B. (1986) Child care and child abuse in early medieval Europe. *Journal of the American Academy of Child Psychiatry, 25*(4), 562–568.

Kronberg, R. (1999). *Coming to grips with the different learning levels in your classroom.* Torrance, CA: Staff Development Resources.

Kronick, D. (1976). *Three families.* San Rafael, CA: Academic Therapy Publications.

Kunc, N. (1992). The need to belong: Rediscovering Maslow's hierarchy of needs. Villa, R., Thousand, J., Stainback, W., & Stainback, S. *Restructuring for caring and effective education.* Baltimore: Paul H. Brookes.

Kunc, N. (1998, July). *Learning to stand still.* Presentation at the Inclusion Summer Institute, Stevens Point, WI.

Kunc, N. (2000, June 27). *Do all kids belong in all classes? Equity or excellence in education.* Presentation at the International Education Summit, Detroit.

Kusche, C., & Greenberg, M. (1994). *PATHS curriculum.* Seattle, WA: Developmental Research and Programs.

Kuttler, S., Myles, B., & Carlson, J. (1998). The use of social stories to reduce precursors to tantrum behavior in students with autism. *Focus on Autism and Other Developmental Disorders, 13*(3), 176–182.

Kwan, G. (1999, November 22). King County Parent Coalition Legislators' Forum, Seattle, WA. Inclusion Daily Express. Retrieved July 1, 2002, from www.inclusiondaily.com.

L'Abate, L., & Milan, M. (Eds.). (1989). *Handbook of social skills training and research.* New York: Wiley.

LaMaster, K., Gall, K., Kinchin, G., & Siedentop, D. (1998). Inclusion practices of effective elementary specialists. *Adapted Physical Activity Quarterly, 15,* 64–81.

Lance, W. (1976). Who are all the children? *Exceptional Children, 43*(2), 66–76.

Lane, P., & McWhitter, J. (1992). A peer mediation model: Conflict resolution for elementary and middle school children. *Elementary school guidance and counseling, 27*(3) 10–15.

Lantieri, L., & Patti, J. (1996). *Waging peace in our schools.* Boston: Beacon Press.

Learning Disabilities Association. (1993, January). *Inclusion: Position paper of the Learning Disabilities Association of America.* Retrieved July 1, 2002, from www.ldaamerica.org/positions/inclusion.html.

Lee, C. (1999). *Learning disabilities and assistive technology.* Atlanta, GA: Tools for Life.

Leone, P. (1991). *Alcohol and other drug use by adolescents with disabilities.* Reston, VA: Council for Exceptional Children.

Lepper, M., & Henderlong, J. (2000). Turning "play" into "work" and "work" into "play": 25 years of Rresearch on intrinsic versus extrinsic motivation. In C. Sansone & J. Harackiewicz (Eds.), *Intrinsic and extrinsic motivation: The search for optimal motivation and performance.* New York: Academic Press.

LeRoy, B. (1990a). *The effect of classroom integration on teacher and student attitudes, behaviors, and performance in Saline area schools.* Detroit: Developmental Disabilities Institute, Wayne State University.

LeRoy, B. (1990b). *Inclusive education in Michigan: A preliminary status report.* Detroit: Developmental Disabilities Institute, Wayne State University.

LeRoy, B. (1995). *Michigan inclusive education initiative: Implementation report.* Detroit: Developmental Disabilities Institute, Wayne State University.

LeRoy, B., England, J., & Osbeck, T. (1994). *Facilitator guides to inclusive education.* Detroit: Developmental Disabilities Institute, Wayne State University.

Levine, K., & Wharton, R. (1995). Facilitated communication: What parents should know. *Exceptional Children, 28*(5), 40–53.

Lewis, B. (1998a). *The kid's guide to social action.* Prairie Village, KS: Center for Understanding of the Built Environment (CUBE).

Lewis, B. (1998b). *The kid's guide to service projects.* Prairie Village, KS: Center for Understanding of the Built Environment (CUBE).

Lewis, R., & Doorlag, D. (1999). *Teaching special students in general education classrooms.* Columbus, OH: Merrill.

Lewis, T. J., Chard, D., & Scott, T. M. (1994). Full inclusion and education of children and youth with emotional and behavioral disorders. *Behavioral Disorders, 19*(4), 277–293.

Lipskey, D. K., & Gartner, A. (1997). *Inclusion and school reform: Transforming America's classrooms.* Baltimore: Paul H. Brookes.

Lofkuist, L., & Dawes, R. (1980). Vocational needs, work reinforcers and job satisfaction. In B. Bolton & D. Cook, (Eds.). *Rehabilitation client assessment.* Baltimore: University Park Press.

Logan, K., Bakeman, R., & Keefe, E. (1997). Effects of instructional variables on engaged behavior of students with disabilities in general education classrooms. *Exceptional Children, 63*(4), 481–498.

Logan, K., & Malone, M. (1998). Comparing instructional contexts of students with and without severe disabilities in general education classrooms. *Exceptional Children, 64*(3), 343–358.

Lovaas, O. (1987). The autistic child: Language development through behavior modification. *Journal of Consulting and Clinical Psychology, 55*(1), 3–9.

Lovett, H. (1996). *Learning to listen: Positive approaches and people with difficult behavior.* Baltimore: Paul H. Brookes.

Ludlow, B., Turnbull, A., & Luckasson, R. (1988). *Transitions to adult life for people with mental retardation: Principles and practices.* Baltimore: Paul H. Brookes.

Ludlum, C. (1993). *Tending the candle: A booklet for circle facilitators.* Manchester, CT: Communitas.

Maag, J. (1997). Managing resistance: Looking beyond the child and into the mirror. In P. Zionts (Ed.), *Inclusion strategies problems.* Austin, TX: Pro-Ed.

Macrorie, K. (1988). *The I-search paper.* Portsmouth, NH: Boynton/Cook.

Maloney, J. (1994/1995). A call for placement options. *Educational Leadership, 52*(4), 25.

Manley, A., & O'Neill, C. (Eds.). (1997). *Dreamseekers: Creative approaches to the African-American heritage.* Portsmouth, NH: Heinemann.

Mann, L. (1997). Designing the learning environment. *Education Update, 39*(6), 1–5.

Manning, M., Manning, G., & Long, R. (1994) *Theme immersion: Inquiry-based curriculum in elementary and middle schools.* Portsmouth, NH: Heinemann.

Manset, G., & Semmel, M. (1997). Are inclusive programs for students with mild disabilities effective? A comparative review of model programs. *Journal of Special Education, 31,* 155–180.

March, R., & Sprague, J. (1999). *Effective behavior support (EBS): A school-wide behavioral support program.* Portland, OR: Institute on Violence and Destructive Behavior, University of Oregon.

Marder, C. (1992, April). *Secondary school students classified as seriously emotionally disturbed: How are they being served?* Paper presented at the meeting of the American Educational Research Association, San Francisco, CA.

Marin, M., Gilpin, M., Goodman, S., & Moses, M. (1996). *Positive behavioral support: An interagency project.* Lansing, MI: Michigan Department of Community Health, Michigan State Training Team.

Marks, S., Schrader, C., & Levine, M. (1999). Para-educator experiences in inclusive settings: Helping, hovering, or holding their own? *Exceptional Children, 65*(3), 315–328.

Marston, D. (1996). A comparison of inclusion only, pull-out only, and combined services models for students with mild disabilities. *Journal of Special Education, 30,* 121–132.

Martin, G., & Pear, J. (1996). *Behavior modification: What it is and how to do it* (5th ed.). Upper Saddle River, NJ: Prentice-Hall.

Maslow, A. (1970). *Motivation and personality.* New York: Harper & Row.

Mayer, G. O. (1995). Preventing antisocial behavior in the schools. *Journal of Applied Behavior Analysis, 28*(4), 467–478.

McAdamis, S. (2001). Individual paths; teachers tailor their instruction to meet a variety of student needs. *Journal of Staff Development, 22*(2), 15–18.

McCarney, S. (1993). *The pre-referral intervention manual.* Columbia, MO: Hawthorne Educational Services.

McClellan, D. (1994). Research on multiage grouping: Implications for education. In P. Chase & J. Doan (Eds.), *Full circle: A new look at multiage education.* Portsmouth, NH: Heinemann.

McClellan, D. & Kinsey, S. (1999). Children's social behavior in relationship to participation in mixed-age or same-age classrooms. *Early Childhood Research and Practice, 1*(1), 22–30.

McCormick, L., Loeb, D., & Schiefelbusch, R. (1997). *Supporting children with communication difficulties in inclusive settings: School-based language intervention.* Boston: Allyn & Bacon.

McDonnell, J., Hardman, M., Hightower, J., & Kiefer-O'-Donnell, R. (1991). Variables associated with in-school and after-school integration of secondary students with severe disabilities. *Education and Training in Mental Retardation, 26,* 243–257.

McDonnell, J., Hardman, M., Hightower, J., & Kiefer-O'-Donnell, R. (1997). Academic engaged time of students with low-incidence disabilities in general education classes. *Mental Retardation, 35*(1), 18–26.

McGinnis, E., & Goldstein, A. (1984). *Skillstreaming the elementary school child.* Champaign, IL: Research Press.

McGonigel, M., Kaufmann, R., & Johnson, B. (Eds.). (1991). *Guidelines and recommended practices for the individualized family service plan* (2nd ed.). Bethesda, MD: Association for the Care of Children's Health.

McGregor, G., & Vogelsberg, T. (1998). *Inclusive schooling practices: Pedagogical and research foundations: A synthesis of the literature that informs best practices about inclusive schooling.* Baltimore: Paul H. Brookes.

McIntosh, R., Vaughn, S., Schumm, J. S., Haager, D., & Lee, O. (1993). Observations of students with learning disabilities in general education classrooms. *Exceptional Children, 60,* 249–261.

McKnight, J. (1995). *The careless society: Community and its counterfeits.* New York: Basic Books.

McLane, K., Burnette, J., & Orkwis, R. (1997). School-wide behavioral management systems. *Research Connections, 1*(1), 1–8.

McLaughlin, M,, & Rouse, M. (2000). *Special education and school reform in the United States and Britain.* New York: Routledge.

McLaughlin, M. J., Leone, P. E., Warren, S. H., & Schofield, P. F. (1994). *Doing things differently: Issues and options for creating comprehensive school-linked services for children and youth with emotional or behavioral disorders.* College Park, MD: University of Maryland at College Park, Center for Policy Options in Special Education.

McLeskey, J., Waldron, N., & Pacchiano, D. (1993, April). *Inclusive elementary school programs: Teachers' perceptions of strengths and challenges.* Paper presented at the Council for Exceptional Children Annual Convention, San Antonio, TX.

McMichael, A., Baghurst, P., Wigg, N., Vimpani, G., Robertson, E., & Roberts, R. (1988). Port Pirie cohort study: Environmental exposure to lead and children's abilities at the age of four years. *New England Journal of Medicine, 319*(1), 468–475.

McVay, P. (1998). Paraprofessionals in the classsroom: What role do they play? *Disability Solutions, 3*(1), 3–14.

McWhirt by McWhirt v. Williamson County School, 23 IDELR 509 (6th Cir. 1995).

Meadows, N. (1996). Meeting the challenges of responsible inclusion. *Preventing School Failure, 40*(4), 139–142.

Medenwaldt, M. (2000). *The role of caring in inclusive practice.* Unpublished paper, Douglas College, Child, Family, and Community Studies, New Westminster, British Columbia, Canada.

Meek, A. (Ed.). (1995). *Designing places for learning.* Alexandria, VA: Association for Supervision and Curriculum Development.

Melaville, A., Blank, M., & Asayesh, G. (1993). *Together we can.* Washington, DC: U.S. Department of Education.

Metz, M. H. (1994). Desegregation as necessity and challenge. *Journal of Negro Education, 63*(1), 64–76.

Meyer, L., Peck, C., & Brown, L. (1991). *Critical issues in the lives of people with severe disabilities.* Baltimore: Paul H. Brookes.

Michigan Department of Education. (1999). *Individualized education program team manual.* Lansing, MI: Author.

Miles, M. (1999). Historical background of educational and social responses to disabilities in Anglophone eastern and southern Africa: Introduction and bibliography. *Disabilities and Childhood in Eastern and Southern Africa.* University of Nijmegen, Nijmegen, Netherlands. Retrieved July 2, 2002, from www.socsci.kun.nl/ped/whp/histeduc/mmiles/aesabib.html.

Miller, B. (1995). *Children at the center: Implementing the multiage classroom.* Eugene, OR: ERIC Clearinghouse on Educational Management. (ERIC Document Reproduction Service No. EA025954)

Miller, D., & Westerman, J. (1995). Reading disability as a condition of family stability. *Family Process, 3*(5), 49–59.

Miller-Lachmann, L., & Taylor, L. (1995). *Schools for all: Educating children in a diverse society.* New York: Delmar.

Modrow, J. (1996). *How to become a schizophrenic: The case against biological psychiatry.* Seattle, WA: Apollyn Press.

Moles, O. C. (1993). Collaboration between schools and disadvantaged parents: Obstacles and openings. In N. Chavkin (Ed.), *Families and schools in a pluralistic society.* Albany, NY: State University of New York Press.

Monda-Amaya, L., & Pearson, D. (1996). Toward a responsible pedagogy for teaching and learning literacy. In M. Pugach & C. Warger (Eds.), *Curriculum trends, special education, and reform: Refocusing the conversation* (pp. 143–163). New York: Teachers College Press.

Moody, S., Vaughn, S., & Hughes, M. (2000). Reading instruction in the resource room: Set up for failure. *Exceptional Children, 66*(3), 305–316.

Moore, A. (1999). *Teaching multi-cultured students: Culturalism and anti-culturalism in school classrooms.* New York: Falmer Press.

Morocco, C., & Zorfass, J. (1996). Unpacking scaffolding: Supporting students with disabilities in literacy development. In M. Pugach & C. Warger (Eds.), *Curriculum trends, special education, and reform: Refocusing the conversation.* New York: Teachers College Press.

Mount, B., Beeman, P., & Ducharme, G. (1988) *What we are learning about circles of support.* Manchester, CT: Communitas.

Murphy, S., & Rogan, P. (1995). *Closing the shop: Conversion from sheltered to integrated work.* Baltimore: Paul H. Brookes.

Murray-Seegert, C. (1989). Nasty girls, thugs, and humans like us. In M. Falvey, *Community-based curriculum: Instructional strategies for students with severe handicaps.* Baltimore: Paul H. Brookes.

Naicker, S. M. (1999). *Curriculum 2005: A space for all: An introduction to inclusive education.* Cape Town, South Africa: Renaissance.

National Association of Protection and Advocacy Systems (2000). *Protection and advocacy systems.* Washington, DC: Author. www.protectionandadvocacy.com/.

National Association of School Boards of Education (NASBE). (1994). *Winners all: A call for inclusive education.* Washington, DC: Author.

National Center for Educational Restructuring and Inclusion. (1995). *National study of inclusion.* New York: Author.

National Center on Accessibility. (2000, November 20). Americans with Disabilities Act (ADA) Accessibility Guidelines for Buildings and Facilities; Play Areas. 36 Fed. Reg., Part 1191

National Commission on Excellence in Education. (1983). *A nation at risk.* Washington, DC: Author.

National Community Building Network. (1995). *Statement of principles.* Oakland, CA: Urban Strategies Council.

National Council of Teachers of Mathematics. (1987). *Curriculum and evaluation standards for school mathematics.* Reston, VA: Author.

National Council of Teachers of Mathematics. (1991). *Professional standards for teaching mathematics.* Reston, VA: Author.

National Institute of Mental Health (2001). *Attention deficit hyperactivity disorder (ADHD): Questions and anwers.* Bethesda, MD: Author. www.nimh.nih.gov/publicat/adhdqa.cfm.

National Law Center on Homelessness and Poverty, (2000). *Separate and unequal: A report on educational barriers for homeless children and youth.* Washington, DC: Author.

Needleman, H., Schell, A., Bellinger, D., Leviton, A., & Allred, E. (1990). The long-term effects of exposure to low doses of lead in childhood: An 11-year follow-up report. *New England Journal of Medicine, 322*(2), 83–88.

Neill, M., Bursh, P., Schaeffer, B., Thall, C., Yohe, M., & Zappardino, P. (1995). *Implementing performance assessments: A guide to classroom, school, and system reform.* Cambridge, MA: National Center for Fair and Open Testing.

Nelson, C. (1992). Searching for the meaning in the behavior of antisocial pupils, public school educators, and lawmakers. *School Psychology Review, 21*(1), 35–39.

Nelson, C. (1996). Rhythms of the racing brain. In T. Hartmann & J. Bowman (Eds.), *Think fast! The ADD experience.* Grass Valley, CA: Underwood.

Nelson, C. (1998, February). *Hyperactive hearts and minds: Toward a unified model of attention difficulty.* Paper presented at the meeting of Mind–Brain Sciences Colloquium, Palm Springs, FL.

Nelson, K., & Dimitrova, E. (1993). Severe visual impairment in the United States and in each state. *Journal of Visual Impairment and Blindness, 87*(2), 80–85.

Nesbitt, N. (1991, March). Cross-age tutoring in mathematics: Sixth graders helping students who are moderately handicapped. *Education and Training in Mental Retardation,* pp. 89–97.

Newmann, F., & Wehlage, G. (1993, April) Five standards of authentic instruction. *Educational Leadership,* pp. 8–12.

Ninness, C., McCuller, G., & Ozenne, L. (2000). *School and behavioral psychology: Applied research in human–computer interactions, functional assessment and treatment.* Norwell, MA: Kluwer.

Nisbet, J. (Ed.). (1992). *Natural supports in school, at work, and in the community for people with severe disabilities.* Baltimore: Paul H. Brookes.

Noddings, N. (1992). *The challenge to care in schools: An alternative approach to education.* New York: Teachers College Press.

Noell, G., & Witt, J. (1999). When does consultation lead to intervention implementation? *Journal of Special Education, 33*(1), 29–35.

North, S., Fontanive, L., Hechlik, J., Lamp, S., Sheehy, J., & Nichols, A. (1995) *Integrating exceptional individuals with diverse needs: A resource guide.* Detroit: Wayne State University.

North Carolina Special Olympics. (2001). *Unified Sports.* Columbia, SC: Author. www.so-sc.org/unified.htm.

Northwest Regional Educational Laboratory. (1998, March). *Catalog of school reform models.* Portland, OR: Author.

Nunley, K. (1998). *The regular educator's guide to layered curriculum.* South Jordan, UT: Kathie Nunley.

Oakes, J. (1985). *Keeping track: How schools structure inequality.* New Haven, CT: Yale University Press.

O'Brien, J., & O'Brien, C. (1992). Members of each other: Perspectives on social support for people with severe disabilities. In J. Nisbet (Ed.), *Natural supports in schools, at work, and in the community for people with severe disabilities.* Baltimore: Paul H. Brookes.

O'Brien, J., & O'Brien, C. (1996). *Members of each other: Building community in company with people with developmental disabilities.* Toronto: Inclusion Press.

O'Brien, J., & O'Brien, C. (Eds.). (1998). *A little book about person centered planning.* Toronto: Inclusion Press.

O'Brien, J., O'Brien, C., & Jacob, G. (1998). *Celebrating the ordinary: The emergence of options in community living as a thoughtful organization.* Toronto: Inclusion Press.

Odom, S. L., Deklyen, M., & Jenkins, J. R. (1984). Integrating handicapped and nonhandicapped preschoolers:

Developmental impact on nonhandicapped children. *Exceptional Children, 51*(1), 41–48.

Office of Special Education and Rehabilitative Services (OSERS). (1991, September 16). *AD(H)D and special education services: Memorandum.* Washinton, DC: U.S. Dept. of Education.

Office of Special Education and Rehabilitative Services. (2000). *A guide to the Individualized Education Program.* Washington, DC: U.S. Department of Education. www.ed.gov/offices/OSERS/OSEP/IEP_Guide/

Office of Special Education Programs. (1998). *20th annual report to Congress.* Washington, DC: Author.

Office of Special Education Programs (1999). *Twenty-first annual report to Congress.* Washington DC: Author.

Office of Special Education Programs. (2000a). *Parent training and information centers.* Washington, DC: U.S. Department of Education. www.taalliance.org/PTIs.htm.

Office of Special Education Programs. (2000b). 22nd annual report to Congress. Washington, DC: Author.

Office of Special Education Programs (2001). *Twenty-third annual report to Congress.* Washington, DC: Author.

Oglan, G. (1997). *Parents, learning and whole language classrooms.* Urbana, IL: National Council of Teachers of English.

Ogle, D., Pink, W., & Jones, B. F. (Eds.). (1990). *Restructuring to promote learning in America's schools.* Columbus, OH: Zaner-Bloser.

O'Halloran, J. (1995). The celebration process. In *Parent articles.* Phoenix, AZ: Psychological Corporation.

Ohanian, S. (1999). *One size fits few: The folly of educational standards.* Portsmouth, NH: Heinemann.

Ohio Developmental Disabilities Council. (1999). *American dreaming: Stories of change.* Worthington, OH: Author.

Oliver, M. (1990). *The politics of disablement: A sociological approach.* New York: St. Martin's.

O'Neill, R. E., Horner, R. H., Albin, R. W., Storey, K., & Sprague, J. R. (1996). *Functional assessment and program development for problem behavior: A practical handbook* (2nd ed.). Pacific Grove, CA: Brooks/Cole.

Orelove, F., & Sobsey, D. (1987). *Educating children with multiple disabilities.* Baltimore: Paul H. Brookes.

Orfield, G. (2001, April 3). *Housing segregation: Causes, effects, possible cures.* Cambridge, MA: The Civil Rights Project, Harvard University.

Orkwis, R., & McLane, K. (1998). *A curriculum every student can use: Design principles for student access.* Reston, VA: Council for Exceptional Children.

Ormrod, J. (2000). *Educational psychology: Developing learners* (3rd ed.). Columbus, OH: Merrill–Prentice Hall.

O'Shea, D., O'Shea, L., Algozzine, R., & Hammitte, D. (2001). *Families and teachers of individuals with disabilities: Collaborative orientations and responsive practices.* Boston: Allyn & Bacon.

Osher, D., & Hanley, T. V. (1996). Implications of the national agenda to improve results for children and youth with serious emotional disturbance. In R. Illback & C. Nelson (Eds.), *Emerging school-based approaches for children with emotional and behavioral problems: Research and practice in service integration.* Binghamton, NY: Haworth.

Osher, D. M., & Osher, T. W. (1996). The national agenda for children and youth with serious emotional disturbance (SED). In C. Nelson, R. Rutherford, Jr., & B. Wolford (Eds.), *Comprehensive and collaborative systems that work for troubled youth: A national agenda.* Richmond, KY: Eastern Kentucky University, National Juvenile Detention Association.

Oswald, D. P., & Coutinho, M. J. (1995). Identification and placement of students with serious emotional disturbance: Part I. Correlates of state child-count data. *Journal of Emotional and Behavioral Disorders, 3*(4), 224–229.

Paley, V. (1990). *The boy who would be helicopter: The uses of storytelling in the classroom.* Cambridge, MA: Harvard University Press.

Paley, V. (1992). *You can't say you can't play.* Cambridge, MA: Harvard University Press.

Palmer, P. (1998). *The courage to teach: Exploring the inner landscape of a teacher's life.* San Francisco: Jossey-Bass.

Parent Education Project. (1998a). *How to build a better IEP.* West Allis, WI: Author.

Parent Education Project. (1998b). *Parent rights, roles, and responsibilities: A look at special education and its impact on your child.* West Allis, WI: Author.

Parrish, T. (1993). *Fiscal policies in special education: Removing incentives for restrictive placements. Policy Paper #4.* Palo Alto, CA: American Institutes for Research, Center for Special Education Finance.

Patriarcha, L., Freeman, G., Hendricks, J., & Swift, C. (1996). *Understanding, improving, and promoting effective co-teaching: Final report.* Lansing, MI: Michigan Department of Education.

Patriarcha, L., & Zago, P. (1997). *Frameworks for maximizing co-teaching: A resource manual.* Lansing, MI: Michigan Department of Education.

Pavan, B. (1992, October). The benefits of non-graded schools. *Educational Leadership,* pp. 22–25.

Pearpoint, J., O'Brien, J., & Forest, M. (2001). *Planning alternative tomorrows with hope.* Toronto: Inclusion Press.

Peck, C. A., Carlson, P., & Helmstetter, E. (1992). Parent and teacher perceptions of outcomes for typically developing children enrolled in integrated early childhood programs: A statewide survey. *Journal of Early Intervention, 16*(1), 53–63.

Peck, S. (1987). *The different drum: Community making and peace.* New York: Simon & Schuster.

Perin, C. (1988). *Belonging in America: Reading between the lines* Madison, WI: University of Wisconsin Press.

Perske, R., & Perske, M. (1981). *Hope for families: New directions for parents of persons with retardation or other disabilities.* Nashville, TN: Abingdon.

Perske, R., & Perske, M. (1988). *Circles of friends: People with disabilities and their friends enrich the lives of one another.* Nashville, TN: Abingdon.

Peterson, M. (1996). Circles of support. *The responsive community, 6*(3), 58–63.

Peterson, M. (1998). Teacher focus group. Unpublished field notes. Detroit, MI: Wayne State University.

Peterson, M. (1999). Unpublished field notes of observations of mainstreaming and inclusive education, Wayne State University, Detroit.

Peterson, M. (2000). *Key elements of whole schooling.* Detroit: Renaissance Community Press, Wayne State University.

Peterson, M., Beloin, K., & Gibson, R. (1997). *Whole schooling: Education for a democratic society.* Detroit: Whole Schooling Consortium.

Peterson, M., & Hittie, M. (2000). *Whole Schooling Research Project field notes.* Detroit: Wayne State University.

Peterson, M., LeRoy, B., Field, S., & Wood, P. (1992) Community-referenced learning in inclusive schools. In S. Stainback & W. Stainback (Eds.), *Curriculum considerations in inclusive schooling.* Baltimore: Paul H. Brookes.

Peterson, M., Tamor, L., Feen, H., & Silagy, M. (2002). *Learning well together: Lessons about connecting inclusive education to whole school improvement.* Whole Schooling Research Project Final Report. Detroit: Whole Schooling Consortium, Wayne State University.

Peterson, R. (1992). *Life in a crowded place: Making a learning community.* Portsmouth, NH: Heinemann.

Phillips, W. C., Alfred, K., Brulli, A. R., & Shank, K. S. (1990). The Regular Education Initiative: The will and skill of regular educators. *Teacher Education and Special Education, 13*(3–4), 182–186.

Piers, M. (1978) *Infanticide.* New York: Norton.

Pitsch, M. (1994, October 12). Mississippi learning. *Education Week,* pp. 29–30.

Popham, J. (2001). *The truth about testing: An educator's call to action.* Alexandria, VA: Association for Supervision and Curriculum Development.

Porro, B. (1996). *Talk it out: Conflict resolution in the elementary classroom.* Alexandria, VA: Association for Supervision and Curriculum Development.

Prager, D., & Telushkin, J. (1983). *Why the Jews? The reason for antisemitism.* New York: Simon & Schuster.

President's Committee on Mental Retardation. (1998). *With a little help from my friends: A series on contemporary supports to people with mental retardation.* Washington, DC: Author. www.acf.dhhs.gov/programs/pcmr/help.htm

Price, B., Mayfield, P., McFadden, A., & Marsh, G. (1998). *Collaborative teaching: Special education for inclusive classrooms.* Parrot Publishing. Retrieved July 2, 2002, from www.parrotpublishing.com/Inclusion_Chapter_1.htm

Procedures for evaluation and determination of eligibility, 34 C.F.R. 300.530–300.536 (1999).

Public Agenda. (1997, April). Getting by: What American teenagers really think about their schools. *Education Week,* pp. 20–21.

Puddington, A. (Summer, 1996). *American Educator, 20*(2), 36–42.

Pugach, M. C., & Johnson, L. (1995). Unlocking expertise among classroom teachers through structured dialogue: Extending research on peer collaboration. *Exceptional Children, 62*(2), 101–110.

Pugach, M. C., & Wesson, C. L. (1995). Teachers' and students' views of team teaching of general education and learning disabled students in two fifth-grade classes. *Elementary School Journal, 95,* 279–295.

Putnam, J. (1993). *Cooperative learning and strategies for inclusion.* Baltimore: Paul H. Brookes.

Quigney, T., & Studer, J. (1999). Touching strands of the educational web: The professional school counselor's role in inclusion. *Professional School Counseling, 2*(1), 77–82.

Quina, J. (1995). *Principles of accelerated learning.* Unpublished manuscript, College of Education, Wayne State University, Detroit.

Quinn, M. M., Osher, D., Hoffman, C. C., & Hanley, T. V. (1998). *Safe, drug-free, and effective schools for ALL students: What works!* Washington, DC: Center for Effective Collaboration and Practice, American Institutes for Research.

Rainforth, B. (1992). *The effects of full inclusion on regular education teachers.* San Francisco: California Research Institute.

Rankin, B., & Quane, J. (2000). Neighborhood poverty and the social isolation of inner city African American families. *Social Forces, 79*(1), 139–164.

Rankin, D., Hallick, A., Ban, S., Hartley, P., Bost, C., & Uggla, N. (1994). Who's dreaming? A general education perspective on inclusion. *Journal of the Association for Persons with Severe Disabilities, 19*(3), 235–237.

Reavis, K., & Andrews, D. (1999). *Behavioral and educational strategies for teachers—B.E.S.T.* Salt Lake City, UT: B.E.S.T. Project.

Reeves, L., & Stein, J. (1999). Developmentally appropriate pedagogy and inclusion: Don't put the cart before the horse. *Physical Educator, 56,* 2–7.

Rhodes, L., & Dudley-Marling, C. (1996). *Readers and writers with a difference: A holistic approach to teaching struggling readers and writers.* Portsmouth, NH: Heinemann.

Richardson, J. (1994, Novermber 9). Adventures in learning. *Education Week,* pp. 25–28.

Riester, A. E. (1998). *A guide for developing IEPs for students with behavioral and emotional disorders.* San Antonio, TX: Psychological Corporation.

Roach, V., with Ascroft, J., & Kysilko, D. (1995). *Winning ways: Creating inclusive schools, classrooms, and communities.* Alexandria, VA: National Association of School Boards of Education.

Roberts, C., & Zubrick, S. (1992). Factors influencing the social status of children with mild academic disabilities in regular classrooms. *Exceptional Children, 49,* 192–202.

Rogers, J. (1993). The inclusion revolution. *Phi Delta Kappan Research Bulletin, 11,* 1–6.

Rohd, M. (1998). *Theatre for community, conflict, and dialogue: The hope is vital training manual.* Portsmouth, NH: Heinemann.

Romberg, T. (1995). *Reform in school mathematics and authentic assessment.* New York: State University of New York Press.

Rosenberg, S., McKeon, L, & Dinero, T. (1999, October). Positive peer solutions: One answer for the rejected student. *Phi Delta Kappan*, pp. 114–118.

Ross, H., Bernstein, G., & Rifkin, H. (1983). Relationship of metabolic control of diabetes mellitus to long-term complication. In M. Ellenberg & H. Rifkin (Eds.), *Diabetes mellitus: Theory and practice*. New Hyde Park, NY: Medical Examination Publishing.

Roth, M., Bartlinski, A., & Courson, P. (1994). *Modifying essential curriculum for the typical classroom*. Baltimore: Maryland Neighborhood Inclusion Project.

Rothman, D. (1990). *The discovery of the asylum: Social order and disorder in the new republic*. Boston: Little, Brown.

Routman, R. (1996). *Literacy at the crossroads: Crucial talk about reading, writing, and other teaching dilemmas*. Portsmouth, NH: Heinemann.

Rowlye-Kelly, F., & Regel, D. (1993). *Teaching the student with spina bifida*. Baltimore: Paul H. Brookes.

Rudolph, A., & Kamei, R. (1994). *Rudolph's fundamentals of pediatrics*. Norwalk, CT: Appleton & Lange.

Rusch, F., & Mithaug, D. (1980). *Vocational training for mentally retarded adults: A behavior analytic approach*. Champaign, IL: Research Press.

Russell, H. (1998). *Ten-minute field trips: A teacher's guide to using the school grounds for environmental studies*. Arlington, VA: National Science Teachers Association.

Rutter, M. (1977). Protective factors in children's responses to stress and disadvantage. In M. W. Kent & J. E. Rolf (Eds.), *Primary prevention of psychopathology: Vol. 3. Social competence in children*. Hanover, NH: University Press of New England.

Rydeen, J. (May, 1999). Universal design. *American School and University, 71*, 56–62.

Ryndak, D. L., & Alper, S. (1996). *Curriculum content for students with moderate and severe disabilities in inclusive settings*. Boston: Allyn & Bacon.

Ryndak, D. L., Downing, J. E., Jacqueline, L. R., & Morrison, A. P. (1995). Parents' perceptions after inclusion of their children with moderate or severe disabilities. *Journal of the Association for Persons with Severe Handicaps, 10*(2), 147–157.

Ryndak, D. L., Morrison, A., & Sommerstein. L. (1999). Literacy before and after inclusion in general education settings: A case study. *Journal of the Association for Persons with Severe Handicaps, 24*(1), 5–22.

Sacks, O. (1989). *Seeing voices: A journey into the world of the deaf*. Berkeley, CA: University of California Press.

Sage, D. (1997). *Inclusion in secondary schools: Bold initiatives challenging change*. Port Chester, NY: National Professional Resources.

Saha, N., Enright, B., & Timberflake, M. (1996). *Schools as inclusive communities: Training seminar series*. Orono, ME: Center for Community Inclusion, University of Maine.

Saint-Laurent, L., & Lessard, J. C. (1991). Comparison of three educational programs for students with moderate or severe disabilities. *Education and Training in Mental Retardation, 26*(4), 370–380.

Saint-Laurent, L., Glasson, J., Royer, E., Simard, C., & Pierard, B. (1998). Academic achievement effects of an in-class service model on students with and without disabilities. *Exceptional Children, 64*(2), 239–253.

Salend, S., & Duhaney, G. (1999). The impact of inclusion on students with and without disabilities and their educators. *Remedial and special education, 20*(2), 114–126.

Salisbury, C., Palombaro, M. M., & Hollowood, T. M. (1993). On the nature and change of an inclusive elementary school. *Journal of the Association for Persons with Severe Handicaps, 13*(1), 41–53.

Sapon-Shevin, M. (1994a). Celebrating diversity, creating community: Curriculum that honors and builds on differences. In S. Stainback & W. Stainback (Eds.), *Inclusion: A guide for educators*. Baltimore: Paul H. Brookes.

Sapon-Shevin, M. (1994b). *Playing favorites: Gifted education and the disruption of community*. Albany, NY: State University of New York Press.

Sapon-Shevin, M. (1994/1995). Why gifted students belong in inclusive schools. *Educational Leadership, 52*(4), 64–69.

Sapon-Shevin, M. (1999). *Because we can change the world: A practical guide to building cooperative, inclusive classroom communities*. Boston: Allyn & Bacon.

Sarasson, S. (1974). *The psychological sense of community*. San Francisco: Jossey-Bass.

Schaefer, N. (1997). *Yes! She knows she's here*. Toronto: Inclusion Press.

Schiller, L. (1998). *Increasing the success of your sixth grade students: Writing and reading strategies that work: Resource handbook*. Bellevue, WA: Bureau of Education and Research.

Schilling, M., & Coles, R. (1997). From exclusion to inclusion: A historical glimpse at the past and reflection of the future. *Journal of Physical Education, Recreation and Dance, 68*, 22–24.

Schlechty, P. (1990). *Schools for the 21st century: Leadership imperatives for educational reform*. San Francisco: Jossey-Bass.

Schleien, S., Ray, T., & Green, F. (1997). *Community recreation and people with disabilities: Strategies for inclusion*. Baltimore: Paul H. Brookes.

Schmidt, C. (1999). Poisoning young minds. *Environmental Health Perspectives, 107*(6), A302–A307.

Schulte, A. C., Osborne, S. S., & McKinney, J. D. (1990). Academic outcomes for students with learning disabilities in consultation and resource programs. *Exceptional Children, 57*(2), 162–172.

Schum, J. S., Vaughn, S., & Leavell, A. (1994). Planning pyramid: A framework for planning for diverse student needs during content area instruction. *The Reading Teacher, 47*(8), 608–615.

Schwartz, D. (1992). *Crossing the river: Creating a conceptual revolution in community and disability*. Cambridge, MA: Brookline.

Schwartz, D. (1997). *Who cares: Rediscovering community*. Boulder, CO: Westview Press.

Schwartz, S., & Pollishuke, M. (1990). *Creating the child-centred classroom*. Toronto: Irwin.

Scotch, R. (1984). *From good will to civil rights: Transforming federal disability policy*. Philadelphia: Temple University Press.

Scruggs, T. E., & Mastropieri, M. A. (1994). Successful mainstreaming in elementary science classes: A qualitative study of three reputational cases. *American Educational Research Journal, 31*(4), 785–811.

Sensory Access Foundation. (2000). *Access technology.* Sunnyvale, CA: Author. www.sensoryaccess.com/ .

Sergiovanni, T. (1990). *Value-added leadership: How to get extraordinary performance in schools.* San Diego, CA: Harcourt Brace Jovanovich.

Sergiovanni, T. (1994). *Building community in our schools.* San Francisco: Jossey-Bass.

Sexton, M., Harris, K., & Graham, S. (1998). Self-regulated strategy development and the writing process: Effects on essay writing and attributions. *Exceptional Children, 64*(3), 295–311.

Seyler, A., & Buswell, B. (2001). *Individual education plans: Involved effective parents.* Colorado Springs, CO: PEAK Parent Center.

Shaffer, C., & Anundsen, K. (1993). *Creating community anywhere: Finding support and connection in a fragmented world.* New York: Putnam.

Shane, H. (1994). *Facilitated communication: The clinical and social phenomenon.* Florence: Thompson Learning.

Shapiro, J. (1993). Separate and unequal. *Newsweek,* December 13, 1993, 46–60.

Shapiro, J. (1993). *No pity: People with disabilities forging a new civil rights movement.* New York: Times Books.

Sharpe, M. N., York, J. L., & Knight, J. (1994). Effects of inclusion on the academic performance of classmates without disabilities. *Remedial and Special Education, 15*(5), 281–287.

Shaywitz, S., & Shaywitz, B. (1988). Attention deficit disorder: Current perspectives. In J. G. Kavanagh & T. Truss Jr. (Eds.), *Learning disabilities: Proceedings of a national conference.* Parkton, MD: New York Press, 369–523.

Sheereneberger, R. (1983). *A history of mental retardation.* Baltimore: Paul H. Brookes.

Sheets, L., & Wirkus, M. (April/May, 1997). Everyone's classroom: An environment designed to invite and facilitate active participation. *Closing the Gap.* Retrieved July 2, 2002, from www.closingthegap.com/cgi-bin/lib/libDsply.pl?a=1050 +b=4&c=1.

Shelton, T., Jeppson, E., & Johnson, B. (1992). *Family-centered care for children with special health care needs.* Bethesda, MD: Association for the Care of Children's Health.

Sheppard, S., & Kanevsky, L. (1999). Nurturing gifted students' metacognitive awareness: Effects of training in homogeneous and heterogeneous classes. *Roeper Review, 21*(4), 266–272.

Shores, R. E., Gunter, P. L., & Jack, S. L. (1993). Classroom management strategies: Are they setting events for coercion? *Behavioral Disorders, 18*(2), 92–102.

Short, K. G., Harste, J., & Burke, C. (1996). *Creating classrooms for authors and inquirers.* Portsmouth, NH: Heinemann.

Siegel-Causey, E., & Allinder, R. (1998). Using alternative assessment for students with severe disabilities: Alignment with best practices. *Education and Training in Mental Retardation and Developmental Disabilities, 33*(2), 168–178.

Sinclair, E., & Alexson, J. (1992). Relationship of behavioral characteristics to educational needs. *Behavioral Disorders, 17*(4), 296–304.

Simpson, E. (1999, June 23). Passing life's tests: Hard work and persistence pay off in a regular diploma for a student with Down syndrome. *Virginian–Pilot,* p. E1.

Sizer, T. (1996). *Horace's hope: What works for the American high school.* New York: Houghton Mifflin.

Skiba, R., & Grizzle, K. (1992). Qualifications v. logic and data: Excluding conduct disorders from the SED definition. *School Psychology Review, 21*(1), 23–28.

Skrtic, T. (1994). *Democracy and special education.* New York: Bantam.

Smith, A. (1998, December). *Inclusive education: An international perspective.* Annual Conference of The Association for Persons with Severe Handicaps, Chicago.

Smith, D. (1998). *Inclusion: Schools for all students.* Boston: Wadsworth.

Smith, F. (1997). *Reading without nonsense.* New York: Teachers College Press.

Smith, F. (1998). *The book of learning and forgetting.* New York: Teachers College Press.

Smith, O. (1997). *Case study of an elementary student with severe learning disabilities.* Unpublished study, Okemus, MI.

Smull, M., & Harrison, S. (1992). *Supporting people with severe reputations in the community.* Alexandria, VA: National Association of State Mental Retardation Program Directors.

Snell, M., & Janney, R. (2000). *Collaborative teaming.* Baltimore: Paul H. Brookes.

Snow, J. (1998a). Centering on people: A quiet revolution. *Impact, 11*(2), 1, 26–27.

Snow, J. (1998b). *What's really worth doing and how to do it: A book for people who love someone labeled disabled (possibly yourself).* Toronto: Inclusion Press.

Sobsey, R., & Doe, K. (1991). Patterns of sexual abuse and assault. *Sexuality and Disability, 9*(3), 243–259.

Society for Developmental and Behavioral Pediatrics (2001). *Education programs.* Cleveland, OH: Author. www.sdbp.org/education/index.cfm.

Sommerfield, M. (1992). Micro-society schools tackle real-world woes. *Education Week, 12*(13), 1, 8.

Spear-Swerling, L., & Sternberg, R. (1998). *Off track: When poor readers become learning disabled.* Boulder, CO: Westview Press.

Stacey, R. (1992). *Managing the unknowable.* San Francisco: Jossey-Bass.

Stainback, S., & Stainback, W. (1994). *Inclusion: A guide for educators.* Baltimore: Paul H. Brookes.

Stainback, W., & Stainback, S. (1984). A rationale for the merger of regular and special education. *Exceptional Children, 51,* 102–112.

Stainback, W., Stainback, S., Moravec, J., & Jackson, H. J. (1992). Concerns about full inclusion: An ethnographic investigation. In R. Villa, J. Thousand, W. Stainback, & S. Stainback (Eds.), *Restructuring for caring and effective education: An administrative guide to creating heterogenous schools.* Baltimore: Paul H. Brookes.

Staub, D., Schwartz, E., Gallucci, C., & Peck, C. (1994). Four portraits of friendship at an inclusive school. *Journal of the Association for Persons with Severe Handicaps, 19*(4), 314–325.

Staub, D., Spaulding, M., Peck, C. A., Gallucci, C., & Schwartz, I. (1996). Using nondisabled peers to support the inclusion of students with disabilities at the junior high school level. *Journal of the Association for Persons with Severe Handicaps, 21*(4), 194–205.

Stein, D. (1999). *Ritalin is not the answer: A drug-free practical program for children diagnosed with ADD or ADHD.* San Francisco: Jossey-Bass.

Steinfeld, E. (1994). *The concept of universal design.* Center for Universal Design. www.ap.buffalo.edu/~idea/publications/free_pubs/pubs_cud.html.

Stepien, W., & Gallagher, S. (1993, April). Problem-based learning: As authentic as it gets. *Educational Leadership,* pp. 25–28.

Sternberg, R., & Grigorenko, E. (1999). *Our labeled children: What every parent and teacher needs to know about learning disabilities.* Reading, MA: Perseus.

Stevahn, L., et al. (1996). Effects on high school students of intergrating conflict resolution and peer mediation training into an academic unit. *Mediation Quarterly, 14*(1), 21–36.

Stolov, W., & Clowers, M. (1981). *Handbook of severe disability: A text for rehabilitation counselors, other vocational practitioners, and allied health professionals.* Fed. Reg. 65,083 (December 29, 1977). Washington, DC: U.S. Government Printing Office.

Strickland, K. (1995). *Literacy not labels: Celebrating students' strengths through whole language.* Portsmouth, NH: Boynton/Cook.

Susman, J. (1994). Disability, stigma and deviance. *Social Science and Medicine, 38*(1), 15–22.

Swaggart, B., Gagnon, E., Bock, S., Earles, T., Quinn, C., Myles, B., & Simpson, R. (1995). Using social stories to teach social and behavioral skills to children with autism. *Focus on Autistic Behavior, 10*(1), 1–15.

Szabo, J. (2000). Maddie's story: Inclusion through physical and occupational therapy. *Journal of Teaching Exceptional Children, 33*(2), 12–18.

Tarrant, K. (1993). *Teachers' beliefs about literacy, the instructional needs of special education students, and inclusion.* Paper presented at the Annual Meeting of the American Education Research Association, Atlanta, GA.

Tarrant, K. (1999a, June 22–24). *Building communities of practice between general and special education: Teachers and students working together to enact an early literacy curriculum inclusive of all students.* Presentation at the Whole Schooling Summer Institute, Wayne State University, Detroit.

Tarrant, A. (1999b). *Learning disabilities.* Unpublished paper. Kalamazoo, Western Michigan University, College of Education.

Tarrant, K. (1999c). *The collaborative implementation of an early literacy curriculum in a full-inclusion primary grade classroom: Co-teachers and students working together to accomplish literacy goals.* Doctoral dissertation, Michigan State University.

Tashie, C., Shapiro-Barnard, S., Donoghue-Dillon, A., Jorgenson, C., & Nisbet, J. (1993). *Changes in latitudes, changes in attitudes: The role of the inclusion facilitator.* Durham, NH: Institute on Disability, University of New Hampshire.

Taylor, D., Coughlin, D., & Marasco, J. (Eds.). (1997). *Teaching and advocacy.* York, ME: Stenhouse.

Taylor, S. (1988). Caught in the continuum: A critical analysis of the principle of least restrictive environment. *Journal of the Association for Persons with Severe Handicaps, 18*(2), 75–83.

Taylor, S., & Searl, S. (1987). The disabled in America: History, policy, and trends. In P. Knoblock (Ed.), *Understanding exceptional children and youth* (pp. 5–64). New York: Little, Brown.

Thomas, C., Correa, V., & Morsink, C. (1995). *Interactive teaming: Consultation and collaboration in special programs.* Englewood Cliffs, NJ: Prentice-Hall.

Thurlow, M. (2000). Including special needs students in standards-based assessments. In *Including special needs students in standards-based reform: A report on McREL's Diversity Roundtable III.* Aurora, CO: Mid-continent Research for Education and Learning.

Tomlinson, C. (1999). *The differentiated classroom: Responding to the needs of all learners.* Alexandria, VA: Association for Supervision and Curriculum Development.

Townsend, B. (2000). Standards-based school reform and culturally diverse learners: Implications for effective leadership when the stakes are even higher. In *Including special needs students in standards-based reform: A Report on McREL's Diversity Roundtable III.* Aurora, CO: Mid-continent Research for Education and Learning.

Treadwell, S., & Roxborough, L. (1991). Cerebral palsy seating. In M. Letts, (Ed.), *Principles of seating the disabled.* Boca Raton, FL: Council for Exceptional Children Press.

Troia, G., Graham, S., & Harris, K. (1999). Teaching students with learning disabilities to mindfully plan when writing. *Exceptional Children, 65*(2), 235–252.

Turnbull, A., & Turnbull, R. (1997). *Families, professionals, and exceptionality: A special partnership.* Columbus, OH: Prentice-Hall.

Turnbull, A., Turnbull III, H., Bronicki, G., Summers, J., & Roeder-Gordon, C. (1989). *Disability and the family: A guide to decisions for adulthood.* Baltimore: Paul H. Brookes.

Turnbull, R., Turnbull, A., Shank, M., Smith, S., & Leal, D. (2002). *Exceptional lives: Special education in today's schools.* Columbus, OH: Merrill/Prentice-Hall.

Tyack, D., & Cuban, L. (1995). *Tinkering toward utopia: A century of public school reform.* Cambridge, MA: Harvard University Press.

United Cerebral Palsy Association. (1993). *Policy on full inclusion of individuals with disabilities.* Washington, DC: Author.

United Nations Educational, Scientific and Cultural Organization (UNESCO), (1994, June 3). *The Salamanca statement and framework for action on special needs education.* Document produced at the World Conference on Special Needs Education: Access and Quality, Salamanca, Spain.

U.S. Congress. (1988). Technology-Related Assistance Act, Pub. L. No. 100-407, § 3.1.

University of Alberta. (2000). *Inclusion listserv archives.* Retrieved July 2, 2002, from www.ualberta.ca/htbin/lwgate/INCLUSION/

University of Oregon. (1999). First step to success. In *Success Stories of the Center for Effective Collaboration and Practice.* Portland, OR: Author. www. air-dc.org/cecp/resources/success/firststep.htm.

Vargo, S. (1998, January/February). Consulting: Teacher to teacher. *Teaching Exceptional Children,* pp. 54–55.

Varin, R. (1998). *Autism and its history in education: An outline of past and current effective educational options.* New York: Teaching Remarkable Children. Retrieved July 2, 2002, from home.earthlink.net/~varin/infopub/infopub/in01002.htm.

Vaughn, S., Bos, C., & Schumm, J. (1997). *Teaching mainstreamed, diverse, and at-risk students in the general education classroom.* Boston: Allyn & Bacon.

Vaughn, S., Gersten, R., & Chard, D. (2000). The underlying message in LD intervention research: Findings from research syntheses. *Exceptional Children, 67*(1), 99–115.

Vaughn, S., Moody, S., Schumm, J. (1998). Broken promises: Reading instruction in the resource room. *Exceptional Children, 64,* 211–225.

Vaughn, S., Schumm, J., & Arguelles, M. (1997). The ABCDE's of co-teaching. *Teaching Exceptional Children, 30*(2), 4–10.

Venolia, C. (1988). *Healing environments: Your guide to indoor well-being.* Berkeley, CA: Celestial Arts.

Villa, R., & Thousand, J. (1992). Restructuring public school systems: Strategies for organizational change and progress. In R. Villa, J. Thousand, W. Stainback, & S. Stainback (Eds.), *Restructuring for caring and effective education: An administrative guide to creating heterogeneous schools,* pp. 109–137. Baltimore: Paul H. Brookes.

Villa, R. A., & Thousand, J. S. (1996). *Creating the inclusive school.* Alexandria, VA: Assocation for Supervision and Curriculum Development.

Villa, R. A., Thousand, J. S., Meyers, H., & Nevin, A. (1996). Teacher and administrator perceptions of heterogeneous education. *Exceptional Children, 63*(1), 29–45.

Villa, R. A., Thousand, J. S., Stainback, W., & Stainback, S. (Eds.). (1992). *Restructuring for caring and effective education: An administrative guide to creating heterogenous schools.* Baltimore: Paul H. Brookes.

Vitello, S. J., & Mithaug, D. E. (1998). *Inclusive schooling: National and international perspectives.* Mahwah, NJ: Erlbaum.

Vygotsky, L. (1978). *Mind in society: The development of higher psychological processes.* Cambridge, MA: Harvard University Press.

Wagner, M. (1995). Outcomes for youths with serious emotional disturbance in secondary school and early adulthood. *The Future of Children: Critical Issues for Children and Youths, 5*(4), 90–112.

Wagner, M., Blackorby, J., Cameto, R., Hebbeler, K., & Newman, L. (1993). *The transition experiences of young people with disabilities.* Menlo Park, CA: SRI International.

Wagner, S. (1999). *Inclusive programming for elementary students with autism.* Arlington, TX: Future Horizons.

Waldron, N., & McLeskey, J. (1998). The effects of an inclusive school program on students with mild and severe learning disabilities. *Exceptional Children, 64*(2), 395–405.

Walker, W., Durie, P., Hamilton, J., Walker-Smith, J., & Watkins, J. (1991). *Pediatric gastrointenstinal disease: Pathophysiology, diagnosis, and management.* Philadelphia: Decker.

Walker, H., & Walker, J. (1991). *Coping with noncompliance in the classroom: A positive approach for teachers.* Austin, TX: Pro-Ed.

Walther-Thomas, C., Korinek, L., McLaughlin, V., & Toler Williams, B. (2000). *Collaboration for inclusive education: Developing successful programs.* Boston: Allyn & Bacon.

Wang, M. C., & Baker, E. (1986). Mainstreaming programs: Design features and effects. *Journal of Special Education, 19*(4), 503–521.

Wang, M. C., & Birch, J. W. (1984). Effective special education in regular classes. *Exceptional Children, 50,* 391–398.

Warren, R. L. (1988). The good community: What would it be. In R. Warren & L. Lyon (Eds.), *New perspectives on the American community* (5th ed.). Belmont, CA: Wadsworth.

Weaver, C. (1994a). *Reading process and practice: From socio-psycholinguistics to whole language.* Portsmouth, NH: Heinemann.

Weaver, C. (1994b). Understanding and educating attention-deficit students: A systems-theory, whole language perspective. In A. Flurkey & R. Meyer (Eds.), *Under the whole language umbrella: Many cultures, many voices.* Urbana, IL: National Council of Teachers of English (NCTE) and Whole Language Umbrella (WLU).

Weaver, J. (1994). What I've learned as an ADHDer about the problems and needs of students with ADHD. In C. Weaver (Ed.), *Success at last: Helping students with AD(H)D achieve their potential.* Portsmouth, NH: Heinemann.

Wehman, P. (1993). *The ADA mandate for social change.* Baltimore: Paul H. Brookes.

Weiner-Zivolich, J. (1995). If not now, when? The case against waiting for sheltered workshop changeover. *Journal of the Association for Persons with Severe Handicaps, 20*(4), 311–312.

Weisgerber, R., Dahl, P., & Appleby, J. (1980). *Training the handicapped for productive employment.* Rockville, MD: Aspen.

Werts, M. G., Wolery, M., Snyder, E. D., & Caldwell, N. K. (1996). Teachers' perceptions of the supports critical to the success of inclusion programs. *Journal of the Association for Persons with Severe Handicaps, 21*(1), 9–21.

West, C. (1993). *Race matters.* Boston: Beacon Press.

Westerly Public Schools. (1999). *Westerly system of care.* In Success Stories of the Center for Effective Collaboration and Practice. Retrieved July 2, 2002, from cecp.air.org/resources/success/westerly.htm.

Wheelock, A. (1992). *Crossing the tracks: How "untracking" can save America's schools*. New York: New Press.

White, A., & White, L. (1992). A collaborative model for students with mild disabilities in middle schools. *Focus on Exceptional Children, 24*(9), 1–12.

Wiedmeyer, D., & Leyman, J. (1991). The house plan: Approach to collaborative teaching and consultation. *Teaching Exceptional Children, 23*(2), 6–10.

Wilcox, B., & Bellamy, T. (1987). *A comprehensive guide to the activities catalogue: An alternative curriculum for youth and adults with severe disabilities*. Baltimore: Paul H. Brookes.

Wilhelm, J. D. (1995). *"You gotta be the book": Teaching engaged and reflective reading with adolescents*. New York: Teachers College Press.

Will, M. (1986). *Educating students with learning problems: A shared responsibility*. Washington, DC: Office of Special Education and Rehabilitative Services, U.S. Department of Education.

Williams, D. (1994a). *Like color to the blind*. New York: Times Books.

Williams, D. (1994b). *Somebody somewhere: Breaking free from the world of autism*. New York: Times Books.

Williams, W., Fox, T., Monley, M., McDermott, A., & Fox, W. (1989). *Individual program design series*. Burlington, VT: University of Vermont.

Willis, S. (1995, February). Mainstreaming the gifted. *Education Update, 37*(3), 4–5.

Winzer, M. (1993). *The history of special education from isolation to integration*. Washington, DC: Gallaudet University Press.

Winzer, M. (1998). The inclusion movement and teacher change: Where are the limits? *McGill Journal of Education, 33*(3), 229–247.

Wise, M. (1999, February/March). Participating in high school and beyond: A six-pack for success. *Closing the Gap*. Retrieved July 2, 2002, from www.closingthegap.com/cgi-bin/lib/libDsply.p1?a=1180&b=2&c=2.

Wolf, D. (1989). Portfolio assessment: Sampling student work. *Educational Leadership, 46*(7), 35–39.

Wolfensberger, W. (1972). *Normalization: The principle of normalization in human services*. Toronto: National Institute on Mental Retardation.

Wood, J. (1994). *Reading the hard to teach*. Midlothian, VA: Judy W. Wood.

Wood, J. (1998). *Adapting instruction to accommodate students in inclusive settings*. Upper Saddle River, NJ: Merrill/Prentice-Hall.

Wood, M. (1998). Whose job is it anyway? Educational roles in inclusion. *Exceptional Children, 64*(2), 181–195.

Wood, P. (1981). *International classification of impairments, disabilities, and handicaps*. Geneva, Switzerland: World Health Organization.

Wright, S. (1999, September 10). Mixed ability dance troupe. Available in archives at www.ualberta.ca/htbin/lwgate/INCLUSION/archives/Inclusion.1999-09/subject/

Yager, R. (1987). Assess all five domains of science. *The Science Teacher, 54*(7), 33–37.

Yager, R. (1990). Science, technology, and society (STS): Thinking over the years. *The Science Teacher, 57*(3), 52–55.

Yoe, J., Santarcangelo, S., Atkins, S., & Burchard, J. (1996, March). Wraparound care in Vermont: Program development, implementation, and evaluation of a statewide system of individualized services. *Journal of Child and Family Studies, 5*(1), 23–29.

York, J., Kronberg, R., Medwetz, L., & Doyle, M. (1993). *Creating inclusive school communities*. Minneapolis, MN: University of Minnesota.

York, J., Vandercook, T., Mac Donald, C., Heise-Neff, C., & Caughey, E. (1992). Feedback about integrating middle-school students with severe disabilities in general education classes. *Exceptional Children, 58*(3), 244–258.

Young, K. (1994). *Constructing buildings, bridges, and minds: Building an integrated curriculum through social studies*. Portsmouth, NH: Heinemann.

Young, M. (1995). *Restorative community justice: A call to action*. Washington, DC: National Organization for Victim Assistance.

Zahn-Waxler, C. (1993). Warriors and worriers: Gender and psychopathology. *Development and Psychopathology, 5*(2), 79–89.

Zemelman, S., Daniels, H., & Hyde, A. (1998). *Best practice: New standards for teaching and learning in America's schools*. Portsmouth, NH: Heinemann.

Zigmond, N., & Baker, J. (1995). Concluding comments: Current and future practices in inclusive schooling. *Journal of Special Education, 29*(2), 245–250.

Zigmun, N., Jenkins, J., & Fuchs, L. (1995). Special education and restructured schools: Findings from three multiyear studies. *Phi Delta Kappan, 76*, 531–540.

Zionts, P. (Ed.). (1997). *Inclusion strategies for students with learning and behavior problems: Perspectives, experiences, and best practices*. Austin, TX: Pro-Ed.

Zoccolillo, M. (1992). Co-occurrence of conduct disorder and its adult outcomes with depressive and anxiety disorders: A review. *Journal of the American Academy of Child and Adolescent Psychiatry, 31*(3), 547–556.

Korinek, L., 128, 131, 132, 134, 137
Koroloff, N. M., 82
Kortering, L. J., 303
Kostelny, K., 40, 358, 360, 361, 373
Kovalik, S., 131, 226, 251, 441, 442
Kozleski, E., 211
Kozol, J., 15, 49
Kretzmann, J. P., 79, 80, 82, 84, 134, 322, 323, 443
Kroll, J., 4
Kronberg, R., 145, 169, 192
Kronick, D., 199
Kunc, N., 4, 28–29, 323, 327, 356, 358, 362, 366, 367, 369, 384, 406
Kusche, C., 369
Kuttler, S., 369
Kwan, G., 313
Kysilko, D., 480

L'Abate, L., 369
Lakin, C., 208
LaMaster, K., 252
Lance, W., 6
Lane, P., 30
Lantieri, L., 40, 329, 358, 360, 375
Leaf, P. J., 302
Leal, D., 394, 412
Learning Disabilities Association, 201
Leavell, A., 169
LeDoux, J., 327
Lee, C., 203
Lee, M., 329
Lee, O., 16, 36, 39
Leicester, N., 38, 201
Leone, P., 301
Leone, P. E., 303
Lepper, M., 355
LeRoy, B., 21, 109, 111, 235
Lessard, 91, 38
Levin, H., 49, 162
Levine, K., 460
Levine, M., 141
Leviton, A., 412
Levitz, J., 208
Lewis, B., 444
Lewis, R., 203, 393, 394
Lewis, T. J., 39, 303
Leyman, J., 147
Lipskey, D. K., 20, 21, 24, 27, 42, 485
Lloyd, J., 40
Loeb, D., 387, 388, 389
Lofkuist, L., 258
Logan, K., 211, 228
Long, R., 131, 333, 334, 347
Lopez, M., 300
Lovaas, O., 312
Lovett, H., 365, 380

Lowenbraun, S., 37, 39
Luckasson, R., 112
Ludlow, B., 112
Ludlum, C., 343

Maag, J., 365
McAdamis, S., 46
McCarney, S., 96
McClellan, D., 126
McCormick, L., 387, 388, 389
McCuller, G., 11
McDermott, A., 103
MacDonald, C., 41, 392
McDonnell, J., 38, 40, 211, 392
McFadden, A., 274, 275, 282
McGinnis, E., 307, 369
McGonigel, M., 118
McGregor, G., 36, 41
McIntosh, R., 12, 36, 39
McKenzie, B., 215–216
McKeon, L., 371
McKinney, J. D., 202
McKnight, J., 10, 11, 64, 79–80, 82, 84, 134, 289, 322, 323, 443
McLane, K., 358, 373, 452
McLaughlin, M., 27
McLaughlin, M. J., 303
McLaughlin, V., 128, 131, 132, 134, 137
McLeskey, J., 36, 37, 38, 39, 40
McMichael, A., 412
MacMillan, D., 302, 312
Macrorie, K., 172
McVay, P., 140, 141
McWhitter, J., 370
Madge, S., 37, 39
Madsen, S., 322
Maher, C., 230
Mahoney, B., 37
Malone, M., 228
Maloney, J., 154
Mank, D., 118
Manley, A., 234
Mann, L., 424
Manning, G., 131, 333, 334, 347
Manning, M., 131, 333, 334, 347
Manset, G., 37, 39
Marasco, J., 485
March, R., 40, 306, 308
Marder, C., 299
Mariage, T., 201, 203
Marin, M., 355
Marks, S., 141
Mars, A., 311
Marsh, G., 274, 275, 282
Marston, D., 37
Martin, G., 355
Martin, J., 109, 212

Maruyama, G., 38
Maslow, A., 326
Mason, J., 340
Masterson, C., 41
Mastropieri, M. A., 39, 41
Mayer, G. O., 303
Mayfield, P., 274, 275, 282
Mazlish, E., 356, 367
Meadows, N., 40, 288, 305, 308, 309
Medenwaldt, M., 255, 256, 1611
Medwetz, L., 145
Meek, A., 420, 423, 424, 425, 426
Melaville, A., 82, 85
Metz, M. H., 302
Meyer, L., 356, 360, 378, 379, 390, 392
Meyer, L. H., 37, 38, 391
Meyer, R., 321
Meyers, H., 41
Michigan Department of Education, 96, 97, 99
Mikus, K., 60, 68
Milan, M., 369
Miles, M., 27
Miles, P., 302
Miller, B., 126
Miller, D., 199
Miller, R., 109, 212
Miller-Lachmann, L., 195, 196
Miner, B., 251
Mirenda, P., 395, 451, 460, 462
Mithaug, D., 208
Mithaug, D. E., 27
Modrow, J., 303
Moles, O., 60, 62, 73, 77
Monda-Amaya, L., 171
Monley, M., 103
Moody, S., 16, 36, 202
Moore, A., 195, 196
Moravec, J., 21, 39
Morocco, C., 171, 172
Morrison, A., 211, 228
Morrison, A. P., 38, 41, 68
Morsink, C., 137
Moses, M., 355
Mount, B., 18, 343
Mulick, J., 460
Mullen, L., 373
Mundy, F., 37
Murphy, S., 208
Murray-Seegert, C., 342
Muscott, H., 40, 304, 305, 308, 309
Myles, B., 369
Myree-Brown, G., 41

Naicker, S. M., 27
National Association of Protection and Advocacy Systems, 84

Credits